THIRD EDITION

NATION

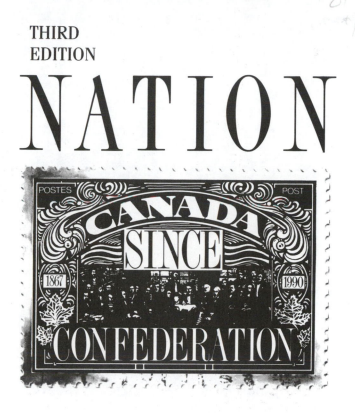

12/21

THIRD
EDITION

NATION

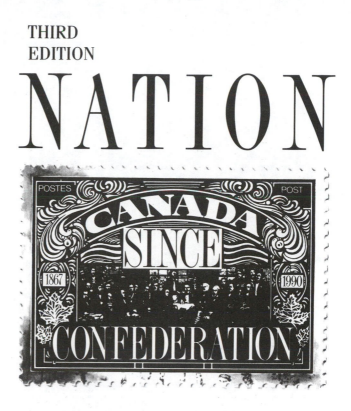

J.L. GRANATSTEIN
York University

IRVING M. ABELLA
Glendon College, York University

T.W. ACHESON
University of New Brunswick

DAVID J. BERCUSON
University of Calgary

R. CRAIG BROWN
University of Toronto

H. BLAIR NEATBY
Carleton University

McGRAW-HILL RYERSON LIMITED
Toronto   Montreal   New York   Auckland
Bogotá   Caracas   Hamburg   Lisbon   London
Madrid   Mexico   Milan   New Delhi   Paris
San Juan   São Paulo   Singapore   Sydney   Tokyo

NATION: CANADA SINCE CONFEDERATION, THIRD EDITION

Formerly **Twentieth Century Canada**, Second Edition
© McGraw-Hill Ryerson Limited, 1990, 1986, 1983. All rights reserved. No part of this publication may be reproduced, stored in a data base or retrieval system, or transmitted, in any form or by any means, electronic, mechanical, photocopying, recording, or otherwise, without the prior written permission of McGraw-Hill Ryerson Limited.

ISBN: 0-07-549801-4

67890 MP 9876543

Printed and bound in Canada

SPONSORING EDITOR: CATHERINE O'TOOLE
SUPERVISING AND PRODUCTION EDITOR: ROSALYN STEINER
PERMISSIONS EDITOR: NORMA CHRISTENSEN
COVER AND TEXT DESIGN: SHARON MATTHEWS

Canadian Cataloguing in Publication Data
Main entry under title:
Nation : Canada since Confederation
3rd ed.
Earlier eds. published under title: Twentieth century Canada.
Includes bibliographical references.
ISBN 0-07-549801-4

1. Canada – Politics and government – 20th century.
2. Canada – History – 20th century.*
I. Granatstein, J. L., 1939. II. Title: Twentieth century Canada.
FC600.N37 1990 971.06 C90-093501-4 FI033.N37 1990

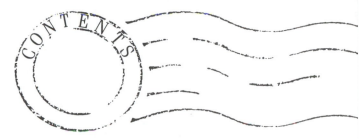

CONTENTS

 PREFACE

In the years since Confederation, Canada has developed and prospered. Most of its people, wherever they originated and however brief their residency, have the opportunity for an education, a job, and a decent standard of living. Not without difficulty, the state has put in place and thus far maintained a safety net of social security, assuring all its inhabitants most of the basic necessities of life. The harsh and repressive attitudes that stifled cultural development earlier in our history and the bitter prejudices that oppressed the lives of women, immigrants, and native peoples have eased substantially, notwithstanding sudden, sometimes vicious, reappearances.

How did we get to this point? The purpose of this book is an attempt to answer that question. The contributors of *Nation: Canada Since Confederation* aimed to convey the basic history of Canada and its peoples since 1867. But they also wanted to do something more. By focusing in detail on six major themes – creation of the industrial order, political process and leadership, the rise of labour, immigration, foreign policy, and the new Quebec – they set out to add a new dimension to Canadian history texts. The chronological chapters lay out the basic facts of political, economic, and social development simply and clearly; the theme chapters allow an in-depth look at important subjects. This approach necessarily results in some duplication, but we make no apology for this. Some users of the text will only read the chronology; others might only use one or two themes. In the authors' view, it was best to allow the repetition to stand so that every student could get a fair and relatively complete account.

A generation ago there was very little research into the areas covered in the theme chapters. Canadian historians were just beginning to venture tentatively into social history, to study trade unions or business attitudes, to consider the exploitation of immigrants and the racist attitudes that lay behind government policies, or to move behind the facade of speeches and political posturing to study the party machinery or the bureaucracy that kept the wheels of government spinning. The idea that Quebec might be a worthy area of study, that provincial struggles for power could ever be anything more than dry-as-dust disquisitions on Oliver Mowat and the provincial boundary struggles of the late nineteenth century, say, seemed almost incredible to all but a few specialists. But events change history, and they change historians, too. There is a vigorous process of healthy revisionism underway, and this book in each of its chapters reflects it. The bibliographical footnotes, carefully updated to be as current as possible, point to the newest and best work available so that readers can readily pursue specialized topics.

The themes that are studied here and that help to shape the approach of all the chapters of this book represent some of the newest work of the most accomplished generation of Canadian historians. Professor T.W. Acheson of the University of New Brunswick recently published a massive study of the city of Saint John and was one of the first historians to explore the complex processes of industrialization in Canada. Professor R. Craig Brown of the University of Toronto is the biographer of Sir Robert Borden and the co-author of *Canada, 1896-1921*, the best study of that period, and he is now carefully studying the Canadian experience during the Great War. David Bercuson of the University of Calgary is one of the country's pioneer labour historians, the author of the foremost studies of the Winnipeg General Strike and western unionism, and he is currently working on a biography of Brooke Claxton, one of the leading mid-century Liberals. Irving Abella of Glendon College, York University, is also a labour historian, but one who has recently turned his full attention to the study of immigration policy. His book, *None Is Too Many*, examines the ways the Canadian government kept Jewish refugees from Hitler out of this promised land, and he is now in the midst of a major study of the Canadian Jewish community. H. Blair Neatby of Carleton University is the official biographer of Mackenzie King, the author of a notable study of Laurier and Quebec, and is currently working on a study of university education in Canada. And J.L. Granatstein, the co-ordinating author of this book, has written on politics, foreign policy, and conscription and is the author of the final volume in the Centenary series, *Canada, 1957-1967*. The writers are all active and prolific published scholars and teachers, deeply immersed in the process of trying to discover more about this country. All assume a collective responsibility for this book and its approach.

January 1990

MAKING THE NATION

The noon sun broke through the late summer sky as the steamship *Queen Victoria* entered Hillsborough Bay. It was September 1, 1864. Along the shore and as far back as the eye could see stretched the low terrain and rich red soil of the Island countryside peppered with neat white farm houses and outbuildings. Very soon, the city of Charlottetown appeared on the horizon. On shore, expectant Islanders gathered to view the arrival of the newcomers. "The Canadians are coming" was the cry in the streets. Aboard the ship, the eight Canadian political leaders and their families, who had travelled more than three days from Quebec, prepared to disembark. The leaders of the coalition government of Canada were about to engage in the most important adventure of their careers: they had come to persuade the executive councillors of Nova Scotia, New Brunswick, and Prince Edward Island to extinguish their self-governing colonies in order to create a new British nation in North America. The Nova Scotian and New Brunswick leaders were in Charlottetown to discuss Maritime Union. It was the mission of the Canadians to divert them into the larger union.

The Canadians worked hard to secure their objective. A week of discussions, intrigues, gala social events, and eating and drinking worked to their advantage. At the centre of the negotiations was John A. Macdonald, the small Scottish-born Conservative lawyer from Kingston. Witty, gregarious, possessed of a marvellous facility for remembering names, Macdonald struck the compromises, suggested the possibilities, and kept the discussions rolling. Inexorably, with a skill born of long

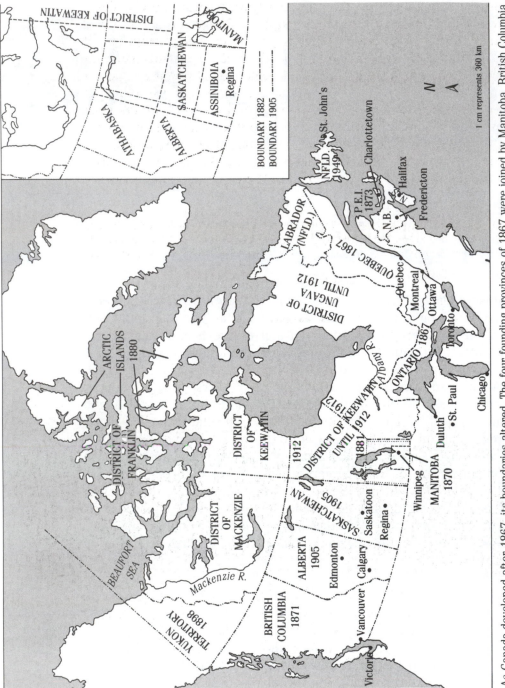

As Canada developed after 1867, its boundaries altered. The four founding provinces of 1867 were joined by Manitoba, British Columbia, and Prince Edward Island; Britain ceded the Arctic islands in 1880; Alberta and Saskatchewan received provincial status in 1905; and Newfoundland joined Confederation in 1949.

ADAPTED FROM *THE KINGDOM OF CANADA* BY W.L. MORTON, PUBLISHED BY MACMILLAN OF CANADA. P.404.

experience in measuring men, he drew the Maritimers into the scheme. By September 6, they agreed to the principle of a larger union, provided satisfactory terms could be arranged. These included promises of railways and subsidies to the colonies and personal advancement for their leaders. The parties then began an inspection through the Lower Provinces – Halifax, Saint John, Fredericton – and finally reassembled at Quebec on October 10. There they were joined by two observers from Newfoundland. Over the course of the next 16 days, they hammered out a series of resolutions that would form the basis of the new union.

The next two years proved anticlimactic to the heady optimism created by the events of the autumn of 1864. An agreement on the

The process of achieving Confederation was difficult, with regional, racial, religious, and personal interests all at stake. The delegates at the Quebec Conference of 1864 look suitably solemn at the responsibility they bear. (Macdonald is fourth from the left in the first row.)

C-16588/NATIONAL ARCHIVES OF CANADA.

Quebec Resolutions had been achieved only among the members of a small political elite and, even within this group, serious reservations remained, especially on the part of some Maritime leaders. Selling the proposition to legislators and electors proved considerably more difficult. Newfoundland and Prince Edward Island withdrew from the undertaking, the latter arguing that the terms were unfair to the Island. When Leonard Tilley called a general election on the issue in the winter of 1865, the electors of New Brunswick rejected him and returned an anticonfederation government. Only with the defeat of that government in the spring of 1866 did the momentum for union resume.

The next winter, a handful of political leaders from Canada, New Brunswick, and Nova Scotia arrived in London with the blueprint for a new federal state that they hoped to create in the northern half of North America. With the assistance of a sympathetic British government, the appropriate legislation was pushed through the British Parliament. The new state created by the British North America Act was born on July 1, 1867. And it was named Canada. The name was important. It reflected the fact that the new state was an extension of the old central Province of Canada, which remained the dominant element in the new system. Not all inhabitants of the new nation supported its creation. Many preferred the status quo, while others had different visions of colonial destiny. In the end, however, Canada was created when Canadian and British needs coincided following the American Civil War.

Canadian needs in the 1860s were both political and economic in nature. The root of the political problem can be traced to the legislative union of the English-speaking colony of Upper Canada and the predominantly French-speaking colony of Lower Canada, a union imposed on Lower Canada by the British government. The political life of the union was marked by a series of confrontations, many of them cultural in origin, and, by 1864, it was obvious even to the most optimistic observer that the existing constitutional arrangement was unworkable. At the same time, no matter how much English- and French-Canadians differed in culture and outlook, it was clear that the St. Lawrence - Great Lakes basin, which they shared, was a single commercial system centred on Montreal. Its division into two competing political jurisdictions – a return to the pre-1840 situation – was perceived as unthinkable by the commercial interests of the colony. What was required was a larger union that could accommodate cultural differences within a federal system. Such a union might also satisfy the demands of many leaders from western Ontario who wished that agricultural lands of the British prairies might become part of their patrimony. Freed from internal crisis, the new state could negotiate with the imperial government for access to the West. The ambition of many leaders was to integrate most of the Second British Empire in North America into a single self-governing state, a "dominion" rather than a kingdom as the founders called it in deference to American sensibilities, paralleling the state created to the south by the Americans. It was Canadian needs and particularly Upper Canada's needs that provided the major incentive for the new federal union.

At the same time, it is difficult to exaggerate the importance of the British role in the 1867 union and in the subsequent expansion of the Canadian state. The expansion of the old colony of Canada from its St. Lawrence heartland eastward into the Maritimes and westward to British Columbia was the result of a series of orderly negotiated takeovers accomplished through the midwifery of British cabinet ministers, British company executives, and British viceroys. The British decison to withdraw from North America was partly the effect of a "Little England" anti-imperialist sentiment that had been growing among English liberals throughout the nineteenth century and partly the result of the American Civil War. That war convinced most British political leaders that a significant British presence in North America was impossible in the face of growing American strength unless the British were willing to face the possibility of waging a land war in the interior of the continent. On the other hand, the Americans would tolerate a self-governing British dependency that would pose no threat to American interests. So the British government supported Canadian initiatives to take over the imperial responsibility for the far-flung and thinly populated North American empire. The British influence was decisive in the process; without it Upper Canada's dream of a greater Canada would never have become reality.

The 1867 Confederation had been accomplished quickly but not easily. Negotiations had been carried out by small political elites representing the dominant political groupings in each of the five British colonies in northeastern North America. Those from Newfoundland and Prince Edward Island had refused to accept the terms of the union and had withdrawn. In the end, approval for the proposals had been given by the legislatures of Canada and Nova Scotia. Only New Brunswickers were given the opportunity of voting on the issue and they had approved the scheme on the second ballot by a narrow margin, and only after the full weight of the imperial government had been brought to bear in favour of Confederation. Indeed, there is not much evidence that any of the political minorities in the new state – French-Canadians, New Brunswickers, or Nova Scotians – accepted the union with enthusiasm despite the benefits that each was to receive in the new constitutional order. French-Canadians had been offered a provincial government that they could control. New Brunswick and Nova Scotia had been offered the crucial railway link with the interior and a third of the senators in the new Parliament, an arrangement that would provide parity of representation with Ontario and a means of defending their interests.

The genius of the new constitutional arrangement could be found in its federal nature. That system offered the solution to many of the problems faced by the old union. The English and French sections of the old Canadian colony would once again be assigned their own geographic spheres of influence. New Brunswick and Nova Scotia would continue to deal with the purely local concerns of their region. All local matters such as those relating to municipalities, local business, roads, public lands, and the maintenance of order were handed to the new provincial legislatures. As well, they were given responsibility for all those sometimes-contentious matters that might be defined as cultural: language, education, religion, social welfare, marriage, and civil rights. The central government at Ottawa was assigned matters of general concern, particularly those relating to the economy. Thus, in addition to the traditional imperial responsibilities for defence and the care of the native peoples, Ottawa assumed responsibility for banking and currency, tariff and trade policies, navigation, and interprovincial trade and business. Most important, all matters not specifically assigned to the provinces were reserved for the jurisdiction of the central government. To further ensure the primacy of the central government, Ottawa retained the power to appoint the lieutenant governors and Supreme Court judges in all provinces and to disallow provincial legislation. Even in spheres that were clearly within provincial jurisdiction, such as education, the central government was given the authority to intervene on behalf of religious minorities.

These constitutional arrangements were only partly effective in producing a strong union. Demands for repeal and for better terms continued throughout the generation following 1867. Nova Scotians were particularly bitter about the annexation that obliterated their nascent nationality. To that problem was added serious religious and ethnic controversies. For many English Canadians the union was to be a definitive solution to the seemingly intractable problems of French and Roman Catholic identities. In their view, Quebec was an area in which the French culture could flourish; the remainder of the state would be English and Protestant except for a limited recognition of Catholic educational rights in Ontario. Efforts to create or preserve French or Roman Catholic culture outside Quebec were fiercely resisted. Even the federal arrangement itself was called into question as provincial rightists challenged Ottawa's authority to intervene in any area of provincial jurisdiction and eventually propounded a theory that argued for the Canadian state as a federation of sovereign provinces. Most of these issues centred on the nature of the Canadian nationality. The 1867 union created a constitutional arrangement that offered possibilities but no conclusions. It could create the Canadas but not a Canada. In 1838, following the rebellions of the previous year, Lord Durham wrote that he had found two nations warring in the bosom of a single state. Sixty years later, that situation had changed little.

Yet the union had its successes as well as its failures. Its survival in 1896 was one of these. In part that survival may be attributed to the national policies of economic development implemented between 1868 and 1886. The acquisition of the West, the transportation links from Nova Scotia to British Columbia, the drive to industrialization and economic integration all contributed to an expanding economy and to a considerable degree of social integration. If the nation still remained undefined in 1896, the state had come to fulfill the function planned for it in 1864.[1]

State of the Nation

The Dominion of Canada in 1867 contained about 3½ million people scattered from Cape Breton to Lake Superior. In the West, most people lived in the St. Lawrence River valley, along the north shore of Lake Ontario, and in the broad sweep of southwestern Ontario. Its central geographic characteristic was the St. Lawrence River, which until the mid-nineteenth century made Canada East and Canada West a single

---

[1] There are several surveys of the Canadian experience in the generation following Confederation. For an overview, see W.L. Morton, *The Critical Years: The Union of British North America 1857-1863* (Toronto, 1964) and P.B. Waite, *Canada 1878-1896: Arduous Destiny* (Toronto, 1971). The best regional study is Gerald Friesen, *The Canadian Prairies: A History* (Toronto, 1984). A fine overview of the Quebec experience is Paul André Linteau, René Dorocher, and Jean-Claude Robert, *Quebec: A History, 1867-1929* (Toronto, 1983).

commercial region. The construction of the Grand Trunk Railway from
Montreal to Sarnia reinforced that natural route. The integrity of the
Laurentian system was increasingly challenged after 1825, first by the
Erie Canal, then by the construction of the Great Western Railway,
which linked Hamilton, U.C., to the American transportation network.
Yet, despite this threat, so long as control of the state remained in the
hands of Montreal business interests, nature and a fiscal policy ensured
that the commerce of Canada West would move through Montreal and
that the market of the region would be largely dominated by its
merchants and manufacturers. The economic geography of the two
Maritime provinces stood in sharp contrast to that of Quebec and
Ontario. New Brunswick and Nova Scotia were extensions of the
Appalachian system of New England, and settlement clustered in the
narrow river valleys of New Brunswick and on the coastal areas of both
provinces. The narrow bands of water-based settlement meant that the
region had only a limited geographic focus. No city in the region could
play the role in the East that Montreal held in the West.

TABLE 1

POPULATION AND POPULATION DENSITY 1871

	Total	Ontario	Quebec	New Brunswick	Nova Scotia
Area in acres	215 million	65 million	120 million	17 million	13 million
Population	3 485 761	1 620 857	1 191 516	285 594	387 800
Acres per Person	62	40	101	61	35

CENSUS OF CANADA. 1871. 1881. 1891.

The dominant motif in Canadian society was its rural and essentially
agricultural nature. Two-thirds of all Canadians lived in rural communities and perhaps half the remainder were found in villages that existed to
service the inhabitants of the rural countryside. About half of all gainfully
employed Canadians claimed to make a living from agriculture, but
another large segment of the population worked at other primary
occupations or provided for the needs of those who lived in rural
communities. The farm was the basic unit of production. Nearly 90
percent of farmers owned their farms. As a result, they generally
possessed the franchise, although their adult sons living at home did not.

The centrality of farms and of the rural community is important in understanding the attitudes of the constitution-makers regarding social policy. Most farmers possessed the means for subsistence, but hard cash for taxes was often more difficult to come by, and their payment was resented. Families should care for their elderly, their sick, and their handicapped. If they could not, then the local parish would reluctantly assume the cost and the expenses would be assessed on the parish freeholders. The initiative toward Confederation was strongly supported by those farmers of Canada West who saw the Prairies as a source of good farm land for their second and third sons. The paucity of good farm land for the growing population of rural children was rapidly reaching a crisis in all four provinces.

The living standards of rural families were directly related to the quality of soil and climate in the area they inhabited and to the opportunities for working in other extractive industries, such as forestry, fishing, or mining. The most extensive commercial agriculture was practised in western Ontario where good land made possible the production of large quantities of surplus wheat, much of which could be sold outside Canada. In Quebec, New Brunswick, and Nova Scotia, most farm produce was used to supply family needs. Surpluses of butter, meat,

TABLE 2

FARMS AND FARM OUTPUT 1870

	Canada	Ontario	Quebec	N.B.	N.S.
Farm occupiers	367 900	172 200	118 000	31 200	46 300
owners	89%	84%	93%	93%	95%
tenants	11%	16%	8%	7%	5%
Acres per farm	99	94	93	122	108
Improved acres per farm	47	51	48	39	35
Wheat (bu. per farm)	45	82	18	6	4
Oats (bu. per farm)	115	128	128	96	48
Barley (bu. per farm)	31	55	14	3	7
Buckwheat (bu. per farm)	10	4	14	39	4
Potatoes (bu. per farm)	129	99	152	211	121
Hay (tons per farm)	10	10	10	10	9
Butter (lb. per farm)	202	218	206	164	156
Timber (cu. ft. per farm)		196	206	122	89
Logs (cu. ft. per farm)		41	73	151	30

CENSUS OF CANADA, 1871, 1881, 1891.

hay, oats, and potatoes in these provinces were sold in local or regional markets. Timber and lumber, and sometimes fish, also provided important cash crops in most rural areas; in the eastern provinces they frequently were more valuable than agricultural commodities.

The villages and small towns scattered across the Canadian countryside contained the merchants and shopkeepers who controlled the wholesale and retail trade of the district, the artisans who produced a limited range of consumer and producer goods, the mills for processing the grain and timber produced in the countryside, the professionals offering services to the people of the district, and the day-labourers and servants who found casual employment in a variety of menial tasks. Increasingly, too, villages and towns housed those who worked on the railways, which were slowly but fundamentally altering the economic shape of the country. In their turn, the people of the towns were bound by ties of credit or employment to the cities.

In 1870, Saint John, N.B., was a small but bustling city with handsome buildings. The horses, which drew carts of people and goods, created a difficult sanitation problem.

NEW BRUNSWICK MUSEUM.

Cities were the financial, commercial, intellectual, and administrative centres of the country. In many important ways, they defined the regions they headed. Only Montreal, standing at the centre of the Laurentian commercial system and containing more than 100 000 people, had achieved the status of a major city. Toronto and Quebec were at the second stage of the urban hierarchy. The remaining Quebec and Ontario cities, small communities like Drummondville, Kingston, Hamilton, and London, were clearly satellites of either Montreal or Toronto. In the East, Saint John and Halifax dominated their largely independent economies. They possessed their own banking systems and, through their legislatures, they had been able to control the fiscal policies of their regions for more than a generation. Only about one Canadian in nine lived in a city, although the proportion of city dwellers varied considerably from province to province.

Cities were the most socially diverse communities in the Dominion. As well as business, political, religious, professional, and intellectual groups, they contained the mass of poor immigrants who survived as day-labourers in the urban centres and were the refuge for large numbers of women who found life as servants and seamstresses more congenial than the limited opportunities offered in the rural environment. Increasingly, too, as manufacturing industries expanded to take shape, the urban communities began to absorb the surplus population from the countryside.

Canadians, however, were more than parts of an economy. Their identity was shaped by the powerful cultural forces of ethnicity and religion. Canada in 1867 was a state, but not a nation. There was no recognizable ethnicity called Canadian. Language, the most fundamental element of culture, separated a million francophones, and small numbers of Indians, Mennonites, and Gaelic-speaking Scots and Irish from 2.5 million anglophones. The Canadiens of Quebec and Ontario, the Acadians of New Brunswick and Nova Scotia, and the tiny Indian and Mennonite communities functioned as distinct societies, each containing elites that mediated between their own and the larger society. The anglophone majority, although it shared a common language, was far from being culturally homogeneous. For one thing, in sharp contrast to the Indians and francophones, the anglophones were relative newcomers. Most adult anglophones in 1867 either were born in the British Isles or were children of British emigrants, a factor of some significance when Canadians came to consider the nature of their identity. Moreover, British emigrants themselves were of diverse backgrounds. Although two-thirds of the population of the British Isles were English, two-thirds of the British emigrants who settled in Canada had come from the Celtic fringe. The Irish were the largest ethnic group in Ontario and New Brunswick, while Scots played the same role in Nova Scotia. To further complicate the ethnic pattern, a majority of Irish-Canadians were Protestants, while a small minority of Scots were Roman Catholics.

TABLE 3

ETHNICITY AND RELIGION OF CANADIANS 1871

	Canada	Ontario	Quebec	N.B.	N.S.
	3 485 761	1 620 851	1 191 576	285 594	387 800
Ethnicity		%	%	%	%
French	1 083 000	5	78	16	8
Irish	846 000	35	10	35	16
English	706 000	27	6	29	29
Scots	550 000	20	4	14	34
German	203 000	10	0.7	2	8
Dutch	30 000	1	–	2	1
Indian	23 000	0.8	0.6	0.5	0.4
Black	22 000	0.8	–	0.6	2
Religion		%	%	%	%
Roman Catholics	1 492 000	17	86	34	26
Methodists	562 000	29	3	9	10
Presbyterians	545 000	22	4	14	27
Church of England	494 000	20	5	16	14
Baptists	239 000	5	0.7	25	19

CENSUS OF CANADA, 1871, 1881, 1891.

Where people of a particular ethnic group settled in sufficient numbers, they were usually able to establish the institutions and maintain the family connections that sustained an ethnic identity. Since most emigration was family-centred, migrants from a single British family or village usually became a magnet drawing others from the same family or district into their Canadian settlement. Such settlement patterns were most obvious in rural areas, but they were also evident in the ethnic ghettos of towns and cities. Ethnicity was particularly influential where it was buttressed by religious tradition. Catholicism was a central feature of the French-Canadian identity and a powerful influence in many Irish and Scottish communities. Being French-Canadian was almost as synonymous with being Catholic as being English was with being Protestant. But both Irish-

and Scottish-Canadians were deeply divided along religious lines, and Irish and Scottish Catholic minorities usually lived apart from their Protestant compatriots.

In many ways, religion was the primary cultural institution. It defined the values and world view of its adherents. Intermarriage, particularly between Protestants and Catholics, was frowned upon and was uncommon. And while Quebec was a pillar of Catholic strength, the presence of Methodists, Free Presbyterians, Baptists, and low Anglicans in Ontario, New Brunswick, and Nova Scotia created a powerful evangelical Protestant influence in those provinces, one capable of dominating the debate on any public issue of the day.

These cultural patterns defined the ideological disputes and cultural confrontations that had shaped the politics of the 1850s. So too in the new country. The ultimate significance of ethnicity, particularly when coupled with religious tradition, was its capacity to generate a genuine nationality. Within the Canadian state of 1867, both Protestant British-Canadians and Catholic French-Canadians possessed that capacity. Much of the history of Canada's first half-century is the story of the efforts of both groups to achieve that goal.

Politics and Power

Political parties were the principal integrative element in the new Canada. The political party brought competing interests and groups together and forged the consensus necessary to govern the state. Even in 1867, only a coalition or party that could claim the allegiance of significant groups in every region and among the principal cultural groups could claim to be "national." By that definition, there was only one national political grouping in 1867, the Confederation or Liberal – Conservative Party headed by John A. Macdonald.

The colonies of British North America had traditionally contained political groupings that might be described as "court" and "country" – divisions based on the relationship that voters had to the central-governing elites in the colonial capitals. The court party in all four colonies had been Tory, established around the premises of loyalty to the British connection (both to the Crown and to political traditions), and in commitment to both a highly stratified society and an established Church of England. This official establishment had reflected the circumstances of the early Loyalist tradition following the American Revolution. Opposition to this tradition, when it emerged, was generally centred on "outsiders" in the society who saw themselves the objects of discrimination. The Reformers or Liberals appealed to colonists who differed from those who governed in the Loyalist tradition. These usually included people of particular religious and ethnic groups, often from particular statuses or occupations, and sometimes those from certain localities.

Even so, the differences between the parties were ones of emphasis rather than fundamental ideological divergence. For example, despite the insurrections of the 1830s, by 1864 no major political grouping in anglophone British North America challenged the British connection. The necessity of appealing to adult male freeholders and prosperous townsmen, the two groups that comprised the great majority of electors, led all parties to a similarity of viewpoint on such fundamental issues as national identity and the rights of property. The political heirs of the Upper Canada Tories, known as Conservatives by 1864, had jettisoned their insistence on an established Church of England (although they never embraced the principle of the separation of church and state), and they distinguished themselves from their Liberal opponents by a greater willingness to use the power of the state to promote economic development. The older traditions still persisted, however. Liberals were more likely to receive the support of adherents of the "free" churches – Methodists, Baptists, and Free Presbyterians who had opposed a Church of England establishment.

Only in Canada East did the pattern differ. There, from the 1840s, the dominant political tradition had been that of the bleus, a political organization dedicated to the preservation of a French Catholic society in the St. Lawrence valley. The ideals of the bleu stood in opposition both to those anglophones who wished to integrate the francophone into an anglophone society and to the rouge, a francophone liberal party with tendencies toward anticlericalism and republicanism.

The government of the Province of Canada before Confederation usually had consisted of a coalition of bleus, who represented a clear majority (often a large majority) of the members from Canada East, and Conservatives, who constituted a minority of those from Canada West. It was this unequal alliance that provoked cries of "French domination" in Canada West and created the political instability that made the first Canadian union so unstable. The situation changed dramatically in 1864 when Liberals, who commanded a majority in Canada West, joined in a coalition with the bleus and the Conservatives to create the government that set about to achieve a confederation of the colonies of British North America. The leaders of these parties – George Brown, George-Étienne Cartier, and John A. Macdonald – the first a passionate Free Presbyterian and Scottish-born owner of the Toronto *Globe*, the second a francophone

Montreal corporation lawyer, and the third a Scottish-born Kingston lawyer, were the principal architects of the new federal union. Although Brown and a number of Liberals withdrew from the coalition after Confederation, this coalition remained the core of the first Canadian national party.

The political parties of New Brunswick and Nova Scotia were similar to those of Canada West. A Liberal administration, drawing heavily on country support, "free" church adherents, prohibitionists, and new wealth, wrested power from the respectable New Brunswick Tory patricians in the 1850s. This mildly reformist government of new men, headed by Charles Fisher and Leonard Tilley, retained power until the first Confederation election of 1865. In Nova Scotia the Conservatives, drawing heavily from the towns and from Anglicans and Baptists, succeeded in toppling Joseph Howe's Liberals in 1862. Under the leadership of Charles Tupper, an Amherst physician, they held power until Confederation had been achieved. The process of Confederation profoundly altered the party system of the Atlantic colonies. The unity of the New Brunswick Liberals was shattered when Tilley and most of the party supported Confederation; a minority joined the Tory opposition to create the short-lived anti-Confederation government that governed New Brunswick in 1865-66 before it too disintegrated into pro and anti-Confederation factions. Most Nova Scotia Confederationists were Conservatives but they were supported by a number of Liberals.[2]

The dominant pro-Confederationist alliances in all three colonies came together in a single nationwide party in 1867. In the election of that year, the party elected majorities from the representatives of all provinces except Nova Scotia. Arrayed against this party was a collection of provincially based opposition parties, some of which had to carry the claim that they were disloyal to the new Canadian state. Successful in the first national election, the Liberal–Conservative Party dominated the politics of Canada for a generation following Confederation. Macdonald's great political strength was his ability to conciliate and bring a number of diverse and sometimes antagonistic groups together in the political arena. His party was a coalition of these interests, held together in part

---

[2] Peter Waite's *The Life and Times of Confederation* (Toronto, 1964) remains the best overview of the Confederation period. For background on political parties in the uniting colonies see J.M.S. Careless, *The Union of the Canadas* (Toronto, 1968) and W.S. MacNutt, *The Atlantic Provinces: The Emergence of a Colonial Society, 1712-1857* (Toronto, 1965). On Macdonald and party organization, see Gordon Stewart, "John A. Macdonald's Greatest Triumph," *CHR* (1982). On ethnicity, religion, and occupational structure see A.G. Darroch and M.D. Ornstein, "Ethnicity and Occupational Structure in Canada in 1871: The Vertical Mosaic in Historical Perspective," *CHR* (1980).

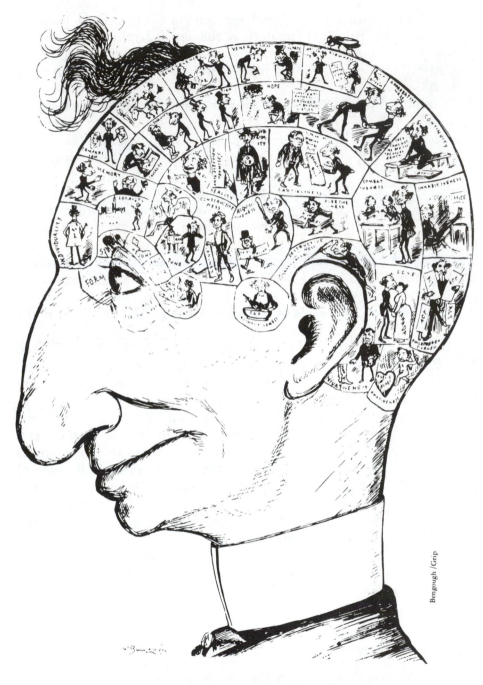

Phrenological Chart of the Head of the Country

by a commitment to the constitutional and social status quo and in part by the promise of a place in public life and a share of the jobs and contracts that were government patronage. Macdonald, for example, could assure Catholic bishops that a fair proportion of public positions would go to Catholics and that their nominees for the position would be given favourable consideration. Through effective use of patronage, Macdonald forged a powerful national organization linking every community with the centre.

John A. Macdonald became prime minister of the Dominion of Canada on July 1, 1867. Although the new constitution was the product of compromise, its central tenets – and notably those that conferred great powers on the federal government while restricting those of the provinces – faithfully reflected Macdonald's vision of the new state. With the instruments of state at his disposal, Macdonald used patronage to build a powerful party organization. The power was exercised in several ways. It sometimes consisted in the conferring of material benefits such as honours, jobs, or contracts on the faithful. In another form, it simply conferred privilege of association – the right to approach and advise those in positions of power. At the level of the interest group, it offered a sense of security that the party (and through it the state) would protect the welfare of the group. Patronage committed individuals and interests to the leader and to the party.

With 72 senatorships to confer and a new cabinet to build, the possibilities were extensive, even at the highest levels of the government. Macdonald's first cabinet was selected to reflect the new country's major regional, ethnic, and religious groups. Four cabinet ministers were named from each of the Maritimes, Quebec, and Ontario. An Irish Catholic was appointed from the Maritimes and an anglophone Protestant from Quebec. The other Maritime and Ontario ministers were Protestants and the remainder from Quebec were Catholics. With the exception of Brown (who had left the coalition) and Tupper, the Confederation leaders from each province had a seat in the cabinet along with all the government leaders of the former colonies. Tupper was omitted to provide a place for a Maritime Catholic. The cabinet also contained representatives of all the pre-Confederation Reform and Conservative parties in Ontario and Nova Scotia. Both New Brunswick ministers had been Reformers. All of the francophone members had been bleus.

Having formed a government, Macdonald went to the electorate in the late summer of 1867. His government won 101 seats in the House of

Commons to 80 for the opposition parties. The government party won in Ontario, won overwhelmingly in Quebec, and split New Brunswick. It lost Nova Scotia 18 to 1.

Expansion and Consolidation

In the wake of Confederation, people talked of doing great things. Newspaper editors and public figures wrote and spoke of creating a nationality and of duplicating the American achievements of nation building. The first few years produced the fervent idealism of a few young men from Ontario and Nova Scotia, united in a movement they called Canada First, which dreamed of promoting a Canadian national feeling and of creating a great British nation in North America. The economy was buoyant and the British and American markets for Canadian food and wood products remained strong. The idea of creating a state that would integrate all the remnants of the Second British Empire from the colony of Newfoundland to the colony of Vancouver Island into a single nation was central to all of the discussion.

Completing Confederation was the first task of the new government. The British North America Act anticipated the inclusion of the other British colonies, and the drive to the West began within months of the Dominion's creation. Unlike eastern expansion, the move into the West was unencumbered by the presence of strong autonomous colonies that first had to be conciliated.

Control of the vast interior of northern North America rested in the hands of the Hudson's Bay Company, a British chartered company that had been given a trading monopoly over Rupert's Land in 1670. Rupert's Land consisted of all the territory drained by rivers flowing into Hudson Bay, and in 1867 it was home to about 70 000 people, nearly 60 000 of whom were Indians. The commercial economy of the territory was centred on the fur trade, which the Hudson's Bay Company conducted through an intricate trading network with the various Indian peoples. Most of the non-Indians in the territory were the Métis offspring of French or Scottish men and Indian women. Traditionally, they acted as intermediaries between the company and the Indians. By the time of Confederation, most of the Métis had settled in parishes along the Red and Assiniboine rivers near the company headquarters at Fort Garry (Winnipeg). There, they settled in two geographically extended communities, one French and Catholic, the other English and Protestant. These constituted the only concentration of population in Rupert's Land. The Red River settlement was augmented by a few thousand British, mostly employees or former employees of the company, and by a small colony of Canadians on the western edge of the settlement. Some settlers engaged in small-scale agriculture, but for most residents of Rupert's Land, the economy rested on the buffalo hunt and the fur trade.

A Riel Ugly Position

In December 1867, Parliament passed a joint address of the House of Commons and the Senate requesting the transfer of the North West to Canada. The British government, anxious to shed responsibility for a continental territory already under pressure by the westward expansion of the United States, was only too ready to comply. Two cabinet ministers, Cartier and William McDougall, were dispatched to England to arrange the terms of the transfer. In exchange for £300 000, a grant of 1/20 of the lands of the southern prairies, and a monopoly of the fur trade, the Hudson's Bay Company yielded a territory more than 2 000 000 square miles (5 200 000 km²) in size. In June 1869, Parliament created a provisional government for the Northwest Territories (formerly Rupert's Land) consisting of a governor and an appointed council. McDougall was appointed governor and set out for Fort Garry to take possession of the territories on December 1, the date on which the transfer was to occur.

The rapid Canadian advance into the West came to an abrupt end before McDougall arrived. The acquisition of the territory had been a tripartite arrangement involving Canada, the company, and the imperial government. In the West, as in the East, the wishes of the local population had never been considered. To make matters worse, the Canadians at Red River treated the impending annexation as a triumph. Led by John Christian Schultz, the Canadian Party had the support of the Canada First movement and of George Brown's *Globe*. Surveyors from Canada entered the settlement even before the transfer was completed and began the process of marking off the land for settlement without regard for the rights of existing settlers. The French Métis of the area, alarmed at the implications of the Canadian takeover, shared the fears of their missionary clergy, most of whom had been recruited in France, that the new order would undermine the Roman Catholic faith. In the absence of their bishop, A. A. Taché, who was attending the First Vatican Council, leadership of the French Métis passed to Louis Riel. A few years earlier, Riel had returned from Montreal where he had studied theology and law. Under his leadership, armed French Métis resisted the takeover of their land by Canada and turned McDougall back at the border on October 31. Three days later Riel's men seized Fort Garry. When the Canadian settlers at Red River attempted to oppose the seizure, in response to a proclamation by McDougall, they were captured and imprisoned by Riel's men. At this point, the Canadian government refused to accept transfer of the territories until order had been restored.

Louis Riel, seen in an 1868 photograph taken in Montreal when he was 24, sparked two rebellions in the West.

GLENBOW ARCHIVES, CALGARY/NA-2631-1.

Having acted with violence, the Métis leadership now tried desperately to consolidate their precarious position. First, Riel attempted to win the support of the other half of the settlement by inviting the Scottish "half-breeds" to send representatives to a convention that would determine the future of the settlement. The convention then prepared a bill of rights setting out its terms for annexation by Canada. At the urging of Donald Smith, the chief factor (general manager) of the Hudson's Bay Company, the convention also named delegates – all of whom were members of Riel's provisional government – to go to Ottawa to discuss union with the Canadian government. The bill of rights was then amended by Riel, by the delegates, and by the Catholic bishop of St. Boniface, to include demands for provincial status and for state-supported Roman Catholic schools.

Meanwhile, the Canadians rallied once more and attempted to take Fort Garry. The effort was easily thwarted, and the Canadians imprisoned. One of the prisoners, Thomas Scott, a young Irish Protestant settler from Ontario, so irritated his captors that he was put to death by Riel's order. The news of Scott's murder rekindled all the ethnic and religious tensions of the pre-Confederation period and poisoned the atmosphere in which the admission of the North West was carried through.

Nonetheless, the delegates from the Red River met with the Canadian government in the spring of 1870. The central personality was Cartier. He insisted that the new territories not be simply cultural extensions of Ontario. There would be a small province centred on the Red River settlement, and the constitution of that province would resemble that of Quebec rather than Ontario, New Brunswick, or Nova Scotia. The subsequent Manitoba Act (1870) provided for the equality of the English and French languages in the legislature and courts of the new province and for public support for both Protestant and Roman Catholic schools. The Métis were to receive 1 400 000 acres (566 580 ha) of land, and, in the meantime, each head of household received land scrip worth $160. With the passage of the Manitoba Act, the Hudson's Bay Company transferred its rights to the British Crown, and the Crown, by order-in-council, transferred the entire territory of Rupert's Land to Canada on July 15, 1870. This was followed by the dispatch of a largely British military expedition to the Red River settlement and the formal annexation of the territory. Riel fled, and the organization of the new province proceeded peacefully. The issue of the Red River settlement had been resolved. Manitoba, a tiny "postage stamp" province, obtained its own

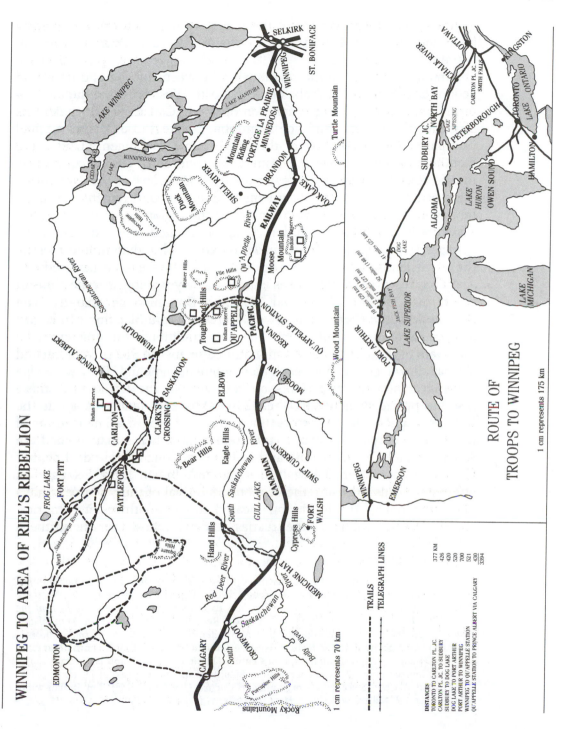

WINNIPEG TO AREA OF RIEL'S REBELLION

LAKE WINNIPEG

CEDAR LAKE

LAKE WINNIPEGOSIS

LAKE MANITOBA

SELKIRK

WINNIPEG

ST. BONIFACE

Turtle Mountain

Riding Mountain

PORTAGE LA PRAIRIE

MINNEDOSA

BRANDON

OAK LAKE

Duck Mountain

SHELL RIVER

Porcupine Hills

RAILWAY

Moose Mountain

Indian Reserve

Qu'Appelle River

Beaver Hills

File Hills

QU'APPELLE

QU'APPELLE STATION

PACIFIC

REGINA

Wood Mountain

Saskatchewan River

PRINCE ALBERT

Indian Reserve

HUMBOLDT

SASKATOON

Touchwood Hills

Indian Reserve

CARLTON

CLARK'S CROSSING

ELBOW

South Saskatchewan River

FROG LAKE

FORT PITT

BATTLEFORD

Bear Hills

Eagle Hills

GULL LAKE

SWIFT CURRENT

CANADIAN

MOOSE JAW

North Saskatchewan River

Eagle Hills

Hand Hills

Cypress Hills

FORT WALSH

MEDICINE HAT

EDMONTON

Red Deer River

South Saskatchewan River

Saskatchewan River

CALGARY

CROWFOOT

Belly River

Bow River

Porcupine Hills

Rocky Mountains

1 cm represents 70 km

TRAILS

TELEGRAPH LINES

ROUTE OF TROOPS TO WINNIPEG

OTTAWA

CHALK RIVER

KINGSTON

CARLTON PL. JC.

SMITH FALLS

NORTH BAY

SUDBURY JC.

LAKE NIPISSING

PETERBOROUGH

TORONTO

LAKE ONTARIO

HAMILTON

ALGOMA

LAKE HURON

OWEN SOUND

DOG LAKE

PORT ARTHUR

JACK FISH BAY

11 miles (17 km)

25 miles (40 km)

19 miles (31 km)

17 miles (27 km)

29 miles (46 km)

LAKE SUPERIOR

LAKE MICHIGAN

WINNIPEG

EMERSON

1 cm represents 175 km

DISTANCES

	KM
TORONTO TO CARLTON PL. JC.	377
CARLTON PL. JC. TO SUDBURY	426
SUDBURY TO DOG LAKE	420
DOG LAKE TO PORT ARTHUR	520
PORT ARTHUR TO WINNIPEG	700
WINNIPEG TO QU'APPELLE STATION	521
QU'APPELLE STATION TO PRINCE ALBERT VIA CALGARY	430
	3394

government. The remainder of the north-western territories was to be governed by a Canadian viceroy who would serve as Ottawa's agent in opening the Prairies.[3]

Land was the key to the relationship between Canada and its newly acquired territories. Manitoba and the North West provided the agricultural base for the coming generation of young Canadians. To make this possible, the Crown lands of Manitoba, unlike those of the original provinces, were retained by the Dominion Government. Under the Dominion Lands Act, every legitimate head of family could acquire title to 160 (64.75 ha) acres of Crown land in Manitoba or the Northwest Territories after three years' settlement. Every encouragement was given to Canadian and European settlement of the region.

Before this new social order could be created, the old had to be displaced. Arrangements were made to extinguish Indian title to most of the fertile lands of the southern Prairies. Indians were to be gathered into scattered reserves where, it was expected, they would learn the skills of the farmer. Between 1871 and 1877 the Dominion negotiated seven treaties with the Crees, Chippewas, Ojibways, and Blackfoot. In return for the surrender of all claims to their traditional hunting grounds, members of these tribes received initial payments of $12 per person and annual allowances of $5 for each man, women, and child. They were also granted communal land rights on reserves. In the fertile belt, these reserves provided about 640 acres (259 ha) for each family. Why did the Indians acquiesce to this destruction of their way of life? The traditional prairie economy had rested on the great buffalo herds that roamed the American and Canadian grasslands. These had long been in decline, but by the 1870s they had largely disappeared. Indian leaders sought an alternate means to ensure the economic survival of their people. Chiefs like Crowfoot of the Blackfoot, located in the southwestern Prairies, could see no alternative to the treaties. And even those in more northern

---

[3] The American threat to the West is discussed in A.C. Glueck, *Minnesota and the Manifest Destiny of the Canadian North West* (Toronto, 1966). On eastern views of the West see Douglas Owram, *Promise of Eden: The Canadian Expansion Movement and the Idea of the West, 1856-1900* (Toronto, 1980). On the first Riel Rebellion see W.L. Morton, *Manitoba: A History* (Toronto, 1957); "Introduction" to *Alexander Begg's Red River Journal* (Toronto, 1960), and George Stanley, *The Birth of Western Canada* (Toronto, 1936). On the Manitoba Act, see Donald Creighton, *Canada's First Century* (Toronto, 1970); Ralph Heintzman, "The Spirit of Confederation: Professor Creighton, Biculturalism and the Use of History," *CHR*, (1971), and Alastair Sweeney, *George-Etienne Cartier* (Toronto, 1976). On Indian-white relations see J.R. Miller, *Skyscrapers Hide the Heavens* (Toronto, 1989).

areas, like Big Bear and Poundmaker of the Crees, who at first refused to accept the treaties, were at length driven by hunger into the government's net.

Even as the integration of the Prairies into a Canadian social order began, the completion of a transcontinental state drew near. The two British colonies on the Pacific Coast – Vancouver Island and British Columbia – had united in 1866. Despite its large size and extensive natural resources, the united colony contained only about 25 000 Indians settled in the coastal areas and scattered through the interior, and 10 000 non-Indians, concentrated in coastal areas around Georgia Strait. The Vancouver Island settlement was dominated by the Hudson's Bay Company. On the mainland, the gold rush of the 1850s had receded, leaving only a small residue of the former population, numerous abandoned settlements, and a public debt of more than one million dollars. For all intents and purposes, the colony was bankrupt.

The colony did not have responsible government, and authority was exercised by a British governor and a legislative council composed of both appointed and elected members. In the circumstances, the imperial government took the initiative for confederation of British Columbia and Canada. In 1869, a new governor, Anthony Musgrave, was dispatched to the colony. His instructions, published shortly after his arrival, declared the intention to promote a union with Canada. The colonists had little choice but to comply. Following a protracted debate, the legislative council acquiesced to the imperial decision, and Musgrave appointed three delegates to go to Ottawa to negotiate the terms of the union. With the largest per capita debt in British North America, the colony desperately needed external resources to carry the debt and to provide capital for colonial development. For the latter, a transportation link to the East was essential.

Ottawa was generous. The British Columbians got agreement from the federal government to assume the public debt of the province, to undertake a public works program, to provide an annual subsidy, and to begin construction of a transcontinental railway line within three years. The latter was to be completed within ten years, although there was general agreement among the delegates that the completion date was flexible. British Columbia would also have six members of Parliament instead of only the two or three members to which it was entitled by population.

The railway proposal provoked a storm of controversy in the East. Even the Ontario caucus of the Conservative Party threatened to vote against the project when the agreement came to Parliament for ratification. That incipient mutiny was only quelled after Cartier intervened and threatened to bring down the government if the agreement did not pass. British Columbia duly became part of Canada on July 20, 1871. In just four years the western strategy had been completed.[4] In 1880, the imperial government transferred its remaining Arctic territory to Canada.

Expansion and consolidation eastward took much longer. From the beginning, opposition to the Confederation scheme had been centred in the eastern colonies. Newfoundland and Prince Edward Island had refused to enter the union. Moreover, though a majority of the Nova Scotia assembly had acquiesced in the union, the assembly did not reflect the popular will of Nova Scotians. Following Confederation the furious anticonfederates summoned Joseph Howe, the old "tribune of the people" and former Liberal premier, to their cause. In the summer of 1867, they set about to repeal the union. In the federal and provincial elections of that season they won 18 of the 19 seats in the House of Commons and virtually all of those in the Nova Scotia assembly.

Early in 1868, Howe went to London with a petition from the assembly demanding repeal of the union. There was no possibility that the imperial government would agree. Howe was, nonetheless, a problem. An ardent imperialist who had advocated the union of Nova Scotia into the United Kingdom, he could claim the support of a considerable segment of influential English public opinion. It was in the interests of both the Canadian and British governments, therefore, that Howe's anticonfederation influence be neutralized as soon as possible. The colonial secretary brought Howe and Tupper together in London for a series of meetings. Howe had to face the reality that Britain would do nothing to placate Nova Scotia. The option of an autonomous Nova Scotia within the British Empire did not exist. The only alternatives were to remain within the Dominion or to engage in an act of rebellion against the Queen. While the anticonfederate attorney-general of Nova Scotia was prepared to consider just such a course of action, Howe would not contemplate it. Under the circumstances, he acquiesced. So, just as the colonial secretary was arranging the transfer of Rupert's Land to Canada,

---

[4] The best study of British Columbia in the period of Confederation is still Margaret Ormsby, *British Columbia: A History* (Toronto, 1958).

he was also assuring the defeat of the Nova Scotia repeal movement. In September 1868, Howe accepted the federal government's offer of better terms – a $19 000-a-year increase in the federal subsidy to Nova Scotia – and entered Macdonald's cabinet as secretary of state for the provinces. His defection undermined the repeal movement, and several anticonfederate members of Parliament eventually moved to support the government. The repeal movement continued as an undercurrent in the political life of Nova Scotia, but it never again captured the popular imagination as it had in 1867–68.

Prince Edward Island posed a different sort of problem to Canadian interests. It contained a population nearly as large as that of Manitoba, the Northwest Territories, and British Columbia combined, and possessed a significant agricultural economy. Even more important was its strategic location in the Gulf of St. Lawrence. In the hands of an unfriendly power it had the capacity to seriously threaten Canadian economic and strategic interests. The possibility of such action occurred in 1869 when the Island government attempted to form a free trade area with the United States, which would have given the Americans access to the major Maritime fisheries. Congressional representatives were received with full public honours by the provincial government, much to the displeasure of the imperial government whose response was to promote the integration of the Island into Canada. In 1869, the governor-general of Canada arrived on the Island, accompanied by Cartier and Tilley who offered a new financial arrangement to entice it into Confederation. The Island's Liberal government, after requesting the meeting, refused the terms. Nothing further developed until 1870 when the government of PEI decided to construct a railway using the public credit. Within two years, the Island was deeply in debt. At the critical moment in 1872, London refused to give further guarantees for Island bonds, and the major British creditors withdrew from the market. An embarrassed Island government was forced to approach the Canadian government and ask for terms. Canada agreed to assume the railway debt, to complete the process of buying out the Island's non-resident proprietors, to pay an annual subsidy, and to guarantee the communications link with the mainland. The arrangement was considerably less generous than that negotiated two years earlier with British Columbia. Moreover, the Island, with nearly three times the population of British Columbia, was given the same number of parliamentary seats as the western province. Prince Edward Island entered confederation on July 1,

1873. Its acquisition completed the nineteenth-century confederation process; periodic discussions with Newfoundland proved fruitless.[5]

British influence and authority had been central to the creation of the new Dominion. From the initial British efforts in New Brunswick in 1865 to the final intervention in PEI in 1873, imperial policy had aimed to create a Canadian state that would consolidate and assume responsibility for British interests in North America. The one remaining British responsibility was to ensure that the new state could live in a relatively harmonious relationship with the United States. There were a number of outstanding issues to be resolved. British sympathy for the South during the Civil War had left a legacy of bitterness toward Britain and British interests in the minds of many Americans. In addition, a number of boundary issues posed potential problems between Canada and the United States, including the use of the St. Lawrence River and Canadian canals, the settlement of the boundary in the Straits of San Juan de Fuca in British Columbia, and fishing rights in shared coastal waters.

The British and American governments agreed to discussions in Washington in 1871 to try to resolve these outstanding issues. A commission of four American and four British delegates was appointed and, as a matter of courtesy, Macdonald was invited to join the British delegation. Most issues dealt with by the commissioners related to Canada, but little consideration was given to the views of the Dominion. The imperial government was primarily concerned with conciliating American interests and with creating an environment in North America that would permit the peaceful development of the new Dominion. In this, subsequent events would show that the British largely succeeded.

Macdonald's goal was more specific: to achieve a reciprocity agreement with the Americans in return for permitting American access to Canadian fisheries. He failed in this; instead, the Americans were granted access to the fisheries and given unhindered navigation of the St. Lawrence River. Canadian gains were limited to free access for fish to American markets and navigation of Lake Michigan and the rivers of southern Alaska. American claims for damages arising out of British activities in the Civil War were referred to an arbitration procedure that

---

[5] On Nova Scotia, see Kenneth Pryke, *Nova Scotia and Confederation 1864-1874* (Toronto, 1979) and D.A. Muise, "Parties and Constituencies: Federal Elections in Nova Scotia 1867-1896," *CHAR* (1971). The standard work on P.E.I. is Francis Bolger, *Prince Edward Island and Confederation* (Charlottetown, 1964).

ultimately decided in favour of the Americans. The Treaty of Washington was finally ratified in Ottawa, but only after the British government agreed to compensate angry Canadians for most of the costs that the treaty imposed on the Dominion. The passage of the treaty, however, made it possible to withdraw the British troops who traditionally had garrisoned the forts and most of the major urban centres of British North America. The empire remained intact. But by 1871 its major costs and responsibilities in North America had been transferred to the new Dominion.[6]

Railways

The British and Canadian partnership in nation building had effectively ended by 1873. Thereafter, the development of the new state passed to the Canadian government. At first there was no clear consensus among Canadian leaders on development strategy. In 1870, for example, all shades of political opinion would have agreed that reciprocity with the United States was a desirable end, but legislators doubted the feasibility of constructing a transcontinental railway system ahead of settlement. A distinctive development policy for Canada only emerged in response to the political and economic issues of the 1870s. That policy was firmly established by 1885 and was not seriously challenged for half a century.

The one area where there was general agreement prior to 1873 was prairie settlement. The government's determination to achieve this old Upper Canadian dream was evident in the negotiations for the North West, in the retention of public lands in Manitoba, and in the passage of the Dominion Lands Act in 1872. To this had been added the guarantee, imposed over the opposition of much of the Conservative caucus, that a railway line would be constructed to British Columbia – someday.

The Macdonald government acted on the railway issue in 1872. In this, as in other great matters of state in the first Macdonald administration, the initiative was taken by Cartier. The line, it was decided, would be constructed privately but with public incentives sufficient to entice

---

[6] The theme of British withdrawal has been addressed by a number of scholars, most notably W.L. Morton in *The Critical Years* and C.P. Stacey in "Britain's Withdrawal from North America," *CHR* (1955).

capitalists to invest in such a dubious undertaking. Two groups of investors competed for the right to undertake the construction: a Montreal syndicate under the leadership of Sir Hugh Allan and one at Toronto formed by a close friend of Macdonald's, Senator David MacPherson. For political reasons, Macdonald repeatedly tried, without success, to bring the two syndicates together. In the spring of 1872, Cartier introduced the Canadian Pacific Railway bill into Parliament. It provided that a railway line would be constructed from Nipissing, Ontario, to the Pacific within 10 years. The company prepared to undertake this contract would receive $30 million in public funds and 50 000 000 acres (20 235 000 ha) of public lands.

Within months of passage of the CPR bill, Macdonald went to the country for the first test of his mandate. The election was fought on the issues of the great cost of the new railway and the humiliation suffered by Canada in the Treaty of Washington. The Conservative Party barely escaped electoral defeat in the election of 1872. Macdonald managed a stand-off with the opposition in New Brunswick and Nova Scotia (actually a considerable improvement over his 26-8 defeat in 1867), carried Quebec 38-27, and lost Ontario 38-50. That threw the election into the West and the Conservatives' final six-vote majority was entirely found in British Columbia where the province's voters returned six Conservatives and saved their eastern patron.

Macdonald remained in power long enough to complete the work of his first term. In the autumn, the CPR charter was given to Sir Hugh Allan and a syndicate having representation from across the country. In 1873, the government created a Department of the Interior and established the North-West Mounted Police – designed to administer the Northwest Territories – and admitted Prince Edward Island. Then a series of catastrophes rocked and finally destroyed the government.

Early in 1873, the Liberals charged that the Conservative Party, through Cartier and Macdonald, had received significant financial benefits from Sir Hugh Allan. At almost the same time Cartier, the most able member of the cabinet, died. Macdonald appointed a royal commission to examine the Liberals' charges that the Conservative Party had received $320 000 from Allan during the 1872 election. The commission upheld those charges and revealed that the syndicate's principal backers were American, a fact Macdonald would almost certainly have been aware of throughout the negotiations. To make a bad situation worse, the beleaguered Allan syndicate surrendered its charter. The governor-general advised the government to resign. Macdonald, still hoping for the support of the Commons, met the House on October 23. On November 5,

"WE IN CANADA SEEM TO HAVE LOST ALL IDEA OF JUSTICE, HONOR AND INTEGRITY."—THE MAIL, 26TH SEPTEMBER.

C-8449/NATIONAL ARCHIVES OF CANADA.

in the face of defections even from his own party, he submitted his resignation.

The Liberals won the election of 1874, taking nearly two-thirds of the Commons' seats. The new prime minister, Alexander Mackenzie, was a Scottish-born Ontario stonemason and a veteran of the pre-Confederation political wars in the Province of Canada. A Grit and a friend of George Brown, Mackenzie was one of a group of Liberals who had

Alexander Mackenzie, the first Liberal prime minister, was a dour stonemason, honest, incorruptible, and ordinarily no match for Macdonald.

C-20052/NATIONAL ARCHIVES OF CANADA.

followed Brown out of the Great Coalition. Ontario Liberals were generally Confederationists, but their allies in Quebec and Nova Scotia included a number of former anti-Confederationists from among the rouges of Quebec and the repealers of Nova Scotia. To all these were joined a number of anti-Conservative candidates recruited in the wake of the Pacific Scandal. The dominant figures in the government were from Ontario: apart from Mackenzie, there was the caustic finance minister, Richard Cartwright, descendant of Kingston Loyalists and a former Conservative member of Parliament; and the enigmatic Edward Blake, brilliant son of a Low-Church Irish parson. Blake and Mackenzie had both served in the Ontario cabinet. The evangelical origins of the party's leader were reflected in his political style: stuffy and somewhat self-righteous, but honest. He and his party stood in sharp contrast to the general pattern of Canadian public life, which had been characterized by patronage and often by corruption.

In fact, there were few policy differences between the Conservatives and the new Liberal coalition. Mackenzie's commercial policy, like that of Macdonald, was to seek reciprocity with the United States. One of his first acts after assuming power was to dispatch George Brown to Washington to negotiate a reciprocity agreement in return for American use of the Canadian fisheries. The proposed treaty would have covered a wide range of natural and manufactured products. In the end the arrangement failed because the American administration would not push it through the Senate.

Liberal railway policy also differed little in principle from that of the Conservatives. Railways were the key to consolidation and development. The Liberals inherited major Conservative railway commitments designed to integrate the eastern and western sections of the country with the centre. To the East, the Intercolonial Railway, linking Halifax to Rivière du Loup, was about two-thirds completed by 1874. A substantial part of its construction cost had been guaranteed by the British government, and its purpose was to link two well-settled regions with significant domestic markets. The Liberals completed construction and opened the line in 1876. In the West, the Liberals recognized Manitoba as a potential area of settlement and were prepared to begin construction of a rail line linking northwestern Ontario to Winnipeg. They probably would have preferred that construction be undertaken by a private firm, but after 1873 there was no consortium willing to take the risks. So western railways, like those in the East, became public undertakings. The Pacific Railway Act was passed in 1874. It provided that the all-Canadian route would run by water from southern Ontario to Fort William. From there, a complex of railway, lakes, and rivers would link the head of Lake Superior to Winnipeg.

The one line the Liberal government ignored was that to British Columbia. The proposal to run a railway through 1500 miles (2400 km) of empty land across mountain ranges seemed preposterous, an exorbitant charge to the Canadian taxpayers. The contract with British Columbia would be honoured only when circumstances permitted. Neither pressures from London nor demands from British Columbia could move the government from this position, and there the matter stood until 1878. In the end, Mackenzie accepted a compromise in which the deadline for completion of the line was extended to 1890, and the government agreed to construct the Esquimault and Nanaimo railways as compensation. Many Liberals, including Blake, objected even to that commitment.

The Liberals were also concerned with political and civil rights. Under the influence of Blake, they introduced the use of the secret ballot to replace the old tradition where each elector voted by publicly stating his preference to the poll clerk. They also established the Supreme Court of Canada and made it the final court of appeal for most Canadian court cases. Finally, they passed the Canada Temperance Act, which permitted voters in each municipality to determine whether or not their district would prohibit the sale of alcoholic beverages.[7]

The Liberal failure to make greater use of public enterprise, particularly in the construction of railways, was only partly a question of principle. The financial capacity of the government was constrained by the severe economic downturn that began in the autumn of 1874 and, as a result of bad harvests and the failure of international markets, persisted throughout the next four years. The value of domestic exports began to fall in 1875 and continued until 1879. The value of imports also fell, as did federal government revenues, more than 70 percent of which were raised through import duties. Inevitably every part of the Canadian economy felt the impact, and every commercial operation suffered. Federal revenues, which had reached $20.4 million in 1874, fell to $17.5 million in 1876.

---

[7] The political history of this period is best told through the biographies of its principal players: Dale Thomson, *Alexander Mackenzie: Clear Grit* (Toronto, 1960); J.M.S. Careless, *Brown of the Globe: Statesman of Confederation* (Toronto, 1963); Joseph Schull, *Edward Blake: The Man of the Other Way* (Toronto, 1975); Donald Creighton, *Sir John A. Macdonald: The Old Chieftain* (Toronto, 1955). See also W.R. Graham, "Liberal Nationalism in the 1870's," *CHAR* (1946), and A.A. Den Otter, "Nationalism and the Pacific Scandal," *CHR* (1988).

By 1878, the Liberal government faced an increasingly disgruntled electorate. Urged by some of his party to resort to a protectionist policy to defend Canadian manufacturing interests against foreign competition – and incidentally to increase revenues – Mackenzie refused. The last Liberal budget continued the policy of low tariffs and low taxation. It was this decision that provided the formerly discredited Macdonald with the opportunity to appear as the defender of the Canadian national interest. The National Policy, as it was called, was a description of the fiscal position that the Liberals had left open to the Conservatives. Although he had toyed with the idea for sometime, Macdonald's decision to espouse the policy was made only after the Liberals brought down the 1878 budget. The policy was not very clearly defined before the election. It seemed more a general philosophy than a conceived course of action. In its broadest terms, the National Policy proposed to protect Canadian producers from "unfair" foreign competition, to create an integrated and largely self-sufficient economy, and to develop an industrial economy. If Canadians could not have reciprocity with Americans, then they would replicate the American economy.

This was a blatant appeal to self-interest in the name of national honour, and it succeeded. The election of 1878 reversed the results of 1874: the Conservatives were returned with almost two-thirds of the seats in the House of Commons. Macdonald's third government consisted essentially of the same people. Cartier's absence was a decided loss, although Hector Langevin would assume his mantle as Quebec chief within the cabinet. Cartier had played the leading policy role in the first government; Charles Tupper, the leading Nova Scotia Confederate, and Samuel Tilley, his New Brunswick counterpart, would be the principal architects of the National Policy. They monopolized the principal financial offices of cabinet throughout most of the 1880s.

The government quickly proceeded to implement its policy of economic nationalism. Tilley invited producers to tell him what they needed, and they did. Out of a welter of sometimes conflicting advice, requests, and demands, Tilley constructed a budget and presented it in March 1879. Commodities not produced in Canada, such as cotton and cotton mill machinery, generally were admitted duty free. Most products manufactured in Canada were given protection ranging from 20 percent to 35 percent of value. Many agricultural products, such as wheat and butter, and natural products, such as coal, were also given very substantial protection. Regional interests received special consideration. Nova Scotia coal would heat the houses of Montrealers, while Maritimers would eat Ontario flour. The beauty of the system seemed to be that, even though consumers might pay more for their products, the system would provide markets and security for the producers who were also the majority of consumers. It seemed to succeed as economic conditions improved after 1879 – although the Opposition suggested other factors were responsible – and Tilley gradually raised tariffs and expanded the variety of commodities on which they were imposed in successive budgets between 1880 and 1885. The tariff undoubtedly accomplished many of its ends. While there was some import substitution, many commodities continued to be imported and the higher tariffs yielded higher and higher federal revenues. Dominion receipts rose from $18.3 million in 1879 to $29.3 million in 1882, providing the resources that permitted the federal government to play a more active role in the economy.

Meanwhile, Macdonald contended with the problem of the transcontinental railway. The Conservative leadership had never accepted the Liberal policy of building the line to British Columbia only as public revenues permitted. Rapid completion of the line required a private consortium with a large public subsidy. It was, however, difficult to find any group of capitalists willing to risk the necessary resources in the face of the continuing recession. That problem was resolved in 1880 when Montreal Conservatives arranged a meeting between the prime minister and a group of Scottish-Canadian Montreal businessmen headed by George Stephen, president of the Bank of Montreal, and his cousin, Donald Smith, chief factor of the Hudson's Bay Company, who had played a mjaor role in the Red River crisis. Both Stephen and Smith had made sizable fortunes in western American railway speculations.

The new syndicate struck a hard bargain. They would build a railway from Lake Nipissing to Fort William and from Winnipeg to Kamloops. In return they wanted incorporation as a private company that would own the railway. The government would provide a subsidy of $25 million and 25 million acres (10 million ha) of arable land, a territory larger than the combined areas of New Brunswick and Prince Edward Island. In addition, the company was to receive the already-completed government railways in Ontario and in British Columbia, together valued at over $30 million. No federally incorporated railway was to run southeast of the main line of Canadian Pacific Railway. The railway property was to be free from taxation forever. Again, as in 1872, even the Conservative backbenchers were unhappy with the generous terms of the contract. This time, it was Tupper who whipped them into line. Against bitter opposition, the Canadian Pacific Railway bill finally became law in February 1881.

The construction of the CPR main line quickly took on the appearance of a great national feat. An American railwayman, William Van Horne, was brought in to supervise construction, and work proceeded apace from both east and west. At the same time, the company bought several Ontario lines to give it access to a number of eastern markets and allow it to compete with the Grand Trunk. But the costs were enormous. By late 1883, despite the heavy public subsidies and the sale of stock on the British and European markets, the railway was virtually bankrupt. When Stephen approached Macdonald for a loan of $30 million, the prime minister's worst fears seemed realized: the line would be a bottomless pit that would consume the public credit of Canada without yielding any return. Edward Blake's almost pathological opposition to the line seemed justified. Conservative members of Parliament – this time from Quebec and the Maritimes – were opposed to granting further subsidies. In the end, Tupper got the bill authorizing the loan through Parliament, but only by granting subsidies to railway lines in Quebec and to projects in the Maritimes.

It was not enough. Within a year Stephen was back, desperate for more money. Macdonald beat his own caucus into submission only by threatening to resign as prime minister. To appease the 50 Quebec and 27 New Brunswick and Nova Scotia Conservatives, the CPR agreed to make terminuses of Quebec City and Saint John by buying or constructing a railway between Montreal and Quebec and by constructing a short line from Montreal to Saint John. This last injection of public capital made completion of the railway possible in November 1885. The railway was thus the creation of a complex integration of public and private initiative and capital. Although the government perceived the CPR as an integral and essential part of national development, it remained a private corporation operated for private profit. The political process necessary to its completion, however, transformed it from a Montreal-Vancouver railway to a transcontinental line reaching eastward to Quebec City and Saint John.[8]

------

[8] The view of the development of the National Policy and the CPR from the perspective of the leader is given in Donald Creighton's *Sir John A. Macdonald: The Old Chieftain* (Toronto, 1955). On the National Policy see Benjamin Forster, *A Conjunction of Interests: Business, Politics and Tariffs, 1825-1829* (Toronto, 1986); John Dales, *The Protective Tariff in Canada's Development* (Toronto, 1966); John Dales, "Protection, Immigration and Canadian Nationalism," and Craig Brown, "The Nationalism of the National Policy," both in Peter Russell, ed., *Nationalism in Canada* (Toronto, 1966). On the CPR see Heather Gilbert, *Awakening Continent: The Life of Lord Mount Stephen*, vol. I (Aberdeen, 1965), and the popular accounts by Pierre Berton, *The National Dream* (Toronto, 1971) and *The Last Spike* (Toronto, 1972).

Even the 1885 political negotiations that permitted completion of the line might have failed had Van Horne not been able to demonstrate that the CPR was indispensable to the national interest in the North-West Rebellion. The underlying causes of that rebellion were found in the relationship between the Northwest Territories and the federal government. Ottawa governed the Territories as a colony through a lieutenant-governor and a council responsible to the minister of the interior. There had been many complaints from the Indians and Métis and from new settlers that Ottawa and its western bureaucracy were unresponsive to the needs of the inhabitants of the Territories. There was even talk of rebellion in the newspapers of Edmonton and Prince Albert.

Feelings ran particularly high among the several thousand Métis living along the South Saskatchewan River. Most were emigrés from Manitoba who had built farms around a settlement at Batoche. In 1884, a delegation headed by Gabriel Dumont, a man of exceptional organizational abilities, journeyed south to Montana and persuaded Louis Riel to return to join his people in their coming struggle. Although now an American citizen, the charismatic Riel quickly established his leadership among the Métis. Even the church did not oppose his claim. Riel believed that God had created the Métis as a chosen people and called him to create a nation in the middle of North America. In March 1885, he proclaimed the formation of a provisional Métis government at Batoche. The North-West Mounted Police superintendent at Fort Carlton, 20 miles (32 km) away, responded by sending 100 men to Duck Lake to prevent the Métis from seizing arms and ammunition located there. Dumont met the force at Duck Lake. In the ensuing skirmish, 12 members of the Mounted Police party were killed and 11 others wounded. News of the Duck Lake "massacre" reached Ottawa during discussions over the last CPR loan, and Van Horne offered to transport Canadian troops to the Saskatchewan within 11 days.

The defeat of the Mounted Police encouraged a number of young men among the Cree bands of the North Saskatchewan area to take up arms. The Cree had long been unhappy with the treaties of the 1870s because they had been provided with widely separated reserves that divided their people. Added to this grievance was the final destruction of the buffalo herds. The Indian Act of 1876 completed the process, making the Indian peoples effectively minor wards of the state under an often unsympathetic Indian service. By 1880, the Indian bands were dependent on the food supplied by Indian agents. The principal Cree chiefs, Big Bear and Poundmaker, tried to restrain their people, but the fighting men of the bands were caught up in the fever. Within four days of the defeat at Duck

JAMES PETERS/NATIONAL ARCHIVES OF CANADA. C-3453.

All Canada rallied behind the military expedition sent west to put down the 1885 rebellion. Military commander General Fred Middleton, the corpulent figure seen standing at the right (above), was no strategist. His men, shown relaxing in camp (below), were largely untrained; they won out through weight of numbers and pluck.

SASKATCHEWAN ARCHIVES/N-A-444.

Lake, the Mounted Police abandoned Fort Pitt on the North Saskatche-wan and moved to Battleford, which was under virtual seige as hundreds of Cree warriors pillaged the surrounding countryside. A more serious event occurred on April 2 when warriors from Big Bear's band attacked the Hudson's Bay Company post at Frog Lake and killed nine men in the assault.

For weeks, it seemed as if the authority of the Canadian state in the West might disintegrate. In retrospect, such a view was absurd. Riel's Métis numbered no more than three or four thousand people, and even the Indians in the southern territories were considerably outnumbered by the rapidly expanding European population. A crucial factor in the rebellion was the decision of Crowfoot and the powerful Blackfoot Confederacy to remain neutral. Still, the reaction throughout the country was shock and, on the Prairies, fear. The Canadian government moved with uncharacteristic speed to quell the rebellion. Within days some 8000 men were called into service. The first reinforcements for the police were already on their way at the time of the Duck Lake massacre. More followed on the new Canadian Pacific Railway. Three Canadian forces were sent into the North-West: one to Batoche, one to Battleford, and one to Edmonton and Frog Lake. The main force, under General Middleton, left Qu'Appelle on April 6 and took Batoche on May 12. Riel surrendered three days later. Poundmaker surrendered on May 26 and Big Bear on July 2. The North-West Rebellion was over.

On May 23, Riel was brought to Regina for trial. He was found guilty of treason on July 31 and, despite appeals for royal clemency, was hanged on November 16, 1885. Riel's execution has been at the centre of a major debate among historians. A federal government, which had often ignored and neglected the native peoples of the Prairies, seems to have gone to extraordinary lengths to procure the death of the man who spoke for the neglected. Riel was an American citizen, and he may have been insane; nonetheless, he was convicted of high treason and his insanity ignored. He was tried before an all-white jury in the Northwest Territories rather than in Winnipeg. Many eastern anglophones still saw him as the murderer of Thomas Scott and as the leader of a savage band of frontierspeople. There can be no doubt that deep prejudices were involved in the debate following the rebellion.

The reasons for Riel's execution are as compelling as those against it. His responsibility in precipitating the rebellion was never in doubt. Many had died defending the authority of the Canadian state, and a small army had been required to re-establish its authority. The only legal defence for

Riel's actions was insanity, but Riel himself undermined that defence and, indeed, the evidence of insanity may reflect a highly ethnocentric view of normality on the part of his defenders. Certainly from the government's perspective Riel's death was a very satisfactory outcome. Macdonald's main concern was that Riel would provoke a general Indian uprising. When that did not occur, Macdonald was quite happy to permit the judicial system to dispose of the troublemaker. Certainly there would be no pardon. At first, Riel was viewed simply as a rebel by Eastern Canada. Differences in ethnic responses to Riel emerged after the North-West Rebellion, and, more than anything else, they reflect the influence of the media in shaping a coherent public opinion. As the Ontario press portrayed Riel as a francophone and a Catholic, the

The completion of the CPR in 1885 united the country from "sea unto sea." Donald Smith, later Lord Strathcona, drove the last spike in the line at Craigellachie, B.C.

C-3693/NATIONAL ARCHIVES OF CANADA.

Quebec press moved more and more to his defence. The transformation of Riel into a French-Canadian symbol occurred in the months following his trial. The growing crisis over the execution was reflected in the parliamentary vote on a motion, in March 1886, which deplored Riel's execution. Although the motion was defeated 146 to 52, the government lost the support of a majority of French-Canadian members and gained that of a significant number of anglophone Liberals. The real victims of the 1885 rebellion were the Indians. Eight joined Riel on the scaffold. For the rest the rebellion marked the end of their ability to influence the events that were shaping their future.[9]

The year 1885 marked the high water mark of the Conservative national policy. The CPR was finished, the only physical threat to federal authority had been eliminated, and the protective tariff seemed to be fulfilling the promises of its founders. The Conservatives remained in power for another 11 years but their major policies were completed by 1885. It was the Liberal Party that suggested new directions in the later eighties.

Leadership of the Liberals had passed in 1880 from Mackenzie to Edward Blake, who opposed the Pacific railway, the protective tariff, and the execution of Riel. A brilliant and conscientious man, he never fully accepted the venality, ferment, and compromises of political life. After having fought and lost the elections of 1882 and 1887, Blake determined to leave politics. His choice as a successor was a young Quebec Member of Parliament, Wilfrid Laurier. Blake's choice was not popular with many in the Liberal caucus, but it reflected the growth of Liberal support in Quebec in the election of 1887. Blake had his way, however, and in 1887 Laurier assumed the leadership of a divided and often dispirited party.

Division was most obvious in the debate over the execution of Riel, which had been opposed by Blake and Laurier but supported by most of the Ontario party stalwarts including Mackenzie and Cartwright. But rifts also appeared over fundamental economic policies. Blake was increasingly reconciled to a moderate protective tariff, while Cartwright from Ontario and J.W. Longley from Nova Scotia argued for a free trade arrangement with the United States, embodied in a concept called

---

[9] Riel's execution has been one of the most controversial issues in Canadian writing. See George Stanley, *The Birth of Western Canada* and *Louis Riel* (Toronto, 1963); Thomas Flanagan, *Louis "David" Riel: Prophet of the New World* (Toronto, 1979); Douglas Owram, "The Myth of Louis Riel," *CHR* (1982); and J.R. Miller, "From Riel to the Métis," *CHR* (1989). On the North West campaign see Desmond Morton, *The Last War Drum* (Toronto, 1972).

"commercial union." The arrangement would make Canada and the United States a single free trade area with a common tariff on the products of all other nations, including those of Great Britain. The whole idea was anathema to many older Liberals, including Mackenzie and Blake. To make the idea more palatable proponents of free trade turned to the policy of "unrestricted reciprocity" – the free flow of all Canadian and American-produced products across the border – as an alternative.

Liberal leader from 1880 to 1887, Edward Blake was an intellectual in politics. His lengthy speeches could sometimes empty the House of Commons.

PA-13010/NATIONAL ARCHIVES OF CANADA.

Although the proposal was less popular among Quebec Liberals than those of Ontario, Laurier accepted the idea as the basis of a creative and distinctively Liberal policy of development. Besides, in the economic climate of 1888, the proposal seemed a viable alternative to a stalled and failing Conservative National Policy. The years after 1885 had not been kind to the Canadian economy. After a prosperous start in the early 1880s, economic growth noticeably slowed in the latter half of the decade. The time for a free trade alternative seemed favourable. The Liberals introduced their proposal in the Commons in 1888. It was defeated 124-67 with a number of Liberals abstaining. But this was only a first round. Unrestricted reciprocity remained the commercial policy of the Liberal Party until the election of 1891.

Meanwhile, the Conservatives continued to press for reciprocity in primary products. The government had never abandoned the hope that American access to the Maritime fisheries could be exchanged for a limited reciprocity agreement. After years of negotiations and threats – the Canadians seized hundreds of American fishing boats in 1886 and 1887, and the Americans responded by empowering the president to cut off commercial relations with Canada – the American and British governments agreed to the creation of a Joint High Commission in Washington in 1887. Again, as in 1871, the Canadians hoped for some form of reciprocity in primary products. Again, they were disappointed. The commission agreed that the Americans would give up using Canadian inshore fisheries. In return for allowing American fishers the use of Canadian ports, Canadian fishers could sell fish in the United States.

In 1890 another Canadian attempt at reciprocity occurred when the new Republican administration in the United States introduced a high tariff bill to protect American farm products. The American secretary of state accepted the Canadian request to hold confidential exploratory talks with the British ambassador in Washington concerning the matter. When knowledge of these talks threatened to become public, the Americans, who feared political embarrassment among their own electorate, denied that they had occurred. This latest failure took place on the eve of the 1891 general election in Canada.

Having failed to achieve reciprocity with the Americans and confronted with an American administration determined to protect American markets through a tariff system significantly higher than that in Canada, the Macdonald government wrapped itself in the symbols of the Canadian state and prepared to do battle with those who would betray

Free trade with the United States was the hot issue of the late 1880s and early 1890s, and everyone, including cartoonists, had an opinion. Some saw Macdonald as dishonest in running on ''loyalty''; others praised the Old Chieftain for the benefits brought by the tariff and denounced the Grits for trying to sell out Canada.

JACKDAW NO. C3 CANADA VOTES.

their country to the enemy. Unrestricted reciprocity was denounced as a fraud and as the road to commercial union and annexation. The Conservative rhetoric was spurious, a mask for the fact that this was an aging government lacking any significant policy initiatives. Nonetheless, the electorate was provided with the opportunity of choosing between two economic visions for Canada. Appropriately, the principal beneficiaries of the National Policy – the CPR and the manufacturing interests – provided solid supoort for the Conservative cause. Van Horne boasted that the Conservatives carried every riding through which the main CPR line ran. Equally important, however, was the loyalty cry. The Conservatives were particularly strong in those communities where the imperial connection remained a potent influence. Although they increased their popular vote over that of 1887, the Conservatives

C-6541/NATIONAL ARCHIVES OF CANADA.

returned fewer members to Parliament. The two parties divided Ontario and Quebec almost equally. In the end, the party of the National Policy won the election in New Brunswick and Nova Scotia where it captured 29 seats to 8 for the Liberals. The day following the election, Blake published a letter to his former West Durham constituents in which he denounced his party's policy of unrestricted reciprocity; within the next two years, the Liberals quietly followed his lead and abandoned the idea of a continental economy.[10]

Provincial Rights

The architects of Confederation had seen the federal system as a means of accommodating local concerns and regional peculiarities. Indeed, the creation of a province able to protect the distinctive culture of French-Canadians had been the only condition under which the leaders of francophone Quebec could consent to Confederation. The system had the advantage of enabling the central government to avoid divisive cultural issues of language, religion, education, and civil rights. At the same time, Ottawa retained the power to intervene in provincial matters when this was deemed necessary. In fact, the instruments given to the central government seemed to give substance to the assumption of some founding fathers that the provinces were little more than municipalities. The lieutenant-governors of the provinces were agents of the central government and had the authority to withhold royal assent to any provincial legislation. Ottawa also named all judges of the higher courts of the provinces. The federal cabinet could disallow any provincial legislation deemed to intrude into areas of federal jurisdiction; that jurisdiction was seen as covering anything relating to the general welfare of Canada. Even in areas of provincial jurisdiction, provincial powers were sometimes constrained. The power of a province to legislate in regard to education, for example, was limited by safeguards for all educational systems that had existed before 1867 and by the federal right to intervene in protection of the educational systems of cultural minorities within a province. Moreover, individuals could serve as

---

[10] See R. C. Brown, *Canada's National Policy 1883-1900: A Study of American-Canadian Relations* (Princeton, 1964), J.W. Lederle, "The Liberal Convention of 1893," *CJEPS* (1950), and Donald Creighton, *Sir John A. Macdonald: The Old Chieftain.*

members of both Parliament and the provincial legislatures of Ontario and Quebec, and Macdonald made a serious effort to link the provincial executives with the federal cabinet. For example, it was difficult to distinguish between the provincial and federal Conservative parties in Quebec. Finally, the revenue sources available to the provinces were strictly limited. In the case of Quebec, federal transfers accounted for over half the provincial revenue. This severely restricted the capacity of the Quebec government to undertake new policy initiatives or to act in opposition to the wishes of the federal government.

Yet, as the American experience had shown, federal systems were notoriously unstable. Every provincial government could become the focus of the first loyalty of its inhabitants, and when the province was dominated by members of a particular culture or interest, it could even supplant the central government. Indeed, some would argue that each province was fully a state, sovereign within its fields of jurisdiction and thus equal to the federal government.

Macdonald always attempted to maintain control over the provinces. The easiest way was to ensure that Conservative governments were elected in all the provinces. Federal support, both in terms of manpower and patronage, was always available to ensure this end. Macdonald was generally able to achieve this in the early years. Conservative governments were returned in Ontario and Quebec in 1867. In New Brunswick, where most of the anti-Confederationists belonged to the Conservative party, the Liberal government appeared as an ally. Only in Nova Scotia did an overtly hostile Liberal administration achieve power.

In Quebec and Ontario, the federal and provincial Conservative parties were closely linked at Confederation. That situation began to change in 1871 when Blake's provincial Liberals captured control of the Ontario legislature. When Blake entered federal politics the following year, Oliver Mowat assumed the mantle of power and began a reign that would last until 1896.

As master of a province containing 44 percent of the Canadian population and more than that proportion of Canada's resources, Mowat's goals were to expand the physical area of his province, assert its sovereignty over areas of provincial jurisdiction, and limit the activities and expenses of the federal government on the assumption that the largest share of any federal expense would come from Ontario. Mowat claimed much of the territory that had belonged to the Hudson's Bay Company before 1870, an area larger than the province in 1867, and one which Macdonald argued should go to Manitoba. Mowat nearly achieved his wish in 1878 when a commission, jointly appointed by Mowat and Mackenzie, recommended that Ontario should receive everything Mowat asked for. The Mackenzie government was defeated before the arrangement could be completed, and Macdonald refused to ratify the accord. Eventually in 1884 the whole matter was referred to the Judicial Committee of the Privy Council in London, and Mowat won the case that year.

More serious than the boundary dispute, however, were Ontario's challenges to the sovereignty of the Dominion government. In the years immediately following Confederation, Macdonald's government had functioned as if the legislation of provincial governments could be disallowed at will. Ottawa disallowed 52 pieces of provincial legislation before 1887, most of them from Manitoba and British Columbia. The presumptions of the founders were eventually undermined by the judicial system, which was responsible for interpreting the constitution. The highest judicial authority in the Empire was the Judicial Committee of the Privy Council. Up to 1880, the J.C.P.C. upheld the federal authority over the provinces in a series of appeals. Beginning in 1881, however, it handed down a number of decisions that fundamentally altered the relationship between the two levels of government. Decisions in 1881 and 1882 limited the power of the Dominion to regulate trade and commerce within a single province. In the famous 1883 case, *Hodge v. The Queen*, the J.C.P.C. held that the provinces were sovereign within the powers granted to them in the British North America Act. The implication of this decision – developed in subsequent cases – was that the provinces could exercise their powers as fully as Ottawa could exercise its jurisdiction under the act.

This expansion of provincial powers coincided with the decline of Conservative provincial fortunes after 1880. After briefly capturing the government of Nova Scotia, the Conservatives lost it to the Liberals in 1882. Two years later, W.S. Fielding assumed the premiership. Feeling the pinch of the economic downturn that began in 1885, Fielding introduced a resolution in the assembly calling for the repeal of Confederation and the creation of a Maritime state shortly before the end of his mandate in 1886. The motion carried. He then dissolved the legislature and went to the people, winning a 29-8 victory. The Liberals carried those constituencies in which the traditional economy of wood, wind, and sail remained the strongest. In fact, the Liberal Party was divided between those who wanted repeal and those who wanted better terms from Canada. Having achieved such a notable victory, Fielding did not know what to do. Although Nova Scotians seemed to have voted for repeal, they had also elected 15 Conservatives to 6 Liberals in the federal election of 1882 and would return the Conservatives federally again in 1887. The BNA Act provided no exit clause. The British government, faced with an Irish home-rule movement of its own, had little sympathy with Nova Scotia secessionists. What alternative did that leave? A unilateral declaration of independence would be an act of rebellion. Faced with this possibility, Fielding did nothing. The legislature that had been elected to challenge Confederation duly continued to function within the constitutional framework of a Canadian provincial legislature.

Quebec posed a more serious threat to Ottawa's authority. The Quebec Conservatives had long been divided between the bleus and the ultra-Catholics known as the ultramontanes. The execution of Riel in 1885 provided the Quebec Liberal leader, Honoré Mercier, with the opportunity to lead a French-Canadian crusade against those whom he depicted as the enemies of the French-Canadian people. Forming the Parti national in 1886, Mercier attracted the support of many ultramontanes to his Liberal Party and took control of the Quebec government in 1887.

Mercier lost no time in challenging Ottawa by mobilizing other unhappy provincial governments. Liberal governments ruled the four most populous Canadian provinces in 1887. The Conservative government in a fifth, Manitoba, smarted under repeated federal disallowances of its railway legislation and harboured no love for the Macdonald government. When Mercier called an interprovincial conference at Quebec in that year to discuss provincial demands, all the provinces except Prince Edward Island and British Columbia were represented. The conference agreed, among other things, on abolition of the federal power to disallow provincial legislation, on the principle that senators should be chosen by the provinces rather than Ottawa, and on restructuring the financial terms of Confederation in a way that provided greater resources for the provinces. Soon after, the provincial legislatures dutifully approved the resolutions prepared at this second Quebec Conference. As with the Nova Scotia resolution of the previous year, no one then knew what to do. Macdonald had refused to participate at Quebec and would not accept the validity of the provincial resolutions. In the end, they came to nothing.

In the final analysis the provinces were powerless to alter the constitutional relationship between themselves and the federal government. That could only be accomplished by the Judicial Committee of the

Privy Council. The eventual enlargement of provincial powers generally benefited the government of Ontario, which possessed the financial resources to exercise them. Ontario became the principal regionalist in the country, a curious situation since the Confederation proposition had been an Ontario idea. Yet, soon after Confederation, it became obvious that, even with nearly half of the population of the new state, Ontario could not alone dominate the union but that it was going to have to bear the largest part of the financial costs of any federal initiative. The rivalry between Mowat and Macdonald continued throughout the period. Provincial rights in Quebec emerged only in the 1880s, and under Mercier they had a distinctly ethno-religious flavour, one much more capable than the Nova Scotia repeal movement of sustaining a genuine nationality. In Nova Scotia, repeal in 1887 did not have the power of repeal in 1868. Increasingly, Nova Scotia had been politically, socially, and economically integrated into Canadian society in the interval. Nova Scotians, too, had shared the Canadian experience for two decades. Some of them had shared the ideals of that early group of Canadian nationalists, the Canada First movement. Many of them had participated in the 1885 campaign against Riel and the Métis. Many of them – perhaps most – expressed their national ideas in imperial terms, but increasingly, they shared, along with the majority from Ontario, a view of nationhood that was British North American and Protestant.[11]

Religion in Society

The provinces were the preserve of those who wished to retain the values of institutions and cultural groups. Difficulties arose when cultural majorities within a province captured control of the province and attempted to use it to create the social institutions that would identify

---

[11] On views of the nature of federal authority see Peter Waite, "The Political Ideas of John A. Macdonald," in Marcel Hamelin, ed., *The Political Ideas of the Prime Ministers of Canada* (Ottawa, 1969), and Ramsay Cook, *Provincial Autonomy, Minority Rights and the Compact Theory, 1867-1921* (Ottawa, 1969). On Ontario, see J.A. Morrison, "Oliver Mowat and the Development of Provincial Rights in Ontario," *Three History Theses* (Toronto, 1961), and Christopher Armstrong, *The Politics of Federalism: Ontario's Relations with the Federal Government 1867-1942* (Toronto, 1981). On Quebec, see René Durocher et.al., *Quebec: A History 1867-1929*, and H.B. Neatby and J.T. Saywell, "Chapleau and the Conservative Party in Quebec," *CHR* (1956). On Nova Scotia, see Colin D. Howell, "W.S. Fielding and the Repeal Elections of 1886 and 1887," *Acadiensis*, 1979. On religion, see J.W. Grant, *The Church in the Canadian Era* (Toronto, 1972).

their particular concerns with those of the state. Nowhere was this more obvious than in the domain of public education. There is nothing surprising about this. Traditionally most children received little formal education, and that which they had was paid for and arranged by their parents. The transfer of education from the private to the public arena occurred in nineteenth century. By 1880, it was a free public service provided to and required of every child. Increasingly, it joined transportation as a central function of the new Canadian provincial states. Increasingly, too, it came to symbolize the distinction between two modern world views: a Protestant view influenced by a utilitarian program of public education and a Catholic view that tended to emphasize the essentially religious nature of all education. What values, skills, and knowledge should form the basis of a compulsory state-supported educational system?

The divisions were most obvious in Ontario and Quebec. The former had a common education system designed by the Reverend Egerton Ryerson, a leading Methodist clergyman, and a separate Roman Catholic system, each supported by the state. Quebec also possessed two religious-based systems, one Catholic and one Protestant, the latter almost always conducted in English. Neither New Brunswick, Nova Scotia, Prince Edward Island, nor British Columbia had fully supported compulsory public schools at the time of Confederation, and the common schools, which existed by law in each parish and town, were only partly funded by the provinces. When Manitoba entered Confederation, the Manitoba Act was patterned on Quebec rather than Ontario and provided for both publicly supported Protestant and Catholic school systems and for schools in both the official languages of the province. The Manitoba decision of 1870 reflected the almost-equal division of population in the Red River settlement at the time.

Behind the debate over public education was the growing influence of two powerful religious movements. The characteristic religious movement in Canadian Protestantism in the nineteenth century was evangelicalism. Its moral equivalent among Canadian Catholics was ultramontanism. Ultramontanism had developed within nineteenth-century European Catholicism in response to growing secular threats to the faith. Its influence was felt in most Canadian Catholic communities but was particularly strong in French Canada.

The particular bête noire of ultramontanes was modern liberalism with its secularism and its emphasis on the autonomy of the individual. Ultramontane leaders, like Bishop Ignace Bourget of Montreal, had been at war with political liberalism since mid-century. The ultramontanes were a significant force within the parti bleu, the major element in the Quebec wing of the Conservative Party, and their spokesman was Hector Langevin. Prior to the 1871 provincial election, a number of ultramontanes prepared a "Catholic Program," which demanded that candidates for election to the Quebec assembly agree to subordinate the interests of the state to those of the church. The strategy failed – they succeeded in electing only one member – but the movement remained a powerful force in Quebec politics.

The strength of the movement rested on the strong support it received from ultramontane bishops and clergy. Under the influence of Bishop Bourget, many priests threatened to withhold the sacraments from parishioners who supported the Liberal Party. The Conservatives found themselves bound both provincially and federally to these awkward allies. Although Cartier was not an ultramontane, neither he nor the provincial government, which the provincial Conservatives controlled for all but one year between 1867 and 1887, could afford to ignore them. In 1875, the Conservative government under Charles Boucher de Boucherville abolished the Department of Public Instruction and turned control of the education systems over to the Catholic bishops and to Protestant churchmen. The government had abdicated its responsibility for public education.

The ultramontanes suffered a setback in the late 1870s when Quebec Liberals led by the young Wilfrid Laurier and Honoré Mercier, and with the support of the more liberal clergy, persuaded the papal legate to Canada that Canadian Liberals did not pose a threat to the influence of the Catholic Church. This curbed the direct influence of the clergy in the Conservative interest, but the ultramontanes remained a powerful group within the party. The Catholic values and institutions for which the ultramontanists contended were an important part of the culture of French-Canadians; indeed, many would have argued that they were the central element. And many French ultramontanists were quite prepared to come to the aid of coreligionists among the English-Canadians in their efforts to establish distinctive Catholic institutions within other provinces.

The Protestant counterparts to the ultramontanes were the evangelicals. By the mid-nineteenth century, they were the dominant influence among Methodists, Baptists, Free Presbyterians, and Low-Church Anglicans. Evangelicalism had arisen in the eighteenth century as a movement of spiritual renewal in Europe in response to the spirit of scepticism and

materialism that characterized the age. That much evangelicals shared
with ultramontanes. Like ultramontanists, too, evangelicals were suspicious of certain tendencies in secular liberalism, but these were
submerged in their fears of what they perceived as the authoritarianism
of the Roman Catholic Church, a fear they shared with powerful secular
movements such as the Orange Order and liberalism. Evangelicals were
found in both major political parties, but the movement had rarely been
part of an established church, and evangelical mistrust of state power
more often put them in the Liberal Party. In this respect, they differed
from the secular defenders of Protestantism, the Orangemen, who were
generally political Conservatives.

Protestant concerns over Catholic aggression surfaced periodically
throughout the Confederation era. Its most significant early manifestation occurred in the public school crisis in New Brunswick in 1871. In
that year the Liberal government of New Brunswick determined to create
a compulsory free public school system. "The Methodist pope and his
Presbyterian and Baptist College of Cardinals," as opponents dubbed
Lieutenant-Governor L.A. Wilmot and his executive council, invited the
Ontario Methodist, Egerton Ryerson, to assist in planning the new
system. Their proposal was for a common school system modelled on
that of Ontario, one which was Christian but nonsectarian, where the
Bible had to be read each day, but where no religious symbols were
allowed. Catholic leaders in the province protested, arguing that there
had been Catholic public schools before Confederation. In fact, it is
highly unlikely that such an interpretation could be sustained – the 1858
schools act passed by Tilley's government provided only for Bible
reading without commentary – but the attempt to deny a system to the
Catholic third of the province's population was politically unwise,
socially divisive, and highly embarrassing to the federal government.
Nonetheless, the Catholic minority lost its appeal before the provincial
Supreme Court, which ruled that the province had acted within the
constitution.

The situation proved even more divisive at the federal level. Tilley had
been a member of the Liberal government that had passed the 1858
Schools Act, and he wanted no federal intervention. Bishop Bourget
pressed the government to suspend the legislation. Quebec members
were sympathetic to the plight of their coreligionists, but they were also
concerned about establishing the precedent of federal intervention into
fields of provincial jurisdiction. The House of Commons passed a
resolution asking the New Brunswick legislature to provide Catholic

schools. In the end, Parliament contented itself with paying the cost of an appeal to the Judicial Committee of the Privy Council. That court sustained the legality of the New Brunswick legislation.

In the provincial election of 1874, the New Brunswick government was overwhelmingly sustained and the opposition was reduced to five members. The following year, an attempt was made to amend the BNA Act to provide guarantees for Catholic schools in New Brunswick. The proposal failed, however, when Mackenzie's Liberal government refused to support the resolution. The crisis culminated in the Caraquet Riots of 1875 where a mob, some of whose members were armed, attempted to intimidate both Protestants and Catholics who were prepared to obey the school law. When a sheriff's posse later attempted to apprehend some of the rioters, a melee erupted, resulting in the deaths of two men. In the end, the issue was resolved by administrative fiat. In 1876 the school regulations were amended to provide for religious instruction in public schools outside of regular school hours, and members of religious orders were permitted to teach. Essentially, the common school system remained intact.

Similar debates over education haunted Ontario politics throughout the late nineteenth century, but constitutional guarantees to the separate school system held. Under Mowat, a Presbyterian and president of the Evangelical Alliance, a majority of Ontario citizens demonstrated in election after election their willingness to live with the status quo. Toronto, however, was the centre of anglophone and Protestant communications networks. Developments in the country's major Protestant denominations parallelled those in the state. In 1875, several major Presbyterian churches united to form a single national Presbyterian Church. The Methodists accomplished the same thing in 1884. The administrative centre for both national churches was Toronto. When the Protestant way seemed threatened in some fashion, the reaction to that threat was usually led by Ontario. The most conspicuous example occurred as a result of the Jesuits' Estates Act. That crisis had its roots in the decision to execute Riel in 1885.

The execution cost the Conservatives dearly in Quebec. There were, by 1885, three distinct francophone political groupings in the province: the rouges, the bleus, and the ultramontanes (often called the castors). The latter two groups formed the Conservative Party. The Liberal leader, Honoré Mercier, used Riel's execution to whip up francophone passions against the federal government. Mercier's appeal was to Conservative ultramontanes and, despite Riel's apostasy, the appeal was effective.

Ultramontanes sought the defence of their faith and purity in public life; many felt they had found neither in the Conservative Party. In the provincial election of 1886, they supported Mercier's nationalist appeal and succeeded in returning a Liberal government. Mercier then rewarded them by deciding to recompense the Jesuit Order for the confiscation of its property a century before. Although the order had no legal title to the property, Mercier offered to pay the Catholic Church $400 000, the disposition of the money to be decided by the pope. In addition, the Protestant Council for Public Instruction was to receive $60 000.

Protestant response to the act was immediate and negative. The Evangelical Alliance demanded that the federal government disallow the act. By the end of 1889, Equal Rights Associations had been organized in Ontario, and a few years later a secret Protestant Protective Association was formed. The cry for disallowance was taken up by the Ontario press. In March 1889, a resolution requesting disallowance was introduced into the House of Commons. The motion was defeated 188-13. The leading figure of the "Noble 13," as they were promptly dubbed in the press, was a prominent Conservative, Dalton McCarthy, a man who had been touted as a possible successor to Macdonald. Arguing that the issue was one of whether Canada was to be English or French, McCarthy insisted on supporting the resolution.

McCarthy quickly emerged as a cultural hero in large parts of the country. He carried his crusade to save English civilization across Canada. In August 1889, he spoke at Portage la Prairie on a platform with Manitoba Attorney-General Joseph Martin. Martin and the local crowd enthusiastically embraced McCarthy's opinions. This outburst reflected the fundamental changes that had occurred in the fabric of Manitoba society since 1870. The old dualism of religion and language had broken down in the face of successive waves of immigration, most of it from Ontario. In spite of repeated efforts to encourage Quebeckers to settle the Prairies, few French-Canadians came. By 1891 there were more than 150 000 people in Manitoba, the overwhelming majority of whom were anglophone and Protestant. In 1888, a Liberal government, the first in the province's history, had been elected under Thomas Greenway. Even before McCarthy's arrival at Portage la Prairie, the Greenway government had decided to abolish Manitoba's Catholic school system, which they viewed as costly, inefficient, and divisive. After McCarthy's speeches or, more precisely, after witnessing the popular reaction to McCarthy's proposals, the government determined to remove both the bi-confessional school system and the bilingual character of the province's political institutions.

In 1890, through the Manitoba Schools Act, the legislature created a single free and compulsory common school system, which, like that of New Brunswick 19 years before, was modelled on the Ontario common

Sir Mackenzie Bowell became prime minister after Thompson's death. But the heightened racial and religious tensions made it no time for a nonentity.

C-696/NATIONAL ARCHIVES OF CANADA.

schools. Manitoba Catholic leaders demanded that Macdonald disallow the legislation, but the prime minister, who had refused to disallow the Jesuit Estates Act, felt he could not do so. Instead, he urged judicial redress through the courts. A test case on behalf of the Catholics was rejected by the Manitoba courts, upheld on appeal by the Supreme Court of Canada, and finally rejected by the Judicial Committee of the Privy Council. The court held that Catholic educational rights had been given only after the Manitoba Act.[12]

The Manitoba Schools Question and Politics

Macdonald's electoral victory in 1891 was his last. The Old Chieftain died within three months, after serving as prime minister for 19 of the 23 years following Confederaton. The Conservative government he left behind was in disarray with no logical successor. Dalton McCarthy was now unacceptable to the Quebec wing. Hector Langevin would have been a reasonable choice, but he was implicated in a railway scandal involving bribery and the misappropriation of public funds. The most able cabinet member was John Thompson, a Halifax lawyer, but Thompson was a Methodist who had married a Catholic and converted to Catholicism. The choice in the end was Senator John Abbott, an elderly Montreal lawyer, who acted as caretaker for 17 months. He was succeeded by Thompson who governed effectively and restored credibility to a government badly damaged by charges of corruption. But Thompson suddenly died at 50 in 1894, and the succession passed to a compromise candidate, Mackenzie Bowell, a Belleville, Ontario, newspaper editor and a prominent Orangeman. Bowell was a conciliatory but essentially weak leader, incapable in a crisis of holding the diverse elements of the party together. After a long period of bitter dispute within the cabinet, he was forced to resign in 1896 in favour of Sir Charles Tupper, who had left the cabinet in 1888 to serve as High

---

[12] On New Brunswick schools see William M. Baker, *Timothy Warren Anglin: Irish Catholic Canadian* (Toronto, 1977). On Quebec see René Durocher, *Quebec: A History 1867-1929*; Barbara Fraser, "The Political Career of Sir Hector Langevin," *CHR* (1961); H.B. Neatby and J.T. Saywell, "Chapleau and the Conservative Party in Quebec," *CHR* (1956), and Brian Young, *George-Etienne Cartier: Montreal Bourgeois* (Montreal, 1981). On Jesuits' Estates see J.R. Miller, *Equal Rights: The Jesuits Estates Act Controversy* (Montreal, 1979).

Commissioner in London. His return to active politics in 1896 at the age of 75 demonstrated the desperation of the Conservative Party.

The issue that haunted this administration was the Manitoba schools question. Having failed in their first appeal against the abolition of their schools, Manitoba Catholics appealed to the governor-general-in-council on the basis of section 93 of the BNA Act. That section would permit the federal government to intervene in Manitoba to restore Catholic schools through remedial legislation. In so doing, however, Ottawa would be challenging provincial authority on a highly emotional issue, something no political party wanted to do. The cabinet referred the issue to the Supreme Court of Canada to determine whether or not Ottawa had the jurisdiction to act in this case. The Supreme Court said it did not. A further appeal of that question was made to the Judicial Committee in London, which in January 1895 reversed the decision: Ottawa did indeed have the authority to intervene on behalf of Manitoba's Catholic minority. At first, Bowell tried to persuade the Manitoba government to restore Catholic schools. Greenway and attorney-general, Clifford Sifton, refused to budge. Then followed a great debate within cabinet and a growing determination first on the part of Bowell and then, in the spring of 1896, by Tupper to enforce remedial legislation on Manitoba. Before such legislation could be passed, however, the 1896 election intervened.

The question of schooling was an important issue in the 1896 election. Yet the results suggest that many partisans on both sides of the issue did not believe the public declarations of their leaders. On the one hand, the Protestant Tupper promised remedial legislation to Manitoba Catholics. On the other, the Catholic Laurier defended provincial rights and argued that he could secure Catholic rights by reasoned dialogue with the Liberal government in Manitoba. The Catholic hierarchy of Quebec came out in support of the Conservative Party, but many francophones felt that the hierarchy was not united in that support. At the same time, there was a general feeling among anglophone Conservatives that a Tupper government would not coerce Manitoba. This confusing situation produced some curious electoral results. A majority of voters outside Quebec supported the Conservatives. Within Quebec, however, large numbers of bleu Conservatives swung their support to their native son, Laurier and, together with traditional Liberals, gave Laurier an overwhelming majority of the seats in the province. This new bleu-rouge alliance in Quebec was to remain the basis of Laurier's strength.

The responses of English- and French-Canadians to the Manitoba schools question illustrate very well the different ideas of nationality that informed the two linguistic groups. At Confederation, most Quebec francophones would have defined their nation as the French Catholic society of the St. Lawrence. National purpose consisted of the preservation and nurturing of that society. That idea was still prevalent a generation later. Among many of the province's influential petite bourgeoisie, however, there was a growing sense of identification with francophone minorities in other parts of the country in the belief that French Canada should survive in any part of Canada.

English-Canadians were more divided on the matter of national purpose, but the dominant nationalism by the 1890s was clearly found in the rising tide of imperial sentiment that was spreading through Great Britain and the Dominions. There was nothing surprising in this. It was, after all, the British connection that provided the common bond among all Canadians throughout the Confederation period, and the sense of that identity was powerful among British-Canadians and particularly among Protestants. In the face of the threat of continentalism, the committment was re-inforced. But the Canadian imperialism that emerged in the 1880s was not an ideology of inferiority. Imperialist theorists like George Parkin dreamed of an imperial unity in which Canadians would participate as equals in an imperial Parliament, maintain a Pax Britannica through an imperial army and navy, and participate in an imperial free trade area. In the fullness of time, they hoped, Ottawa might become the centre of what was seen as the greatest civilization in human history. At a less grandiose level, imperialism provided a powerful sense of English-Canadian nationalism, with an outward, optimistic world view and national purpose that contrasted sharply with that of French Canada.[13]

So ended the age of Macdonald. It had begun with the move away from Europe and with the consolidation of a continental state. It ended with a demand for re-integration into a worldwide network. In the interval, it had failed to achieve the integration of its two nations, although, in both nations, this was probably viewed as a good thing. It had failed to produce the dazzling growth of population that had been predicted a

---

[13] See Lovell Clark, "The Conservative Party in the 1890's," *CHAR* (1961); Carl Berger, *The Sense of Power* (Toronto, 1970); J.I. Cooper, "The Political Ideas of George-Etienne Cartier," *CHR* (1942); Arthur Silver, *The French-Canadian Idea of Confederation* (Toronto, 1982), and Paul Crunican, *Priests and Politicians: Manitoba Schools and the Election of 1896* (Toronto, 1974).

generation earlier. There were perhaps 5 million Canadians in 1896, up from 3.5 million at Confederation. And the road from Confederation was littered with the dashed hopes and expectations of those who had opposed its progress. Still, substantial achievements had been witnessed. The completion of Confederation and the implementation of the policies of economic development might be counted among these. Most significant, perhaps, was the increase in the material well-being of Canadians. The gross national product produced by Canadians probably more than doubled between 1870 and 1896. Put another way, the actual output per person rose from some $120 in 1870 to $170 in 1890. The structural changes that had made this growth possible were gradually remaking the societies that composed the Canadian state.

BUILDING THE INDUSTRIAL ORDER

About one Canadian in six lived in towns and cities in 1871. Thirty years later that proportion had risen to one in three. The implications of this shift suggest much of the social change that occurred in the generation following Confederation. Industrial growth in the form of manufacturing and railways were the most important elements in the growth of towns: the value of manufacturing output in constant dollars more than tripled during this time; the number of industrial workers increased by more than 130 percent; rail lines in Canada increased from 2000 to 17 000 miles (3200 to 27 350 km). It is important to remember, however, that this generation did not witness a sudden and unexpected industrial revolution. A considerable manufacturing sector had been gradually developing throughout most of British North America in the decades leading up to Confederation. The industrial process accelerated in the generation following Confederation, partly the result of political policies and partly as a continuation of this earlier development.

What distinguished much post-Confederation industrialism from earlier developments were location and size of producing unit. Mid-century manufacturing had not been a particularly urban activity. Most rural areas contained a number of small producers capable of supplying a considerable part of the local needs for agricultural implements, horse shoes, boots, barrels, and even cloth. Grist mills and sawmills were as often found in the countryside and village as in town. Even an activity as labour intensive as shipbuilding was frequently a village undertaking. There were a number of large producing units in the colonial cities, but the overwhelming majority of industrial workers, even in urban centres, were found in the small shops that produced most of the industrial output of the colonies.

TABLE 1

URBAN AND RURAL POPULATION

	Population	Rural	Urban (under 30 000)	Urban (over 30 000)
1871	3 689 000	83%	11%	6%
1881	4 324 000	78%	14%	8%
1891	4 833 000	70%	17%	13%
1901	5 371 000	65%	20%	15%

This situation gradually altered after 1867 and changed rapidly after 1879. By 1900, most Canadian industrial output was being produced by large firms, usually in factory settings. The larger units were generally more efficient than shop production, and prices for most consumer and producer goods declined in the last third of the nineteenth century. The larger units also had far greater capital requirements. These needs were often met by re-investing profits over a number of years, a financial arrangement that often happened in family-owned firms. More often, the necessary capital was raised through the creation of joint-stock companies owned by numerous shareholders, controlled by boards of directors, and run by teams of professional managers who did not own the concerns they were running. After 1885, the joint stock corporation was frequently used as a device to consolidate several producing units of a particular industry under the control of a single board of directors. Eventually it became the technique through which most of the output of entire industries could be controlled by one or two large consolidations.

This development was stimulated at first when businesspeople responded to the opportunities of a growing market and to a political determination to create a Canadian industrial economy through tariff stimulation. Later, the growing consolidation movement was both a defensive measure, designed to protect the market against the effects of excess production, and a means through which certain business interests could reap large profits through speculation in the stock of the newly formed concerns.

The effects of the development were felt in every aspect of Canadian life. Virtually all of it was either town-based or resulted in the creation of towns where only villages had existed before. Small-scale rural manufacturing retreated in the face of advancing large development. Village producers had seen their world in terms of the village or, at most, the parish. The new industrial forms were designed to serve a regional or even a national market. The growth and eventual consolidation of these firms contributed to the emergence of a wider Canadian economy and to the growth of a Canadian society, as opposed to local or regional societies. The new firms not only fostered the growth of towns but they also restructured the relationships of the groups that had traditionally occupied the towns. Most production in colonial towns had taken place in shops where a small number of skilled journeymen had worked with and under the supervision of a master. Masters were owners, and in most industries in most towns, there were a large number of them. Many journeymen remained employees all their working lives, but for the ambitious or the lucky, the prospect of owning a shop was a reasonable expectation. Much of this shop tradition disappeared in the late nineteenth century. Technological change and factory organization made much of it obsolete. The development of the industrial servicing machine and the shoe factory, for example, sounded the death knell for the widely scattered cobbling trade in the Dominion. Technology and organization also made possible the use of a wide range of labour. Much factory work was tedious, but not heavy, and required only limited skills. Increasingly, women and children were employed to do factory work in work places increasingly controlled by managerial bureaucracies. Towns had always been the special habitats of women – they had always comprised sizable majorities of the population of colonial towns – but now they offered a wide variety of employment opportunities, almost all of them characterized by low wages and few chances of advancement. The same limited opportunities drew large numbers of rural migrants to the towns. This movement was largely a reflection of the growing rural population and declining rural opportunities.

As towns grew and the urban industrial structures became more complex and increasingly impersonal, the possibilities for identities based on class interest continued to grow. There had been colonial traditions of collective identity and occasionally collective action, especially on the part of artisans and among dock workers. This tendency was strengthened in the late nineteenth century in the new industrial systems that employed masses of labour: in the factories, in the railways, and in the coal mines of Nova Scotia and British Columbia. It was stimulated by the presence of craftsmen who felt that their traditional status was being undermined by the new technology and industrial organization and by large numbers of immigrant workers from England and Scotland whose attitudes reflected a long experience in the cradle of industrialism.[1]

The Rural Economy

The Canadian economy in 1870 was dominated by primary producers. About half the gainfully employed made a living as farmers, while another large proportion were lumberers, fishers, or miners – all rural occupations. Most of this rural population was only partially integrated into the commercial economy. In some measure, farms continued to produce most of the necessities of life for their occupants until the end of the nineteenth century. This was particularly true in the Maritimes, Quebec, and eastern and northern Ontario, but was true as well even in the principal areas of commercial agriculture in Ontario. Fuel and a variety of foods were found on every farm, and many farmers produced significant quantities of woollen cloth. For many the farm was a little commonwealth assuring a stability and a status not easily found elsewhere. For women, too, it has been argued, farming provided a role and an equality of function that could not be found in an urban setting. Women's control of such income-generating activities as butter making, egg gathering, and cloth weaving, as well as their roles as labour producers and homemakers, made them absolutely indispensable, albeit overworked, members of these little commonwealths. And in an age when pensions did not exist and the only alternative to self-support was the ignominy of life in a poorhouse, the farm offered a refuge and support, perhaps the only security, to both the aged and the widowed.

However, the culture and the future of these little commonwealths were in doubt by 1870. The best arable land in all provinces had been occupied for at least a generation. New farms in the Maritimes, Quebec, and Ontario had to be developed on increasingly marginal lands that required greater effort to achieve lower yields. Yet even the best lands,

---

[1] Aspects of the Canadian industrial experience are surveyed in J.M. Bliss, *Northern Enterprise: Five Centuries of Canadian Business* (Toronto, 1987); Alison Prentice et al., *Canadian Women: A History* (Toronto, 1988); and Bryan Palmer, *The Working Class Experience: The Rise and Reconstruction of Canadian Labour* (Toronto, 1983).

those that had been subject to decades of unrelenting wheat production for export, faced declining levels of output. The wheat sector, traditionally the principal element of Canadian commercial agriculture, came under increasing pressure from the competition of the American midwestern wheat belt following the Civil War. Slowly but surely, eastern Canadians lost the battle for the British wheat markets, first to Kansas, then, by the century's end, to Manitoba. Under these circumstances, the acquisition of the East at Confederation was as important as the West to the Ontario farmer. New Brunswick and Nova Scotia had been the largest export markets for Ontario wheat in 1867, and the imposition of a substantial tariff on American flour in 1879 preserved this traditional market for Ontario farmers in the face of the American threat.

The principal cash crop of most rural communities in the Maritimes and Quebec was the harvesting and processing of timber. However, the international market for wood products was in decline by the mid-1870s and, while it later recovered, it remained unstable until the end of the century.

Farmers traditionally had had large families, in part at least, to provide a source of labour for the many tasks required for their successful operation. By Confederation, many of the most labour-intensive farm operations utilized hay rakes and mowers, reflections of the technological innovations that were remaking nineteenth-century farms into increasingly efficient producing units. Farmers and farm wives responded to these developments by reducing their number of children. Even so, as the 1871 census revealed, most farm families possessed a "full quiver" of dependent young men, women, and children, all of whom would have to be provided for in the next few decades. Under these demographic pressures, farmers in all five eastern provinces continued to open new farms on more marginal land, improved still more land on their own farms, and shifted production from grain to livestock and dairy produce. In areas where large-scale commercial agriculture was possible, farms became increasingly mechanized, and machinery replaced manual labour. In more self-sufficient areas, where opportunities were more limited, farming continued to be more labour-intensive. In either case, farmers in all eastern provinces became increasingly commercial in their operations. The salvation of eastern agriculture was found in the growing British market for meat and dairy produce. The value of Canadian cheese exports, for example, rose from $3.9 million in 1880 to $20.6 million in 1901, at which point it was the largest single Canadian export commodity.

These developments could not accommodate the large population of potential farmers already present on Canadian farms in 1871. To do so, the number of farms and quantity of farm land in each province would have had to double in a generation. Instead, the number of farms in Quebec increased by 50 percent and those of Ontario and the Maritimes by 25 percent by 1891 before entering a gradual decline. For most farmers' children, there would be no little commonwealth. Indeed, it is probable that many of those in the older areas of subsistence agriculture in the Maritimes and Quebec were no longer willing to accept the satisfaction of the farm in the face of the material advantages that the commercial economy had to offer. Tens of thousands left, a large proportion the children of farmers. Large numbers were drawn to the towns where they formed a reservoir of unskilled and semi-skilled labour. Even larger numbers were drawn away from their native provinces. In all, perhaps 200 000 Maritimers, 250 000 Quebeckers, and 230 000 Ontarians left their provinces between 1881 and 1901. Many of those from Ontario moved westward (Ontario-born Manitobans were the dominant group at the time of the passage of the Manitoba Schools Act), but Maritimers and Quebeckers generally followed their traditional migratory trails to Boston and the surrounding New England states.

The rural population within the whole of Canada was essentially stagnant between 1880 and 1900. The slow decline of eastern rural communities was barely offset by the growth of those in the Prairies. And that stagnation extended to the villages and institutions that serviced those eastern rural communities. Effectively, all of the growth that occurred after 1880, and most of that which occurred after 1870, took place in urban settings. The population of urban places nearly tripled between 1871 and 1901. The most spectacular growth occurred in cities containing over 100 000 people (Montreal in 1871, Toronto in 1901), although the rise should not be allowed to obscure the fact that most urban Canadians in 1901, as in 1871, lived in centres of fewer than 30 000 people. Most urban growth was the result of migration. Rural migrants joined large numbers of overseas arrivals in Canadian towns. British migration to Canada continued unabated through the late nineteenth century, although the proportion of the English among the migrants was far greater than it had been earlier in the century. In addition, small numbers of Icelanders, Chinese, Germans, Italians, Scandinavians, Poles, Jews, and German Mennonites from Russia began to supplement the traditional migrant groups in the 1870s and 1880s. Through the 1890s, these groups came to comprise a more significant part of the migrant flow, although the great majority of newcomers were still British. On average about 30 000 overseas migrants arrived each year in the 1870s, about 80 000 in the 1880s (reflecting the opportunities available in railway construction), and about 40 000 in the 1890s. While large numbers of these newcomers passed through to the United States, most probably remained in Canada and most of those probably became urban settlers. They, too, became part of the personnel who staffed the developing industrial sector. Their presence was important because many were products of the English industrial and urban experience, and they brought the skills that were essential to the industrial transition.

TABLE 2

REGIONAL AGRICULTURAL GROWTH

	Farms ('000s)			Improved Land ('000s of acres)			Milk Cows ('000s)		
	1881	1891	1901	1881	1891	1901	1881	1891	1901
Maritimes	106	112	105	3 731	4 222	3 394	287	294	290
Quebec	138	175	140	6 410	8 071	7 440	491	550	734
Ontario	207	216	204	11 294	14 258	13 266	782	876	1 018
Prairies	10	31	55	279	1 267	5 573	20	83	134
B.C.	3	6	7	185	58	474	11	18	22

Industrial Organization

Manufacturing industries developed in British North America from the time of the foundation of the colonies. Virtually every locality possessed a blacksmith and other small producers, while a large part of the population of villages and towns consisted of artisans capable of supplying a wide variety of consumers' needs. The other large group of manufacturing industries were those processing lumber, flour, and ships for export to other colonies or to the United Kingdom.

Technologically more complex manufacturing began in the 1820s with the development of iron foundries, usually for the purpose of providing iron implements and manufacturing steam engines for use in ships and sawmills. The expansion of railways in the 1850s provided a major impetus. Although rails were imported, the construction of steam engines and rolling stock became an important enterprise. Even more important were the facilities needed to maintain the rolling stock and the railways. Iron foundries and equipment construction for the growing gas light industries of the period required large, organized firms, a skilled labour force, and a large capital investment. Within the framework of British North American industry in 1867, these constituted only a small part of colonial output, but, together with the few daily newspapers and the few small cotton mills, they were suggestive of a process that was soon to become dominant within the economy of the new Dominion.

The large new enterprises, not surprisingly, were located in the cities. Montreal, Quebec, Toronto, Saint John, and Halifax all contained examples of the new firms. They possessed a large local market, integrated business communities – which provided greater access to credit and banking facilities – and an immigrant population that offered easy access to a great variety of skills. This was particularly true in Montreal with a population of 100 000 by 1871 where the process was

Credit was necessary if industry was to expand, but banks and bankers, as this 1890s photograph demonstrates, were intimidating.

THE BANK OF NOVA SCOTIA ARCHIVES.

most advanced. Montreal had the further advantage of being the *entrepôt* that controlled the distribution and transportation facilities into southern Ontario.

George Stephen and Hugh Allan were in Montreal. Stephen had been a Scottish village boy brought to Montreal by his mother's cousin to work as a clerk in a small Montreal dry goods firm. He eventually took over the firm, developed it into a major wholesale business, and went on to become a director of the Bank of Montreal. He then joined other dry goods owners in the development of textile mills in the towns around Montreal, invested in American railway enterprises, and joined other businesspeople like Hugh Allan in the creation of joint stock manufacturing firms in the city.

The joint stock company had been used a number of times in nineteenth-century British North America, mainly for the creation of banks, canals, railways, mining companies, and other enterprises that had capital requirements larger than any individual could raise. Ownership of the company was in the hands of its stockholders. Each stockholder bought shares in the company and, through this means, large sums could be raised for the purchase of land and equipment and the provision of operating capital. In the event of failure, no stockholder was liable for more than the value of his own shares. Company policy was set by its board of directors, but the actual running of the firm was in the hands of professional managers. Joint stock firms were usually large and could develop complex organizations of managers, department heads, and supervisors whose job was to increase efficiency of production.

This form of business organization stood in sharp contrast to that of most pre-1870 manufacturing enterprises. Traditional shops were the property and product of a single individual, usually one who had acquired the skills of the craft through some form of apprenticeship and then had worked as a journeyman in the trade. The shop would typically employ two or three journeymen and perhaps a labourer or a young apprentice. Even larger firms, like foundries, tanneries, or shipyards, followed the same industrial model. The owners were the managers, and they usually possessed the skills required to produce the output. Capital required for the firm was generated internally. Where the capital requirements were large, two or even three tradespeople might enter a partnership. Above all, and this was particularly true of the larger firms, they were family-oriented. Sons were first recruited, as were nephews and even cousins. Capital requirements were small even by the standards of the 1860s. Many, perhaps most, shops operated on as little as $500 or $1000. Even most large partnerships were valued at less than $100 000. By comparison with leading merchants or railway entrepreneurs, the principal manufacturers of British North America were a poor lot.

The tendencies evident in pre-Confederation industry continued through most of the decade following 1867. The commercial prosperity of the period permitted the development of larger and more complex units of production, particularly on the part of textile wholesalers like the Stephens in Montreal and foundry owner Edward Gurney of Hamilton. Then in 1873-4 the depression came. For four years, virtually every manufacturing enterprise suffered the effects of this worldwide downturn. Demand for wood and agricultural products declined, limiting the capacity of their producers to share in the commercial economy. Many wood producers and processers were driven into bankruptcy. To further exacerbate the situation, the wooden shipbuilding industry, long an important staple in the economies of the Maritimes and eastern Quebec, effectively collapsed. The situation was nearly as serious in most other manufacturing industries. Confronted by the same depression, many American producers responded by dumping products onto the Canadian market, often below cost. Hundreds of Canadian firms, producing everything from paper to furniture to iron castings, were driven into bankruptcy, and thousands of labourers into unemployment. The seriousness of the recession was reflected in its length; as the situation worsened year by year, many came to feel that its final effect would be the destruction of all Canadian industry.

In the face of this threat, the manufacturing interests of the country mobilized in defence of their businesses. Their first appeal was to the state for protection. There was nothing new or unusual in this appeal. The same groups had appealed to the New Brunswick legislature in the 1840s and to the Canadian in the 1850s. In both cases, they had been able to achieve a measure of success, most notably with the Canadian tariff of 1857-58, which provided a general duty of up to 20 percent. Twenty years later manufacturers were a stronger and more unified interest group. In 1874, Ontario manufacturers formed an organization soon known as the Canadian Manufacturers Association, which provided a powerful lobby. The leaders of the movement were owners of larger firms located mainly in Montreal, Toronto, and Hamilton; some of them, like George Redpath, the Montreal sugar refiner, had strong ties with the Conservative Party. The peak of their campaign came in the 1878 election, one of the most decisive in Canadian history. Manufacturers supported the Conservatives, campaigned for the Conservatives, ran for the Conservatives, and used their influence to persuade their employees and associates to vote for the Conservatives. There were a great number of manufacturers in Canada – nearly 40 000 in 1871 with over 180 000 employees – and they certainly boosted the Conservative campaign. However, the size of the Conservative victory was so great that it is impossible to credit the victory simply to the manufacturing interest. It was the most decisive in Canadian history before 1935. Fighting on a high-tariff platform against the low-tariff Liberals, the Conservatives carried every province except New Brunswick by majorities of at least two to one. In a country where farmers controlled the vote in the majority of constituencies, it seems clear that most voters chose a policy of economic nationalism.

Manufacturers and those dependent on manufacturing industries were the immediate beneficiaries of the National Policy. The new government asked manufacturers what they needed for protection and generally granted it. The impact of the policy was immediate and, in conjunction with the economic activity generated by the construction of the Canadian Pacific Railway, it produced a period of unprecedented prosperity between 1879 and 1885. The opportunities provided by the National Policy provoked a rush of development in towns and cities across the country. Civic leaders sensed the importance of attracting new industry to their communities and offered various incentives in the form of grants and tax holidays. Leading manufacturers and other business-people in numerous towns and cities combined efforts to raise capital and create significant units of production within their communities. The latter device was commonly employed in towns and smaller cities. Existing enterprises were expanded and new ones established. Textile mills, a principal beneficiary of the 1879 tariff, sprouted in towns across the Dominion. The textile protection had been intended for the Montreal textile entrepreneurs, but business leaders from Halifax, Moncton, Yarmouth, Saint John, St. Stephen, Marysville, Brantford, and Hamilton, as well as Montreal, responded to the incentive. Secondary iron and steel manufacturers were another major beneficiary. Foundries expanded from New Glasgow to Sarnia, and small agricultural implements producers like Hart Massey began major expansions. A host of consumer goods ranging from shoes and leather to glass, sugar, rope, and paper received protection. The effect of the expansion was to spread the factory system and the industrial joint stock corporation into every part of the Dominion. Numerous middling enterprises were expanded using this device, and the ownership and, incidentally, the risk of the business was spread over a far greater number of people.

TABLE 3

GROWTH RATES OF REAL MANUFACTURING OUTPUT

	Gross Value (constant $)	Output per person
1870	$271 million	$ 73
1880	$422 million	$ 97
1890	$674 million	$139
1900	$856 million	$159

TABLE 4

PROVINCIAL MANUFACTURING OUTPUT PER PERSON (Current $)

	B.C.	Manitoba	Ontario	Quebec	N.B	N.S.	P.E.I.
1870	–	–	$ 70	$ 63	$ 60	$ 31	$ 30
1880	$ 56	$ 50	$ 81	$ 75	$ 58	$ 41	$ 38
1890	$117	$ 60	$110	$ 94	$ 75	$ 64	$ 24

The most extensive expansion in terms of capital, output, and employment was found in Quebec and Ontario; in relative terms, however, the National Policy had its greatest impact in the Maritimes. As the wooden shipbuilding industry declined and the lumber industry stagnated, entrepreneurs from many parts of the region turned to the promise of the National Policy. The communities that did so were those that had already experienced considerable industrial development and possessed significant entrepreneurial and financial resources, as well as an adequate labour force. St. Stephen was typical of these. At the head of the St. Croix drainage basin, it had long been the second sawmilling centre in New Brunswick. Devastated by the decline in the wood industries, its businesspeople made the transition to secondary industries, which led to the development of a major cotton mill, candy factory, soap factory, and axe factory. A similar development at New Glasgow, a traditional ship-building town, gradually transformed the community into Canada's first integrated steel centre. Since the region possessed the only major coal deposits in Eastern Canada, the expectation of many community leaders of the 1880s that it might become the Pittsburgh of Canada did not seem unrealistic.

Mechanization could make work easier and less labour-intensive, and advertising, by the 1880s, was becoming one way to sell new machinery.

PORTABLE GRIST MILLS AND SAW MILLS.

George Book writes, St. Anns, Ontario, June 17, 1879, regarding his 16-horse power Champion Sawmill:

"Last week, on Monday morning, three men of us commenced to tear up mill to move it. We tore up, moved three miles, set it up and on Tuesday at three o'clock sawed a log with it. Not quite two days. In one week we moved and set it up as mentioned, and sawed twenty thousand feet. I will write full particulars soon. We sawed six hundred feet in twenty-nine minutes—1-inch lumber."

2 sizes built—12 H. P. using 44 in. saw, Capacity 3 to 4,000 per day. 16 H. P. using 48 in. saw, Capacity, 4 to 5,000 per day. Most simple, efficient and portable mill of its size in the world.

WATEROUS ENGINE WORKS CO., BRANTFORD, CANADA.

THE FIRE PROOF CHAMPION IN THE BARN YARD

WATEROUS ENGINE WORKS CO., BRANTFORD, CANADA.

THE FIRE PROOF CHAMPION

WATEROUS ENGINE WORKS CO., BRANTFORD. CANADA.

SEE OUR NEW IMPROVED Sectional Boiler! Made expressly for the GREAT NORTH-WEST.

Can be taken apart and cleaned thoroughly every week with little trouble. The only way to overcome the effects of *alkaline* water is to keep a boiler clean. *This can only be done with our improved Sectional Boiler.* Send for Circulars.

The industrial transition of the whole century is contained in the career of James Harris, who trained as a blacksmith in his native Annapolis, set up a blacksmith shop in Saint John in 1825, and later formed a partnership to expand his shop into a foundry. A successful manufacturer of railway rolling stock in the 1860s, Harris incorporated his firm into a joint stock company and developed a large plant in the early 1880s capable of producing more railway cars than any other firm in the country.

The major areas of industrialization in the region focused on a number of towns clustered in a crescent beginning at Yarmouth and extending through Halifax, Cape Breton, New Glasgow, Amherst, Moncton, Saint John, Fredericton, and St. Stephen. Most of the remainder of the region remained committed to the traditional staples economy. In the short run, in the Maritimes as in Quebec and Ontario, the rapid expansion

Saint John remained the industrial and commercial heart of New Brunswick. The South Market Wharves, shown here around 1870, were a major trans-shipment point for the whole province.

NEW BRUNSWICK MUSEUM, SAINT JOHN.

decentralized the industrial sector. Traditionally, most manufacturing in New Brunswick had been centred on Saint John; the National Policy scattered it over the southern half of the province.

Not surprisingly, much growth in the decade following the implementation of the National Policy occurred in the Montreal area. The city was already the centre of the footwear and clothing industries. These were consolidated and expanded. As well, a wide variety of secondary industries developed including rubber, leather, and especially cloth. Montreal was the centre of the Canadian distribution network for dry goods.

From the mid-nineteenth century, Montreal entrepreneurs had begun to organize the industrial structure of the surrounding hinterland. After Confederation, Cornwall, Almonte, Valleyfield, Sherbrooke, Magog, and a number of other surrounding towns became the centres of growing Montreal-controlled enterprises that experienced rapid development in the decade following 1879. Most of this development resulted less from the creation of new industry than the expansion of existing enterprises, a reflection of the political influence of Montreal businesspeople in shaping tariff policy. Most of this development was directed by a great bourgeoisie of anglophone businesspeople, although a small group of francophones participated as well. This bourgeoisie included many of the people who participated in the organization of the Canadian Pacific Railroad corporation. The construction of that railway enriched contractors and sub-contractors, and many of these participated in the opportunities offered by the industrial expansion of the period. Some of them participated, as well, in the early consolidation movement that was led by the Montreal bourgeoisie and that gradually centred control of a number of industries in Montreal.

The most spectacular growth in the 1880s occurred in the manufacturing industries of Ontario. Throughout the decade, the value added by the manufacturing process increased by nearly 65 percent. While some significant growth occurred in eastern Ontario, the expansion was centred on a cluster of towns extending from Toronto west and southwest to Hamilton, Guelph, Brantford, and Berlin, in a wide variety of industries, including such traditional activities as food and wood processing. The cutting edge of development was in the secondary iron and steel industries of the Lake Peninsula. Characteristic of this expansion was the activity of the agricultural implements manufacturer, Hart Massey, who moved the family firm to Toronto in 1880, where he was offered a large tract of land in the west end of the city and, stimulated by the promise of a 30 percent protective tariff, built one of the largest industrial concerns in the country. Although Toronto was less an industrial centre than Montreal, the Queen City was the largest centre in a region containing the greatest concentration of manufacturing establishments in the country.

The industries of the still largely frontier West were little affected by the general development after 1880. Manufacturing in both the Prairies and British Columbia was centred on the processing of grain, fish, and wood before 1890. Nonetheless, the combination of rich natural resources and small population gave British Columbia the highest per capita output of any province in Canada in 1890.

The high, heady period of expansion was over by 1887. Canadian manufacturers had been given control of the Canadian market, and there is evidence that their produce replaced many products that had previously been imported. But the Canadian market was limited in size – there were fewer than 5 million people in 1891 – and the producing capacity of many industries considerably exceeded their demands. As competition became more and more fierce and prices fell, leaders in a number of industries attempted to achieve stability by acquiring control of most of the producers in order to fix prices.

Developments in the cotton mill industry were typical of those occurring in many industries. The principal Montreal dry goods wholesalers, who already marketed a substantial part of the cloth consumed in the Dominion, bought up control of most Canadian cotton mills at depressed prices and amalgamated them into two cotton combinations, Dominion Cotton Mills and Canada Coloured Cottons, both controlled by a board of directors in Montreal. The various factories of the companies were operated at the local level by professional managers. The new companies acted as near-monopolies, setting prices and driving smaller competitors out of the market by reducing prices below cost in the competitors' market. A similar merger occurred in western Ontario where the two largest agricultural implements manufacturers, Massey and Harris, united in an effort to prevent competition. In the process, control of that industry became centred in Toronto. Dozens of similar mergers occurred in the nineties.

The effect of these mergers was to concentrate control in the hands of small numbers of directors and professional managers, usually located in Montreal or occasionally in Toronto. The answers to the critical questions of any producer (what to sell or buy, who to sell to or buy from, at what price) could be made by a few individuals who were, in effect, capable of controlling the market and setting a price that would yield a profit without fear that a competitor would drive them from the field. The federal government attempted to protect the consumer from price fixing by merchants and manufacturers through passage of an Anti-Combines Act in 1889. That legislation may have calmed public apprehension of price fixing, but it was so broadly conceived that it was virtually impossible to obtain a conviction under it.

The development pattern established in the 1880s would be repeated in each successive decade. Tariff protection was offered to a group of industries. This was followed by a sometimes dramatic expansion of industry and a significant increase in the number of firms and producing units. There was a period of strong competition as each firm fought for a larger market share. Then there was a consolidation of the industry into a few major corporations that were able to control the market and establish stable prices. Throughout this process, Canadian industrial output slowly diversified.

When the pace of industrial expansion slowed in the mid-1880s, attention turned to the production of primary iron and steel. The leading edge in the 1890s was the development of the massive Nova Scotia Iron and Steel Co. at New Glasgow, Dominion Coal, and Dominion Iron and Steel at Cape Breton, the forerunners of the Steel Company of Canada at Hamilton, Algoma Steel at the Sault, and the development of electricity and electrical equipment and chemicals. Throughout the decade these companies would undergo the same process as had the textile and agricultural implements industries earlier. Only in these cases, the technology was more sophisticated, the capital requirements greater, and the consolidations more grand.[2]

---

[2] The major themes treated in this discussion are discussed in the following: Hugh Aitken, "Government and Business in Canada: An Interpretation," *Business History Review* (1964); T.W. Acheson, "The National Policy and the Industrialization of the Maritimes 1880-1910," *Acadiensis* (1972); "The Social Origins of the Canadian Industrial Elite 1880-85," in D.S. MacMillan, ed., *Canadian Business History: Selected Studies 1497-1971* (Toronto, 1972); L.D. McCann, "The Mercantile-Industrial Transition in the Metal Towns of Pictou County, 1857-1939," *Acadiensis* (1981); A. Faucher and M. Lamontagne, "History of Economic Development," in M. Rioux and Y. Martin, eds., *French-Canadian Society* (Toronto, 1964); Heather Gilbert, *Awakening Continent: The Life of Lord Mount Stephen, 1824-1891* (Aberdeen, 1965); Michael Bliss, *A Canadian Millionaire: Life and Business Times of Sir Joseph Flavelle 1858-1941* (Toronto, 1978); and *A Living Profit: Studies in the Social History of Canadian Business* (Toronto, 1974); Jacob Spelt, *Urban Development of South-Central Ontario* (Toronto, 1971); H.V. Nelles, *The Politics of Development: Forests, Mines, and Hydro-Electric Power in Ontario, 1849-1941* (Toronto, 1971); Christopher Armstrong and H.V. Nelles, *Monopoly's Moment: The Organization and Regulation of Canadian Utilities* (Baltimore, 1986); W. Kaye Lamb, *History of the Canadian Pacific Railway* (New York, 1977); and G.R. Stevens, *Canadian National Railways* (Toronto, 1960, 1962).

~~~~ Industrial Organization and the Worker

There was no single model of industrial organization in Canada in 1880. Apart from the shops, in which a majority of producers worked, there were a variety of increasingly complex industrial forms. Perhaps the most primitive was the putting-out system in which women worked on garments at home and were paid for piece work. Many dry goods wholesalers also had large workshops, sometimes employing a hundred people, where ready-made garments were prepared on sewing machines under the direction of supervisors.

The classic factory was a large three- or four-storey brick building containing machinery powered by steam engines. The plant was divided

Lumber workers lived well away from civilization, often in cramped conditions. But the food was plentiful, and none of this crew look anything but happy.

ARCHIVES OF ONTARIO (ACC. 6693-S11476).

into sections in which specialized functions were performed by a work force that prepared a certain number of parts at a particular rate of output. At the end of the process a number of completed items would emerge. This system existed in many shoe factories and textile mills where operators tended machines and performed specialized functions under the eye of an overseer. In these operations, there was a chain of command reaching to the works manager and a carefully defined set of operating procedures. A similar but more primitive system existed in cigar factories where much of the work was carried out by hand, and the procedure was completed by teams of individuals working around single tables.

Most of this factory system – including the physical design, the machinery, the supervisor, and the regimen – was imported from England or New England. It generally assumed work that was tedious but not too strenuous and employed a largely semi-skilled work force that was highly disciplined. Many supervisors preferred to hire women and children in preference to men, not only because they could be paid much less but because they could be much more easily disciplined and moulded to the demands of factory work. Children and sometimes even women might be physically punished if they broke the rules. Failure to do a task properly could result in fines or dismissal. Tardiness could result in a person being denied entry to the workplace for the morning. Hours were long – usually 60 a week for women and youths and 60 to 70 for men.

Yet this was only one model of industrial organization, one that did not affect most skilled craftspeople who comprised a large part of the industrial work force. Indeed, even cotton mills were places where dozens of different crafts and skills were found, and even here, there was a clear hierarchy of labour: machinists, who kept the plant in working order, could make four times the wages of women spinners and were not subject to the same discipline. The more technical trades were generally able to resist much of the pressure to conform to a central discipline. In many foundries, for example, moulders and other highly skilled trades-people retained a considerable degree of independence from the larger organizations. In some cases, they effectively acted as subcontractors, hiring their own crews and independently performing their function within the system. A similar independence was found in many coal-mining operations where crews often exercised a high degree of control within the workplace.

A few trades continued to function within an unchanging organization;

most were re-organized in very different ways. The small bakeries in towns gradually developed into plants, while their candy-making functions were directed into separate factories. Furniture makers gradually became piece workers in larger mills. Shoemakers survived only in repair shops; those who entered shoe factories found their functions reduced to a few repetitive tasks and their expectations limited to the possibility of becoming a supervisor in the new system. For such people, the new organization meant reduced status, limited expectations, and, over the long haul, lower incomes.

New industrial workers also came to discover what every nineteenth-century resident had long experienced: the instability of urban employment. Traditionally, a large part of the urban labour force had been unemployed throughout much of the winter. The factory provided more stable employment for those who might otherwise have been general labourers, but production needs often resulted in considerable season-

The development of electric streetcars made the urban workers' lot easier. But the tracks and wires running through Montreal scarred the city's face.

COURTESY OF *LA PRESSE*.

able fluctuation in factory employment levels. Wages were sufficiently low that the unemployment or illness of the breadwinner generally spelled disaster for the family. No insurance against the exigencies of the urban environment was provided. Increasingly, two or three members of a family were seeking work in one place to improve their financial situation. To the employer's advantage, the discipline of the mill was reinforced in the home.

The condition of the industrial worker was in part a function of the community in which he or she worked. Most workers lived within walking distance of the workplace because, apart from a few large cities, public transportation facilities were limited before 1890, and where they did exist they were often too costly for the budget of a small wage earner. In large cities such as Montreal and Toronto this led to overcrowding, deplorable housing, and unsanitary living conditions for those in the most poorly paid industrial occupations. For skilled tradespeople and petty managers, it often meant life in sombre but not uncongenial row housing on the English model. As the cities expanded, residential areas became more and more segregated. Yet industrial workers rarely lived or worked in isolation. Whether the workers were local tradespeople, labourers, farm migrants, or recent arrivals from England, they would soon be joined by people whom they knew or to whom they were related. They would probably work and settle with such people. Some employers, like Boss Gibson at Marysville near Fredericton and Hart Massey in west Toronto, built houses that they rented to their workers. Others would maintain dormitories for single women. By and large, industrial workers were probably better off in towns than in cities. Housing was cheaper, access to work easier, and inexpensive farm produce was nearby. Water supplies were usually less contaminated, and sewerage was less a problem. Conditions in the worst industrial slums of large cities could be frightening: Montreal had the highest rate of infant mortality of any city in North America, largely the result of contaminated milk supplies and inadequate sewerage facilities.

Although many suffered economically as a result of the industrial transition – it is very difficult to judge whether living standards were rising or falling – the general trend of industrial wages between 1870 and 1890 moved slightly upward. However, this was an age of deflation and prices for most commodities declined steadily after 1874.[3]

---

[3] See Gregory Kealey, ed., *Canada Investigates Industrialism* (Toronto, 1973) and Terry Copp, *The Anatomy of Poverty: Conditions of the Working Class in Montreal 1897-1924* (Toronto, 1974).

TABLE 5

___

GROWTH OF INDUSTRIAL WORKERS

	Employees	Average Annual Wage
1870	181 000	$215
1880	248 000	$229
1890	351 000	$268

TABLE 6

___

WHOLESALE PRICE INDEX

	1870	1880	1890	1900
Vegetable Products	88	89	72	59
Animal Products	75	68	61	65
Textiles	105	95	76	68
Wood Products	36	35	53	56
Iron Products	106	99	82	79

Women and Industry

The process of industrialization had a unique impact on the condition of women. Some scholars agree that the net effect of that process was not to the benefit of most women. The farm, they would argue, was more of a partnership of the sexes where women and women's functions were accorded greater dignity and recognition than in the towns. For most women at Confederation, the pattern of life had changed little throughout the nineteenth century.

There were more than a million women in Canada over the age of 14 in 1871. Over half were married at that time and about 90 percent would marry at some point in their lives. Those who were middle-aged in 1871 would typically have married in their early 20s; those who married in the 1870s would wait until 25 or 26. A majority of the native-born were farmers' daughters, and most would marry farmers or other rural residents. As farm wives, they would keep house, weave cloth, cook, milk cows, churn butter, and help with the field labour at seedtime and harvest. Dairying was particularly significant for farm women because they made and sold most of the surplus butter. Most important, middle-aged women in 1871 would have borne six or seven live children – slightly more if they were French-Canadians and slightly less if they were Nova Scotians – and probably would have buried one or two of them before the child reached five. In old age, they would remain on the homestead either as the mistress of the home or as the grandmother sharing a home with a daughter-in-law and grandchildren. In the event of their being widowed – there were twice as many widows as widowers in 1871 – they would normally be assured, either through dower rights or through their husband's will, a place in the homestead.

A farm could be a source of security in an unstable world, but the rural environment offered few other opportunities for women. A few women farmed, a number of young women took service in the homes of neighbours, and some became school teachers, increasingly a women's occupation as local school trustees found they could meet the expanding educational requirements of their district by employing women who were paid smaller salaries than men. For women desiring other means of employment, many more opportunities could be found in the towns.

Young women sometimes outnumbered young men by as much as three to two in some towns. Such was the case in 1871, and the trend was to persist for many years. The employment that women found in the towns was almost always poorly paid. The most common job was that of live-in household servant. Live-in servants received free room and board and perhaps $5 a month in Montreal and $6 in Saint John and Toronto in the late nineteenth century. The work was confining and endless. Servants were on call 24 hours a day. Every aspect of life was regulated by the employer, and sexual exploitation was common. Although more than 40 percent of employed women were servants in 1891, it was not an occupation that most women would choose. Most young women worked in these situations until they married, at which time they usually stopped working outside the home. Others sought employment in the garment factories. Some widows, deserted women, and poor married women took in piece work at home where they worked long hours since wages were directly dependent on output. But the environment was generally more pleasant, and two or three women from the same household could work together. Although the hourly wage was greater in the factory, the often-harsh factory discipline for efficiency was absent. Some women at home might rent accommodations and take in boarders. Others taught. A few owned their own businesses.

Without a secure and adequate income, life in the towns was more precarious than in the countryside for women. Overcrowding was common, especially in districts where those with low incomes could find accommodation. Sanitary facilities were often deplorable in those same areas. Summers were usually more pleasant because wages and employment were higher, but winters – when unemployment rose, wages fell, and heating costs added great burdens to small incomes – could be very difficult times. Most women who had to support themselves in the towns were among the poorest inhabitants of the community.

These women and others who grew up in or migrated to the towns provided an important source of labour for the industrial expansion of

The disparities between rich and poor were enormous, as these contrasting photographs demonstrate. The poor were crowded and cramped while the well-off had space and every sign of turn-of-the-century culture on display.

the late nineteenth century. A significant part of that expansion required the services of a docile, disciplined workforce composed of people possessing limited skills who were prepared to work for low wages. Most of the new employment opportunities in textile mills and in garment

PA-30820/NATIONAL ARCHIVES OF CANADA.

manufacture were for women. So too were many in the tobacco and shoe industries. Wages for women in these industries were about half those paid to men. Indeed, cotton mill proprietors sometimes spoke of the high standard of living that family income could provide, and in both New Brunswick and Quebec farm families, who always earned less than townspeople, were recruited to the towns to work in the mills. Despite the low wages and long hours and tedious work, women frequently saw the new industry as an advance over the older urban opportunities. The pay might not be as secure, but it did bring the employee into the market economy and, despite the fears of some prominent Canadians that the factory system would lead to the sexual exploitation of female employees, it provided a freedom not afforded to those who worked as servants in the houses of other people.

The impact of the expanding industrial order on women's work was clearly seen in Montreal where in some wards the proportion of factory-employed women between the ages of 10 and 20 rose from 10 percent in 1861 to 30 percent in 1881, while the proportion of servants among the same age group declined from 15 percent to only 5 percent.

The industrial working life of most young women was comparatively short. Most married by their mid-twenties and became either full-time housewives or else engaged only in part-time work outside the home. The choosing of a husband was a most serious matter for both rural and urban women of all social levels. The first mark of a man's respectability was his ability to provide a steady, decent wage to support his family. When he could not do this, his wife returned to the labour market. For most women, however, the child-bearing years were spent at home. However, they were forced to find work when divorced (a most uncommon event), deserted, or widowed. The latter, especially, was a real possibility: research in the working-class districts of Montreal suggests that nearly a third of all women over 40 were widows. Life for most elderly widows in a wage economy was usually much more difficult than for those on farms.

The most significant and dangerous activity in the lives of most nineteenth-century women was childbirth, the leading cause of death among women of child-bearing age. Five of every thousand women giving birth in 1900 died. While these odds may seem very small, they meant that a woman giving birth to seven children (the average at mid-century) faced odds of 1 in 28 of dying as a result.

The growing urbanization of the population and the declining need for labour in rural areas was reflected in the falling birth rates of the last half of the nineteenth century. Among every 1000 women in Canada between the ages of 14 and 45, about 190 gave birth to children in 1871. This proportion fell to 160 by 1881 and to 145 in 1901. The average number of children born to fertile married women fell from 7 to 3.5 between 1850 and 1900. Such a decline was clearly the result of deliberate decisions by women and men to limit the size of their families. The most obvious means to accomplish this was by postponing marriage and, indeed, women's average age at marriage rose from 23 at mid-century to between 26 and 27 in 1891. Other means of birth control – apart from sexual abstinence – were less effective. Douches and pessaries were available, but manuals describing natural birth control methods were notoriously inaccurate. The declining birth rate provoked fears among many Canadians that current trends would lead to the demise of the Canadian people, or at least of its anglophone elements. That fear was sufficiently widespread that Parliament in 1892 incorporated a provision into the Criminal Code that anyone who sold or advertised anything designed to prevent conception or cause abortion was guilty of an offence punishable by two years imprisonment.

Urbanization and industrialization radically altered the lives of a large proportion of Canadian women in the last half of the nineteenth century. They encouraged the development of a home-centred woman's sphere and contributed to declining birth rates. Even so, by 1891, over one-quarter of all manufacturing jobs in Canada were held by women. In that same year, most servants were women and so, too, were about 40 percent of all professionals. In all, about one woman in seven between 14 and 60 worked for wages.[4]

----

[4] The following studies illustrate the role of working women in this period: Suzanne Cross, "The Neglected Majority: The Changing Role of Women in Nineteenth Century Montreal," *Histoire Social/Social History* (1973); Susan Trofimenkoff, "One Hundred and Two Muffled Voices: Canadian Industrial Women in the 1880s," *Atlantis* (1977); Marta Danylewycz, Beth Light, and Alison Prentice, "The Evolution of the Sexual Division of Labour in Teaching: A Nineteenth-Century Ontario and Quebec Case Study," *Histoire Social/Social History* (1983); Marjorie Cohen, "The Decline of Women in Canadian Dairying," *Histoire Sociale/Social History* (1984); Genevieve Leslie, "Domestic Service in Canada 1880-1920," in Janice Acton et al., *Women at Work: Ontario 1850-1930* (Toronto, 1974); Bettina Bradbury, "The Fragmented Family: Family Strategies in the Face of Death, Illness and Poverty, Montreal 1860-1885," in Joy Parr, ed., *Childhood and Family in Canadian History* (Toronto, 1982); "Women and Wage Labour in a Period of Transition: Montreal 1861-1881," *Histoire Sociale/Social History* (1984), Beth Light and Joy Parr, eds., *Canadian Women on the Move 1867-1920* (Toronto, 1983); Angus McLaren and Arlene McLaren, *The Bedroom and the State: The Changing Practices and Politics of Contraception and Abortion in Canada* (Toronto, 1986); and Ellen McGee, "Marriage in Nineteenth Century Canada," *Canadian Review of Sociology and Anthropology*, 1982.

The Labour Movement

The growth and integration of Canadian industry was paralleled by the growth and integration of a labour movement designed to protect the interests of those caught up in the new industrial structures. Organizations for the protection of wage workers had existed long before Confederation. Traditionally the sense of belonging to a common enterprise had been strongest among the artisans in each trade. Tailoring and printing had been brotherhoods whose practitioners were linked by the knowledge and skills of their craft. The tailors of a town sometimes negotiated with the masters of their trade to establish wages and working conditions. Occasionally, some journeymen tailors would withhold services from the master tailors in order to achieve their ends. In such cases, the dispute concerned members of a trade in one locality dealing with the division of profits from that trade. Occasionally, too, day labourers working on the docks, the canals, railways, or in the larger sawmills might engage in collective action to better their lot. But these

Immigrant workers in Toronto often lived in boarding houses with few amenities. Many had come to Canada intending to make their fortunes and return home, but large numbers stayed.

CITY OF TORONTO ARCHIVES/RG 8 32-58.

were usually spontaneous reactions to particular situations; only rarely had they any institutional basis.

The workforce of most Canadian cities possessed little cohesiveness. The continual influx of immigrants from the British Isles created a large pool of unskilled labour that depressed wages and gave the advantage to the employers through most of the year. Day labourers, moreover, were a mobile band moving from place to place seeking opportunity. That mobility tended to create an unstable workforce. Coupled with this disadvantage were the ethnic, religious, and racial divisions inherent in any immigrant community. In some workplaces, all the workers belonged to one ethnic or religious group because others would not be tolerated. Irish workers sometimes would not accept French, and Irish

Unions scored few gains among labour-hardened lumber workers; city workers seemed more receptive to protecting and enhancing their rights through union organization.

NOTMAN PHOTOGRAPHIC ARCHIVES, McCORD MUSEUM OF CANADIAN HISTORY.

Catholics would rarely tolerate Irish Protestants. Blacks lived and worked as a separate caste. Links of family, kinship, and traditional prejudices tended to strengthen these patterns of division.

The strongest sense of collective identity was found among the craftsmen, particularly printers and those in the metal trades. Their world, like those of most wage labourers of the period, was being altered by the new forms of industrial organization. However, they possessed specialized skills that gave them an advantage with their new masters. Tradesmen, however, often did not perceive themselves as part of a social group that included the more poorly paid day labourers and the women and children who occupied the very bottom of the wage pyramid. Taken together, these divisions and perceptions posed a formidable problem to anyone attempting to regulate the labour market and the workplace on behalf of the wage earners.

Attempts to ameliorate the lot of the wage worker achieved some success in periods of economic prosperity and generally collapsed during periods of depression. The years immediately following Confederation were relatively prosperous. By 1872, trade unions in a number of southwestern Ontario towns had organized central town unions, each of which could speak for wage earners in a variety of trades. Representatives from several of these town unions, including those of Hamilton, Toronto, Brantford, and Dundas, organized a central union for the region that soon became known as the Canadian Labour Union.

The major goal of these central unions was the achievement of the nine-hour work day. The nine-hour movement was embraced by the Toronto printers and the Hamilton metal trades in 1872. The most famous confrontation was between the printers at the country's leading daily newspaper, the Toronto *Globe*, and their employer, the former Liberal leader George Brown, who fiercely resisted any attempt at collective bargaining. Union activity to secure better wages had always been inhibited in British North America by a common law doctrine that viewed collective bargaining as a conspiracy or combination designed to restrain trade. Anxious to secure support among the growing body of industrial wage earners, Macdonald passed the Trade Union Act of 1872, which freed unions from the threat of prosecution for conspiracy. The printers lost the strike, but the act ushered in a period of labour participation in the Conservative Party that lasted until the end of the century. Despite the best efforts of the most influential unions in the country, the nine-hour movement failed to achieve its objectives. By 1874, it was effectively dead.

The recession that gripped Canada for the five years after 1874 destroyed most of the gains achieved by the labour movement in the previous decade. Any efforts at collective action beyond the local trade disappeared, and the Canadian Labour Union collapsed.

A revival began in 1879. In 1883 delegates from unions mainly from Toronto formed the Trades and Labour Congress of Canada, an umbrella organization designed to bring both skilled and unskilled labour into a single organization. The congress and its city counterparts acted as pressure groups in labour's dealings with the federal and provincial governments. The Trades and Labour Congress grew rapidly for several years, and by 1890 it represented significant groups of unions in a number of towns and cities.

The largest organization in the congress was the Knights of Labour. The Knights were the most remarkable labour organization to appear in Canada in the National Policy period. Imported from the United States where it had been active since 1869, the Knights differed from the dominant craft unions in several important ways. They were more broadly concerned with bettering the condition of all wage earners than were the more narrowly based craft unions. They organized workers by plants, thus cutting across the craft divisions that might see a dozen different unions in a single factory. They were the only union to admit women. They also admitted craft unions. They placed considerable emphasis on education and on the use of political pressure to persuade the traditional parties to provide legislation beneficial to wage workers. While they would and did organize strikes, they were more willing to work toward conciliation than were most craft unions.

The Knights spread very rapidly in the 1880s. While local assemblies were found from Vancouver Island to Cape Breton, their numbers and influence were centred on a corridor running from Montreal into the Lake Peninsula. While they initially encountered some opposition from the Catholic Church in Quebec, that was soon removed, and the Montreal district had 64 local assemblies divided into French-speaking and English-speaking district assemblies in the late nineteenth century. There were 252 local assemblies in Ontario with nearly 22 000 members at one time in the 1880s. The Knights were particularly effective in providing a voice for the unskilled and semi-skilled labourers and for women caught up in the factory system. In British Columbia, they spread among coal miners and rallied the white workers against the Chinese who had been imported as strike breakers by some British Columbia employers. In the main, however, the Knights managed for a time to bring a unity to the labour movement that had never been seen before.

The Knights dominated the congress and its Toronto and Montreal subsidiaries. The organization and many of its members were politically active: Knights ran for and several were elected federally and provincially in Quebec and Ontario in the 1880s. In the main they worked within the Conservative and Liberal parties. Although it is difficult to judge the influence that they had within the government, Knights did sit on the federal Royal Commission on the Relations of Labour and Capital in 1887 and were able to produce a majority report favourable to their views.

Still, their success was short-lived. Their decline began after 1886 as their relations with the craft unions became increasingly strained. Many craft unions were linked to their American counterparts in what became known as "international" unions. In the late 1880s, many craft unions came to view the Knights' emphasis on the welfare of the whole working class and their recruitment of craftsmen as threats to their welfare and status. The economy entered another recession in the mid-1890s and, once again, the union movement suffered. The Trades and Labour Congress survived as the representative for organized skilled and unskilled wage workers, but its activities and influence diminished through much of the decade.

A movement similar to the Knights emerged among the Springhill miners of Nova Scotia in 1879. The Provincial Workmen's Association soon spread to include glass and foundry workers, shoemakers, as well as a variety of general labourers. For a generation, it remained the principal labour movement in Nova Scotia. Its influence was mainly centred on the coal miners, but through its efforts miners in the province fought a number of industrial actions, entered the political arena, and received Premier Fielding's support. It maintained a high degree of work-place control throughout the period.

As prosperity returned and the pace of industrial change increased after 1879, so too did the self-confidence and organization of the workers. The instances of collective action and industrial confrontation grew dramatically in every region of the country. Most of the several hundred strikes in the 1880s were fought over attempts by employers to reduce wages, to mechanize trades, or to interfere with the traditional ways in which the workplace had been organized. All of these problems reflected the tensions created by the new industrial organizations, by the changing relationships between tradespeople and managers, and by the growing proletariat of the unskilled.

Apart from the fact that they probably represented a genuine concern for the working class – though they not possess much sense of class conflict – the Knights of Labour did much to bring the most serious problems of the new industrial order to the consciousness of society as a whole. At the same time, they could not hold together the diverse elements that comprised the industrial workforce. By 1900 the labour movement was small and fragmented.[5]

At Century's End

At century's end, Canada provided an interesting study in contrast. On the one hand, the majority continued to live in rural areas and farm. Many of those farmers, like their parents before them, continued to exist on the margins of the commercial economy. In the villages and urban places of the country, thousands of small producers – like the ubiquitous blacksmith – practised their trades in little shops typically employing two people. To an outsider crossing the countryside by road, little would seem to have changed in a generation.

On the other hand, there existed the great business organizations that had already reshaped the lives of a substantial minority of Canadians. The CPR, with its tens of thousands of employees performing hundreds of functions in dozens of communities across the country, epitomized the new order. And that structure was found on a lesser scale in other railways like the Grand Trunk and the Intercolonial. It was reflected, too, in the smoke stacks towering over hundreds of towns and cities, in the growing presence of nationwide retailers such as Eaton's, and in the branch-banking system that was slowly consolidating financial control of most banking resources in a small number of chartered banks. Even the farms of the new prairie wheat culture seemed extremely large, mechanized, and organized in comparison with their more traditional eastern counterparts.

The process was gradually integrating larger and larger numbers of people into larger organizations whose parameters were national rather than local or regional. The social implications of the process were

---

[5] See Gregory Kealey and Bryan Palmer, *Dreaming of What Might Be: The Knights of Labour in Ontario* (New York, 1982); Bernard Ostry, "Conservatives, Liberals and Labour in the 1870s," *CHR* (1960); Bryan Palmer, *A Culture In Conflict: Skilled Workers and Industrial Capitalism in Hamilton Ontario 1860-1914* (Montreal, 1979); Gregory Kealey, *Toronto Workers Respond to Industrial Capitalism, 1867-1892* (Toronto, 1980); Peter DeLottinville, "Trouble in the Hives of Industry: The Cotton Industry Comes to Milltown, New Brunswick, 1879-1892," *Historical Papers* (1980); "Joe Beef of Montreal. Working-Class Culture and the Tavern, 1869-1889," *Labour/Le Travail* (1981-82); and Ian McKay, "By Wilson, Wile or War: The Provincial Workingmen's Association and the Struggle for Working-Class Independence in Nova Scotia, 1879-97," *Labour/Le Travail* (1986).

For prosperous Canadians, such as this Fredericton businessman of the Confederation era, life was full of opportunities.

profound. Large agglomerations of capital placed control of most dynamic elements of the economy in fewer hands while lengthening the social distance between those who owned and those who worked for these organizations. It doubtless contributed to a growing self-consciousness on the part of many workers. At the same time, it opened a number of opportunities. A class of professional managers commanded most of the mills, factories, banks, and railways and headed the specialized departments that were beginning to emerge in the larger organizations.

While many skilled workers suffered, it still remains unclear whether women and other unskilled workers viewed the new order as less palatable than the alternatives. And the most depressing element in industrial development was the growing regimentation of this workforce and the decline in the quality of its living and working environment.

1896-1911:
THE LAURIER YEARS

On Tuesday evening, June 20, 1893, Ottawa, whose basic industry was politics, was agog with excitement. The carriages and drivers outside the large old Rideau Rink had brought the Liberal faithful from Parliament Hill, from the provincial capitals, from constituencies across the land to the arena. Inside, the workers had finished their chores; the chairs had been set out in rows with military precision and draped Union Jacks, freshly cut boughs and early summer blooms were in place. On the platform sat the potentates of the Liberal Party in strict order of prominence and seniority. The main event of the first national political party convention ever to be called in Canada was at hand.

The man standing at the podium was known to all of the delegates, alternates, newspeople, and visitors who had crowded into every cranny and corner of the rink. And – it was only one of his remarkable talents – he knew most of them, had probably given many a kindly word of greeting or encouragement at some time, in some place, during the seven years he had been party leader. He was 52: tall, erect, handsome, his flowing hair starting to grey, his warm smile balancing the alert, piercing gaze of his deep-set eyes. His dress, the high, white collar, the silk cravat, the high-buttoned coat, was formal. About his bearing there was a formality, an aristocratic touch, befitting a leader. But the delegates also knew him as a friendly man whose approach to politics, and life, was seemingly easy-going, almost lazy, though governed by a deep commitment to moderation, conciliation, and tolerance.

Wilfrid Laurier, the son of a land surveyor of modest means, had been born in L'Assomption County, Lower Canada, in 1841. His early schooling at a classical college was followed by studies in law at McGill University. After admission to the Lower Canada Bar in 1864 he practised his profession in Montreal for two years and then took up the editorship of a small newspaper, *Le défricheur*, in Arthabaska County. The radical politics of the Institut Canadien and parti rouge, of which Laurier had been a member in his student days, found expression in the journal, incurring the profound displeasure of the very conservative Bishop Laflèche. It was the first of a lifelong series of ideological conflicts between the liberal-minded Laurier and the superiors of his church over the role of the Catholic Church and churchmen in the affairs of state. Within months, *Le défricheur* was banned. By then Laurier was again practising law in Arthabaskaville.

The briefs and busy work of a small law office were not enough to contain his ambition. That ambition found its outlet in politics where, as he told a friend, his goal was "making my ideas triumph." In 1871, Laurier won election to the Legislative Assembly of Quebec. Three years later, he was elected for the first time to the House of Commons in Ottawa. Laurier was quickly recognized as a young man of uncommon talent and in 1877 he joined the cabinet of Alexander Mackenzie's Liberal government and became leader of the federal Liberals in Quebec. When Mackenzie retired after Sir John A. Macdonald's victory in the 1878 election, Edward Blake, the new leader of the Liberal Party, depended heavily upon Laurier as a friend and adviser. Then, when Blake himself retired in 1887, the Liberal caucus chose Laurier as their national leader.

The early years of Laurier's leadership had been neither easy nor rewarding. His reputation for fairness and moderation in addressing the great and decisive questions of English-French relations in the 1880s, the Riel question, and the use of the French language in the Northwest Territories, was firmly established. However, many English-Canadian members of the party worried as much about Laurier's Roman Catholicism and his defence of the rights of French-Canadians as French-Canadian members fretted about his tendency to compromise what they perceived to be the essential rights and privileges of French-Canadians in Confederation. Moreover, when he assumed the leadership, Laurier knew that his party was desperately in need of a policy alternative to the Macdonald government's National Policy of tariff protection to promote industrial and agricultural development. He quickly embraced unrestricted reciprocity, with its demand for complete free trade with the

United States and, in the 1891 election, was charged with disloyalty by Macdonald and humiliatingly defeated.

The Ottawa convention had been called two years later to restore party confidence, to encourage party organization and, Laurier hoped, to adopt a new program that would at last put the Liberals on the path to victory. As Laurier waited for the cheers that greeted him to die, he noted the bold banners displayed throughout the hall. Like all the other convention arrangements, they had been carefully prepared to draw the delegates' attention to a single point:

Protection is a National Folly and a National Crime.
The Tory Tariff Oppresses the Farmer.
Millions for Necessity – Not a Cent for Monopoly.
Protection is Legalized Robbery.
Liberty to Commerce.

Delegates were being reminded of 15 years of Tory protectionism, of courting the big interests, of neglect of farmers and workers. Macdonald, the Father of Confederation, the champion of the National Policy, was dead. But the Conservatives still ruled on Parliament Hill, and it was easy enough on that warm summer evening for Laurier's followers to believe that baneful Tory policies were the cause of the depressed trade and low farm prices which wracked Canada in the mid-1890s.

That was Laurier's theme. "One of the plagues of Egypt took away the first-born of each family," the Liberal press reported him as saying, "but under Canada's National Policy the whole issue of the people was being taken away. (CHEERS) The ideal fiscal system was the British system of free trade. (GREAT APPLAUSE) It was the policy of the Liberal party to get as near that ideal policy as the requirements of revenue would permit. Free trade was the goal toward which they should struggle. (CHEERS) He was, before all things, a Canadian. TARIFF REDUCTION AND RECIPROCITY ought to form the two main planks in the platform of the party. (GREAT APPLAUSE)."

Ever so skilfully the banners, Laurier's speech, and the resolutions adopted the next day began to move the party away from total reliance on the dangerous doctrine of unrestricted reciprocity and toward a new tariff policy that would accommodate the manufacturing and commercial interests that the National Policy had nurtured. The "requirements of revenue" could cover many concessions to these interests. The "goal" of free trade – *freer* trade with Great Britain and the United States was the way the tariff resolution put it – held out hope to the farmers.

Another Adventurous Inventor

Performer Laurier: "Yes, my friends, I'm going over in this machine – my own invention – I feel sure it will take me safely through."

KAHRS/*DAILY MAIL AND EMPIRE.*

No less carefully, the banners, the speech, and the resolutions of the convention were silent on the other great issue that bedeviled Canadian politics in the 1890s, the Manitoba schools question. At that moment the issue was before the courts and that was an excuse for silence. More important, members of the Liberal Party, like their opponents, were deeply divided on the issue. There was little that could be said that would not offend one or another faction of the party whereas silence, and deflection of the party's interest to other issues, like the tariff, would promote party unity.

The Liberal Party Convention of 1893 marked the turning point in Wilfrid Laurier's political fortunes. The next general election was still a few years away, but the convention stimulated party loyalty and organization and established the strategy and the programs that the Liberals would carry into the contest. Over the months ahead Laurier would keep his counsel on the schools question and reassert, again and again, the party's safe if ambiguous trade policy. When followers strayed away and urged him to take a stand on the schools issue, they were brought back into line. "Let us bring back public opinion to the tariff," he told a Liberal editor in Ontario in 1895.

This position could not be sustained as the Manitoba schools question dominated Parliament and the election of 1896. But the flexibility and political shrewdness the confident Laurier had demonstrated in resolving the splits in his party over tariff policy inspired confidence among his followers that the Liberal leader could somehow find a method of resolving the schools question too. Laurier got his chance when the voters gave his Liberal Party a comfortable majority of 30 seats in the general election. The Conservative Party's dominance over federal politics had been broken. The Laurier era, the Liberal century, had begun.

Laurier in Power[1]

It was a propitious time to begin a new regime. An impressive upswing in the economy was well underway and confidence in the future seemed pervasive. Everyone, an English visitor noted, "is preaching, praising, prophesying." Everyone was also counting; counting every imaginable measure of progress, because numbers lent "scientific" credibility to the rhetoric of progress. Government clerks in Ottawa, and in the provincial capitals, eagerly compiled mountains of statistics to illustrate the increasing productivity in growing grain, in livestock husbandry, in peat

[1] The most comprehensive survey of the Laurier years is Robert Craig Brown and Ramsay Cook, *Canada, 1896-1921: A Nation Transformed* (Toronto, 1974). A major study of developments in Quebec is Paul André Linteau, René Durocher, and Jean-Claude Robert, *Histoire du Québec Contemporain: De la Confederation à la crise, 1867-1929* (Québec, 1979). The standard biography of Laurier is O.D. Skelton, *Life and Letters of Sir Wilfrid Laurier*, 2 vols. (Toronto, 1921). Other accounts include Joseph Schull, *Laurier: The First Canadian* (Toronto, 1965); Richard Clippingdale, *Laurier, His Life and World* (Toronto, 1979); J.S. Willison, *Sir Wilfrid Laurier and the Liberal Party*, 2 vols. (Toronto, 1903); and J.W. Dafoe, *Laurier, A Study in Canadian Politics* (Toronto, 1922). A masterful analysis of Laurier's political career is H. Blair Neatby, *Laurier and a Liberal Quebec: A Study in Political Management* (Toronto, 1973).

moss mining, in the export of bicycles, and the number of telegraphic messages sent every year. Not to be outdone, businesspeople and boomers rivaled politicians and civil servants in their glowing recitations of Canada's potential for greatness.

Much was made of Canadian progress in education, "religious and moral interests," the arts and music, and literature and journalism, lest anyone feared that the Dominion of the North lagged behind in the development of all the elements of Victorian sophistication. But the focus of attention was on material progress, and nowhere more so than in Ottawa. "Official Ottawa shows nothing of the sedate dignity of a Government capital," another visitor wrote. "Her clubs and offices are tense with the spirit of the 'boom.' "[2] Keenly appreciating the political value of good times, Laurier boasted that "the twentieth century shall be the century of Canada and of Canadian development." Development was good politics, good for the new government, good for the party. It contrasted sharply with the stalemate, confusion, and acrimony of the last years of Tory rule. It caught the imagination of a confident nation yearning for self-realization.

There were some worries about the new government. How, business-people asked, would the Liberals deal with the tariff? A letter was quickly sent to John Willison, editor of the Toronto *Globe*. "The tariff should not be reformed," Laurier wrote, "until there has been ample discussion with the businessmen. . . ." Another positive signal was sent to the manufac-turers whose interests had been so assiduously protected by the National Policy. Sir Richard Cartwright, the long-time Liberal financial critic and an ardent advocate of unrestricted reciprocity, was relegated to the secondary Ministry of Trade and Commerce. And Laurier's "cabinet of all talents" included many new faces sympathetic to the protectionist principles of the National Policy. Most important was the new minister of finance, William S. Fielding who, as Premier of Nova Scotia, had courted Amercian financial interests to develop the coal resources of his province. Quebec's delegation included Joseph Israel Tarte, a former Tory with strong protectionist sympathies, and Richard Dobell, a Quebec City Conservative who had been elected with Tory support. Ontario's members included Sir Oliver Mowat, former premier, and William Paterson, a manufacturer who became minister of customs. Both were

---

[2] A lively account of Ottawa in these years is Sandra Gwyn, *The Private Capital: Ambition and Love in the Age of Macdonald and Laurier* (Toronto, 1984).

protectionists. Soon Clifford Sifton, Manitoba's attorney general, would join them as the new minister of the interior. Sifton led the western delegation in the cabinet, and he knew that for Westerners free trade was second only to the Gospels as a sacred principle of life. But he was no champion of free trade, which could destroy an entrenched interest group that could pay rich political dividends to the Liberal Party. He bluntly told a constituent that "I would consider that to so construct the tariff as to wantonly destroy the industries that have been built up under it, would be utterly unjustifiable from any standpoint of reason."[3]

In April 1897, Fielding announced the new government's tariff policy. There were a few concessions to the farmers who had been the backbone of the party and the staunchest advocates of free trade: a reduction in duties on implements, binder twine, and a few other goods essential to agricultural production. The prospect of freer trade also existed in the innovative feature of Fielding's policy: the adoption of a two-tier tariff. Canada would offer a 12½ percent preference immediately, to be increased to 25 percent in the next year, to any nation that lowered its duties against Canadian goods by an equivalent rate. Because of its free trade policy, the United Kingdom, a major market for agricultural exports, automatically qualified for the preference, and British goods, as a result, would be allowed into Canada more cheaply than American products.

Beneath the preference, however, the solid structure of protection remained intact. Laurier's assurances to the business community had been fulfilled. And, apart from Britain, the onus of moving further toward free trade had neatly been shifted from Ottawa to Canada's trading partners. So it would remain until the very last days of the Laurier administration. Ten years after the first Fielding tariff, in 1907, another modification was introduced: a third "intermediate" schedule of duties between the general tariff and what had become the British preference.

---

[3] On the National Policy see O.J. McDiarmid, *Commercial Policy in the Canadian Economy* (Cambridge, 1946); J.H. Perry, *Taxes, Tariffs, and Subsidies: A History of Canadian Fiscal Development*, 2 vols. (Toronto, 1955); and J.H. Dales, *The Protective Tariff in Canada's Development* (Toronto, 1966). The origins of the National Policy are explored in Ben Forster, *A Conjunction of Interests: Business, Politics, and Tariffs, 1827-1879* (Toronto, 1986). R.C. Brown examines "The Nationalism of the National Policy" in Peter Russell, ed., *Nationalism in Canada* (Toronto, 1966). See also Michael Bliss, "Canadian American Business: The Roots of the Branch Plant," in Ian Lumsden, ed., *Close the 49th Parallel: The Americanization of Canada* (Toronto, 1970). A valuable retrospective is "The National Policy, 1879-1979," *Journal of Canadian Studies* XIV, Fall, 1979.

This quickly led to limited reciprocal trade agreements with France, Japan, and Italy. Still, protectionism remained the keystone of tariff policy, as it would for decades to come. The significance of the modifications of the Laurier government was that it modernized the National Policy. It retained the protective principle but added additional schedules to the tariff to give the government flexibility in its efforts to entice foreign customers to buy an ever-increasing flow of Canadian products for export.

The other worry was the schools question in Manitoba. How would Laurier handle it? There were few clues in his campaign speeches leading up to the election: the advocacy of "sunny ways" only hinted, but significantly so, at conciliation. It was true that Manitoba might have to be coerced. But Laurier knew that compulsion would only intensify distrust between French- and English-Canadians on this most sensitive of Canadian problems. A face-saving compromise, quietly arranged between Liberal governments in Ottawa and Winnipeg, was a much better solution. By November 1896, it was in place. Manitoba's public school system would remain intact and Catholics would have to support it with their tax dollars. But religious instruction by clergy could take place during the last half-hour of the school day and public school trustees would have to provide a Catholic teacher for every 25 Catholic pupils in rural districts and every 40 Catholic students in urban areas. Moreover, in schools where 10 or more students spoke French or any other language than English, instruction had to be provided in French or such other language, as well as in English.[4]

The Laurier-Greenway compromise did not satisfy the clerical leadership in Manitoba and Quebec. The hierarchy had always been suspicious of Laurier, of his rouge background, of his unwavering espousal of the principles of English Liberalism. Laurier always seemed too ready to yield to English-Canadian arguments that separate schools perpetuated

---

[4] Paul Crunican, *Priests and Politicians: Manitoba Schools and the Election of 1896* (Toronto, 1974), is a detailed analysis of the Manitoba schools question. David Hall gives another perspective on the issue in Manitoba in *Clifford Sifton*, Volume One: *The Young Napoleon, 1861-1900* (Vancouver, 1981). A useful collection of documents is Lovell Clark, *The Manitoba School Question: Majority Rule or Minority Rights?* (Toronto, 1968). A related issue is explored in Manoly R. Lupul, *The Roman Catholic Church and the North-West School Question: A Study in Church-State Relations in Western Canada, 1875-1905* (Toronto, 1974). See also W.L. Morton, "Manitoba Schools and Canadian Nationality, 1890-1923," *Canadian Historical Association Annual Report, 1951*; and Ramsay Cook, "Church, Schools and Politics in Manitoba, 1902-1912," *Canadian Historical Review* XXXIX (1958).

religious prejudice and prevented the social homogeneity essential in a democracy. However, for the clerics Catholic schools were a matter of survival, survival of the race and its rich cultural heritage in and outside Quebec, survival of the religious convictions that were the foundation of a Christian society. The clerics appealed to Rome for intervention against Laurier's compromise with Manitoba's "godless" school system. When, in December, 1897, the papal encyclical *Affari Vos* advised acceptance of the Manitoba settlement, the clergy obeyed, very reluctantly.

Still, opposition to Laurier's policy continued to smoulder among his clerical critics. For his part, the prime minister remained an enthusiastic champion of school systems "where the young children of the land are taught Christian morals and Christian dogmas." It was not enough. The Roman Catholic clergy correctly perceived that the prime minister was charting a new course, trying to accommodate the traditional role of the Catholic school in French-Canadian society, so deeply rooted in the history of Quebec and embodied in the Manitoba Act of 1870, to the demographic and political realities of the emerging West that had been crystallized in the Manitoba Schools Act of 1890. Unlike his critics, Laurier did not believe that the survival of French-Canadian culture rested upon the preservation of entrenched guarantees for separate schools. He had a more optimistic faith in his people, in their talent of survival. "The salvation of the French race is not in isolation," he told a member of his caucus, "but in struggle. Give our children the best education possible, put them on equal footing with those of the other race, and give them the legitimate pride which they will have in such a struggle. There is salvation. There is autonomy."

Immigrants Are Welcome

Clifford Sifton, the minister of the interior, provided the innovative spark to the new Laurier administration. The astonishing success of his aggressive programs to promote immigration laid the foundations for the government's breathtaking national development policies. The goal of his immigration policy was to attract experienced farmers to Canada to exploit the rich soil of the prairie West, and the improved economic conditions of the Laurier era made Sifton's policies all the more attractive to prospective immigrants. Prices for food products rose rapidly, the price of wheat in the British market increasing by 35 percent between 1896 and 1913. At the same time cost increases for new, labour-saving farm implements like the chilled steel plow, the improved harrow and seed-driller, and the threshing machine were more moderate. Transportation costs, both ocean freight rates and railway rates, dropped in Canada. In 1897, for example, the government negotiated the Crow's Nest Pass Agreement with the Canadian Pacific Railway. The agreement stipulated that in return for government assistance in building a branch line through the difficult terrain of the Crow's Nest Pass, the railway would reduce its freight rates for westbound articles necessary for agricultural production and for eastbound shipments of grain. In addition, federal government scientists and technicians promoted improved farming techniques, such as dry farming, and experimented with new strains of wheat, such as Marquis, developed by Dominion cerealist C.E. Saunders, which would mature more rapidly in the short growing season of the prairie West. Taken together, these developments transformed the Canadian Prairies into a land of promise for future settlers.[5]

The chief impediments to immigration had hitherto been erected by the Government of Canada. Railway construction had been assisted by the grant of huge blocks of land to the railways, tying up many of the most fertile areas in the Prairies. Sifton pressured the holders of grants to select their land and put it on the market. Administration of lands policy under the Dominion Lands Act of 1872 was simplified and centralized in Ottawa. Most important, the Department of the Interior embarked upon an unprecedented promotion of Canada as a land of opportunity, not just in the United Kingdom, the traditional focus of Canada's immigration effort, but also in the United States and in Europe.

The timing was right. But Canada was competing with Australia, Argentina, and the United States for the potential migrants from Britain and Europe. Success required vigorous and continuous promotion of Canada. Immigration work, Sifton observed, "has to be carried on in the same manner as the sale of any commodity; just as soon as you stop advertising and missionary work the movement is going to stop."

Canada did not recruit just anyone. Immigration policy was, in

---

[5] For Sifton's immigration policy see Hall, *Clifford Sifton*, vols. I and II (Vancouver, 1981 and 1985). Other studies include M.F. Timlin, "Canada's Immigration Policy, 1896-1910," *Canadian Journal of Economics and Political Science*, XXVI (1960); George Woodcock and Ivan Avakumovic, *The Doukhobors* (Toronto, 1968); Robin Winks, *The Blacks in Canada* (New Haven, 1971); Peter Ward, *White Canada Forever: Popular Attitudes and Public Policy Toward Orientals in British Columbia* (Montreal, 1978); Joy Parr, *Labouring Children* (London, 1980); and Donald Avery, *"Dangerous Foreigners": European Immigrant Workers and Labour Radicalism in Canada, 1896-1932* (Toronto, 1979).

intention if not always in practice, selective. City folk, especially labouring men and mechanics, were not wanted. They were, Sifton wrote, "the most helpless people in the world when they are placed upon the Prairie and left to shift for themselves." Canada wanted farmers who were accustomed to working the grain lands of Europe and the United States where conditions were similar to those of the Prairies. Between 1896 and 1905, 58 000 immigrants arrived from Austria-Hungary, 32 000 from Russia and 8000 from Italy. The burning issue of the Laurier years, especially in Western Canada, focused on how Canada could absorb and make loyal citizens of these hordes of "strangers," including almost 12 000 Chinese immigrants who had concentrated in British Columbia. For the Chinese and other Asians, the answer seemed clear enough: cut off further immigration. As early as 1899 the government of British Columbia tried to impose a $500 head tax on Asian immigrants,

Canada sought immigrants; but if they were unfit, like the boy on crutches, they were ordinarily denied entry.

but the B.C. legislation was disallowed in Ottawa. After 1905, when Frank Oliver succeeded Sifton as minister of the interior, immigration policy became increasingly restrictive. By then curtailing Asian immigration had become a prominent political issue and, in 1907, in the wake of rioting against Asian immigrants in Vancouver, the government concluded a "gentlemen's agreement" with Japan to limit Japanese migration to Canada sharply. The following year the Immigration Act was amended to require immigrants to come to Canada by direct passage from their home country, and this further curtailed Asian immigration. By the end of the Laurier years, the full force of the Department of the Interior's administrative machinery was also being applied to discourage further immigration of blacks, who had made up 9 percent of the 303 680 immigrants from the United States who came to Canada by 1911.

Previous waves of immigration, especially in the mid-nineteenth century, had come largely from the United Kingdom. But now there were huge numbers of immigrants on railway construction gangs, in factories and mines, and on the Prairies who had emigrated from Europe. Their foreign ways, many Canadians worried, would undermine Canadian society. The editor of the *Canadian Magazine* described them as "rude, barbarous and uncultured." Sifton believed that the key to assimilating the immigrants was getting them on the land. Dominion lands policy, in addition to "proving up" required that homesteaders become British subjects before the issue of the final patent to the land. By 1911, 45 percent of the foreign-born had become British subjects. As Sifton's Winnipeg paper, the *Free Press* put it, "if you get the immigrant on the land he becomes at once naturalized and nationalized."

Sifton and many other Canadians also believed that the public school system was a vital instrument of assimilation. "One of the best ways of Canadianizing, nationalizing, and turning all into intelligent citizens," a Protestant minister argued, "is by means of a good English education." If title to land would tie the immigrants to Canada, the schools would be the means of transforming their children into loyal Canadians. This became the fundamental factor in a new school issue in national politics. Between 1891 and 1901 the population of the Northwest Territories had increased by 66 percent. In response to demands from politicians in the Territories for provincial status, Laurier promised to create new provinces in his 1904 election campaign. In February 1905, bills creating the provinces of Saskatchewan and Alberta were introduced in the House of Commons.

Laurier was amazingly popular in both English and French Canada. This superb photograph shows the prime minister mainstreeting during the 1908 election.

C-932/NATIONAL ARCHIVES OF CANADA.

When the Territories were organized by the Dominion Government in 1875, separate and equal Catholic and Protestant school systems had been established. Over the years Territorial Ordinances had dramatically altered the educational system, partly in response to the need for greater efficiency and partly in the desire to "Canadianize" the growing foreign-born population which, by 1900, was more than 27 percent of the populace. All schools had become public schools, with the same regulations and curriculum. Religious instruction was permitted only at the end of the school day, and the majority in each district determined whether Catholic or Protestant teachers were hired.

Conscious of the lingering distrust of the administration by the Catholic clergy and of a growing concern among French-Canadians that Sifton's immigration policy was excluding them from their rightful share

To eastern Canadians the West was ranches and rodeos; the reality, however, was often a sod hut and appalling conditions.

GLENBOW ARCHIVES, CALGARY/NA-1255-31.

BUILT OF SOD

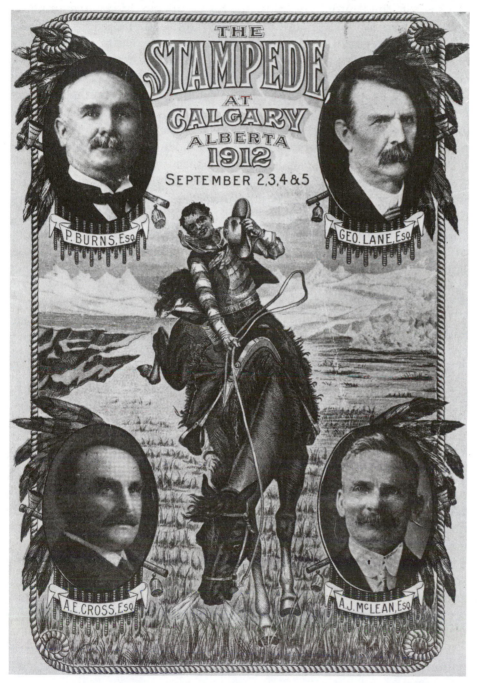

in western development, Laurier gave the task of drafting the education clauses of the autonomy bills to his minister of justice, Charles Fitzpatrick from Quebec, and to the M.P. from Labelle, Henri Bourassa. Sifton, who remained adamantly opposed to separate schools, was excluded. When the bills were introduced, the ambiguously worded education clauses conveyed the impression that the government was going to restore the separate school system of 1875 and impose it on the new provinces.

The clauses provoked a heated debate in the House of Commons, one that threatened to split both parties on religious and racial lines. Robert Borden, who had become leader of the Conservative Opposition in 1901, was forced to allow his caucus a free vote on the issue. For his own part, Borden firmly argued that the education clauses would deny the new provinces the right to determine their own education policies. It was a telling constitutional and political point. Liberals, after all, had long prided themselves on their respect for provincial autonomy. And what province had more to fear from the precedent of Dominion interference in its educational system than Quebec?

Far more damaging to the government was the resignation of Sifton as minister of interior and the threatened resignation of Fielding. Laurier, taken aback, denied that his purpose had been to present Sifton with a fait accompli. But he did not urge Sifton to rejoin the cabinet. He did, however, entrust him with the responsibility for redrafting the education clauses. The new version, accepted by Parliament, recognized only the miniority rights that remained in the 1901 Territorial Ordinances.

Laurier had kept his election promise to create the new provinces, but at great cost. Once again the more militant clergy, now joined by a small but growing number of French-Canadian nationalists such as Henri Bourassa, argued that the prime minister had surrendered sacred principles to placate the English-speaking majority in Parliament. "In constituting the French-Canadian, who has lived in this country since its discovery, the equal in rights and privileges to the Dukobor [sic] or the Galician who has just embarked," one critic said, "we have opened a gulf between eastern and western Canadians which nothing will fill." The speaker was Armand Lavergne, another nationalist. He, with Bourassa and Sifton, had lost faith in Laurier. These three, with their diametrically opposite visions of the future of Canada, would all play prominent roles in Laurier's defeat in 1911.

For the immigrants the quarrels in Parliament and the tensions of national politics scarcely mattered. Their daily concerns were more prosaic. Agriculturists had to find a piece of land, erect a dwelling, make provision for the families who accompanied them or would soon follow, and cope with a strange language, different customs, and, not least, the elements. Add to that the corrosive factors of distance and loneliness. In time the telephone, improved roads, and motor vehicles would all help and account, in part, for the extraordinary numbers of social groups, from church societies to baseball teams, that settlers joined. But still the loneliness persisted. E.B. Mitchell, in his book on Western Canada before the war, noted that the "loneliness of many parts is extreme. The farms are large, a quarter square mile at the least. In three districts I knew, blocks of empty 'Company land' were constantly intervening, breaking up the settled country and harbouring gophers." It was especially hard on the women. "A woman alone in the house all day may find the silence deadly; in the wheat-farming stage there may not even be a beast about the place. Her husband may be tired at night, and unwilling to 'hitch up' and drive her out 'for a whimsy'; or the husband may be willing and sympathetic, but she may grow shy and diffident, and not care to make the effort to tidy herself up and go to see a neighbour – any neighbour, just to break the monotony."

TABLE 1

INTENDED DESTINATION OF IMMIGRANTS TO CANADA, 1901-1911

	Maritime Provinces	Quebec	Ontario	Manitoba	Saskatchewan and Alberta	British Columbia and Yukon Territories	Canada
Total number 1901-1911	73 501	258 820	403 899	309 623	516 832	188 571	1 751 246
%	4.3	14.8	23.0	17.7	29.5	10.7	100.0

SOURCE: *CANADA YEAR BOOK*, 1913.

The government's terms for homesteaders were generous. On Dominion lands, as distinct from the land granted to the railways or the Hudson's Bay Company, the settler was entitled to a free quarter-section if he lived on it and "proved it up" over a period of three years. He was also allowed a pre-emption to purchase an additional 160 acres (65 ha) of land. But often this was not enough for wheat farmers, especially in the more arid regions of the prairie West. In addition, the process of settlement was costly, whether the settler came from Britain, Europe, the American Midwest, or an Ontario or Nova Scotia farmstead. Estimates varied from $250 to as much as $1500 for start-up costs, depending upon the degree of deprivation a settler would tolerate for a new life. Cash was only part of the cost. There was the painful labour of breaking the prairie sod or clearing parkland, and the risk of hailstorms and early frost that could destroy a year's work in a matter of minutes. And, again, there was the loneliness. Still the settlers came, and almost 60 percent of those from abroad told immigration officials that they were bound for the West.[6]

Every province except Prince Edward Island experienced a growth in population between 1901 and 1911. And a massive internal migration

TABLE 2

POPULATION OF CANADA AND THE PROVINCES, 1901-1911

	1901	1911	% change
Nova Scotia	459 574	492 338	7.1
New Brunswick	331 120	351 889	6.3
Prince Edward Island	103 259	93 728	−9.2
Quebec	1 648 898	2 003 232	21.5
Ontario	2 182 947	2 523 274	15.6
Manitoba	255 211	455 614	78.5
Saskatchewan	91 279	492 432	439.5
Alberta	73 022	374 663	413.1
British Columbia	178 657	392 480	119.7
CANADA	5 371 315	7 206 643	34.2

SOURCE: *CANADA YEAR BOOK*, 1913, p. 51

---

[6] There is a splendid account of the opening of the West in Gerald Friesen, *The Canadian Prairies: A History* (Toronto, 1984). An excellent analysis of settlement of a particular area in Alberta is Paul Voisey, *Vulcan. The Making of a Prairie Community* (Toronto, 1987); and R.C. MacLeod examines an important aspect of settlement in *The North-West Mounted Police and Law Enforcement, 1873-1905* (Toronto, 1976). Other studies include J.B. Hedges, *Building the Canadian West* (New York, 1939); A.S. Morton and Chester Martin, *History of Prairie Settlement and Dominion Lands Policy* (Toronto, 1938); W.L. Morton, *Manitoba, A History* (Toronto, 1967); and Margaret Ormsby, *British Columbia, A History* (Toronto, 1958). Also see Donald Swainson, ed., *Historical Essays on the Prairie Provinces* (Toronto, 1970); and Carl Berger and Ramsay Cook, eds., *The West and the Nation, Essays in Honour of W.L. Morton* (Toronto, 1976).

supplemented immigration from abroad. Also spurred by better times and new economic opportunities, patterns of internal migration varied from region to region. Some Maritimers sought better jobs close to home in another province in the region. Tens of thousands of French-Canadians moved into eastern and northern Ontario to work in the lumber camps and mines of that rapidly developing area. In general, however, the flow of migration was clearly from east to west. By 1911 more than 12 percent of all those born in Ontario lived between the Red River and the Pacific Ocean. They were joined by large numbers from the Maritimes and Quebec, and all of them exerted their heavy influence upon the developing institutions and cultural attitudes of Sifton's "New Canada."

TABLE 3

BIRTHPLACES OF POPULATION BY PROVINCE IN 1911 (PERCENTAGES)

	Canadian Born		Immigrants	
	Born in province	Born in another province	British-born	Foreign-born
Nova Scotia	90.2	2.5	5.1	2.2
New Brunswick	90.7	4.1	2.9	2.3
Prince Edward Island	95.4	1.8	1.8	1.0
Quebec	91.1	1.6	3.6	3.7
Ontario	76.6	3.3	14.2	5.9
Manitoba	37.5	20.6	20.9	21.0
Saskatchewan	20.7	29.8	16.5	33.0
Alberta	19.7	23.6	18.6	38.1
British Columbia	21.5	21.6	30.1	26.8
CANADA	70.2	7.8	11.6	10.4

SOURCE: *CANADA YEAR BOOK*, 1913. Data Rounded Off.

The Peoples' Lives

It would be a mistake to assume that all of the migrants were or even intended to be agriculturalists. Thousands of Canadians and immigrants found new jobs in the forest industries of northern Ontario, Quebec, and British Columbia, in the hardrock mines of Ontario and British Columbia, and in the newly opened coal shafts in the Rocky Mountains. The number employed in those occupations increased by 156 percent and

119 percent, respectively, between 1901 and 1911. And, among the gainfully employed, the proportion of farmers, despite the emphasis in immigration policy, steadily declined from 45 percent in 1891 to 40.2 percent in 1901 and 34.3 percent in 1911.

As significant as the development of the West was the growth of cities in the Laurier years. Not until after 1921 would more Canadians live in urban communities than in rural areas, but between 1901 and 1911 every major city except Charlottetown grew in size, with the western cities of Winnipeg, Regina, Saskatoon, Edmonton, Calgary, and Vancouver leading the pack. Much of the internal migration, especially in Eastern Canada, was from farm to city as young people sought jobs in the industrializing and expanding urban areas. This expansion was heavily supplemented, across Canada, with immigration from abroad. Thousands of mechanics and workers were assiduously sought out by the owners of factories and mills, and both craftsmen and common labourers provided the labour force for the booming construction industry of the era. Sometimes immigrants were encouraged to come because they had special skills required for the industrialization of Canada. More often, the immigrant factory workers and the "foreign navvies" who manned the railway construction gangs were hired because they would accept lower wages than Canadian workers.[7]

These men were joined by an army of girls and young women. As the numbers of businesspeople and professionals in the workforce increased, more and more of the young women were employed as domestic servants. There never seemed enough to go around in these years. Henry

---

[7] Contemporary accounts of urban life include Herbert Brown Ames, *The City Below the Hill* (Toronto, 1972); C.S. Clark, *Of Toronto the Good: A Social Study* (Montreal, 1898); and J.S. Woodsworth, *My Neighbour* (Toronto, 1972). A.F.J. Artibise and Gilbert A. Stelter have edited the valuable collection, *The Canadian City: Essays in Urban History* (Toronto, 1977). Artibise is also the author of a major urban history, *Winnipeg: A Social History of Urban Growth, 1874-1914* (Montreal, 1975). Major studies of industrial development include H.V. Nelles, *The Politics of Development: Forests, Mines, and Hydro-Electric Power in Ontario, 1849-1941* (Toronto, 1974); Christopher Armstrong and H.V. Nelles, *Monopoly's Moment. The Organization and Regulation of Canadian Utilities, 1830-1930* (Toronto, 1988); Duncan McDowall, *Steel at the Sault: Francis H. Clergue, Sir James Dunn, and the Algoma Steel Corporation, 1901-1956* (Toronto, 1988); J.H. Dales, *Hydroelectricity and Industrial Development, Quebec, 1898-1940* (Cambridge, 1957); W.J. Ryan, *The Clergy and Economic Growth in Quebec, 1896-1914* (Quebec, 1966); H.G.J. Aitken, *American Capital and Canadian Resources* (Cambridge, 1961); and K. Buckley, *Capital Formation in Canada, 1896-1930* (Toronto, 1955). Also see Ian M. Drummond, *Progress Without Planning: The Economic History of Ontario from Confederation to the Second World War* (Toronto, 1987).

Morgan and Lawrence Burpee's 1905 book, *Canadian Life in Town and Country*, intended to promote Canada for a British audience, noted that domestic service was "one of the chief occupations of women." But, they added, "In Canada, as elsewhere, the servant problem becomes more serious every year. The demand is always far in excess of the supply."

Women accounted for just over 13 percent of the Canadian workforce in both 1901 and 1911. In 1901 the largest number, 69 percent, were employed as "operatives" in the industrial sector, in factories and mills, and in the sweatshops of the clothing industry. By 1911 the proportion had dropped slightly to 66 percent, a hint of a dramatic change taking place in the employment of women. By 1921 female "operatives" made up only 49 percent of employed women. The trend was already clear by 1911; both the numbers of female owners and managers (a small percentage of the whole) and of clerks and sales persons (much larger) increased substantially. In the two decades after 1901, the number of women in the professions grew from 40 201 to 92 973, and just short of 19 percent of all employed females in 1921 were in the professions. In that year, as Michael Piva notes, women made up almost 30 percent of the workforce in Toronto, and nearly all the new jobs for women since 1901 in Toronto were in white-collar occupations – teaching, sales and clerical positions, telephone operators. None of this meant that working women in Toronto, or elsewhere, had necessarily improved their economic status in comparison with men in the workforce. Almost everywhere women continued to be paid lower wages for similar work. But it did mean that, as the number of women employed as "operatives" declined, more and more working women gained improvements in their working conditions.

Similar trends are evident in the male workforce. The proportion of farmers and "operatives" declined, while the proportion of owners, managers, clerks, and sales persons increased. Together, these important changes in the total workforce indicated the impact of industrialization and urbanization on the Canadian economy.

For working people, especially blue-collar workers, city life could be as harsh as it was for the farmers "proving up" homesteads in the West. The attention of urban governments was on expansion and growth, the management of street railway, street light, and telephone franchises, and the costly business of giving tax concessions and bonuses to new industries. Many basic services lagged far behind the growth of population. The enforcement of public health regulations, where they existed, was shockingly deficient. Electricity and telephone lines spread quickly through industrial and business districts and into middle- and upper-class areas. They seldom penetrated the working-class wards of Halifax, Montreal, Toronto, Winnipeg, and Vancouver. A persistent shortage of low-cost housing forced thousands of people to live in the deplorable conditions described by a Toronto civil servant in 1904: "in stables, tents, old cars, sheds (others in damp cellars), where we would not place a valued animal, let alone a human being."

TABLE 4

POPULATION OF SELECTED CITIES, 1901–1911

	1901	1911	% change
Halifax	40 832	46 619	14.2
Saint John	40 711	42 511	4.4
Charlottetown	12 080	11 203	-7.3
Quebec	68 840	78 710	14.3
Montreal	328 172	490 504	49.5
Ottawa	59 928	87 062	45.3
Toronto	209 892	381 833	81.9
Hamilton	52 634	81 969	55.7
Winnipeg	42 340	136 035	221.3
Regina	2 249	30 213	1 243.4
Saskatoon	113	12 004	10 523.0
Edmonton	4 176	31 064	643.9
Calgary	4 392	43 704	895.1
Vancouver	27 010	100 401	271.7
Victoria	20 919	31 660	51.3

SOURCE: *CANADA YEAR BOOK*, 1922-23, p. 171

In time governments at all levels responded to the social and economic pressures of urban growth and the opening of virgin territory. In the cities welfare services, traditionally the responsibility of the churches and private charities, were gradually taken over by municipal governments. To control the "diseases" of urban life, prostitution, drunkenness, vagrancy, and juvenile delinquency, cities modernized their police forces and passed hefty lists of more restrictive bylaws. (As a result, between 1901 and 1911 the number of convictions for offences by juveniles and other minor crimes skyrocketed from 32 000 to 94 000 per annum.) By the end of the Laurier years some cities had begun to experiment with commission government and other formulas that, urban reformers promised, would wipe out ward politics and corruption and bring efficient administration and balanced budgets to city governments.

At the provincial level new departments, bureaus, and branches of provincial administration multiplied as the provinces tried to cope with growing demands for public services. Particular attention was paid to education where both educators and social reformers demanded tighter regulations for school attendance and substantial revisions to the curriculum to make it more "practical" and responsive to the needs of a complex society and diversified economy. Domestic science and technical and agricultural education were but three of the new subjects being taught in public and secondary schools by the end of the Laurier years. Similarly, increasing emphasis on pure science, engineering, social science, forestry, and agriculture was evident in university faculties across the land. But the universities, whether privately funded or provincially supported, remained small, elite institutions open only to the few. Only 7437 students were enrolled in universities in 1904, and graduating classes ranged in size from 25 at the University of New Brunswick and 65 at Dalhousie to 210 at McGill and 424 at Toronto. Among the few, women were fewer still. As late as 1921, a decade after Laurier's defeat, females accounted for less than 30 percent of the university students in Canada.

At the national level the Laurier government tinkered with the great social issues of the day. A referendum on the prohibition question in 1898 revealed a decisive split between French and English Canada, reason enough to bury the issue. After a divisive debate, the government passed the Lord's Day Act in 1906, but delegated the responsibility for enforcement of the Sunday legislation to the provincial governments. In part the Dominion response was dictated by the British North America Act. Like education, jurisdiction for most of the pressing social questions of the period was assigned to the provinces. But the hesitant response of the Liberals was also a measure of their very conservative attitude on all social issues, especially women's rights, and of the explosive potential of federal initiatives in areas where English- and French-Canadian attitudes were so different.

Far safer, and much more popular with the electorate, was the heavy investment by every level of government in transportation and public utilities. As cities expanded their street railway systems, provinces like Ontario and Alberta chartered railways to frontier areas to promote resource development and joined other provinces in offering land grants and bond guarantees for the construction of branch lines. Responding to pressure from municipalities in southern Ontario, the Whitney government took the first steps toward the creation of a publicly owned hydro-electric system in 1908. In Manitoba and Alberta the telephone systems were already publicly owned.

Living conditions in urban Canada were often fearfully crowded and unsanitary. This Toronto housing was far from the worst available in the early years of the new century.

CITY OF TORONTO ARCHIVES. RG 8 33-65.

The most spectacular plunge was taken by the Dominion government. As soon as large numbers of settlers began to spread across the prairie and parkland of Manitoba and the Territories, it became obvious that the Canadian Pacific Railway would not be adequate to service the transportation needs of the new homesteaders. By 1901, the owners of the Canadian Northern Railway, William Mackenzie and Donald Mann, who already had a line to the Lakehead and were building westward from Manitoba, announced their ambition to construct another transcontinental line. The Grand Trunk, long established in the East, also was interested in building a new railway to the Pacific. Here were the obvious elements of a partnership in a new transcontinental railway. But the two

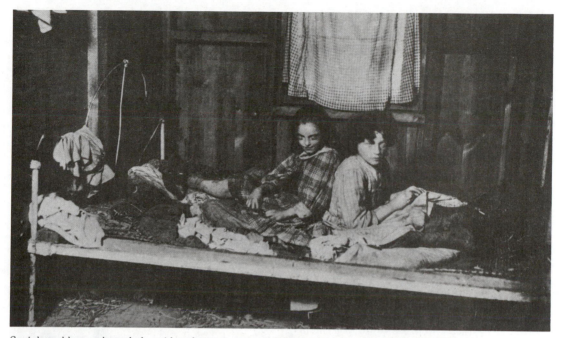

Social problems abounded amidst the prosperity of Edwardian Canada. This photograph, taken in Winnipeg in 1912, was entitled "The One-Room Home" and carried the apt caption, "The Shame of Large Cities . . ."

C-30936/NATIONAL ARCHIVES OF CANADA.

companies could never agree to terms, and Laurier shied away from the role of honest broker. Instead, he cast his lot with the Grand Trunk while refusing to discourage the plans of Mackenzie and Mann. In effect, and over the opposition of his minister of railways, A.G. Blair, who wanted one new publicly owned transcontinental line, Laurier sanctioned two new railways from coast to coast.[8]

The Grand Trunk drove a very hard and advantageous bargain. A subsidiary company, the Grand Trunk Pacific, would build the line (in many places parallel to and in sight of the Canadian Northern) from Winnipeg to Prince Rupert, British Columbia. In return, the government

---

[8] The pioneering history of the C.P.R. is H.A. Innis, *A History of the Canadian Pacific Railway* (Toronto, 1971), which can be supplemented by the more colourful books of Pierre Berton, *The National Dream* and *The Last Spike* (Toronto, 1970 and 1971). G.R. Stevens, *Canadian National Railways*, 2 vols. (Toronto, 1960 and 1962), and T.D. Regehr, *The Canadian Northern Railway: Pioneer Road of the Northern Prairies, 1895-1915* (Toronto, 1976), are impressive studies.

would guarantee 75 percent of the company's bonds. But the Grand Trunk wanted no part of the construction of the politically rewarding but unprofitable link from Winnipeg across northern Ontario and Quebec, through Quebec City to Moncton. Instead, that 3000 km line, called the National Transcontinental, would be built by the Government of Canada and, when completed, leased to the G.T.P. at 3 percent of its cost per annum. Blair resigned when the scheme was announced in Parliament. (Laurier quickly appointed him to the Board of Railway Commissioners.) The leader of the Conservative Opposition, Robert Borden, argued for a publicly owned line, making it the chief issue in his unsuccessful 1904 election campaign. Laurier dismissed charges of extravagance and, with Finance Minister Fielding, pooh-poohed the potential costs of the plan. The future was limitless, the government was accumulating unprecedented surpluses in its public accounts ($14 million in 1903, $15 million in 1904) and such concerns could be harboured only by the faint-hearted. "This plan may scare the timid and frighten the irresolute," Laurier said. "But I may claim that every man who has in his bosom a

These workmen were building a railway trestle for the Canadian Northern near Ernsted, Alberta, in late 1912.

MR. AND MRS. PERCY HITCHCOCK COLLECTION.

stout Canadian heart will welcome it as worthy of this young nation, for which a heavy task has no terrors, which has strength to face grave duties and grave responsibilities." That was magnificent, but it was most imprudent; by 1911 neither of the new railways was finished and both were in financial trouble. Borden, the new prime minister, was eventually forced to take them over as major components of the publicly owned and operated Canadian National Railways system.

Railway schemes were especially attractive to politicians. The costs were distant and indirect, tucked away in long-term bond guarantees. The benefits were widespread and immediately apparent. Farmers and land speculators, often one and the same person, reaped the rewards of the railway boom in rising land prices and improved access to foreign markets. So too did the railway contractors and, in a very different way, the immigrant and native labourers who found steady but hard and often dangerous employment constructing the new railways. The manufacturers of iron and steel products, of the components of railway cars, and the hundreds of other goods necessary to build a modern railway were also major benefactors. And the payoffs spread still wider to the producers of the thousands of items pictured in the retail store catalogues so popular at the turn of the century. Orders for boots and corsets and tools and stoves and pianos could be sped over the new lines from big city warehouses to distant customers.

By 1910 the amount of capital invested in manufacturing and the value of manufactured products produced had both exceeded one billion dollars. The value added by manufacturing, a more exact indicator of the contribution of manufacturing to the economy, increased by 163 percent between 1900 and 1910. The growth of the number of empoyees by product groups within the manufacturing sector gives one indication of the fastest growing areas of manufacturing. Vehicles for land transport, which by 1910 included an expanding automobile industry, led the list, and developments in iron, steel, other metals, and chemicals all pointed toward a quickly maturing industrial economy.

The growth of investment in manufacturing, 179 percent between 1900 and 1910, was marked at the end of the Laurier years by a very substantial consolidation movement. Financiers in Montreal and Toronto promoted vertical or horizontal integrations of major areas of manufacturing from iron and steel to cement, bakery products, and canned foods. The returns were usually handsome for investors and promoters alike.

With some exceptions for skilled workers and tradesmen, industrial workers did less well. The approximate annual wage in manufacturing rose 44.5 percent between 1900 and 1910, but this figure, calculated on full-time employment, must be put in broader perspective. Wage increases varied significantly from group to group. The textiles, food, and tobacco sectors, which employed large numbers of women, paid their female workers substantially lower wages than males earned. Equally important, employment in many manufacturing groups was seasonal, ranging from a few months to three-quarters of the year. Year-round employment in a factory was the exception in the Laurier era.[9]

The Dominion Department of Labour calculated that the cost of food, laundry starch, fuel, lighting, and rent of a six-room dwelling was $9.38 per week ($490 per annum) in 1900. By 1910 these selected items in a family budget, which excluded clothing, transportation, and other costs, had increased more than 31 percent to $640 per annum. In neither year did approximate annual wages in the manufacturing sector match these costs or afford the factory worker any surplus for the other necessities and incidentals of family life. Based on departmental surveys in sixty cities across Canada, these estimates strongly suggest that for many working-class families, at least two and often more members of the family had to work for as many weeks as they could to make ends meet. The wages of workers grew in the boom times of the Laurier period, but so too did prices, and whether workers improved their standard of living is still much debated by scholars. Eleanor Bartlett, in a study of real wages and living standards in Vancouver in the period, concluded that "inflation often outweighed the benefits which rapid growth brought the skilled and unskilled, the organized and unorganized." Similar conclusions are reached by Terry Copp in his study of Montreal workers and by Michael Piva in his analysis of the working class in Toronto. In short, it appears that there is little evidence that the working men and women of Canada earned enough to improve their standard of living in the Laurier years.

Beyond that, the working environment in the forest, factories, and especially in mines, was hard, dangerous, and sometimes deadly. The 10- or 12-hour day and the 64-hour week was normal; the "8-hour-day" movement was just beginning to attract attention at the end of the

---

[9] See Eleanor A. Bartlett, "Real Wages and the Standard of Living in Vancouver, 1901-1929," *B.C. Studies* 51, 1981; T.J. Copp, *Anatomy of Poverty: The Condition of the Working Class in Montreal, 1896-1929* (Toronto, 1974); Jacques Rouillard, *Les travailleurs du coton au Québec, 1900-1915* (Montréal, 1974); and Michael Piva, *The Condition of the Working Class in Toronto* (Ottawa, 1979); and Drummond, *Progress Without Planning* (Toronto, 1987).

Laurier era. Factories and mines were dirty, noisy, and dangerous places. Owners provided little protection for workers from heavy, fast-moving machinery. Provinces like Ontario, which did have rudimentary safety regulations in place, employed too few factory inspectors to ensure that the rules were enforced.

TABLE 5

NUMBER OF WAGE EARNERS AND APPROXIMATE ANNUAL WAGE BY MANUFACTURING GROUP, 1900 and 1910

Manufacturing Group	Employees			Approximate Annual Wage		
	1900	1910	% change	1900	1910	% change
Food Products	42 401	52 730	24.2	$189	$275	45.5
Textiles	59 324	72 672	22.5	258	368	42.6
Iron & Steel	24 766	48 558	96.0	397	531	33.8
Timber, Lumber, & Wood Products	75 704	110 049	45.4	250	358	43.2
Leather & Products	19 204	22 742	18.4	315	425	34.9
Paper & Printing	15 413	22 894	48.6	369	474	28.5
Liquor & Beverage	3 208	4 688	46.1	397	563	41.8
Chemicals & Allied Products	2 868	5 274	83.9	357	452	26.6
Clay, Glass, & Stone Products	10 765	17 699	64.4	256	435	69.9
Other Metals & Products	9 358	17 502	87.0	414	559	35.0
Tobacco & Products	6 329	8 763	38.5	306	378	23.5
Vehicles for Land Transport	14 866	35 778	140.7	424	546	28.8
Vehicles for Water Transport	2 587	4 414	70.6	324	530	63.6
Miscellaneous	21 084	38 537	82.8	356	480	34.8
Hand Trades	605	8 826	1358.8	413	466	12.8
All Manufacturing	308 482	471 126	52.7	290	419	44.5

SOURCE: *CANADA YEAR BOOK*, 1913.

Exploitive and dangerous working conditions invited the intervention of the trade union movement. Even though workers lacked governmental recognition of such elemental rights as collective bargaining, trade unionism had deep roots in nineteenth-century Canada. The trade union movement was tiny in 1900, claiming only some 20 000 organized workers. Over the next decade it experienced phenomenal growth. By 1911 about 130 000 workers were members of union locals. Lists of union locals compiled by the Department of Labour strongly suggest that most unionists worked in traditional crafts in the building trades and printing, and in transportation, mining, and lumbering. The expansion of trade unionism in the first years of the new century was remarkable, but organization of the industrial workplace had barely begun.

Moreover, the union movement was deeply divided both regionally and culturally in 1911. Almost 90 percent of Canadian trade unionists were members of international unions affiliated with Samuel Gomper's conservatively oriented American Federation of Labor in the United States. Equally conservative was the Provincial Workman's Association, the major trade union force in Nova Scotia, though its influence was waning under the challenge of American miners' unions. A very different American union, the radical Western Federation of Miners, had established a foothold in British Columbia. At the beginning of the century the American-based Knights of Labour had a relatively strong base in Quebec, but over the decade a growing number of workers came to support an emerging French-speaking Catholic union movement in the province.[10]

Industrial warfare was rampant in the mines, in factories, and on the railways. More than a thousand disputes were recorded between 1901 and 1911. In most strikes the basic issue was wages, frequently supplemented by the fundamental issue of union recognition. Often the response of government was to call out the militia in aid of the civil power to suppress violence between strikers and scab labour. Administratively, the problem of strikes and lockouts was complex. Except in a few industries under Dominion jurisdiction such as the major railways, labour questions were the responsibility of the provinces and very few provinces had the administrative capacity or the political inclination to deal with them adequately. In 1900 the Laurier government created a Department of Labour under the authority of the Conciliation Act. The department was charged to provide assistance in the prevention and settlement of strikes and to enforce a fair wages policy – within Dominion jurisdiction. Seven years later Parliament passed the Industrial Disputes Investigation Act, the brain child of the then deputy minister of labour, William Lyon Mackenzie King. A tiny element of compulsion was included in the act: strikes and lockouts in the mines or public utilities were prohibited until the dispute had been investigated by a three-man

---

[10] Major studies of working people and labour include Gregory S. Kealey, *Toronto Workers Respond to Industrial Capitalism, 1867-1892* (Toronto, 1980); Bryan Palmer, *A Culture in Conflict: Skilled Workers and Industrial Capitalism in Hamilton Ontario, 1860-1914* (Montreal, 1979); and Paul Craven, *An Impartial Umpire: Industrial Relations and the Canadian State, 1900-1911* (Toronto, 1981). Also see Janice Acton et al., eds., *Women at Work: Ontario 1850-1930* (Toronto, 1974); Robert Babcock, *Gompers in Canada: A Study in American Continentalism Before the First World War* (Toronto, 1974); and David Jay Bercuson, "Labour Radicalism and the Western Industrial Frontier, 1897-1919," *Canadian Historical Review* LVIII, no. 2 (1977).

board. But conciliation remained the essence of Ottawa's labour policy. Thorough investigation and public revelation of grievances, King believed, should be enough to bring reasonable men to their senses.

Even this hint of government intervention caused alarm among some businesspeople. However, the more tough-minded accepted the I.D.I.A. for what it was, a potentially useful device to persuade the parties in an industrial dispute to reach a settlement. Of course, because neither party was compelled to accept the recommendations of the board of investigation, management's prerogatives remained unchallenged and the rights demanded by workers unrecognized. Owners and managers remained confident of public – or at least political – support. Neither the Laurier government nor its provincial counterparts displayed any desire to interfere with business. After all, aided by incentives and development policies at every level of government, businesspeople were as much nation builders as were politicians. And so they saw themselves. Left to their own devices, they argued, they were exploiting neither workers nor consumers. Instead, theirs was a noble mission. The President of the Canadian Manufacturers Association put it best in 1903:

We are not manufacturers merely of articles of wood and stone, and iron and cotton and wool, and so on; we manufacture enthusiasms; we manufacture Canadian sentiment; . . . we manufacture a spirit of independence, a spirit of national pride.

The Life of the Mind

With a confidence spurred on by prosperity, it seemed as if everyone was in the business of manufacturing the Canadian identity during the Laurier years. Some Protestants toyed with the idea of church unification as an expression of a uniquely Canadian Protestantism. When the idea came to flower in the postwar years, one of its proponents explained that "the heritage of the Gospel we have in common with fellow-Christians the world over, but we have also the heritage of the Canadian spirit and this will find in the new Church an expression and an instrument peculiarly its own." In Quebec the Catholic Church, intensely concerned over the growing secular influences in French-Canadian society and the increasing Americanization of the economy, gave enthusiastic support to a traditionalist and nationalist student movement, the Association Catholique de la Jeunesse Canadienne-Française. A founder of the movement summarized its tenets as:

... l'amour de la race canadienne-française et de la mission spéciale que la Providence lui destine; c'est aussi l'amour du sol que lui est échu, avec ses ressources suffisantes à la formation d'une grande nation.

The militia, with broad support in English Canada and rather less influence in Quebec, actively promoted the cadet movement in schools to encourage preparedness and patriotism, and laboured mightily to Canadianize – and mythologize – the history of Canadian arms. Their patrons in Ottawa, led by Sir Frederick Borden, Laurier's minister of militia and defence, struggled to revitalize the militia and wrest its control away from British-appointed commanding officers.

Among the most interesting efforts of self-discovery was the experimentation by writers and artists with subject matter and techniques that would reveal distinctively Canadian art forms. In Winnipeg, for example, the Reverend Charles W. Gordon, as Ralph Connor, used the challenging environment of the Prairies as the setting for most of his melodramatic novels. A fascination with the Canadian landscape, with its uniqueness and its challenging harshness, was even more evident in the work of Montreal painters J.W. Morrice, Maurice Cullen, and Clarence Gagnon. The trend was more self-conscious in Toronto where the artist Charles Jefferys observed that "it is inevitable that a country with such marked physical characteristics as Canada should impress itself forcefully upon our artists."

If the land was one source of inspiration, the past was another. In the academies the first serious efforts at research in Canadian history were underway, and before the Laurier years were over an impressive list of multi-volume projects had been launched. At l'Université Laval Thomas Chapais completed his studies of Talon and Montcalm and began work on his eight-volume *Cours d'histoire du Canada: 1760-1867*. Lionel Groulx returned to Valleyfield Seminary from studies in Europe and started his research on a history of French Canada that would contrast sharply with Chapais's in its nationalist interpretation. In 1897 a University of Toronto historian, George M. Wrong, started the *Review of Historical Publications Relating to Canada*. He was also one of the founders of the Champlain Society in 1905, and with H.H. Langton, the university librarian, Wrong organized the 32-volume *Chronicles of Canada*. Pelham Edgar of Victoria College and Duncan Campbell Scott, poet and Dominion civil servant, launched the biographical series, *The Makers of Canada*. Most impressive as a monument to sound scholarship was the majestic 23-volume *Canada and its Provinces: A History of the Canadian People and Their Institutions*, edited by Adam Shortt of the

Civil Service Commission and A.G. Doughty, the Dominion archivist. Doughty's archival work was equally important. He collected documents in London and Paris, provided scholars with ready access to historical records, and initiated a series of archival publications that began in 1907 with *Documents Relating to the Constitutional History of Canada: 1758-1828.*

The search for the meaning of Canada by artists, writers, and historians added authenticity and perspective to the maturing Canadian nationalism of the Laurier years. It sharpened the awareness of Canada's dual cultural heritage and documented the role Canada had played in the British Empire. It also defined the very significant differences in culture, attitudes, and political systems between Canada and the United States. But this heady exercise created its own problems. Foremost among them was the revelation that there were many different realities in the Canadian identity. For many English-Canadians in the older provinces, the nation's destiny rested squarely upon its imperial foundations. As Principal Grant of Queen's University put it, "We are Canadian, and in order to be Canadian we must be British." Most French-Canadians were no less attached to Canada's inherited British political institutions but took a much more detached attitude to the Empire and the aggressive imperialism of late Victorian Britain. "All our patriotism, all our love, all our aspirations, all our memories, all our soul attaches us to the Canadian land," the newspaper *La Patrie* proclaimed. "It is our only Fatherland." If eastern Canadians found their identities in the past, western Canadians posited their destiny on buoyant assumptions about the future. "In western Canada there is seen today that most fascinating of all human phenomena, the making of a nation out of breeds diverse in traditions, in ideals, in speech, and in manner of life, Saxon and Slav, Teuton, Celt and Gaul, one people is being made," Ralph Connor wrote in his immensely popular novel, *The Foreigner.* "The blood strains of great races will mingle in the blood of a race greater than the greatest of them all."[11]

---

[11] Carl Berger, *The Sense of Power: Studies in the Ideas of Canadian Imperialism, 1867-1914* (Toronto, 1970), is a brilliant analysis of imperialist and nationalist ideologies in Canada. For a different perspective see R.G. Moyles and Doug Owram, *Imperial Dreams and Colonial Realities: British Views of Canada, 1880-1914* (Toronto, 1988). The ideas of the foremost French-Canadian nationalist, Henri Bourassa, are examined in Joseph Levitt, *Henri Bourassa and the Golden Calf* (Ottawa, 1969) and in Robert Rumilly, *Henri Bourassa* (Montreal, 1953). For an incisive analysis of French-Canadian nationalism see Ramsay Cook, *Canada and the French-Canadian Question* (Toronto, 1966), which can be supplemented by his *French-Canadian Nationalism: An Anthology* (Toronto, 1970).

The Imperial Tie

Each perspective and its several variations informed arguments and shaped decisions on the domestic issues of the day, great and small. Each perspective also had to be recognized and accommodated in the Laurier government's approach to external relations. Canada's relations with foreign states, in law and in practice, were the responsibility of the Foreign Office in London. Only gradually was the Government of Canada acquiring self-government in external relations, and Laurier was in no particular hurry to hasten the process of autonomy. In part, he correctly reasoned that it would continue to evolve through precedent and circumstance as it had in the Macdonald years with the appointment in 1880 of a High Commissioner as Canada's quasi-diplomatic representative in London. In part, recognizing how potentially explosive issues in external relations could be, given the contrasting perspectives of English- and French-Canadians, retention of responsibility in London provided a convenient focus for blame when Canadians believed (as they very often did) that their interests in imperial and foreign affairs had been mishandled. In consequence, serious, systematic analysis of external problems had a secondary priority in the Laurier government. Foreign affairs were seen as something to be considered when occasion demanded, and even then policies were governed more by abstract perceptions of Canada's place in the Empire than by tough-minded scrutiny of practical issues.[12]

A clear example was Laurier's cautious and circumspect approach to the Colonial Conferences in London in 1897 and 1902, where delegates from the self-governing colonies gathered under the chairmanship of the colonial secretary, Joseph Chamberlain, to discuss a wide range of imperial problems. Chamberlain was an ambitious champion of the aggressive imperialism that characterized late Victorian Britain and he

---

[12] The best survey of Canadian external affairs is C.P. Stacey, *Canada and the Age of Conquest,* vol. 1, *1867-1921* (Toronto, 1977). Carl Berger, ed., *Imperial Relations in the Age of Laurier* (Toronto, 1969), is an important collection of essays. Political relations with Great Britain are studied in J.E. Kendle, *The Colonial and Imperial Conferences, 1887-1911* (London, 1967). Aspects of defence and military relations are surveyed in Desmond Morton, *Ministers and Generals* (Toronto, 1970); Richard Preston, *Canada and "Imperial Defence"* (Toronto, 1969); and Kenneth Bourne, *Britain and the Balance of Power in North America* (Berkeley, 1967). Norman Penlington, *Canada and Imperialism, 1896-1899* (Toronto, 1965), is important for the South African War as is the introduction to Paul Stevens and John T. Saywell, eds., *Lord Minto's Canadian Papers,* vol. 1, *1898-1900* (Toronto, 1981). The naval question is explored in G.N. Tucker, *The Naval Service of Canada,* 2 vols. (Ottawa, 1952), and in Robert Craig Brown, *Robert Laird Borden: A Biography, 1854-1914,* vol. 1 (Toronto, 1975).

had set himself the goal of efficient management of imperial affairs by encouraging participation of the colonies in the policy-making process in London. Chamberlain was thoroughly confused and frustrated by Laurier's ardent declarations of faith in British political institutions and his eloquent praise of the British connection. To Laurier these were the bedrock of Canada's freedom of action and absence of prior commitment in external affairs. Chamberlain, however, misinterpreted Laurier's rhetoric as an indication of sympathy with his own centralizing vision. Laurier acknowledged, as he told the House of Commons in 1900, that *if* Canada were compelled to share all of the burdens of empire, then Canada would have the right to say to the imperial Government, "Call us to your councils." But such was not the case. And Laurier would have none of Chamberlain's centralizing schemes. His stance, as he put it in 1902, was that imperial relations "are generally satisfactory under the existing condition of things." At the 1902 conference, Laurier adroitly sidestepped a proposal of colonial contributions to an imperial naval force with a vague promise to establish in due course a Canadian navy. This elusive approach angered Chamberlain and other centralists. "That dam' dancing-master," a South African representative remarked, "bitched the whole show." So he did, deliberately. Laurier did so because he believed that for Canada the maintenance of the imperial connection depended not on contrived centralization but upon the silken bond of sentiment and freedom of choice.

When the Laurier government came to power the area of immediate concern in external affairs was relations with the United States. They were not in good repair and, shortly after Laurier returned from the 1897 Colonial Conference, he secretly slipped off to Washington to propose negotiations on all outstanding questions. An Anglo-American Joint Commission, the last of a series that had begun before Confederation, finally met over the fall and winter of 1898-99. It was in this realm, where Canadians could convincingly argue that they knew their own problems far better than British diplomats, that Canada's developing autonomy in external affairs was most evident. For example, in 1871 Sir John A. Macdonald was one of three British representatives on a similar commission, taking his instructions from London. In 1898-99 there were four Canadians and one British member, and all took their instructions from Ottawa.[13]

---

[13] Robert Craig Brown, *Canada's National Policy, 1883-1900: A Study in Canadian-American Relations* (Princeton, 1964), is an analysis of the relationship of external policies to domestic politics. C.S. Campbell, *Anglo-American Understanding, 1898-1903* (Baltimore, 1957), and

The list of problems on the Joint Commission's agenda was long. Included were a number of minor problems characteristic of neighbouring states with close commercial, financial, social, and cultural links to each other. The major items included trade relations and disputes about fishing rights on both the Atlantic and Pacific coasts. Most immediate and contentious was the argument over the delineation of the boundary in the Alaskan panhandle. Here Canada pinned its ambition to control the exploitation of the gold fields of the Yukon upon claims for access across the panhandle to the sea. When the Canadians, led by Laurier, could not win the diplomatic concessions to overcome their shaky legal claims, they held out for an all-or-nothing settlement and the Joint Commission collapsed. Looking back, it is clear that the commissioners tried to do too much, to balance too many delicate trade-offs and compromises in one negotiating package. Laurier, however, explained the diplomatic failure in strongly nationalistic terms. A mature Canada, he explained, no longer had to make diplomatic concessions to senior partners in the North Atlantic triangle.

Laurier's argument, as appealing as it was, ignored the very real limits on Canada's freedom of action in external relations. By 1903 the Foreign Office and the State Department had agreed that the boundary question would be resolved by a tribunal that would meet in London. As the tribunal waded through the contending legal arguments, President Theodore Roosevelt's administration in Washington pointedly informed the Foreign Office in Whitehall that it would not tolerate a decision contrary to its claims. The tribunal award, with the two Canadian members dissenting, generally concurred with the United States' case. And, in the bargain, at the last moment, the British member of the tribunal, Lord Alverstone, changed his mind and sided with the Americans on the drawing of the boundary around a group of tiny islands at the southernmost tip of the panhandle. Lord Alverstone's decision touched off a furious reaction in Ottawa, rekindling old charges that the British always sacrificed Canadian interests when they dealt with the untrustworthy Yankees.

Even before the Alaskan award some thoughtful Canadians argued that Laurier's ambiguous status quo stance in imperial relations was

---

A.E. Campbell, *Great Britain and the United States, 1895-1903* (London, 1960), look at Canadian-American relations in the context of Anglo-American diplomacy. An important essay is A.C. Gluek, Jr., "Pilgrimages to Ottawa: Canadian-American Diplomacy, 1903-1913," *Historical Papers, 1968*. A standard account of the reciprocity agreement of 1911 is L.E. Ellis, *Reciprocity, 1911* (New Haven, 1939).

endangering Canadian interests. If Canada expected firmer support from the British at the negotiating table, then Ottawa had to be prepared to take a more active role in imperial affairs. Moreover, involvement in the empire had become a matter of national honour. Canada was no longer a weak, struggling, self-governing colony. The Dominion, imperial nationalists believed, was a rapidly industrializing, powerful nation, fully capable of participating in the development and execution of imperial policy. This argument gave substance to the clamorous demand, in the fall in 1899, for Canadian participation in the South African War.

Laurier was fully prepared to give his moral support to the British effort to suppress the Boers who were alleged to have persecuted British subjects in the Transvaal. "To me," he wrote some months later, "it is clearly and manifestly a war for religious liberty, political equality, and civil rights." But sending troops – that was another matter. His initial response to a call from Chamberlain for soldiers was to temporize, arguing that no action could be taken without summoning Parliament into session. Within a matter of days, however, Laurier was forced to reconcile the English-Canadian demands for troops with an obvious reluctance in the French-language press and the opposition of his French-speaking ministers to a contribution. His policy of necessity became a carefully constructed compromise. Canada would raise a volunteer contingent of one thousand men and transport it to South Africa where the British Government would assume financial support for the soldiers. To placate French-Canadian critics, Laurier resorted to legal contrivances. The order-in-council authorizing the contingent firmly declared that the policy would not be "construed as a precedent for future action." Another contingent went forward in December 1899, and still more Canadians fought in South Africa in unofficial contingents. In all, some seven thousand Canadians eventually saw service in South Africa.

Neither English- nor French-Canadian nationalists were satisfied with Laurier's policy. The English believed that the prime minister's voluntarist compromise was a clever but unworthy evasion of responsibility. The French argued that he had made a binding commitment to participation in all of the empire's military adventures in the future. "The precedent," Henri Bourassa observed with impeccable logic, "is the accomplished fact." Nevertheless, Laurier kept the overwhelming support of his caucus throughout the conflict. He believed that the South African War clearly illustrated the danger of prior commitments in imperial relations and the necessity to have freedom to act or not to act, depending upon the circumstances of the moment. Of course, the extremists were not satisfied. They never were with compromises. But compromise was the essence of Canada, the glue of national unity. "If we had refused our Imperial duty," Laurier observed, "the most dangerous agitation would have arisen, an agitation which, according to all human probability, would have ended in a cleavage in the population of this country upon racial lines. A greater calamity could never take place in Canada."

Steering a cautious middle course between the demands of his critics remained the foundation of Laurier's imperial policy. After 1905, when the Liberals came to power in Great Britain, much of the agitation for colonial participation in the administration of the empire abated. The British Government was as reluctant to share the responsibility as

The South African War roused imperial patriotism in English Canada, and departing contingents were feted across the land.

GLENBOW ARCHIVES, CALGARY/NA-3052-4.

Laurier was to have a share in it. Then the agitation was revived in the winter of 1908-09 when an apparent acceleration in the rate of construction of German capital ships threatened the margin of superiority the Royal Navy maintained in dreadnaughts. The "naval scare," like the South African War a decade earlier, aroused the English-Canadian press to demand a Canadian contribution.

But of what kind? Should Laurier be forced to make good his long-delayed promise to create a Canadian navy? If so, what aid could a Canadian force provide? Was not a financial contribution to the Admiralty's dreadnaught construction program the most obvious and effective solution? In the spring of 1909 Liberals and Conservatives in the House of Commons joined together to pass a resolution favouring the building of a Canadian navy and rejecting *regular* financial contributions to the Admiralty. What was left out of the text was as important as what was included. In the eyes of some, an unmentioned *emergency* contribution remained an option for the Laurier government.

Laurier's policy was announced in January 1910. The Canadian navy would have a complement of five cruisers and six destroyers, manned by a volunteer force. A naval college would be established to train officers. The navy would be under Canadian command but, in the event of war, it could, with the consent of Parliament, be placed under imperial control. It was another compromise: a major step toward autonomous responsibility in external policy coupled with a recognition that in time of war unified command of the Empire's naval resources was a necessity.

Robert Borden's Conservative Opposition, pushed hard by the imperially minded Tory premiers of British Columbia, Manitoba, and Ontario, had two major objections. Laurier's navy would take years to build, especially with the meagre annual appropriations being proposed by the penny-pinching minister of finance. The Opposition supported the building of a Canadian navy, but it was no contribution at all in the present crisis. Therefore, an emergency contribution was also in order. In addition, the arm's-length relationship between the Canadian and the Royal navies, dictated by the provision that Parliament would decide the extent and mode of participation in the event of war, made Laurier's force an "order-in-council" navy. That was doubly dangerous; it was tantamount to a declaration of independence from the Empire, and it left open the possibility that Parliament, especially a Laurier Parliament, would decide not to participate at all!

That last charge was a deliberate misreading of Laurier's intentions. The consent of Parliament was a formality, but it was also an important assertion of Canada's autonomy *within* the British Empire. As Laurier explained to a Montreal audience, if a major war broke out, his government would not hesitate to come to Britain's aid.

Nous ne sommes obligés de prendre part à aucune guerre, mais cependant je déclare que, s'il y avait des guerres . . . s'il y avait une guerre dans laquelle la suprématie navale de l'Empire serait mise en péril, je serais d'opinion moi-même, – et je ne veux pas que d'autres en soient blâmés, parce que j'en prends la responsabilité – je crois que nous devions aider l'Angleterre de toutes nos forces.

After fierce and fractious debate Laurier mustered his majority and the Naval Service bill was passed. A short while later two old British cruisers, the *Niobe* and the *Rainbow*, were acquired as training ships for the new Canadian Naval Service.

Again the Quebec nationalists complained. Since the South Africa War, their forces had grown considerably. They now posed a much

Touring the West in 1910, Sir Wilfrid Laurier spoke to many crowds such as this one in Wetaskiwin, Alberta. He was startled to learn how strong the demand was for reciprocity with the United States; the next year, he would offer it to Canadians.

GLENBOW ARCHIVES, CALGARY/NA-3592-6.

Henri Bourassa led *nationaliste* forces in Quebec against Laurier. His newspaper, *Le Devoir*, had small circulation but substantial influence.

C-27495/NATIONAL ARCHIVES OF CANADA.

greater threat to the leaders of both political parties. On the Conservative side, Borden's small contingent of French-Canadian M.P.s, led by Frederick Monk, and deeply influenced by the growing nationaliste sentiment in Quebec, had bolted from party ranks and demanded a referendum before any naval policy was adopted. Borden's challenge paralleled Laurier's – to find some middle ground between them and the contributionist Tory premiers. He argued that, in addition to a Canadian navy and an emergency contribution, any contribution to imperial defence had to be matched by a Canadian voice in the determination of imperial foreign policy.

Many strong-minded imperialists in the Liberal camp also grumbled that Laurier's policy did not go far enough. But a more immediate threat came from his former protegé, Henri Bourassa. In 1907 Bourassa had resigned his House of Commons seat to begin an angry campaign against Laurier Liberalism, all its works, and all its hangers-on in Quebec City and Ottawa. By 1910 his creed was being expounded in an influential new journal, *Le Devoir*. In the fall a by-election was called in the Drummond-Arthabaska riding, once Laurier's own seat. While the Quebec Tories watched from the sidelines, all of Bourassa's followers rallied to the support of a nationalist candidate who narrowly beat out the Liberal party candidate. For Laurier, the result, in one of the safest Liberal seats in Quebec, was an ominous warning. For Borden, it was a delicate and dangerous opportunity. If Laurier's stranglehold on Quebec could be broken, if an alliance could be cemented between Monk and Bourassa, and if the imperial extremists among the English Tories could be kept in check, Laurier's long reign of power would be threatened as never before.

The political consequences of Laurier's external policies had begun to accumulate. Since 1907, in a broadly based effort to "clean the slate" of unresolved problems with the United States, the several issues left in dispute by the Anglo-American Joint Commission were separately and successfully resolved. In addition, in 1909 a Boundary Waters Treaty was signed, establishing the Canada-United States International Joint Commission to deal with future problems in the sharing of boundary water resources. And in the same year the Laurier government took a significant step toward formalizing the administration of its external policies when it established the Department of External Affairs.

The most contentious and sensitive problem in Canadian-American relations, trade policy, remained a divisive political issue. Canadian farmers had not been satisfied with the minor concessions they had been given in the 1907 tariff. Especially in the West, where agrarians had formed powerful farmers' organizations, the tariff was the potent symbol of the "new feudalism," of the class bias and regional favouritism of the Laurier government's economic policies, of its toadying to the monopolists, the banks, and the railways, and of its abject subservience to the political strength of Quebec and Ontario. On a three-month-long whistle-stop tour of the West in the summer of 1910 Laurier discovered that the demand for free trade was stronger than ever. Then, in December, an angry delegation of farmers besieged Ottawa, pressing its case for relief from the oppression of protectionism.

In fact, reciprocity negotiations with the United States were far advanced. In January 1911, Finance Minister Fielding astonished the House of Commons when he announced a comprehensive trade agreement with the United States. Ottawa and Washington had agreed to free trade in the natural products of either country. In addition, other schedules lowered the duties on selected lists of manufactured goods originating in one or the other nation. Equally important, the agreement was not in the form of a treaty. Rather, it would come into force only after it had been approved by the legislatures of both nations. By the summer the sanction of Congress was in place.

At first, as Robert Borden later recalled in his *Memoirs*, the Tories were utterly dismayed. Here was the trade agreement with the United States that Canadian governments, Conservative and Liberal, had sought in one form or another since Confederation. On the face of it, reciprocity, with so many obvious benefits to Canadian consumers – and voters – was hard to oppose. The wily old fox of Canadian Liberalism seemed assured of another term in office. And it was, in fact, only a disastrous split among Laurier's followers that soon brought the Opposition to its senses. Clifford Sifton and an influential group of eighteen Liberal Toronto businessmen – "certain hysterical women of the male sex," Sir Richard Cartwright called them – discovered a traitorous continentalist drift in Laurier's policy. They joined the Ottawa Conservatives to denounce the inner meaning of reciprocity. So encouraged, Borden's men filibustered the reciprocity bill in the House until July when Laurier finally accepted the challenge, prorogued Parliament, and called a general election.

Like the Liberal businessmen, who threw the full weight of their dollars and their organizational and promotional skills into the campaign, the Tory premiers rallied behind Borden. Both groups professed strong imperialist loyalties, agreed with Borden that the issue was "continentalism or Canadianism," and regarded Laurier as dangerously equivocal on the imperial connection. For them the defeat of reciprocity was a matter of both pocketbook and the heart, and an opportunity to punish Laurier for his Naval Service Act. For French-Canadian nationalists the election was also an opportunity to seek revenge for the Naval Service Act, for the long list of other sellouts of French-Canadian interests the Laurier government had accumulated, and for the cynical manipulation and callous patronage that, they believed, was the secret to Laurier's power.

Laurier's power, in fact, was by no means as great as it appeared. Behind the facade of incalculable influence every governing party carried into an election, the Liberals' organization, in the hands of smugly confident but used-up party chieftains, was a shambles. By contrast, over the ten years of Borden's leadership, the Opposition Conservatives had slowly but steadily strengthened their local and provincial party machines. Now the last bit of strategy fell into place, and a quiet, effective arrangement was made with Bourassa.

On election day, September 21, 1911, the unthinkable happened. The popular vote was very close: 666 074 for the Tories, 623 554 for the Grits. But it was seats in the House of Commons that counted. "Follow my white plume!" Laurier had said in the campaign. In too many constituencies too few Liberals were still listening. The Conservatives scored a stunning triumph, winning 134 seats to 87 for the Liberals. In Quebec the nationaliste alliance yielded a gain of 16 seats for Borden. In Tory Ontario, the Liberals won only 13 of 86 seats. The Laurier years were over. Robert Borden, the shy, earnest lawyer from Halifax, awaited a summons from the governor general.

Sir Wilfrid Laurier was the political architect of modern Canada, the eloquent spokesman and gallant defender of the transformation of the Dominion into a twentieth-century industrial state. Paradoxically the success of Laurier's policies proved his undoing. The pride and confidence in the reawakening of Canada that took place during his term of office were the prerequisites of the nationalist challenge to his policies that grew in both French and English Canada. The settlers who came by the thousands to build the West forced his government into the fatal pact with Washington.

There is another paradox. Laurier, the champion of twentieth-century Canada, was the last of the great nineteenth-century politicians to serve as prime minister. He had scant sympathy for many of the political reforms, bureaucratic procedures, and regulatory practices that his policies stimulated. His beliefs, his political style, and his solutions to political problems were deeply rooted in an earlier day, in the laissez-faire Liberalism of his long term as Opposition leader, in the comfortable hierarchical society of Victorian Canada, and most of all, in the subtle compromises between the aspirations of French- and English-Canadians that had made Confederation possible in 1867. Most of the great political issues of the Laurier years were old issues, perennial problems with schools, tariffs, railways, and imperial relations. And so were Sir Wilfrid's solutions to them.

PARTIES ARE NOT PERFECT ORGANIZATIONS

The top storey of the old Marché St-Pierre in Quebec City was poorly lit, full of shadows, gloomy. It was here that Laurier came with friends and followers on the evening of September 21, 1911, to await the results of the general election. Like the humblest junior member of the House of Commons, on election day the political fortunes of the prime minister of Canada rested in the hands of his constituents. Not that anyone in the cheerful crowd doubted the result. Laurier had first won the favour of the voters of Quebec East in a by-election in November 1877, after accepting cabinet office in Alexander Mackenzie's government. They had returned him to Ottawa ever since and would do so again this night. Early results from other constituencies were equally promising.

Then came the news that Labelle, long a Liberal seat, had fallen to the Opposition. Then Brome, the seat of Sydney Fisher, Laurier's minister of agriculture since 1896, succumbed. In Nova Scotia the seats of two other cabinet ministers, William S. Fielding and Frederick Borden, were captured by the Tories. In all, seven of Laurier's cabinet colleagues, including William Paterson, George Graham, and the young, ambitious William Lyon Mackenzie King from Ontario, were beaten. Now the shadows seemed ominous, the room, a journalist recorded, "full of fear." The hangers-on had drifted away. Laurier was alone with his loyal followers. In the gloom they raised their voices in a brave cheer to their leader and moved close to the platform where he stood. "Sir Wilfrid spoke briefly," the journalist wrote, "perhaps being unwilling to trust himself too far, then sat down at the table with the look of a man who has said good-bye."[1]

The Electoral System

Looking back on it, the 1911 election was a classic political confrontation, illustrating the assets and liabilities that both parties carried into the contest. On the Liberal side, Wilfrid Laurier had devoted his whole life to the Liberal Party. And, more than any other person, he had shaped and defined the party's principles. He was a disciple of the great British liberal reformers, of Fox, of Russell, of Gladstone. He was, he said in the Manitoba schools debate, "a Liberal of the English school. . . . I believe in that school which has all along claimed that it is the privilege of all subjects, whether high or low, whether rich or poor, whether ecclesiastics or layman, to participate in the administration of public affairs, to discuss, to influence, to persuade, to convince – but which has always denied even to the highest the right to dictate even to the lowest." Canadians, he had remarked shortly before entering Mackenzie's cabinet, "are a free and happy people, and we are so owing to the liberal institutions by which we are governed, institutions which we owe to the exertions of our fore-fathers and the wisdom of the mother country." It was the policy of the Liberal Party to protect, defend, and extend those institutions: "It has no other."

Laurier recognized that in the electoral process some ways of influencing and persuading voters were more legitimate than others and that parties were as prone to human frailty as individuals. "Parties are not perfect organizations," he once told a friend, "but after all, constitutional government founded on the existence of parties is still the best system which has been invented by man."

---

[1] For information on Laurier's political career see Paul Stevens, "Wilfrid Laurier, Politician," in Marcel Hamelin, ed., *Les Idées Politiques des Premiers Ministres du Canada* (Ottawa, 1969); the essays by John T. Saywell, "The 1890s," and H. Blair Neatby, "The 1900s," in Robert Craig Brown and J.M.S. Careless, eds., *The Canadians, 1867-1967* (Toronto, 1967); the appropriate chapters of P.-A. Linteau, R. Durocher and J.-C. Robert, *Histoire du Québec Contemporain* (Montréal, 1979); and J.S. Willison, *Reminiscences, Political and Personal* (Toronto, 1919). More generally, all students of Canadian political history must consult *Morang's Annual Register of Canadian Affairs, 1901*, edited by J. Castell Hopkins, and Hopkins' series of volumes of *The Canadian Annual Review, 1902-1937*. The Conservative bias of Hopkins' volumes is more than balanced by the mine of information in his annual accounts of national and provincial political events and personalities.

Parties at the turn of the century were complex, delicately balanced machines, ever needful of attention and care. At the top, the party leader was chosen by the caucus, the members of the party sitting in the House of Commons or the Senate. He was at once expected to represent their views and to be the spokesperson and leader for the whole of the party. For their part, as representatives of their party in Parliament, members of the party caucus jealously guarded their right to speak for the interest of their constituents on all public matters great and small. At the same time they were expected to adhere to party policy in Parliament and on the hustings. They were also expected to keep the faithful in the constituencies organized and ready to destroy the enemy at any moment. And in the constituencies the same delicate balances had to be maintained. A member of Parliament who casually neglected his constituents' interests could expect decisive retribution at the next election.

The task of influencing and convincing the electors had become increasingly difficult since Confederation. One reason was that the number of potential voters grew steadily with the growth of population. At the time of the second Dominion general election in 1872, there was one representative in the House of Commons for every 18 500 Canadians. By 1891 each M.P. represented about 22 500 Canadians. By 1911 there was one representative for every 30 800 Canadians.

That did not mean that each constituency had the same, or even approximately the same, population. The relationship between the number of members in the House of Commons and the population was much more complicated than that. Generally speaking, the process of distribution of seats began with the assignment of 65 seats to the Province of Quebec in the British North America Act. The ratio of seats to population in Quebec then was used to determine the number of seats relative to the population of each of the other provinces. Within each province the distribution of seats and the size and boundaries of each constituency were quite literally the object of the partisan manipulation of the governing party at the redistribution following each decennial census.

At no time was the ratio of seats to population in Quebec more than a rough guide to the population of each constituency represented in the House of Commons. For example, after the 1892 redistribution of seats, which established the constituencies for the elections of 1896 and 1900, 46.6 percent of the constituencies had populations greater than the Quebec standard. Similarly, after the 1903 redistribution, only 32 of the 208 constituencies had populations equal to the Quebec standard. There were many reasons for this. Most important was the agreement among the politicians that urban seats should have larger, in some cases much larger, populations than rural constituencies. In short, rural Canada should be overrepresented in the House of Commons. Thus, in 1904, Brome, Quebec, Sydney Fisher's rural seat, had a population of 13 400, while Laurier's Quebec City seat had a population of 40 000 people.[2]

In addition, the number of people eligible to vote in each constituency grew rapidly as the population increased and the election laws became more liberal. The first general elections after Confederation used the various provincial franchise laws to determine voter eligibility, and each provincial franchise contained some kind of property or other qualification for a man to become a voter. In 1885 Sir John A. Macdonald's government enacted a separate federal franchise that governed the eligibility of voters in the 1887, 1891, and 1896 elections. It also contained a property qualification – $300 in cities and towns and $150 in rural areas – and a host of other provisions that, as one scholar put it, was "an astonishing hodge-podge that discriminated between provinces, social classes and racial groups." Laurier was determined to do away with the 1885 federal franchise, and in 1898 the Franchise Act returned control of the franchise to the provinces. By no coincidence, Liberal regimes were in power in every province but British Columbia at the time. (The first party government in Victoria came to power in 1903 and was Conservative.) The result was a culling of the swollen federal lists in Nova Scotia, Quebec, Manitoba, and most dramatically, in Ontario. At Queen's Park the friendly, i.e., Liberal, Ross government reduced the number of eligible voters from 650 000 in 1896 to 482 000 in the 1900 general election.

At the same time, the more general effect of returning control of the franchise to the provinces was to eliminate property qualifications for voter eligibility and establish the principle of universal male suffrage, paving the way for universal suffrage in the next decade.

During the Laurier years the number of eligible voters grew by 34 percent and the number of voters who cast ballots rose by 45 percent from the 1896 to the 1911 election. Naturally enough, the largest increases in the number of eligible voters occurred in the western provinces where population growth was so rapid in the Laurier years.

---

[2] Norman Ward, *The House of Commons: Representation* (Toronto, 1950), is an indispensable guide to the history of representation.

This election advertising card for a Conservative candidate was distributed for a 1902 by-election. Note that there is no party specified, although the reverse of the card sets out Wallace's platform – One Policy, One Country, One Empire, One Flag – and identifies his party implicitly. Wallace lost to his Liberal opponent.

The number of eligible voters participating in elections varied from election to election and province to province. On election day voter participation was affected by a huge number of variables including weather, ease of access to the local poll, party organization and strength within the constituency, cheating, impersonation, intimidation, and other forms of illegal electoral manipulation. Party bosses, acutely aware of these variables, recognized that elections were risky ventures. An election, therefore, was seldom called without the most thorough preparation to convince the voters, by fair means or foul, to vote for the governing party. For all that, participation in the five general elections between 1896 and 1911 was remarkably high, averaging 75 percent across the nation.

The governing party (the Liberals throughout this period), with an infinite range of patronage at its disposal, was usually thought to have the upper hand in the contest. The battle in the British Columbia constituency of Yale-Cariboo in 1900 illustrates how a government could come to the aid of a local candidate. The Liberals feared they might lose the seat and the candidate was desperately short of funds. Cash always seemed to be in short supply everywhere in an election but the minister of the interior, Clifford Sifton, himself a strict prohibitionist, did control the issuance of liquor permits in the Yukon area. The candidate was promised a permit and agreed to contribute one dollar per gallon from the proceeds to the party treasury. A permit for 5000 gallons (22 700 l) was issued and the support of another Liberal backbencher in the next Parliament was secured.

The support of sympathetic provincial governments was also critical for the federal administration, as we have seen. Laurier had been careful to have Liberals named as premiers of the new provinces of Alberta and Saskatchewan in 1905 because he recognized the assistance that co-operative local politicians could offer his government at election times. On the other hand, the premiers, whatever their political allegiance, ordinarily tried to stay on good terms with Ottawa, the fount of every province's revenue. In this era before income taxes, when the provinces received much of their funds from a variety of licence fees, when their budgets were tiny and their civil services generally small and inadequately trained, Ottawa's fiscal support was critical. Successful premiers, men such as Nova Scotia's W.S. Fielding (1884-96), New Brunswick's A.G. Blair (1883-96), and Ontario's Oliver Mowat (1872-96), knew this all too well. They could fight with Ottawa, sometimes with amazing virulence, but nothing that ultimately jeopardized federal financial support could be tolerated.

For we who live in an era of big government, the limited range of provincial government activities around the turn of the century was nothing short of incredible. The provinces controlled education, but put very little money into it, leaving local ratepayers to carry the burden; inevitably, most municipalities spent as little as they could. The social welfare system was effectively nonexistent, again the municipalities having to shoulder the load, and most provincial government funds went to the provision of asylums and prisons. Agriculture received some limited support in all the provinces, but roads in the pre-automobile era were also virtually nonexistent. Canada was a small country in the years before the Great War, and the governments of all its provinces were small and ineffectual.

The Party Press

If government revenues and expenditures were small, members of Parliament were well paid. Each M.P. received a sessional indemnity of $1500 ($2500 after 1905), a handsome sum for the day. But their expenses for travel, accommodation in Ottawa, constituency services, and other demands were correspondingly high. That, in part, accounts for the very substantial proportion of financiers, lawyers, manufacturers, and merchants in the Parliaments of the Laurier years. These people were better able to afford to spend several months each year in Ottawa attending to the public's business, they were not solely dependent upon the indemnity paid to members of Parliament, and they were better able to bear the risks of the insecurity of political careers. They also could afford the expense of elections. Time and again throughout Clifford Sifton's long political career a multitude of election expenses were borne by his ample pocketbook. And, being one of the most skilful managers of the art of politics in the Laurier era, he left nothing to chance. It was said that Sifton made a practice of knowing the political leaning of every voter in his Brandon constituency. But this was not enough. When he learned that far more Brandon families were reading the Opposition's newspaper than his own *Free Press*, he quickly arranged for 1000 copies of his paper to be distributed to homes in his constituency for several months prior to the election of 1900.

The support of a vigorous party press was thought to be a key to the survival of the political parties in the Laurier years. As historian Paul Rutherford put it, "The typical politician saw newspapers as essential vehicles of publicity, indeed a surrogate for organization, which could confound foes, strengthen party discipline and morale, and educate electors." The educative process was subject to formidable manipulation. Even editorial support could never be taken for granted. Throughout his long career, Laurier continually had to remind the editors of party journals to adhere to the party policy on every issue. But, as Sifton recognized, management of the news was even more important. A properly written news story, extolling the insight and propriety of the Liberal Party and eliminating or belittling the view of the Opposition, could have the desired impact on the reader. A journalist of those years recalled that "the government news, official announcements and what not was exclusive to the Liberal correspondents . . . no correspondent in the confidence of the Government had anything like the latitude which was open to his competitors. He could not indulge in intelligent anticipation or, indeed, in any kind of anticipation, but was bound and gagged by the responsibilities of a partisan journalist connection."

The symbiotic relationship between the party and its party press waxed and waned with the fortunes of the party. At the heart of the matter was patronage, government advertising, and printing contracts upon which many small party journals depended for survival. A change in government was the despair of many a publisher. For example, between 1891 and 1896, when there was a Conservative government in Ottawa, the Tory Halifax *Herald* received $33 951.75 in government business, and the Liberal Halifax *Chronicle* received $38. Between 1896 and 1901, with a Liberal government in Ottawa, the *Chronicle* received $27 811.31 and the *Herald* $1152.73. Likewise in Montreal, the Liberal *Herald* received $105.83 between 1891 and 1896 and $97 796.57 between 1896 and 1901.

An ominous warning to both parties of changing times was the growing popularity of the independent press, especially in urban Canada. By 1900 independent dailies and weeklies accounted for 46 percent of the circulation of Canadian newspapers. The independents threatened traditional modes of influencing the voter in two ways: they could not be relied upon for partisan support and, equally damaging, the whole thrust of their treatment of information was toward local issues, problems, and happenings and away from partisan politics and national issues. At the very time that the number of voters was growing, so too was the probability that more and more electors were acquiring their news and views of the world from independent newspapers. The role of the party press as a surrogate for party organization was slipping away.[3]

Two other well-established ways to influence the voter were elaborate and expensive programs for economic development and extensive use of government patronage. As we have seen in the preceding chapter, the Laurier government was especially adept at the former. Investigations of the Departments of Marine and Fisheries, Interior, Militia and Defence, and Railways and Canals between 1906 and 1909 revealed that it was equally skilled in the latter. Marine and Fisheries, for example, had paid $10 000 for $2800 worth of pemmican for the exploratory voyage of the *Arctic* to Hudson Bay. Some other items purchased for Captain Bernier's expedition had been acquired in quantities sufficient for a 30-year voyage. The whole issue of corruption in government was argued out in

---

[3] A classic analysis of electoral politics in Canada, published in 1906, is André Siegfried, *Le Canada, les deux races: problèmes politiques contemporains*; a recent English edition is Siegfried, *The Race Question in Canada* (Toronto, 1966). Norman Ward, ed., *A Party Politician, The Memoirs of Chubby Power* (Toronto, 1966), gives a glimpse of politics in Quebec in the Laurier years. Paul Rutherford, *A Victorian Authority: the Daily Press in Late Nineteenth-Century Canada* (Toronto, 1982), contains a superb analysis of the party press. The same subject is discussed in Norman Ward, "The Press and Patronage: An Exploratory Operation," in J.H. Aitchison, ed., *The Political Process in Canada* (Toronto, 1963).

bitter debates engineered by the Conservative Opposition in the parliamentary sessions of 1906, 1907, and 1908, and scandal charges were the centrepiece of the Tory campaign in the 1908 election.[4]

The net effect was to discredit the party system as much as the Liberal government in the minds of many voters. "There is no more any difference between the two so-called parties in the House," wrote a young Montreal lawyer.

They are alike in the scandals in which members of them participate. They are alike in the maxims by which they are content to be guided. They are alike in their utter contempt of arguments that are founded not upon expediency but upon right. They are alike, therefore, through and through, in their political barrenness; and in need of a complete new birth, if they are not to become an absolute danger to the country.

J. Castell Hopkins, editor of the *Canadian Annual Review*, agreed. "The great principles of the past have died out," he observed after the 1908 election, "and been replaced by political organizations whose distinctive features are those of the ins and outs."

The Opposition

Robert Borden, the Conservative Party leader, was much more receptive to this kind of criticism than Laurier. He could afford to be. As Laurier observed with steely realism, "Reforms are for Oppositions. It is the business of governments to stay in office." Staying in office, as we have seen, involved alliances with provincial governments of the same political stripe at election time, the widespread distribution of patronage, the initiation of development projects that had a beneficial impact on large numbers of voters, and the nourishment and manipulation of the party press.

The Leader of the Opposition possessed none of this heavy weaponry of political warfare. Only in the last years of Borden's Opposition leadership did powerful Conservative governments reign in a number of the provincial capitals. Only then could they exercise their influence

---

[4] John English, *The Decline of Politics: The Conservatives and the Party System, 1901-1920* (Toronto, 1977), includes an incisive analysis of patronage and political corruption in the Laurier years. See also Robert Craig Brown, "The Politics of Billingsgate," in Carl Berger and Ramsay Cook, eds., *The West and The Nation*, and Norman Ward, "The Bristol Papers: A note on Patronage," *Canadian Journal of Economics and Political Science* XII (1946).

over voters' lists or distribute largesse in favour of the federal Tories as well as of their own machines. Borden had no policies to implement, only promises – some vague, others remarkably like the Laurier government's programs – of what his party would do if called to power. He had to rely upon party loyalty and his own powers of persuasion to keep the Conservative press faithful. Neither paid the bills for editors' and correspondents' loyalty or for the tons of newsprint required by a big city daily.

Party loyalty, in the absence of constant nourishment, could be unreliable indeed. Like many politicians who assume leadership in Opposition, Borden had a dual challenge: to retain and consolidate his support within the party and to shape its policies to attract enough additional voters to supply the margin of victory. Support within the party began with the parliamentary caucus that elected him leader, and the Conservative caucus, in Borden's day, was an especially fractious body representing Protestant Orangemen, a small group of French-Canadians with growing nationaliste sympathies, veteran Tory members wedded to the ideas and practices of the Conservatism of Macdonald, and young bloods demanding new approaches to both policy and party organization.

Borden himself was a remarkably successful and extraordinarily ambitious self-made man who had risen from very modest beginnings on an Annapolis Valley farm to wealth and a distinguished reputation at the Nova Scotia bar. He had entered politics at the personal request of Sir Charles Tupper in 1896. Five years later Tupper and his son, Sir Charles Hibbert Tupper (Borden's former law partner), had engineered his selection as party leader. Naturally enough, many of the veteran members of the caucus regarded Borden both as a novice and as a mouthpiece for the Tuppers. The French-Canadian members viewed him, correctly, as a moderate on the sensitive issues of English-French relations but also as a man who had less understanding of and sympathy for their special role in Canadian politics than they desired. Although Borden was also distrusted by many militant Protestants in the party and by old-style Conservative loyalists steeped in Macdonald's National policy, the newer men welcomed his fresh approaches to policy, such as his advocacy of government ownership of the new transcontinental railway in 1904, and his desire to build a new organizational structure for the Conservative Party. As he established himself as a leader, Borden challenged the view that the Conservative caucus was the repository of all wisdom on party policy, the mediator between the leader and the voters, and the centrepiece of party organization.[5]

A characteristic example of Borden's style of leadership was his announcement of the "progressive" Halifax platform in 1907. It attacked the problem of corruption in government by promising the honest appropriation and expenditure of public monies and the more advanced proposition of a thorough overhaul of the civil service, as well as the appointment of public officials on the merit principle. In its tariff plank Borden eliminated the cherished term "protection" and suggested a more systematic and efficient tariff policy to promote the production of Canadian goods. Borden also called for government regulation of telephones and express companies as well as railways and for the eventual establishment of a system of national telegraphs and telephones. Defending his platform, Borden argued that natural resources, national franchises, and public utilities had to be seen as "the property of the State, and they must be administered and exploited for the public benefit." That could best be done, he said, by "Government ownership or operation."

Heady stuff for Premier Rodmond Roblin, whose recently elected Conservative government in Winnipeg administered a public telephone system; also, in some measure, for Premier James Pliny Whitney in Ontario, whose government was moving toward the establishment of Ontario Hydro. But Borden's views were dangerous and frightening to party contributors on Montreal's St. James Street and to many veteran members of the caucus. Caucus members also thought the way Borden inaugurated the Halifax platform still more threatening. After elaborate consultation with a selected group of Conservative M.P.s, with some prominent businesspeople, and with the Conservative provincial premiers, Borden simply announced the platform in a major address in

---

[5] The standard biography of Borden is Robert Craig Brown, *Robert Laird Borden, A Biography, 1854-1937*, 2 vols. (Toronto, 1975 and 1980). Borden's own account is Henry Borden, ed., *Robert Laird Borden: His Memoirs*, 2 vols. (Toronto, 1938). Another collection of Borden's views, Henry Borden, ed., *Letters to Limbo* (Toronto, 1971), contains many insights on Borden's life and career. See also Robert Craig Brown, "The Political Ideas of Robert Borden," in Hamelin, *Les Idées Politiques des Premiers Ministres du Canada*. An interesting perspective on Borden's problems as a party leader in the early years may be gained by comparing the above with Lovell Clark, "Macdonald's Conservative Successors, 1891-1896," in John Moir, ed., *Character and Circumstance: Essays in Honour of Donald Grant Creighton* (Toronto, 1970). English, *The Decline of Politics*, is an excellent analysis of Borden's party, and Arthur Ford, *As the World Wags On* (Toronto, 1950), is a delightful reminiscence of the era.

Halifax. The parliamentary party was not consulted, nor was it given the opportunity to debate and endorse the platform. Borden, in short, had bypassed party structures, courted and received advice beyond the parliamentary party, and taken a major step toward building an independent power base in the party. Significantly, in the 1908 general election, the Halifax platform was given far less prominence than the charges of scandal in the Laurier government. It is probable that discontented M.P.s were sending a signal to the leader from the hustings that consultation and co-operation between Borden and his parliamentary colleagues was a two-way street.

Borden's attitudes and actions indicated his dissatisfaction with the Conservative Party's traditional procedures and practices. But that did not mean that Borden questioned either the principle or the efficacy of party government. He echoed Laurier in his commitment to government by party: "Government by party is more in the interest of the great mass of the people than any other system which has been devised by human wisdom up to the present time." Critics of his Halifax platform had raised the spectre of incompetent or corrupt administration against his advocacy of government ownership. But, Borden countered, should private enterprise be condemned for insurance frauds or business failures? "The principle of state ownership is no more to be condemned for its defects or errors of administration than is the general principle of responsible government. The remedy is to amend the methods." The defence of the party system was exactly the same. Like many other institutions, it was noble in purpose and replete with faults in administration. "The remedy is to amend the methods."

Borden's attitude toward party business differed from that of many of his colleagues. This was neatly illustrated by his acceptance of the new special allowance to the Leader of the Opposition of $7000 per session, the equivalent of a cabinet minister's payment, which was introduced by the Laurier government in 1905. Borden recognized that party leadership was expensive. That limited the party's choice of leader to the wealthy who were willing to make a personal financial sacrifice to the cause, or required a subscription to a fund by the rich people in the party to support the leader, as had been done for Macdonald and many other party leaders before and since. When the special allowance came into effect, disgruntled Tories suggested Borden had become "a payee of the Government of the day" or "an unattached member of the Administration." They believed that the party should fund the leader. Not so, Borden replied. The expenses of leadership:

. . . should come as a provision from the country for public service [rather] than as a contribution from party funds. In the latter case the leader is in effect a pensioner of a few men of wealth within the ranks of the party. This condition is obviously not a desirable one. It does not seem to me that the independence of a leader is in any way affected by a special indemnity payable out of the Exchequer. The independence of members in Opposition is surely not affected by an indemnity paid in the same way.

Remedying the method of party government went far beyond the payment of Borden's leadership expenses. A prominent Montreal businessman and Conservative M.P., Herbert Brown Ames, argued that critics of partyism and corruption were firing at the wrong target when they trained their guns on the party machine. The way to clean up politics, he proclaimed, was to impose the principles of business efficiency and business management upon the party's organization, thus relieving the party of the baneful influences of special interests and allowing it to "claim the services of the noblest men" who would give Canada "pure and honest administration." That idea, which confidently identified the business and industrial elite as the leaders in the modernization of Canada, was the most popular cliché of the day, as much a cure-all for the sickness of party politics as it was for the building of city sewers, the growing of wheat, or the education of young Canadians. But Borden and other progressively inclined politicians firmly believed it. And they had a point. Just as efficient methods and skilful management were enabling industry to produce more and better products for an expanding market, the time had come to apply the same principles to an ever-expanding electorate. Properly organized and properly administered, the party machine could be made to run for the people rather than for the business and industrial interests.

The problem was that a parallel party structure, elaborate in organization, with elected party officials at every level from the constituency district to the national committee of advisers to the leader, could impair the influence and authority of the member of Parliament both in his constituency and with the party leader. Borden never resolved this, and his attempts to build a tightly controlled, carefully managed organization for the Conservative Party received only lukewarm support in the caucus and in the growing provincial party organizations across the country.

The focus of party attention upon systematic organization, however, did have its rewards. Party organizations appropriate to local conditions and designed in close co-operation with provincial leaders were created or revived and given a new sense of purpose. The total Conservative vote increased steadily during Borden's leadership. It increased by 7.2 percent from 1900 to 1904, another 14.3 percent from 1904 to 1908, and another 21.3 percent from 1908 to 1911. Overall, the Conservative vote increased by almost 61 percent from 1896 to 1911, the Liberal vote by 54 percent.

The Reciprocity Election

Nonetheless, the Liberals approached the 1911 election with supreme confidence. They had much to be confident about. The party, after all, had compiled a remarkable string of victories under Laurier's guidance and Laurier was widely acknowledged as a masterful leader. As the architect of the social and economic changes that had transformed Canada in the past fifteen years, Laurier was immensely proud of his accomplishments. More than that, there was, as his biographer put it, "an indefinable touch of authority" about Laurier that had proved compelling to voters in the past. The party counted on that image of mastery and statesmanship to work its magic on the voters again in 1911. So did Laurier.

Confidence also rested upon the fact of power. Properly managed, the power of the governing party could be decisive in an election. Liberal principles were important, and a commitment to Liberalism was deep in the hearts of generations of Canadian voters. But, as Laurier, ever the realist, once remarked, "It is always more easy to govern if, besides appealing to their best nature, we can also show them some substantial advantage." Never was the axiom more true than at election time. Then a wharf, a bridge, a post office, a few judiciously placed printing contracts, or a new customs shed with its attendant jobs more often than not provided the margin of victory in a host of constituencies. Some studies of elections even suggest that these substantial advantages and the constituency organizations are more important than great issues in persuading a majority of electors to vote for a governing party's candidate. But in 1911 the great issue for the governing party itself promised a substantial advantage to electors: cheaper binder twine would cut farmers' production costs; cheaper food would benefit urban workers. That, as the Liberals saw it, was the issue and the compelling promise of the 1911 election.

So attractive was the package that there was more than a hint of complacency in the Liberal ranks. Always more comfortable with proven formulas than with untried experiments, Laurier seemed wedded to the approaches and appeals that had worked in previous elections: a winning record, his own reputation, an attractive issue, the support of Liberal governments in the provinces, and the distribution of largesse. The turning point may well have come in late April when Borden announced the "uncompromising hostility" of the Tories to the reciprocity bill and Laurier countered with his party's "uncompromising support" and determination to see it through Parliament. Borden was threatening to use the procedures of the House of Commons to tie up the bill indefinitely while Laurier was anxious to bring it to a final vote so that he could leave for an Imperial Conference in London. Unwilling to compromise with Borden on any point, Laurier refused his offer of a two- or three-month adjournment and the vote of interim supply. A deadlock had been reached. Then, early in May, the government did decide to adjourn Parliament, with the reciprocity bill in limbo, for two months. Laurier left for England. Borden rushed off to Western Canada to try to convince prairie farmers that reciprocity was not the panacea that many of them believed it to be. The threat to tie the House of Commons in procedural knots earned Borden a precious two months of time to campaign while Laurier was out of the country.

The day before the party leaders exchanged challenges in the House of Commons, Hartley Dewart, a worried young Toronto Liberal, published an ominous letter in the Toronto *Globe*. To ritual denunciations of the Conservative Party he added the warning that "the Liberal Party in Ontario today, while strong in its constructive policy, is lamentably weak in the matter of organization." The blame rested with Laurier's Ontario ministers and especially with Allen Aylesworth, the minister of justice, who was senior among them. "A Commander-in-Chief," Dewart wrote, "even if he be as brilliant and skilful as Sir Wilfrid Laurier undoubtedly is, cannot be expected to achieve the success that he should without able tacticians between himself and the men in the ranks." Whatever the other talents of Laurier's lieutenants, they had neglected their crucial organizational roles in the province with the largest number of seats in the House of Commons. And Dewart was not a lone complainer. Long before his letter appeared, Laurier had been told that Liberals would not follow his cadre of Ontario ministers. As one correspondent put it, "With the present organization it would be impossible to elect St. Peter to any one of our seats." It added up to this: while no election had been called, the Conservatives had offered the government a choice of a vote or a filibuster and still the Liberal election machine was in storage, its gears awaiting grease, its fixtures needing polish, its drivers unpopular.

Not so the Conservative side. In mid-April J.D. "Doc" Reid, a veteran Ontario M.P. and sometime discontented member of Borden's caucus, prepared a long memorandum for the leader reporting the results of the most recent meeting of Ontario organizers. By then the Ontario Tory machine was moving into high gear and it may be safely assumed that the same was also true in the Conservative provinces of British Columbia and Manitoba. (New Brunswick's Conservative government, led by lethargic Douglas Hazen, plagued by uncertainty, and short of cash, lagged behind.) Reid reported that 36 of the present 50 Conservative seats were "absolutely sure": the remainder would be fiercely contested by the Liberals. Of the 36 Grit seats in Ontario, the Conservatives would concede only 14. In the remaining 22 a "vicious attack" was planned. "A good man" or "the best available man" had already been nominated or was slated for nomination in half of the seats. The Tories were ready.[6]

When first announced in January, the reciprocity agreement with the United States had thrown Borden and his colleagues into despair. But Borden, by nature a cautious and deliberative leader, slowly but surely discovered the fatal flaws in the government's policy. From Winnipeg and Queen's Park came signals that reciprocity had struck a severe blow at "Canadian national development" (the protective tariff policy) and "sane imperialism" (the imperial connection). That was the theme of Borden's response in the House of Commons in early February and it was echoed in the anti-reciprocity manifesto of 18 Toronto entrepreneurs a few days later. The components of Borden's election strategy were falling into place.

The first part of the plan was to capitalize on the outrage of the business community and especially to hold out a welcoming hand to Liberal capitalists whose imperialist sentiments had been offended by the Naval Service Act and who viewed reciprocity as yet another blow to national dignity and purpose – and their own financial holdings. Borden had always believed that a successful party leader had two equally important duties. One was to retain, consolidate, and strengthen his

---

[6] Many of the political and organizational factors in the 1911 election are covered in R.D. Cuff, "The Conservative Party Machine and the Election of 1911 in Ontario," and "The Toronto Eighteen and the Election of 1911," *Ontario History*, LVII (1965); W.M. Baker, "A Case Study of Anti-Americanism in English-speaking Canada: The Election Campaign of 1911," *Canadian Historical Review*, LI, 1970; and in Paul Stevens' valuable collection of documents and readings, *The 1911 General Election: A Study in Canadian Politics* (Toronto, 1970).

electoral support among voters who were loyal to the party through thick and thin. The other, and this was the key to victory, was to "seek to reach and influence men of moderate opinion who vote now with one and now with the other party." For election purposes people in business fit neatly into this category. Most had probably supported Macdonald in his day and it was certain that most had rallied behind Laurier's revamped and more successful National Policy since 1896. Now they might be moved again, but nothing could be left to chance. If business-people believed that reciprocity could be turned back by a few meetings and a manifesto, they were "living in a fool's paradise," Borden told Premier Whitney. They had to be brought into active partnership in the Tory campaign.

Businesspeople agreed. Very quietly – at first not even Borden was privy to what was afoot in "another organization" – the "nonpartisan" Canadian Manufacturers Association set up the Canadian Home Market Association with headquarters in Toronto and branch operations in Montreal and Winnipeg. Lavishly funded by annual subscriptions from its member firms, the C.H.M.A. was in fact a huge propaganda machine organizing the preparation of anti-reciprocity pamphlets distributed by a front organization, the Canadian National League, and of editorials and "news stories" sent in boiler plate for regular printing in hundreds of country dailies and weeklies from Nova Scotia to British Columbia. By late August the C.H.M.A. had sent out 9.5 million pieces of its material and was dispatching another 20 000 each day.

The blitz of the country papers was not a substitute for, but a potent supplement to, party organization. Here, in the absence of a strong national party structure, the key was wholehearted co-operation between the Ottawa Tories and the four provincial Conservative govern-ments. Borden had courted the Tory premiers for years and had won their support. Imperialists to a man, the affront of reciprocity now added fervour to their support. In Manitoba Robert "Hon. Bob" Rogers, Roblin's minister of public works and unofficial "minister of elections," quickly put the provincial civil service on combat status as Conservative soldiers. Roblin also assigned Rogers, who had close ties to most French-Canadian Conservatives and Montreal financiers, to part-time duty as bagman for the national party.

Similarly, Rogers' counterpart in Ontario, "Silent Frank" Cochrane, the minister of mines, was brought into the Ontario campaign. He was a key figure in the organizational meetings Doc Reid was attending. Reid's memorandum to Borden revealed the fullness of Premier Whitney's

Before the Great War, the campaign for women's suffrage made little headway, as this cartoon illustrates. But the war would change all that.

COURTESY OF *THE COUNTRY GUIDE*/R-A-369.

commitment. Several of the nominees chosen to contest tough Liberal seats were members of Whitney's caucus, M.P.P.s who had been ''given'' to Borden by Whitney because they were the most likely candidates to capture the Liberal constituencies. Beyond that, Whitney had played a critical role in negotiating the alliance between the Borden Conservatives and the Toronto businesspeople, and Borden relied upon Whitney for advice on matters great and small throughout the campaign.

Another alliance, unofficial, unannounced and, as Liberals charged, unholy, was at work in Quebec. William Price, lumberman and member for Quebec West, was given major organizational responsibilities in Quebec and New Brunswick. He soon discovered that he was not completely in charge in his own province. Frederick Monk, sometime leader of the Quebec Conservatives in Parliament, "has again put us into a most horrible mess," Price wrote in alarm. "He has made a definite alliance with Bourassa and the Nationalists, and this new combination is calling itself an Independent Conservative Party, under the leadership of Monk. They will not be able to obtain much funds for organization, but they will, at any rate, take several seats from the Liberals."

An arrangement between Borden, Monk, and Bourassa was not as strange as it seemed at first sight. During the last year of Borden's first term as M.P. he had boarded with Bourassa in Ottawa and each had developed a strong respect for the intelligence and integrity of the other. Their views on English-French relations and, to a large extent, on imperial questions were poles apart. But on other major issues, especially on questions of political reform and progressive approaches to the relations between the state and private enterprise, they were at one. In 1908, when Bourassa campaigned on a reform platform against the Liberal government of Lomer Gouin in Quebec, he received support from important Quebec Conservatives and proposed an "alliance – not open, but real" with Borden's party. Then, as in 1911, the heart of the matter was Bourassa's detestation of Laurier and Laurier Liberalism in Quebec City and in Ottawa, detestation of its endless compromises, its scruffy deals and cynical politics. If Monk and Bourassa could take seats away from Laurier in his own fortress, Borden was more than willing to give his silent consent to their arrangement.

Winning the support of disenchanted Liberal capitalists, working closely with the Conservative provincial premiers, and encouraging the independent campaign of Monk and Bourassa in Quebec were, then, the components of Borden's election strategy. Slowly and carefully developed, they were all in place long before July when Laurier finally called the general election. They were specially significant because each of the elements was an arrangement with a group outside the caucus, a manifestation of Borden's belief that the road to victory was paved with alliances with political forces not represented in the parliamentary party.

That made some members of caucus very, very nervous. In 1910 Borden's neglect of the tender sensibilities of caucus had led to an abortive but widely publicized revolt. In March 1911, the discontent resurfaced over Borden's courting of his new allies. Even though it was quickly squashed by Borden the revolt left some of the dissidents – among them were Reid, Price, and Monk – "very frightened." That within weeks each of these three men was playing a major role in the Conservative campaign revealed much about the fevered intensity of Opposition politics and the astute leadership of the party by Borden. In the end he put together a powerful combination of political forces that exploited the negative responses to the Laurier government's policies and marched to battle in carefully organized formation.

The effectiveness of Borden's strategy was obvious on election night. There were minor increases in the Conservative popular vote in Prince Edward Island and Nova Scotia but more than an 11 percent increase in Hazen's New Brunswick. The "horrible mess" in Quebec paid handsome dividends. Whether interpreted as a Conservative vote, a Conservative-nationaliste vote, or simply as an anti-Laurier vote, the Opposition candidates in Quebec tallied 37.8 percent more votes in 1911 than they had in 1908. And the close working relationships with the provincial governments in Ontario, Manitoba, and British Columbia yielded 13 percent, 15 percent, and 46 percent gains in Tory support in those provinces. For the Liberals, the largest gains came in Saskatchewan, with a 56 percent increase, and in Alberta, with 61 percent. There Liberal provincial governments reigned and farmers' support for reciprocity was most intense. Fractional increases in the Liberal popular vote in Quebec and Nova Scotia were offset by minor losses in Prince Edward Island and New Brunswick and a significant 5 percent drop in Ontario. The Liberals also won major gains in the popular vote in Manitoba and British Columbia, but it was not enough to influence the results in either province. As elsewhere, the popular vote in those provinces provided one gauge of the people's support for the Liberal Party.

What really counted, however, was the contest for seats constituency by constituency. There the provincial control of electoral lists and the strengths and weaknesses of local party organization came into play. The Liberals lost seats in six of the nine provinces: Prince Edward Island – one; Nova Scotia – three; New Brunswick – three; Quebec – 16; Ontario – 25; and British Columbia – two. Their only gain was in Alberta, where they picked up two seats. Clearly, the close co-operation between Borden and his provincial colleagues had paid off most handsomely in

Ontario, and the Conservative-nationaliste arrangement in Quebec had cut deeply into Laurier's support in his home province.

A Liberal candidate from a constituency that included a large manufacturing town in Ontario reflected upon his losing campaign after the election:

I fought a good fight on a cause I did not believe in and which I will never do again. Fighting for the "full dinner pail" and the "farmer" is poor policy – neither appreciate your efforts on their behalf, and are controlled by their employer when it comes down to the finally final.

"I am neither laughing nor weeping," he concluded. "I am just thinking – what damn fools we were." The Liberals in 1911 relied too much on past accomplishments, too much on their leader's personal prestige and popular appeal, too much on a seemingly attractive policy. The problem with reciprocity was that it undercut the carefully modulated but solid support for protectionism that had characterized Liberal policy since 1896. It threatened, or seemed to threaten, too many economic interests that had flourished under that tariff policy. And, in the eyes of too many Canadians, it challenged the very essence of Canada's identity and future. The Liberal leadership, smugly satisfied with the reciprocity agreement Fielding had engineered in Washington and convinced that his panacea from the past was the magic formula for retaining power, was much too slow off the mark in the campaign of persuasion. The Liberals never did marshal enough force to turn back the assault of Conservative propaganda against the "inner meaning" of reciprocity.

It was equally significant that in the latter years of the Laurier regime the party's organizational talent, so evident in earlier elections, had been allowed to wither away. That was the point of Hartley Dewart's outburst in April 1911. But by then it was much too late to act; many of Laurier's cabinet colleagues who were charged with organizational responsibilities were old and tired, but they could not be replaced on the eve of an election. The ossification of the Liberal machine had already become evident in the 1908 election, but the prime minister, intensely loyal to long-time, trusted colleagues like Aylesworth, refused to replace them. Alexander Smith, veteran party organizer in Ontario, made the point in a letter to Laurier after the 1911 election. "Warnings, suggestions, directions and offers of assistance were all resented," he wrote, "and the result was that you had not the support of the lineal descendants of those who were proud to see you elected in 1896 and followed you until old age denied their ardour."

Laurier received the letter in November, two months after the election. Smith, who had been at the centre of electoral organization in Ontario since 1896, was sorting and burning correspondence that contained the deeper secrets of party activity in federal and provincial elections over 15 years. The exercise stirred many memories and gave Smith a unique perspective on the state of the Liberal party in 1911. Two sentences from his letter were a telling epitaph on the death of Laurier Liberalism.

We had nobody in charge. It was like playing marbles with marbles made out of ordinary roadside mud.

The Keys to Political Success

A general election is the beginning- and the end-point of the Canadian political system. Each election, federal or provincial, is fixed in time and place, conditioned by the circumstances of the day, and shaped by the personalities and activities of all the actors from the party leader to the local poll captain. But many factors that were important in the 1911 election are constant and worth remembering as we continue our study of twentieth-century Canada.

The foundation stones of the political process are deeply imbedded in the past. The parliamentary system, which confounds facile comparison between Canadian and American politics, grew out of the earliest European colonies in British North America and evolved alongside the "mother of Parliaments" in London. Party government grew out of the rebellions in the Canadas in 1837 and the gradual establishment of responsible government in the 1840s. Together, the parliamentary system and party government created the liberal-democratic political institutions that were as much the beacon for Robert Borden's "progressive" Conservatism as they were for Sir Wilfrid Laurier's Liberalism.

Later twentieth-century political parties faced many of the same difficulties and challenges that confronted Laurier's Liberals and Borden's Conservatives. The number of potential voters to be influenced and persuaded grew, especially with the adoption of female suffrage – which began in the English-speaking provinces in the years of the Great War and ended in federal female suffrage – and the return of the control of the federal franchise to Ottawa in 1918. So too did the average size of each constituency grow, to 34 500 by 1958 when John Diefenbaker's Progressive Conservative Party swept the nation and captured 208 (79 percent!)

of the 265 seats in the House of Commons. Over the decades the rules governing the conduct of elections were tightened. In time regulations affecting party funding were adopted, in part by legislation, in part by

Sir Robert Borden.

C-18632/NATIONAL ARCHIVES OF CANADA.

codes formulated by the parties themselves. Both tended to curb the more imaginative schemes to manipulate the electoral process so freely used by men like Sifton, Rogers, Reid, and Cochrane – or at least to make their application more discreet. For all the changes, however, the party leaders of the 1930s or the 1970s faced the same fundamental challenge as Laurier and Borden – to persuade more voters in each constituency to vote for their party than for their opponents.

The most significant change was the gradual acceptance by electors of third parties. The effect in some provinces was practically to displace one or the other of the traditional parties. Alberta from the 1920s to the 1970s and Quebec since the 1930s are examples of this process. At the federal level the Social Credit Party was a significant factor in electoral politics for almost three decades, and the Co-operative Commonwealth Federation/New Democratic Party has become a permanent fixture deeply influencing the development of policy by the governing parties and adding yet another complexity to the electoral strategies.

The role of the media in elections has also changed dramatically, partly in response to a growing electorate but even more as the result of remarkable innovations in communications technology, from radio broadcasting to television's hourly transmission of news and information to a mass audience. The party press, as it was known and used by Laurier, has been eclipsed. Generally, "kept" editors and journalists are few in number, and parties have developed more elaborate strategies, from constituency newsletters and the use of advertising agencies to televised national press conferences, to get their news and views directly to the voter. The communications blitz organized by the Canadian Home Market Association in 1911 has been taken over by the parties themselves and developed into a higher art. If the party press is no longer a surrogate for party organization, the management of information and the dissemination of publicity has certainly come to be among the most important and costly activities of the late twentieth-century Canadian political party.

All of these changes have made the need for broadly based, vital, party organizational structures more imperative. In a sense the process had begun before 1896, with the first national party convention staged by the Laurier Liberals in 1893. Borden had also toyed with the convention idea but held back, arguing that a well-organized party structure in each province was a necessary antecedent to a national convention. The Conservatives did not convene a convention until 1927. For their part, the Liberals called another convention in 1919.[7] It was most significant because that convention not only charted future party policy but also elected the party leader, William Lyon Mackenzie King. The transfer of the selection of the party leader from the caucus to a national party convention was a fundamental step in the democratization of the political party, and it set the pattern for regularly scheduled party conventions, leadership elections, and even leadership reviews that today characterize the business of all political parties in Canada.

The gloom in the Marché St-Pierre contrasted sharply with the scene in the Union Bank Building in Halifax on the night of September 21, 1911. Borden arrived at his constituency headquarters early. The initial results were not encouraging and for a time Borden wondered if his carefully planned election strategy had backfired. By the time the news of the triumph in Ontario was announced it was late, and later still when the sweep of British Columbia was known. By then the rooms were crowded with shouting, cheering, backslapping party workers. Borden, among old friends and acquaintances, was joyful and confident. The decade-long test of party leadership in Opposition was over; his policies and his political strategy had been vindicated. He planned to spend a day or so at the family homestead in Grand Pré. Then he would go back to Ottawa to test the opportunities, and the limits, of power.

As party organization developed into an elaborate operation with its own leadership figures and councils and committees, the opportunities for disagreement and tension between the party and the caucus multiplied. Borden's problems in this area pale into insignificance compared to those of Mackenzie King, John Diefenbaker, Joe Clark, Pierre Elliott Trudeau, and Brian Mulroney. As the chief of both the party and the caucus, the party leader, as Borden's career illustrated, must walk a fine line. Unlike Borden or Laurier, the modern political leader is the creature of his party, not his caucus. But, as John Diefenbaker's leadership demonstrated, a party leader who loses the loyalty and daily support of his caucus is in very great trouble.

Finally, leadership is a determining factor in the health of every political party and of the vitality of the political process in Canada.

---

[7] On the Liberal party conventions of 1893 and 1919 see J.W. Lederle, "The Liberal Convention of 1893," *Canadian Journal of Economics and Political Science*, XVI, (1950), and "The Liberal Convention of 1919 and the Selection of Mackenzie King," *Dalhousie Review*, XXVII (1948).

Obviously, the style and tone of the party will be influenced by the leader's personality and character. But successful party leaders have had several common attributes: a deep commitment to the integrity of the democratic political process, an ability to follow as well as to command, patience, a keen instinct for compromise, and a high level of ambition. Laurier put it best in his analysis of the reason why Alexander Mackenzie was a notably lacklustre leader: "He has no zest to carry a party on." Laurier, Borden, R.B. Bennett, Mackenzie King, M.J. Coldwell, and Diefenbaker, among others, had zest in abundance. Their party members responded to it. So too did that body of electors Borden thought so significant – citizens "of moderate opinion who vote now with one and now with the other party."

1911-1919:
TO VIMY RIDGE AND
BACK

The men of the First Canadian Division left Canada in October 1914 with bands playing and flags flying; all hoped for a short and glorious war and to be home by Christmas. But Christmas came and went with the troops mired in the muck of Salisbury Plain during one of the wettest English winters in memory. They were not well-enough trained, their British superiors judged, to be sent quickly into battle and, besides, the rapid movement of armies that had marked the outbreak of war the previous August had quickly given way to the stalemate of the trenches. The Canadian Division did not reach the battle lines in Belgium until February 1915. There they found a world of mud, filth, stink, bad food, little sleep, and sheer boredom alleviated only briefly in early March when they were ordered to provide fire support for a British attack at Neuve Chapelle. That boredom ended with deadly speed late on a warm and sunny afternoon on April 22, 1915, near the Belgian town of Ypres.

As the Canadian troops lolled in the sun below, a reconnaissance pilot flying over the battlefield noticed a large cloud of yellowish smoke drifting toward the Allied trenches from the German lines. He quickly dove for his airfield to report what he had seen. At about the same time, French colonial troops on the left flank of the Canadians saw a wall of smoke rising about a metre from the ground and behind it, higher than a man's head, a greenish-yellow cloud drifting toward them. An intense German barrage began falling on their trenches. In their positions the Canadians took note of the shellfire and hunkered down. Soon German shells began falling near their positions as well, and the men noticed a greenish tinge around the sun. They began coughing and choking, their lungs filling with chlorine, their eyes tearing from the stinging gas. They grabbed their rifles and prepared to defend their trenches in the greenish murk, unaware that they and the French colonial troops to their left had been picked for the singular honour of suffering the first German gas attack of the war.

Canada entered the war as part of the British Empire at midnight on August 4, 1914; it was the greatest struggle in the short history of the young country. When the fighting finally ended on November 11, 1918, 60 000 Canadians had been killed in action and tens of thousands more had been wounded, many badly maimed and scarred for life. It was the supreme test that marked Canada's coming of age, and it challenged Canada's leaders with political, social, economic, and moral problems that dwarfed the troubles of bygone times. It brought Canada's prime minister, Robert Laird Borden, to the pinnacle of his career at home and abroad while, at the same time, it brought him close to resignation and placed burdens on him that no Canadian leader had ever had to bear before. He had been elected prime minister three years before the outbreak of war during sunny days of optimism and peaceful expansion; he was destined to lead Canada through dark days of division, despair, and death.

Borden in Power

Borden and his Conservative Party were swept into office on September 21, 1911, in the eleventh general election since Confederation. He was neither colourful, flamboyant, nor charismatic, and his speeches, even on the most dramatic of occasions, were uninspiring. He was a lawyer by occupation and temperament, a careful, honest man, loyal to his friends, and reluctant to make the hard decisions sometimes demanded of a leader. Borden's watchwords were duty and sacrifice, qualities that would be essential in the years ahead.[1]

---

[1] On Borden as a political leader and on the Conservative Party after 1911, see Robert Craig Brown's *Robert Laird Borden*, Vol. I (Toronto, 1975), and Vol. II (Toronto, 1980). Conservative politics are covered in John English, *The Decline of Politics: The Conservatives and the Party System* (Toronto, 1977). The stories of two leading Liberal politicians in this period are told in Margaret Prang, *N.W. Rowell, Ontario Nationalist* (Toronto, 1975), and O.D. Skelton, *The Life and Letters of Sir Wilfrid Laurier* (Toronto, 1921), which is dated but still the

Borden came to office with many important national issues unan-swered. It was clear that reciprocity was dead, but the future trade and financial relationship with the United States was still uncertain. Western farm demands for greater social reform and government intervention in the grain marketing and transportation system were unresolved. Demands from urban progressives for civil service reform, votes for women, aid for the poor, and the assimilation of Canada's masses of new immigrants remained unsettled and problematic. How Quebec national-ism – so important to the outcome of the 1911 election – was to be accommodated in a government committed to the defence of the British Imperial connection was an enigma.

Borden's first task was to form a government, and in the weeks following the election victory he busied himself with the difficult and delicate work of sorting out claims to positions in his new cabinet. There were more seekers than posts and Borden was forced to weigh ability against political muscle. He had many political debts to pay. There were Quebec Tories such as F.D. Monk who had supported Borden on the naval issue, renegade Liberals such as W.T. White who had opposed reciprocity as a member of the "Toronto 18," and the party faithful such as Sam Hughes, who had backed Borden in his long years as Opposition leader despite his defeat in two federal elections. Borden also had to follow the time-honoured tradition of including in the Cabinet represen-tatives of the French and the English, of Catholics and Protestants, and of all the regions in Canada. Sometimes it no doubt seemed to him that ability was not a very important factor in building a cabinet. One Conservative observer noted: "There was hardly a member of the party who did not rush to him and say he had to make him a cabinet minister. It was a most humiliating spectacle."

While Borden was in the process of selecting his ministers, Conserva-tive Party leaders were beginning to hand out government jobs. In every riding people who had supported the Conservatives for years clamoured for positions from postmasterships to judgeships as rewards for faithful service. Patronage was normal in Canadian politics and many govern-ment jobs were ordinarily filled by political appointments. This was one of the first reforms Borden had pledged to make – but only after the usual orgy of pork barrelling.

---

best work on Laurier. W.R. Graham, *Arthur Meighen*, Vol. I (Toronto, 1960), covers the story of an important Conservative minister and Borden's successor as leader and prime minister up to 1920.

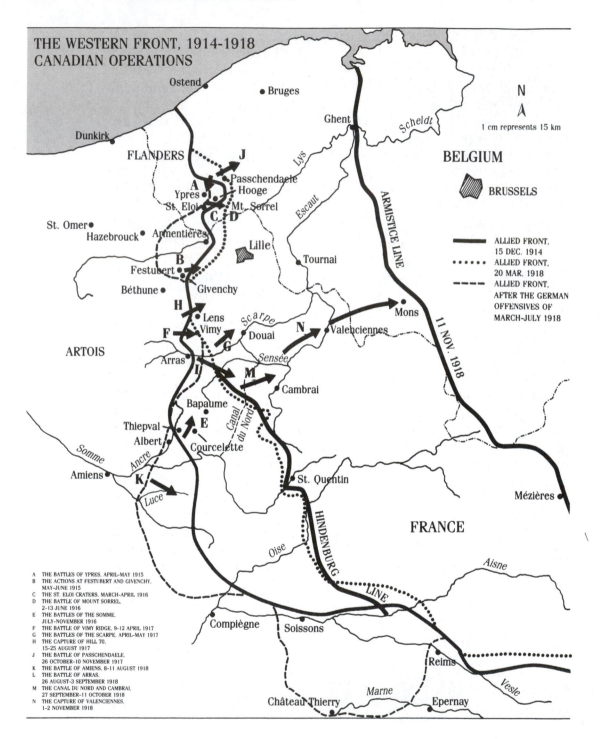

THE WESTERN FRONT, 1914-1918
CANADIAN OPERATIONS

Ostend
Bruges
Dunkirk
Ghent
Scheldt
FLANDERS
J
BELGIUM
Passchendaele
A Hooge
Ypres
St. Eloi Mt. Sorrel
C D
St. Omer
Hazebrouck Armentières
Lille
Tournai
B
Festubert
Béthune Givenchy
H
Lens
F Vimy Scarpe
Douai
Arras Sensée
ARTOIS L
M
Bapaume Cambrai
E
Thiepval Canal du Nord
Albert
Somme Courcelette
Amiens Ancre
K St. Quentin
Luce
FRANCE
Oise
Compiègne Soissons
Aisne

BRUSSELS

1 cm represents 15 km

N

ARMISTICE LINE
11 NOV. 1918

Mons
N Valenciennes

HINDENBURG LINE

Mézières

Reims
Vesle
Château Thierry Marne Epernay

—————— ALLIED FRONT,
15 DEC. 1914
• • • • • • ALLIED FRONT,
20 MAR. 1918
– – – – – ALLIED FRONT,
AFTER THE GERMAN
OFFENSIVES OF
MARCH-JULY 1918

A   THE BATTLES OF YPRES, APRIL-MAY 1915
B   THE ACTIONS AT FESTUBERT AND GIVENCHY,
    MAY-JUNE 1915
C   THE ST. ELOI CRATERS, MARCH-APRIL 1916
D   THE BATTLE OF MOUNT SORREL,
    2-13 JUNE 1916
E   THE BATTLES OF THE SOMME,
    JULY-NOVEMBER 1916
F   THE BATTLE OF VIMY RIDGE, 9-12 APRIL 1917
G   THE BATTLES OF THE SCARPE, APRIL-MAY 1917
H   THE CAPTURE OF HILL 70,
    15-25 AUGUST 1917
J   THE BATTLE OF PASSCHENDAELE,
    26 OCTOBER-10 NOVEMBER 1917
K   THE BATTLE OF AMIENS, 8-11 AUGUST 1918
L   THE BATTLE OF ARRAS,
    26 AUGUST-3 SEPTEMBER 1918
M   THE CANAL DU NORD AND CAMBRAI,
    27 SEPTEMBER-11 OCTOBER 1918
N   THE CAPTURE OF VALENCIENNES,
    1-2 NOVEMBER 1918

Borden took more than two weeks to construct his cabinet. It was sworn in on October 9, 1911, a mixture of old-party supporters and some recent converts. W.T. White was given the important post of minister of finance, not only as a reward for his opposition to reciprocity but also in recognition of the expertise he had gained as general manager of National Trust. One appointment that would later haunt Borden was his selection of Colonel Sam Hughes as minister of militia and defence. Hughes had been an unrelentingly loyal supporter of Borden, but he was a potential troublemaker for his leader. He was cantankerous, arrogant, and opinionated. He thought little of the professional officers in the army and did not hesitate to tell them so. On the other hand he considered himself a genuine military hero (demanding at least one and possibly two V.C.s for his feats in the South African War) and a logistical and organizational genius. As long as Canada was at peace, Hughes, responsible for a small peacetime militia and an even smaller professional army, was harmless. Once the war began, however, he would prove a serious obstacle to the organization of the war effort.

Hughes was not the only weak spot in Borden's cabinet. Another was Frederick D. Monk, minister of public works and the acknowledged leader of the Conservative Party in Quebec. Borden had little choice but to appoint Monk, but if he expected him to be a source of strength and leadership in Quebec, his hopes were misplaced. Monk was a weak and hesitant man and he was often incapable of making important decisions and sticking by them. His support for Borden's external policies was never more than lukewarm and he failed entirely to keep Borden in close touch with Quebec opinion or to act as a bridge between Ottawa and his native province as other leading French-Canadian Conservatives had done before him since the days of George-Etienne Cartier. Monk had neither the strength of character nor the vision of his predecessors.

Borden and his cabinet soon turned their attention to the business of government. As far back as 1907 Borden had advocated government intervention in and regulation of many commercial and economic activities such as railway transportation and had allied himself with others who appeared to share his views. He had also pledged to reform the federal bureaucracy by replacing the patronage system with a merit system. This would mean setting up an independent commission to hire civil servants and to decide questions of pay and advancement.

These views were shared by a growing number of people in both Canada and the United States who considered themselves progressives. They were upset by the poverty and labour strife that rapid industrialization and immigration had produced and were convinced that reform of the capitalist system was absolutely necessary if social strife and even revolution were to be avoided. They usually advocated measures to make government more efficient and democratic and to bring both capital and labour into a more harmonious balance with the general needs of society. Reform measures as different as votes for women and government ownership of the railways were all a part of this progressive tradition.

Borden did not forget his reform promises and in December 1911 his government appointed a royal commission to make a thorough investigation of the public service. Sir George Murray, a former permanent secretary to the British Treasury, was appointed to come up with the answers. He recommended that ministers no longer involve themselves with the day-to-day operation of their departments but instead give their ministries broad political direction. He also recommended competitive examinations to fill civil service posts and urged tighter control over appointments and promotions. Murray's report anticipated a vastly improved and more efficient civil service but, aside from some minor changes to the Civil Service Act in 1912, the Borden government did little to carry out Murray's suggested reforms until the spring of 1918. There was too much opposition to change within the cabinet and the Conservative Party. Patronage was too deeply rooted in the Canadian Party system to be eradicated overnight, especially since many politicians were convinced that patronage attracted and kept the allegiance of party supporters and unified the party.

Borden had good intentions, but his reform record in the prewar period was distinctly uneven. He failed to carry out a major reform of the civil service, he failed to change the machinery for setting and regulating tariffs, and he failed to bring the railways under public control. But he did have some important successes. The government passed the Canada Grain Act in 1912, which established a Board of Grain Commissioners to supervise grain inspection and to regulate the grain trade. The act also gave the government the authority to own and operate terminal elevators and went far to meet farmers' complaints about elevator monopolies and shoddy grain grading and inspection practices that robbed them of a fair return for their labour. Other measures were introduced to aid farmers, including federal assistance to the provinces for the upgrading of agricultural education, free rural delivery of mail, and federal funds for provincial highway construction.

Borden's attempts at progressive reform suffered both from opposition within his own party and from the Liberal majority in the Senate, which did not hesitate on several occasions to reject bills passed by the Conservative majority in the Commons. At the same time, growing tensions in Europe forced Borden to pay less attention to domestic affairs and more to imperial defence questions, particularly the naval issue. The naval debates of 1909 and 1910 had been bitter. They had not resulted in a Canadian navy but rather in a "Laurier navy," and soon after taking office in March 1912, Borden announced that he would submit a new naval policy to Parliament. He believed that Canadian participation in British naval expansion ought to bring a greater Canadian role in the shaping of imperial defence and foreign policy, and he was convinced that if Canada and the other dominions had a duty to help Great Britain defend the Empire, they must also share in making those decisions that would determine peace or war.

Borden had little time to plan his new naval policy because, almost as soon as he had made his announcement, word came from the British government that their naval-building program was going to be stepped

While the naval question divided Canadians, new technology was changing the future. The Silver Dart, designed and flown by J.A.D. McCurdy in 1909, was the first successful aircraft in the British Empire.

up to match an accelerated German fleet expansion. The British wanted an emergency contribution from Canada. Borden was forced to postpone his own plans to develop a naval policy, devote his attention to the British request and, at the same time, try to keep the government united on the issue. That would not be easy since Conservatives in Quebec had very different ideas from those in the rest of Canada on the question of imperial defence.

In June 1912, Borden led a Canadian delegation to England to study the naval emergency. The group left in late June and spent two months in England examining the problems of the Empire's defence and other imperial issues. While there, Borden was able to convince British Prime Minister Herbert Asquith that the dominions should be allowed representation on the Imperial Defence Committee when dominion defence matters were being discussed. This was far short of the overall consultation Borden had sought, but for the moment, it was all he could get.

Borden returned to Canada at the end of August and waited for secret admiralty reports to spell out, in detail, the extent of the naval crisis. When they finally arrived at the end of September, Borden revealed them to the cabinet and sought support for an immediate cash contribution to Britain. Monk refused to agree and insisted that the government hold a plebiscite before aid was extended to the British, a position he had taken as far back as 1909 when the Laurier naval bills were being discussed. Fearing an angry reaction from English Canada, Borden refused, and in mid-October Monk resigned. These serious divisions were likely to split the government, and Borden tried to secure the backing of other French Conservatives and *nationalistes* by stressing the concessions he claimed to have won from the British on consultation. He gained some French support, but a significant number of his Quebec members still refused to go along.

In early December 1912, Borden introduced his emergency naval aid bill into the House of Commons. Canada would give the British an immediate contribution of $35 million for the construction of dreadnaughts to be placed at the disposal of the British for the common defence of the Empire. Borden stressed the emergency nature of the contribution and claimed that the British had agreed to consult with Canada and the other dominions on imperial foreign policy in future. In fact, the British had made no such promise and had only pledged to consult with the dominions on matters that directly concerned them. Borden's attempts to placate the Opposition were a total failure, and a bitter five-month debate followed that ended only in May 1913, when the Conservatives invoked closure for the first time in Canadian history.

The measure, devised by Borden's young solicitor-general, Arthur Meighen, in 1912, ended debate, and the naval bill finally passed on May 15. By the end of the month it had been defeated in the Liberal-dominated Senate. Borden was incensed at this latest example of Liberal obstructionism in the Senate and began to devote more attention to reforming it by making it elective, an idea he had thought about for years. But other, more important matters, soon demanded his attention.

Canada's apparently endless economic expansion ended abruptly in the fall of 1913 as the worst depression in two decades gripped the country. The most direct cause was a rapid withdrawal of British investment capital from Canada. These funds had largely financed the commercial, industrial, and real estate expansion of the previous decade. A war had broken out in the Balkans and many investors con-cluded – correctly – that a major European war was just around the corner. If that happened, money would be needed in Britain to pay for the war. Many investors had also lost confidence in the Canadian economy, and Canada, with little surplus capital of its own to invest, was caught short. By early 1914 tens of thousands of Canadians were out of work, and trade unions began to demand an immediate end to immigra-tion and the establishment of government measures to help the unem-ployed. Despite these demands, the federal government did little to help, while immigration continued at an accelerated rate – 400 000 immigrants entered Canada in 1913.

The cities bore the brunt of the depression. Many farmers, in debt and cut off by their banks, abandoned their farms to move to the cities where they competed for work with the urban unemployed whose ranks were already swollen by newly arrived immigrants. Some city governments, like the one in Toronto, did all they could to help the unemployed with the few resources available. Others showed little or no sympathy: the mayor of Winnipeg told the jobless in that city to "hit the trail." Despite reforms introduced by progressives, most upper-class Canadians and their political representatives still believed that periodic depressions were to be expected and that little could, or should, be done to help those who suffered. Social welfare was a matter for private charity, not for governments, they claimed.

The depression was eventually ended by war. On the morning of June 28, 1914, in Sarajevo, a young Serbian nationalist shot and killed the Archduke Franz Ferdinand, heir apparent to the Austrian throne. The killing sparked off a chain of events that sent the major powers of Europe marching against each other. Austria attacked Serbia, which was allied to

Russia, while Germany, allied to Austria, prepared to attack both Russia and its ally, France. The intrigues of European diplomacy had created a net of secret alliances and agreements that quickly dragged millions into what became the most murderous war in history. Britain and its empire were not to be spared because Britain had ties to France and, for at least a century, had guaranteed the neutrality of Belgium. When German forces crossed the Belgian border as part of a sweeping attack into France, Britain declared war on Germany.

The British declaration of war was made by King George V on behalf of all his subjects. Canada was bound by this declaration because it was still a colony, with almost no control over its own foreign affairs and no autonomous status within the Empire. Few Canadians worried about this lack of status in 1914; most threw themselves into the war in a great burst of enthusiasm. Canada may have had no choice as to its participation, but Canada alone would decide the degree of its involvement. Canadians generally seemed to agree with Liberal leader Sir Wilfrid Laurier that their country should give "assistance to the fullest extent of [its] power." For one thing, most believed the war would be short and glorious and would afford a good opportunity to demonstrate what the young dominion could accomplish on the battlefield. For another, a majority of Canadians were still either British-born or of British origin, and the sentimental and emotional ties to the mother country, as well as the economic and constitutional ones, were strong. To many of these people, Canada was little more than a self-governing district of a great and unified Empire that spanned the globe bringing order, British civilization, and Christianity to the darkest corners of the world. These were the sort of people who had clamoured for Canadian participation in the Boer War in South Africa. As the oldest self-governing dominion, therefore, Canada was bound to do its duty. To this end Laurier pledged that the Opposition would do everything possible to assist the government in the smooth operation of the war effort. Laurier was in every respect a British Liberal, and it was no surprise that he would rally to the side of his philosophical homeland.

Canada at War

In the first weeks of war, the government moved quickly to give itself extraordinary powers to govern in this time of national crisis. A War Measures Act was drawn up and passed into law, giving sweeping authority to the government to be used to meet the war emergency.

There had never been anything quite like it in Canadian history. It granted Ottawa the power to use orders-in-council in a broader and more

Vol. II. No. 6.   OTTAWA, FEBRUARY, 1915.   Ten Cents

BOTH WILL SERVE THE EMPIRE IN THE FIELD

The Canadian who enlists to fight the foe and the one who remains to feed the friend.

sweeping fashion than during peacetime, even, in some cases, to bypass the normal legislative process that required passage of bills through the Commons and Senate and the approval of the governor general. It effectively suspended the right of habeas corpus by allowing government officers to order arrests and detentions without having to bring specific charges before a judge. It gave the government power to deport without trial and power to regulate or interfere in any area of society or the economy that was considered necessary for the prosecution of the war. Matters that were defined by the constitution as provincial areas during peacetime could pass under federal jurisdiction during times of war. The act, in the words of one political scientist, made Canada into a "democratic dictatorship."

At first few of these emergency powers were used except those that allowed the government to control the movements of "enemy aliens." These were immigrants – roughly a half million – who had come to Canada from Germany or Austria-Hungary and who had not yet become British subjects. There was substantial fear that they might work secretly for a British defeat and sabotage the war effort, even though very few of them harboured pro-German or pro-Austrian sympathies. The fear was not based on actual threats but on a war-created xenophobia that caused Canadians to suspect the loyalty of those different from themselves. In many cases this feeling was just an extension of the anti-immigrant attitudes that had grown rapidly in Canada in response to the flood of immigrants who had arrived after 1896. Enemy aliens were required to carry special identity cards and to report at regular intervals; 8300 of them were interned in four detention camps in isolated parts of the country. The government also established a chief press censor, whose job it was to examine magazines and newspapers and order the deletion of articles and stories that he judged harmful to the war effort. Most of the Canadian press co-operated fully with him because the editors were, as a rule, solidly behind the war and anxious to show their loyalty. They could not do this and at the same time fulfull their responsibility to the public to act as a watchdog on government. Thus Canadians, like Britons and others, learned little about the incompetence of both generals and politicians and about the failures of strategy and equipment that led to the slaughter at the front. As United States Senator Hiram Johnson said in 1917, "The first casualty when war comes is truth."

When the war began Canada's army was too small, too ill-equipped, and too poorly trained to make an immediate contribution to the Allied cause. Plans for the quick mobilization of a division of approximately

25 000 men had been drawn up by the army in 1911, but they were scrapped almost immediately by the minister of militia, Sam Hughes. Hughes was too much the megalomaniac to trust mobilization to army commanders around the country or to army headquarters itself. He was a militia man and had never got along well with the officers of the regular army whom he considered little more than barroom loafers. He alone would direct the raising of troops. Hughes sent out telegrams to militia units across Canada calling on them to prepare lists of volunteers. These lists were to be sent to Ottawa for final approval. This and just about every other job in the complicated mobilization process was to be handled by Hughes himself or a trusted subordinate. It was a most inefficient way of mobilizing a large force and would have failed but for the enthusiasm of the tens of thousands of young men who clamoured to join the fray. A very large number of those men were British immigrants or Canadians who felt strong ties to the British cause. At institutions such as McGill University and the University of Toronto the Anglo-Saxon males of Canada's middle and upper classes were expected by friends, family, and school to do their duty and join up in the same way they were expected to join fraternities or play rugby. But the volunteers did not all volunteer out of patriotism. Many were also unemployed workers who needed a roof over their heads, clothing, and three meals a day.

The men were brought to a new army camp at Valcartier, Quebec, which was thrown up, complete with sewer lines, water mains, and a rail link to Quebec City, in thirty days. There thousands of tents were set up while mess halls, latrines, rifle ranges, and drill fields were laid out. By the third week in August, the first of the men began to arrive; eventually more than 33 000 were housed there. This huge, combined training and manpower supply depot was Hughes's brainchild, and he had a brick bungalow and an office built on a hill overlooking the camp so that he could survey the scene like a medieval lord. He tried to direct almost every aspect of the camp's operations and interfered in virtually everything. This, plus the constant arrival of troop trains, the comings and goings of construction crews, and a continuing flow of V.I.P. visitors, caused tremendous confusion.[2]

On October 3, 1914, 30 000 Canadian troops sailed for England from

---

[2] The mobilization of the initial Canadian contingent is described in Ronald G. Haycock, *Sam Hughes: The Public Career of a Controversial Canadian, 1885-1916* (Waterloo, 1986). See also A.M.J. Hyatt, *General Sir Arthur Currie: A Military Biography* (Toronto, 1987), which describes the mobilization from Currie's perspective.

Gaspé Basin in the largest convoy ever assembled at the time. They arrived less than two weeks later and were soon encamped on Salisbury Plain where they spent a cold, wet winter in training, fighting mud, discomfort, and disease before being transferred to France. By the middle of February the Canadian Division, as it was designated by the British War Office, had taken its place in the lines on the western front near the Belgian town of Ypres.

In the spring of 1915 the Canadian Division was only one unit of the British V Corps, commanded by Lt.-Gen. Sir Herbert Plumer, a man described as "a soldier's soldier." The division was led by Gen. E.A.H. Alderson, a British officer. At one point during the initial mobilization, Hughes himself seemed to have considered taking command of the Canadian troops, but Borden would not allow this while Hughes was minister of militia. Hughes chose to keep his job in the cabinet. Although he played an important role in Alderson's selection, he was suspicious of British officers, constantly tried to interfere in the day-to-day operations

The machine gun was a powerful battlefield weapon, and these Canadians were quick to set up their weapons to consolidate the successful capture of Vimy Ridge. Note the German prisoner in the left rear.

PA-1017/NATIONAL ARCHIVES OF CANADA.

of the Canadian army in England, and missed no opportunity to try to place his favourites in command positions. This caused continuing problems because Canadian officers were simply not ready, at that stage of the war, to command at the divisional level.

Sir Sam Hughes.

C-20240/NATIONAL ARCHIVES OF CANADA.

The Canadians found a war that few were prepared for. The initial German assault into France in August 1914 had been stopped by the French and British armies, and the fighting had settled down to the deadly stalemate of trench warfare. Army commanders on both sides were unprepared and slow to adopt new offensive tactics that could overcome the strong defences of the trenches. Instead, both sides dug complex defences of their own, usually consisting of three or more parallel lines of trenches connected by other trenches dug at right angles to the main lines. The defence systems combined trenches, tunnels, dugouts, and deep underground shelters with minefields, barbed wire, and sandbags. Machine guns with sweeping fields of fire were placed at carefully sited key positions, and the artillery was positioned behind the lines to allow each side to pound the enemy's front with continuous and deadly barrages. There was little drama in this type of warfare, just a steady toll of lives.

The trenches were a dark, subterranean hell, and the men in them endured a cramped existence. Water from rains or from the seeping ground water of Flanders flooded the bottoms, creating a thick mud, collapsing trench walls, and making life one long, soggy battle to stay clean, warm, and dry. Rats were everywhere, growing fat on the flesh of dead horses and dead men and scurrying over the living during the nights as a constant reminder of the fate that might await them all. The stench of rotting flesh from unburied bodies mixed with the stink of sweat, filthy bodies, and latrines. By day all movement was careful and crouched – a head above the trench line was too easy a target for enemy snipers. By night men stumbled down ragged trenches with no light to guide their way. There were diseases – from trench foot to pneumonia – and boredom, and lice and nits. Men soon learned the exacting art of picking lice from their clothes and bodies. A gallows humour developed that summed up the bitter irony of the situation. In one section of a trench the hand of a corpse stuck out from the mud, and each new man joining the unit was obliged to shake it. Nothing expressed the aimless cruelty of trench warfare as much as a soldiers' ditty, sung to the tune of "Auld Lang Syne," which gave a worm's eye view of the lofty purposes for which they were suffering and dying:

◀ This famous cartoon appeared in Punch to celebrate the Canadian capture of Vimy. Five years later it made a fine cover for the program of a reunion dinner.

TORONTO TELEGRAM COLLECTION. YORK UNIVERSITY ARCHIVES.

We're here because we're here because
We're here because we're here
We're here because we're here because
We're here because we're here . . . [3]

The futility of the war and the gratuitous waste of human life proved to be a severe trial of faith for those who believed in a personal and merciful God. Of the 426 Methodist ministers who served overseas, 39 resigned from the ministry on returning to Canada and another 113 relinquished direct ties with the church. The destruction, the suffering, the apparent aimlessness of the entire war experience, and the inability to alleviate the soldiers' pain clearly affected these ministers. Rev. S.D. Chown, General Superintendent of the Methodist Church, wrote after the war: "In many minds the war shook with the violence of a moral and intellectual earthquake the foundations of Christian faith. It shattered many structures of belief in which devout people found refuge from the storms of life." One front line army chaplain put it more succinctly: "When we sen[d] out men to slaughter other men, to thrust bayonets into them and to experience all the carnage and deviltry of war, don't you imagine it will make spiritual beings out of them because it won't."

In April 1915, the Germans began to mount limited offensives on the western front which were intended to hold the British and French at bay while they devoted their attention to defeating the Russians and knocking them out of the war. One of these assaults was the gas attack of Ypres on April 22. Although the Allied High Command had received indications that the Germans were about to unleash this new and terrible weapon, the staff had failed to warn the front lines or to provide for an adequate defence; when the choking, green clouds were carried by the wind over the French colonial troops in the trenches, they panicked and ran. The Canadians did not receive the full brunt of the initial German

---

[3] For life and death on the western front, see John Keegan, *The Face of Battle* (New York, 1976), which describes the Somme campaign, and John Ellis, *Eye Deep in Hell: The Trenches, 1914-1918* (London, 1975). The effect of the war on the psyche of those who fought in it is analyzed by Paul Fussell, *The Great War and Modern Memory* (New York, 1975). There are many memoirs of those who were there. A Canadian work is Charles Yale Harrison, *Generals Die in Bed* (Hamilton, 1975). Three books which relate Canadian experiences at home and at the front are William B. Mathieson (ed.), *My Grandfather's War: Canadians Remember the First World War 1914-1918* (Toronto, 1981); Grace Morris Craig, *But This Is Our War* (Toronto, 1981); and Gordon Reid (ed.), *Poor Bloody Murder: Personal Memoirs of the First World War* (Oakville, 1980). On the overseas war experiences of Methodist ministers and probationers see David B. Marshall, "Methodism Embattled: A Reconsideration of the Methodist Church and World War I," *Canadian Historical Review*, LXVI, (March, 1985), pp. 48-64.

General Sir Arthur Currie.

TORONTO TELEGRAM COLLECTION, YORK UNIVERSITY ARCHIVES.

assault nor of the gas. When the chlorine began to drift over the Canadian positions, word quickly spread that a cloth soaked in urine and held up to the face would provide some protection from the deadly fumes. These factors, combined with the quick reaction of Canadian officers such as Brigadier-General R.E.W. Turner, commander of the 3rd Canadian Brigade, and Colonel Arthur W. Currie, commander of the 2nd Brigade, enabled the Allied High Command staff to send troops northward to try to fill the gap in the line while they prepared for a counterattack. For the next three days the Canadians and the British fought tenaciously to restore the Allied lines, although casualties were brutal because of repeated German assaults supported by massive artillery fire and more chlorine gas. The Germans were eventually pushed back, but at a devastating cost. When the Canadian troops were withdrawn from the battle on April 25, less than half were left. Out of an initial frontline strength of 10 000 men, 1850 Canadians had been killed, 3411 had been wounded, and 776 had been taken prisoner.

Turner and Currie showed great promise at Ypres — Currie at one point even left his brigade headquarters at the height of the confusion to personally search out reinforcements. Turner was 43 at the outbreak of war and had seen action in the Boer War. Currie, on the other hand, was the epitome of the citizen-soldier. He had received no formal officer's training before the war and had been a businessman in Victoria. After making a good living in insurance and real estate, he was almost wiped out in the 1913 depression, and he used funds earmarked for uniforms for his militia unit to pay off part of his debts. The possibility of exposure and scandal hung over him for most of the war. He might have remained an unknown failure but for his continuing interest in soldiering. In the militia he soon gained a reputation as an able organizer, respected for his fairness and strength of character, and for his ability to generate loyalty among the troops. He rose rapidly through the ranks and was appointed commanding officer of the 50th Victoria Regiment in January 1914. When war broke out he was offered command of a brigade in the Canadian Division.

While the Canadian Division was receiving its introduction to battle, tens of thousands back home continued to volunteer for army service. The recruiting was carried out with a flourish of patriotic propaganda exhorting Canada's young men to heed the call of honour. The clergy, prominent politicians, and leaders of women's organizations took part in the drive. Despite the growing realization that the war would not be short, increasing numbers of volunteers joined up during 1915. A Second Canadian Division was formed in May 1915 and moved to France in September where it joined with the First Division to form the Canadian Corps under the overall command of General Alderson who was promoted from command of the First Division. Currie replaced Alderson and Turner was given command of Second Division.

As volunteers continued to pour into recruiting centres – a monthly peak of 30 000 was reached in March 1916 – and the realization took hold in Allied capitals that the war was going to be very long and costly, Prime Minister Borden continued to raise the authorized force levels. In early 1916, the overall size of the army was set at 500 000 men. This included rear echelon and supply troops – the "tail" – as well as front line combat troops – the "teeth." Two new divisions were formed – the Third in December 1915 and the Fourth in August 1916 – and sent to the front while the Fifth was kept in reserve in England. Thus by late 1916 the Canadian Corps consisted of four divisions, approximately 80 000 troops, fighting together virtually all the time. It was commanded by Lieut.-Gen. Julian Byng who had taken over from Alderson following a Canadian failure to hold the St. Eloi craters during a battle in early April 1916.

The Home Front

For the first time in Canadian history a massed army of citizen-soldiers was taking to the field. They left behind thousands of dependent wives, mothers, and children. This posed a serious question: With the men gone, who would take care of their families? At first the answer appeared to be private charitable organizations. They tried to provide a basic income for the immediate families of men overseas. Most of the work was voluntary, supported by individual and corporate donations to charities such as the Canadian Patriotic Fund, incorporated by the federal government in August 1914. The fund undertook to pay as much as $30 per month to the families of soldiers living in Eastern Canada, with $10 more for those living in the West, where the cost of living was recognized to be higher. Later in the war, the basic payment was raised to $50 per month and was supplemented by federal widows' and dependants' pensions.

Other organizations distributed food, cigarettes, and clothing to the men in Europe, and service groups such as the Y.M.C.A. maintained gathering places for men on leave in Great Britain and Canada. These activities were supported by the time and money voluntarily contributed by thousands of Canadians. In the first years of the war, when the expeditionary force was small and enthusiasm great, they helped considerably to ease the strain on soldiers' families.

In the long run, however, it was not enough – voluntary effort was insufficient. The war apparatus became too massive and the amounts of money needed to support soldiers' families too great for voluntary contributions to fill the need adequately. This was true not only of the campaign to support soldiers' families but of virtually every other area of war organization from the attempt to convince food suppliers not to raise prices in a time of shortages to the campaign to persuade employers to treat their workers fairly. It became increasingly evident, as early as the first months of 1916, that government action would have to be used to organize the war effort. This move from voluntarism to compulsion to solve a range of social and economic problems produced an interventionist state such as Canadians had never known before. It was parallelled by a growing sentiment among Canadians that this was not simply an Empire war but also Canada's war. The young nation's mettle was being tested not only on the field of battle but also in its ability to run an efficient war effort.

Canada's contributions on the battlefield were considerable but only part of the total Canadian war effort, which included the supply of millions of tons of foodstuffs to the Allies and the production of hundreds of millions of dollars in munitions and other war necessities. In this area as in others, Canada started virtually from nothing. When war broke out there was only one factory in the country capable of producing artillery shells, and its capacity was limited to about 75 shells per day. Artillery was particularly important in trench fighting and the guns could fire millions of shells in a single battle. Britain produced much of this but Canada was also called upon to help. The war production was initially directed by the Shell Committee, an arm of the British Ministry of Munitions headed by a Canadian officer, Lt.-Col. Alexander Bertram. The Shell Committee included several prominent Canadian manufacturers and was responsible for placing contracts for the production of shells with Canadian manufacturers on behalf of the British government. At the start of the war the committee offered lucrative contracts to induce Canadian factories to change to war production. Contracts to make shells went to companies with experience in metal manufacturing such as railway shops, farm implement factories, bedspring manufacturers, and structural iron works all across Canada. For the system to work smoothly the companies were forced to learn new methods of organizing production and new and more exacting techniques for manufacturing according to strict specifications. When a fuse manufactured in Winnipeg and an explosive charge from Toronto were placed inside a shell casing from Hamilton, everything had to fit perfectly. This was a new challenge for managers and workers alike.

The manufacturing process went smoothly, but the operation of the Shell Committee did not. By the fall of 1915 considerable evidence had piled up that committee members were making fat profits through shady deals. After consultations between the British and Canadian governments, the Shell Committee was disbanded and replaced by the Imperial Munitions Board – also an arm of the British government – headed by Toronto pork-packing magnate, Joseph Wesley Flavelle. Flavelle was rather conservative in his outlook, unfriendly toward trade unions, and a superb organizer and businessman. There was never a whiff of scandal in the I.M.B., though there was considerable controversy over working conditions and industrial relations questions in factories working on I.M.B.-awarded contracts.

Flavelle was soon the virtual czar of Canadian munitions manufacturing which, by the third year of the war, set new production records in terms of both quantity and variety. At first the Canadian munitions industry was limited to the manufacture of shells, but it soon expanded to include production of explosives, guns, ships, aircraft, aircraft engines, and many other implements of war. By 1917 the I.M.B. was establishing "national factories," directly owned and controlled by the board, to produce war equipment that private corporations were unwilling or unable to handle. Thousands of Canadians from coast to coast were engaged in war work and were, in effect, working directly or indirectly for the I.M.B.

Since the munitions industry was expanding at the same time that the Canadian army was being enlarged, industry and the army were competing for recruits. The unemployment that had marked the prewar depression began to disappear; by late 1915 there was a labour shortage. This labour shortage gave Canadian workers, especially those in the munitions industry, the economic leverage to demand better wages and working conditions and to organize trade unions to advance their interests. When skilled workers were scarce it was difficult for employers to dismiss workers who organized unions or demanded higher wages. This gave munitions workers advantages that workers in depressed industries such as construction did not have.

Workers faced tremendous difficulties during the war, but their leaders were rarely consulted by the federal government when it sought solutions to problems directly affecting them, such as increases in the cost of living, the establishment of minimum wages in war industries, and the maintenance of decent working conditions in munitions plants. There were many complaints from workers that employers were reluctant to improve plant conditions or raise wages, but the thorniest problems arose when workers organized unions only to have employers refuse to bargain or sign contracts with them. Many strikes during the war were caused directly by this refusal to recognize unions. Even though workers in war industries enjoyed higher wages and better working conditions than many other industrial workers in Canada, they lived in constant fear that employers were only waiting for a good chance to destroy their unions and roll back their wages.

Employers tried to end the labour shortage by hiring unskilled workers, particularly East European immigrants, to take the place of skilled men who had joined the army and by opening the doors of heavy industry to women for the first time. Women were not new to the industrial workforce – thousands had been employed in the textile and other light industries at least as far back as the 1880s – but they had traditionally been barred from work in heavy industries and from jobs

The war offered women new opportunities. The three nursing sisters are representative of those who went overseas; many more became factory workers, such as these munitions-makers on their lunch break.

PA-24439/NATIONAL ARCHIVES OF CANADA.

that demanded special skills, such as those in machine shops and metal foundries. This changed by 1916, when industries desperate for labour hired some 30 000 women for munitions plants, shipyards, and agricultural implements factories across Canada. At first the labour movement protested, but eventually the unions began to consider a special campaign to organize these new workers into unions. However reluctant, this was a change for a labour movement dominated by male leaders who were usually markedly unsympathetic to the needs of working women. Most of these leaders were skilled workers of Anglo-Saxon background who believed it was unmanly for a male not to be able to support his

PA-6783/NATIONAL ARCHIVES OF CANADA.

household through his own efforts. Their wives, like those of the middle class these workers hoped to emulate, were not supposed to work.

It became easier for women to enter the industrial labour force in the Great War, but it was never simple. No special efforts were made to open day-care centres to assist working mothers, and women's pay was almost always considerably lower than male workers doing similar work. In most factories they found poor sanitary facilities; in many cases no toilets were set aside for them. From the beginning it was made clear to women that they would not be wanted after the war and that their work was a departure, made necessary by the war, from their traditional tasks of domestic work, child rearing, and taking care of their husbands' needs.

Despite this bias, women played an active and vigorous role in the war effort. They filled jobs traditionally held by men. They participated actively in recruiting leagues, the Patriotic Fund, and organizations such as the Y.M.C.A. to give aid and comfort to soldiers far from home. Housewives who provided wholesome meals on reduced family budgets, despite inflated food prices and the scarcity of some goods, may have contributed as much to the war effort as did single girls labouring in shell plants. Many women campaigned for reforms that would allow them full political rights. Women's special contributions to the war were rarely acknowledged – except in war propaganda that exhorted mothers to send their sons to the field of battle – and women's rights received little attention.

Making an Army

The rapid expansion of the munitions industry and the growth of the industrial work force created many difficulties on the domestic front. At the same time, problems arising from poor administration of the Department of Militia and Defence were beginning to undermine the morale of the troops abroad. The trouble was attributable in no small measure, to Sir Sam Hughes and was exemplified by the scandal over the Ross rifle, a weapon designed and built in Canada and used primarily for hunting and target shooting. It had been tried and rejected for service use by the North-West Mounted Police before the war because of its unreliability in field conditions – it jammed easily. This did not bother Hughes, however, who considered it superior to other available weapons and decided that it must be used by the Canadian army. Thus, soldiers going overseas in the first years of the war were armed with a weapon whose unreliability became evident as they entered the front lines. They threw Ross rifles away by the thousands and unofficially re-equipped themselves with the British-manufactured Lee-Enfield rifle by raiding British arms dumps or stripping weapons from dead Britons on the battlefield. Complaints to Ottawa about the Ross produced no results until the Battle of the St. Eloi Craters in the spring of 1916, when large numbers of Ross rifles jammed during the fighting. An official British War Office investigation followed, and the Canadian cabinet finally stepped in to overrule Hughes and re-equip the troops with Lee-Enfields.

The Ross rifle fiasco was the most dramatic proof of Hughes's inability to co-ordinate the Canadian war effort, but it was not the only evidence. From the beginning of the war, he had tried to run the army as a one-man show. What he could not oversee personally was done by friends appointed to various high positions in England; their chief job was to watch and report to Hughes. The most obvious example of this was the appointment of Sir Max Aitken, a Canadian-born entrepreneur who had moved to England in 1910, as government "eyewitness" at the front. He and other friends of Hughes interfered constantly both with the operations of the army's General Headquarters (GHQ) in England and with the efforts of Canadian High Commissioner Sir George Perley to convey Canadian government views on army matters to the British. Canadian commanders in France began to feel as if they were serving two masters at once – Hughes and GHQ.

As the war dragged on, Borden became increasingly aware of Hughes's shortcomings, but he was reluctant to dismiss him, partly because he had often supported Borden in the past. Instead of sacking Hughes, Borden undermined his power by taking important areas of responsibility from him and placing them under the control of other ministers. The most important salvo came in October 1916 when Borden created the Ministry of Overseas Military Forces, located in London and headed, at first, by Perley who also continued on as High Commissioner. Perley assumed control of the army in Europe, thereby stripping Hughes of much of his authority. (One year later Perley was replaced as minister of overseas forces by Sir Edward Kemp.) By the time Hughes resigned from the cabinet in November 1916, his departure had little effect on the management of the war.

The Canadian government was responsible for recruiting, training, transporting, equipping, and paying for Canadian troops overseas, but it had almost no control over the deployment and use of its own soldiers. Canadian commanders were only responsible for tactical decisions to achieve objectives that were assigned by their British superiors at higher levels of command. No Canadian commander assumed any responsibility throughout the war for deciding overall strategy. That was the job of the Imperial General Staff, operating in conjunction with the French. The commander of the imperial forces was General Sir Douglas Haig, who showed little imagination or originality in his tactics and strategy. Haig, like other Allied strategists, was slow to adapt to trench warfare and slower still to realize that new methods of assault had to be found to overcome the formidable obstacles of multiple rows of trenches, barbed wire, and machine guns. Until they did learn, countless lives of Allied troops, Canadians among them, were thrown away in massive battles such as those of the Somme campaign, which began on July 1, 1916.

The Battle of the Somme was intended to be a co-ordinated assault of the British and French armies aimed at smashing through the German defences near the French town of Albert, located approximately 100 km southeast of the port of Boulogne. It was badly planned and poorly executed. The initial focus of the assault was a position in the German lines that the Germans had strongly fortified and that they defended in great depth. It was chosen only because it lay opposite the point in the Allied lines where the British and French armies joined. British and French guns bombarded the German lines for days before the attack because Allied commanders believed that a massive bombardment would wipe out the German defenders. Instead, the Germans simply went deeper into their concrete bunkers, fully alerted to the attack by the bombardment. When the barrage lifted, the German soldiers reappeared to take their places in their trenches and gunpits. They were astonished to see tens of thousands of British troops walking slowly over open ground in the full light of the morning encumbered by heavy field packs and entrenching equipment. The defenders opened fire with a hail of machine-gun bullets that tore up the ranks of the British attackers. In the *first day* of fighting 20 000 British soldiers were killed and 37 000 more wounded. The Newfoundland regiment, caught in a crossfire in front of the village of Beaumont Hamel, lost 700 men in about 30 minutes. Despite the heavy losses, Haig continued to throw fresh troops into the attack, including the Canadian divisions, for several more months. The Canadians went into action in September, capturing the village of Courcellette and suffering 7230 casualties in one week's fighting. By the time the offensive was called off in November, British and French troops had advanced 13 km over a 20 km front at a cost of 600 000 casualties. The Canadian divisions, pulled out of the line in October, suffered 8000 dead and 16 000 wounded for a total gain of 2800 m.

The Somme fighting exemplified the Great War. An entire generation of young men from the countries at war were moulded by the horrific experiences of trench warfare and traumatized by murderous battles such as the Somme campaign, which wasted an appalling number of lives. Villages, neighbourhoods, counties, and parishes lost their young men to the shells or the choking, burning gas.

For much of the war countless numbers of men lived in a world whose horizons were the muddy walls of their trenches. Forests were replaced by twisted and gnarled trees, shorn of leaves by the whistling shrapnel. Grass gave way to mud, and sunrise and sunset became nothing more than times for renewed attack and killing. Many staff officers were incompetents whose mistakes, perhaps confined to columns of numbers in a balance book during peacetime, now cost thousands of lives. They seemed to forget everything and learn nothing while they tested their theories of battle with real soldiers. A generation of cynics climbed from the trenches after the war, men whose faith had been eroded, men who no longer took anything for granted or trusted as readily as before. For millions, this war marked the end of innocence.

There was, however, still a place for pride in the accomplishments of arms. And for the Canadians, the testing ground became Vimy Ridge, a German-held salient that poked into the British lines between Lens and Arras. The ridge was used by enemy observers to keep watch over a large area and call down deadly artillery fire on troop movements. It had been assaulted repeatedly by Allied troops since 1914 with no result except the loss of 200 000 men. The Canadian Corps, four divisions strong by late 1916, was transferred to the lines opposite Vimy after the Somme battles had ended. There the four Canadian divisions were to fight together for the first time in yet another attack on the ridge, as part of the left flank of a larger British offensive aimed at the German lines south of Arras.

By the spring of 1917 both German and Allied generals were beginning to develop new techniques to overcome the stalemate of trench warfare. The Germans were experimenting with defence in depth – leaving the front lines lightly defended while concentrating the bulk of their defence troops to the rear of the front lines. The British and the Germans were studying lightning assaults following short but intense artillery barrages to assist attackers with the element of surprise. The British were developing new weapons such as the tank, and both sides were beginning to realize that aircraft had tremendous potential when used to attack the enemy's forward positions with machine guns and bombs in co-ordination with ground assaults. In 1917 trench warfare began to give way to mobile warfare.

Despite these new developments, General von Falkenhausen, in command of the German troops at Vimy, based his defences on the tried and, he thought, still true concepts of wire, trenches, and artillery support. Although he placed his reserves well back, the bulk of his troops were entrenched at the top of the ridge. His artillery was sited on the far side of the ridge out of sight of British and Canadian observers. The four Canadian divisions were assigned to attack this force with a total of 30 000 men. Preparations for the assault were painstaking in detail. A large clay model of the ridge was built and carefully studied by the officers, while a full-scale mockup, with German defensive positions marked, was used to familiarize the troops with their objective. Royal Flying Corps surveillance photographs were studied to determine shifts in the German positions that might necessitate changes in the assault plans. The German guns were located using new sounding devices and were systematically destroyed by British and Canadian counterbattery fire. Tunnels were dug from rearward positions to the front lines to enable the Canadians to move forward out of sight of German observers. Huge mines were placed under the German positions to be detonated as the attack began. Plans were laid for a creeping artillery barrage that would lay a curtain of fire ahead of the attacking troops and be moved forward at 90 m intervals every five minutes.

In the early morning hours of Easter Monday, April 9, 1917, the explosive charges under the German lines were blown and the artillery began a massive barrage that was concentrated on specific German targets. Guns, fortified positions, and wire entanglements were levelled as the first line of German trenches disappeared in a rain of shellfire. Then the creeping barrage began and the Canadian attackers moved out of their forward positions and began their assault on the ridge. The German defenders were stunned. The communications to their artillery were cut, and there were too few guns left to give them much support. The attack rolled forward; only on the extreme left flank did the Fourth Division run into difficulties in an assault on Hill 145, where many Canadian soldiers were cut down by massed machine-gun fire. Elsewhere the attack was a brilliant success, and before long the Canadian soldiers were standing on the heights of Vimy Ridge looking down at thousands of German troops in headlong retreat. Some German guns had been left behind, and these were turned against their former operators by specially trained troops. The sight was one few Canadian soldiers had ever seen because the land that lay before them, once behind the front lines, was almost untouched by war. It looked as if a tunnel had been driven through hell to the peace of heaven on the far side.

The Vimy victory marked a shift in the attitude of many Canadians about themselves and about the war. The war was speeding Canada's passage from colony to nation, and pride in the Vimy victory was a key to that transformation. Canadians were coming to believe that they were not simply fighting as a colony of the British Empire, but as a nation in its own right. With that belief came a determination almost everywhere, except in Quebec, that the entire resources of the country had to be mobilized at home and at the front.

The victory of Vimy Ridge had been costly – 10 602 Canadian casualties, 3598 of them fatal – but for once that cost had returned positive results. The German lines had been pierced, and an important enemy position had been captured. Fighting as a unit for the first time, the Canadian Corps had proved itself second to none, and Canadian officers, particularly Arthur Currie, commander of the First Division, had demonstrated that they were capable of planning and carrying out a well-co-ordinated attack. The Canadians' new prowess in the art of war was fittingly symbolized by Currie's promotion to commander of the Canadian Corps in June 1917. After the Vimy battle it was obvious that there was no longer any need to fill staff ranks with British officers as there had been at the beginning of the war; by the time of Currie's promotion there were only a tiny handful of them left in the entire Canadian Corps.

Currie was an unlikely success as a soldier. He appeared awkward in uniform, almost pear-shaped, and he sat a horse badly. He was stiff and formal when speaking to large groups of men on parade. When he exhorted his men with the words "to those who will fall I say, 'You will not die but step into immortality' " during the 1918 German offensive, the battle-hardened men jeered. Such words seemed hollow by that time, but they were a genuine reflection of Currie's sentimentality; he cared deeply about his men. He took great pains to keep casualties low and was sensitive to the new technological developments and attack techniques that were changing the nature of the war. There were few Allied generals who could match him in tactical planning. At the same time, he passionately believed in the national mission of the Canadian Corps and strongly opposed periodic efforts by his British superiors to detach Canadian units from the corps.

Currie's career was dogged with controversy. In June 1917, just after his appointment as corps commander, the Militia Council in Ottawa was finally apprised of Currie's misappropriation of funds in 1913. The matter was quickly brought to Perley's attention and through him to Borden. The potential for a major public scandal was obvious; Perley resolved to demand an explanation from Currie and offered to pay half the debt himself if Kemp, the minister of overseas military forces, would pay the other half. Borden even considered having the Militia Department pay the debt and recover the money from Currie after the war. Currie, apparently unaware that the matter had been brought to Borden's attention, solved the problem himself by beginning to repay the debt at about the time that his superiors were made aware of the situation.

Billy Bishop.

PA-1654/NATIONAL ARCHIVES OF CANADA.

The victories of the Canadian divisions swelled national pride (most particularly among English-speaking Canadians) but so, too, did the exploits of those individual knights of the air who flew into battle with the Royal Flying Corps or Royal Navy and who captured the imagination of a generation. By the end of the war almost every schoolboy could recite the stories of Canadian flyers such as Raymond Collishaw, "Wop" May, Billy Barker, Roy Brown, and the most famous of all, Billy Bishop, a dashing former cavalryman from Owen Sound, Ontario. Bishop claimed 72 German fighters before the war ended, but his most famous exploit was undoubtedly his solo attack on a German airfield near Cambrai on June 2, 1917, which won him the Victoria Cross.

At 3:00 a.m. on that cold and drizzly morning Billy Bishop awoke in the dark, pulled his flying suit on over his pyjamas, gulped a quick cup of tea, and climbed into the cockpit of his waiting Nieuport fighter. He gunned his motor and was soon climbing through the fog and rain in the general direction of the German lines. The cloud and darkness made navigation almost impossible, but when Bishop descended he found himself over a German airfield at Estourmel, where the day's flying activities had not yet begun. Bishop dropped low, to perhaps 15 m or less, and roared over the field firing at parked enemy planes, their pilots and mechanics, and dodging anti-aircraft fire. Two German fighters struggled into the air, but Bishop swung behind them and shot them down in quick order. A third and fourth German fighter then came after the Canadian flyer, and Bishop shot one of these down before running out of ammunition. He was then forced to change his ammunition drum while keeping his plane level and evading the other German fighter. With his gun reloaded he fought off his attacker by firing his full drum of 99 rounds in one long burst and then dove down and headed for home. This was the first low-level raid of its type in the war. Bishop had destroyed at least three German fighters and pioneered a new type of aerial tactic.[4]

The war stimulated national feeling in Canada and forged a shape and a direction on Canadian culture. Several famous Canadian painters – Frederick Varley and A.Y. Jackson of the Group of Seven and David Milne among them – became war artists in a program designed to record the exploits of Canada's troops on canvas. The experience left deep impressions in each case. Varley, for example, developed a sombre style that reflected the tragedy and decay of the battlefield. At one point he wrote to Arthur Lismer, another member of the Group of Seven, to describe the horror of the western front. "You pass over swamps on rotting duck boards, past bleached bones of horses with their harness still on, past isolated crude crosses sticking up from the filth, and the stink of decay is flung all over." His painting ever after reflected his war experiences.

Literature too was changed by the war and came to reflect the cynicism of the soldiers in the trenches. One of the great, but generally

---

[4] The story of the Canadian Army in the war is told in several works, including G.W.L. Nicholson, *The Canadian Expeditionary Force: 1914-1919* (Ottawa, 1962), which is the official history, and D.J. Goodspeed, *The Road Past Vimy: The Canadian Corps, 1914-1918* (Toronto, 1969), a short, popular account. Another popular account is John Swettenham, *To Seize the Victory* (Toronto, 1965). The story of the Canadians in several major battles including Ypres and Passchendaele is told in Daniel Dancocks, *Spearhead to Victory: Canada and the Great War* (Edmonton, 1987) and *Welcome to Flanders Fields* (Toronto, 1988). The Vimy battle is highlighted in Kenneth Macksey, *Vimy Ridge* (New York, 1972) and Pierre Berton, *Vimy* (Toronto, 1986). Exploits of Canadian pilots are related in Edmund Cosgrove, *Canada's Fighting Pilots* (Toronto, 1965), a short, popular account and S.F. Wise, *Canadian Airmen and the First World War* (Toronto, 1980), the official history. The story of Billy Bishop is told in his son's *The Courage of the Early Morning* (Toronto, 1965). On the manner in which the government organized Canada's war-fighting capability, see Desmond Morton in *A Peculiar Kind of Politics: Canada's Overseas Ministry in the First World War* (Toronto, 1982).

unknown, Canadian novels to come out of the war was *Generals Die in Bed*, by Charles Yale Harrison, a Philadelphia-born newspaper reporter who served with the Royal Montreal Regiment. His book, first published in 1930 when the public was beginning to read novels such as *All Quiet on the Western Front* and *A Farewell to Arms*, was hailed by the *New York Evening Post* as "the best of the war books." In deliberately simple prose, it told the story of a group of Canadian soldiers and the brutalizing impact of war on them. Harrison's soldiers were far removed from the glories of a spit-and-polish war fought for king and empire:

We have advanced about a hundred yards. There is no enemy fire. It is nearly dawn. A blue grey light appears. Renaud walks by my side. His face is red with excitement now. To my left Anderson and Fry walk together. Legs and arms in grey rags lie here and there. The trenches are almost flattened. In the smoke-murk I step on something. It is soft. I look down. It is the ripped open stomach of a German. We walk on.

In a later period, pacifists such as F.R. Scott, whose older brother Harry was killed at the front, would draw on wartime memories to explain their antiwar views. In "Lest We Forget," Scott wrote:

The British troops at the Dardanelles
Were blown to bits by British shells
Sold to the Turks by Vickers.
And many a brave Canadian youth
Will shed his blood on foreign shores,
And die for democracy, freedom, truth,
With his body full of Canadian ores. . .

REPRINTED BY PERMISSION OF MCCLELLAND & STEWART LTD., THE CANADIAN PUBLISHERS.

The Hothouse of War

Canadian society changed to meet the challenges of this most terrible conflict. In British Columbia the demand for ores and ships kept the mines and smelters of the interior working at full tilt and stimulated a rapid expansion of local shipyards. In some coastal communities, a high rate of enlistment created acute manpower shortages that could only be filled by women and hitherto unskilled immigrants, though the rate of female participation in the workforce was low compared to that of central Canada because of the relative lack of heavy war industry.

On the Prairies high rates of enlistment, especially in Manitoba, produced labour shortages, although communities with substantial numbers of Eastern European immigrants in their populations did not experience the same problem. To take advantage of high grain prices, farmers expanded their production by buying new land, much of it marginal in quality, and paying for it with money borrowed at high wartime interest rates. They also turned increasingly to mechanization, although the horse remained the chief power supply for farm equipment for at least two decades after the war.

Farmer interest in political reform did not end after the defeat of reciprocity in the 1911 election. It was kept alive by leaders such as John Kennedy, vice-president of the Manitoba Grain Growers' Association, who campaigned actively for the formation of a third, farm-based, party in federal politics. For the most part, however, western farmers concentrated on provincial politics in the first three years of the war where two key reform issues – prohibition and votes for women – were at stake.

The farmers were joined by middle-class progressives in the cities who pushed ahead with demands for change and reform and linked those demands to the war. This was, they claimed, a war fought at great sacrifice to defeat a cruel enemy and bring about an improved world. What better time was there to reform Canadian society and what better way than to involve government much more deeply in bringing about change? This too was a sign of the evolution from voluntarism to compulsion that marked the Canadian war effort and that paralleled and was linked to the growth of the Canadian army and the increasing importance of the Canadian Corps at the front. The crusade for temperance and prohibition, for a fair system of taxation, for greater government regulation and ownership, and especially for women's suffrage, intensified as the war dragged on.

Although progressives campaigned hard for the female franchise all across Canada, the movement found some of its strongest and most imaginative leaders in Manitoba. There, the Manitoba Political Equality League, led by early Canadian feminists such as E. Cora Hind, agricultural editor of the *Manitoba Free Press* since 1901, had pressed its case vigorously for years. In 1914 it had organized a Women's Parliament intended to embarrass the Conservative government of Rodmond P. Roblin into granting women the vote. Novelist Nellie McClung acted as the "premier" and presided over a "parliament" which voted down a male request to be granted the vote.

The women's movement in Manitoba was linked to similar movements across Canada. Organizations such as the Women's Christian Temperance Union, the National Council of Women of Canada, and the Canadian Suffrage Association had first appeared in the 1870s dedicated to the enlightenment of women and to the improvement of their place in society. Many of these organizations believed that women's emancipation was directly linked to general social improvement and advocated a range of other reforms from temperance to universal suffrage. Some female reformers believed that women were more moral and upright than men and that granting the vote to women would somehow produce a more moral and pacifist society. Others had no such illusions, however, and campaigned for the vote using the argument that governments could scarcely govern in the interests of women and their families if only men cast ballots. In that campaign, the issue was pressed by a broad coalition of reformers – male and female – who also wanted to use the powers of the state to remedy the myriad ills of the nation. But it was the women who led the suffrage struggle, as Nellie McClung, Francis Marion Beynon, Flora Macdonald Denison, E. Cora Hind, and hundreds of others demanded women's just rights. By September 1917, the fight had begun to pay off: women had been granted the right to vote in provincial elections in Ontario, Manitoba, Saskatchewan, Alberta, and British Columbia.

One tangible result of this rise of progressivism on the Prairies was the election of an unabashedly reformist Liberal government in Manitoba in 1916 under the leadership of T.C. Norris. Norris introduced prohibition, the female franchise, laws to improve working conditions, a minimum wage for women, and an industrial conciliation and collective bargaining law for the trade unions. Under Norris, Manitoba quickly gained a reputation for having one of the most enlightened governments in the country. Norris's victory was a sign of what was to come elsewhere at the end of the war.

The rise of progressivism was also based on the direct impact of the war on Canadian society. The effects of the war were felt most strongly in Ontario and Quebec. Both provinces were heavily industrialized, and both experienced rapid growth in war-related industries and the towns and cities that contained them. There were increased demands for electricity and municipal services as well as for political and social reforms. The process of rural depopulation away from the farms and small country towns and villages to the big cities accelerated, adding to fears that already existed in both provinces that the rural values that had dominated social and political mores for so long would be undermined and perhaps even destroyed.

In Atlantic Canada, coal mining and ship building were the industries most directly affected by the war, and production in both increased dramatically, creating new demands for skilled labour and stimulating rapid increases in wages. Warring union factions in the Nova Scotia coal industry finally united under the banner of the Amalgamated Mineworkers of Nova Scotia, the forerunner of the United Mine Workers of America's District 26, which was established in the coalfields by 1919. Halifax, always a busy port town, became the port of departure for the Atlantic convoys organized by the Royal Navy to protect shipping from German submarines, and local businesses thrived on the demands for goods and services created by the merchant ships that stopped here before joining eastbound convoys to Britain. Halifax also suffered terribly because of this role. On the morning of December 6, 1917, the French ship *Mont Blanc*, carrying more than 2000 tons of explosives and explosive chemicals, was steaming slowly into Halifax harbour toward Bedford Basin when it was struck by the Belgian vessel *Imo* in the narrows opposite the northwest portion of the city. Fire broke out on the ammunition ship and the crew hastily abandoned the vessel and made for shore. The *Mont Blanc* then drifted toward the docks. At 9:05 a.m. the French ship blew up with a roar heard 320 km away and a force that devastated Halifax. Close to 2000 people were killed, 9000 were injured, and thousands more were left homeless. Food, medicine, building materials, and other relief supplies began to pour into Halifax from

The Halifax explosion of December 6, 1917, caused extensive devastation.

C-19945/NATIONAL ARCHIVES OF CANADA.

across the country and from the northeastern United States while rescue parties searched among the smouldering ruins for the dead and the living. It was the worst single disaster ever to befall a Canadian city.[5]

Becoming a Nation

The devastation of the Halifax explosion and the charge under fire at Vimy Ridge were dramatic examples of the high cost Canadians were paying for the country's new maturity and self-confidence. However, it was obvious even before the Vimy assault that Canada was making an important contribution on the battlefield and paying a heavy price to do it. By 1918, almost one-third of the British Empire forces on the western front were from the self-governing Dominions such as Canada and Australia or from the dependent Empire. This growing contribution of the Dominions was recognized in late 1916 when British Prime Minister David Lloyd George invited Borden and the other Dominion premiers to London to sit as members of the newly constituted Imperial War Cabinet and to attend an Imperial War Conference. Lloyd George was not simply making a magnanimous gesture to reward the Dominions for their effort; he knew that Britain did not have the resources to sustain the massive output of men and material that the war required and he hoped the Dominions could help make up the shortfall. Borden arrived in London in late February 1917 and immediately busied himself studying the vast documentation compiled by the British War Cabinet – a small inner group of the United Kingdom cabinet that was responsible for directing the British war effort. For the first time, Borden had access to the whole canvas of Britain's war machine and its foreign relations. He and the other prime ministers were about to achieve the consultation in foreign and defence matters that Borden had sought at least as far back as the 1910 naval crisis.

---

[5] The Halifax explosion is documented in Graham Metson, ed., *The Halifax Explosion: December 6, 1917* (Toronto, 1978), and a fictional account is presented in Hugh MacLennan, *Barometer Rising* (Toronto, 1941). For the impact of the war on Canadian society see Barbara M. Wilson, ed., *Ontario and the First World War* (Toronto, 1977), Leslie Frost, *Fighting Men* (Toronto, 1967), and John H. Thompson *The Harvests of War* (Toronto, 1978). On women see Carol Lee Bacchi, *Liberation Deferred? The Ideas of the English Canadian Suffragists, 1877-1918* (Toronto, 1982); Veronica Strong-Boag, *The Parliament of Women: The National Council of Women of Canada* (Ottawa, 1976); and Catherine L. Cleverdon, *The Woman Suffrage Movement in Canada* (Toronto, 1950). On the reform movement generally see Robert Craig Brown and Ramsay Cook, *Canada: 1896-1921, A Nation Transformed* (Toronto, 1974). The impact of the war on one aspect of Canadian culture is found in Maria Tippett, *Art at the Service of War: Canada, Art and the Great War* (Toronto, 1984).

The Imperial War Conference opened on March 20, 1917, and it was soon evident that the Dominions were being asked to pay a further price for the new equality that the British were extending to them: more men. Lloyd George bluntly told the Dominion leaders that Germany was strong and growing stronger and that a renewed effort was needed for victory. Borden supported this and backed the British leader in his belief that the Empire must bring its total military power to bear in the struggle.

The Dominion prime ministers learned much at the London meetings, even though their opinions on military matters counted for little with the Imperial General Staff who were directing military operations in Europe. Nevertheless, the meetings were significant to the increased national feelings so much in evidence in Canada and the other Dominions. The foundation of the modern Commonwealth was laid when a resolution was adopted that declared that the constitutional status of "the component parts of the Empire" should be discussed at a special imperial conference to be held immediately after the war. Until then the British and Dominion governments placed on record their belief that this new constitutional status "should be based upon a full recognition of the Dominions as autonomous nations of an Imperial Commonwealth" with the right to "an adequate voice in foreign policy and in foreign relations" and with "effective arrangements for continuous consultation" in imperial questions of common concern. It was obvious that the Dominions would no longer be mere self-governing colonies in the British Empire but would, instead, become partners in a newly structured Empire Commonwealth. The resolution was "the brainchild of Borden and [his adviser] Loring Christie" and reflected the changed attitude of Canadians that they were now fighting this war as a nation, fully committed to victory, and determined to mobilize the money, the people, and the resources needed for the task. Canada was a colony no longer.[6]

---

[6] There is much work, mostly in article form, on Canada's imperial and foreign relations during and after the war. Two document collections that are particularly useful are R.M. Dawson, *The Development of Dominion Status: 1900-31* (Hamden, Conn., 1967), and *Documents on Canadian External Relations*, published by the Department of External Affairs. Volume I covers the period 1909-18, and Volume II is devoted solely to the Paris Peace Conference of 1919. The Borden biography by Brown gives the best overview. See also R.C. Brown, "Sir Robert Borden, the Great War and Anglo-Canadian Relations," in J.S. Moir, ed., *Character and Circumstance* (Toronto, 1970); Brown and Robert Bothwell, "The 'Canadian Resolution,' " in M. Cross and R. Bothwell, eds., *Policy by Other Means* (Toronto, 1972); L.F. Hardinge, "Hughes, Borden and Dominion Representation at the Paris Peace Conference," *Canadian Historical Review*, 1968; G.P. de T. Glazebrook, *Canada at the Paris Peace Conference* (Toronto, 1942); and C.P. Stacey, *Canada and the Age of Conflict*, Vol. I (Toronto, 1977).

Borden stayed in England until early May 1917, and he used every spare moment to visit as many Canadian soldiers as he could at the front and in the barracks and hospitals in England. He had done this on an earlier trip to England in 1915, and he was again deeply moved by the sacrifice of these citizen-soldiers. He was more convinced than ever that Canada must support these men by providing sufficient reinforcements to allow the four Canadian divisions to continue to function as effective fighting units. That would not be easy. Voluntary enlistment was falling off rapidly from the peak it had reached in the spring of 1916; by December of 1916 only 5200 men had volunteered for service. Losses were now outstripping replacements in the Canadian Corps. In November 1916 there were only about 80 000 fit men serving with the Canadian army in England. That was estimated to be enough to sustain the Canadian Corps through one more year at current force levels.

Borden was sensitive to Lloyd George's plea for more men from the Dominions to shore up the forces already in the field. He was buoyed by the thought that the recent entry of the United States into the war against Germany would add tremendous new resources of military and industrial power to the struggle, but he worried about a total collapse on the Russian front. A new provisional government, headed by Alexander Kerensky, had been established following the overthrow of the czar in February 1917. Although it had chosen to continue the war against Germany, the decision was not popular in Russia, and some of Kerensky's left-wing opponents were loudly demanding peace with Germany. On the passage back to Canada, therefore, Borden made up his mind to propose conscription to his cabinet in order to raise an additional 100 000 men. He also decided to try to create a coalition government to bring this about.

Conscription and Regulation 17

Borden and many other Canadians had been considering conscription since early in the war. Borden's first inclination was to reject it, and he declared himself against compulsory enlistment in 1914. The political cost was too high to justify it, especially in Quebec where most French-Canadians were adamant against being forced to serve in foreign

Appeals to the glorious history of New France failed to move most French-Canadians to enlist, ▶ and conscription, when it came, was resisted fiercely on individual and collective levels.

wars and had helped defeat Laurier over such an issue. Besides, voluntary recruiting had worked very well at the beginning of the war when there were more volunteers than were immediately needed. As the war dragged on, however, the conditions that had created a surplus of volunteers disappeared: war factories, farms, and mines needed more workers than ever; the bulk of eligible British-born men had already enlisted; the government had raised the ceiling on the forces to 500 000. Once again, compulsion seemed to provide a better answer, and more and more voices were raised to demand an end to voluntary recruiting and the introduction of conscription. This reflected the growing belief that voluntary enlistment alone would not provide sufficient reinforcements to enable the Canadian Corps to carry on.

Did Canada really need conscription in 1917? Borden certainly thought so, although Australia, the other major Dominion, never introduced conscription; compulsory military service was defeated by Australian voters in two national plebiscites, and there were strong feelings against conscription in the Australian Expeditionary Force. Although much smaller in population, Australia fielded an army almost as large as Canada's and had nearly as many battle casualties. It was true that battle casualties were outstripping recruits in Canada by early 1917, but it is possible that the reinforcement problem lay not in the number of fit reserves stationed in England but in the time it took for them to trickle into units at the front. Before resigning, Hughes had formed a fifth division in England, in part to make his son Garnet a divisional commander, and had even promised a sixth. Conditions there had been chaotic from the start of the war because of the crosscurrents that resulted from Hughes's action. This could only impede the flow of replacements. By the time the war ended in November 1918, only 124 588 conscripts had actually been added to the CEF's rolls and approximately 24 000 of these were actually at the front. It is likely, however, that many more would have seen action if the war had lasted longer.

Conscription, however, was never simply about numbers; it was an issue arising out of the major differences that separated English- and French-Canadians in their attitude toward the war; it was also about national duty in fighting it. As well, it was an attempt by the majority to force its view on the minority without regard for the damage this might do to the development of a national consensus. Put simply, French-Canadians were not enlisting at anywhere near the rate of other Canadians, and many English-Canadians were determined to change this.

The French-English battle over conscription was rooted in other crises such as the Riel affair and the Manitoba schools question, which stretched back at least to the mid-1880s. The latest of these quarrels was over Ontario Department of Education Instruction 17 – popularly referred to as Regulation 17. Issued by Ontario's Conservative government in 1912 to severely restrict French as a language of instruction in the province's schools, including those in regions with large French populations, the regulation was a response to fears that the rapidly expanding Franco-Ontarian population might one day become the majority in Ontario. These fears were unreasonable, but they were fed by the claims of some francophone leaders that the high French-Canadian birth rate would constitute a "revenge of the cradle." Regulation 17 provoked an angry reaction from Franco-Ontarians who were forced to turn to the federal Liberal Party for aid because the provincial Liberal Opposition, headed by Newton W. Rowell, refused to take up their cause. In 1916 Quebec M.P. Ernest Lapointe introduced the matter into Parliament with a motion that Ottawa "respectfully suggest to the Legislative Assembly of Ontario the wisdom of making it clear that the privilege of the children of French parentage being taught in their mother tongue be not interfered with."

Though there was some sympathy for the Franco-Ontarian cause among French members of Borden's cabinet, the prime minister refused to touch this political hot potato. Borden was convinced there was nothing he or his government could do, and he was not willing to risk a split with the Ontario government in the midst of a war. Once again, as on the emergency naval contribution issue, Borden showed a decided lack of understanding of French Canada and placed other matters higher on his list of priorities. Once again French-English antagonism increased. For many Quebeckers, particularly those with nationaliste sympathies, the fight over Regulation 17 was every bit as important as the war in Europe. Ontario's restriction of French in its schools was denounced as "Prussianism" at home.

It is hard to know what effect Regulation 17 had on recruiting in Quebec because there were other important factors that discouraged a higher rate of voluntary enlistment there. Much of the recuiting was done by the English elites of Montreal and Quebec City who traditionally had little contact with French-Canadians and who tended to look down on them. Indeed, Protestant clergymen sometimes acted as recruiters in predominantly French-Catholic areas when no curé could be found to do the job. Those French-Canadians who did sign up were often shunted to garrison duty in quiet backwaters of the war, while others were placed in

English-speaking units. Few completely French-speaking battalions were formed, and thus French-Canadian soldiers were not even able to communicate with their comrades in times of danger. For French-Canadians, the war was not an emotional struggle in support of a mother country as it was to many English-Canadians, especially those who had arrived recently from Britain, or who were only one generation removed from it. There were few, if any, emotional ties to bind French-Canadians to France, which had abandoned Quebec in the 1760s and then turned republican and anticlerical during the French Revolution. Many Quebec Catholics believed, in fact, that the Church was oppressed in France while liberals, socialists, and other anti-Christian groups were allowed to run rampant. After so many years of physical and spiritual separation from the land of their ancestors, Quebeckers could not be moved to enthusiasm for a crusade designed to save France from German aggression, even though the Church in Quebec formally supported the war effort.

These factors were important impediments to recruitment, but, essentially, Quebec at this time was largely an inward-looking culture, conservative and religious in orientation, untrusting of immigrants or social and economic developments that appeared to threaten its Catholic, agrarian character. It was not Laurier, Bourassa, nor even his *nationaliste* followers of the turn of the century who represented the soul of Quebec. Their vision had been of a changed and forward-looking Quebec that would play an active role in a larger Canada and Empire. Most Quebeckers were better represented by thinkers such as Jules-Paul Tardivel, a Quebec City journalist who had died in 1905 after devoting his life to the cause of a conservative, church-dominated Quebec, separate from Canada, living sublimely apart from the money-grubbing Protestant-Jewish world that North America had, in his opinion, become. For those who shared that view, then, the war could not be an affair of the heart.

French-Canadians were not alone in their opposition to conscription, however, because many workers and farmers in English-speaking Canada also opposed it. Workers feared that conscription for military service would lead to conscription for industrial service as well, forcing them to stay at one job in one plant for the duration of the war. This would rob the trade unions of virtually all their leverage. Farmers worried that conscription would deprive them of the labour of their sons or their hired hands, at a time when commodity prices were soaring, and force them to cut back on production. In the belief that the burden of war should be equally shared by all, they joined the workers in demanding that the government consider "conscription of wealth" – the nationalization of banks and industries for the duration of the war – if it conscripted manpower.

Although Borden did not make a final decision on conscription until May 1917, his government had been moving toward a change in recruiting policy since the fall of 1916. In August 1916 the National Service Board had been established to survey the labour force in the country and to try to increase recruiting while, at the same time, avoid the withdrawal of much-needed skilled work from war industries. There had been some difficulty in finding a chairman for the board, but the prime minister eventually settled on R.B. Bennett, a Calgary lawyer and fellow conservative M.P. In January 1917, the board sent a registration card to every male of military age in Canada, asking for information on age, health, job status, and other factors to help it determine how many men eligible for military service remained in the country. At the time, Borden insisted that registration was not intended as a first step toward conscription, but he refused to give assurances to labour leaders that conscription would never be used. In fact, he made it quite plain that

FORRESTER/*CALGARY EYE OPENER.*

Suicide?

Forrester

conscription would be resorted to if other means of increasing the number of recruits failed. Once Borden made up his mind in favour of conscription, nothing else – French-Canadian anger, the resentment of the workers and farmers, the survival of the Conservative Party – was

PUBLISHED BY *LE DEVOIR* IN 1917.

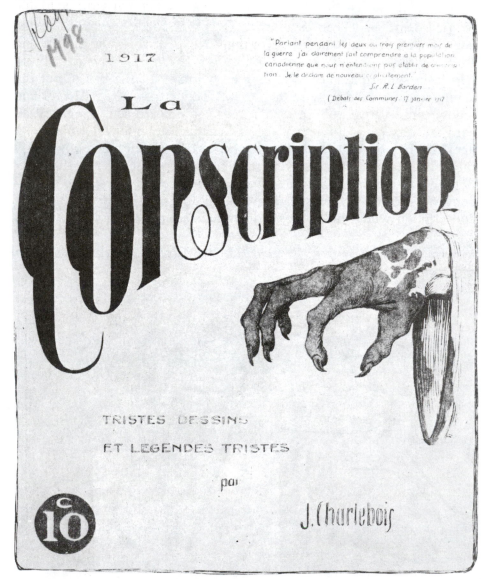

allowed to take a higher priority. Borden was absolutely determined to do whatever was necessary to ensure the success of conscription.[7]

The prime minister announced his government's new policy to the House of Commons on May 18, 1917 (an actual bill was not presented until the following month), and then prepared to approach Laurier with a proposal to establish a coalition government. Coalition, the temporary joining together of the Liberal and Conservative parties inside the government, had been suggested in some quarters since early in the war to ensure a united nonpartisan war effort. Both parties had shied away from it, thinking they would lose much and gain little from such an arrangement. However, in 1916, when Lloyd George assumed power in Great Britain, he forged a coalition that included all the major political parties. This spurred many Canadians to renew their call for a national coalition and, when Borden decided to introduce conscription, he attempted to forge a union of his party with the Liberals to provide bipartisan support for the contentious measure.

The approach to Laurier was made on May 25, one day after rioting in Montreal underlined the implacable opposition of French Canada to conscription. Borden proposed that the Liberals join a new government with half the cabinet positions reserved for Liberal ministers. Borden was to remain prime minister. Laurier did not reject the proposal but instead asked for time to consult with his political advisers. This was undoubtedly only a delaying tactic because he knew that any French-Canadian who supported conscription was committing political suicide. Laurier represented Quebec in the House of Commons in Ottawa, but he knew well that Henri Bourassa and the *nationalistes* were waiting in the wings and would profit from the destruction of the Quebec Liberals that would follow if Laurier joined a conscriptionist coalition. Although Borden approached Laurier a second time less than a week later to sweeten the pot by promising to hold back on conscription until after it was confirmed by a general election, Laurier refused to give in. Borden now knew that, if there were to be a coalition, the leader of the Liberal Party and whoever remained loyal to him would have to be left out of it.

The Military Service Act was introduced into the House of Commons in June 1917, debated throughout the summer, and passed and signed

---

[7] Conscription is covered in J.L. Granatstein and J.M. Hitsman, *Broken Promises: A History of Conscription in Canada* (Toronto, 1977). An older but still valuable work is Elizabeth Armstrong, *The Crisis of Quebec: 1914-1918* (New York, 1937). Several articles on the subject can be found in Carl Berger, ed., *Conscription 1917* (Toronto, n.d.)

into law at the end of August. Many English-speaking Liberal M.P.s bolted party lines to support it, proof that a considerable number of Liberals outside Quebec might have been willing to break with Laurier and join Borden in a coalition. Some acted purely out of support for the war but others, particularly those from Ontario and Western Canada, were Liberals eager for a chance to undermine Laurier's power in the party. They knew he had little sympathy for progressivism and they did not believe that the Liberal Party could reflect their objectives as long as he was leader and as long as the party rested upon the support of conservative-minded voters in Quebec. They reasoned that if they could join with Borden, their survival in the next general election would be ensured because of their support for conscription. They could break with the Conservatives after the war to re-create a more progressive Liberal Party less dependent on Quebec.

Managing the War

Though Borden spent most of his time in the spring and summer of 1917 on the fight for conscription and coalition, his government was also wrestling with growing social and economic problems.[8] It was apparent by 1917 that voluntarism was not working and that government intervention in, and regulation of, broad areas of social and economic activity were needed. Conscription was the bellwether of the change; once the government assumed the power to compel men to fight, there could be little philosophical reason for opposing the extension of compulsion to other areas of Canadian life. In 1917, therefore, government control in Canada was extended through direct taxation of incomes and the control of supplies of food and fuel.

Inflation was one of the government's most pressing problems. When

---

[8] There are few works that focus directly on government intervention and regulation during the war. A good overview is Robert Cuff, "Organizing for War: Canada and the United States during World War I," *Canadian Historical Association Report, 1969*, which should be supplemented with reading from the Borden biography by R.C. Brown, and Brown's and Cook's *Canada: 1896-1921*. On the Imperial Munitions Board see Michael Bliss, *A Canadian Millionaire: The Life and Business Times of Sir Joseph Flavelle, Bart, 1858-1939* (Toronto, 1978). There are several books that cover railway nationalization, including the Graham biography of Meighen. The most complete account is found in T.D. Regehr, *The Canadian Northern Railway* (Toronto, 1976). A good analysis of business attitudes is Tom Traves, *The State and Enterprise: Canadian Manufacturers and the Federal Government, 1917-1931* (Toronto, 1979).

TO WIN THE WAR
THIS HOUSEHOLD IS PLEDGED
TO CARRY OUT CONSCIENTIOUSLY THE ADVICE AND DIRECTIONS OF THE
FOOD CONTROLLER

By 1918 Canada was increasingly well organized for the war as government extended its controls into the public sector. These cards were put in the windows of houses or displayed in restaurants.

ALL persons in ordering their food ought to consider the needs of Great Britain, the Allies and the armies for wheat, beef and bacon. The Food Controller requires the public to do everything in their power to make these commodities available for export by eating as little as possible of them, by using substitutes and by avoiding waste.

war broke out in August 1914, the country was in the midst of a depression; wages and prices had been falling steadily since late 1913. The war brought with it munitions production and the beginning of recruitment. By the end of 1915, labour shortages had forced wages up in industries most closely connected with the war. At the same time, shortages began to show up in supplies of food and raw materials because a large army had to be fed, food was needed by Canada's European allies, and war factories demanded massive amounts of metals, textiles, wood, chemicals, and other materials. These shortages, combined with a rise in labour costs caused by a growing labour shortage, created some inflation, but the government's fiscal policies made it worse. Ottawa spent hundreds of millions of dollars on the war effort, far more than it raised through taxation, and it had to borrow at home and abroad to pay the bills. For the first time in Canadian history, the government borrowed large sums from private investors in the United States through the sale of bonds. This borrowing added to inflation by driving up interest rates, which in turn increased production costs. The rise of living costs began in the last months of 1915 and became noticeable by early 1916. By 1917 many Canadians were complaining bitterly about inflation, pointing out that their living standard was dropping because wage increases were not, in most cases, keeping up with rising prices. Soon there were charges that "food pirates and price manipulators" were gouging Canadian consumers. The government first took action in 1916, when a cost-of-living commissioner was appointed to investigate complaints about increasing prices. He found no conspiracies. In 1917 food and fuel controllers were appointed to attack inflation in these two basic areas, while a Board of Grain Supervisors was formed with total control over wheat sales in Canada and abroad. Thus the free market system for buying and selling wheat was suspended for the duration of the war.

One of the most revolutionary means of government intervention in the economy was direct taxation, which began in 1916 with the establishment of a business profits tax, a tax levied directly on businesses by the federal government to raise revenue and decrease the enormous profits that many businesses were making from the war. The minister of finance, W.T. White, declared that since some businesses were doing so well compared to other Canadians, it was only "just that a portion of their advantage should be appropriated to the benefit of the state." One year later, in July 1917, White introduced direct taxes on the personal incomes of all Canadians (still relatively few in number) who earned more than $2000 per year.

The government's new activism was also obvious in its solution to the deepening financial troubles that plagued several large Canadian railways; because of the war, they could not borrow the money needed to keep themselves running. The Canadian Northern Railway was in the worst shape and had approached the federal government for loans several times in the early stages of the war. Finance Minister White was forced to warn the cabinet that failure to extend aid would force the railway into bankruptcy and possibly cause it to be dismembered by its creditors. This would be a heavy blow to the confidence of foreign investors in Canadian securities and thus to the war effort itself. When the railway came to the government again in 1916, White proposed an extension of government aid but coupled it with a proposal to establish a commission of experts to examine the situation of the major Canadian railways and report to the government on suggested courses of action. In July a royal commission of three was appointed – A.H. Smith, president of the New York Central Railroad, W.H. Acworth, an expert on British railways, and Sir Henry L. Drayton, chief commissioner of the Canadian Board of Railway Commissioners. The three spent months studying the structures, finances, and prospects of Canada's major railways and reported to the government in the spring of 1917.

The commissioners were divided in their recommendations. Smith proposed that in future the Grand Trunk Railway operate the eastern section of its own and the Canadian Northern tracks, while the Canadian Northern operate its own western section together with the entire Grand Trunk Pacific network. The government would then operate the section connecting the two systems or turn it over to a private company. He admitted that Canada had too many major railways but was optimistic that a solution could be found to this problem without radical changes to the existing system. Drayton and Acworth, on the other hand, recommended that the Canadian Northern, Grand Trunk, and Grand Trunk Pacific Railways be consolidated into a single corporation managed by a board to be appointed by the government. This was to be a private company managed by a self-perpetuating board. Neither plan was fully acceptable to the government, which instead presented a plan to Parliament to begin nationalizing all of the major railways, except the C.P.R., beginning with the purchase of the Canadian Northern. The nationalization was but the first step in a process that eventually resulted in the formation of Canadian National Railways. This issue, involving vast sums of money, remained a front-ranking political crisis for years.

Although Borden had favoured some sort of government ownership of major Canadian railways as far back as 1904, the railway nationalization of 1917 was not ideologically motivated. Nor was the government's new interventionism in areas such as the marketing of grain or the introduction of income taxes (a measure demanded by progressives for years). Borden was a progressive, but the apparent progressivism of the government up to the December 1917 federal election was rooted in the need to solve war-created problems, not in philosophical principles. In a very real sense, therefore, most of these measures were intended to be ad hoc solutions that would be dismantled when more normal times returned. In the long run, of course, some, such as the income tax, remained permanent.

The Conscription Election

While the government made significant headway in its efforts to bring major areas of the economy under its direct control in 1917, it made little initial progress on the coalition question. Laurier's refusal to join the cabinet meant that overtures had to be made over Laurier's head to other Liberals who supported conscription and who were unhappy with his leadership. In fact, many Liberals believed their party stood a good chance of winning a federal election because of the Ross Rifle and other scandals, the rising cost of living, growing social unrest, and the unwavering support of French-Canadians and others opposed to conscription. There was little doubt about how the soldiers would vote, but some Liberals believed it would be extremely difficult to collect and count the soldiers' ballots while the fighting raged.

Elected in 1911, the government's normal parliamentary term of five years had already expired. In 1915 and again in 1916 Laurier and Borden had agreed to one-year extensions of the government's life to avoid a wartime vote. However, in 1917 the Liberals (and many Conservatives) were opposed to another extension. There was also a possibility that the war, which had lasted far longer than most had ever expected, would continue indefinitely. Borden was unwilling to push for another extension without the consent of the Opposition and was forced to schedule the election for December 17, 1917. As the date neared, the political manoeuvring over a coalition intensified.

Borden was determined to win the election at any cost because losing would mean the downfall of conscription. He had made his pledge to the troops and he was willing to resort to almost any measure to guarantee victory, despite the political consequences. This reasoning culminated in the Military Voters Act, proposed to the House of Commons in mid-August as the debate over the Military Service Act was reaching its conclusion, and the Wartime Elections Act, tabled in mid-September.

In 1917 Borden's government claimed to represent the national purpose, but the Liberals, looking at the actions of Bob Rogers, minister of public works, saw more of the same patronage games.

THE CANADIAN LIBERAL MONTHLY

VOL. IV. No. 10.   OTTAWA, JUNE 1917.   TWO CENTS

WE HAVE WITH US AGAIN

The first gave the vote to all members of the armed forces, male or female, no matter how long they had lived in Canada, and stipulated that they were to vote for or against the government and not for individual candidates in their home ridings. If military personnel could not name their home riding, their votes could be allocated to whatever riding the electoral officer saw fit. The second bill gave the vote to all Canadian women who were mothers, wives, sisters, or daughters of servicemen and took the vote away from all immigrants from enemy countries who had settled in Canada after 1902 as well as from all conscientious objectors.

The two bills were drawn up by Arthur Meighen, a Portage la Prairie lawyer who was appointed solicitor general in 1913, an office without a cabinet seat, and who entered the cabinet two years later. Meighen had a brilliant mind, a sharp tongue, and considerable oratorical powers. He was didactic and sharply logical in his reasoning; although he was conservative in both philosophy and temperament, he did not allow his ideological proclivities to stand in the way of his duty, as he interpreted it, to party, country, and Empire. He was also the author of the controversial legislation to nationalize the Canadian Northern Railway, thus earning for himself the enmity of much of the Montreal business establishment. Meighen was openly contemptuous of equivocal politicians and seemed to thrive on destroying their arguments in the parry and thrust of Commons debate. He was a man of great skill, little warmth, and even less compassion, or so, at least, he seemed in public.

When added together, Meighen's bills assured the government of a distinct advantage in the forthcoming election. Many immigrants, who traditionally voted Liberal because they had settled in Canada during Laurier's time as prime minister, would not be able to vote, while women who were close to men at the front and who could, therefore, be depended upon to vote in favour of the government and its conscription policy, would vote in a federal election for the first time. A large bloc of Liberal votes had been cancelled and a large bloc of government votes had been created. The soldiers' vote, which could also be counted on to favour the government, could now be apportioned to those constituencies where close battles between Conservatives and Liberals were expected.

The women's movement was badly divided by the government's decision to grant the vote to only some women. The act divided women in two ways: many immigrant women would be barred from voting and

Anglo-Saxon women not related to soldiers would also be barred from voting. Before introducing the Wartime Elections Act the Borden government had sounded out a number of proconscription women to try to determine what the reaction of the women's movement might be. It had decided that a large number of "active" women – leaders of women's groups who were apt to reflect the views of Canadian elites – were more concerned about the fate of conscription than about the discrimination inherent in the act. Nellie McClung, for example, believed that even a "partial franchise" was "better than none" because it opened the door to a full franchise later on. But McClung was chastised for this by Francis Marion Beynon, another Manitoba leader, who believed that a grave injustice would be done if foreign-born women were denied the vote. Beynon, a columnist for the *Grain Growers' Guide*, had opposed the war from the start and was forced to resign her position at the *Guide* in 1917 because of her stance. She moved to the United States as a result and remained there for the rest of her working life.

Most leaders of women's organizations in 1917 were Canadian- or British-born and strongly supported the Wartime Elections Act. Mrs. A.E. Gooderham, president of the Independent Order of the Daughters of the Empire, Mrs. L.A. Hamilton, president of the National Equal Franchise Union, and Mrs. F.H. Torrington, president of the National Council of Women, endorsed the measure. But voices were raised in opposition. At the Ontario Women's Christian Temperance Union annual convention in 1917, a blunt motion was passed stating that "we resent the action of the government in creating an arbitrary distinction among the women of Canada by placing on the books the Wartime Elections Act." The division in the ranks was not closed until March 1918 when the Borden government extended voting rights to all women in Canada on the same basis as men.

The Wartime Elections Act and the Military Voters Act weighted the vote in favour of the government, but there was still significant opposition to conscription outside Quebec among workers and farmers who thought it unfair of the government to conscript a man's body while so many businesses in Canada were thriving on war-generated profits. Some labour leaders, particularly in Western Canada, wanted to organize a national general strike in opposition to conscription, but the national convention of the Trades and Labour Congress of Canada in September 1917 decided instead to launch a political campaign and to support labour candidates in the upcoming federal election who entered against the government. Farmers were already angry with Borden because of the ceilings imposed on the prices of farm products and resisted any notion that their sons and farm hands should be forced to join the army. How could they produce the food the government wanted without help? But in a shrewd move to undermine this opposition the government issued an order-in-council two weeks before the election to exempt agricultural labourers from compulsory military duty.

After months of being wooed by Borden, a number of important proconscriptionist Liberals agreed to enter a coalition with the Conservatives by early October. Most of these men were connected to provincial Liberal parties, because Laurier's hold on the federal party was still strong: in two conventions of federal Liberals – in Toronto in July and Winnipeg in August – support for him was re-affirmed. The most prominent of the proconscription Liberals were Alberta Premier Arthur Sifton, leader of the Ontario Liberal Opposition Newton W. Rowell, and farm leader T.A. Crerar. A Manitoban, Crerar had been president of The Grain Growers' Grain Company, a farmer-owned co-operative since 1907. He represented those progressive Liberals who were hoping to force a political re-alignment in Canada through a temporary arrangement with the Conservatives. The new coalition, called the Union Government, was sworn in on October 12.

There was little doubt about the outcome of the election when the fact of the new coalition was added to the Wartime Elections Act and the Military Voters Act, but the country remained deeply divided. Government election propaganda claimed that a vote for Laurier was a vote for the Kaiser and against the boys in the trenches. Even though the new Union Government was armed with a broad platform of progressive campaign promises – temperance, votes for all women, civil service and tariff reform – most of the electioneering centred on conscription. Traditional Conservatives concentrated on conscription as the one issue sure to bring victory, while Unionist Liberals, as they were called, concentrated on it because they feared that many of their traditional supporters would not otherwise follow them in their desertion of Laurier. Laurier and his followers were, ironically, also preoccupied with conscription. They concentrated on the issue not because they thought they could win on it – it was clear by late October that they would not – but to avoid coming to grips with the Union Government's progressive and state-

The Union Government of 1917, here pictured in an election advertisement, included only two ▶ French-Canadians, and neither survived the election.

CRERAR PAPERS, QUEEN'S UNIVERSITY.

interventionist policies to which Laurier was opposed. Campaigning on conscription was good old-fashioned politics, and it allowed Laurier to keep his loyal Liberals behind him to await the end of the war and the collapse of the Unionist coalition at which time the party could be reconstituted. On election night all three groups achieved their aims. The Unionist coalition swept the country outside of Quebec (when the military vote was taken into account), while Laurier captured all of French Canada. Within the coalition, the Unionist Liberals did well, capturing one quarter of the government's 152 seats.

Union Government in Power

Following the election, the government began to fulfill its campaign pledges and oversee the operation of conscription. One of the first reform measures it enacted was prohibition. Many progressives viewed alcohol as evil and used the opportunity created by the war to claim that drink undermined the war effort. Borden responded by imposing a prohibition on the manufacture, import, and transportation of almost all alcoholic beverages within a week of the election. In February 1918, the War Trade Board was set up as a subcommittee of the cabinet in response to the desire of many businessleaders that more government direction of the war economy be introduced to cut down on "wasteful" competition and to promote co-operation between government and business. The board had power to supervise imports and exports, prevent wastage of labour and raw materials, direct the distribution of fuel, electricity, and raw materials, and encourage economic co-operation between Canada and the United States. It could also negotiate contracts for the government and, before the war ended, started to regulate the production of pig iron, an essential component in the manufacture of steel.

In the six-week session of Parliament that opened on March 18, 1918, the government revealed the full extent of its reform program. A Civil Service Act was passed that placed almost all civil service jobs under the control of the Civil Service Commission, thus taking a large patronage plum out of the hands of the government. This fulfilled Borden's 1911 election pledge. The vote was granted to all Canadian women who were not still disenfranchised by the Wartime Elections Act. The Department of Soldiers' Civil Re-Establishment was set up, belatedly, to begin

Union Government election propaganda worked very hard to equate a vote for Borden with ▶ patriotism. This flyer was more restrained than most.

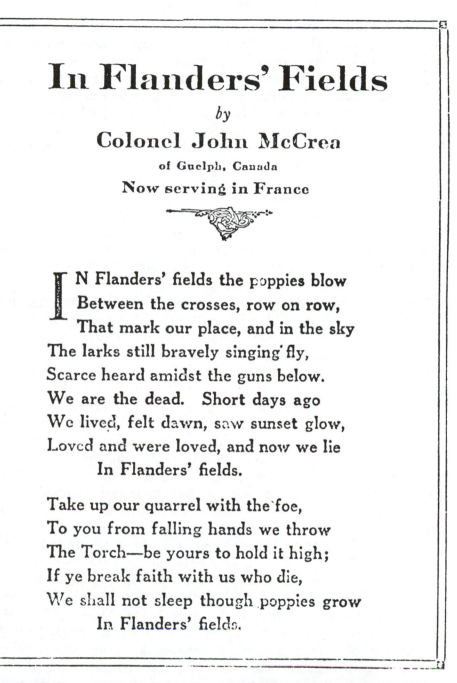

In Flanders' Fields

by

Colonel John McCrea

of Guelph, Canada

Now serving in France

IN Flanders' fields the poppies blow
Between the crosses, row on row,
  That mark our place, and in the sky
The larks still bravely singing fly,
Scarce heard amidst the guns below.
We are the dead.   Short days ago
We lived, felt dawn, saw sunset glow,
Loved and were loved, and now we lie
    In Flanders' fields.

Take up our quarrel with the foe,
To you from falling hands we throw
The Torch—be yours to hold it high;
If ye break faith with us who die,
We shall not sleep though poppies grow
    In Flanders' fields.

VOTE UNION GOVERNMENT

planning for the re-integration of soldiers into civilian life upon their return to Canada. The government was acting quickly now, but not quickly enough for western farmers or organized labour.

The West had played an important role in the triumph of the Union Government and had placed great store in Unionist promises for sweeping reforms. One area that concerned farmers was the tariff, and they believed they had a good case for its abolition on farm machinery during the war. But the protectionist faction in the government was strong, and no tariff relief was offered. Coupled with the government's sudden cancellation of conscription exemptions for all classes of labourers aged 20 to 22, the result, Borden claimed, of a need for rapid reinforcement of Canadian troops because of a massive German offensive on the western front in March, western farmers felt betrayed. They began to look for a political alternative to both the Liberal Party, which was still dominated by Laurier and his followers, and the Union Government, which had stabbed them in the back.

For organized labour the Unionist reforms were too little too late. Labour leaders had warned Borden in 1916 that his government had an obligation to "prevent employers from taking advantage of the war to increase the exploitation of their employees," and, by the spring of 1917, they had put together a long list of complaints about low wages and bad working conditions in war industries. The government did little to help other than extend the Industrial Disputes Investigation Act (a measure unpopular with Canadian trade unionists) to war plants. Labour leaders, unlike business leaders, were not called upon to help the war effort and were rarely, if ever, taken into the government's confidence. The unions had been thwarted in an attempt, launched early in the war, to have fair-wage clauses inserted into war contracts to protect the wages of war workers, and they had been defeated over conscription. Their anger and frustration grew and, as it did, they began to strike more frequently.

Work time lost from industrial disputes was very low in 1915, but it climbed steadily and reached a new peak during 1917 with strikes in many major war industries. But 1917 was peaceful compared with 1918. During that year strikes broke out in West Coast shipyards, Winnipeg metal-working shops, and the postal service. In May a strike of Winnipeg city employees spread to almost a general one before it was ended by the intervention of Senator Gideon Robertson, a vice-president of the railway telegraphers union who was sent to restore peace as the personal representative of Prime Minister Borden. A dispute between the major Canadian railways and their repair and maintenance workers threatened to paralyze the Canadian rail transport system in July and was averted only when the Borden government threatened to conscript the workers and force them to work under army supervision on army pay.

Although these disputes were instigated by workers trying to force their employers to recognize their unions or by demands for higher pay to keep up with increases in the cost of living, the government did little or nothing to solve the basic problems affecting Canadian workers. Instead it issued orders-in-council in the summer and fall of 1918 banning strikes and lockouts, forbidding the public use of "enemy" languages such as German, Ukrainian, and Czech, and declaring 14 radical unions and left-wing political parties illegal. The government had become convinced that radicals and revolutionaries were behind the unrest and were trying to undermine the war effort. These beliefs were supported by C.H. Cahan, a Montreal lawyer appointed director of public safety by Borden in the fall of 1918, who conducted an inquiry into the growing unrest and concluded that Bolshevik ideas were strongly affecting Slavs, Russians, Austrians, and Ukrainians. There was little evidence to support such a theory and much to suggest that inflation, thwarted worker aspirations, and the irresponsible actions of some employers were at fault; nevertheless, the government chose to believe that the unrest was connected with foreign movements such as the Bolshevik revolution that broke out in Russia in November 1917, toppling Alexander Kerensky's provisional government.

The Final Battles and the Making of Peace

After the Bolsheviks seized power in Russia, they sued for peace with Germany, and the Germans were able to concentrate their resources on the western front. The Kaiser's officers decided to deal the Allies one massive knockout blow before the full strength of the United States, still mobilizing a vast army, could be brought to bear. On March 21, 1918, Germany launched a massive attack in the West. This was different from any large assault previously mounted by either side on the western front. The Germans used every tactic they had learned about surprise and about mobile warfare since the great stalemate battles of 1916. Their troops quickly overran Allied forward positions under the cover of fog and supported by accurate shellfire. They overran Allied strongpoints and cut Allied lines of supply and communication. Using aircraft, mobile machine guns, trucks, and other vehicles, they advanced rapidly toward Paris, concentrating the bulk of their assault on the British Fifth Army and the French First and Third armies.

The main German axis of attack was south of the positions occupied by the Canadian Corps, stationed near Vimy. It was not long before Haig dismantled the Corps and placed the individual Canadian Divisions under different British commands. To Haig this was a simple matter. The Allied front was collapsing and he was determined to shore it up with every available man wherever he was needed. Canadian sensibilities were not high on his list of priorities while the outcome of the war lay in the balance. Currie was left without troops to command.

Currie recognized the gravity of the situation but fought hard to get his Corps re-united. He fired off a message to his superiors entreating them to keep the Corps together because, he claimed, Canadians fought best when they fought together: "I know that necessity knows no laws and that [Haig] will do what he thinks best, yet for the sake of the victory we must win, get us together as soon as you can." Within 24 hours, two of his divisions were back under his command and a third was returned to him two weeks later. The last was re-united with the Corps at the beginning of July.

The German attack – there were four successive assaults between March 21 and mid-June – was eventually thwarted by stubborn Allied resistance. This offensive, together with the heavy Allied losses in the Battle of Passchendaele in late 1917, became the chief topic of discussion at the meeting of the Imperial War Cabinet in the summer of 1918. Borden was appalled at the casualty rate, accused the Imperial General Staff of incompetence, and backed a strenuous effort by Lloyd George to bring the military under the direct control of the Imperial War Cabinet. The year before, Canada and the other Dominions had finally won British agreement, in theory, to consult them on foreign policy and defence matters; at the 1918 meeting the Dominions won that agreement in practice by taking part in the determination of future war strategy for the combined imperial forces.

Although the German offensive had been costly to both sides, the Germans suffered more. Allied blockades of Germany were beginning to have a direct impact on food supplies and on civilian morale both in Germany and at the front. In addition, the Germans had lost thousands of troops in their offensive, losses that were becoming almost impossible to replace. Large numbers of Americans were beginning to arrive at the front, augmenting Allied ranks. The time was right for a major push using

The Canadian Corps ended the war at Mons, Belgium, the very place where the British army had first met the Germans four years before. The corps had built a proud reputation for ferocity and efficiency, but its men were eager to resume their civilian lives.

TORONTO TELEGRAM COLLECTION, YORK UNIVERSITY ARCHIVES.

planes, tanks, and all the new techniques of mobile warfare to knock the Germans out of the war. In early August 1918, a massive combined offensive was launched by American, British, and French forces with the Canadian Corps and the Australians acting as shock troops. The offensive rolled forward recapturing much of the French and Belgian territory taken by the Germans in the first months of the war. The German armies were on the verge of collapse, and the Kaiser was forced to abdicate in favour of a republican administration headed by Social Democrats. As the Allied armies neared the borders of Germany, the new German government pressed for an armistice. The Allies agreed, and all fighting on the western front ended at 11 a.m. on November 11, 1918.

Although the fighting had ended on the western front, Canadian soldiers and airmen were still in action far from home. From the time of the Bolshevik Revolution in Russia, Britain had tried to intervene there militarily to shore up the eastern front, to protect British interests in places such as the Caucasus oilfields, and to help counter-revolutionaries in their campaign to topple the Communists. They sought and received help from Canada. The first Canadian contingent of 28 men was dispatched in February 1918 with a larger British force to Baku on the Caspian Sea, by way of Iraq. A second group, consisting of 16 men, accompanied a British expedition to Murmansk, in north Russia, in June. The largest Canadian group, about 5000, was sent to Siberia in October as part of a much larger force of Japanese, American, and British troops.

The interventions in Russia caused Borden no end of trouble at home. The bulk of the Siberian force were conscripts who had seen no action on the western front, and many Canadians could not understand why their soldiers were fighting in a civil war far from home, especially after the Armistice of November 11. Union leaders, political progressives, and liberal newspaper editorials began to demand their withdrawal. Borden had never been enthusiastic about the intervention in the first place but he hoped Canada could gain some commercial advantage from the escapade in the event that the Allies carved Siberia up into spheres of influence. By early 1919 he had concluded that the adventure was no longer worth pursuing and he informed the British that Canadian troops would be back in Canada by April.

Canada and the other Dominions had made substantial progress toward full autonomy during the war, and Borden was determined to preserve these gains during the peace-making process; Lloyd George appeared determined, however, to undo much that had been done. It was not that the British prime minister wanted the Dominions to revert to their prewar colonial status. But he jealously guarded the prerogative of the major Allies – Britain, France, the United States, and, to a lesser degree, Italy – to shape the peace without the interference of lesser powers. Thus, to placate the Imperial War Cabinet without offering them any substantial representation among the ranks of the Allied peace negotiators, Lloyd George proposed that Borden represent the Dominions as one of five British Empire delegates at the peace conference in Paris.

Borden refused. He wanted nothing less than full representation for each Dominion as part of the British delegation; he claimed no right or desire to speak for the others. Borden had to contend not only with the British but also with the Americans, who initially balked at the idea that the Dominions should be separately represented at the peace negotiations, even though it was clear that they would also be part of the British delegation. U.S. Secretary of State Robert Lansing wondered aloud what business Canada had in the settlement of European affairs, ignoring the large Canadian contribution to the war and the 60 000 Canadian dead. However, in mid-January, President Woodrow Wilson proposed a compromise to allow two delegates each from Canada, South Africa, Australia, and India, and one from New Zealand (but none from Newfoundland) to take part in the peace conference. Despite this, the Dominions contributed very little to the actual formation of the peace treaty, which was written almost exclusively by the major powers.

The Paris Peace Conference set the terms of the peace settlement and established the foundation of the League of Nations, an organization of countries to guard peace and punish aggressor nations. Borden was able to secure separate Canadian representation in the league and eligibility for membership on the league's governing council, as well as separate Canadian representation on the league's International Labour Organization. However, he was decidedly unhappy over the collective security arrangements as outlined in Article 10 of the League of Nations charter. This stipulated that its governing council had the power to tell members what action to take in case of a threat to peace. Borden thought the article imposed unreasonable obligations upon league members. He had, in any case, more faith in a British-American alliance to keep peace around the globe than in any action the league might take. Borden stayed in Paris until mid-May 1919 but took little real part in the deliberations except for a brief stint on the commission established to set the boundaries of the Balkan countries.

While Borden was trying to help forge a new international peace in Paris, there was turmoil at home. Canadians in all walks of life had made sacrifices to win the war, but none matched that of Canada's 650 000 men and women who had served in the armed forces. Sixty thousand had died and 173 000 had been wounded. Some of the survivors had returned to Canada even before the war ended, but the coming of peace brought a virtual flood of veterans eager to take their place in civilian life again. The Department of Soldiers' Civil Re-Establishment orchestrated efforts to integrate the veterans into society by spearheading a campaign that urged private businesses to hire returning soldiers, while the government gave them preference in hiring for the civil service. In addition, a limited pension scheme was set up, homestead land was made available, and veterans' hospitals were built at government expense to care for the critically wounded and sick. But these measures did little to meet veterans' demands for tangible rewards for their long and faithful service. They wanted a cash bonus payable to every veteran, based on length of service; the government refused to give it to them. Unrest mounted, and in the winter and spring of 1919 veterans across the country staged brief riots and attacked aliens and leftist political organizations (seen both as "slackers" and/or anti-British), and business- es that employed foreigners. On January 26, 1919, an angry crowd of veterans attacked the headquarters of the Socialist Party of Canada in Winnipeg. They stormed up the stairs, broke through the door, and smashed up the furniture, crashing a piano through the window onto the street below. They showered books, leaflets, and pamphlets down on the shattered piano and then set the whole pile ablaze. For the next two days, they demonstrated against employers who hired aliens rather than returned soldiers. In the spring, veterans attacked socialist and labour organizers in British Columbia's interior, throwing several out of mining towns such as Trail, Silverton, and Cranbrook. One union organizer thought that "the time [had] arrived when a working man [needed] a bodyguard as well as a King." Probably the worst incident took place in Drumheller, a small Alberta coal-mining town where crowds of veterans attacked the homes of striking miners in early August and forced many of them to flee with their families into the hills for safety.

The unrest among the veterans parallelled the growing unrest among Canadian workers. Many had suffered a decline in their living standard because of inflation, while others feared a return to prewar depression once the war-related prosperity ended. Although some had resorted to strikes during wartime, many had not, out of a sense of patriotism, and they expected matters to improve after the war. They, like the other Canadians, had been promised a better society after the killing was over. Now they waited impatiently for the government to make good on its promises.[9]

---

[9] Discontent among veterans is described in Desmond Morton and Glenn Wright, *Winning the Second Battle: Canadian Veterans and the Return to Civilian Life, 1915-1930* (Toronto, 1987). Labour unrest during and after the war is covered in David J. Bercuson, *Confrontation at Winnipeg: Labour Industrial Relations and the General Strike* (Montreal, 1974), and *Fools and Wise Men: The Rise and Fall of the One Big Union* (Toronto, 1978). On radicalism see A.R. McCormack, *Reformers, Rebels and Revolutionaries: The Western Canadian Radical Movement, 1899-1919* (Toronto, 1977), and Martin Robin, *Radical Politics and Canadian Labour: 1880-1930* (Kingston, 1968). Several articles on the labour unrest of 1919 can be found in *Labour/Le Travail* (Spring, 1984).

THE YEARS OF LABOUR RADICALISM

Winnipeg: Saturday, June 21, 1919. The day began as a typical summer Saturday in the main shopping area of Canada's third largest city. As the sun rose higher in the sky, shop owners and storekeepers opened their doors, and crowds of people began to stroll up the sidewalks of Main Street and along Portage, some to window shop and some to buy. It was much cooler than it had been a few weeks earlier and promised to be a good day to loll in the sun in Assiniboine Park.

There was, however, a sense of unease in the air. Almost everyone knew that First World War veterans – "returned men" they were called – who supported the general strike that had gripped the city since May 15 had called for a demonstration that afternoon; almost everyone also knew that Mayor Charles F. Gray was determined to stop them. By about 11:00 a.m., the normal crowd of shoppers began to thicken as pro-strike veterans (most in civvies) and curious onlookers began to gather in Main Street, not far from City Hall. As their numbers grew, they became more raucous and Police Chief Newton, watching from City Hall, started to worry. He telephoned Gray, who was at the Royal Alexandra Hotel meeting with local anti-strike leaders, federal Minister of Labour Gideon D. Robertson, and pro-strike veteran leaders, to tell him that the crowd was getting out of hand and to get back to City Hall immediately.

At about 2:30 p.m., a streetcar appeared moving south on Main. The resumption of streetcar service several days earlier had prompted the

The Winnipeg general strike frightened Ottawa and many Canadians. A street car tipped over was one thing, but an assault on the values of the nation, for so organized labour unrest seemed to many, could not be tolerated.

MANITOBA PROVINCIAL ARCHIVES/N 2762.

pro-strike veterans to call for a demonstration; as this particular streetcar moved slowly through the milling crowd, men close to the tracks began to jeer and shake their fists at the motorman and the conductor. Suddenly two or three men climbed atop the car and pulled its trolley off the wires, stopping it dead. Within seconds other men began to smash its windows. Then, hundreds of others pushed at the side of the car, trying to tip it over. When this proved impossible, another man ran inside, slashed the seats and set the interior ablaze. What Gray and others had feared from the very start of the general strike was now happening – a mob was running loose in the heart of Winnipeg.

Gray did not witness the arson taking place in front of City Hall, but not long after Newton's phone call he had arrived to look the situation over. When Newton told him that his men could not restore order, the two men made their way to the headquarters of the Royal North-West

Mounted Police to request assistance. That was granted and Gray and Newton hurried back to City Hall.

Within minutes, sounds of clattering hoofs were heard and a squad of Mounted Police galloped on to the main street from a connecting avenue. There were as many as 50, by some accounts, their revolvers in their holsters and their batons in their hands. They galloped through the jeering crowd and stopped to regroup. For a few moments the police and the demonstrators watched each other uneasily. Then the police spurred their horses and charged again; this time the crowd reacted by throwing bricks, stones, and bottles. None of the Mounted Police was seriously hurt and after completing their charge through the crowd, they wheeled about and charged back. Again they rode through a rain of missiles, and again they turned to the charge, but this time they did not escape unharmed. One horse stumbled over a piece of streetcar fender that had been torn off and left lying in the street. The rider was thrown from the saddle, but his foot caught in the stirrup, and he was dragged along the street until a man leaped from the crowd, grabbed him, and started to beat him. When other policemen saw this, they turned around quickly and rode toward the crowd with "revolvers cocked in their hands." Their commander gave the order to fire and a volley of shots punctuated the jeering and the yelling.

Bullets ricocheted off brick and concrete, and the crowd broke in panic. One man was killed instantly, shot through the heart, and another was mortally wounded, while others sustained less serious injuries. Hundreds ducked down side streets and alleys trying to escape the deadly fusillade and were met by cordons of club-wielding police who beat them back. Scores were arrested. Within minutes, trucks carrying heavy machine guns bolted to their flatbeds, and soldiers armed with rifles and bayonets began to roll into the heart of the city. The militia moved in to occupy the downtown core.

The confrontation that occurred in the streets of Winnipeg that June day has gone down in history as "Bloody Saturday." It was the climax of the Winnipeg General Strike, which paralyzed the city for six long weeks. The strike was the focus of a workers' revolt that swept Canada from coast to coast in the spring and summer of that year. Though Canadians have come to think of themselves as a peaceful people, settling their internal disputes with reason, discussion, and conciliation, in reality they have had, as one historian has noted, "a record of labour unrest and industrial conflict, with illegal and violent overtones, second only to the United States, and far greater than that of most west European countries."[1] If this is true of the twentieth century in general, it is certainly true of the period from 1911 to 1921.

The Rise of Unionism

Before the Great War, Canada was still primarily an agricultural country, and more Canadians lived on farms and in small country towns than in the cities. The 1911 census showed that more than three out of ten working Canadians were farmers or farm labourers, the largest single group in the country's labour force. Other Canadians worked in manufacturing (18 percent of the labour force), trade and commerce (10 percent), transportation (10 percent), building and construction (9 percent), domestic and personal service (8 percent), and a large variety of other occupations such as mining, fishing, and government service. Although many of these workers were highly skilled craftspeople who had served long apprenticeships and who earned good, steady wages, a very large number were unskilled labourers who earned very little. The workforce in the heavy manufacturing, transportation, and mining industries was almost exclusively male, but women workers dominated the labour force in cotton and woolen mills, in tailoring shops, in the larger retail establishments, and in the growing number of telephone exchanges. Large numbers of women also earned their keep as domestic servants, laundresses, housekeepers, and hotel and restaurant employees. Women made up slightly more than 20 percent of the non-agricultural workforce. In the poorest of homes, children, too, were often forced to work.

For many Canadian workers – men and women – workplaces were unsafe, unhealthy, and uncomfortable. In July 1911, a typical month, 92

In 1912, family economic necessity and the turning of a blind eye by employers combined to let ▶ young children like this boy of 14 do hard and dangerous jobs. The child was working in a coal mine.   C-30945/NATIONAL ARCHIVES OF CANADA.

---

[1] The statement comes from S.M. Jamieson, *Times of Trouble: Labour Unrest and Industrial Conflict in Canada, 1900-1966* (Ottawa, 1971). The two most recent texts presenting overviews of Canadian labour are Desmond Morton with Terry Copp, *Working People* (Ottawa, 1984) and Bryan D. Palmer, *Working-Class Experience: The Rise and Reconstitution of Canadian Labour, 1800-1980* (Toronto, 1983). A number of important Canadian strikes are described in I.M. Abella (ed.), *On Strike: Six Key Labour Struggles in Canada, 1919-1949* (Toronto, 1974).

Canadian workers were killed on the job. An iron worker in Davenport, Ontario, was crushed by shifting iron rails; a brakeman in Saskatoon was caught between two box cars; a coal miner in Sydney Mines, Nova Scotia, was buried by falling rock; a lock tender in Montreal was drowned. The toll was always heavy among railway workers, sailors, and miners, as well as farmers and farm labourers. For every one killed there were others who survived industrial accidents with mangled limbs, pain-wracked bodies, or sightless eyes. Friends, relatives, fellow union members, or private charities supported many of these victims of industrial accidents for the rest of their lives because there was at the time no government-operated compensation plan anywhere in Canada, and provincial laws were almost entirely ineffective in forcing employers to pay compensation.

When physical survival was not directly threatened, economic survival was still a basic question for Canadian workers. Few unskilled workers in factories, on construction sites, or in track-laying gangs earned enough to support themselves in anything but a hand-to-mouth existence. An unskilled Hamilton factory worker, for example, had to work two hours to earn enough to buy a pound of coffee and more than 80 hours to pay for one month's rent. Skilled workers, such as bricklayers or carpenters, earned enough to raise families and sustain a relatively high standard of living, but others were much worse off. However, even the skilled were insecure because their work was often seasonal; carpenters, for example, could expect many months of unemployment during the winter. There was no unemployment insurance in 1911. The skilled too suffered greatly if their working days were cut short by sickness, accident, or prolonged unemployment.[2]

---

[2] Conditions of work and life for Canadian workers in specific cities can be found in Terry Copp, *The Anatomy of Poverty: The Condition of the Working Class in Montreal, 1897-1929* (Toronto, 1974); Michael J. Piva, *The Condition of the Working Class in Toronto: 1900-1921* (Ottawa, 1979); and Alan F.J. Artibise, *Winnipeg: A Social History of Urban Growth, 1874-1914* (Montreal, 1975). Women in the labour force are covered in Barbara Latham and Roberta Pazdro (eds.), *Not Just Pin Money: Selected Essays on the History of Women's Work in British Columbia* (Victoria, 1984); Marie Lavigne and Yolande Pinard (eds.), *Travailleuses et féministes: Aspects historiques* (Montreal, 1977); Janice Acton et al. (eds.), *Women at Work: Ontario, 1850-1920* (Toronto, 1974); Meg Luxton, *More Than a Labour of Love: Three Generations of Women's Work in the Home* (Toronto, 1980); Pat Armstrong and Hugh Armstrong, *The Double Ghetto: Canadian Women and their Segregated Work* (Toronto, 1984); and Linda Kealey (ed.), *A Not Unreasonable Claim: Women and Reform in Canada, 1880s-1920s* (Toronto, 1979). Canadian attitudes toward the unemployed are found in James Struthers, *No Fault of Their Own: Unemployment and the Canadian Welfare State, 1914-1941* (Toronto, 1983).

Trade unions helped improve the wages and working conditions of some Canadian workers and aided them in times of distress with a variety of union-financed insurance schemes to cover sickness, accident, and death. But few Canadian workers were members of unions and even fewer of these were women. In 1911, 1 560 000 Canadians worked for wages as part of the nonagricultural workforce, but only 133 000 of them, roughly 8.5 percent, carried union membership cards. Most union members were usually highly skilled workers who could not easily be replaced by an employer who ordinarily might have fired them for joining a union. In 1911 there were no laws protecting workers from harassment for union activity, and unskilled workers who were easily replaced in shop or factory were usually fired on the spot for joining a union. Some employers insisted that their workers, skilled or not, sign contracts stipulating that they would never join a union.

Union attitudes to women workers were ambivalent at best. Unions in Canada were exclusively led by males, often British born, who believed, quite simply, that a woman's place was in the home and that her most noble calling was to be a wife and mother. They recognized that some women had to work, but they saw this as one of the failures of the capitalist system that would have to be rectified in due course. They could not accept that women might want to work, to make careers, and to enjoy doing it. The conventional trade union wisdom was that women worked only to prevent themselves from starving and that as soon as they could cease working, they would or should do so. Women were looked on as unskilled competitors for male jobs – not unlike immigrants – whose presence in the workforce tended to drive wages down. When male-dominated unions were called upon by women workers to help in strikes or organizing drives, therefore, they rarely responded with anything more than words. Their objective was not to improve working conditions for women, but "to abolish . . . female labour in all branches of industrial life," as a 1907 resolution passed by the Trades and Labour Congress of Canada (T.L.C.) proclaimed. Women were to be helped – helped to get out of the labour force.

Most unions in Canada were affiliated with the T.L.C., which was itself affiliated with and dominated by the American Federation of Labor (A.F.L.) and its president, Samuel Gompers. Gompers was born in Britain in 1850 to immigrant Jewish parents and in 1863 came to the United States, where he took up the trade of cigar maker. He joined the Cigar Makers Union and soon began to play an active part in local and then national union politics. He took part in the founding of the American Federation of Labor and became president of that organization in 1886.

The A.F.L. was a loose federation of unions, most of which were craft unions uniting workers of one particular skill. (A small number of industrial unions such as the United Mine Workers of America, which brought together all workers within one industry, were also affiliated.)

Gompers came to personify the A.F.L. and espoused its philosophy in government hearings, at labour conventions, and in the pages of the *American Federationist*. This philosophy was based on the notion that workers should use their economic power – strikes and boycotts – to lever more wealth out of the capitalists in the form of higher wages, fewer hours, and better fringe benefits and working conditions. In this way a slow but steady redistribution of wealth would take place in society until the workers achieved their rightful position in the industrial and economic hierarchy. The highly skilled were to be organized first as the vanguard of the working class, and they were to be organized in craft unions wherever possible. Unions were especially warned not to engage in partisan political activities such as supporting one party or another because this could divide the workers along party lines. Instead, unions were to concentrate on the immediate improvement of working and living conditions. Trying to foment revolutions or build utopian workers' or socialist societies was a waste of time and precious resources, according to Gompers. Chasing these will-o-the-wisps had destroyed the once-powerful Knights of Labor, which had risen to prominence in the United States after the Civil War, by distracting workers from the more practical task of winning the daily struggle for more bread and butter.

When the Trades and Labour Congress formally affiliated itself to the A.F.L. in 1902, the Gompers philosophy was given a powerful boost among Canadian trade unionists. But, although many skilled Canadian workers seemed ready to embrace that faith, others were not. James Watters, elected to the presidency of the T.L.C. in 1911, was a former miner from British Columbia who believed that the craft unions should actively involve themselves in the fight to create a democratic socialist society in Canada and that industrial unionism was an effective organizational form for workers in certain industries such as mining, logging, and transportation. The man he succeeded, Alphonse Verville, a Montreal plumber, had been prepared to follow Gompers's line on organizational questions, but he opposed the A.F.L.'s antipolitical philosophy. He was, in fact, elected to the House of Commons in a 1907 by-election on a Labour ticket. However, both men were rather weak and indecisive and were reluctant to lead the T.L.C. in a more independent direction. Besides, they had to contend with P.M. Draper, T.L.C. secretary, throughout this period. He believed staunchly in the basic philosophy of the American Federation of Labor, though he wanted the Canadian labour movement to have more autonomy. His views were close to those of John A. Flett, A.F.L. organizer and former T.L.C. president, who strongly backed Gompers and the A.F.L. and who worked hard for the subordination of the Canadian labour movement to that of the United States. Flett, from Hamilton, was a forceful speaker and effective organizer and remained very influential in the Trades Congress after his presidential term ended in 1904.[3]

There were some Canadian workers who scorned the A.F.L. altogether and instead supported organizations such as the Industrial Workers of the World, a United States-based revolutionary industrial union. Founded in 1905, the I.W.W. aimed to organize all workers in society into one highly centralized union. Once this was accomplished, it intended to call a massive general strike that would bring capitalism crashing down. The I.W.W. in Canada attracted few skilled workers and concentrated on the unskilled labourers in the harvest fields, lumber camps, and track-laying gangs. Its most spectacular efforts were concentrated in Alberta and British Columbia where it organized free speech demonstrations, unemployed marches, and bush workers' and track-layers' strikes. In the spring and summer of 1912, close to 9000 railway construction workers employed by the Canadian Northern and Grand Trunk Pacific Railways in the British Columbia interior took part in I.W.W.-organized strikes for higher wages and better working conditions. The strikes were eventually broken by the railways with the help of the federal government, which allowed immigrant strike-bearers to enter the area, and by the provincial government, which used the provincial police to arrest strike leaders.

The opposition of employers was by no means limited to radical unions such as the I.W.W. Few employers willingly recognized or bargained with unions, and even those that did rarely agreed to the wage demands of their workers. Strikes to force employers to recognize unions

---

[3] On Samuel Gompers, see his autobiography, *Seventy Years of Life and Labor* (New York, 1925). Gompers's impact on the labour movement is found in Harold C. Livesay, *Samuel Gompers and Organized Labor in America* (Boston, 1978). Gompers's ideas are analyzed in William Dick, *Labor and Socialism in America: The Gompers Years* (Port Washington, 1972). A good overview of Gompers's thought is Fred Greenbaum, "The Social Ideas of Samuel Gompers," *Labor History* (Winter, 1966). The A.F.L. takeover of the T.L.C. is explained in Robert H. Babcock, *Gompers in Canada: A Study in American Continentalism Before the First World War* (Toronto, 1974).

and strikes for higher wages and better working conditions were frequent in all industries. Moreover, in the early part of the century, many employers had started to re-organize their factories to make them more efficient; this was the beginning of assembly-line production. They embarked on a campaign to break the stranglehold skilled workers had on important parts of the production process; the workers reacted by striking.

In the labour newspapers of the day, employers were sometimes pictured in cartoons wearing top hats and tail coats, with money spilling out of their pockets, evil grins on their faces, and their white-gloved hands clutching instruments of torture to crush, flay, or otherwise destroy the workers. Like workers, however, employers' attitudes and motives varied greatly. Some of the largest employers of the late nineteenth and early twentieth centuries were self-made individuals who had, through intelligence, skill, daring, and luck, risen from the lower ranks of society. They had a special talent for organizing and mobilizing capital; they were artists who created corporations instead of paintings or sculpture. The accumulation of money was often unimportant to them as an end in itself; it was the creation of giant corporations, smoothly efficient factories, or continent-spanning merchandizing establishments that posed the real challenge.

These people tended to judge their fellow human beings as harshly as they judged themselves and their colleagues. They believed that only weak and incapable men and women needed to unite to advance themselves, while those of real talent had no need for trade unions or collective action. As a rule, then, unions were scorned by entrepreneurs such as Robert Dunsmuir, a British Columbia mine owner, who proclaimed his beliefs to a royal commission in 1903: "[The workers] can belong to a union if they like – I don't care. . . . I have my rights. I can hire them if I like and they can work if they like." Other employers across the country, from T.R. Deacon of the Manitoba Bridge and Iron Works in Winnipeg to Joseph W. Flavelle of the William Davies Company in Toronto, readily agreed with Dunsmuir's views, though perhaps not with his willingness to proclaim them to the public. This condemnation of collective action did not, of course, extend to those businesspeople who combined with other entrepreneurs to advance their own interests. Such combination went on all the time. The Canadian Manufacturers Association and the Canadian Bankers Association were two of the most powerful lobby groups in Canada while the joining together of smaller companies into large trusts and monopolies – the formation of Canada Cement and Stelco were prime examples – was a prominent feature of corporate life during this period.

Given the determination of the trade unions to expand and increase their economic power, clashes between the unions and employers such as Dunsmuir were inevitable. Some of the longest and most violent strikes in the prewar era involved coal miners who were members of the United Mine Workers of America (U.M.W.). In Alberta and eastern British Columbia, the U.M.W. had succeeded in winning recognition from the Western Canada Coal Operators Association in 1907, but this did not smooth the way for an easy relationship between them. Strikes over wages were called in 1909 and 1911, and unresolved grievances and bitterness continued to sour the air in the coalfields.

On Vancouver Island, employer-employee relations were even worse. There, miners had tried without success to win union recognition since the 1880s, and a continuing legacy of violence and hatred poisoned all attempts at conciliation. In September 1912, Canadian Collieries (Dunsmuir) Limited at Cumberland and Ladysmith struck. Three thousand miners left work for a variety of reasons, including the issue of union recognition and fears that the company was negligent in enforcing mine safety regulations. The strike spread in the following months, but the company, using strikebreakers, succeeded in restoring production to two-thirds of the pre-strike level. The union reacted with a general strike of all Vancouver Island miners, but this made little impact on coal production. Union members then launched a series of attacks on strikebreakers' houses and mine entrances, and in one night of violence, gunfire and dynamite punctuated the darkness at South Wellington, Nanaimo, Ladysmith, and Extension. The provincial government sent in the militia, which quickly arrested 250 miners to break the strike.

In Cape Breton, Nova Scotia, two unions vied for the loyalty of the coal miners – District 26 of the U.M.W. and the Provincial Workingmen's Association, a local organization founded in 1879. When the U.M.W. first moved into the Cape Breton coal fields in 1908, the P.W.A. allied itself with the Dominion Coal Company to keep the U.S.-based union out. Early in 1909, the company began to dismiss U.M.W. miners, prompting the union to call for a federal board of conciliation. This was a mistake because the board refused to uphold union claims of discrimination and, instead, proclaimed that "foreign officials . . . should not have the power to decree that Nova Scotia miners . . . must stop working." From then until July, relations between the company and the U.M.W. deteriorated further until the union finally struck on July 6. In some collieries, the strike, punctuated by frequent violence, dragged into the spring of 1911. Despite the resolve of the men, however, the U.M.W. was fighting the company, the P.W.A., and the provincial government at the same time – a powerful combination. When the strike petered out, the U.M.W. temporarily lost its foothold in the Nova Scotia coalfields.

Strikes were usually a mark of boom times, when there were accompanying labour shortages and inflation; Canada experienced plenty of these starting in the mid-1890s. However, in the fall of 1913 the economy ran out of steam, and a severe depression began. The effect on Canadian working people was immediate and dramatic. National trade union membership dropped from approximately 176 000 in 1913 to 143 000 in 1915, a decline of more than 18 percent. Unemployment rose quickly as construction slowed and heavy industry laid off thousands of workers. In the pre-unemployment insurance days, a worker without work received no money for the basics of life. Without a job, there might not be food, clothing, or shelter. Private charities provided a patchwork system of soup-kitchen relief, and city governments opened employment agencies to try to steer workers to available jobs, but such measures were far from adequate. Over the winter of 1913-1914 unemployment grew, despair deepened, and economic disaster stared hundreds of thousands in the face.

The War and Labour

The outbreak of war in Europe in August 1914 signalled the start of a shift in Canadian manufacturing that eventually led to better economic times for many Canadian workers. The voracious Allied war machine needed armaments, particularly artillery shells, and the British Ministry of Munitions was soon enquiring if Canadian manufacturers could help fill that demand. A Shell Committee was established in Canada to place British war orders, and soon structural steel companies, railway repair shops, and metal-working establishments of all kinds were in the shell-making business. From a total shell-producing capacity of about 3000 shells per year in 1914 Canadian production reached almost 20 000 000 shells in 1916. At the same time, Canadian factories began to produce an ever-expanding range of other war-related products from aircraft engines to acetone. As these factories expanded, the war labour force grew apace. By 1916, 185 000 Canadians were directly employed in munitions manufacturing alone. The expansion of the munitions industry and the demand for munitions workers, coupled with enlistments in the Canadian Expeditionary Force, helped ease the job shortage and banish the depression. By the end of 1915 unemployment was a thing of the past; labour was in short supply.

The labour shortage gave the unions their best opportunity in years to recruit new members, and trade union membership grew from 143 000 in 1915 to 249 000 by 1918 – an increase of approximately 74 percent. The organizing drives that brought these new members into the unions tended to increase worker militancy, but this was tempered at first by a conviction held by many labour leaders that workers and their unions should not disrupt the war effort with strikes. Patriotism muffled militancy.

The patriotic approach was soon undermined by the rapidly rising cost of living that quickly surpassed the inflation rate of the predepression period. The country's need to feed, clothe, and equip a large army, together with the pressure to export food to European allies, and the ever-increasing requirements for raw materials for Canadian munitions plants created new demands on the Canadian economy that could not be met. Demand outstripped supply, and prices rose accordingly. In the period from 1915 to 1918, the average family budget in Canada rose by 50 percent, while the average hourly wage increased by only 44 percent, thus causing a decline in real wages of about 2 percent per year. However, these figures are averages, and in some parts of Canada, particularly the West, the increase in prices was usually higher than in the rest of the country, while wages of workers in nonmunitions industries, such as construction and urban transportation, rose much more slowly than the national average. Thus inflation affected some parts of Canada much more than others and seems to have been especially acute in the West and the Maritimes. The unions complained bitterly about inflation and flung charges of price manipulation and food profiteering about, but, in fact, there was little evidence that scheming was behind the inflation. It was, quite simply, a case of the federal government's unwillingness, especially during the early years of the war, to introduce the compulsive measures such as rationing that might have cured the problem.

For the first time in Canadian history, a federal government was trying to manage a major war effort that involved a large-scale mobilization of both people and resources; it learned only slowly how to go about the task. The most important lesson that Borden and his colleagues eventually learned was that a war effort of this magnitude could not be sustained on a voluntary basis. It was simply not enough to trust to the good intentions and patriotic feelings of the majority of Canadians. It was only toward the end of the war that the government began to move more quickly to enact compulsory measures such as regulating the prices of important war-related commodities to guide the war effort. This was part of the overall move from voluntarism to compulsion that paralleled the growing belief that the war was Canada's to fight as an independent nation and not Britain's alone.

Despite the lessons it did learn, government did not learn how to rally the labour movement behind the war; from beginning to end, the government failed to treat labour as an important partner in the war effort. Organized labour was held at arm's length, almost as if the unions were considered an impediment to the war effort, while the business community was made part of the war management team. There was little consultation between the government and labour leaders on measures that directly affected labour, and labour's most reasonable request – for a fair-wage clause in war supply contracts, something it enjoyed on all other federal public works – was not granted. Although organized labour hated the Industrial Disputes Investigation Act and believed it was weighted against them, the government's sole response to labour complaints in the early part of the war was to extend that very act to cover war industries in March 1916. By this time, it was dawning on labour leaders that, although they were trying to co-operate with the government, the government was not co-operating with them.

Borden and his cabinet were not entirely at fault for the growing disaffection of organized labour. Joseph Wesley Flavelle must surely share part of the blame. Flavelle, the Toronto pork-packing magnate who became chairman of the Imperial Munitions Board in late 1915, was a devout Methodist and a rugged individualist who was determined to run the I.M.B. as efficiently as possible with one goal in view – increased munitions production. He bristled at the idea that unions should use the war to climb a few more rungs up the ladder of official recognition or that workers should use the labour shortage to better their economic position. That thousands of businesspeople in Canada were doing just that either did not occur to him or did not bother him. In the final analysis, it was Flavelle who blocked government action on fair-wage clauses in munitions contracts.[4]

In the spring of 1916 workers' growing frustrations finally sparked off

---

[4] Some of the difficulties experienced by organized labour during the war can be found in David J. Bercuson, "Organized Labour and the Imperial Munitions Board," *Industrial Relations/Relations Industrielles* XXVIII (1973); Myer Siemiatycki, "Munitions and Labour Militancy: The 1916 Hamilton Machinists' Strike," *Labour/Le Travailleur* (1978); Michael Bliss, *A Canadian Millionaire: The Life and Business Times of Sir Joseph Flavelle, Bart., 1858-1939* (Toronto, 1978); and Daphne Read, et al., *The Great War and Canadian Society: An Oral History* (Toronto, 1978).

strikes in munitions plants in Toronto and Hamilton. In both cities, the International Association of Machinists had been active organizing munitions workers, and in March and April the I.A.M. presented wage demands to factory owners. Many Toronto plants agreed to the union's demands, but the Canada Foundry Company did not and its workers struck. The plant manager, Colonel Frederick Nichols, responded with a complete lockout and a declaration that he would never submit to organized labour. The I.A.M.'s answer was to threaten a general strike of all Toronto munitions workers. In Hamilton, the employers, all members of the Canadian Manufacturers Association, organized a special committee to oversee labour relations in the city and co-ordinate the campaign to block the I.A.M. Union demands for higher wages and shorter hours were met with accusations that the workers were "in the pay of the Kaiser" and declarations that unions had no right to exist inside the factories.

Faced with a serious disruption in the flow of shells, the federal government intervened to appoint a royal commission under Judge Colin Snyder to examine labour problems in the Toronto and Hamilton war plants. When the commission reported in May, it fully endorsed the demands of the I.A.M., but the Hamilton employers, including such major concerns as the Steel Company of Canada, Canadian Westinghouse, and the National Steel Car Company, refused to implement the royal commission's recommendations. Thus, on June 12, 1916, close to 2000 munitions workers at more than 30 Hamilton war plants went on strike. Although the munitions workers received the moral support of the Toronto machinists, it was not nearly enough to ensure victory. Their own leaders clearly felt somewhat disloyal in countenancing a strike and urged their followers "to act honourably." If they did, they were the only ones who were. The federal government ordered the chief press censor to stop news of the strike from spreading, and the employers brought in strikebreakers. In a little over one month, the strike petered out and the union was defeated.

The strike in Hamilton should have provided a clear warning to the federal government and to Flavelle that war workers were absolutely determined to win significant improvements in their wages and working conditions and were starting to disregard appeals to patriotism. But it did not. There were no bold, new initiatives to improve working conditions or to invite labour into the government's confidence, and there was no change of heart on the part of Flavelle or the country's war industry employers. Things continued as they were, and the unions grew more desperate and more angry.

In the spring of 1917, the Trades and Labour Congress presented a list of complaints to the federal government charging that wages and working conditions were substandard in I.M.B.-controlled war plants from coast to coast. The T.L.C. also accused the I.M.B. of deliberately snubbing union officials and allowing "the unnecessary dilution of labour by the introduction of female labour" and the "substitution of cheap semi-skilled labour . . . because of their willingness to accept less than trade union rates." In other words, employers working on I.M.B. contracts were replacing highly skilled, well-paid workers going off to war with women, immigrants, and labourers from the countryside who, though unskilled, were perfectly able to perform the tasks of assembly-line shell production at much lower wages. The unions naturally feared that this practice would undermine and destroy established wage standards.

Organized labour's attitudes toward women workers was glaringly revealed in this petition. It was plain that the unions preferred shortages of skilled males to develop in war industries, thus driving up wages, to offering war employment to women. This was a direct carryover from the attitudes of prewar days. It is no wonder that the unions were reluctant to attempt to organize women workers until late in the war, even though an increasing number of women were entering heavy industry in munitions and other war-related plants. The unions saw these workers as a temporary aberration, not as a permanent new development. In this the unions echoed the attitude of the federal government, which refused to provide incentives to make industrial labour more attractive to women even in matters as basic as providing separate washrooms for women in I.M.B. factories. It was clear that when Johnny Canuck came marching home, Sally Canuck was going to return to the kitchen.

The T.L.C. warning that workers across Canada were growing more militant went unheeded and Canada paid the price in 1917 when more than 1.1 million working days were lost in work disruptions, an increase of 374 percent over 1916. Almost every industry was affected including shell manufacturing, but the most serious disputes erupted in the coal mines of British Columbia and Alberta. There coal was dug not only to heat homes but to operate the transcontinental railways and to fire the smelters of the British Columbia interior, particularly at Trail, which did considerable business for the Imperial Munitions Board.

Inflation was the direct cause of the troubles in the western coalfields: miners' wages were not keeping up with the increasing cost of living.

From the summer of 1916 until April 1917, a number of short strikes for war bonuses or wage increases broke out, in each case involving from 3000 to 6000 miners. Both the federal government and the international leaders of the miners' union watched these events with growing alarm and intervened to get the men back to work. For several months they managed to maintain a shaky peace, but in April 1917, 7000 miners were locked out in a dispute with the coal operators that touched off a strike/lockout, paralyzing the coalfields for three months. Once again the federal government intervened, this time by appointing a director of coal operations for eastern British Columbia and Alberta. W.H. Armstrong of Vancouver became a virtual czar of the western coal industry. He was given power to determine wages, working conditions, and fuel prices in what was an obvious end to voluntarism in the western coal industry. He quickly ordered the mines reopened, granted an immediate wage increase and, shortly after, established a commission to continually examine the cost of living and to adjust wages every four months in line with inflation.

One of labour's biggest fights in 1917 was against conscription. When the federal government announced a voluntary national registration program in December 1916, the T.L.C. sought assurances from the prime minister that conscription would never be introduced. Borden refused to give such a guarantee, but he did assure T.L.C. president James Watters that this particular program of voluntary registration was not intended as the first step of a new conscription policy. Watters and the congress then mildly endorsed the program, even though some labour leaders, particularly in Western Canada, denounced the congress and urged their followers not to co-operate.

Canadian labour leaders were divided by the war. A minority loudly opposed Canada's participation in it and lost no opportunity to denounce it as a capitalist dance of death. Others publicly endorsed the war and worked to ensure the co-operation of their unions in the war effort, sometimes at the sacrifice of the economic interests of their members. In the spring of 1917, after the United States entered the war, this latter group found a vocal leader and supporter in Samuel Gompers who fervently threw himself behind the United States's war effort and urged his Canadian followers to do the same.

Whatever their views on the war, however, almost all Canadian labour leaders opposed conscription. They feared it might be followed by industrial conscription, as it had in Britain, which would tightly regulate workers' freedom to change jobs or to strike for improvements in wages or working conditions. This would put workers more directly under the thumb of employers and it would greatly undermine the unions' ability to protect their members' interests or to attract new members. Conscription, in other words, was viewed as a grave and direct threat to the viability of the trade union movement and to collective bargaining during wartime.

Western Radicalism

When Borden announced the imminent introduction of conscription in May 1917, the T.L.C., lulled by his earlier assurances on registration, was caught by surprise, and labour responded with a howl of protest. A campaign to take direct action to counter the draft gained momentum through the spring and summer of 1917, with union leaders in Eastern and central Canada urging an electoral campaign, and those in the West advocating a national general strike. At the T.L.C. convention in September 1917, the advocates of political action won out, and a decision was taken to launch a coast-to-coast electoral effort in the forthcoming federal election campaign. This was to be done under the auspices of an umbrella organization known as the Dominion Labour Party, a loose, poorly financed amalgam of socialists, labourites, pacifists, and even, in some cases, Laurier Liberals, who had little in common aside from their opposition to the draft. It was an uphill battle against a government that used the basest appeals to patriotism and that painted its opposition as advocates of the Kaiser's cause. The Dominion Labour Party was certainly not helped by Samuel Gompers, who came to Canada in the fall of 1917 to endorse conscription. Every party candidate was defeated.[5]

The conscription fight not only embittered the labour movement and further soured relations between it and the Borden government but also aggravated the continuing disagreements between the majority of organ-

---

[5] Most attention paid to labour in politics in this period has focused on radical movements such as the Socialist Party of Canada. An exception is Craig Heron, "Labourism and the Canadian Working Class," *Labour/Le Travail*, Spring, 1984, pp. 45-75. For earlier works see Martin Robin, *Radical Politics and Canadian Labour: 1880-1930* (Kingston, 1968); Gad Horowitz, *Canadian Labour in Politics* (Toronto, 1968); Kenneth W. McNaught, *A Prophet in Politics: A Biography of J.S. Woodsworth* (Toronto, 1959); A.R. McCormack, *Reformers, Rebels and Revolutionaries: The Western Canadian Radical Movement, 1899-1919* (Toronto, 1977); and Ian Angus, *Canadian Bolsheviks: The Early Years of the Communist Party of Canada* (Montreal, 1981).

ized workers, who lived in Eastern and central Canada, and those in the West over the policies, direction, and the fundamental nature of the labour movement. Western workers tended to be more radical, more oriented toward industrial unionism and more captivated by dreams of a socialist paradise than those in the East who hewed more closely to Gompers's line. The divisions had been apparent for years prior to the war. There had been occasional flare-ups of secessionist fever in Western Canada whenever workers there judged that the eastern majority at T.L.C. conventions was directly undermining the vital interests of western union members.

Although a generation of Marxist labour historians has tried to prove that workers across Canada were as radical as those in Western Canada – that they were as willing to support the complete overthrow of the capitalist system – the evidence shows a different story. It is certainly true that workers from coast to coast grew more militant as the war dragged on, more willing to strike, more inclined to break laws and challenge the actions of government. They also voted more heavily for labour parties and for working-class candidates. This does *not* mean, however, that they were all equally radical and that they all wanted to destroy capitalism. It does mean that they were highly discontented, that they were angry, and that they wanted changes in the capitalist system, some of them far-reaching according to the standards of the day. Only in the West, however, did parties that espoused the total destruction of capitalism, as opposed to its reform, routinely command the allegiance of large bodies of workers, including major established unions such as the United Mine Workers of America District 18. There, true socialist parties such as the Socialist Party of Canada and the Social Democratic Party of Canada dominated labour politics. That is the true test of radicalism. To prove that workers across Canada struck with equal frequency for higher wages and better working conditions scarcely proves that they were equally dedicated to the overthrow of capitalism or were equally radical. To assert that it does is to misunderstand the nature of radicalism and to confuse radicalism with militancy.

The West's lean toward radicalism is explained by a variety of factors. There were a larger number of immigrants in the West on a per capita basis than anywhere else in Canada, and many of these men and women, particularly those from Great Britain or the United States, had strong labour and socialist backgrounds. Other immigrant groups such as the Finns, Ukrainians, Jews, and Italians, also brought strong leftist traditions. The backbone for many of the West's plethora of socialist parties was provided by a mixture of immigrant radicals, usually headed by British socialists who were, of course, far more articulate in the language of their adopted country.[6]

Working conditions also played a part. The coal and hardrock mines of the West were dangerous places where workers were regularly killed at rates that far surpassed those of mines in other parts of North America. At various times in the years 1900 to 1920, for example, the number of men killed per tonne of coal mined was considerably higher in Alberta and British Columbia than it was in Nova Scotia. Logging and railway construction were little better. Wages were usually higher in the West than elsewhere because the cost of living was higher, a result of more expensive transportation costs on everything from fruit to furniture. It was apparent to many of the industrial workers who had immigrated to Western Canada that there was little immediate chance for them to improve their social or economic station in life. Thus frustrated expectations also played a part in the western workers' growing commitment to radicalism.

The structure of western unions was a contributing factor toward radicalism. The Canadian labour movement was largely constructed in the image of the American Federation of Labor with its craft-union base. There were more than one hundred unions affiliated with the A.F.L. This fragmentation of the labour movement was not so serious in the United States because the A.F.L., at the beginning of the First World War, counted more than two million members; even small unions had enough members to be viable. In Canada, there were fewer unions – 88 reported to the Department of Labour in 1913 – but there were also far fewer members (128 652 in 1913), and many of the craft unions were small and ineffective. This was particularly true in Western Canada, which had only about 40 000 union members in 1913. Many western union leaders concluded that their bargaining strength was seriously eroded by the craft-union structure and favoured industrial unions, which would combine smaller unions into larger ones with more members and more strength. Industrial unionism was bitterly opposed by American and central Canadian union leaders who supported the policies of Samuel

---

[6] Several works describe aspects of immigrant radicalism including Donald Avery, *"Dangerous Foreigners": European Immigrant Workers and Labour Radicalism in Canada, 1896-1932* (Toronto, 1979) and *Canadian Ethnic Studies* No. 2 (1978), which devotes an entire issue to immigrant radicalism. See also Ivan Avakumovic, *The Communist Party in Canada: A History* (Toronto, 1975) and William Rodney, *Soldiers of the International: A History of the Communist Party of Canada, 1919-1929* (Toronto, 1968).

Mining, as these British Columbia workers knew all too well, was very dangerous. Safety standards did not exist, explosives were unstable, and the mine owners fiercely protected their rights and privileges.

BRITISH COLUMBIA ARCHIVES AND RECORDS SERVICE (BCARS) HP761.

Gompers. Radical labour organizations such as the I.W.W. and the United Brotherhood of Railway Employees, which stood outside the A.F.L., adopted the industrial union model.

The West's growing militancy and radicalism became obvious in the spring and summer of 1918. In April of that year several groups of employees of the City of Winnipeg approached the municipal government to demand wage increases. The city administration refused and offered them a war bonus to tide them over until peacetime, when a new schedule of wages could be negotiated. The unions rejected the proposal and called their members out on strike on May 7. The city government, backed by the press and the business community, took a hard line and threatened to remove its employees' right to strike. The Winnipeg Trades and Labour Council also took a hard line and called upon its member unions to support the strikers. Workers all over the city, in public service and private business, began to strike in sympathy with the civic workers, and the civic strike spread into a general strike. After three weeks the federal government intervened out of fear that Winnipeg, which was a key rail junction and the commercial centre for all of Western Canada, would be paralyzed. Senator Gideon Robertson, a vice-president of the Order of Railway Telegraphers (and described by Flavelle as a "sane, wise, labour leader"), was sent to Winnipeg by the prime minister to settle the dispute. A staunch Conservative who subscribed to the basic principles of Samuel Gompers even though his union was not affiliated with the A.F.L., Robertson especially opposed strikes during wartime, but within three days of his arrival, he hammered out an agreement that represented a substantial victory for the unions in both increased wages and the confirmation of their right to collective bargaining.

Robertson had been largely responsible for the shape of the settlement, but it was the sympathetic strike that had given labour the power to force its demands upon the city. The lesson was not lost on labour radicals in Winnipeg and elsewhere who declared that the power of individual unions acting alone to "enforce their economic demands" was slipping away as the "master class" united. The answer had now been demonstrated in the form of the general strike. Industrial unionism was also given a boost because of the belief that such unions were better organized to call general strikes. Militancy appeared to pay off in Winnipeg and just a few weeks later in West Coast shipyards as well. In May, 5000 shipyard workers employed by firms engaged in work for the Imperial Munitions Board went on strike for union recognition and higher wages despite appeals to their patriotic duty. The workers were accused of disloyalty, and pressures upon them from press and politicians alike mounted. However, they stayed united and continued to support their leadership until Robertson arrived to bring an end to the strike. Although the unions did not score as clearcut a victory as the civic workers had done in Winnipeg, they made obvious gains and appeared well satisfied with the final settlement.

The strikes in Winnipeg and on the West Coast had been localized, but another dispute was brewing in the spring and summer of 1918 that had the potential of seriously threatening, if not paralyzing, the entire Canadian war effort from east to west. It began in late April 1918, when unions representing 50 000 shop-craft workers on all the major railways began negotiations for a new wage agreement with the Canadian Railway War Board. The board had been formed by the major railways to promote more efficient rail transportation during the war. The shop-craft workers, who repaired and maintained the trains, had joined their different craft unions together in a bargaining federation known as Division 4 of the Railway Employees Department of the American Federation of Labor and had armed their representatives with a strike vote. When negotiations opened, the workers demanded substantial wage increases: these were promptly rejected by the railways, which claimed they could not increase pay because the government would not allow them to raise freight rates during the war. As negotiations dragged on and the prospect of failure loomed, the federal government granted the railways higher freight rates and they, in turn, increased their wage offer to match those paid for the same work by railways in the United States. The new wages were a significant improvement over the old, but the unions were still not satisfied and threatened to strike.

The federal government was determined to prevent the unions from acting. Although a shop-craft strike would not immediately shut down rail service – engineers, firemen, and other running trades workers would still operate the trains – it would soon come to a complete standstill because maintenance and repair work could not be done. Nothing would move in Canada, and the economy, not to mention the war effort, would be stopped. A strike was out of the question, and the government announced that it would conscript the shop-craft workers and force them to work on army pay if they should walk out. At the same time, the U.S. leaders of the shop-craft unions threatened to suspend or revoke the charters of union locals that quit work. At the negotiating table in Montreal, the Division 4 negotiators split; the eastern and central Canadian representatives voted to accept the new wage rates, while the westerners walked out of the negotiations in disgust. They attacked the "weak-kneed" retreat of their eastern brothers even though they had gained wage parity with the United States for the first time. That victory had come, once again, from union militancy.

Both the growing East-West split and the tendency of workers to believe that militant action would invariably produce good results were reinforced by a national letter carriers' strike in July. These workers had been trying, since 1917, to win wage increases from the government to match increases in the cost of living. When all else failed, the union called a strike and stopped postal service throughout Canada. After a few days, the federal government issued a vague promise to investigate the postal workers' grievances, and the predominantly eastern leadership of the union ordered its members back to work. Some complied, but the western members did not, staying off the job until the government announced that the Civil Service Commission would examine their grievances and promised them full pay for the time they had been on strike.

The growing labour unrest prompted Labour Minister T.W. Crothers, probably in conjunction with Gideon Robertson, to design a new war-labour policy that was proclaimed to the nation in early July. It was, in many respects, an enlightened policy that represented a clear advance over the thinking of men such as J.W. Flavelle. It urged a number of principles and policies on workers and their employers, including a ban on work stoppages during the war, a recognition of the right of employees to organize trade unions without interference from their employers, and the right to "negotiate with employers concerning working conditions, rates of pay, or other grievances." Crothers's plan also suggested that workers had the right to a decent wage, reasonable hours of work, and safe and healthy working conditions. Women employed at jobs ordinarily performed by men should receive "equal pay for equal work." To ensure peace in industry, workers and their employers were asked to use the machinery of the Industrial Disputes Investigation Act and a new Board of Appeal, composed of two representatives of organized labour, two representatives of the employers, and a neutral chairman. The board would decide appeals against the findings of the conciliation boards normally established under the I.D.I.A.

This policy might have gone far toward restoring labour peace in Canada, but it was flawed in one major respect: it was, in the words of Senator Robertson, "permissive rather than compulsory as no penalty is provided for failure to comply." This meant that it was voluntary; unions and employers were free to follow it or disregard it at will, and, in the increasingly poisoned atmosphere of 1918, it was practically useless. One official of the Imperial Munitions Board considered it "spineless cowardice and double-faced action." Even though the government had learned by the summer of 1918 that voluntarism did not work, it was too timid (or too conservative) to force collective bargaining on Canadian employers.

Despite the noncompulsory nature of the policy, trade unionists throughout Canada took it as a sign that the government was planning to impose a complete ban on strikes. Thus the policy accomplished virtually nothing positive and actually stimulated further labour unrest. Workers in Vancouver, for example, did not hesitate to conduct a short general strike in August to protest the killing – allegedly by accident – of labour leader and draft evader Albert "Ginger" Goodwin in the woods near Comox by a Dominion policeman. (The Dominion Police later merged with the Royal Canadian Mounted Police.) Many of their leaders, and others from the West, were determined to force drastic changes in the policies and practices of the T.L.C. when it met in its annual convention at Quebec City in September 1918.

The T.L.C. convention became a battleground between East and West. While the congress leadership was busy congratulating itself for the new spirit of co-operation it had forged with the federal government, radicals, led by western delegates, issued a scathing condemnation of the executive's relations with Ottawa and brought forward a long list of resolutions calling for a restructuring of the congress and a redrafting of its policies. Every one of the resolutions, from those condemning the jailing of opponents of the war to those seeking the transformation of the congress into an industrial union, were defeated. To add insult to injury, congress president J.C. Watters, from British Columbia, was defeated in his bid for re-election by Thomas Moore, a Niagara Falls carpenter and a faithful follower of Samuel Gompers.

The westerners were badly outnumbered at the Quebec City convention – they had 45 delegates out of more than 400 – and needed a new strategy. A caucus chaired by Dave Rees, a British Columbia official of the United Mine Workers, decided to organize a meeting of western delegates prior to the next T.L.C. convention to co-ordinate strategy and exchange views on policy and tactics. A committee was formed, chaired by Rees and Vancouver Trades Council secretary Victor Midgley, to handle correspondence and organize the meeting. The caucus claimed that this was not intended to be a first step toward secession of western unions from the T.L.C. and the A.F.L.

Since the new War Labour Policy announced in July did little to stem the growing labour unrest, the federal government decided to take further action. Montreal lawyer C.H. Cahan was appointed director of public safety in the Department of Justice with a mandate to bring radicalism to heel. Cahan quickly concluded that radical and alien influences were behind the growing labour unrest and recommended strong measures to crush what he thought of as incipient revolution. In September 1918, in response to his recommendations, the cabinet issued orders-in-council that prohibited the public use of "enemy alien" languages and banned ethnic associations, unions, and political parties, including the I.W.W. and the Social Democratic Party, both of which contained many immigrant members. Two weeks later, another order-in-council was issued banning strikes and setting heavy penalties, including fines and imprisonment, for its violation. The government also proclaimed that anyone violating the order would be immediately drafted and made subject to military law for the duration of the war.

Organized labour reacted angrily to the orders-in-council; even T.L.C. president Moore cautioned the government against taking labour for granted. But his reproaches were nothing compared to those of western union leaders who pledged to defy the strike ban. In fact, a strike of freight handlers in Calgary broke out five days after the ban was declared, and, when several of the strikers were arrested for breaking the law, trades councils across the West began to poll their members on the question of whether or not to call a general strike to back the arrested men. However, before this strike was called, the court inexplicably released the strikers without imposing either fines or imprisonment. The ban on strikes increased the atmosphere of hate and recrimination and accomplished nothing. The strike ban was rescinded shortly after the fighting in Europe ended on November 11.

The Red Scare

The months following the armistice brought no relief from the rising cost of living, even though war production came to a quick halt. To make matters worse for Canadian workers, returned soldiers began to enter the job market in the winter of 1918/19, causing an increase in unemployment and spurring fears that the prewar depression was returning. At the same time, many employers embarked on a drive to erase labour's hard-won gains in increased wages and improved working conditions and roll matters back to the "bad old days." The working class had given its all to win the war in the plants and factories and at the battle front in the belief that the end of the war would bring an era of social justice and popular democracy. Their political leaders had spurred them to great endeavour with pledges to build a "new Jerusalem" after the "holocaust of blood." Instead of a new Jerusalem, there was a rising cost of living, increasing unemployment, and no significant changes in the social or economic status quo. The working class had been shortchanged.

For many returned soldiers, there was only bitterness and despair. Politicians and the press initially showered the heroes of Vimy, Passchendaele, and Mons with praise and adulation, but old jobs were usually already filled, and new ones were hard to come by. The Department of Soldiers' Civil Re-establishment urged private employers to hire veterans, and the government gave them preference in filling civil service vacancies, but this produced little steady work over the hard winter of 1918/19. The government also set up a limited pension plan for disabled veterans but refused veterans' demands for a cash bonus based on length of service. They feared such bonuses would induce the "pension evil" – laziness among veterans who would come to rely on such bonuses instead of working. Hospitals were built and homesteads were offered, but these measures served the needs of only a few.

Disappointed and bitter, many veterans took matters into their own hands and roamed the streets of Canadian cities attacking people who looked like aliens and tried to force employers to fire immigrant workers to create job vacancies. In several parts of Canada, veterans vented their anger on those who had opposed the war and conscription. But many of these same veterans drifted toward the socialists in a search for leadership and a desire for social change. No less a figure than A. Bowen Perry, the commissioner of the Royal North-West Mounted Police, worried that veterans would begin to support revolutionary movements and urged the cabinet to resolve veterans' grievances quickly and with sympathy and consideration.

Perry and other government officials were worried about both domestic and foreign radical influence. Even though no evidence has ever been unearthed to confirm that foreign agents were attempting to foment revolution in Canada in early 1919, Perry and others thought that Canadian workers might be inspired by the example of revolutionary movements abroad. All over the world in the closing months of the war and in the immediate postwar period, the news was dominated by revolutions, attempted revolutions, general strikes, and worker uprisings.

This news strengthened a growing fear among many Canadians that was rooted in the belief that revolutionaries were capable of monstrous deeds. During the war, Allied governments had orchestrated a propaganda campaign aimed to convince their populations that Germans were violating every code of decent human conduct. The Kaiser's troops were accused of raping, murdering, and plundering their way across Europe committing unspeakable crimes from bayoneting babies to raping nuns. When Lenin and the Bolsheviks came to power in Russia in 1917, these same governments, followed by the press and many religious groups, tarred him and his regime with the same brush. After all, he had been helped by the Germans because they knew that if he were successful he would end the war on the eastern front, freeing German troops to face the Allies in the West. The Bolsheviks, therefore, were placed in the same camp as the Germans and accused of the same crimes. When the war ended, the abdication of the Kaiser removed him as an immediate object of hatred, but Lenin remained; as country after country seemed to explode in Bolshevik-inspired revolutionary violence, many people in Canada and the United States panicked and concluded that the tide of revolution was about to sweep North America. Thus was born the Red Scare.

The committee appointed by the western delegates at the T.L.C. convention of 1918 began its work against this backdrop. Headed by Dave Rees and Victor Midgley, they set to work contacting trades councils and union locals across the West to line up support for the western caucus, but their task was complicated by the growing radicalism among western workers. Many western union members had concluded that T.L.C. reform was a lost cause and began to think of seceding from the congress prior to setting up a new revolutionary union organized along industrial lines. These workers were led by members of the Socialist Party of Canada, including fiery radicals such as Robert Boyd Russell, a Scottish-born machinist who headed the S.P.C. in Winnipeg and who was a power to be reckoned with among western shop-craft workers. Russell and his colleagues in the United Mine Workers and in the Alberta and British Columbia Federations of Labour worked behind the scenes to ensure the triumph of a radical platform at the forthcoming caucus. They eventually succeeded in having the very notion of a caucus set aside in favour of a full conference of western trade union representatives, and any others who wished to attend from the rest of Canada, to be held in Calgary in March 1919.[7]

The General Strike

The Western Labour Conference that met on March 13, 1919, was one of the most radical labour conventions in Canadian history. Most of the

---

[7] No book on the Red Scare itself has yet appeared in Canada, but a good survey of this phenomenon in the United States is Robert K. Murray, *Red Scare: A Study in National Hysteria, 1919-1920* (New York, 1964). There is a chapter on the Red Scare in Canada in

delegates were fired by the rising tide of radical and revolutionary movements around the world and loudly proclaimed their belief that a new workers' paradise was at hand. They passed resolutions against political lobbying and in favour of the abolition of capitalism, secession from the T.L.C. and the A.F.L., and the formation of a new industrial union to be named the One Big Union, or O.B.U. The O.B.U. would organize all workers into one union that would be able to call general strikes to enforce workers' demands. The conference decided to hold two referenda, one on the question of conducting a general strike to back demands for a national 30-hour work week and the other to determine if Canadian workers favoured secession from the T.L.C. and the establishment of the O.B.U. The meeting also proclaimed its support for various European revolutionary movements, including Lenin's Bolshevik regime, and condemned the Borden government. When the conference broke up, the work of conducting the votes on the general strike and secession began.

The Western Labour Conference further fueled the Red Scare. Following the Calgary meeting, politicians, newspapers, and church leaders alike rallied Canadians against the forces of radicalism and revolution. Newspaper headlines proclaimed "Red Bolshevism Declares War On World At Large," while government reports warned that Bolsheviks might use new and secret weapons to cause blindness in their campaign for world domination. The Bolsheviks in Russia were accused of "nationalizing" women to provide sexual services for Red soldiers and of destroying the foundations of civilization. Nothing was too evil to pin on the Reds.

Although some members of the federal government were all too ready to take part in the anti-Red hysteria and to blame labour unrest on bolshevism, others took a more moderate approach. They were well aware that labour-management relations had taken a new turn since the start of the war and that the growth of unionism and the increased sophistication and strength of industrial capitalism were creating greater antagonism between labour and capital. The task, as they saw it, was to create a new system of industrial co-operation between workers and their bosses that would make confrontation obsolete and increase productivity while bringing peace to the workplace. A middle ground was needed before it was too late.

David J. Bercuson, *Fools and Wise Men: The Rise and Fall of the One Big Union* (Toronto, 1978), while other accounts can be found in Robin, *Radical Politics and Canadian Labour* and McCormack, *Reformers, Rebels and Revolutionaries.*

The search began with the appointment in mid-April of the Royal Commission to Enquire into Industrial Relations in Canada, headed by Chief Justice Mathers of Manitoba. The commission began its hearing in Victoria, B.C., on April 26 and completed its work in Ottawa on June 13, hearing 486 witnesses in 28 communities. Many labour radicals chose to ignore the commission, especially in Western Canada, but other trade unionists, as well as employers and consumer groups, appeared or sent representatives. It was apparent from the hearings that the labour movement was in the throes of a re-examination of its traditional approaches to industrial relations and that it had many complaints about living costs, working conditions, and, perhaps most significant of all, the tremendous difficulties unions encountered in winning recognition from employers. The employers, for the most part, claimed the right to operate their plants and shops without interference from organized labour, and it was clear that many of their attitudes had changed little from the early days of industrialization and laissez faire in Canada.

When the commission issued its report in mid-June, it confirmed the widespread labour unrest in the country, especially in Western Canada, but it insisted, nevertheless, that the majority of workers and owners in Canada were interested in a middle way. That direction was outlined in the commission's recommendations, which included a sweeping program of social welfare reforms such as minimum wage and maximum hours laws, state insurance against unemployment, sickness, disability, and old age, and the legalization of collective bargaining. To bring peace to the workplace, the commission recommended a system of joint plant and industrial councils, composed of representatives chosen by management and labour, to determine wages and working conditions, to settle grievances, and generally to regulate labour-management relations in the shop. Such councils already existed in Great Britain, where they were known as Whitley Councils, and in the United States, where they were generally patterned after the industrial representation plan of the Colorado Fuel and Iron Company. (This latter scheme had been established in 1914 by the former minister of labour, William Lyon Mackenzie King, while he was acting as a private consultant for the Rockefeller Foundation.) These recommendations were supposed to serve as the basis for a National Industrial Conference held in Ottawa in September. Called by the federal government, the conference was attended by representatives of labour, employers, and the general public. It was a complete failure, largely because the bitterness between the unions and the bosses was, at that point, too great to overcome, especially against the backdrop of the summer of strikes that had just preceded it.

The first and the most important of those strikes broke out in Winnipeg on May 15, 1919. There, trouble between labour and many local manufacturers and employers had been brewing for years. Winnipeg's spectacular growth since the 1880s had been based on the grain trade, the railways, and agricultural service industries. A vigorous group of business people worked hard for decades to make Winnipeg the Chicago of Western Canada. Only the unions seemed to stand in their way. Those unions derived most of their support from the thousands of railway workers who settled in Winnipeg after the 1890s to work in the city's repair shops, round houses, and marshalling yards. They were led mostly by British immigrants, veterans of the labour and socialist movements in their native land. They were determined to win a share of the power, influence, and wealth of the city and soon challenged the bosses and their allies in city government. Industrial unrest marked by violence was evident as far back as a street railway strike in 1906 when troops were called out to maintain order in downtown Winnipeg. Labour's wartime grievances increased the unrest among Winnipeg's workers and led to the growth of militancy and radicalism. By the spring of 1919 the city was polarized into two camps and ready for a major confrontation.

It came following two strikes; one in the metal trades over union recognition, which began May 2, the other in the building trades over higher wages, which started one day earlier. The striking workers approached the Winnipeg Trades and Labour Council for help, and the council responded by polling its members to see if they favoured a general strike. The membership was overwhelmingly in favour, and the strike began May 15. Within days every union local in the city was on strike, and private businesses, municipal offices, and even federal government services such as mail delivery were paralyzed. Only the city police stayed on the job. The Strike Committee, organized to run the strike by the Trades and Labour Council, had asked them to remain at work and maintain law and order to forestall government intervention. The Strike Committee was composed of radicals such as R.B. Russell and moderates like Ernie Robinson, a faithful craft unionist who had been secretary of the Winnipeg Trades and Labour Council for many years.

Almost from the beginning, the strike was opposed by the federal government, represented by Senator Gideon Robertson, now minister of labour, and by the acting justice minister, Arthur Meighen, both of whom proclaimed that the strikers had no legitimate cause for the walkout but were aiming to build up the One Big Union, destroy craft unionism, and, at bottom, foment revolution. Robertson and Meighen were joined in this view by the Citizens' Committee of One Thousand, a body composed of business and industrial leaders and supported by Winnipeg's upper crust.

The Citizens' Committee co-operated with the militia, the federal, municipal, and provincial governments, and the employers and co-ordinated strike-breaking activities. On the strikers' side, the walkout was supported by close to 20 000 nonunion workers, many of whom were recent immigrants, who finally had a chance to vent the anger that had been building for years. It appears as if the general strike made Winnipeg a divided city, but in reality it had been divided for a long time, and the strike merely demonstrated this.

A city cannot live without essential services. Shortly after the strike began, the Strike Committee, meeting with the Citizens' Committee and the city government, devised a plan to allow essential services to operate. Placards were printed up that proclaimed that essential services, such as milk and bread delivery, were "permitted by order of Strike Committee," thus informing striking workers that the services were not being run by strike-breakers. The wording was an error; the placards gave the impression that the Strike Committee was running Winnipeg instead of the legally constituted city government. This confirmed fears in some quarters that Act I of the Canadian Bolshevik revolution was being played out at the junction of the Red and Assiniboine rivers.

As the strike began, the Twenty-seventh Battalion of the C.E.F., recruited in Winnipeg, arrived home from Europe and was demobilized. This added to the thousands of returned soldiers who were already roaming the streets of the city seeking work. The veterans began to involve themselves in the strike: a minority, generally from the upper class of the city, opposed it and a majority, many former trade unionists among them, supported it. The pro-strike veterans were an especially active lot and soon began to parade in the streets of Winnipeg to show their support for the strike. The strike leaders did not want this – they begged their followers to sit tight, be quiet, and not provoke the authorities – but they had no control over the veterans. Once the pro-strike veterans began to parade, the anti-strike veterans took to the streets also. After a clash between the two groups was narrowly averted, Winnipeg's mayor, Charles F. Gray, issued a proclamation banning all public demonstrations.

Gray was different from most Winnipeg mayors before him in that he was not a wealthy member of the business establishment but a career engineer. He was a moderate, mild man who generally favoured liberal and progressive solutions to social problems and, like most progressives, had avoided taking sides during the growing confrontation between capital and labour that preceded the strike. He tried to stay neutral immediately after the walkout began, but the strike appeared to challenge his authority and that of the constituted city government, and this led him toward the employers' camp. As the strike dragged on, that lean became more pronounced until he completely supported the Citizens' Committee.

Gray's first ban on public demonstrations restored order for a time but was defied on June 10 when a minor riot erupted between strike supporters and a band of Special Police in the centre of downtown

These mounted police were dispersing a crowd on Portage Avenue in Winnipeg.

C-26782/NATIONAL ARCHIVES OF CANADA.

Winnipeg. The Special Police had been recruited by the Citizens' Committee in conjunction with the city council, mostly from students and returned soldiers, at the suggestion of Major General H.D.B. Ketchen, commanding officer of Military District 10. Strike opponents had feared that the regular city police would not enforce the law against strikers because they themselves were union members and had, indeed, voted to go on strike. At one point, city council ordered them to break their ties with the union or be dismissed, but the ultimatum could not be enforced because doing so would leave Winnipeg without a police force. The Special Police were then recruited to replace them and were given clubs and white arm bands for identification. A small mounted contingent was also set up, equipped with draft horses donated by the T. Eaton Company. When there was a sufficiently large force of Specials, the regular police were again told to quit their union, and when many refused, they were fired. The Specials took over the responsibility for keeping order in Winnipeg, but they had no training, and, when the mounted contingent tried to clear a small crowd from the sidewalk on the afternoon of June 10, fighting broke out and they were routed. Gray then issued his second ban on public demonstrations, the mounted contingent was disbanded, and the city agreed to keep the Specials as inconspicuous as possible to avoid provoking more trouble.

Although the Citizens' Committee was a formidable opponent, the federal government was far more powerful, and it threw its full weight against the strikers. Meighen and Robertson intervened from the beginning by ordering postal workers back to their jobs and then firing them when they refused to return within 48 hours. Robertson and Meighen also orchestrated the build-up of militia and police forces in the city and worked in conjunction with the minister of immigration to ram an amendment through Parliament in less than half a day, giving the government power to deport British subjects suspected of revolutionary activities. In the fifth week of the strike, the government arrested Russell and several other radical strike leaders in the hope that the moderates who remained in charge of the Strike Committee would end the strike on a conciliatory note. These arrests, and the return of Winnipeg's streetcars to the streets, led to the events of Bloody Saturday and the collapse of the strike.

On Friday evening, June 20, an angry crowd of strikers and pro-strike veterans gathered in Market Square, near City Hall. Speaker after speaker reviewed the events of the preceding days, demanded that the veterans be allowed to meet in the Industrial Bureau's exposition building, and called for an end to streetcar service within 48 hours. The crowd then decided to parade to the Royal Alexandra Hotel the next afternoon to listen to Senator Robertson address them. They were in an ugly mood. The strike had dragged on for almost six weeks with no break and no sign of a settlement. Savings had long since disappeared, cupboards were bare, nerves were frayed. Now popular strike leaders had been arrested, and the streetcars had returned to service, a highly visible symbol of the weakening resolve of some strikers and the growing strength of the city and the employers. Had this long, hot spring been wasted? The crowd was determined that it had not, and it would demonstrate in defiance of Mayor Gray's ban. The mayor, backed by Robertson, the Royal North-West Mounted Police, and the militia were equally determined to stop them.

The next morning, Gray, Robertson, and representatives of the Citizens' Committee and the R.N.W.M.P. met a delegation of pro-strike veterans to hear a recapitulation of the demands that had been voiced at Market Square the previous evening. Gray stood firm and told the veterans that he would stop the demonstration "peacefully if possible," but if not, "other measures would have to be taken." The militia and police were alerted. When several men attacked a southbound streetcar on Main Street, Bloody Saturday moved to its inexorable and violent climax. When the shooting and rioting were over, the strikers' determination collapsed completely, and the walkout was called off in return for a promise from the provincial government to appoint a royal commission to examine the causes of the strike.

The Winnipeg General Strike had been the product both of local conditions, rooted in the history of the city's development, and of national unrest growing out of wartime circumstances. It provided a focus for Canadian labour unrest in the summer of 1919, but it was also the cause of much unrest. From coast to coast workers were released from the restraints that patriotism had imposed during wartime and revolted against government repression, the high cost of living, and the general condition of powerlessness of the working class. Over three million worker days of labour were lost in more than 420 strikes, the greatest number in relation to the size of the workforce in Canadian history.

The causes of these strikes were many and varied. In May and June, for example, workers in many urban centres, especially in the West, struck in sympathy with their brothers and sisters in Winnipeg. Some of these sympathy strikes – those in Calgary, Edmonton, and Vancouver are the best examples – were organized by leaders of the One Big Union and quickly collapsed because they did not arise out of local conditions. But most strikes were not sympathy strikes; they were rooted in battles over basic issues such as wages and union recognition. Whatever their causes, few of these strikes were successful and those that were politically motivated were abysmal failures.[8]

The O.B.U.

The One Big Union had played no role in the Winnipeg General Strike despite the accusations of Senator Robertson, Arthur Meighen, and the Citizens' Committee. In fact, the O.B.U. was born rather quietly in Calgary during the third week of the strike when a handful of O.B.U. representatives met to write a constitution and proclaim the establishment of their new union. The referendum ordered by the Western Labour Conference in March had demonstrated overwhelming support for creation of the O.B.U. in Western Canada, and the decision was consequently made to go ahead with the founding of the new organization despite the strike in Winnipeg.

The One Big Union grew rapidly in the following months, reaching a peak of perhaps 70 000 members, concentrated mostly in the West, but with several thousand in Montreal, Northern Ontario, Nova Scotia, Chicago, San Francisco, and the state of Washington. The leaders of the O.B.U. were dynamic, dedicated, and hard-working, and they had earned the respect of trade union members throughout the West because of their long and active involvement in the unions and in socialist political parties. In Vancouver Victor Midgley, O.B.U. executive secretary, was a lathe operator by trade who had supported socialism and industrial unionism since 1911. He was helped by William A. Pritchard, a fiery Socialist Party of Canada member who had arrived in Canada in 1911 to

---

[8] There is much on the Winnipeg General Strike. Norman Penner (ed.), *Winnipeg: 1919, The Strikers Own History of the Winnipeg General Strike* (Toronto, 1973) is a reprint of a book first published by the strikers just after the event. An early scholarly treatment was D.C. Masters, *The Winnipeg General Strike* (Toronto, 1950). A later treatment is David J. Bercuson, *Confrontation at Winnipeg: Labour, Industrial Relations and the General Strike* (Montreal, 1974). Religion's role in the strike and the social gospel movement is found in Richard Allen, *The Social Passion: Religion and Social Reform in Canada, 1914-1928* (Toronto, 1971). A Marxist view of the labour revolt of 1919 is presented by G.S. Kealey in "1919: The Canadian Labour Revolt," *Labour/Le Travail* (Spring, 1984).

become one of the S.P.C.'s star attractions on the West Coast. Pritchard pushed the O.B.U. cause as far south as Seattle and as far east as Winnipeg. In Edmonton Carl Berg, a Swedish-born immigrant who had worked at everything from fruit picking to railway construction, carried the O.B.U. banner along with Joe and Sarah Knight. In Winnipeg R.B. Russell, the perennial radical, led the O.B.U. forces – after being released from his jail cell in Stony Mountain Penitentiary in December 1920.

These people were not short on ability, drive, or intelligence but neither were they united in their goals and aspirations. This proved to be fatal for the One Big Union. Its demise was as rapid as its meteoric climb; by the end of 1922 there were 5000 members left in the entire country and most of these were in Winnipeg. The leaders of the O.B.U. could not agree on the kind of union they wanted or on basic issues of strategy and tactics. Some wanted true industrial unionism, others wanted revolutionary syndicalism; some wanted the union to support political action, others were opposed to it; some wanted all members to be members of the O.B.U. only, others wanted members to adhere to the O.B.U. through separate industrial unions such as the loggers union. The problems of internal disunity were made worse by attacks upon the O.B.U. from employers and governments, usually in league with each other and sometimes in league with the craft unions. In Alberta and eastern British Columbia, for example, the government was best man at the marriage of the coal operators and the United Mine Workers to keep the O.B.U. out of the coal fields. In the days before collective bargaining laws, it was perfectly legal for any employer to bargain with a craft union and ignore the O.B.U., even if a small minority of his workers supported the craft union and a heavy majority were O.B.U. members. Finally, after Winnipeg and other sympathetic and general strikes that swept across Canada in the spring and summer of 1919, workers had little strength and few financial reserves left to use in a strike for recognition of the O.B.U. Since the workers received little direction from the O.B.U. and gained little from it, they soon deserted it, bringing about its virtual collapse.

The 1919 strikes may have brought few tangible rewards and many crushing defeats to Canadian workers, but they increased the labour movement's awareness of the need to elect labour representatives to all levels of government. In almost every province in Canada, labour representatives contested elections and scored greater successes than ever before in their history. In the 1919 Ontario election, eleven Independent Labour Party members were elected to form a coalition government with the 44 members of the United Farmers of Ontario. In the following year, eleven labour members were elected to the Manitoba legislature, including three – William Ivens, John Queen, and George Armstrong – who were serving jail sentences after having been arrested during the Winnipeg General Strike. In other provincial elections held that year, four labour members were elected to the Nova Scotia legislature, three in British Columbia, and two in New Brunswick. In 1921 four were elected in Alberta and one in Saskatchewan. And in the federal election held in December 1921, one labour man who had been connected with the Winnipeg General Strike, James Shaver Woodsworth, was elected to represent the constituency covering the working-class districts of North Winnipeg.

Labour's political offensive marked a new class awareness for workers across the country, but it did little to stall an employers' counter-offensive that was mounted toward the end of 1919. Spearheaded by groups such as the Canadian Manufacturers Association, the Canadian Reconstruction Association, and local employers' associations, management set out to roll back the gains that unions had won during the war in increased wages, better working conditions, and union recognition. Many employers' associations insisted their members sign pledges that bound employers to each other in establishing a common front against trade unions in their districts. Employers were aided in their campaign by a labour disunity that pitted craft unions against the O.B.U. and Catholic unions in Quebec against craft unions. All across Canada wages were cut, particularly in the mining and transportation industries; unemployment increased, and trade union membership, which had reached a peak of 378 000 in 1919, began to decline until it dropped to 260 000 by 1924, a loss of more than 30 percent. Employers also resorted to the increased use of joint plant councils or industrial councils along the lines of those earlier designed by Mackenzie King. The anti-union campaign was ironically aided by the depression that began to grip the Canadian economy in the fall of 1920: it was the most severe economic downturn since 1913. Although many businesses suffered drastically while the depression ran its course until 1922-23, business-people were able to take advantage of growing unemployment and falling prices to undermine union membership and cut wages.

In Quebec the employers' counter-offensive was given a tremendous boost by the founding of the Canadian and Catholic Confederation of Labour in December 1920. This was a highly centralized federation of Catholic unions that had been growing in the province since the turn of the century. The unions were based on the ideas of social Catholicism first enunciated by Pope Leo XIII in the papal encyclical *Rerum Novarum* toward the end of the nineteenth century, which exhorted Catholics to strive for social justice within a general framework of Catholic humanism. Catholics were warned not to forget that social harmony and Christian brotherhood, even between employers and workers, was more important than economic gain. Thus the Catholic union movement put protection of the Catholic ideals of its members ahead of economic advancement and condemned the use of strikes or other direct action methods. In Quebec the unions were largely led by priests who negotiated with the employers, kept the books, and guided the union in

Working conditions continued to be unsafe in many trades. These workers, rebuilding a stretch of the Rideau Canal locks north of Kingston, Ontario, in the early 1920s, stood a good chance of being hurt on the job.

MR. AND MRS. PERCY HITCHCOCK COLLECTION.

setting out strategy and tactics. The Catholic unions attacked the materialism of the craft unions and considered them little better than Communists. And although the craft unions continued to hold the allegiance of the better educated and more highly skilled Quebec workers, particularly in the construction trades, the Catholic unions were a direct threat, especially when employers, for obvious reasons, preferred to deal with them rather than with the strike-oriented craft unions.

In the Atlantic provinces, the employer counter-offensive was most acutely felt by the miners in the Cape Breton coalfields. There the British Empire Steel Corporation, a holding company founded in 1920 by Montreal entrepreneur Roy Wolvin, aimed to improve its market position by increasing efficiency of its mines and steel mills and by cutting worker wages. It was bitterly opposed by the United Mine Workers, which, by 1917, had emerged from its earlier battles with the Provincial Workingmen's Association to dominate unionism in the coalfields. The U.M.W. was led by J.B. McLachlan, who had emigrated to Nova Scotia from his native Scotland in 1902. A fiery radical, he had been elected secretary-treasurer of District 26 of the U.M.W. in 1909. When Wolvin attempted to push through the first of a series of wage cuts in 1921, his actions sparked a bitter labour war that was still raging five years later. At various points during that half decade, McLachlan was jailed, the union was put under the trusteeship of U.M.W. headquarters in the United States, and federal troops were dispatched to the coalfields both to keep the peace and to help break the workers' resolve. When the labour war ended, workers' wages had been drastically eroded and BESCO was in deep financial difficulty.[9]

The Condition of Labour, 1920

By the end of the Borden era, it must have been obvious to many workers across Canada that the struggles and trials of the war period had brought

---

[9] On the Nova Scotia coal industry and the development of militancy among the miners, read David Frank, "The Cape Breton Coal Industry and the Rise and Fall of the British Empire Steel Corporation," *Acadiensis* (Autumn, 1977) and Donald Macleod, "Colliers, Colliery Safety and Workplace Control: The Nova Scotian Experience, 1873 to 1910," *Historical papers/Communications historiques* (1983). An overview is presented in Paul MacEwan, *Miners and Steelworkers* (Toronto, 1976). Some background to the development of the Catholic labour movement in Canada is in Babcock, *Gompers in Canada*. A recent study of early Catholic unionism is Jacques Rouillard, *Les Syndicats Nationaux au Québec de 1900 à 1930* (Québec, 1979). The memoir of an important Catholic union leader is Alfred Charpentier, *Ma conversion au syndicalisme catholique* (Montréal, 1946).

TABLE 1

NUMBER OF HOURS OF WORK NEEDED TO PAY FOR BASIC COMMODITIES IN HAMILTON: 1911 and 1920

| | Hours of Work to Buy | | | | | | | | | | | | | |
| | Hourly Wage | | Month's Rent | | Ton Coal | | 1 lb Coffee | | 1 lb Flour | | 1 lb Butter | | 1 lb Sirloin | |
	1911	1920	1911	1920	1911	1920	1911	1920	1911	1920	1911	1920	1911	1920
Bricklayers	.50	1.03	30	25	13.5	14	.7	.5	.06	.07	.5	.6	.4	.4
Carpenters	.40	.85	37.5	30	16.9	17	.9	.6	.07	.08	.6	.7	.5	.5
Sheet-Metal Workers	.35	.85	42.9	30	19.3	17	1	.6	.08	.08	.7	.7	.5	.5
Machinists	.32½	.73	46	36	20.8	20	1.1	.7	.09	.1	.7	.8	.6	.6
Bldg. Labourers	.27½	.55	54.5	47	24.5	26	1.3	.9	.11	.1	.9	1.0	.7	.7
Factory Labourers	.17	.41	88	63	40	35	2	1.2	.18	.13	1.4	1.1	1.1	.7

SOURCE: COMPILED FROM MONTHLY FIGURES IN *LABOUR GAZETTE*, 1911-1920, AND IN CANADA DEPARTMENT OF LABOUR, *WAGES AND HOURS OF LABOUR IN CANADA*, 1902-1920 (OTTAWA: 1921).

little in the way of social advancement, economic improvement, or the acceptance of trade unions and collective bargaining as legitimate institutions in Canadian life. An examination of some cost-of-living and wage statistics collected by the Department of Labour in 1920 tends to bear this out. If a group of workers in Hamilton, Ontario, a leading industrial centre, is taken as typical, the table above shows there was little increase in their real wages between 1911 and 1920, and in some cases there was an actual decrease. The table gives the hourly wages for a cross section of workers in 1911 and 1920 and also shows how many hours of work were needed by each group of workers to pay for rent or basic commodities. If less work was required to buy a particular item in 1920 than in 1911, that worker's buying power had increased. If more work was required, buying power had been eroded. These Hamilton workers clearly paid less for rent in 1920 but almost as much, and sometimes more, for other items. After nine years, therefore, their living standard was only slightly higher despite all the strikes and lockouts, the sacrifices of war, and the advances in industrial technology.

More Canadians were employed in 1921 than ten years before, reflecting the general increase in population, but their distribution in the different sectors of the economy had changed little since the war. The ratio of men to women had not changed much, and the distribution of women had also stayed about the same because the vast majority of women who entered heavy industry to work on munitions during the war went back to more traditional occupations afterwards. In many cases they had little choice, whatever their inclination. Men did not want to work with them, and the unions, for the most part, were interested in restoring their male members to their usual spots on the factory floor. Besides, government and society made it clear that women's place was in the home, raising and caring for the family, and nothing was done to make industry more hospitable to female workers.

Trade union membership reached a peak in 1919 but began to decline with the onset of the depression in 1920. Nevertheless, the ratio of organized to unorganized workers in the nonagricultural workforce had changed over a ten-year period. Union members in 1921 accounted for roughly 17 percent of nonagricultural workers, doubling since 1911. However, it appears from an examination of the wage and price trends, as reflected by the preceding table, that the unions were able to do little to improve the living standards of the labour force over this period. Despite the sacrifices of war, little had changed for most Canadian workers in the basic struggle to eke out a living, raise a family, and provide a small cushion for old age. The 1920s have become known as the Roaring Twenties – an era of bathtub gin, fast cars, radio, daring fashions, and loose morals. This was the great blowout after the war, a return to the good life with a vengeance. The picture is true as far as it goes; a small number of middle- and upper-middle-class Canadians did enjoy that Great Gatsby kind of life. For most Canadian workers, however, there was a different reality to be faced every day – a reality of poor wages, periodic unemployment, unsafe and unhealthy living and working conditions, and a battle to rise above poverty. The war had made a nation of Canada, but most Canadian workers had still not found their place in the sun. The 1930s, just around the corner, were to be even worse for the vast majority.

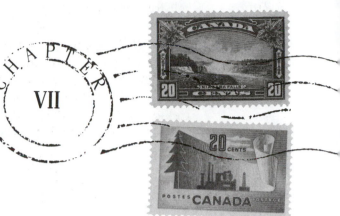

1919-1939:
THE YEARS OF BOOM
AND BUST

The On-to-Ottawa trekkers clambered out of the boxcars and blinked in the early morning light. This was Regina in June 1935, and there was still a chill in the morning air although the sun was already bright. The leaders formed the men into ragged ranks and marched them off through the streets to the Exhibition Grounds. To the surprise of some of the trekkers, the citizens of the city seemed friendly, and some of the major streets were actually lined with cheering crowds. For the unemployed, that was not the usual reception.

After some food – and after the issuance of relief vouchers – the trekkers settled back to wait on events. It did not take long before two cabinet ministers arrived from Ottawa as emissaries of the prime minister, R.B. Bennett. Mr. Bennett would accept a delegation, the trekkers' leaders were informed, and the delegation of eight could proceed to Ottawa on first-class rail tickets with meals provided. That was a victory for the unemployed men – for five years they had been trying without success to get the government to negotiate about their plight. At last, success.

But not for long. When the trekkers' representatives were ushered in to see the prime minister, his officials, and the press, the meeting quickly blew up. Bennett began to attack the leaders of the trek as radicals and trouble-makers, and he singled out Slim Evans, one of the major organizers of the event. "We know you down here, Evans! You are a criminal and a thief!" Bennett's bluster had frightened many men, but Evans was not intimidated. "And you're a liar, Bennett," he shouted back at the portly, red-faced prime minister, "and what is more, you are not fit to run a Hottentot village, let alone a great country like Canada." The delegation was hustled out, and the negotiations were over.

Two days later, the Royal Canadian Mounted Police attacked the trekkers and broke up the On-to-Ottawa Trek. It was Dominion Day, the middle of the Great Depression.

Grievances

The social and political unrest and the personal dissatisfaction and frustration that followed the end of the Great War were not confined to industrial workers or returned soldiers. Among farmers there was bitter disappointment that Borden's Unionist colleagues had not produced the legislative results that they had believed would follow the 1917 election victory, especially in the area of lower tariffs. Some farmers had understood the government's need to cancel military service exemptions in March 1918, but all had hoped that this violation of a solemn pledge would be balanced by progressive measures in other areas; all felt betrayed when it was not. The one place where their demands were met was in the marketing of grain. When the war ended the demand dropped, and prices of wheat and other cereals fell accordingly. Many western farmers had overextended themselves during the war to produce as much as they could and had bought new machinery and new land, paying high prices and borrowing money at high interest rates. Now, left high and dry, they demanded government price supports. In response, in the summer of 1919 the Canadian Wheat Board was established to buy up all the grain and sell it at the highest possible price. After one year, it was disbanded.

Understandably, western farmers were angry; and so were farmers in Ontario, who faced different problems. They were worried about the growth of cities, the consequent shift of political power and influence from country to city, and about rural depopulation, the slow but steady movement of young people away from farming and agricultural communities into the big cities. A popular song of the time explained it all. It asked the unanswerable question about farm boys just returned from war: "How ya gonna keep 'em down on the farm, after they've seen Paree?" The shift brought with it a diminution of prestige and status. In the popular mind the once stalwart farmer, pillar of the community, was being reduced to a country bumpkin. Enraged and humiliated, the farmers demanded that the Ontario government pay more attention to them and to their problems. They wanted ready and easy access to city markets via electrically powered railways and the maintenance and improvement of rural services such as schools and roads.

In the Atlantic provinces, farmers, workers and even businesspeople were complaining loudly about the federal government's total lack of concern for their problems. "Drastic action" would be necessary, warned a Halifax newspaper, unless changes were made and unless the rest of Canada began to take their "Maritime cousins" seriously. Indeed, nowhere was there more unhappiness with federal policies than in the Maritimes. Overwhelmed by their apparently insoluble economic problems and even more by a sense that they were inexorably losing whatever status and influence they had enjoyed to the rapidly rising West and the dominant urban centres of central Canada, many in the Atlantic provinces threw their support behind a full-fledged regionalist movement. "Maritime Rights" was their slogan; it was an expression of their economic and social frustrations. They were determined to restore their position within Confederation and to force an apathetic Ottawa to take note of their legitimate grievances.

The country was seething with unrest. Canadians had expected the war to change their lives, and instead all they received were the same old answers. New people and new ideas were needed.

Grits, Tories, and Progressives

Sir Wilfrid Laurier died in February 1919. By refusing to join a conscriptionist coalition, he had succeeded in preserving the Liberal Party. Now the Liberals were faced with the dual task of finding a worthy successor and reuniting the party. Many Liberal supporters also wanted their party to branch out in new directions. They believed that a united and reinvigorated Liberal Party would be able to find a solution to the labour problems that plagued the country and put forward new initiatives in social reform legislation.

In August 1919, the Liberals met in convention and constructed a platform that placed the party solidly behind state intervention in social and economic affairs. They promised comprehensive pension legislation, a national health care insurance scheme, unemployment insurance, and, in keeping with their new direction, elected a 44-year-old bachelor, William Lyon Mackenzie King, as party leader. During his years as deputy minister and then minister of labour in the Laurier government, as consultant for the Rockefeller Foundation on the labour problems in Rockefeller's Colorado coalfields, and as the author of *Industry and Humanity*, published in 1918, King had become widely known as a labour expert and progressive thinker. This book outlined the need for a social welfare program much like that adopted at the Liberal Party convention. King was a man of mixed motives. Highly religious and morally upright to the point of pompous stuffiness, he also projected, at least in his first years as leader, an image of youthful vigour and forward thinking. The power of public opinion, he believed, could do away with evils such as overcrowded factories or unsafe mines. At the same time, he had a keen appreciation of the ability of wealthy and powerful men, such as Rockefeller, to either speed up or block reform. He saw himself, always, as the great healer, divinely ordained to maintain Canadian unity across class, region, and ethnic and linguistic divisions, and this mission was always his first priority.[1]

Despite its new leader and new platform, the Liberal Party made little headway with those, like the farmers, who were the most dissatisfied with the current social and economic state of affairs. In Ontario and throughout the West, the agricultural leaders were arguing and debating political issues and organizing into political action groups. They had discussed direct political action for years and, in 1910, had first formulated a program that they called the Farmers' Platform or – pointedly, with a jab in the direction of the old one – the New National Policy. This demanded greater government intervention in the economy, public ownership of transportation and basic utilities, regulation of the grain trade, and lower tariffs. Abandoning the Liberal Party, many farmers had supported the Unionist government in 1917 because,

---

[1] There is much material by and about King that gives a good picture of his career up to his assumption of the Liberal leadership in 1919. His own work, *Industry and Humanity*, has appeared in several editions, the most recent with an analysis and introduction by David J. Bercuson (Toronto, 1973). See also King's *The Secret of Heroism: A Memoir of Henry Albert Harper* (New York, 1906). Books on King include R.M. Dawson, *William Lyon Mackenzie King: A Political Biography, 1874-1923* (Toronto, 1953); H.S. Ferns and Bernard Ostry, *The Age of Mackenzie King: The Rise of the Leader* (London, 1955); and Paul Craven, *An Impartial Umpire: Industrial Relations and the Canadian State, 1900-1911* (Toronto, 1980), which details King's career as a labour arbitrator. A psychohistory is Joy E. Esberey, *Knight of the Holy Spirit: A Study of William Lyon Mackenzie King* (Toronto, 1980). A United States view of King's involvement with the Rockefellers is contained in George S. McGovern and Leonard F. Gittridge, *The Great Coalfield War* (Boston, 1972).

unlike the Liberals, it promised change. But the Unionists had delivered little; worse, they had cancelled conscription exemptions in the bargain. Though reluctant to return to the Liberal fold, the farmers could no longer support the Unionists. Their answer was to launch their own parties, which, they believed, would most closely reflect their needs.[2]

The first break came in October 1919, in Ontario, where farm candidates running under the banner of the United Farmers of Ontario captured the provincial government, a result that surprised them as much as anyone else. When the ballots were counted, they had won 43 seats to 28 for the Liberals and 26 for the Conservatives. Although in the minority, they were able to form a government with the help of members of the Independent Labour Party and took office under Premier E.C. Drury. In Canada's most urbanized and industrialized province, the farmers ruled.

Four months later, a national farm party began to emerge out of the Unionist coalition. Under the leadership of the former Unionist agriculture minister, T.A. Crerar, a group of western M.P.'s began to caucus together in Ottawa. This led to the birth of the National Progressive Party, which was fully endorsed by the Canadian Council of Agriculture in December 1920. Crerar intended to unite progressive Canadians into one political organization that would not have to rely on the power of Montreal and Toronto bankers and businesspeople or conservative voters in French Canada.

The rising political consciousness of the farmers was further reflected in the Manitoba provincial election at the end of June 1920. The Liberal government of Premier T.C. Norris, an administration that had passed much progressive legislation on such issues as temperance, votes for women, a minimum wage, and workers' compensation, sought a renewal of its mandate. Despite its reformism (or because of it, some said), the Norris government lost considerable ground to farmer and labour

---

[2] The farm protest movement has been well covered. Early works that are still useful include Paul F. Sharp, *The Agrarian Revolt in Western Canada: A Survey Showing American Parallels* (Minneapolis, 1948); W.L. Morton, *The Progressive Party in Canada* (Toronto, 1950); and W.K. Rolph, *Henry Wise Wood of Alberta,* (Toronto, 1950). For Ontario see E.C. Drury, *Farmer Premier: The Memoirs of E.C. Drury* (Toronto, 1966), and L.A. Wood, *A History of Farmers' Movements in Canada: The Origin and Development of Agrarian Protest, 1872-1924* (Toronto, 1975). Recent works on the subject include John H. Thompson, *The Harvests of War: The Prairie West, 1914-1918* (Toronto, 1978); John Kendle, *John Bracken: A Political Biography* (Toronto, 1979); and Gerald Friesen, *The Canadian Prairies* (Toronto, 1984). On Maritime grievances, see E.R. Forbes, *The Maritime Rights Movement* (Montreal, 1979).

candidates. The United Farmers of Manitoba elected 12 members to the legislature while labour candidates accounted for 11 seats, throwing the Norris government into a minority and the legislature into a deadlock.

Farm support had been one of the major building blocks of the Unionist coalition and it was obvious, by early 1920, that the farmers were turning away from the Borden government. The coalition was in deep political trouble. In Quebec, it had no support outside the English-speaking community of Montreal. In the West, the government's failure to lower tariffs and complete the nationalization of the railways cost it much support, and farmers were starting to back the Progressive Party.

In the Maritimes, under the "Maritime Rights" banner, Progressive candidates were beginning to appear and – even worse from the old parties' point of view – were beginning to win elections. In reality, the coalition had never truly united conscriptionist Liberals and Conservatives, as both had continued to maintain their identities and had rarely worked together. After Mackenzie King was elected leader and put a light in the window for all Unionist Liberals, no questions asked, many of them found it easy to abandon the coalition and return to the fold. Borden's long absences overseas and his apparent lack of interest in domestic political matters did not help Unionist fortunes. He had been in active politics as leader of the opposition and prime minister for 19 years, and he was ill and tired. It seemed as if the greatest political triumph of his life – the election of 1917 and the successful introduction of conscription – had both exhausted him and soured him on politics. In early July 1920, he resigned as party leader, and in elections among the Unionist caucus in the House of Commons and the Senate, Arthur Meighen was chosen to succeed him. At the same time, the party dropped the name Unionist and renamed itself the National Liberal and Conservative Party, attempting with this cumbersome label to claim descent from the wartime coalition.

As the Unionist name passed from the scene, farm protest continued to rock the traditional party structure in the country. Farm candidates were elected to the Nova Scotia legislature in July and to the New Brunswick legislature in October; in the latter province they even held the balance of power. Another major victory for the farm parties was scored in the Alberta provincial election of June 1921, when the United Farmers of Alberta swept to office with a majority, defeating the Liberals. Here, as in Ontario, the victory came as a surprise, and the U.F.A. was hard pressed to find a suitable candidate for premier. They eventually settled on Herbert Greenfield, vice-president of the U.F.A.

Now it was Meighen's turn to face the people – and the music. The election campaign began in September 1921, amidst much popular grumbling. The depression that had been expected after the war had begun in earnest in late 1920 when the government and the banks decided to put an end to inflation by calling in loans and tightening up on credit and borrowing. Once again unemployment lines grew while wages fell. The government offered the people little except a promise that it would continue the National Policy and keep tariffs high. Meighen, with his didactic mind, tried to face the issue of conscription in Quebec and received a polite reception, but few votes. Nor was he much more successful in the West or in Ontario, where the back roads and concessions were still buzzing with talk of independent political action. Meanwhile, Mackenzie King and the Liberals ran on their reform platform and his reputation as a conciliator, a man who could bind up the many wounds of the nation. When the voting was over, Meighen's government had been reduced to 50 seats while the Liberals won 116.

GLENBOW ARCHIVES, CALGARY NA-3055-31.

Bringing Cheer to the Western Farmer

Crerar's Progressive Party scored the campaign's major upset by placing second with 65 seats – 21 in Ontario, one in New Brunswick, five in British Columbia, and 38 on the Prairies. A decade of Conservative leadership had ended, and the Liberal domination of Canadian political life in the twentieth century, begun by Laurier, was about to resume.

Prime Minister Authur Meighen, 1920-21, and 1926.

C-4967 (204-30-3)/NATIONAL ARCHIVES OF CANADA.

Mackenzie King in Power

The Canada that emerged from the election of 1921 seemed ungovernable. As the astute editor of the *Manitoba Free Press*, J.W. Dafoe, remarked at the time, ". . . any person who holds office . . . at any time during the next five years is entitled to a measure of sympathy." Never since Confederation had the country been so divided; never had the political map been in such shambles. Meighen's party had ceased to exist as a national party in any representative sense, for it had failed to elect a single member from six out of the nine provinces. The Liberals had won everything in Quebec, Nova Scotia, and Prince Edward Island but only three seats on the Prairies, while the newly created Progressives emerged as a new national threat, having elected members in six provinces (but tellingly, only one east of the Ottawa River).

It was a House of Commons unlike any other ever elected. Many of the members were in Ottawa for the first time, speaking for groups that had for too long been under-represented, if represented at all. Chief of these was, of course, the agricultural community, which now had some 65 members to voice its concerns. Among these was a young school teacher from Ontario, Agnes MacPhail, the country's first woman member of Parliament, elected, appropriately, in the first federal election in which women were officially distinguished from the insane and the imprisoned by being given the right to vote. Even the labour movement had its representatives in the House. As William Irvine informed the Speaker at the beginning of the session, "I wish to state that Mr. Woodsworth is the leader of the labour group . . . and I am the group." Then with a wicked nod at Prime Minister King, he added, "But even if we are small I would like to say without any presumption whatsoever that a small living seed, however small it may be, is greater than a dead trunk."

King was likely too concerned with other things to have noticed. After all, he was now the first prime minister in Canadian history elected without a majority in the House. He faced a double task: governing and reconstructing the country while rebuilding his own Liberal Party, which was, despite the election results, in ruins almost everywhere outside of Quebec. To remain in office he would be compelled to rely on the support of the Progressives.

And how ironic it was that just at the time the farmers were making their first concerted attack on the political system in 1921, the census takers were making their rounds. Their findings merely bore out what farmers had felt for some time: the rural and agricultural elements of

Canadian society had had their day. They no longer made up the majority of the Canadian population. Canada was fast becoming an urban nation; about half of those surveyed in the census lived in the rapidly expanding cities and towns of an increasingly industrial society. The hour of the farmer was fast passing and most of them knew it. This was their last chance to make the Canada they wanted.

The response to this challenge from the leaders of the two old-line parties was typical of both men. To Meighen, the leader of the Conservatives, there were only two sides to every question: his own and the wrong one. He was a brilliant man who was seemingly aware of all facts but the facts of politics. Attack, to him, was the only legitimate form of defence. Deciding to confront the farmers head on, he told them that they were "backward" and "blazing madmen," and refused to listen to them. Mackenzie King, on the other hand, could not do enough for the farmers. He told them their policy was his and that he shared their objectives. Infinitely more shrewd than Meighen, at least in politics, King strove to defuse the farmers' rebellion by promising what they wanted in order to woo them back into the Liberal Party from which many of them had come. King succeeded. The revolt soon petered out, and many of the farmer-politicians headed back to the farm and the Liberal Party.

Much of the problem was caused by the Progressives themselves. They were hopelessly split on ideological issues. Some wished to rid the country of its party system and replace it with the innovation of an erratic American farmer, Henry Wise Wood, who had settled in Alberta and brought with him ideas taken from the Populists south of the border, blended with some thoughts he claimed to have got from the Russian Revolution. His was a theory of representation based on conflicting occupational and class groups. "Group government" as it was called, was based on the premise that each "group" in society would elect parliamentary groups to represent its interests and to "cooperate with other groups to serve justice." The larger section of the party, led by T.A. Crerar of Manitoba, simply wanted to reform the party system by lumping all the progressive groups in the country into one large political party that would exclude only the "big and powerful interests."

They believed that only minimal changes in federal policy would satisfy the West's requirements. All the Liberals had to do, argued Crerar, was to rid themselves of their big business ties and drop the hated protective tariffs. What united these two elements was their hostility to high tariffs and high freight rates and their feeling of being left behind; their complaints were often more psychological than material. But they could not agree on strategy, and their nominal leader, Crerar, refused to become the leader of the Opposition. Indeed, the Progressives even refused to become the official Opposition.

After a time, Crerar succumbed to the blandishments of King and rejoined the Liberal Party he had left in 1917. In 1922 the United Farmer government of Ontario came to an end, none too soon for the people of the province if the results of the 1923 provincial election were any reflection of the mood of the people: the party was savagely rebuffed, winning just a handful of seats.

Though the farmers hung on grittily to power in Alberta, by the mid-1920s the farm-power movement had lost its momentum in federal politics. It had blossomed almost overnight, but progressivism had neither the leadership nor the program for a permanent place in the political spectrum. The movement was badly handicapped from the first by the individualism of the farmer and his suspicion, and even jealousy, of his own leaders. Above all, it came up against an obstacle it could not overcome: the political wizardry of a master of the craft, Mackenzie King.

By now in his late forties, shy, lonely, and dumpy-looking, King was already being recognized as the master tactician that he was. It was a

DALE/*WINNIPEG FREE PRESS.*

disorganized and ambiguous country he had been elected to rule, and as an observer later remarked, his greatest talent was for dealing with the disorganized and the ambiguous. His was not simply the politics of opportunism. Though he was the perfect pragmatist and compromiser, there was more to King than that; there was more to his policies than simple expediency. The grandson of the great Canadian rebel whose name he bore so proudly, the son of a weak, inadequate father and a crushingly possessive mother, King was determined to make his mark on the country that had treated his grandfather so shabbily. And he would make his mark through his party. The Liberal Party would provide, in King's mind, a home for all progressive Canadians; it would embody all their needs and concerns. It would be the party of national unity, regional interests, provincial rights, and French-Canadian nationalism, no matter how contradictory and antipathetic these were. "The whole farmers movement," he told a friend, "is a real liberal movement and . . . as such should be sympathetically viewed by the Liberals. . . . We should openly co-operate and . . . combine our forces in the face of the common enemy." The latter, of course, were the hated Tories, who, he felt, had divided Canada, turned race against race and region against region.

More important even than the farmers and the West in King's scheme were the French-Canadians. Unity, he knew, depended on them. After the wrenching trauma of the conscription experience, their commitment to Confederation, he felt, was tenuous. Anything that would reassure them, that would strengthen their Canadianism, he would do. He was determined to preserve national unity at all costs. New *nationaliste* leaders were arising in Quebec who were promising to take their followers along new paths which would eventually lead out of Canada. Another false step, another crisis such as that of 1917, might forever sunder the delicate bonds tying the sensitive French-Canadians to the rest of Canada. In any case, over half of King's following in the House came from Quebec. It was the Quebeckers' support and allegiance that were crucial both to his leadership and his ability to govern; he could do nothing to offend them. In the hands of these members lay, in King's mind at least, the key to Quebec. Ernest Lapointe, a large, swarthy man with unmatched eloquence in both English and French, was given the responsibility of keeping Quebec happy. He could do anything he wished in the province, both in patronage and policy, so long as he strengthened the forces of federalism, and especially of liberalism, in Quebec. For the next two decades King and Lapointe worked in tandem to retain the loyalty of French-Canadians. The prime minister rarely acted without the advice of his French-Canadian lieutenant, lest any of his policies alienate a substantial number of the people of Quebec.[3]

The Prosperous Twenties?

When King took office following the election of 1921, the surprising postwar boom had come to a sudden end. The Canadian economy was in a severe slump. In 1921 well over 15 percent of the Canadian workforce – about 300 000 men and women – found themselves without work. Many others were either underemployed or reduced to part-time labour at low wages. The haughty Canadian Manufacturers Association did not take the depression very seriously; however, it blamed the unemployment problem on the "large influx of labour to the cities who previously followed agriculture for a livelihood . . . [and who were] attracted to the city by the hope of finding easier work at higher pay and enjoying the excitement of city life." But to the men and women looking for work, the problem was indeed serious. Many of these were veterans who expected – and certainly deserved – far better.

Unhappily, the new King government, committed to appeasing the rural areas of the nation, did little for the unemployed. Both the Liberals and the Progressives were determined to slash government spending and to lower tariffs. Any large-scale assistance to the victims of the depression would, in their eyes, only exacerbate the problems of rural depopulation by making the cities more attractive. The crisis to them was in any case rural in nature. With the end of the wartime boom, commodity prices moved steeply downward. As late as 1920, with wheat selling at the unheard-of price of three dollars a bushel, western farmers had confidently (and as it turned out, recklessly) expanded their productive capacity by borrowing heavily from the all-too-willing banks. The prairie West had become the world's breadbasket during the war, and few saw any reason why it should not remain so. However, the government's decision to do away with the Wheat Board, which had stabilized the price of wheat, coupled with the decision of banks to call in

---

[3] There are a number of books on the politics of the 1920s. See Dawson's biography of King and also Roger Graham, *Arthur Meighen*, vol. II (Toronto, 1963). Other studies include Ramsay Cook, ed., *The Dafoe-Sifton Correspondence* (Altona, 1966); John Kendle, *John Bracken: A Political Biography* (Toronto, 1979); and Morton's study of the Progressives. An excellent overview of the interwar period is John H. Thompson with Allen Seager, *Canada 1922-39: Decades of Discord* (Toronto, 1985).

loans and raise interest rates, brought about a collapse in the wheat economy. Prices plummeted as markets dried up, and wheat was soon selling for less than half of what it had brought only a few years before. Canadian export prices in general dropped almost as badly. And when the agricultural sector suffered, so did the manufacturing sector. Without funds, farmers made bad customers. The demand for consumer goods fell sharply, adding to the unemployment problems in Ontario and Quebec.

However, by the middle of the decade, the worst was over. Markets for Canadian goods reappeared, prices rose, and Canadian wheat was again king, its export far surpassing the record shipments of the war years. Investment was flowing in, and huge capital projects were being undertaken. New industries were being built to service what promised to be a growing and affluent population. The boom was back, or so it seemed. The world appeared to need Canada's wheat, lumber, and nickel. Large pulp and paper mills were springing up throughout Northern Ontario and British Columbia. The completion of railway lines into the Precambrian Shield, where huge deposits of gold, copper, iron, zinc, and nickel had earlier been discovered, allowed an army of miners, prospectors, and businessmen to exploit the area. By 1928, over a billion dollars worth of metals and lumber products were being extracted from the Shield alone. And to fuel the boom – while at the same time ensuring that wages would not skyrocket – the government again adopted an open-door immigration policy. Nothing united Canadian industrialists and farmers more than their demand for more and cheaper immigrant labour. In response to cries from both farm and factory, the King government accepted hundreds of thousands of immigrants.

What was noteworthy about this economic upsurge, though few noted it at the time, was the growing importance of American markets and investments. The United States had, for the first time, displaced Great Britain as Canada's most important trading partner. Canadian trade was rapidly being redirected south from its historic transatlantic flow. But perhaps of greater significance were the huge sums in United States dollars that were pouring into Canada to pay for businesses, factories, mines, and smelters. Much of the economic activity of the period, particularly in the mining sector, was dependent on these American funds. The Canadian patrimony was finding its way into the hands of American entrepreneurs. No one seemed to mind; in the heady 1920s there seemed to be plenty for everyone.

Prosperity in Canda was mostly the result of a spillover of wealth from

Railway nationalization – and the costs involved – frightened many, as this cartoon from *Bob Edwards's Summer Annual* of 1922 suggests.   GLENBOW ARCHIVES, CALGARY/NA2920-9.

the United States. The introduction of new products into North American life was largely responsible for this boom. For example, between 1920 and 1930, more than a million cars and trucks were bought in Canada, and automobiles needed rubber and gasoline, roads and garages. For the first time, North Americans were buying radios, electric appliances, and a host of other consumer products. Canadians alone acquired 500 000 telephones in these years. At the same time, to keep pace with the growing demand for energy, close to $700 million was spent on building new electrical power plants. According to many observers, for the middle and upper classes at least, the Roaring Twenties was an age of pleasure, with moving pictures, radio, the Model T Ford, and a more sophisticated amusement called the stock market. Everybody seemed to be playing it – and making huge profits. The rich seemed to be growing richer and some of the poor less poor. The symbols of the period, according to one historian, were hip flasks, raccoon coats, short skirts, Ford roadsters, and dollar signs.

There were, of course, many segments of society to whom the 1920s were anything but golden. Most farmers did not share in the prosperity of the decade. Life for the farmer was still drab and unrewarding. And even worse, rubbing salt in his economic wounds, was his feeling of being unaccountably left out of the gay, carefree, and affluent life of the cities he heard and read about. Thousands packed their bags and left behind their dull lives on the farms and in the small towns of rural Canada for the glitter of life in the big cities. Most were disappointed. The jobs and money they thought readily available were hard to come by, and the conditions of life – and work, if they found any – were not much better than they had been on the farm.

Worst of all was the lot of the workers. The twenties hardly roared for them. These were the lean years for the Canadian working class. Buffeted first by inflation at the beginning of the decade and then by the sudden deflation that cost many of them their jobs, they soon found themselves competing for jobs with the thousands of hungry immigrants landing monthly in Canadian ports. These hapless newcomers found themselves in the most pitiable conditions of all. Promised jobs and security, they arrived in Canada and found neither. Many were penned up in company towns and slums and forced to work in horrific conditions for abysmally low wages. Threatened with deportation if they protested, most stayed at their jobs and said nothing. They had nowhere to turn for succour; the country's trade unions were both too weak and too insensitive to help.

Women workers especially suffered. They were clustered in particularly low-paying sectors of the economy – domestic service, teaching, clerical work, and the clothing industry. Thousands of young girls, many under the age of 15, were forced to work in order to save their families from destitution. As for single women, they were expected to live at home with relatives and to turn over most of their paltry wages. Indeed, many of the jobs that had opened for women during the war, in government and in manufacturing, were suddenly closed. For women, wholesale dismissals became routine in order to make room for returning soldiers. After all, men had families to support; women did not. Only a few women were able to rise above the restrictions of a largely misogynist society.

Certainly the trade unions were of no help. Most dismissed the idea of women's organizing despite much evidence in industries such as garment making and textile production to the contrary. As a result, less than one percent of all the women workers in the country were organized.

No decade was more disappointing for the Canadian labour movement than the 1920s. Throughout the twenties union membership plummeted in the face of an unparalleled anti-labour onslaught by business.

Organizers were blacklisted and fired; strikes fell into disuse as companies had armies of strike-breakers on hand to deal with any disruptions. Taking their cue from their counterparts in the United States, Canadian employers began loudly demanding open shops and right-to-work laws that would bar unions from their plants. Others simply replaced unions with their own company unions. The crushing defeat of the Winnipeg General Strike had set a pattern for unholy alliances of business and government against unions all across Canada, but especially in the West. The labour movement was paralyzed, its leadership demoralized, its radicalism and vitality sapped.

There were some fresh initiatives, but their effect was limited. In Quebec a new labour federation, the Canadian and Catholic Federation of Labour, came into being in 1921 at the behest of the Church. Some years later, in 1927, a number of English-Canadian workers also broke with the internationals to form the All-Canadian Congress of Labour, an organization of unions committed to industrial and national unionism. Finally, at the end of the decade, the Communists, who since their founding meeting in Canada in 1921 had been determined to gain control of the labour movement and had failed abysmally, created the Workers' Unity League, an aggressive, militant organization, bent on organizing not only the unorganized, but the unemployed as well.

However, still dominating the Canadian labour scene in those years was the conservative, craft-dominated Trades and Labor Congress. It seemed totally unprepared to do anything for workers outside its fold. The rise of mass production industries called for different and more aggressive methods of organization. But organizing the unskilled was, to the T.L.C. leadership, anathema. Even though these new industries could not be accommodated within their existing craft structures, both the T.L.C. and its American parent organization, the A.F.L., were unwilling to adopt different structures. They were select organizations whose membership made up the elite of the labour movement; they wanted nothing else but to maintain their status and to be left alone.

Much of the labour militancy in the 1920s occurred among the miners of Cape Breton Island, where almost 50 percent of Canada's strikes took place. Reacting to a series of pay cuts initiated by the new owners of the Sydney coal mines, the British Empire Steel Corporation, thousands of miners went out on strike. When half the cut was restored, they went back to work. But over the next few years violent strikes became a way of life among the steelworkers and miners of the island. Troops and police were permanently stationed around the mines and steelmills.

Beatings and arrests were the order of the day. When a delegation of miners met with the prime minister to plead for pensions for their disabled colleagues, all they received from him was a copy of his book, *Industry and Humanity*. Miners and their families were eventually starved into submission. Twelve thousand survived only on rations provided by local relief committees. "Even the sparrows," reported one newspaper, "have a hard time to live in the Sydney Mines and Glace Bay districts." In the face of such adversity – even their own union, the United Mineworkers of America, disowned them – those miners who still had jobs went back to work, defeated but not humbled. Their leader, the fiery Scot, J.B. MacLachlan, was even sent to jail for "seditious libel." His crime? He had openly criticized the brutality of the provincial police in putting down the strike. Telling the truth, the stern Nova Scotian judge lectured MacLachlan, was no defence. "The truer the statement," said the province's attorney general, "the worse the libel." With such justice, could anyone wonder why the miners gave up their futile struggle and went back to the mines?[4]

The one industry that was thriving throughout this decade was smuggling. In the 1920s a large number of Canadians were making a living – and a very good one at that – by transporting liquor across the border. In the United States, the burning domestic political question of the times was whether or not people had the right to buy a drink. It turned out they did not: under the Eighteenth Amendment, the Volstead Act of 1919, all of America had suddenly gone dry. But with the help of Al Capone and his bootleggers, and thousands of Canadian rumrunners, millions of Americans got drunk – unconstitutionally.

Prohibition forces were almost as potent in Canada. By the end of the war every single province had introduced some form of legislation prohibiting the consumption of alcohol. But because of various lobbies and pressure groups, the provinces kept changing their regulations. As one wag put it, "Prohibition, semi-prohibition and the open bar raced back and forth through the statute books of the nine provinces like the lights on a busy switchboard." For example, to placate Niagara grape growers, the government of Ontario allowed the production and sale of

---

[4] On the economics of the 1920s, see W.L. Marr and D.G. Paterson, *Canada: An Economic History* (Toronto 1980); W.A. Mackintosh, *The Economic Background of Dominion-Provincial Relations* (Ottawa, 1939); and C.F. Wilson, *A Century of Canadian Grain* (Saskatoon, 1978). Dozens of additional studies can readily be found in the chapter by J.M. Bliss in J.L. Granatstein and P. Stevens, eds., *A Reader's Guide to Canadian History*, vol. II (Toronto, 1982).

wine. Using this loophole, the province's wineries were soon producing wines that were up to 25 percent proof, and this in a province that had just voted overwhelmingly to bar the sale of beer containing 2.5 percent alcohol. As the forces of good fought the forces of Demon Rum in each province, only one thing remained constant: no matter how dry a province was, it was still legal to produce and store alcoholic beverages for the export market. The returns from this enterprise were far too remunerative for any government to consider ordering it stopped. And in any case, the temperance groups were too concerned about saving their own citizens from drink to worry about foreigners. It was common knowledge that every night barges, schooners, launches, even canoes and sailboats left their berths in Halifax, Vancouver, Windsor, and scores of other tiny harbours for a quick trip across the border to unload cases of scotch, rye, gin, and whatever else the overworked distilleries of Canada were producing. In addition, on the Prairies, enterprising Canadians were crossing the border in cars, trucks, airplanes, and even on bicycles to unload their goods. This traffic, noted a Toronto newspaper, was helping give Canada a favourable trade balance. And even better, it was legal: the rumrunners were breaking no Canadian law. Though the Americans set up a so-called "dry navy" of motorboats to patrol the Great Lakes and the Atlantic and Pacific coasts, few Canadians were caught. Trade in spirits continued unabated.[5]

Throughout the 1920s Canadian rumrunners and the American coast-guard were fighting a full-scale war. And the Americans meant business as the ill-fated crew of the small Canadian ship *I'm Alone* discovered. For two days the tiny Canadian rumrunner tried desperately to escape pursuing American patrol vessels. Finally, 390 km out at sea, well in international waters, her engines failing, she was caught and destroyed by cannon fire from the American cutters. And she was not the only Canadian ship sunk. But while the guns blazed, bootleggers and corrupt officials on both sides of the border lined their pockets.

Unfortunately, the fully loaded boats and vehicles that left Canada often did not return empty. Instead they smuggled back into Canada goods, especially textiles and tobacco products, worth millions of dollars annually. And only when manufacturers in these industries complained did the King government attempt to put a halt to this illicit trade. But by

---

[5] For colourful examinations of this trade see C.W. Hunt, *Booze, Boats and Billions*, (Toronto 1988), and James H. Gray, *Booze: The Impact of Whiskey on the Prairie West* (Toronto, 1972).

then it was too late, at least for the prime minister. An investigation of the Customs Department and its minister, the genial, ineffective Jacques Bureau, was begun and would eventually have very grave political repercussions.

～～～ The King-Byng "Wing-Ding"

Presiding over all these rapid changes and developments in the country and apparently oblivious to them all was Mackenzie King. He had taken office in 1921 with a limited but critical objective – to restore national unity. And by the end of his first term as prime minister in 1925 he had succeeded brilliantly. Not only was Quebec no longer isolated but many English-Canadians were again beginning to feel that the province, through its massive representation on the government side of the House, had too much influence, that Lapointe, rather than King, was, in the words of one Toronto newspaper, "calling the shots on all important matters." Clearly, the conscription wounds, at least in French Canada, had been healed. Similarly, King's masterful and leisurely digestion of the rural protest movement seemed to have eased the crisis in the West. The Liberal Party, so badly dispirited when King replaced Laurier, was again united. Normalcy, it seemed, had returned to Canada far sooner than most expected.

But if King expected the gratitude – and the votes – of the Canadian people for his achievements, he was sadly disappointed. Though he himself admitted that his government's legislative record was not spectacular, he had given the country four years of calm and respite, and he certainly had provided adequate, though not spectacular, government. But events were not turning his way. The Conservatives had made a remarkable recovery from the 1921 election, which many had thought to be a fatal blow, and under the vigorous leadership of a renewed Arthur Meighen they were providing forceful opposition in the House.

On October 29, 1925, the people of Canada went to the polls. The campaign had been as dull as any in Canadian history. King ran on his record, Meighen on his eloquence. The people of Canada were not impressed with either. The Conservatives swept Ontario and the Maritimes; the Liberals, Quebec. Both shared the West with the Progressives. As a result of the vote, the Conservatives won 116 seats, the Liberals 99, the Progressives 24, with 6 going to independents, including Woodsworth and his "labour group" of one.

The election had been a personal disaster for the prime minister. Not only had his policies and his party been rejected at the polls, but he had suffered a personal defeat in his own York North riding. At 52 his once-promising political career seemed over. But King's greatest political ally, Luck, did not desert him. The Progressives had lost two-thirds of their members but were now paradoxically in a stronger position. Their 24 seats put them in a commanding position in the next House. No government could be formed without their support. And on most issues of importance to them, they were far closer to King than to Meighen.

After many days of indecision, during which King consulted the governor general, Baron Byng of Vimy, as well as his mother and father who had died years before ("The whole family in Heaven," he wrote in his diary, "are guiding and directing me."), the prime minister decided to stay in office until the Commons met. And he set about at once to get ready. He assured the Progressives of his support for their programs. To Woodsworth and his "labour group" he promised to introduce old-age pension legislation as soon as Parliament met. Meanwhile, Meighen, confidently expecting to become prime minister, sat tight, made no promises, courted no one, and played right into King's hands.

On January 7, 1926, with the prime minister of Canada looking on from the gallery, the House met. The fate of his government now depended on the uncertain support of the Progressives, Woodsworth, and a handful of independents. He had made them promises. Would their gratitude be translated into enough votes to support the government? Under the firm guidance of Ernest Lapointe, the Liberals and their allies held firm and beat back every Tory effort to defeat the government. But a political time bomb was inexorably ticking away in the files of a former grocer who now sat as a Conservative member from Vancouver. H.H. Stevens had come into possession of the results of the investigation launched into the activities of the Customs Department and was waiting for the opportune moment to release its explosive contents to the House.

Finally the moment arrived. On February 2 Stevens rose and for the next few hours delivered his indictment of the government's corruption and criminal behaviour. He charged that King, Lapointe, and various other ministers knew "that the grossest violations of customs laws were being perpetrated in this country," but did nothing. Officials involved in smuggling were kept in their jobs, or even worse, promoted. Known criminals had been kept out of jail in return for contributions to Liberal Party war chests. There was hardly a crime, cried the enraged Stevens, of which this debauched government had not been guilty. What was necessary, he declared, was that a parliamentary committee be set up to investigate. The Liberals and the dazed Progressives had little choice but to go along. An all-party committee of nine was set up to look into Stevens's charges.

In June the committee reported. Its conclusions were not entirely what the Tories had expected. Instead of condemning the government, the report simply stated that the Department of Customs was guilty of inefficiency, and its minister had "failed to appreciate and properly discharge the responsibilities of his office." This was clearly inadequate for the Tories. At once, Stevens moved an amendment condemning the entire government. Thus began one of the most crucial debates in Canadian parliamentary history. For four days the House argued whether to censure the King administration. If it did, the government would fall and very likely King's own career would be destroyed. When it became evident to the prime minister that some of his Progressive

Mackenzie King spoke at Brampton, Ontario, during the 1925 campaign. The two microphones suggest that some people were listening at home on their radios.

ARCHIVES OF ONTARIO (ACC. 3117 2).

Viscount Byng, commander at Vimy Ridge and later governor general of Canada.

C-39555/NATIONAL ARCHIVES OF CANADA.

supporters were deserting him, King played his trump card. Refusing to be the first prime minister to be censured by his colleagues, King decided to dissolve Parliament and call new elections. Since a request for dissolution had never before been rejected by a governor general, he expected no trouble from Lord Byng. He was in for a rude shock.

The governor general had been convinced by the results of the election of 1925 that King should have resigned. He pointed out to him that he *"had lost* seventeen seats, while the Leader of the Opposition had gained sixty-seven." In Byng's soldierly mind there was no moral justification for King remaining in office. Thus, when the prime minister approached him on a June weekend, without ever having suffered a major defeat in the House, to ask for a dissolution, Byng's sense of justice was outraged, and he refused. Three times the two men met, and each time King tried to convince the obdurate Byng that in a responsible government the governor general had no legal right to reject the demands of a democratically elected prime minister. Each time Byng stood firm, convinced that King wanted dissolution simply for partisan reasons – so that he could go to the people as the prime minister, still not repudiated by the House, and could, for the purposes of the campaign, control the electoral and patronage machinery.

For the past two generations historians, politicians, lawyers, and constitutional experts have argued the merits of what one Canadian humorist has called "the King-Byng-wing-ding."[6] Who was right? Did the governor general have the right arbitrarily to reject the request of the prime minister and refuse dissolution? Most scholars agree that Byng was right, although some argue that he made the right decision for the wrong reasons. In any case, under the Canadian system of government, the governor general represented the Crown and the Constitution, and even if what he did was wrong, it was, nonetheless, law. King had no choice but to return to the House, announce his resignation, and tell the country that Canada no longer had a government.

Within days, Byng called upon Meighen to form a new government. It was the biggest mistake in the Conservative leader's error-filled political life to accept the request. He probably had no choice. To refuse would have disgraced the governor general, since Byng would then have been

---

[6] On the King-Byng affair, the starting point should be H.B. Neatby, *William Lyon Mackenzie King*, vol. II (Toronto, 1963), and Graham on Meighen, vol II. Graham's collection of documents, *The King-Byng Affair, 1926* (Toronto, 1967), is very useful and recourse may be had to Eugene Forsey, *The Royal Power of Dissolution of Parliament in the British Commonwealth* (Toronto, 1943).

forced to call again on King to form a government. In any case, Meighen believed that the governor general had acted correctly. Furthermore, Meighen had every confidence that, as leader of the largest party in the House, he would have no problem in forming a viable government. And he might have succeeded, had it not been for some strange parliamentary procedures.

As the law stood then – it was changed several years later – a member of the House who accepted a cabinet position was forced to resign to seek re-election. Thus, as soon as Meighen became prime minister, he lost his seat in the House. Like King at the beginning of the session, he was forced to conduct his government's business from a parliamentary gallery. Even worse, to carry on the business of government and yet to keep enough members in the House, he was forced into the embarrassing position of appointing "acting" cabinet ministers. But without the powerful presence of Meighen on the floor of the House, the Conservatives were hard put to withstand the Liberal onslaught. Concentrating on the appontment of an "acting ministry," King and his men charged that the new government was illegal, that it had usurped the Constitution and was making nonsense out of a thousand years of British history. If it was a legitimate cabinet, he argued, its members had no right to sit in the House; if it was illegitimate, it had no right to transact business. Furious words were hurled across the House for three days and nights as both parties prepared for the ultimate test. Finally, in the early morning hours of July 2, the House was ready to vote on whether the new government was legal. By one vote, 96 to 95, the Commons decided it was not. Only after the roll call did a sheepish Progressive arise to inform the House that, so excited had he become during the debate, he had inadvertently voted against the government. In fact he had been paired with a member who was absent and had committed himself to abstain. Thus the three-day-old Meighen government collapsed because of a mischance. As one historian later commented, "Meighen's evil star had betrayed him again. King's infallible good luck had rescued him from the greatest gamble of his life – rescued him for two more decades of power."

The governor general now had no alternative but to grant Meighen the dissolution he had refused King. For the second time in less than a year the Canadian people were required to go to the polls. Each side was convinced it had the winning issue. The Conservatives campaigned full-out on the corruption issue; the Liberals on the constitutional issue. King argued that what was at stake in this election was what his grandfather had fought for a century before – responsible government.

The Conservative leader charged that the Liberals had provided the most corrupt government in Canadian history, and King's attempt to hang on to the premiership, "like a lobster with lockjaw," had dealt a severe blow to Canadian democracy. In the end, nationalism won over corruption. But in fact neither issue caught fire. Though they lost seats, the Conservatives actually polled more votes than they had the year before. However, the Liberals again won most of Quebec as well as a substantial part of the Progressive vote in Ontario and the West and emerged decisive winners, 128 seats to the Conservatives' 91 and the Progressives' 20.

King had been vindicated. Through political ingenuity he had turned the greatest crisis of his political life into one of his greatest successes. He was now unchallenged as a political figure, the true heir of Wilfrid Laurier. Stable government had been restored and prosperity returned; the western protest movement had collapsed, and national unity had been regained. In the prime minister's mind, all his major domestic objectives had been achieved. And even better, Arthur Meighen, his great nemesis, seemed to be finished as a major political figure. Shortly after the election of 1926, Meighen announced his resignation as Conservative leader and was replaced by a lesser man, but one who would prove to be a better political match for King, Calgary lawyer R.B. Bennett. However, for the foreseeable future King seemed unassailable. What could threaten his government except some great national calamity? And who could imagine such a disaster as the affluent 1920s drew to a close?

"Parliament Will Decide"

Certainly not the prime minister, though if there were to be trouble, he believed it would most likely come from Europe, its traditional source. King did not particularly dislike European statesmen; he just distrusted them. He had learned from the experiences of Sir Wilfrid Laurier that nothing divided Canadians faster than foreign policy. The domestic impact of the Boer War and the Great War was not lost on him. An enterprising, aggressive foreign policy must be avoided at all costs since it seemed incompatible with national unity. He was a strong autonomist, but he also retained a close attachment to the British Commonwealth. He fought for a greater Canadian voice in the League of Nations; yet once he got it, he found he had nothing to say for fear he might say too much. Words preceded commitments; thus words should be shunned. For him it was important that Canada have a place among the nations of the world; but there was nothing he wished to do once he got there. He wanted recognition without obligation, status without responsibility, consultation without commitment. No one could decide for Canada, not the British cabinet, not the Commonwealth, not the League of Nations. The Parliament of Canada alone could decide, but only after King and his cabinet had handed down their decision. Parliament could always veto that decision, but King knew it never would.

In King's mind there was one overriding goal: full Canadian autonomy. Its achievement and extension were to be his greatest contributions to his country. Without autonomy, he knew, national unity was impossible; only with full autonomy was a national consensus on foreign policy possible. And only by standing up to the British and resisting their cajolery for a common imperial policy – obviously to be decided upon at Westminster rather than Ottawa, Canberra, or Pretoria – could autonomy be attained.[7]

It was not long after he had first taken office that the opportunity arose to show the British that a new day had dawned for the Empire. On August 26, 1922, the Turks attacked the Greeks. It seemed that another of the interminable Balkan wars was about to break out. Few in Canada, including the prime minister, gave it a second thought. However, by the Treaty of Sèvres, one of the treaties that ended the Great War, the British had committed themselves to keeping the Straits of the Dardanelles demilitarized. Now only a tiny British garrison in the small Turkish village of Chanak stood between the Turkish army, led by the charismatic Mustapha Kemal, and the Straits. At once the British cabled the dominions for help. Unfortunately, on its arrival in Ottawa on September 15, the message was mislaid, and its contents were not made known to the prime minister until the following day, after King had read about the conflict in the morning newspapers. He also read that New Zealand had already agreed to send troops to the Balkans.

To the indignant King the affair reeked of imperial arrogance. He was

---

[7] For foreign policy in the interwar years, see the King and Meighen biographies, J.L. Granatstein, *The Ottawa Men: The Civil Service Mandarins, 1935-57* (Toronto, 1982), and Granatstein's *A Man of Influence: Norman A. Robertson and Canadian Statecraft, 1929-68* (Ottawa, 1981). See also Philip Wigley, *Canada and the Transition in Commonwealth: British-Canadian Relations, 1917-26* (Cambridge, 1977), and Claude Bissell, *The Young Vincent Massey* (Toronto, 1981). On defence questions, see James Eayrs, *In Defence of Canada*, vols. I, II (Toronto, 1964, 1965).

convinced that the British were testing the waters to see how the dominions would respond. Now that the British had thrown down the gauntlet, King was anxious to fling it back in their faces. He was appalled at the bad manners of the British in publicly announcing a policy involving Canada before the Canadian prime minister had been informed. He was, as he wrote in his diary, annoyed, and he let the British prime minister, Lloyd George, know it. More significantly, after meeting his cabinet he informed the British that he would not think of sending troops to Chanak without first consulting Parliament. And he had no intention, yet, of calling it into session. In effect, King was announcing that Canada's automatic commitment to fight at Britain's side anywhere and at any time the British demanded was finished for good. He was not going to ask Canadian boys who had just come home from four bloody years in Europe to go back and fight the Turks for reasons neither they, nor he, understood. "I am sure," he confided to his diary, "the people of Canada are against participation in this European war."

Arthur Meighen was less sure. To a Toronto audience, he stated categorically that he stood with the British. "When Britain's message came," he said, "then Canada should have said: 'Ready, aye Ready; we stand by you.' " Nor was the Conservative leader alone. The Toronto *Globe* thundered, "If the Turk attacks Constantinople he attacks Canada." But before this "Oriental imbroglio," as it was described by Henri Bourassa, could blow up into a full-scale foreign crisis, cooler heads prevailed. A peace conference was hurriedly called to meet at Lausanne, Switzerland, and a settlement was reached which seemed to please everyone – including Mackenzie King, since, to his great relief, Canada was not invited.

But the prime minister had only begun. At the Imperial Conference in London in 1923, King formally rejected the idea of a united Commonwealth policy determined by the British. Canada, he said, through its Parliament, would decide on its own course of action. And though this did not necessarily preclude Canada from joining with the British, it also did not obligate it to do so. King was less concerned with devising a distinctive Canadian foreign policy than he was with making sure that Britain did not devise one for Canada. Reluctantly the British accepted the new King formula; they had little choice. Already the Canadian prime minister had shown that he intended to push forward his country's new independent status at every opportunity. By signing a fishing agreement, the Halibut Treaty, with the United States in March 1923, Canada had indicated that it was capable of negotiating its own treaties without British involvement.

The Imperial Conference of 1925 formally recognized that a new Commonwealth had emerged in which all members were autonomous, equal in status, and "in no way subordinate one to another in any aspect of their domestic or external affairs." Joined by the leaders of South Africa and Ireland, King would accept nothing less. Under his quiet prodding, the structure of the Commonwealth was revamped, and the Statute of Westminster, in 1931, declared Canada's new status for all to see. Canada now had her own diplomatic identity within the Commonwealth. As befitted that new status, by 1929 Canadian legations were opened in Washington, Paris, and Tokyo, and a British high commissioner had appeared in Ottawa. No longer would the governor general act as a channel of communications between the British government and the dominions. King had got his revenge on the hapless Byng.

If King's dealings with the Empire were his greatest triumph, those with the League of Nations were his greatest failure. Though for a time he thought of the League as a symbol of civilized diplomacy, by the mid-1920s he saw it simply as a debating society. Even worse, he felt it was a harmful organization; there would have been no Second World War, he wrote much later, "if the League of Nations had never existed." He fully shared the sentiments of his representative to the League, Senator Raoul Dandurand, that Canada was "a fire-proof house, far from inflammable materials." Thus, from the beginning, the King administration (much like Borden's before it) strenuously opposed all efforts to strengthen the collective security arrangements of the League; it was not, in King's mind, a law enforcement agency. Without the security arrangements embodied in Article 10 of its covenant, the League of Nations was weak. If it could not deter aggression, then what could it do? It could debate. And the Canadian government believed in these years that public debate would resolve disputes. Canada refused to sign any agreement that implied that it might be committed to come to the aid of any nation under attack. European disputes were essentially that: European. Canada did not wish to become involved. In this it shared the views of the United States, which had refused even to join the League. It was clear that, despite the efforts of Canadian leaders to achieve some sort of status on the world scene, they were not prepared to use that status in any positive way. All they were prepared to do was to join with those who were busily emasculating the League, so that when the crises of the 1930s arose, the League was impotent.

The Dirty Thirties

Few Canadians in the 1920s gave more than a passing thought to the League, to the imperial relationships, or even to the questions of status and autonomy. They had had their fill of Europe in the previous decade, and now they wished to be left alone to share in the prosperity of the decade. And indeed, at least in the latter years of the 1920s, rapid economic growth in both industry and agriculture led many to believe that at last Laurier's prediction was coming true: the twentieth century would be Canada's. Typically, there was only one foreign event that captured the imagination of the Canadian people. At the 1928 summer Olympic games in Amsterdam, Canadian women were competing for the first time. And what a debut they made! Not only did they win medals, but they captivated appreciative European fans with their new uniforms, which many considered risqué. For Canadian women this was not the sole triumph of the decade. Though women were beginning to make their mark in such professions as law and medicine, on the whole their conditions of work had improved little. Though more were being educated than ever before, and more were in the labour force, women were still largely restricted to traditional occupations. The workplace remained an area of great inequality. What had changed significantly was the legal status of women. On October 18, 1929, a Supreme Court decision that women were not persons and therefore not eligible for Senate appointments was overturned by the Judicial Committee of the Privy Council in Great Britain, then the highest court of appeal. Their lordships concluded that "the exclusion of women from all public offices is a relic of days more barbaric than ours. . . . To those who ask why the word [person] should include females the obvious answer is why should it not?" A few months later, the country's first woman senator, Cairine Wilson, was appointed by Mackenzie King.

Less than two weeks after the Privy Council decision, that triumph was almost forgotten in the general gloom. On October 29, Black Tuesday, the great boom of the 1920s came to an end. On that day, after several false alarms, the New York Stock Market collapsed. "Playing the market" had been the national sport of the decade, but suddenly, for reasons economists are still debating, everybody lost confidence in the market at the same time. Everyone wanted to sell, and no one wanted to buy. Within days, thousands had lost their life savings and were destitute. Within weeks, the value of shares on the market had gone down by thirty billion dollars.

The collapse of the market was only the beginning. Consumer spending declined drastically, and without customers, stores and factories and banks were soon closing all over North America. Within a year, millions of middle-class Americans and Canadians were without work or money. The impact of the collapse of the American economic system on the rest of the world was devastating. The gigantic American market was closed off by punishing tariffs; American investment abroad ceased; and American bankers began recalling their loans. International trade slowed to a halt, dropping by 50 percent within three years, and unemployment spread throughout the world.

Most desperately affected was Canada, which was inextricably linked to the American market. The Canadian economy was geared to export markets in minerals, lumber, newsprint, fish, and especially wheat. As early as 1928, for those astute enough to see them, the warning signs abounded. Prices for Canada's most important exports, newsprint and wheat, had begun to sag, and there was a general oversupply of most products. But instead of cutting back, production actually increased. Even worse, expecting higher wheat prices, Canadian wheat pools kept much of their harvest off the market in 1929. By the time they realized their tragic miscalculation, it was too late: there was no market for their wheat anywhere. By the end of the year nearly two hundred million bushels remained unsold. Since Canada derived one-third of her national income directly from abroad, she was drastically affected by the decline in trade and foreign investment. Construction ground to a halt. There was no demand for new homes, stores, factories, or mines. Throughout the country, hundreds of thousands were on the street without jobs, without money, without security, and, even worse, without hope. For these hopeless men and women there was no relief, no social welfare, no unemployment insurance. Many men were forced to abandon their families to join the huge army of hoboes travelling by freight from place to place, looking for work, for food, indeed for anything to keep them alive.

Of course, not everyone suffered. Those on pensions or fixed salaries suddenly found their money would now buy much more. And it was a wonderful world for those who were still wealthy. As the young John David Eaton, scion of the affluent Eaton family, later recalled, the Depression for him was a grand time since he could spend an entire evening dining and dancing at a posh restaurant for less than ten dollars. Expressing the view of his class, Eaton added that the Depression was a worthwhile experience since it taught men the value of a job.

Certainly everything was cheap – if you had the money. A good pair of shoes could be had for a dollar or two; a huge sirloin steak for 20 cents; a solid brick home in Montreal for under $5,000; a brand-new car for less than $500. The problem was that almost no one had the money to pay for these bargains. And since few could afford luxuries – or even necessities – stores and factories shut down and jobs disappeared. Worse, even though governments kept raising taxes, the collapse of economic activity meant there were less taxes to collect. Income, imports, and consumption declined; property taxes went unpaid. Just when they needed more revenues than ever before to alleviate distress, governments had far less than they had ever had. None was far-sighted enough to realize that the remedies recommended by a little known British economist, John Maynard Keynes, might work: governments should spend their way out of the depression by increasing deficits. Governments' goal, a balanced budget, simply prolonged both the economic downturn and the suffering of the Canadian people.

Though the Depression affected the whole country, some regions were hit harder than others. The worst by far was Saskatchewan. In the 1920s, that province was among the most prosperous farming communities in the world; by the 1930s it was among the least, for the Depression there was aggravated by natural disaster – grasshoppers, rust, drought, and drifting soil. No province was so completely dependent on one staple as Saskatchewan. And when the market for wheat collapsed, so did the entire economy of the province. In two years the total income of Saskatchewan's farmers fell by close to 90 percent. Wheat sold for $1.65 a bushel in 1929 was, by 1931, selling for under 30 cents. Thousands of farmers left the province, and more would have followed had neighbouring provinces not warned indigent farmers from Saskatchewan to stay away. Others were forced to go on whatever relief existed; but so strapped for funds were relief agencies that they could not provide fruits or vegetables for the hungry. For the first time ever, scurvy appeared on the Prairies. And if that were not bad enough, swarms of grasshoppers, "so dense," in the words of one farmer, "that they obscured the sun," ate their way through large parts of the province. So terrible was their rampage that they stalled buses and trains, clogged car radiators, and almost choked a patient to death in a dentist's chair by lodging in his throat while he had his mouth open to have a tooth extracted. And what the grasshoppers left behind, windstorms blew away. Millions of hectares of topsoil disappeared; much of southern Saskatchewan ended up in North Dakota and the American Midwest.

The economic depression in Saskatchewan was compounded by a disastrous drought that produced dust storms and drifting soil. This 1936 photograph shows a typical scene near Ponteix.

TREE NURSERY INDIAN HEAD/SASKATCHEWAN ARCHIVES, R-A17,005.

Though Saskatchewan was the most desperately affected by the Depression, her sister Prairie provinces also suffered, though not as drastically. Neither relied so heavily on wheat, and neither experienced such ravages from natural forces. The most recently settled province, Alberta, was the least well prepared to cope with the problems of the Depression. Of all the farmers in Canada those in Alberta could least afford high interest rates; yet theirs were the country's highest. Thus, Alberta's major problem was one of debt rather than destitution. In Manitoba, the suffering was worst among the residents of Winnipeg. Because it was totally dependent on East-West trade, when that collapsed, the economy of the city went down with it. Not only were most of the city's workers unemployed but they were joined by thousands of needy farmers and labourers pouring in from rural areas looking for jobs that weren't there. The situation in British Columbia was not much better. Like its prairie neighbours, it depended largely on the export trade for its wealth. Unemployed miners and forestry workers poured into Vancouver from the interior of the province. They were joined by thousands of penniless prairie farmers searching for work and a milder climate; they found only the latter. In the words of one disgusted citizen, Vancouver had become "just a blamed summer resort for all the hoboes in Canada."

Economic depressions were not unfamiliar to the Maritimes – or to Ontario and Quebec, for that matter. But none had ever known any so unrelenting and savage. Unemployment was particularly severe in southern Ontario and Montreal, both of which had relied heavily on western trade for their prosperity. The huge manufacturing complex of Canada's industrial heartland ground to a halt. Countless thousands were without jobs; many were evicted from their homes. They had nowhere to go and nothing to do.

Faced with such widespread destitution and hardship, the federal government was paralyzed. With the onset of the Depression even the usually unflappable Mackenzie King was shaken, though less, it seems, by the calamity itself than by his failure to correct the situation. He was a born conciliator, and he had no reason to doubt that he could negotiate his way out of this economic downturn. It was, he believed, only a "temporary seasonal slackness." His remedies were as useless as they were naive: balancing the budget and slashing government expenditures. These were typical Liberal solutions to a problem that had no solution; all they did was exacerbate the crisis. In any case, the prime minister was convinced that the Depression was a political rather than an economic problem. Thus, when he received desperate requests from provincial and municipal governments for financial assistance to cope with the horrendous difficulties confronting them, King passed them off as nothing more than a Tory plot to undermine his government. If these governments wanted to spend money, he told Parliament, they should collect it themselves. He would give them none. Why should he? As King told the House of Commons in April 1930: "As far as giving moneys out of the federal treasury to any Tory government in this country for these alleged unemployment purposes . . . I would not give them a five cent piece."

Though later that evening he confided to his diary that he had gone too far and should never have made that statement since it made him appear "indifferent to the conditions of the unemployed," it was too late to do anything about it. Whatever he meant to say, the Tories did not let the country forget that the prime minister had publicly vowed not to give a nickel for unemployment relief and to help only those who lived in provinces with Liberal administrations. This slip of the tongue would cost him dearly.

Totally oblivious to how unpopular he and his policies were with the Canadian people, the supremely confident King decided to call an election in the fall of 1930. What he had not taken into account – and could not because he did not understand it – was the impact of the Depression on the Canadian electorate. As well, he seriously underestimated the abilities of the new Conservative leader, R.B. Bennett.

Bennett in Command

Born in New Brunswick of Loyalist stock, the ambitious Bennett went to Calgary at the age of 26 and began a lucrative career in law and business. Unlike the flabby prime minister, Bennett was tall, imposing, and immaculately groomed, though somewhat paunchy. In his later years he spent much time on the masseur's table in a vain attempt to control his

R. B. Bennett.

C-7731/NATIONAL ARCHIVES OF CANADA.

weight. The alternative, to limit his voracious appetite to three meals a day, either never occurred to him or was unacceptable. He was a millionaire and he looked the part; he was rarely seen without his tophat or bowler, tail coat, striped trousers, expensive patent leather shoes, gloves, and cane. A fiery speaker – he was known as "Bonfire" Bennett, once having been clocked at 220 words per minute – he was more than King's match on the hustings.

Bennett's campaign was a classic. The less the prime minister talked about the Depression, the more Bennett emphasized it. And unlike King, he had a solution; he would "use tariffs to blast a way" for Canadian goods into world markets. The tariff was his panacea; it would restore prosperity to businesspeople, farmers, and workers.

This was the first federal election fought on the issue of unemployment, and despite King's unstinting efforts to ignore it, he could not. Even though approximately 14 percent of the workforce was unemployed, King did not think it a serious political matter. "Men who are working," he said, "are not going to worry particularly over some of those who are not." Everywhere he went he became the target of wooden nickels or shouts of "Five-Cent Piece." And he received little help. With the Conservatives in control of most of the provinces, the Liberal election machine, which relied on provincial party support, was in total disarray. Liberals everywhere were overwhelmed by the Tory campaign. Bennett seemed to have all the answers; King had none. This was also the first federal campaign in which radio was extensively used by the candidates, and Bennett proved to be far superior to King as a communicator. However, neither was as popular as "Amos 'n' Andy," an American comedy show that captured the vast bulk of the radio audience during the political broadcasts.

Not surprisingly, in their desperation, thousands turned to the new saviour. Bennett had promised to solve the economic problems or "perish in the attempt." By a landslide, Canadians voted to grant the Conservative leader his somewhat morbid wish. The Tories won 137 seats, including a remarkable 24 in Quebec; the Liberals won 91. The Depression would now be Bennett's problem to solve, and he threw himself into the task with enormous energy.

But even in defeat, King's devoted political mistress, Lady Luck, had not deserted him. Aside from the stalemate in 1925, this was the only election he ever lost, and it was the only one worth losing. For now Bennett and the Conservatives would be saddled with the Depression. It was their unenviable task to find the appropriate nostrums. Defeat had saved the Liberals from disaster. As King noted in his diary on election night, "Bennett has promised impossible things and put himself in an impossible situation. . . . My guess is he will go to pieces under the strain."

As usual, King was right. There was no way that someone with Bennett's background and philosophy could solve the problems of the greatest economic crisis in Canadian history. He was a conservative who believed in a sound, hard currency and disliked spending money on massive public works or relief payments. A balanced budget, he was convinced, would protect Canada's credit rating, and this would ultimately help break the back of the Depression. He shared with his American counterpart, Herbert Hoover, the belief that the crisis was largely psychological. As the American President said, "What this country needs is a great big laugh. . . . If someone could get off a joke every ten days, I think our troubles would be over." Bennett was proud that the banks were bulging with money. "There is no shortage of currency," he reassured hungry, unemployed, homeless Canadians. Nor was unemployment a serious problem. "One of the greatest assets a man can have on entering life's struggle," he told a group of students, "is poverty." One of the few positive steps Bennett undertook in his first years in office was to raise the tariff. He did provide more than ten times the amount spent on relief in the entire previous decade to help those out of work, but he emphasized that unemployment was a provincial and municipal responsibility, and neither level of government could count on a continuous flow of funds from Ottawa. As under the previous regime, the provinces and municipalities would have to pay for the ravages of the Depression from their own rapidly dwindling treasuries.

There is no question that Bennett threw himself totally into his job. No prime minister worked harder or took on more responsibility. He was his own external affairs minister and, for a time, his own finance minister, and he delegated very little. In effect he was almost a one-man government, causing one wit to remark that a Conservative cabinet meeting was Bennett talking to himself. But he had only one policy, higher tariffs, and once that failed, he seemed to run out of ideas. He went to London to propose an imperial customs union against the rest of the world but was rebuffed by the British, who saw little in it for them. At the subsequent Imperial Economic Conference in Ottawa in 1932, the British were not much more forthcoming. Bennett did establish the Bank of Canada in 1934 to give greater stability to the country's finances, but he decreed that it would be privately owned and not controlled by the government.

The Depression devastated the country. Unemployed men "rode the rods," fruitlessly crossing the country in search of work. Farmers, such as this Ukrainian family in Edmonton in 1934, were driven off their land by crop failure or the seizure of their land by the banks.

GLENBOW ARCHIVES, CALGARY/ND-3-6742.

The Depression worsened in the terrible winter of 1933, when about one-third of Canada's workforce was unemployed, and nothing Bennett did worked. Canadians were now turning against their saviour, who had promised to get them out of the Depression but, in fact, seemed to be immersing them even deeper. Soon the prime minister became the butt of their bitter humour. An abandoned prairie farm was now known as a Bennett barnyard; a Bennett blanket was a newspaper; and roasted wheat was Bennett coffee. Eggs Bennett? Broiled chestnuts. A Bennett buggy was an engineless automobile drawn by a horse.

And even when Bennett tried something new, it boomeranged. The Depression had spawned a new danger: thousands of homeless, jobless young men riding on freight cars, drifting from one place to another, and looking for work that was never there were seen as a threat by many middle-class Canadians. The "menace of single men" spread across Canada almost like the Great Fear at the time of the French Revolution. They were hounded by police, arrested as vagrants, and then unceremoniously escorted out of town. In the words of Gideon Robertson, the minister of labour, who was asked to investigate the problem, "They are becoming a menace to the peace and even safety of many communities along the lines of railway . . . especially among the women folk."

In response to the demand that something be done about this army of the unemployed roaming throughout the land, "threatening everything

GLENBOW ARCHIVES, CALGARY/NC-6-12955(e).

There had always been hoboes, such as this veteran of the road, but the Depression greatly increased their numbers.

GLENBOW ARCHIVES, CALGARY/NC-6-12955(j).

in their path,'' in the words of one frightened matron, work camps were opened across the country. Most were run by the Department of National Defence under military control and law. They were supposed to help the single homeless persons, as they were euphemistically referred to on the official relief rolls, by providing them with work, food, and shelter. As a side benefit, the chief of the General Staff, Major General A.G.L. McNaughton, reported that these camps were ''directed to the breaking up of the congestion of single homeless men in the principal centres of population . . . otherwise we would have had no recourse [but to use] military forces to suppress disorder.''

Whether the camps were used to benefit them or simply to keep them out of sight made little difference to the 175 000 inmates who at one time or another found themselves as ''guests'' of the government. Though some camps were well run, comparatively comfortable, and treated the unemployed with respect, many were more like prisons or ''slave camps,'' as they were known to the many who passed through them. The pay was an insulting 20 cents a day; the food was terrible; the bedbugs plentiful; the life depressing; the isolation unbearable. Most camps were deep in the bush, far from the cities. And the work was hard – clearing land for highways and airports in swampy, mosquito-infested areas. There was no entertainment: no books, no sports, and of course, no alcoholic beverages.

Frustrated beyond endurance by the conditions in the camps and by the federal government's adamant refusal – or inability – to provide work for real wages, these Royal Twenty-Centers, as they called themselves, eventually rebelled. Thousands left the camps in the interior of British Columbia and congregated in Vancouver to lobby for their cause. There they paraded through the streets, snake-danced down the city's main intersections, crowded in the aisles of department stores, pan-handled their way through the city, and eventually occupied the museum.

The Vancouver City Council did "donate" $1800 to recapture the museum, but when Ottawa failed to respond, the young men, led by their union, the Relief Camp Workers Union, decided to go directly to Parliament Hill to complain. As they headed across the Prairies by freight, the On-to-Ottawa Trek picked up hundreds of reinforcements. But when they arrived in Regina, the RCMP ordered them into the local stadium where they would be billeted and fed, while their leaders went on to Ottawa to meet with the prime minister.

After the collapse of the talks between Bennett and the march leaders on Dominion Day, the order to clear the trekkers out of Regina was given. For two hours, Market Square was a mass of seething humanity as strikers battled both the Mounties and the city police. It was no contest. In short order, the trekkers were cowed. One man, a city detective, was killed, scores were injured, and 130 strikers were arrested. The rest dispersed quietly within a few weeks, some to their camps, others to their homes, but most to begin their lives as hoboes all over again.

To Bennett, these men were agitators and Communists, or at least the pawns of agitators and Communists. He was certain that Canada was on the verge of revolution and was determined to maintain law and order at all costs. In many instances the unemployed who organized were indeed led by Communists. Thus, under the infamous Section 98 of the Criminal Code, invoked in 1931, prominent Communists, including the party's leader, Tim Buck, were convicted of "seditious conspiracy, and belonging to an unlawful organization." Other alleged militants were also jailed and, when possible, deported. Troops were used to put down strikes and break up demonstrations. The prime minister even wanted to send a destroyer full of troops into Vancouver's harbour to prevent a

May Day parade in that city in 1932. The R.C.M.P. was ordered to infiltrate trade unions, organizations of the unemployed, and other such "subversive" groups. Civil liberties were trampled; the right of thousands of hungry men and women to protest was forgotten in the frenzied atmosphere of the time. Teachers were fired for speaking their minds on the situation; foreigners were threatened with deportation if they went on strike or even took part in demonstrations; and union organizers were constantly harassed and always on the verge of being arrested.[8]

The Department of Immigration discovered an ingenious way of fighting the Depression: it would simply threaten to deport immigrants who asked for relief. In 1933 alone over 7000 were expelled. Their crime? Being unemployed and hungry. "Shovelling out the redundant" was popular with municipal authorities who provided federal authorities with the names of foreigners who had asked for relief. Some municipalities even forced applicants for welfare to first sign a document requesting deportation. And though, in the end, not that many were expelled, it was certainly a threat distinctly felt by many immigrants who thought about applying for relief.[9]

The Depression was even more desperately cruel and trying for Canadian women since neither government nor society in general took seriously their plight. After all, men were the breadwinners, the heads of families; it was their wages that provided sustenance to the family. And, as well, unlike women, they were highly vocal, visible, and carried enormous political clout. How could the needs of women compare with those of men?

Or at least that was the predominant attitude of the period. For a woman to take a "man's job" simply was not done, no matter how desperate her situation. How could she brazenly rob someone of his manhood and his family of an income? Every job held by a woman was perceived as one taken away from a man who needed it more. Society's

---

[8] There is a large body of literature on the Depression. On the politics, see Neatby on King, vols. II, III. There is no good study of Bennett. A good survey is H.B. Neatby, *The Politics of Chaos* (Toronto, 1972), while the best economic study is A.E. Safarian, *The Canadian Economy in the Great Depression* (Toronto, 1959). See also Alvin Finkel, *Business and Social Reform in the Thirties* (Toronto, 1979), Michiel Horn, *The Dirty Thirties* (Toronto, 1972) and his *The Depression in Canada: Responses to Economic Crisis* (Toronto, 1988). The best study of unemployment is James Struthers, *No Fault of Their Own: Unemployment and the Canadian Welfare State* (Toronto, 1983).

[9] See Barbara Roberts, *Whence They Came: Deportation From Canada: 1900-1935*, (Ottawa, 1988).

priority was to find work for men, not for women. Thus, most school boards, professional organizations, governments, manufacturers, and retailers stopped hiring women.

In order to survive, many women were once again forced into domestic work, reversing the trend of the previous two decades in which women had been moving in increasing numbers into sales and clerical jobs, and even into the professions. Worse, the wages of domestics were abysmally low, even in a period in which all wages were low. Domestics in 1930, for example, averaged less than $300 a year, while employed males earned three or four times that amount. In some provinces domestics worked for less than $4 a week – and in some cases simply for room and board. According to a government study, between 1921 and 1936 the number of domestics in Canada doubled, while their wages decreased by half.

Ironically, working against women were the minimum wage laws that had been enacted in many provinces specifically to protect them. But since these laws did not apply to men, many companies simply fired the women and hired men and boys at a far lower wage, thus forcing women into occupations with no minimum wage protection, or worse, into unemployment. Two royal commissions of the period – on price spreads and the textile industry – uncovered much evidence of women being displaced by men because of the higher wage employers were required to pay their female workers. And in those industries not covered by legislation, women were paid 60 percent less than men.

Nor were there any specific measures for unemployed women as there were for men – no work camps, no public work programs. Women were supposed to marry and be taken care of by their husbands; and if they were young and single, they were their father's responsibility. And if husbands and fathers could not provide the necessary support, there was always work as a char or a domestic. Sadly, many young women found they could only survive by selling their bodies. As a C.C.F. member of Parliament reported in the House in 1937, many of these single, unemployed women looking for work "ended up in questionable sections of cities [to be] taken advantage of by the touts of the underworld."[10]

---

[10] For the role of women in the 1920s and 1930s see Alison Prentice et al., *Canadian Women: A History* (Toronto, 1988); Victoria Strong-Boag "The Girl of the New Day," *Labour/Le Travailleur* (1979), as well as articles in S. Trofimenkoff and Alison Prentice, eds., *The Neglected Majority*, vols. I, II (1985), and J. Acton et al., eds. *Women at Work: Ontario, 1850-1930* (Toronto, 1974).

An important consequence of the grinding poverty in which most women found themselves was the emergence of a birth-control movement, though the distribution of information and the sale of contraceptive devices were still illegal. Birth control clinics were set up in various places to help working-class women deal with repeated unwanted pregnancies. The trial in 1936 of Dorothea Parker for disseminating contraceptive information to women in the suburbs of Ottawa provided the movement with a platform to sell its message about the need for birth control. Parker's acquittal was a great victory for the movement, though the law remained unchanged for another generation.

There were many prominent Canadians who were opposed to birth control – and not simply for religious reasons. Between 1919 and 1939, the birth rate dropped from almost 30 per thousand to just over 20. The average family now had three children rather than the five or six of a previous generation, thus prompting some, including Dr. Helen MacMurchy, director of the Dominion Division of Child Welfare, to warn that Canada was committing "race suicide."

New Ideas

Ironically, given the hardships and agonies endured by most Canadians, the number of civil disturbances in Canada were remarkably few. Perhaps the Canadian people were too hungry, too busy looking for work, too engrossed in mere survival to have time for rebellion. However, it is certain that the Bennett government overreacted. There was never a threat of revolution in Canada. But what did happen was perhaps as frightening to the Canadian establishment – the politicians, bankers, industrialists, businesspeople, and senior civil servants who felt that they had the moral right to govern. For the first time Canadians began to examine the existing economic, social, and political systems and found them unsatisfactory. Throughout the country there was a clamour for change, culminating in a series of upheavals that altered the political topography of the nation.

Predictably, the most important of these disturbances occurred in Western Canada, a region prone to political eruptions. For some time, the various socialist and labour groups in the West had been chafing in frustration. It was clear that neither of the old-line parties had anything to offer the Canadian people except more of the same failed policies. Something new was needed. In the summer of 1932, in Calgary, something new was created. At a meeting of western labour parties, representatives appeared from various farm groups. It was decided to form a united socialist party with an imposing, if awkward, name: the Co-operative Commonwealth Federation (Farmer Labour Socialist). A year later these somewhat oddly assorted groups met again in Regina and accepted as their canon a manifesto written by members of the League for Social Reconstruction, a body of academics inclined to socialism. The manifesto called for the replacement of the capitalist system, with its inherent injustice and inhumanity, by "a social order from which domination and exploitation of one class by another will be eliminated"; it advocated public ownership of all financial institutions, public utilities, and transportation companies, especially that bête noire of all western farmers, the Canadian Pacific Railway.

Only one man could have united the several disparate farm, urban, labour, and socialist components that formed the C.C.F., and he was acclaimed the party's leader. James S. Woodsworth, the M.P. from Winnipeg, the House leader of the "Ginger Group" composed of Progressive and labour members, had provided much of the impetus for the Calgary and Regina meetings. He was comfortable with, and respected by, workers, farmers, and intellectuals. A former Methodist minister, he was steeped in the social gospel of an activist, caring

Delegates to the founding convention of the C.C.F., held in Regina in July 1933. J.S. Woodsworth is front and centre.

C-29298//NATIONAL ARCHIVES OF CANADA.

J.S. Woodsworth, first leader of the C.C.F.

C-34443/NATIONAL ARCHIVES OF CANADA.

Christianity and saw it, rather than Marxism, as the basis for socialism. Mild, gentle-mannered, extraordinarily patient and honest – his biographer not hyperbolically described him as "a prophet in politics" – he was able to convince many of the doubtful that, in spite of the fire and brimstone of its manifesto, the C.C.F. was actually a moderate reformist party, calling for changes "through orderly and peaceful means."

The C.C.F. made rapid headway, especially in the West. It soon became the official Opposition in British Columbia and Saskatchewan. And in the federal election of 1935 it polled about 400 000 votes and elected seven members. But even then the problems that would block its attempts to become a national force were readily apparent. The C.C.F. made little impact in either Quebec or the Maritime provinces, and it never would. It was shunned by many industrial workers, who preferred to continue voting the old family patterns of Tory or Grit. And to many, its philosophy, no matter how scented by Woodsworth, still reeked of communism. Nonetheless, both as a party and a movement, the C.C.F. made an indelible mark on the Canadian scene, a mark far more enduring than its limited membership and electoral success seemed to warrant.[11]

At the other end of the ideological spectrum, a movement arose in Alberta that would provide its own novel approach to the problems of the time. Social Credit was largely the work of one man, a fundamentalist lay preacher from Ontario, William Aberhart. Every Sunday afternoon throughout the early 1930s, a quarter of a million people in Alberta sat beside their radios listening to his fiery sermons. His, it was said, was the most popular radio program in the province, next to Jack Benny's. And of course, Benny was not running for office; nor was Aberhart at first. He was interested only in spreading the word of the Lord, that is, until he read a book on Social Credit written by a peculiar Scottish engineer, Major C.H. Douglas. It was like a flash of revelation to Aberhart. Overnight he became a monetary as well as a religious fundamentalist and began preaching both the doctrines of Christ and of Social Credit. Taken together, to Aberhart they were the answer to all the world's moral and economic ills. The essence of Social Credit was that since there never was enough money available to buy the always-available goods and services, governments should issue "social dividends," or cash payments, to everyone. This would keep the consumers' ability to buy in balance with the farmers' and manufacturers' ability to produce. Basically this was Social Credit's "A plus B theorem," which most economists dismiss as both semantic and financial nonsense. Nonetheless Aberhart was convinced, and he carried the message into every home with a radio.

It was an especially appealing doctrine in Alberta where there was an abundance of consumer goods but no noney to buy them. Who could argue against a scheme that promised to provide funds to everyone, particularly when it was being sold by a man who was also busy saving

---

[11] On the C.C.F., the basic book is Walter Young, *The Anatomy of a Party: the National C.C.F., 1932-61* (Toronto, 1969). This can now be supplemented by David Lewis, *The Good Fight: Political Memoirs, 1909-58* (Toronto, 1981); Michiel Horn, *The League for Social Reconstruction: Intellectual Origins of the Democratic Left in Canada, 1930-42* (Toronto, 1980); and K. McNaught, *A Prophet in Politics* (Toronto, 1959). On Social Credit, the basic books can be found in the *Social Credit in Alberta* series, most notably the volumes by J.R. Mallory, John Irving, and C.B. Macpherson. The sole biography of Aberhart is by L.P.V. Johnson and Ola McNutt, *Aberhart of Alberta* (Edmonton, 1970). Useful documents are collected by Lewis Thomas in *William Aberhart and Social Credit in Alberta* (Toronto, 1977). On the Communist Party, see Norman Penner, *Canadian Communism* (Toronto, 1988).

souls? The new gospel of Social Credit spread like the ever-present prairie windstorms across the province. Aberhart set up study groups, circulated pamphlets, and made hundreds of speeches, preaching his inflationary message to anyone who would listen. It was only a matter of time before the religious crusade turned into a political one and Aberhart founded a party to contest the next provincial election.

The Alberta election of 1935 could not have come at a better time for Aberhart. The premier of the province, John Brownlee, was charged in a morality suit brought by his housemaid. His minister of public works was deeply involved in a messy divorce case. The government was in a shambles, demoralized, scandal-ridden. With no viable opposition, the Social Credit Party was merely filling a vacuum. It won a stunning victory, carrying 63 seats out of the 70 in the legislature. But as Premier Aberhart soon discovered, Social Credit was easier to preach than to practise. When, after some 18 months in office, he eventually got around to introducing policies based on Social Credit theories, all were disal-

Social Credit was viewed with scorn – outside of Alberta.   DALE/*WINNIPEG FREE PRESS.*

lowed by the federal authorities or by the courts. Aberhart did pass major legislation to reduce debts and mortgages, but in the end, what happened was what Aberhart vowed never would: its fervour spent, Social Credit became just another political party. It would provide Alberta with a solid, free-enterprise, conservative government for the next generation, but its

Elected in 1935, Premier W.A. Aberhart of Alberta was a spellbinding orator who seemed to have the answers to the Depression. His successor, Ernest Manning, sits behind the premier.

W.J. OLIVER/GLENBOW ARCHIVES, CALGARY/NB-16-206.

theories were now only useful as campaign rhetoric. The eternal verities of Social Credit were never to be implemented.

The political ferment of these years was, surprisingly, matched by an unparalleled cultural activity. The 1920s and 30s were perhaps the golden years of Canadian art. In 1920 the Group of Seven was founded by seven of the country's most nationalistic and ground-breaking artists. Lawren Harris, A.Y. Jackson, Arthur Lismer, J.H. Varley, Franklin Carmichael, J.E.H. MacDonald and Franz Johnston captured the imagination of Canadians with their passionate, compelling landscapes, all painted in bright hues evoking for Canadians the mystery, beauty, and grandeur of their harsh land. Other artists such as David Milne, Emily Carr, and A.J. Casson, and after his death in 1917, Tom Thomson, were also making their mark.

In addition, more than 700 Canadian novels were published in these years. Publishing houses such as Ryerson, Gage, Macmillan, McClelland and Stewart, and Musson were actively searching for Canadian authors. Indeed, some of those authors, in particular Frederick Philip Grove, Mazo de la Roche, and Morley Callaghan, were already well known. Inspired by Ringuet's watershed novel *Thirty Acres*, the first full-scale, realistic treatment of the life of the Quebec farmer, a new generation of nationalistic French-Canadian writers came into being. The cauldron of the Depression was also forging a group of young writers who would soon revolutionize Canadian literature – Hugh MacLennan, A.M. Klein, Gabrielle Roy, and Frank Scott, to name a few.

Ironically, though there was more ideological writing than ever before, the typical Canadian novel of the 1930s was escapist – an adventure, a historical romance, or a comedy. The grief of the decade, noted one commentator, was too overwhelming to write about. With the exception of *As For Me and My House* by Sinclair Ross, most of the good fiction about the Depression was written much later, by a younger generation. Clearly those living through it found it difficult to write about. When they could afford it, Canadians flocked to Hollywood movies; more often, they huddled around their radios listening to American comedy and variety shows. Even the formation of the Canadian Broadcasting Corporation could do little to stop the swamping effects of the American cultural juggernaut. In the depths of the Depression people wanted to forget, to be entertained; no one could do it better, it seemed, than the Americans.

One event, however, did allow Canadians to forget momentarily their concerns. In the early morning of May 28, 1934, five identical baby girls were born on a farm near North Bay, Ontario. Within days the Dionne quintuplets became the world's best-known babies and Northern Ontario's prime economic resource. At their peak, according to their biographer, they represented a $500-million asset. Three million tourists made their way to "Quintland" to see the babies. Millions more watched them play on newsreels in theatres across the world. Along with Niagara Falls, they were Canada's greatest tourist attraction. In a decade full of disasters, the quints were good news; their cheerful photographs, the

Tom Thomson, drowned in 1917, inspired other Canadian artists with his paintings of the wilderness.

C-17399/NATIONAL ARCHIVES OF CANADA.

up-beat news stories, and the countless hours of fascinating film footage were a welcome relief to a country suffering through its blackest years.

By 1935 there was still no respite from the ravages of the Depression. With the economy worsening, western sectionalism on the rise again, new parties appearing all over, and with every Conservative provincial government gone, R.B. Bennett for the first time began to doubt his own policies. The champion of the status quo, the darling of the right, the man who advocated crushing Communists under "the iron heel of ruthlessness" suddenly, without warning, moved dramatically to the left. He had been disturbed by the allegations of his minister of trade and commerce, H.H. Stevens, who claimed to have uncovered frightening evidence of price-fixing, starvation wages, and barbaric working conditions, charges later supported by the hastily appointed Royal Commission on Price Spreads. When Stevens went public with his indictment of the outrages of the capitalist system, he was forced out of the Cabinet and shortly thereafter set up his own Reconstruction Party. Nonetheless, the prime minister could not ignore Stevens's popularity and the widespread conviction that captains of industry, with whom he had for so long had a symbiotic relationship, were venal and corrupt. He now began to listen more intently to his brother-in-law, W.D. Herridge, the Canadian minister to the United States, who was urging him to introduce into Canada some aspects of President Franklin Delano Roosevelt's New Deal.

Once convinced, the prime minister did not delay. Early in January 1935, he stunned the public – as well as his cabinet and caucus – with a series of five coast-to-coast radio broadcasts that called for nothing less than a new society. The old order, he announced, was gone and would never return. He advocated unemployment insurance, subsidized housing, and minimum wage legislation. The capitalist system was in desperate need of reform, he charged, and he was prepared to reform it. An unkind observer remarked that Bennett had discovered the evils of capitalism only after he had accumulated his millions. However, true to his word, within a matter of weeks he brought into the House the most far-reaching reform package ever introduced by any Canadian government. Legislation was passed to fix minimum wages and maximum hours, to establish unemployment insurance, and to give the government control over prices, business practices, and marketing conditions. Though not as radical as his radio talks, the legislation was still enough to frighten every Conservative in the country. "There could only be one explanation," said a prominent Tory. "The prime minister has gone mad."

Mad or not, Bennett knew he had to do something to save the country and his own political career. Elections were looming, and he could hardly go to the people on his record. After all, he had won an election five years before by promising to end unemployment. Now he was confronted with the worst unemployment in the country's history. His New Deal was a last, desperate attempt to salvage another term. Radio broadcasts had worked for Roosevelt; in Alberta they were performing miracles for Aberhart. Bennett was convinced they would do the same for him. But it was too late for what Woodsworth called "a deathbed conversion." Bennett had presided over the worst five years in Canadian history. The people of Canada were determined that he would not preside over another five.

On October 14, 1935, they got their chance. In a massive landslide vote the government of R.B. Bennett was swept away. Rarely has so unpopular a government faced an electorate; and it was a government badly divided. Many of his cabinet ministers were opposed to Bennett's new economic and social policies. Tories throughout the country were confused and aghast at the new turn their party had taken. To them Bennett's policy was communistic. Many would stay home rather than vote. In truth, except for a slogan – "King or Chaos" – the Liberals had no platform; they did not need one. With Stevens's Reconstruction Party successfully wooing away 400 000 potential Conservative voters, the Tories were nearly wiped out. They won only 40 seats, compared to the Liberals' 173. Not knowing what to expect from the suddenly unpredictable Bennett, the Canadian electorate took the safe path and opted for the dull, cautious, but eminently reliable Mackenzie King.

Five years in the Opposition seemed not to have changed Mackenzie King in the slightest. The magnitude of the Depression still escaped him. Campaigning in 1935, he sounded like the discredited Herbert Hoover: "What is needed more than a change of economic structure," he said, "is a change of heart." Unemployment was not the result of defects in the system, he claimed. Rather it was caused by human selfishness and greed. It was clear that King was far less likely to tamper with the system than was Bennett. Echoing the Bennett of 1930, he declared that balancing the budget and slashing government spending would start Canada back on the road to prosperity. All he would do to accelerate matters was to lower the tariff and to sign a trade agreement with the United States. To aid the unemployed who were still wandering around the country or sitting out the Depression in the work camps, he could think of nothing better than to close the camps, which he found too expensive. Predictably, an army of 10 000 homeless men were soon again on the march, looking for work and raising old fears of disorder. However, what disturbed him most was the crisis in federal-provincial financial relations. The four western provinces owed the federal government over $115 million and could not pay back a penny. King vowed that they would be making no further raids on the federal treasury.

But how else could the provinces function unless they were funded from Ottawa? They had many responsibilities but no money. Under the British North America Act the provinces had very limited power to tax; yet it was they who bore the burden of the strained times. The Depression had made it clear that the federal system was badly lopsided: the provinces had most of the pressing tasks – welfare services, relief payments, education, highway construction – but few sources of revenue, while the federal government had almost unlimited taxing power but, under the Constitution, could not infringe on the jurisdiction of the provinces. Indeed, much of Bennett's ill-fated New Deal legislation was rejected by the courts because it undertook activities in areas that were exclusively under provincial control. Thus Ottawa, even if it had the will, did not have the power to adopt measures that might alleviate the economic and social disasters that were crippling the nation. With the imminent possibility of some provinces going bankrupt, King was forced into action. He would not grant any more loans to the provinces, since to him it would be "simply sending good money after bad money"; furthermore, it would make it impossible for him to achieve his goal of balancing the federal budget. Instead he appointed a Royal Commission on Dominion-Provincial Relations under the chief justice of Ontario, Newton Rowell, to investigate and make recommendations concerning the constitutional and financial relations between Ottawa and the provinces. The commission did not report until 1940.

Labour Organization

Rather than uniting Canada in a crusade against a common enemy, the Depression had exacerbated regional and provincial disparities. Emboldened by the acute conditions and their growing social responsibilities, the provinces rose up to challenge Ottawa. The provincial premiers of the 1930s were unique products of the Depression. For the most part bitter and resentful of their treatment at the hands of Ottawa, they were colourful, radical, and eccentric, and so were many of their policies. Some, such as Aberhart in Alberta and Maurice Duplessis in Quebec, founded new parties to express their discontent; others, such as T. Dufferin Pattullo in British Columbia and Mitchell Hepburn in Ontario, kept the old party names but undertook programs that had little in common with their traditional party platforms.

Born not too far from Mackenzie King's birthplace in southwestern Ontario, "Duff" Pattullo had made a name for himself in British Columbia as a dynamic entrepreneur. He was elected premier in 1933 and at once attempted to introduce "a little New Deal" policy in British Columbia. "Work and Wages" was his slogan, and it swept the province. His was the most vigorous program of its kind in Canada. But it was dependent on federal funds, few of which were forthcoming from the tight-fisted administrators in Ottawa. Mackenzie King thought he could

Mitch Hepburn (right) and Maurice Duplessis, premiers of Ontario and Quebec, respectively, in the late 1930s.

C-19518/NATIONAL ARCHIVES OF CANADA.

hoard his way out of the Depression; Pattullo wanted to spend his way out. His was a liberalism totally unrecognizable to the prime minister.

Even more unrecognizable, and much more dangerous, was the liberalism of the Premier of Ontario, Mitch Hepburn. An onion farmer from the St. Thomas area, he had come to power on a radical program, promising "to swing to the left" and to fight for "the dispossessed and oppressed." However, it was not long after he took office that he began to fight against them. Under the influence of the industrial magnates of the province, he launched a crusade against a militant American industrial union, the Committee for Industrial Organizations (C.I.O.), which was threatening to organize the province's industries and mines. When King refused to send in the R.C.M.P. to help Hepburn put down a peaceful strike at the General Motors plant in Oshawa, the Ontario premier declared war on the federal government. He organized his own antilabour police force – in Oshawa they were known as "Hepburn's Hussars" or the "Sons of Mitch's" – so he would not have to rely on "cowardly" federal authorities "when the security of Ontario was threatened." King, he said, was a "tin pot dictator" who was "living in a past age, a generation without any hope of betterment." He even thundered that he would push the prime minister through a washing-machine wringer.

Indeed, Hepburn had much to fear from the newly revivified labour movements that were threatening not only to organize workers under the nose of his wealthy cronies, but to turn the industrial relations system of his province – and perhaps of all Canada – upside down. For trade unions, as for everyone else, the Depression had been traumatic. Membership plummeted as jobs disappeared. Long-established locals vanished throughout the country. Never had the union movement been so immobilized. Indeed, only one union, the Workers Unity League, seemed to be functioning.

Created by the Communist Party, the W.U.L. consisted of industrial unions in the garment, lumber, mining, and textile industries. Its scores of devoted organizers provided the leadership for most of the important labour struggles of the period, including the bloody Estevan-Bienfait strike in which police killed three strikers, and the walkout of furniture workers and chicken-pluckers in Stratford, Ontario, which was put down only with the help of troops and armoured cars. By 1935, when it was disbanded on orders from the Soviet Union, it claimed a membership of some 40 000, the majority of whom were not Communists.

In that same year, however, one in which the Canadian labour movement was at its nadir with fewer members than at any time since the end of the war, a new labour organization was being created in the United States that would ultimately revolutionize trade unionism in Canada. Under the leadership of the fiery leader of the United Mine Workers, John L. Lewis, a new labour centre, the Committee for Industrial Organization, began a whirlwind campaign to organize industrial workers. In two short years it had enrolled millions of unskilled, previously unorganized workers in automobile, steel, meat packing, and other plants throughout America.

Enviously eyeing the C.I.O.'s success, Canadian workers – many of them one-time activists in the W.U.L. – began organizing C.I.O. unions north of the border without the permission, or knowledge, of the C.I.O. leadership. Within months, the C.I.O. had hundreds of new members and dozens of new unions it knew nothing about. Not one cent of C.I.O. money, not one C.I.O. organizer, not one note of C.I.O. encouragement had crossed the border to help in this campaign. Canadians were on their own.

The turning point for the C.I.O. in Canada, which changed its rather limited organizing campaign into a passionate crusade, occurred at Oshawa, Ontario, in April of 1937. There, 4000 workers at the huge General Motors plant went out on strike and asked the C.I.O. and its affiliate, the United Automobile Workers, for assistance. They received one organizer and no money. Despite the C.I.O.'s lack of support and despite the desperate efforts of Hepburn to crush the strike and keep the C.I.O. out of Ontario, the strikers persevered and won a dramatic victory. Spurred on by this triumph, the C.I.O. began a vast organizational campaign, largely in the industrial areas of Ontario, and within a year it had organized thousands of workers. A renewed sense of militancy and idealism permeated Canadian labour for the first time since the end of the Winnipeg Strike.

For the workers of Canada, C.I.O. was a magic name. Wherever they heard it, they flocked; whoever used it, they trusted. Canadian workers obviously felt that the C.I.O. magic would rub off on them, that what the C.I.O. was achieving for its members in the United States it would also achieve for its members in Canada. For the first time unions were appearing in industries that were traditionally thought to be unorganizable: there were now unions for steel workers, automobile workers, electrical workers, rubber workers, packing-house workers, pulp and paper workers, lumber and sawmill workers, and mine and smelter workers. The C.I.O. had clearly revolutionized Canadian labour; it had created a powerful, aggressive and, most important, viable industrial union movement. It had, in effect, organized not only the unorganized but also those thought to be unorganizable.[12]

It was largely to destroy the C.I.O. before it became a real threat that Hepburn began exploring the possibility of an alliance with Premier Maurice Duplessis of Quebec. Like Hepburn, Duplessis had come into office promising reform; once in power he conveniently forgot all his promises. The Depression had proved to be a boon for French-Canadian nationalism, for it brought home to the Québécois the fact that the economy of their province was controlled by Americans and English-Canadians. Taking advantage of the situation, Duplessis, the clever and opportunistic leader of the Conservative Party of Quebec, formed an alliance with disgruntled Liberals and the nationalistes and created a new political party, the Union Nationale. By advocating a wide range of economic, social, and political changes, and by holding out hope of restoring control of the province's economy to French-Canadians, the Union Nationale won a smashing victory in 1936. But Duplessis was soon collaborating with American and other foreign capitalists who wished to invest in his province, allowing them to exploit its resources and workers with little government interference. Reneging on his commitments for change, Duplessis exploited anti-Communist sentiment in his province by introducing such measures as the Padlock Law, which made it illegal to use any premises "to propogate communism."

The act however did not define exactly what the term meant. Thus it was used by Duplessis against a variety of labour, unemployed, and radical organizations. Joining Hepburn in what one critic called "Canada's unholy alliance," he accused the federal government of undermining provincial autonomy and threatening the survival of French Canada.

For King, of all the political leaders in the country Duplessis was much the most frightening. As the leader of the forces of French-Canadian nationalism, he was the greatest threat to national unity and to the unity of the Liberal Party; and in the late 1930s, with another European war in the offing, King could think of little else. If war were to come, then Canada must be united. Ironically, because of his concern for Canadian unity, King contributed to making it more likely that there would be a war.[13]

---

[12] For an overview of the labour movement in the period, see Irving Abella, *Nationalism, Communism and Canadian Labour* (Toronto, 1973); Irving Abella, ed., *On Strike* (Toronto, 1974); and Gad Horowitz, *Canadian Labour in Politics* (Toronto, 1966).

[13] On provincial politics, the material is varied and often thin. H.F. Quinn's dated *The Union Nationale* (Toronto, 1963) is still useful. Conrad Black's *Duplessis* (Toronto, 1977) is a good,

~~~~~~ "Ready, Aye Ready" Again

With the rise of Nazism, the coming to power of Adolph Hitler, the growing militarization of Germany, and its stated intent to expand into areas it thought should belong to the Reich, it was clear that trouble was once again brewing in Europe. Yet Mackenzie King publicly took little note of these events. To him foreign policy was divisive.

In October 1935, Italy invaded Ethiopia. At the League, the Canadian delegate, Dr. W.A. Riddell, took a lead in the attempt to apply sanctions against Mussolini's government to force it to withdraw. At the height of the crisis, the Bennett government was defeated. Caught without instructions, the Canadian delegation assumed that the policy would not change and thus proposed that oil be included in the materials under embargo. An oil embargo, as Mussolini later admitted, would have seriously hampered the invasion. If some other country had proposed these sanctions, Canada might have accepted them, but King did not intend to take the initiative. He told a reporter that Riddell deserved "a good spanking," and, when the League committee continued to debate the "Canadian resolution," the exasperated King finally told the press that Riddell had been acting on his own. King was prepared to follow, not to lead, since leadership on such a sensitive matter might cause serious divisions within the country. The Italian dictator, King knew, had many admirers in Canada, especially in Quebec. In the end, the League never did agree to impose oil sanctions, and Italy went on to conquer all of Ethiopia. Soon Hitler was taking over territories in Europe that he thought belonged to Germany.

In the Ethiopian crisis, King likely was a better reflection of Canadian opinion than Riddell. He knew most Canadians were not prepared to fight for the principle of collective security. They were in no mood to save either Ethiopia or the League. Nor were they in any mood to do anything about Hitler. The prime minister himself, after a visit with the Führer, found him to be "a simple sort of peasant, not very intelligent and no serious danger to anyone."

A few Canadians thought differently. Led by John Dafoe of Winnipeg's *Free Press*, they urged the prime minister to take Hitler more seriously. Nazism, they warned, was a danger to world peace. Some Canadians were prepared to use more than words in their fight against fascism. Well

---

very opinionated study. Neil McKenty, *Mitch Hepburn* (Toronto, 1967) is entertaining, while John Kendle's *Bracken* (Toronto, 1979) is thorough. There are no good studies of Maritime premiers for this period, and there is only article literature on the West. See *A Reader's Guide to Canadian History*, vol. II, for details.

over a thousand, many of them immigrants straight out of the relief camps, travelled to Spain in 1936 to fight for the Republican government against the fascist insurgents of General Franco. The Spanish Civil War, to them and to countless others, was a veritable Armageddon, the ultimate confrontation between good and evil, light and darkness. Their fight was heroic but doomed. The bullets and bayonets of the Canadian Mackenzie-Papineau Battalion were no match for fascist bombs and tanks. More than a third of these Canadians never came back. One who did was Dr. Norman Bethune, a genuine war hero, who returned to warn an apathetic country of the evils of fascism. Few listened.

To the very end the Canadian government supported the appeasement policies of the British prime minister, Neville Chamberlain; it was almost the only British policy with which King had agreed since he became prime minister in 1921. Yet in 1938 he refused to allow the Royal Air Force to train its pilots in Canada lest this automatically involve Canada in any forthcoming war. King knew Duplessis and other French-Canadians would have some choice words about British pilots training in Canada. In his battle for national unity, he could not risk Quebec's anger. In this he succeeded brilliantly. When war came in September 1939, the Parliament of Canada – and the country itself – was united behind King. One week after Britain declared war, a technically neutral Canada followed suit. Even though everyone knew that once Britain went to war Canada would go too, the formalities were observed to the very end. After a serious debate, Parliament, without a recorded vote, decided in favour of war. For the second time in a generation, the country was at war, and for much the same reason – the continuing sentimental link with Great Britain. Autonomous Canada might be, but when the mother country was in trouble, "ready, aye, ready" seemed the only possible response.

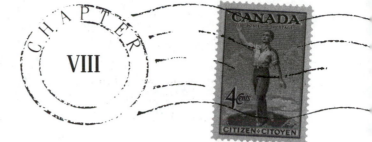

CHAPTER VIII

A NATION OF IMMIGRANTS

       Canada is a peculiar nation. Peopled by immigrants, it is a country that hates immigration. All the historical evidence – including almost every public opinion poll done over the past 50 years – indicates that most Canadians, including immigrants themselves, do not want any substantial increase in the number of people admitted into the country. Given their image of themselves, this attitude may surprise many Canadians; historically, however, it should not.

    Most Canadians take pride in their history, their traditions, their heritage, and especially their myths. And if there is a pervasive Canadian myth, something most Canadians grew up with, were taught in their schools, or were accustomed to hearing from their politicians, it is that theirs is a country of immigrants, a country with a long history of welcoming refugees and dissidents.

    Racism and bigotry, most Canadians were raised to believe, were European, or at least American, inventions that had little part in their country's history, tradition, or psyche. Canada, it has been constantly hammered home to her citizenry, is a country of wide-open space and immeasurable wealth – a country that has always been available to those proverbial huddled masses yearning to breathe free.

    Certainly most Canadians would be shocked to learn that for most of its history, Canada's immigration practices have been racist and exclusionary. It knew exactly what kind of races and people it wanted and how to keep out those it did not. Canada's immigration acts were designed to divide the world in two – the preferred people who were always welcome and the nonpreferred who rarely were. Specifically written into the legislation were those races and peoples in descending order of preference who would be allowed into the country. At the top of the list were British and white Americans who were always acceptable. When economic necessity dictated the admission of non-British, non-American stock, immigration officials were given a list of desirable people. Following the British and Americans were northern Europeans, then central Europeans, and finally southern and eastern Europeans. At the bottom of the list were Jews followed by Orientals and blacks.

Occasionally during economic boom periods these nonpreferred immigrants were acceptable so long as they remained out of sight, risking life and limb in the mines and smelters of the West, holed up in the lumber camps deep in the forest, or packed into stuffy, unventilated sweatshops in various urban centres.

The central problem of Canadian immigration policy for most of its history is that it never had one. In the 122 years Canada has existed as a nation, it has had exactly four immigration acts. Neither now nor in the past has there been any clearly articulated national consensus about what immigration should be or should do. Except for one constant, discriminatory aspect, Canadian policies have had little consistency. Indeed, until the 1970s, Canadian governments did not feel obliged to proclaim clearly defined, long-range immigration objectives – whether demographic, economic, or social. As a result, immigration has been an issue that over the years has divided Canadians far more than it has united them.

Thus it was not until the 1950s, 85 years after Canada became an independent nation and after the country had absorbed millions of immigrants, that a permanent free-standing Department of Immigration with its own minister was created. Until then, responsibilities for immigration were often passed back and forth among various reluctant departments – clearly an indication of how little respect or thought was given to immigration policy. At various times, immigration matters were lumped together with such departments as Agriculture, Interior, and even Indian Affairs and Mines and Natural Resources.

Thus immigration has until recent times largely been in the hands of a small group of bureaucrats. Until the 1950s it was this tiny group that orchestrated Canada's immigration policy – by default. Their historical role was not so much to find ways to encourage people to come to Canada but rather to find ways to keep them out. They were gate-keepers concerned only in opening the gates when economic pressures forced them to, and then, only as narrowly as they could. Their efforts were applauded by successive Canadian governments. Immigration officials were simply doing their job and, in the eyes of most Canadians, doing it well. They were reflecting the nativist, xenophobic attitudes that permeated an earlier period in Canada.

But keeping people out of Canada at the turn of the last century was not a problem. Rather the major concern was to find ways to bring them in.

In 1896, after 25 years of depression and gloom, prosperity returned to Canada. The pessimism of the preceding generation was replaced with an apparently boundless and hopelessly naive optimism. As one breathless historian put it, "In the year in which Laurier Liberalism gained power, Canada was born again." Indeed the prime minister himself was carried away; the twentieth century, he promised the nation, would be Canada's. A speaker to the Canadian Club in Winnipeg reflected the spirit of the times: "In fifty years Canada will have a population of fifty millions and Saskatchewan and Alberta will be greater than Ontario in population and Winnipeg will have surpassed Toronto and Montreal." And why should they not have been optimistic? After two decades of bust, the long-awaited boom had begun.

For many, it was too late. So many Canadians had lost hope that fortune would ever smile on Canada again that well over a million left their farms and homes and made their way across the border to the United States; so many, in fact, that a prominent Liberal politician, Sir Richard Cartwright, was moved to remark that the Dominion of Canada that had begun in Lamentations (the book of the Bible from which the word Dominion was taken) seemed to be ending in Exodus. And with reason. In the twenty years before 1900, more people left Canada than came, 1 600 000 emigrating to the United States and only 1 225 000 arriving from overseas. Who could blame them for leaving? For farmers the great American plains offered better land, to say nothing of a better climate and standard of living. And for thousands of penurious French-Canadians unable to eke an existence out of their marginal lands, the factories and textile mills of New England gave new hope. So long as America remained hospitable, there seemed little reason for Canadians without jobs or with failing farms not to go, and even less reason for European immigrants to come.

However, by the dawn of the new century, events outside of Canada began almost imperceptibly to alter the course of her history. Most of the fertile American land had been settled, and the frontier was rapidly closing. The worldwide depression was lifting, and there were now new markets and higher prices for Canadian goods. With cheap land no longer available in the United States, prospective immigrants for the first time began to look at what Canada had to offer. Except for the criminal, the diseased, and the pauper, Canada was open to anyone – except, of course, for Chinese, who had to pay a $50 head tax. Aside from that, Canada had no immigration restrictions; until 1900 it scarcely needed any. What it needed, rather, were incentives.

Clifford Sifton, the man who encouraged immigrants to populate the West.

PA-27942/NATIONAL ARCHIVES OF CANADA.

 ## Sifton and Immigration

The man appointed by Laurier to provide these incentives and to sell Canada to prospective immigrants was a forceful young businessman, the minister of the interior, Clifford Sifton. Indeed, Sifton saw his task as basically salesmanship. Immigrants, he said, had to be aggressively enticed. "In my judgement . . . the immigration work has to be carried out in the same manner as the sale of any commodity; just as soon as you stop advertising and missionary work, the movement is going to stop," he told the House of Commons. Born in Ontario, Sifton had moved to Manitoba in 1880 to make his fortune. Having done that, he returned to the East with a sense of mission. Determined to convince Ottawa that the future of the nation was dependent on the rapid development of the West, he agreed in 1897 to join the new Laurier administration. Above all, he was committed to bringing into the West the type of settler who could best adapt to the rigours of pioneer life. Like many transplanted easterners, he had become a passionate westerner, and he set about devising an immigration policy that was unashamedly designed to benefit Western Canada. "Our desire," he told the prime minister, "is to promote the immigration of farmers and farm labourers." Urban immigrants, he said, were "undesirable from every standpoint," and would not contribute "in any way whatever to the . . . development of natural resources and the increase of production of wealth from these resources." He specifically ordered Canadian immigration officials to try to prevent the influx of "labouring men and mechanics." The only good immigrant to Sifton was the homesteader. "Agriculture," he argued, was "the foundation of all real and enduring progress on the part of Canada." "Only farmers need apply" was the operating slogan of Sifton's immigration policy.[1]

As soon as he came into office Sifton galvanized the Immigration Branch, for years a backwater of government service. It was, he lamented, "a department of delay, a department of circumlocution, a department in which people could not get business done, a department

---

[1] See on immigration policy in the Sifton period, D.J. Hall, *Clifford Sifton*, vol. I (Vancouver, 1981), and vol. II (Vancouver, 1985); R.C. Brown and R. Cook, *Canada 1896-1921* (Toronto, 1974); K. Bicha, *The American Farmer and the Canadian West 1896-1914* (Lawrence, 1972); and H. Troper, *Only Farmers Need Apply* (Toronto, 1972). General studies include Jean Burnet with Howard Palmer, *"Coming Canadians": An Introduction to a History of Canada's Peoples* (Toronto, 1988), and D.C. Corbett, *Canada's Immigration Policy: A Critique* (Toronto, 1957).

which tried a man to death who undertook to get any business transacted with it." New blood replaced the stodgy time-watchers who had sat at their desks doing nothing under previous administrations. Seemingly limitless amounts of money were poured into the branch to pay for the new appointments, to launch massive advertising campaigns for immigrants in the United States, Great Britain, and continental Europe, and to subsidize tours of Western Canada by foreign journalists. Each new settler was promised 160 acres (65 ha) of free land – though free did not necessarily mean arable, as many colonists were to discover – in Western Canada. Agents were sent to nations with a large pool of potential immigrants to spread the word about opportunities in Canada, and steamship passenger representatives were offered large bonuses for encouraging immigrants to choose Canada. Exhibitions throughout the world often contained large displays outlining the advantages of moving to Canada. There was hardly a method not tried by the creative Sifton to encourage immigrants from those countries he believed would provide Western Canada with the young, hardy, aggressive pioneers it so desperately needed. Indeed, some of his arrangements were highly irregular, though extremely successful. The most notorious of these was the North Atlantic Trading Company.

Many European nations were incensed over the vigorous campaign for their citizens being mounted by the Canadian government. Because many of the settlers Sifton wanted were precisely the ones these countries were loathe to lose, laws were passed to restrict emigration. Some governments even launched their own advertising campaigns to counter the activities of Canadian agents. In France, for example, all government officials, including school teachers and postal clerks, were ordered to warn potential immigrants of the dangers of emigrating to Canada. The greatest ally for most of these countries, the Canadian climate, was continuously used in the struggle to keep Europeans at home. Sifton had even seriously considered banning the publication of prairie temperatures lest they frighten off prospective immigrants. In order to overcome these obstacles, Canadian officials signed a secret agreement with a group of shipping agents calling themselves the North Atlantic Trading Company who agreed to direct agricultural immigrants to Canada. In return, the Canadian government promised to pay a large bonus for each immigrant delivered. In the seven years of its existence, the company brought over 70 000 immigrants to Canada. And much to Sifton's delight, it winnowed the pick of the immigrant crop for Canada. A little bit of flim-flammery was a cheap price to pay for such a large number of high-quality immigrants.

Perhaps Sifton's greatest success was in reversing the tide of emigration to the United States. Prodded by an army of Canadian immigration agents, by a profusion of pamphlets describing the wonders of "the Last, Best West," and by offers of free trips and free land, hundreds of thousands of American farmers crossed the border and took up new homes in the Canadian West. These were, in Sifton's view, "of the finest quality and the most desirable settlers."

Much less successful was his attempt to recruit British agriculturalists. Though every farmer in the north of England and Scotland was sent a brochure graphically outlining the advantages of emigration to Canada, few responded. Rather, much to the interior minister's chagrin, large numbers of British labourers, artisans, and "city types," precisely the people he did not want, decided now was the opportune moment for them to move to the beckoning Dominion. To Sifton, these men, who knew nothing about farming, did not have the "fibre" to be successful pioneers; putting them on the frontier would be "a crime." Crime or not, they came by the hundreds of thousands. In 1907 alone, almost 125 000 Britons arrived, more than ten times the number who had come only eight years before.

The Canadian government emigration offices in London helped supply immigrants during the boom years of the century. C-63257/NATIONAL ARCHIVES OF CANADA.

However, undoubtedly the most innovative and radical of Sifton's schemes was his encouragement of continental European immigration. His ideal immigrant was "a stalwart peasant in a sheepskin coat, born of the soil, whose forefathers have been farmers for ten generations, with a stout wife and a half-dozen children." Sifton did not care whether he was of British stock, so long as he was hale, hardy, and ready to cultivate the soil. Nor did he care whether these immigrants could read or write; for the work he had in mind for them, it did not matter. These Poles, Ukrainians, Slavs, and Russians were slated to open up the vast, isolated, largely unsettled areas of the Canadian West. Sifton's orders were clear:

These Doukhobor women were hitched to a plow, 24 to the team.

C-681/NATIONAL ARCHIVES OF CANADA.

immigration agents were to opt for brawn over brain, strong backs over strong minds. All the eastern European peasant asked for was *vilni zemli* – free land – and a place where, in the words of one, "we do not have to bow our heads to no one." In Canada he got both.

In return these immigrants not only cleared and cultivated huge areas of the Canadian West but they also built the railways, constructed the roads, cut the timber, and mined the coal that allowed the great western boom to continue; though most of them came to Canada to take up land, they were more likely to take up picks and shovels. Despite Sifton's emphasis on agricultural immigrants, many who arrived were neither able nor willing to settle on the land. In order to build up a stake for homesteads, many were forced to become wage labourers; others found they could only survive the first few difficult years of farming by working on railway gangs or construction crews. These immigrants provided the cheap labour many industrialists and government officials thought was necessary for Canada's expanding industrial development.

The Open Door

Ironically, the most important determinant of immigration policy in these years was the business community. They lobbied incessantly and successfully for an open-door policy. Anyone who wanted, so long as he was healthy, unskilled, and preferably illiterate, should be allowed to come to Canada. What industrialists wished above all else was to have a cheap, pliant labour force. And who could possibly be cheaper and more pliant than the hungry, confused, unlettered, docile southern and eastern European immigrants? This vast, apparently limitless source of manpower would assure the business community that labour costs would remain low and that the nascent Canadian trade union movement would be aborted.

In the minds of most Canadians, these immigrants were both unassimilable and unorganizable. They would remain in Canada as long as their work was needed; when it no longer was, they could return home. And indeed, many immigrants shared this belief. They saw themselves as temporary sojourners coming to Canada to earn enough money to return home, in the words of one young Italian labourer, to "live like a prince"; they had arrived in Canada simply to improve their situation at home. So committed were they to returning that many left their families behind in the old country. Unfortunately, most found their wages so low they could barely survive in Canada let alone put some aside for the journey home.

And indeed, in the booming early years of the twentieth century the work of these migrants was essential. Two transcontinental railways were being rapidly pushed across the West. New mines and smelters were opening up all over the country. Factories were producing more than ever before. These were all labour-intensive industries that relied on low-paid workers. The large British immigration of this period could not satisfy this need. Most immigrants from the United Kingdom came with skills and a union background; both were anathema to Canadian employers. According to the president of the C.P.R., Canada needed men who were "accustomed to roughing it." It would be a huge mistake, he warned, to bring in British immigrants "who came here expecting to get high wages, a feather bed and a bath tub." They were not, he and his colleagues agreed, suited to frontier conditions. What Canada needed, the railway men stressed, were more Europeans, particularly Ukrainians. These had proven to be obedient and industrious workers who rarely complained about deplorable work-camp conditions, perhaps because they could not speak English.

Railway magnates were not alone in pushing for unlimited immigration. Eastern manufacturing interests saw a western hinterland full of immigrants as a growing market for their goods, as well as a source of valuable raw materials. Naturally they wanted their own low-cost labour force, particularly because of the inroads organized labour seemed to be making in industrial centres in Ontario and Quebec. But they were also in need of skilled workers, and in 1903 a group of them set up an unofficial Canadian Labour Bureau in London, ironically in the same building as the offices of the Immigration Branch. The latter took only agricultural workers, the former only industrial ones. A frustrated Sifton raged against the attempts to bring in "a lot of helpless people being lodged in cities and towns." Though he attempted to shut down the bureau, there was little he could do. The needs of an expanding capitalist labour market had to be met, and they could not be if Canada were to restrict itself to agricultural settlers.

So great was the demand for unskilled, transient labour – the so-called "navvies" – that some industrialists relied on subcontractors or *padroni* to supply the necessary bodies. These men, through connections overseas, brought over thousands of young Italians, directly from their homeland or from the United States, with promises of work at high wages. Once in Canada, the promises often dissipated, and the migrant workers found themselves at the mercy of callous employers. They were horribly exploited, their pay pitiable and their work back-breaking. But, particularly for railway contractors and mine operators, they were necessary, so long as they were in the bush or in the pits doing their jobs. However, in Canada's cities they were pariahs, totally unacceptable. Thus, when several hundred suddenly appeared without jobs in Montreal in 1904, popular opinion forced a royal commission enquiry into the entire *padrone* system. It achieved nothing; the exploitation continued. Nonetheless, many of the young Italian men who came over were able to return home with a substantial nest egg. All they left behind was their health.

Obviously not all Canadians endorsed an open-door immigration policy. The minister of the interior, Frank Oliver, who took over in 1905 after Sifton's resignation, favoured a more restrictionist policy. Yet even he was unable to stop the flood of newcomers landing almost daily in Halifax, Quebec City, or Montreal. In Oliver's jaundiced view, these migrants were "the off-scourings and dregs of society." But with passenger agents still being paid to divert immigrants to Canada, and with industrialists still in need of workers, even the opposition of the minister responsible for immigration could be overridden.

Most vociferous in its opposition to large-scale immigration was the Canadian labour movement. Though small in numbers, it did have some influence, which it desperately sought to use to limit the number of job-hungry foreigners coming to Canada's shores. Some of these had found themselves being used as strike-breakers; others replaced workers whose pay demands were too high; most were used as an ever-present threat to keep workers' expectations within limits. Frightened, penniless, hungry, they were mercilessly exploited by many employers. The protests of the trade union movement made little headway in government circles. All the labour movement could do was send over representatives to England to warn potential immigrants of the deceptive activities of Canadian shipping and employment agencies.

Few paid them any attention. With the onset of a worldwide depression in 1907, thousands of unemployed British workers decided that the time had come to start their lives anew in Canada, especially since their passage overseas was being covered by local charities who wished to rid themselves of their heavy relief obligations. Many of these were, in the words of Frank Oliver, "a drag on the labour market from misfortune, incompetence or indifference." Indeed, not only did the British urban immigrant face much prejudice on his arrival in Canada – the *Edmonton Journal* warned in 1907 that "their presence [was] a mistake" – but as the depression deepened, the federal government had no hesitation in sending back over a thousand of these newcomers, who made up 70 percent of those deported in 1908.

The labour movement had more success in restricting the flow of an even more worrisome stream of immigrants, the Orientals. No one worked harder and for less than did the Chinese, and no group of immigrants was more in demand by the railway, mining, lumber, and fishing interests of the country, particularly in British Columbia. By 1900 almost 11 percent of that province's population was Asiatic. Legislative efforts to keep Orientals out had proved futile. In 1885 Chinese immigrants were compelled to pay a head tax of $50; fifteen years later it was increased to $100; in 1903 it was raised to a staggering $500. But still they came, lured by the promise of good fortune in the "Land of the Golden Mountains." There was a ferocious anti-Oriental sentiment throughout the province, fuelled by those who feared that British Columbia would soon be taken over by the Chinese. "The yellow hordes," one newspaper warned, would take over "this great big province – a land virtually flowing with milk and honey" and push out the "white British subjects."

More rancorous was the labour press. Not only did the trade unions fear that the Chinese would create a "mongrelized nation," but they worried as well that Orientals would totally undermine the labour movement. "They are . . . fitted to become all too dangerous competitors in the labour market," warned one labour leader. Their "docile servility . . . renders them doubly dangerous as the willing tools whereby grasping and tyrannical employers grind down all labour to the lowest living point." A labour newspaper rhetorically asked, "What is in store for us as an Anglo-Saxon community? With the mongols in our mines, work-shops, forests and on railroads and tilling our farms, what is to become of our white labourers, miners, and mechanics?" Most of the province's white population, with the significant exception of its industrialists, regarded the Orientals as an economic and cultural challenge, as unassimilable, and as severe obstructions to both national unity and a homogeneous society.

These sentiments were fully supported by a royal commission set up by the Laurier government in 1902. The Chinese, it reported, were:

. . . drawn from the poorer classes, reared in poverty where a few cents a day represent the earnings which must suffice for a family; accustomed to crowd together in small tenements or huts, close, unhealthy and filthy, . . . with no desire to conform to Western ideas. They form . . . a foreign substance within, but not of our body politic, with no love for our laws and institutions; a people that will not assimilate or become an integral part of our race and nation . . . they are a continual menace to health . . . their effect on the rest of the community is bad. They pay no fair proportion of the taxes of the country. They keep out immigrants who would become permanent citizens and create conditions inimical to labour and dangerous to the industrial peace of the community. . . . They are unfit for full citizenship. . . . They . . . are obnoxious to a free community and dangerous to the state.

As a result of the furor, the Laurier government clamped down on Chinese immigration. Not to be outflanked, the province's business leaders, led by the C.P.R., began bringing in large numbers of Japanese and East Indians to do the heavy labour once done by the Chinese workers. Labour regarded the Japanese as an even more serious threat since they were more aggressive in going after skilled jobs and were supported by a home government whose good will was being courted by both Canadian and British officials. The arrival of so many Japanese and "Hindoos" (though most of the Indian immigrants were, in fact, Sikhs) offended nativist feeling in the province. Led by the chauvinistic Asiatic Exclusion League, a series of vast demonstrations and parades were held in Vancouver in 1907 to protest the steadily increasing flow of "brown and yellow" immigrants. Sparked by a series of demagogic speeches, a rally on June 7 turned into a full-scale riot as mobs descended on the Chinese and Japanese parts of the city, attacking any helpless Oriental who fell into their hands, breaking windows and destroying property. As a result of this racist violence, the Laurier government placed severe restrictions on the entry of Oriental immigrants into Canada.

The most severe challenge to these restrictions arose in May 1914, when a boatload of 376 East Indians arrived in Vancouver demanding to be admitted. Should these be accepted, warned a Vancouver newspaper, then the remaining 300 million "natives of India . . . who have the same rights as these . . . would have the same claim." Again British Columbia was aflame. For over two months the ship, the *Komagata Maru*, lay in the harbour unable to dock while government officials decided what to do. For the people of British Columbia there was no question what should be done: the East Indians should be sent back home. To allow Orientals in, H.H. Stevens, a Conservative M.P. and later a key minister in the Bennett government, told a large rally, would leave "not a vestige of the civilization of which we are so proud." Canada must go as far as possible, he urged his receptive audience, "to keep [itself] pure and free from the taint of other peoples." Attempts to deport some of the East Indians were foiled when the passengers seized control of the ship and repulsed Vancouver police and immigration officers who tried to board it. As tensions rose on the mainland, the Canadian navy went into action. The training ship *Rainbow*, which had just been acquired for Laurier's navy, pulled alongside the boat and escorted it out to sea while cheering thousands lined the waterfront. British Columbia once again had made it clear that it was going to remain just that – British.

The citizens of Canada's westernmost province were not alone in their concern for their Anglo-Saxon heritage. Throughout the country, questions were being asked about the impact on Canada of the large immigration movements that Sifton had initiated. A Calgary newspaper accused him of trying to build a nation "on the lines of the Tower of Babel, where the Lord confounded the language so that people might not understand one another's speech." To the Canadian economist and humorist Stephen Leacock, European immigrants "were herds of the proletariat of Europe, the lowest classes of industrial society . . . indifferent material from which to build the commonwealth of the future." These voices were not alone. Under Laurier and Sifton, they cried, Canada's ethnic priorities were askew.

Though Canadian governments had divided the world into "preferred" and "nonpreferred" races in the past, it seemed to many Canadians that under Sifton the categories had been reversed; to them the country teemed with Italians, Ukrainians, Jews, Poles, and Chinese. And even the new British arrivals were of the "wrong type." Many were children sent over by British orphanages, among them, of course, the famous Barnardo boys. In addition, in the eyes of a number of Canadians, there were far too many "assisted immigrants," those whose way was paid by charitable organizations or the Salvation Army. Canada, they feared, was being turned into a vast workhouse for the world's poor, a dumping ground for the social casualties of Europe.

Between 1900 and 1914, when immigration was shut off because of the war, more than one million Britons arrived. In addition, 110 000 Italians, 65 000 Jews, 95 000 Poles, 85 000 Russians, and 50 000 Ukrainians, as well as tens of thousands of Germans, Chinese, Finns, Hungarians, Japanese, Swedes, Slavs, and others settled in various parts of the country. Thousands more appeared for short periods of time, laying track, mining coal, or clearing bush before returning to the old country with some money in their pockets. Many who came as settlers found that there was little arable land left, and, forced to colonize isolated areas far from transportation or markets, they also decided to go back home or to the United States. Indeed, since the Canadian government emphasized recruitment at the expense of settlement, most immigrants were forced to fend for themselves. There was little thought given to the foreigner once he arrived and even less assistance. As a result, a high percentage of those who came to Canada in these years eventually returned to Europe or sought entry to the United States. Those who did stay were more likely to become industrial workers than farmers. While the government wanted them hidden away in the bush, on homesteads, in work camps, or company towns, many tended to congregate in teeming, slum-ridden sections of Canada's few large cities, there to become objects of curiosity, often of hostility, and always of prejudice. An editorial in a prominent medical journal referred to the ethnic neighbourhoods as ". . . riff-raff from Europe, colonies of immigrants spreading crime, disease and ignorance." Yet they still continued to arrive. Even the downturn in the economy, which began in 1912, dissuaded few. Indeed, in 1913, the worst year of the depression, more immigrants arrived in Canada than in any year in our history.

Canada had become home to newcomers many thought were both inferior and unassimilable.[2] By 1914 almost a quarter of the Canadian population was foreign-born. The impact of the huge migrations was profound. The population of the country increased by some 40 percent in the years between 1900 and 1914, the fastest rate of increase of any major country at that time. Both the production of wheat and the gross national product more than doubled in these years; millions of acres of new land were cleared and settled; more than 400 000 new homestead applications were approved. Though real wages changed little, hundreds of thousands of new jobs were created. Yet what concerned most Canadians were not the economic results but the social consequences of the arrival of so many immigrants. Could the country absorb and assimilate such large numbers of people with alien ideas, cultures,

---

[2] Useful studies include Donald Avery, *Dangerous Foreigners: European Immigrant Workers and Labour Radicalism in Canada, 1896-1932* (Toronto, 1979); Robert Harney and V. Scarpaci, eds., *Little Italies in North America* (Toronto, 1981); Robert Harney and Harold Troper, *Immigrants* (Toronto, 1977); Jorgen Dahlie and Tissa Fernando, eds., *Ethnicity, Power and Politics in Canada* (Toronto, 1981); J.S. Woodsworth, *Strangers Within Our Gates* (Toronto, 1972); Robert England, *The Central European Immigrant in Canada* (Toronto, 1929); and England's *The Colonization of Western Canada* (London, 1936). Also interesting is J. Burgeon Bickersteth, *The Land of Open Doors* (Toronto, 1976). More recent studies are numerous: K. Adachi, *The Enemy that Never Was: A History of the Japanese Canadians* (Toronto, 1976); Howard Palmer, *Patterns of Prejudice: A History of Nativism in Alberta* (Toronto, 1982) and *Immigration and the Rise of Multiculturalism* (Toronto, 1975); Hugh Johnston, *The Voyage of the Komagata Maru* (Delhi, 1979); Peter Ward, *White Canada Forever* (Montreal, 1978); James Morton, *In the Sea of Sterile Mountains: The Chinese in British Columbia* (Vancouver, 1974); and Frank Epp, *Mennonites in Canada 1920-40* (Toronto, 1982). There are also numerous histories of immigrant groups in the *Generations* series, published by the McClelland and Stewart with the assistance of the federal government.

religions, and languages? How were these foreigners to be "Canadian-ized"? These became the burning issues of the time. For many the only hope lay in the public school system. "If Canada is to become in any real sense a nation, if our people are to become one people, we must have one language," argued J.S. Woodsworth in 1905. "The public school is the most important factor in transforming the foreigners into Canadians."

To people like Woodsworth and John W. Dafoe, the influential editor of Winnipeg's *Free Press*, what was at stake was the future of Western Canada. To them it was still a new, fluid, and insecure society that could hardly be expected to withstand successfully the shock of a huge immigration of people alien in language, religion, and culture. "We must Canadianize this generation of foreign-born settlers," said Dafoe, "or this wll cease to be a Canadian country in any real sense of the term. . . . In a country like ours," he added, "where so many nationalities are settling in our midst, it is imperative that the children of these different nationalities should be taught the same language, the same aspirations, the same ideals of citizenship as our natural-born Canadians."

Others felt that the Protestant churches could play a key role in Canadianization by providing these immigrants with proper religious training and by introducing them to the Canadian way of life. Nonethe-less, in spite of the unremitting efforts of dedicated teachers and ministers, many still clung to their European traditions, insisting on using their mother tongue and attending their Old World churches. Assimila-tion, it was clear, would not come quickly, if at all.

Urban Ghettos?

What concerned substantial numbers of Canadians as well was the problem of the urban immigrants. The ethnic ghettos of Toronto, Montreal, Winnipeg, and various smaller cities across the country were, in the eyes of respectable Canadians, breeding grounds for crime and disease. Overcrowding, unsanitary conditions, hunger, and privation were common in many of these slums. Rather than blaming the system that exploited immigrants to the fullest, Canadians tended to blame the immigrants themselves. They were seen as ignorant, dirty, violent, constantly drunk, and a threat both to individual Canadians and to society as a whole. According to one prominent politician, Canada had become "the dumping ground for the refuse of every country in the world." Some newspapers were warning that Canada faced a future of lawlessness and revolution unless a better class of immigrant replaced those already in the country. Even British arrivals were disparaged as "sparrows," that ubiquitous city pest imported from Europe, or as "broncos" liable to kick over Canadian traditions. "Help wanted" signs reading "No English Need Apply" were common sights in many stores and factories in the years before the Great War.

What most observers ignored in their contempt for the Little Italies, Slavtowns, and Chinatowns that were the hallmark of many Canadian cities, was the incredible vitality of these immigrant communities. Where the Anglo observer saw slums, disease, and poverty, there actually existed a richness of life far beyond his or her experience and understanding. The crowded tenements, the busy street life, the noise were all alien and frightening to native-born Canadians, yet they were all necessary for the integration of the newcomers into Canadian society. To them, the ethnic ghettos were reminders of life in the old country. The streets were full of all sorts of hawkers, stalls, peddlers, street musicians, and promoters. Each area had its own national churches or synagogues to serve the spiritual needs of the immigrants; to meet their other needs there were the local "fixers," usually well-established members of the community, with political connections, who served as a liaison with government officials. There were also fraternal and mutual benefit

To English- and French-Canadians, the recent immigrants, with their colourful street life, seemed almost completely alien. This is a scene from the Toronto Jewish market in 1922.

PA-84811/NATIONAL ARCHIVES OF CANADA.

societies. These offered some protection to the immigrants and provided them with a familiar milieu while they were overcoming the trauma of dealing with alien institutions, a new language, and a vastly different way of life.

For many migrants, especially the countless thousands who landed in Canada without families (in 1908, for example, 4500 Italian men arrived in Toronto, and only 400 women), the boarding house took the place of their far-away families, offering both moral and physical sustenance and camaraderie to ease the pain of loneliness. Most of these homes took in immigrants from the same country – and even from the same region or village back home – thus easing cultural shock. In addition, because there were often seven or eight men sharing one room, the beds occasionally alternating between those on day shifts and those working at night, costs were low. In Toronto, for example, in 1909, the cost per week for room, board, and laundry was just over a dollar; the average weekly wage was about ten dollars. Since most of the migrant workers were in Canada only to send home as much money as possible, these arrangements were quite satisfactory.[3]

Perhaps the most exploited of all the immigrants were the women. Responsible for the home and the children, they were also expected to bring in an outside income. In many households, only the wife's earnings saved the family from total destitution. Large numbers of immigrant women and girls filled the sweatshops, factories, and textile mills of the country; others earned their keep as domestics and charwomen; still others were forced into prostitution. And when a woman could not leave the house because she had small children or because she was widowed, the home became a boarding house. Thus, even those women who were not in the paid work force were still crucially important. As one historian put it, "The ability of these women to operate meagre family budgets successfully was often the condition of survival itself."

Even worse was the life of the immigrant woman homesteading in the West. Often she worked side by side with her husband, clearing the land, removing stumps, building fences, seeding, threshing, or milking, while she alone was responsible for the children and the household chores. And

---

[3] For the urban immigrant experience see John Zucci, *The Italians of Toronto* (Montreal, 1988); Steven Speisman, *The Jews of Toronto* (Toronto, 1979); Robert Harney, ed., *Gathering Places: Peoples and Neighbourhoods in Toronto 1834-1943* (Toronto, 1985); Bruno Ramirez and M. Del Balso, *The Italians of Montreal: From Sojourning to Settlement* (Montreal, 1980); and V. Lindstrom-Best, *The Finnish Immigrant Community of Toronto 1887-1913* (Toronto, 1979).

when her husband was away away at another job, at a political meeting, or visiting with friends (an opportunity most women got only on Sunday at church) she was on her own. As one Ukrainian woman later plaintively described her life to her children:

Your crazy father was often at crazy meetings. I had to cut the ice, bring in water, cut wood, chop wood, bring it in. Who was supposed to do all that? I milked the cows, fed them, cleaned the barn and the chicken coop, gathered eggs. . . .[4]

Some women – particularly Doukhobors – harnessed themselves in teams of up to 20 or 25 to the ploughs because they could not afford horses. And when itinerant threshing crews arrived to help with the harvest, the women had to cook for them as well.

Because of their inhuman working conditions and abysmally low wages, many immigrant workers became actively involved in radical political activity and union organization. Often isolated in far-away railroad, mining, and lumber camps, these men were easy prey for callous bosses. Reluctant to interfere in the private sector, neither federal nor provincial governments provided any protection for the immigrant; alienated and defenceless, he was on his own. Many reacted by joining a union. By far the majority of the members of the revolutionary Industrial Workers of the World, the notorious Wobblies, were immigrant navvies or miners. However, most employers continued to regard immigrants as a docile, helpless workforce. "They are our strength and the weakness of the union," said one mine operator, and he and his ilk often arranged for shifts to include labourers of various nationalities in order to encourage competition and to keep the shifts fragmented. But in fact, many of these immigrants, particularly in the mining towns, displayed a real class consciousness and provided the backbone of much of the militant union activity in Western Canada in this period. Nor should this have surprised the bosses, since large numbers of these immigrants brought to their new home as part of their cultural baggage a long-standing struggle against the state, the landlord, and occasionally even the Church. Once in Canada a small number, particularly Finns, Ukrainians, Russians, and Jews, joined various socialist political parties.

---

[4] On immigrant women, see Rolf Knight, *A Very Ordinary Life* (Vancouver, 1974); B. Caroli et al., eds., *The Italian Immigrant Woman in North America* (Toronto, 1978); Myrna Kostash, *All of Baba's Children* (Edmonton, 1977); and Jean Burnet, ed., *Looking Into My Sister's Eye* (Toronto, 1986).

The presence of so many newcomers in the most militant labour and political organizations in the country simply reinforced the fears of the Canadian gentry about the aliens in their midst. "These people know absolutely nothing of representative government," wrote a leading minister. "Anglo-Saxon institutions are meaningless to them." So concerned were government authorities that in 1910 the Immigration Act was amended to provide for the exclusion and deportation of those harbouring "subversive and anarchistic" views. However, that did not prevent massive strikes among immigrant workers throughout 1912 and 1913. So serious were they that troops were called out because, in the words of one commanding officer, "aliens [are] people without any sense of responsibility of respect for life or property."

The War's Impact

A year later Canadian soldiers were called upon for a more serious struggle. In August 1914, Canada went to war against Germany and the Austrian Empire. The outbreak of war presented the government with a potentially dangerous domestic problem: Canada was now host to some 500 000 enemy aliens. These included most of Sifton's "men in sheep-skin coats" who were born in those parts of eastern Europe ruled by Austria. Some were fired from their jobs for "patriotic reasons"; others were put into internment camps. Indeed, rather than keeping them on the relief rolls, government officials began to divert many unemployed aliens to the camps. There were, in fact, very few acts of sabotage or espionage committed.

For other immigrants the war could not have come at a better time. Many had been left destitute by the depression that had settled on Canada in 1912 and refused to lift. Unemployment had skyrocketed and many newly arrived immigrants found themselves without jobs, money, or homes. For large numbers, soup kitchens and Salvation Army hostels provided life-giving solace. But in some areas of Western Canada, hungry men raided stores and restaurants for supplies to clothe and feed themselves and their families. When war broke out, thousands of these unemployed men, particularly the Britons, rushed to enlist. For others, the demands of the war soon provided new and better-paying jobs and brought prosperity to Canada. With Europe desperately in need of Canadian food, supplies, and munitions, labour was at a premium. Anyone who wanted to could work, and indeed *had* to work, since the government late in the war passed an "antiloafing" law compelling "every male person" to be "engaged in some useful occupation." Many interned aliens were released to feed labour-starved industries.

For some government officials, the outbreak of war came none too soon. It provided them with a convenient opportunity to translate their fears of immigrant radicals into ameliorative legislation. Encouraged by a strong business lobby, a series of laws were passed affecting the rights of aliens and such immigrant pacifist groups as the Mennonites and the Hutterites. In 1917 the Wartime Elections Act disenfranchised Canadian citizens born in enemy countries who had not been naturalized before 1902. While some foreign workers were sent to jail for going on strike, employers were actively warning government officials that more would have to be done to remove the threat of a radical uprising. Already frightened by the rapid rise of organized labour during the war, after the Russian Revolution many Canadians saw radicalism as a real threat.

Capitalizing on the propitious wartime conditions, Canadian trade unions began furious organizing campaigns. Thousands of new members, including many immigrants, were brought into the labour movement. A record wave of strikes swept the nation in 1917 and 1918 as the newly potent union movement flexed its muscles. Even though the vast majority of strikes were caused by labour's frantic attempts to keep pace with inflation, some industrialists warned the Borden government that, for some foreign workers, the major purpose of the strikes was to sabotage the war effort. One mine owner even urged the prime minister "to make the foreigners work at the point of a bayonet." In addition, police and military reports were pouring into Ottawa warning of the growing militancy of foreign workers, particularly Finns, Slavs, Russians, and Ukrainians. A government enquiry, conducted by the Montreal lawyer C.H. Cahan, concluded that many immigrant workers were "being thoroughly saturated with the Socialist doctrines . . . [of] the Bolshevik faction in Russia" and that Soviet agents had arrived in North America "to organize and inflame their comrades." Though there seems to have been little real evidence to support Cahan's revelations, little was really needed. The Borden cabinet had already made up its mind to act against foreign political associations. Immediately following Cahan's report, the Canadian government started banning socialist organizations, suppressing the foreign-language press, and prohibiting meetings where an "enemy" language was used.

To many native Canadians whose contempt and fear of the aliens in their midst had grown exponentially during the war, the government's response was both tardy and insufficient. Many wanted these immigrants deported; indeed, the minister of militia and defence, Sam Hughes, labelled them a menace and initially urged that "they be encouraged to go to the United States." And passions did not subside with the end of hostilities in Europe. Before the last shot was fired, representatives of veterans' groups were already demanding that aliens be rounded up and shipped back home. Newspapers were questioning their worth and their loyalty to the country. Petitions were pouring into Ottawa demanding the deportation of enemy aliens, including Russian immigrants, who were now subject to "Soviet infection." And underscoring the urgency of the situation, confidential police reports were being forwarded to the government warning of the increasing involvement of immigrants in "Bolshevik subversion."

The war greatly heightened ethnic tensions. This cartoon, from the famous *Calgary Eye Opener* of September 1918, shows one cartoonist's attitude to the influx of Mennonites from the United States.

GLENBOW ARCHIVES, CALGARY/NA-2920-1.

Welcome to Our City!

For Canada's immigrant community, as well as for its labour movement, 1919 was a watershed. Never had the labour movement been so
militant and the foreigner so unpopular. There were more organized
workers in the country and more strikes than ever before. The role
played by immigrant workers in these strikes, as well as their prominence in the newly created One Big Union, convinced most government
officials and business people that something had to be done. Many aliens
were deported; police agents were instructed to infiltrate radical organizations; companies began firing their foreign workers; mobs of returning
veterans attacked immigrants with impunity; and a royal commission
was established to investigate the state of industrial relations in the
country and particularly the role played by non-Anglo-Saxon workers.
But it was too late. The Winnipeg General strike ensured that the
problems of both the worker and the immigrant would be met not with
ameliorative legislation but with violence.

Though alien workers had little to do with events either before or
during the strike, they were seen by various establishment groups as the
ultimate villains. The city's major newspaper urged that the government
"clean the aliens out of this community and ship them back to their
happy homes in Europe which vomited them forth." Perhaps worse, not
only were immigrant workers constantly being harassed by government
officials and security forces, but their own allies in the trade union
movement had turned against them. It was unfortunately not uncommon
for vigilante groups of returned soldiers, supported by mainstream
unions, to battle eastern European immigrants who backed the O.B.U.
Eventually the Immigration act was amended so that "dangerous" aliens
could immediately be sent packing. Even without this amendment,
thousands of immigrants, realizing their welcome had been worn out,
returned home on their own. To them, Canada was no longer the land of
freedom or hope.

However, for the vast majority of immigrants, the events of the war
and immediate postwar period were of little note. Very few had the
interest or the time to become involved in politics; they were too
involved in their work and daily lives. Whether as farmers or manual
labourers, as domestics or factory hands, all were consumed by the
unrelenting struggle to survive. Most were only dimly aware of the
heated debates that were to envelope their adopted homeland in the
1920s about their future as well as the future course of the country's
immigration policy. What was no longer in any doubt was that many
Canadians had reservations about the strangers within their gates. These

doubts were not new but were now being officially translated into more restrictive policy.

The Call for Assimilation

The great fear was that the Anglo-Saxon character of the country was being undermined, that the country had already been irreparably "Balkanized," according to a reputable British journal. Paradoxically, the overwhelming majority of those arriving in Canada in this period were from the United Kingdom and the United States. Nonetheless, influential politicians, educators, and journalists, supported by farm and labour groups, maintained a strong anti-immigrant lobby during the twenties. They could point to the patchwork of ethnic settlement across Western Canada that seemed totally impervious to assimilation. These groups, mostly Doukhobors and Mennonites, stubbornly maintained their own traditions, religion, language, and way of life. They resisted all efforts to bring them into the Canadian mainstream.

The predominant ideology of assimilation in Canada in these years was what historians have called "Anglo-conformity." In effect, it demanded of immigrants that they forget their culture, customs, and language and adopt those of the majority Anglo-Saxon group, that they renounce their past and "behave like little Englishmen." Most influential Canadians viewed the "melting-pot" experiment in the United States as a failure. As R.B. Bennett told the House of Commons in 1928, "Every thoughtful man in the United States, every keen observer . . . every author . . . bewails the fact that uncontrolled immigration has been permitted . . . to such an extent that there is now . . . a polyglot population without any distinctive civilization, and one about which many of them are in great despair. . . ." Canada was different, he said, because learning from the American mistake, it was going to make sure "to assimilate these people to British institutions." British civilization, he reminded the House, was "the test by which all other civilized nations are measured." Perhaps no one said it better than the premier of British Columbia in 1923. "We are anxious to keep this a British country. We want [it] British and nothing else."

The attempt to anglicize a large immigrant population was, predictably, not entirely successful. Despite the valiant efforts of countless educators, missionaries, clergymen, and social workers, many foreigners preferred to maintain their own traditions, much to the chagrin of government officials and often to the shame of the immigrants' own children. The conflict between tradition and assimilation was the hallmark of most European families. As the protagonist of John Marlyn's Winnipeg-based novel, *Under the Ribs of Death*, explains to his father:

The English . . . Pa, the only people who count are the English. Their fathers got all the best jobs. They're the only ones nobody calls foreigners. Nobody ever makes fun of their names or calls them bologny-eaters or laughs at the way they dress or talk. Nobody . . . cause when you're English it's the same as bein' Canadian.

Because many felt these newcomers could never become Canadian, much pressure was applied to the government to adopt a far more restrictive immigration policy. Nativist sentiment had already forced the American government to tighten its admission policy. It would shortly do the same in Canada. But even more important than the demands of the xenophobes was the economic situation. The country was suffering from a postwar depression; immigrants were not needed. Canadian immigration policy has always been ethnically selective and economically self-serving. And in the few years following the Great War, it made little political sense for the government to continue its open door policy. The prewar flood of immigrants slowed to a trickle.

One unusual source for restrictionist propaganda was the medical journals of the country. Many of the doctors who conducted the examinations that determined whether newcomers qualified for admission to Canada had distinctly unfavourable attitudes toward immigrant groups. They were constantly warning of the dangerous contagious diseases foreigners might introduce into Canada and were appalled by what they felt were the frightful sanitary conditions of their homes. As the *Canadian Journal of Medicine and Surgery* editorialized in 1919, "Canada has been the dumping ground for thousands of undesirable immigrants. . . . This must stop. Our asylums and jails are over full of degenerates, criminals and mental defectives." Another journal warned, "We cannot melt in our pot certain peoples from Central Europe. They do not fit in. Too many of them have been dumped in already. They already swell our already overcrowded cities and render life in these urban centres most intolerable." The medical profession throughout the 1920s took the lead in agitating for less liberal immigration policies.

Even the most prized newcomers, the British, were not met with open arms. Government officials were even reluctant to accept British immigrants sponsored by the Empire Settlements Act passed by the British

Parliament in 1922 to subsidize those residents of the United Kingdom who wished to emigrate to any of the dominions. Perhaps most noteworthy was the number of British deportees from Canada in these years. As a sop to nativists and other pressure groups, the government ordered the Immigration Branch to be more vigorous in its deportation program. In particular, it had in mind "those foreigners whose presence in Canada was both dangerous and unacceptable." The vast majority of those sent out of the country were, ironically, not continental Europeans but Britons.

Though Ottawa assumed it was satisfying most Canadians with its new restrictive policy, sections of the business and farm communities were annoyed. Mine owners and railway men, in particular, were outspoken in their criticism of the new arrangements. Where, they wondered, were they going to get the workers they so badly needed? Canadians, they argued, even during a depression, had an aversion to the type of work that needed to be done. Some farmers wanted increased access to the large numbers of central Europeans who made up the bulk of the labour force in agricultural communities throughout the West. With the United States now closed to most Europeans, thanks to newly restrictive legislation, increasing numbers of Canadian industrial and farm workers were spilling south across the border to take up jobs usually reserved for European immigrants; and with fewer of these allowed into Canada, industrialists were concerned that there would be, in the words of one, "no one left to do the work." And for the type of work they were offering and the wages they were paying, that was quite understandable. For the railway, factory, and frontier-resource workers in particular, the work was grinding and unremunerative. Railway navvies and loggers were earning up to $5 a day in the 1920s, but after deductions for board, rent, and clothing they were left with very little. At a time when government statisticians were estimating that it required just over $1000 a year to provide a family with the barest essentials, the average earnings of the unskilled worker were less than half that.

In 1925, with the return of prosperity, the "immigration boosters" finally won over the King government, and Canada's immigration doors were flung open again. Canada's railways, the C.N.R. and C.P.R., were given permission to recruit bonafide agricultural immigrants throughout Europe. The King cabinet had convinced itself that immigration was a panacea for the country's economic problems. More settlers would mean more revenue and larger markets. As a shoe manufacturer explained, there were "too many shoes in Canada and not enough feet." To the railways, of course, immigrants were an absolute necessity. There was no problem in Canada, said the president of the C.P.R., that "cannot be solved partially or entirely by new people." These could settle in the West, where the railways fortunately held land and kilometres of unused track, and provide both goods for export and, of course, business for the railways. Though immigration officials attempted to sabotage the arrangement with the railways – they resented the competition and feared that it was, in the words of the deputy minister, a "pernicious attempt to destroy the selective immigration policy" – the railways, nonetheless, brought 200 000 central and eastern Europeans to Canada. Many of these came because they could not get into their land of first choice, the United States.

To offset the large number of continental newcomers, a massive campaign was undertaken to recruit British immigrants as well. Large subsidies and loans were promised to anyone from the United Kingdom who wished to settle in Canada, especially on a farm. In 1928, attempts were even made to ship 10 000 unemployed British miners to Western Canada to act as harvesters. Over 8000 arrived, their way paid by both British and Canadian authorities. Within a short time, 6000 had gone back home. One crestfallen government official opined that it seemed as if "the British race had lost its pioneering instinct." Another, probably more accurately, attributed the failure to the highly advanced British welfare system: "It's the dole that keeps them home," he said. In fact, most of the miners were shipped back home "in locked and guarded trains," according to the historian of this scheme, because officials feared their radicalism and union background might "contaminate the Canadian countryside as they passed through it." The Department of Immigration estimated that while it cost about fifteen cents to recruit a European immigrant, it cost seventeen dollars for each British arrival. And many of these latter, according to some Canadians, were hardly worth the cost. "We do not want mechanics from the Clyde," wrote Clifford Sifton in 1922, "riotous, turbulent and with an insatiable appetite for whiskey." Nor did he want the "trade union artisan who will not work more than eight hours a day and will not work that long if he can help it."

In any event, the immigration procedures of the 1920s satisfied few. Despite the rhetoric of railway representatives who convinced the prime minister in 1925 that there were 25 million acres (40 million hectares) of prime prairie land suitable for at least 300 000 immigrants, the supply of good land had largely run out. Provinces and municipalities were loudly complaining of the large number of unemployed and unassimilable immigrants within their borders. And in Saskatchewan the Ku Klux Klan was successfully recruiting members in reaction to what was perceived as the Liberal government's attempt to populate Canada with Roman Catholic immigrants. Increasing mechanization of both factory and farm meant fewer jobs for the unskilled foreigners. Massive immigration, argued some leading Canadian academics, drove down both wages and living standards and drove out native Canadians. As Professor A.R.M. Lower put it, " 'Cheap men' will always drive out 'dear' men. The men with the higher standard of living cannot compete with the man with the lower." Good English-speaking farmers and workers were thus forced to go to the United States in order to survive. In applying Gresham's famous monetary law – cheap money will drive out dear money – to immigration policy, Lower was not alone; his views were shared by many government officials. Even the British government was perturbed by Canadian policy. In a confidential memorandum in 1928, the Dominions office warned the British prime minister that Canada was fast losing its Anglo-Saxon character, that it was allowing in too many foreigners and was therefore no longer "an appealing home" for British immigrants. Perhaps the Toronto *Globe* expressed these views best in a 1928 editorial. "The country," it said, "cannot go on if its national life is made up of races which fall short of the national standard."

Most dissatisfied with federal immigration policies were the French-Canadians. Many nationaliste leaders saw immigration as a nefarious federal plot to reduce French-Canadian influence in Confederation. Since most new immigrants would undoubtedly assimilate into the English-Canadian culture, few French-Canadians supported an open door policy; for them, immigration obviously was a threat to the country's finely tuned cultural balance. To appease them, efforts were made to bring over numbers of immigrants from France and to bring home those Québécois who had emigrated to the New England textile mills. Neither attempt met with much success.

The King government was fully aware of the political repercussions of its policies. The "nonpreferred immigrants" were acceptable so long as they remained hidden in the farms, smelters, mines, and lumber camps of the North and West. Those who escaped this life for, perhaps, a worse one in Canada's urban centres were less acceptable. As more and more of these drifted toward the cities in the 1920s, the order went out to restrict the immigration of those on the bottom rungs of the ethnic preference ladder. In addition, the federal government agreed to allow provincial premiers to decide how many immigrants their province could accept annually. As well, the freedom of the railways in bringing over colonists was restricted. As the deputy minister of immigration explained, though the economy was still booming, the government was clamping down on "non-preferred country immigrants [since they] had drifted into non-agricultural work almost immediately upon arrival . . . and [were] filling positions that might have been filled by immigrants from the Mother Country." Yet significantly, an enquiry into the immigration policies of the government by a House of Commons committee in 1928 made it quite evident that, while most Canadians wanted fewer "foreign" immigrants, they also did not want any more from Great Britain. Immigrants, it was argued, caused unemployment, and in Western Canada this was a serious problem, especially in winter, when thousands of migrant workers poured into the cities from the farms, forests, and mines looking for work.

The Depression Stops the Flow

By 1929 unemployment was becoming a serious problem in the rest of Canada as well. In that year, just as in 1913, the flood of immigrants peaked precisely at the time the economy was diving into a depression. Just when it needed them least, Canada had more immigrants than ever before. The Liberal government was now coming under severe attack from some of its erstwhile allies because of its immigration policies. The people of Saskatchewan who had voted Liberal since the province entered Confederation in 1905 dealt the provincial Liberals a stunning blow in the provincial election of 1929: one of the major issues of the campaign had been the federal government's "lax" policy in opening Canada to so many foreigners. Now there was a growing clamour across the nation to keep them out. In response, as the economy rapidly deteriorated throughout 1929 and 1930, the King cabinet frantically attempted to close the door. It passed a series of orders-in-council restricting immigration to Canada only to those with enough capital to establish and maintain themselves on farms. In 1931, the new Bennett government took the ultimate step of barring all immigrants who were not agriculturalists with capital and not of British or American stock. For all intents and purposes, Canada had shut herself off from the rest of the world. Immigration throughout the depression-ridden 1930s was at a standstill.

Anti-foreign and anti-Catholic sentiment led to the establishment of the Ku Klux Klan in Canada. The Klan was strongest in Saskatchewan, but this 1927 photograph was taken in Kingston, Ontario.

PA-87848/NATIONAL ARCHIVES OF CANADA.

Predictably, those who suffered worst during the Depression were those who had arrived most recently. Concentrated in the most insecure and vulnerable sectors of the economy, they were the first to lose their jobs, the first to go on welfare, and the first to be herded into the relief camps. Since the country had imported large numbers of unskilled migrant workers for the farms, railways, mines, and lumber camps of the North and the West, the ratio of single, unemployed men was far greater in Canada than in any other western country. Rather than ride out the economic storm in Canada, many of these young men headed back across the Atlantic. Others had no choice; the government simply deported thousands of those without work. Fully two-thirds of the deportees in this period – over 30 000 – were forced to leave because they had become public charges. It was certainly much less expensive to send them back home, argued government officials, than to keep them on the relief rolls. What little money was available for welfare would go to native Canadians.

Never very popular with most Canadians, immigrants were least popular during the 1930s.[5] Not only did many blame them for the unemployment crisis ("If we didn't have so many damn foreigners," said one labour leader, "there'd be plenty of work to go around for everyone"), but they were also seen as a threat to the state. Radical groups proliferated during the 1930s, and none was more feared than the Community Party. It was an "exotic" movement, wrote one academic in the *Dalhousie Review*, "led principally by European immigrants." The Slavs particularly, he added, "contribute to Communist ideas and troubles." Though relatively few recent European immigrants were involved with the party, in the public mind at least, all were; Finns, Jews, Slavs, and Ukrainians were especially suspect. In many places meetings that were conducted in a foreign language were banned; hundreds of foreigners were arrested and many were deported on the flimsiest of evidence. Even some segments of the ethnic press were silenced: how could the government remain immobile, for example, when one Finnish newspaper was described by the *Canadian Annual Review* as "seditious, immoral, anti-Christian, anti-Canadian and anti-British"? It obviously could not; nor could it fail to notice that the most militant union of the period, the Communist-led Workers' Unity League, had a large immigrant constituency. Though the Bennett government attempted to destroy the Communist Party by declaring it illegal and by arresting and deporting its leadership, it failed. The party survived the Bennett administration and would play an important role in the labour movement for the next decade. Similarly, many of the radical immigrants in the Workers' Unity League would surface again as the backbone of the industrial union movement that swept the country in the late 1930s and early 1940s.

Xenophobia

The Canada of the 1930s, overwhelmed by the social effects of the Depression, was a country permeated with xenophobia. In the provinces of Alberta and British Columbia, it took the form of a hardening anti-Oriental bias. Not only were Asian immigrants legally barred from entering the country, but in British Columbia they were disenfranchised

---

[5] On policy in the 1930s, see particularly Irving Abella and Harold Troper, *None is Too Many: Canada and the Jews of Europe, 1933-48* (Toronto, 1982), and Gerald Dirks, *Canada's Refugee Policy* (Montreal, 1977).

and prevented from joining various professions. As an attorney-general of the province once explained, "The *real objection* to the Oriental and the one that is permanent and incurable is the ethnological differences as between the white and Oriental races. . . . In the Divine arrangement of things it was [not] intended that the blood of the Oriental and the blood of the white should mix." In the rest of Canada there were increasing attacks, both physical and verbal, on the "hunky," "bohunk," "uke," and "dago." But perhaps most nefarious was the rapidly spreading anti-Semitism of the period.

This was most apparent in the staunchly Catholic province of Quebec, where the Church led the onslaught against the Jews. Through sermons and articles in Catholic newspapers, the faithful were warned against alien doctrines. In many parishes Jews were regularly denounced from the pulpit as Christ-killers and as exploiters who would cheat and rob the innocent habitant. Many church and *nationaliste* leaders led a movement to boycott Jewish businesses, to keep Jews out of public life and out of Canada altogether. In many popular journals and newspapers, including the prestigious *Le Devoir*, Jews were portrayed as evil, dishonest, dirty, and troublesome.

But anti-Jewish feeling was not restricted to Quebec; it was also strong, though less vocal, in English Canada. Quotas against Jews existed in most universities, professions, businesses, and the civil service. Almost no Jews taught in schools or colleges, worked in anything but the most menial positions in large companies and banks, or played any important role in the legal, medical, or financial communities of this country. Jews were legally forbidden to buy land or homes in many areas, to vacation in certain resorts, or to join various organizations. Anti-Jewish speeches were given regularly by leading Canadian political, religious, business, and labour representatives. There was even some violence as Jews confronted anti-Semites on the streets of Winnipeg, Toronto, and Montreal.

The real tragedy of this anti-Jewish sentiment was that it occurred at the same time that Hitler was persecuting and terrorizing the hundreds of thousands of Jews under his control. There was no popular support, and indeed much opposition, to the proposal that Canada provide a haven for some of these people, most of whom were later murdered at Auschwitz, Treblinka, or the other Nazi death camps. Of all the countries in the western world, Canada had perhaps the worst record of providing sanctuary to the hapless Jewish refugees. While the United States took in 240 000, Great Britain 85 000, tiny Palestine 100 000, Argentina 50 000, and even penurious Mexico and Colombia 20 000 each, Canada allowed in less than 4000.

The Canadian government was fully aware of the extent of anti-Semitism throughout the land, and many of its members shared the prejudice. Thus any program to admit refugees would meet with deep hostility. Mackenzie King was a consummate politician. Had he believed there were votes to be won by allowing Jewish refugees to enter Canada, he undoubtedly would have done so; but he was convinced there were not, so he did not.

Part of the problem lay with the Immigration Branch. Since its heyday under Sifton, it had once again become the backwater of government service. It now found itself attached to the Department of Mines and Resources, reporting to ministers who knew nothing about immigration matters and cared even less. The branch was made up of a handful of civil servants who, according to one critic, thought their job was to keep people out of Canada rather than to let them in. Inspired by their inflexible director, F.C. Blair, who had spent 30 years in the branch, immigration officers all seemed to have a fetish for regulations and were unbending in their application of them. Few could break through the barrier of orders-in-council that now surrounded Canada; few Canadians wanted them to. Except for the ethnic communities themselves, there were no longer any pro-immigrant lobbies in the country. What Canada needed and wanted least during the Depression was more job-hungry immigrants.

Perhaps Canadians felt they had already done their share. In the first 30 years of this century, just under five million immigrants had arrived. In the next 15, barely 200 000 came, far less than previously arrived in one good year during the previous three decades. The arrival of so many new settlers of so many different languages, races, religions, and ways of life had obviously been traumatic to a nation that was itself just finding its feet. To integrate, assimilate, and educate these millions was both essential and enormously difficult. Those who for so long had been calling for a halt, for a period of digestion in which the country could finish absorbing those immigrants who were already here finally got their wish.

Only in 1948, fully 18 years after Canada closed the doors, were they once again opened – selectively. Following the Second World War, a confident, bustling Canada announced to the world that it was once again open for business. Optimism was now in the saddle; boosterism was the order of the day. The spirit of Sifton had finally triumphed over that of Blair. Government officials – indeed probably most Canadians – believed their country was on the verge of greatness. It had wealth, resources, geography on its side; the only thing lacking was people. And so, in 1947, urged on by the business community, the Canadian government unfolded a new immigration policy. In a famous statement read to the House of Commons on May 1, Prime Minister Mackenzie King declared that the policy of the government was "to foster the growth of population by the encouragement of immigration." A large population would create new markets, provide a bigger labour force, develop the resources, and reduce the country's dependence on the export of primary products. But the welcome was not available to everyone. Immigrants, warned King, would "be selected with care." In other words, they would be white, European, and preferably Christian. After all, added the prime minister: "Canada is perfectly within her rights in selecting the persons whom we regard as desirable future citizens."

Over the next two decades, two million immigrants – including thousands of refugees from war-ravaged Europe – arrived in Canada. Still Canada did not abandon its policy of racial discrimination. Indeed, it was not until the late 1960s that Canada finally opened up to immigrants from areas that had never before been recognized as potential sources – the Caribbean, Latin America, Asia, and the Middle East. And ironically, given the restrictionist policy of the first hundred years, the majority of immigrants arriving in Canada since the 1970s have been from precisely these areas.

Over the past two generations, it is obvious that Canada has come a long way in immigration policy and has lurched indecisively between an open door and a closed door, between open-mindedness and narrow-mindedness, between generosity and selfishness. Over the years a whole range of economic, social, political, and demographic factors have determined what Canadian policy would be at a given time. Historically, one significant thing is evident: rarely are Canadian governments prepared to challenge public attitudes, which by and large have been hostile to a large-scale movement of immigrants into this country.

IX

1939-1957: THE LIBERAL ASCENDANCY

When the cabinet met on November 1, 1944, the ministers were tired and quarrelsome. The endless debates over conscription, the tension between Mackenzie King and Colonel J. L. Ralston, the minister of national defence, and the overwhelming weariness engendered in everyone by five years of war had left them all emotionally and physically drained. Conscientious and hard-working, Ralston was sick in body and spirit, his face, with its pugnacious jaw, now looking drawn and gaunt. The minister knew that his time in the cabinet was coming to an end, for he was determined to secure the reinforcements that he believed his men overseas needed to fight the war to its inevitably successful conclusion. And, Ralston knew, the prime minister was no more willing to consider conscription than he had been at any time since 1939. To Mackenzie King, the great issue was national unity, and to him that meant it was absolutely necessary to keep French- and English-Canadians united, something that could not be accomplished if conscription was imposed on a reluctant Quebec by the Anglo-Canadian majority, especially if this took place so late in the war, with victory only weeks or months away.

Mackenzie King called the ministers to order and led them through the statistics that were so familiar to them all. To his surprise, Ralston seemed almost accommodating, prepared to consider measures to avert a break. But to King, determined to remove the cancer of conscription now, this was a trick, "a scheme to make the situation still more difficult for me." The time had come to speak out. "I then said I thought we ought to, if possible, reach a conclusion without further delay." Was there anyone who could "save the government and save a terrible division at this time[?] . . . Was there anyone who could do this[?] . . . If there was, I thought it was owing to the country that such a person's services should be secured. I said I believed I had the man who could undertake the task and carry it out." That was General Andrew McNaughton, the general who had taken the first Canadian troops overseas in 1939 and had built them into the great army that was fighting in Italy and Normandy.

"I then said," King went on, later recording his interpretation of events in his diary, "that the people of Canada would say that McNaughton was the right man for the task, and since Ralston had clearly said that he himself did not believe we could get the men without conscription . . . that I thought if Ralston felt in that way he should make it possible for us to bring McNaughton in at once. . . ." The cabinet members sat stunned as King finished speaking. Ralston rose at his chair, shook King's hand, and left the room, almost without a word.

One of the greatest political gambles in Canadian history had been carried off without a hitch. Mackenzie King had sacked his defence minister because of his attitude to conscription, and he had successfully replaced him with a very popular general – and one who was opposed to compulsory military service. It was a coup, all the more dramatic for being carried out within the confines of the cabinet chamber, and because he had accomplished it so neatly, the prime minister had stunned potentially rebellious ministers into inaction. He had bought precious time with his political victory. However, the irony of the triumph was that within three weeks McNaughton would be driven to appeal to the prime minister for a measure of conscription, and this time Mackenzie King would have no choice except to yield to the political and military powers that demanded it.

The Coming of the War, 1939

Few Canadians felt any excitement as the Second World War began in September 1939. There were no cheering crowds in Montreal singing "La Marseillaise" and "Rule Britannia," as had been the case 25 years before, no enthusiasm, no shouts that the boys would be in Berlin by Christmas. Ten years of depression, unemployment, and hard times had sapped the national will, and there were too many families all across the land who remembered the dead and the maimed from the Great War and who did not underestimate the cost of another struggle with German militarism.

In the circumstances, Mackenzie King's cautious policies fit the national mood. Before the outbreak of war, he had made very clear that no government led by him would support a policy of conscription for overseas service, a promise that had obvious appeal to a French Canada that dreaded the prospect of another confrontation with Ottawa on such an emotive subject. More to the point, perhaps, aside from fire-eating imperialists, in 1939 almost no one in English Canada seemed to believe that conscription was wise – or likely to be necessary. The new Conservative leader, Dr. R.J. Manion, who had replaced Bennett in 1938, made it clear that his party took the same stance, although that was not a position that sat easily with some of his supporters. The prime minister also stated that Canada's policy was to be one of "limited liability" in this war. We were not a great power, we were far from the scene of the action, we had had little part in the events leading up to the struggle against Hitler. In these circumstances, Canada would simply contribute what it could and use the war to rebuild the depression-ravaged Canadian economy. That was not a glamorous position, to say the least; but it was one that seemed to fit the Canadian mood and reflected that of the "phony war," which saw Britain and France glowering at Germany over the Maginot line in a state of armed hostility that produced little actual combat.

Mackenzie King's policy was a natural one for him to follow. King had seen Canada tear itself apart over conscription in 1917; he had watched as the great Laurier was deserted by most of his English-speaking colleagues, and he had sworn that that would not recur. His government would remain intact, his Liberal Party would stay together as the only major national organization that united French- and English-Canadians, and his government would produce a war effort that was decent and honourable. "Everything in moderation" might have been King's slogan. The prime minister was almost 65 years old as the war began, a crafty, experienced politician who had led the Liberals for 20 years and been prime minister for a dozen. His successes had not been spectacular ones to that point – his greatest triumph had been to win election after election and to swallow in the great maw of Liberalism the dissident Progressives. He had led the country through the 1920s and into the Depression, and he had returned to power in 1935 on the slogan of "King or Chaos." But he had been unable to end the Depression (who could?) and had he died on September 1, 1939, he would likely have been remembered by

Canadians only as another in a long succession of sometimes lacklustre leaders. The war was to alter that.

Mackenzie King's first challenges were political. In Quebec, Premier Maurice Duplessis announced to a surprised province that he was going to the people for a renewed mandate in October. The reason? Ottawa was using the war as an excuse to centralize power, to crush the provinces. Cynical observers thought Duplessis' reason for seeking an early election was a combination of the difficulties he was having in borrowing money to keep his Union Nationale government going and the expectation that the war had so alarmed French-Canadians about conscription that they would back a government that was strong on provincial rights. The conscription issue was soon squelched when Mackenzie King's Quebec ministers announced that if Duplessis won they would resign from the federal cabinet, thus leaving Quebec naked and defenceless before the power of the Anglo majority and probably making conscription inevitable. The choice was put clearly to Quebeckers – vote Duplessis and get conscription; vote Liberal and we will protect you. The province responded to this appeal (and probably to Duplessis' very bad record) by tossing the rascals out and electing Adelard Godbout's rouges with a strong majority in the legislature.

One of Ottawa's battles had been won. The second challenge came from the Liberal premier of Ontario. Mitchell Hepburn had never been an admirer of Mackenzie King, and his dealings with the prime minister over the last five years had been acrimonious. The two Liberals had quarrelled about money and the division of powers in the Constitution, about hydro on the St. Lawrence, and about control of the party in the province; gradually, any trust between them had eroded. Now King saw the hard-drinking, womanizing Hepburn as so dissolute that he verged on the insane; the premier looked at King as spineless and, now, soft on the war. Hepburn had convinced himself that Ottawa was running a lackadaisical war effort and letting Britain down, and he put a motion to that effect before the legislature where it was whooped through with the enthusiastic backing of George Drew and the Conservative Opposition. For King, this resolution provided the opportunity he needed. Telling himself that no federal leader could countenance such dissension in Ontario, he advised a surprised House of Commons that he was calling a snap election. The Tories were caught unprepared, Manion and his men having banked on a session of some months to allow them the time to expose the government's weaknesses in fighting the war. The C.C.F. too was in disarray. J.S. Woodsworth, the party leader, had felt obliged to call for neutralism and pacifism in the special war session of Parliament in September 1939, and while that was gallant and honourable, it did his party little good. The Liberals were home free, particularly as the Conservatives converted themselves into the "National Government" party and called for a coalition of "the best brains" in the country. Most of "the best brains" declined to serve under Manion in the unlikely event that he would win, and many French-Canadians apparently believed that the recycled Tories were again putting Union government forward as their platform – and could conscription be far behind? The result, on March 26, was a sweeping Liberal victory. The government was in power for the duration of the war with 181 seats, while the Tories had lost their leader and won only 40 seats, 25 of them in Ontario. The C.C.F. was reduced to eight seats, Social credit won ten, all from Alberta, and independents and others captured six. Any assaults on King's policies could now come only from the press – or from within his own party.[1]

There was little sign of that initially. The cabinet had some strong men, and most of their time was devoted to gearing the nation up for war. At the onset of the struggle, Colonel J.L. Ralston had become minister of finance. A courageous man who had been a battalion commander in the Great War, Ralston was a somewhat dour Nova Scotian with enormous force of will. In June 1940, he would become minister of national defence, a post in which he would be aided by Air Minister Chubby Power, a gregarious, bibulous Irish-Canadian from Quebec City who was one of the ablest men in the ministry, and by Angus Macdonald, the Liberal premier of Nova Scotia, brought to Ottawa by King to be navy minister. That was a first-rate trio. To mobilize the economy, King was fortunate in being able to draw on the organizational talents of C.D. Howe, the grain-elevator builder from the Lakehead. Howe took over responsibility for the new Department of Munitions and Supply in early 1940 and made it the driving force of Canada's industrial contribution to the war. J.L. Ilsley was another of King's ministers who blossomed during the war, and when he succeeded Ralston in the finance

---

[1] Books on the politics of the war include J.W. Pickersgill, *The Mackenzie King Record*, vols. I-II (Toronto, 1960, 1968); J.L. Granatstein's *The Politics of Survival: The Conservative Party of Canada 1939-45* (Toronto, 1967); John Kendle's *John Bracken: A Political Biography* (Toronto, 1979); Granatstein's *Canada's War: The Politics of the Mackenzie King Government, 1939-45* (Toronto, 1975); Neil McKenty's *Mitch Hepburn* (Toronto, 1967); Walter Young, *The Anatomy of a Party: The National CCF 1932-61* (Toronto, 1969); H.F. Quinn, *The Union Nationale*, rev. ed. (Toronto, 1979); and Reginald Whitaker, *The Government Party: Organizing and Financing the Liberal Party of Canada 1930-58* (Toronto, 1977).

portfolio, he became, with his flinty honesty and administrative skill, that most unlikely of creatures, a popular minister of finance. There was also the minister of justice, Ernest Lapointe, a French-Canadian whose special task it was to make sure that Quebec's considerations received their due. It was as strong a cabinet as any that Canada had ever had, and the changes that the war forced on it only strengthened it further.

To formulate and direct war policy, the prime minister created a cabinet War Committee, a grouping of the key ministers. The War Committee's members controlled the major departments, employed the ablest officials in the bureaucracy, and effectively created and directed Canada's war. But even before the War Committee was created in December 1939, the basic outlines of the war effort had been laid down. In September, King announced that Canada would raise a division of infantry for service in Europe, and the 1st Canadian Infantry Division, under the command of Major-General Andrew G. L. McNaughton, had arrived in England by mid-December. The small Royal Canadian Navy was put to work shepherding convoys, a vital if unglamorous task. And the Royal Canadian Air Force was given the job of running the British Commonwealth Air Training Plan, a magnificent and costly enterprise that took advantage of Canada's open spaces and relative safety from the enemy to make this country "the aerodrome of democracy." The B.C.A.T.P. had been conceived by the Canadian and Australian high commissioners in London, and the British government had been quick to accept it. Mackenzie King, however, was appalled at the financial contribution London wanted his government to make, and the negotiations on the plan were bitter. Nonetheless, on December 17, 1939 (not coincidentally King's sixty-fifth birthday), the creation of the B.C.A.T.P. was announced. Soon aircrew trainees from all across the Commonwealth (as well as large numbers of Americans who wanted to get into the war) came to Canada to be turned into pilots, navigators, wireless operators, air gunners, and bombardiers. In Saskatchewan and Prince Edward Island, in Quebec and Manitoba, the trainees learned to fly – and mingled with the local citizens, making the Commonwealth into an objective reality for the first time. It was a splendid plan, and the 131 553 aircrew (of which 72 835 were Canadian) were, arguably, Canada's major contribution to the eventual Allied victory. The cost to Canada was $1.6 billion, three-quarters of the total cost of the B.C.A.T.P.

Canada's modest war effort might have been sufficient had the course of the war followed the plan laid down by Allied staff officers in London and Paris. The war of 1939 was in some respects a continuation of the

Great War – with a 20-year armistice separating the two parts. But there were differences. Italy had switched sides and, although neutral until the summer of 1940, was on the Axis team. So too was Japan, although its

Ernest Lapointe, King's Quebec lieutenant and closest colleague from the early 1920s until his death in November 1941.

C-9796/NATIONAL ARCHIVES OF CANADA.

entry into the war did not occur until Pearl Harbor signalled the conversion of a European war into a world war on December 7, 1941. The Soviet Union was also neutral in 1939, another shift from the course followed by Russia in 1914, and Stalin's nation was a wary partner of Hitler's Germany in the partition of Poland in September 1939. The last great neutral was the United States. President Franklin Roosevelt's country wanted to be free of European entanglements, a traditional attitude but one that had been reinforced by disillusionment after the First World War. However, the president feared Hitler's power and wanted to help the Allies as much as he could, but he was usually constrained by Congress and public opinion.

Britain's Ranking Ally

That American help – and a greater Canadian effort – would be needed became clear in the spring and summer of 1940. The Nazi *blitzkrieg* swept over Denmark and Norway in April and then turned on Belgium, the Netherlands, Luxembourg, and France the next month. The European balance of power changed dramatically in a single month: France was beaten, and England, having rescued its armies at Dunkirk in a brilliantly improvised evacuation, found itself defended only by the Royal Navy, the small but effective Royal Air Force, and a few well-equipped army formations of which the 1st Canadian Division was the best. Hitler was the master of western Europe, and Canada, from being a cautious dominion fighting a war of limited liability, had suddenly become Britain's ranking ally; it remained so until Hitler invaded Russia in June 1941, and the United States came into the war in December 1941.

Increased efforts were undertaken from Ottawa, and limited liability was tossed out the window. Recruiting was stepped up, war production increased (as the British for the first time in the war began to place orders in quantity), and units of infantry, armour, artillery, and R.C.A.F. squadrons were hurried across the ocean. Mackenzie King also gathered his courage and put in place, through the National Resources Mobilization Act, a policy of conscription – but for home defence only. Young men were to be called up for 30 days' training, an attempt, as some army officers saw it, to begin the process of whittling away at 20 years of pacifism. Surprisingly, there was little opposition in Quebec, although Camilien Houde, the mayor of Montreal, was interned for urging his compatriots not to register for the draft. French-Canadians, just as they had always claimed, were willing to serve to defend Canada, and after June 1940, there seemed to be a threat to Canada. Eventually the home defence draft was extended to four months and then, in April 1941, for the duration of the war, but for domestic political reasons the government refused to send the conscripts abroad. The result was the creation of two armies – one of volunteers for service anywhere, and one of draftees (called Zombies after the living dead of Hollywood horror films) who could serve only in Canada and later in Alaska and the West Indies. Two great national crises over conscription, in 1942 and 1944, followed the creation of these armies, and each upheaval almost destroyed the King government. But that was still in the future.

More immediately, the crisis of the summer of 1940 forced Canada to look to its own security. What if Britain fell? What of Canada's defences? What of Canada's trade? Those hard questions were also being posed in Washington by President Roosevelt and his brain trust, and the answers in both countries seemed to demand closer co-operation between them. There had been some movement in this direction even before the war, for Roosevelt and King were friendly, their governments had worked together to negotiate two trade agreements in 1935 and 1938, and there had even been some tentative military staff talks in 1938. Now something more was needed, and in August Roosevelt called the prime minister on the telephone to suggest that the two leaders meet at Ogdensburg, New York. There they agreed to establish a Permanent Joint Board on Defence to plan for the defence of the continent and to co-ordinate the deployment of their forces. It was a historic decision (made, interestingly, without any consultation whatever with Parliament or Congress) and one, in retrospect, that marked Canada's shift from the British to the American sphere of interest. It was also essential, for if Canada had failed to look to its own security, the government would have been foolish indeed. Evidence that the public realized this can be seen in the popular approbation the Ogdensburg Agreement received – and in the harsh words with which Winston Churchill greeted its conclusion. Ogdensburg let Canada go all out to help Britain, but the British prime minister, with his long view of events, recognized the significance of the agreement and its *permanent* defence board.

Canada was also going all out to help Britain economically. But given the limited capacity of Canadian industry, this meant that components, raw materials, and machine tools had to be imported from the United States – at a cost of some $400 million a year, payable in American dollars – and this quickly began to pose difficulties. Before the war Canada could use its surplus earned in trade with Britain to pay for the perennial deficit in trade with the south, but the British barred the exchange of sterling for dollars, and Canada was soon in a bind. The more it tried to help England, the more it had to import and the greater its dollar deficit. Efforts were made to control nonessential imports and holiday travel, notably through the War Exchange Conservation Act of December 1940, but the U.S. dollar shortage increased rapidly, threatening the Canadian economy.

The solution came in April 1941, when Mackenzie King again travelled to see Roosevelt, this time at the president's family home in Hyde Park, New York. If the Americans could buy more raw materials and manufactured goods in Canada, then our difficulties would be eased, King told the president. And if the components that Canada had to import for incorporation into munitions for Britain could be supplied under Lend-Lease and charged to the British account, then the difficulties would disappear altogether. Lend-Lease was the ingenious attempt of a still-neutral America to help Britain secure the supplies for which a nearly bankrupt England could no longer pay. The president, a man who had as long a view as Churchill, readily agreed, and he inscribed the Hyde Park Declaration to say that it had been done by Mackenzie and Franklin on a ''grand Sunday in April.'' It was a grand Sunday for the prime minister indeed, for Canada's economic problems virtually dissolved at a stroke, and the Canadian war economy went from strength to strength. So powerful did industry and agriculture become, in fact, that Canada was soon in a position to give away billions of dollars in munitions and foodstuffs. A great loan of $700 million to Britain was followed by a billion-dollar gift and then by massive Mutual Aid contributions of $2 billion to Britain and other Allies. In total, Canada gave Britain $3.5 billion in aid.[2]

The Condition of the People

The war's transformation of Canada was miraculous. The blighted prairie farms regenerated and began again to produce first-quality wheat in

---

[2] On Canadian-American relations during the war, see S.W. Dziuban, *Military Relations Between the United States and Canada 1939-45* (Washington, 1959); C.P. Stacey, *Arms, Men and Governments: the War Policies of Canada, 1939-45* (Ottawa, 1970); Stacey's *Canada and the Age of Conflict*, vol. II (Toronto, 1981); J.L. Granatstein, *A Man of Influence: Norman A. Robertson and Canadian Statecraft, 1929-68* (Ottawa, 1981); and R.D. Cuff and J.L. Granatstein, *Ties that Bind: Canadian-American Relations in Wartime* (Toronto, 1977).

abundance – and for a good price. The war effort needed every foot of lumber that the British Columbia forests could yield, every fish that the Maritimes could produce, every ounce of ore that the mines of the Laurentian Shield could process. Unemployment disappeared, soon to be replaced by a labour shortage and government controls that required a man or woman to seek permission from National Selective Service before changing jobs. Peace on the labour front was essential if production was to be maintained, and in 1940, the cabinet passed an order-in-council guaranteeing union recognition and bargaining rights to industries under federal jurisdiction. Unfortunately, the Department of Labour did nothing to enforce this order, and labour unrest bubbled away, occasionally erupting in strikes that disrupted war production. Finally, in February 1944, a cabinet that was becoming concerned about its electoral prospects passed P.C. 1003, the National War Labour Order, to guarantee workers in all industries the right to form unions and to oblige employers to bargain with them. This was labour's Magna Carta. The net result was that unionized workers increased over the course of the war from 359 000 in 1939 to 711 000 in 1945. Businesspeople may not have been altogether happy with that development, but the war was a good time for them as well. After the hard years of the 1930s, there was all the work that every factory – if it made goods needed for the war effort – could handle, often on cost-plus contracts that eliminated risks. There was government aid for construction of plants, there were easy write-offs of costs and for depreciation, and, although taxes were high, there was still a good profit. But there were other prices to pay. Unnecessary industries were squeezed out of the marketplace and ordered to convert to war production. Factories that had produced refrigerators in 1939 were making Bren guns or tank tracks by 1941. The state began to intervene in every sphere of life, allocating resources, controlling production, determining wages. Prices and wages were frozen in November 1941, when inflation seemed on the verge of a spiralling increase, and the Wartime Prices and Trade Board, headed by the tough-talking Donald Gordon, a previously little-known officer of the Bank of Canada, became a giant agency that controlled the lives of businesspeople and ordinary citizens alike. Ration cards for scarce foods and for gasoline became the norm; tokens were necessary to purchase meats; car tires became scarce as hen's teeth; and every housewife was urged to grow vegetables in her backyard, to report waste, and to save money, edible fats, and even milkweed for life preservers. Canada was mobilized for the war in a fashion that made the effort of 1914-18 look amateurish.

Astonishingly, despite the great war effort there was enough left over to improve living standards all across the country. Families that had had no breadwinner during the Depression years now found that even if the husband was overseas, the wife and eldest daughter had all the work and overtime they wanted. At their peak of wartime employment in the fall of 1944, more than one million women were working full time, a figure that excluded part-time workers and the 800 000 women on the farms who were doing their share – as they always had – to produce the food that Canada and her allies needed. Approximately 439 000 women worked in the service sector, 373 000 in manufacturing, 180 000 in trade and finance, 31 000 in transportation (including those who drove streetcars and buses in the large cities), and even 4000 in construction. In October 1943, for example, there were 261 000 women employed in war industries where they made artillery pieces, tanks, ammunition, ships,

These army nurses arrived in France very soon after D-Day in June 1944 to staff surgical wards.

PA-128193/NATIONAL ARCHIVES OF CANADA.

and aircraft. "Rosie the Riveter" was a popular American wartime caricature of the female munitions worker – but it was no sham in Canada. Women did much the same work as the men in the factories, and they earned substantially higher wages than were possible in the "traditional" factory jobs they had held before the war. For a time, so desperate were wartime factories for labour, the federal government and several provinces even agreed to finance day-care centres in an effort to entice mothers with young children onto the production lines. There were also a substantial number of women in the army and in the other services (see table on page 385). In all, nearly fifty thousand women enlisted in the Canadian Women's Army Corps, the R.C.A.F.'s Women's

TABLE 1

VALUE OF WAR PRODUCTION ($ MILLIONS)

	1939-40	1941	1942	1943	1944
Merchant ships	–	$29	$183	$232	$170
Naval vessels	$27	73	73	164	204
Aircraft	45	110	232	361	403
Motor transport	119	198	368	435	462
Armoured vehicles	–	21	155	203	146
Guns, small arms	1	20	162	213	156
Ammunition	16	111	257	277	233
Defence construction	94	138	219	194	100
Govt.-financed plant expansion	103	221	185	200	57

SOURCE: *CANADA AT WAR*, NO. 45 (1945)

TABLE 2

PERSONAL INCOME TAXATION

Earnings	Tax in 1939	1940	1941	1943
$1500	–	$14	$35	$24 plus $24 compulsory savings
$3000	$10	97	215	334 plus 334 compulsory savings
$5000	134	427	735	1062 plus 600 compulsory savings
$10,000	738	1921	2710	3346 plus 1200 compulsory savings

(rates for a married man with two children)

SOURCE: *CANADA AT WAR*, NO. 45 (1945)

Division, and the Women's Royal Canadian Naval Service, and almost forty-five hundred more served as nursing sisters in the forces. The war did not emancipate women and give them equality with men – attitudes shaped over centuries could not change so quickly – but it did increase their opportunities.[3]

Certainly the war increased family savings and the country's wealth. The gross national product rose from $5.6 billion in 1939 to $11.8 billion in 1945, an incredible increase, and average wages, personal savings, and government expenditures rose with it. All the while the cost of living remained virtually static, particularly after the imposition of the freeze of November 1941. There was, in spite of high taxes, more money in Canada during the war than there had been for years, but because of war production there was little to buy – except Victory Bonds – and Canadians gave their earnings and savings back to the government by the billions. It was a people's war in Canada, fought by the people with equipment produced by the people and paid for by the people, and for once the people seemed to get some of the benefits.

Overseas, the Canadian army sat in Britain, protecting the little island against the invasion that never came. The army, swollen by late 1941 to more than 250 000 volunteers, was fit, relatively well-equipped, and well-trained by the standards of the day. It was also bored. There was no action for the men of the divisions, since the government and the overseas commander, General McNaughton, insisted that the troops be employed *en bloc*, not used in dribs and drabs.

The Royal Canadian Air Force squadrons in Britain and elsewhere, however, were in the thick of the air war, as were the thousands of Canadians who had been integrated into the Royal Air Force. Some flew Spitfires or Hurricanes in fighter squadrons; others operated Catalina or Sunderland flying boats against the U-boats; still more flew with the army co-operation squadrons that provided tactical air support to infantry and armour in North Africa. The glamorous fighter pilots drew the lion's share of the attention. A Canadian pilot based at Biggin Hill, a famous base near London, wrote after one operation against the Luftwaffe that he had suddenly realized, "This was no joust bound by the rules of chivalry. I had never witnessed such persistent savagery. They were out to kill us by any means possible."

---

[3] The best work on women in wartime is by Ruth Roach Pierson. Her "Canadian Women and the Second World War" (Canadian Historical Association Historical Booklet No. 37, 1983) is a handy summary of women's role, and her book *They're Still Women After All* (Toronto, 1986) is the essential source.

TABLE 3

STRENGTH OF THE CANADIAN ARMY

Year end		Male	Female
1939		63 327	149
1940		117 302	508
1941	Volunteers	256 208	1 958
	N.R.M.A.	16 647	
1942	Volunteers	360 016	4 536
	N.R.M.A.	55 840	
1943	Volunteers	396 867	13 488
	N.R.M.A.	69 299	
1944	Volunteers	411 574	16 581
	N.R.M.A.	63 769	
1945	Volunteers	250 291	10 974
	N.R.M.A.	40 843	
1946	Volunteers	29 684	304
	N.R.M.A.	1 054	

SOURCE: C.P. STACEY, *SIX YEARS OF WAR* (OTTAWA: QUEEN'S PRINTER, 1955), APPENDIX "A."

Canadian pilots did their share of killing. Highly skilled pilots, like George Beurling of Montreal, ran up huge scores. Flying out of Malta after May 1942, "Buzz" Beurling had shot down 7 aircraft by July and 29 by October. He described his success against an Italian Macchi: "One of my shells caught [the pilot] right in the face and blew his head right off. The body slumped and the slipstream caught the neck . . . and the blood streamed down the side of the cockpit." The air war was brutal, but Beurling knew that it was kill or be killed. "You must blaze away whenever you are in a position to get his oxygen bottles or gas tanks," he said.

The bomber war was just as vicious. Huge resources were devoted to the Royal Air Force's Bomber Command armadas that carried the air war into the heart of Germany each night. Tens of thousands of Canadians, serving with No. 6 Group or in RAF squadrons, served in Lancaster or Halifax bomber crews that dropped their payloads of high explosives and incendiaries into the vitals of Hamburg, Frankfurt, and Berlin, and onto the steel mills of the Ruhr. The destruction was enormous. On July 24, 1943, 800 bombers smashed the German port city of Hamburg. Three days later, the bombers were back, dropping incendiaries into the still-smouldering ruins. This raid produced a firestorm with 150 (240 km) mile per hour winds that fanned the flames further. The howling gale sucked people into the air. Fire devoured the oxygen. Those who sought safety in the city's canals sometimes boiled to death. At least 50 000 German men, women, and children died and almost two-thirds of the city lay in ruins.

But the bomber crews did not win a unilateral victory. The German interceptors were skilful and worked closely with searchlight crews, anti-aircraft gunners, and the radar operators to knock them down. Less than one in three bomber crews survived a 30-operation tour, and 8200 Canadians died while serving in Bomber Command.

At sea, the risks statistically were not so high, though the officers and seamen of the Royal Canadian Navy were often in deadly peril. The German U-boats preferred to sink the slow, fat oil tankers or merchant ships, but the Canadian destroyers and corvettes that escorted the lumbering convoys were targets as well. Antisubmarine warfare was a difficult skill to acquire, and the Canadians had to learn it the hard way. In September 1941, two years into the war, the navy was escorting convoy SC-42 toward Britain when a "wolf pack" of U-boats, centrally directed and controlled, fell upon it. The 64 ships in the convoy initially had only one destroyer and three corvettes as escorts, and in the course of a single night 16 Allied ships went down from torpedoes. During the frenzied action, one corvette, HMCS *Moose Jaw*, commanded by Lieutenant Fred Grubb, came upon a U-boat on the surface, and the captain issued that rarely heard order, "Stand by to ram." The little R.C.N. ship fired at the submarine, preventing its crew from using its gun. At one point, the two ships were so close together that the U-boat captain leapt from his conning tower onto the corvette's deck. "See what he wants," Grubb said. The captain surrendered, as did his crew. The U-boat sank, taking with it to the bottom 11 Germans and one Canadian seaman who had boarded the submarine and failed to get clear in time. The sinking of U-501 was the navy's first confirmed U-boat kill of the war. Gradually it learned its deadly and complex craft, and though U-boats sank 654 ships, Canadians manned fully half the escorts for the 2889 convoys that sailed across the Atlantic and sank 29 submarines.

But the victories initially seemed small to the Canadian public. There were few heroes for those who remembered the glorious efforts of the Canadian Corps in the Great War and who nostalgically pined for similar efforts in this war.[4] In vain the Government pointed to the vast air force

---

[4] Some of the best books on the fighting in Europe in which Canadians participated include Murray Peden, *A Thousand Shall Fall* (Stittsville, 1981); Jeffrey Brock, *The Dark Broad Seas*, vol. 1 (Toronto, 1981); C.P. Stacey, *Six Years of War* (Ottawa, 1955) and *The Victory*

and navy; in vain it argued that defending Britain was a vital chore. In vain. Conscription talk – initially disguised as a demand for "total war" – began in earnest in Canada in the summer and fall of 1941, and newspaper editors and politicians alike began to grumble that Quebec was not doing its share in the war. In one sense that was so. Quebec enlistments, while much higher proportionately than in the Great War, *were* less than in the rest of the country, but the N.R.M.A. home defence conscripts, despite popular English-Canadian perceptions, were not all French-Canadian by any means. The mood was becoming ugly as the war dragged on in late 1941 and as Allied defeat followed Allied defeat. Hitler had invaded the Soviet Union in June and his panzer armies were at the gates of Moscow, Leningrad, and Stalingrad; in Africa, General Erwin Rommel toyed with ill-led imperial forces; and on December 7, 1941, the Japanese lashed out at the United States, Britain, and the Dutch East Indies. The attack on Pearl Harbor in Hawaii brought the war close to North America – and created near panic in British Columbia and along the California coast.

The first victims of the growing panic on the coast were the Japanese-Canadians. Some 23 000 men, women, and children of Japanese origin, not all Canadian-born, but mainly citizens, lived in British Columbia, making their livings for the most part from fishing or market gardening. Racism in the province had long been endemic, but the Japanese surprise attack on Hawaii and the fear that the Japanese navy might attack the mainland, something well within its capabilities in early 1942, raised it to a fever pitch. There were instant demands from federal, provincial, and municipal politicians of all parties, the newspapers, alarmed citizen groups, and eventually the army, navy, and air staffs in British Columbia that Ottawa do something. The federal government was repeatedly told by its officials in the capital that the Japanese-Canadians posed no threat, though there were intercepted telegrams from the foreign ministry in Tokyo to the Japanese consulate in Vancouver that demonstrated Japan's intent to make use of spies and saboteurs. The political pressure intensified, not least from Ian Mackenzie, the minister of pensions and national health and the B.C. representative in the cabinet. By February, the government, like the Roosevelt administration in Washington, felt it had to act. Under the authority of the War

---

Campaign (Ottawa, 1960); and G.W.L. Nicholson, *The Canadians in Italy* (Ottawa, 1957), the latter three titles being official histories. The best book on the R.C.N. is Marc Milner, *North Atlantic Run* (Toronto, 1985); the official R.C.A.F. history is W.A.B. Douglas, *The Creation of a National Air Force* (Toronto, 1986).

Measures Act and the Defence of Canada Regulations, Japanese-Canadian men, women, and children were rounded up in the spring of 1942, deprived of their livelihoods, and shunted off to makeshift camps in the mountainous B.C. interior. There was scarcely a voice raised in their defence anywhere in Canada. Many of the evacuees went further east to sugar-beet farms in Alberta or to Manitoba and Ontario. The government also interned under guard some 700 Japanese-Canadians who were considered dangerous in camps in Northern Ontario.

The evacuation of the Japanese-Canadians from the Pacific Coast could at least be defended on grounds of military necessity. There was no attack (beyond the shelling of Estevan Point on Vancouver Island by a submarine and the more frightening Japanese occupation of the Aleutian Islands off Alaska in mid-1942), but had the United States navy not won critical sea battles in mid-1942, there might have been. The Japanese navy was planning for the use of Hawaii as a jump-off point for attacks on the West Coast. Had there been any serious Japanese military incursion, the safety of Japanese-Canadians in all likelihood could not have been protected in the province. Absolutely indefensible were government actions after the evacuation. Japanese-Canadian property was sold at fire-sale prices and, in the latter days of the war the government began to pressure as many Japanese-Canadians as possible to return to Japan. Those efforts continued after the war ended.

The Japanese-Canadians were victims of panic and racism. The treatment meted out to them besmirched the ideals for which Canadians claimed to be fighting, and in 1988, belatedly, the Canadian government formally apologized for the wrongs committed and offered generous monetary compensation.[5]

Conscription Talk

Canadians were frightened then, unhappy and complaining. The Conservative Party, in ruins since the elections of 1935 and 1940, began to press stridently for a greater war effort, and a party meeting in November 1941, turned unexpectedly into a leadership meeting that put Senator

---

[5] Among many titles on the treatment of the Japanese, see T.U. Nakano, *Within the Barbed Wire Fence* (Toronto, 1980); Ken Adachi, *The Enemy that Never Was* (Toronto, 1976); Ann Sunahara, *The Politics of Racism* (Toronto, 1981); and F.E. LaViollette, *The Japanese Canadians and World War II* (Toronto, 1948). One novel is Joy Kogawa, *Obasan* (Toronto, 1981).

Arthur Meighen at the party's helm once again. Meighen had been the draftsman of the Military Service Act of 1917, he had been the "ready, aye, ready" statesman of the 1920s, and his name was anathema in Quebec – and to Mackenzie King. With his great intelligence and acid tongue in debate, Meighen clearly frightened the prime minister, and his return to the scene altered events.

One immediate change was the government's decision to seek release from its promises against overseas conscription through a plebiscite. The electorate of all Canada was to be asked to release King from his pledge to Quebec that this war was to be different. French-Canadians were outraged. Nationalistic groups denounced the government and declared that Ernest Lapointe, dead of cancer in November 1941, would never have permitted such a thing. Lapointe's sucessor in the riding of Quebec East and as minister of justice, Louis St. Laurent, a distinguished Quebec City lawyer, spoke against the mounting hysteria in his province, but he was as yet unknown, his prestige not nearly as great as Lapointe's and his and his cabinet colleagues' efforts against the forces campaigning for a *non* vote on the plebiscite were ineffectual. There were no such problems in English Canada, where the Meighen-led Tories and the C.C.F. found themselves in the uncomfortable position of being obliged to support King's plebiscite. The result was a great national split, as virtually all French-Canadians, wherever they were in the country, voted on April 27, 1942, not to release the government from its pledge, while the great majority of English-Canadians voted yes to the referendum. In Quebec, 72.9 percent voted no; in Ontario, by contrast, only 17.7 percent did so. The exceptions to the general trend in English Canada were constituencies that were heavily French-Canadian, German-Canadian, or Ukrainian-Canadian – which amounted to a few ridings in New Brunswick, Ontario, Alberta, and Saskatchewan.[6]

Mackenzie King now faced a dilemma (one that had been eased somewhat by the surprising and decisive defeat of Meighen by Joe Noseworthy, an unknown high school teacher and the C.C.F. candidate, in a Toronto by-election on February 9). If he did not act to enforce conscription, now that the national majority had declared for it, he would be in difficulty with the electorate, the media, and strong elements within

---

[6] On conscription, see Pickersgill, *Mackenzie King Record*; Stacey: *Arms, Men and Governments*; J.L. Granatstein and J.M. Hitsman, *Broken Promises: A History of Conscription in Canada* (Toronto, 1985); André Laurendeau, *La crise de la conscription, 1942* (Montréal, 1962); and W. Denis Whitaker and Shelagh Whitaker, *Tug of War* (Toronto, 1984).

his cabinet, must notably Colonel Ralston and Navy Minister Macdonald; if he did impose conscription for overseas service, he could split the country and perhaps destroy his party's base in Quebec irrevocably. His solution was characteristically clever – too clever, his critics argued. Legislative action, in the form of Bill 80, which deleted the restrictive geographic clause of the National Resources Mobilization Act, would be taken to make overseas conscription possible, but conscription would never be enforced unless and until it was necessary to do so. Not necessarily conscription, the prime minister told a bewildered and bemused House of Commons and nation, but conscription if necessary. One senior Quebec minister, P.J.A. Cardin, resigned, and Ralston, too, almost left in disgust, but the government survived, and the crisis of 1942 passed uneasily into history.

The Boys Overseas

Perhaps the increasing casualties overseas snapped some Canadians back to reality. The Japanese attacks of December 1941 had included an assault on the British Crown Colony of Hong Kong, an indefensible patch of Chinese mainland and an island to which the government, at Britain's request, had dispatched two battalions of infantry and a brigade headquarters late in 1941. The 1975 troops from Manitoba and Quebec fought better than might have been expected, given the fact that their vehicles had not reached Hong Kong before the attack, but they and their 12 000 British and Indian comrades were overwhelmed, killed, or captured by the Japanese attackers. On Christmas Day 1941, Hong Kong was lost, all the Canadians with it. Two hundred and ninety died in the fighting, and almost 500 suffered wounds, a high casualty rate that attested to the heavy fighting. Worse was yet to come for the survivors who were thrown into appalling prisoner-of-war camps in Hong Kong or in Japan. More died of maltreatment, and at the end of the war in 1945 only 1428 survivors returned to Canada. Many of them never recovered their health.

The next action of the Canadian army came in Europe, and it too was disastrous. In August 1942, most of the 2nd Canadian Division launched an amphibious assault against the French port of Dieppe. The port was heavily defended by the German Wehrmacht, and the Dieppe beaches were dominated by high cliffs from which the defenders rained fire on the helpless invaders. Worse, on the main beach in front of the town, the

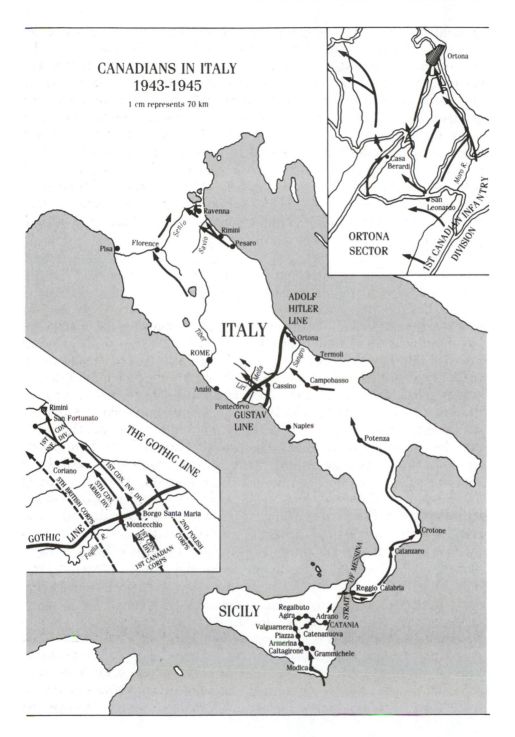

CANADIANS IN ITALY
1943-1945

1 cm represents 70 km

ORTONA
SECTOR

Ortona

Casa
Berardi

San
Leonardo

1ST CANADIAN INFANTRY DIVISION

Moro R.

Ravenna

Rimini

Pesaro

Pisa

Florence

Senio

Olivo

ADOLF
HITLER
LINE

ITALY

Tiber

ROME

Anzio

Liri

Melfa

Ortona

Sangro

Termoli

Campobasso

Cassino

Pontecorvo

GUSTAV
LINE

Naples

Potenza

Rimini

San Fortunato

1ST CDN
INF. DIV.

THE GOTHIC LINE

1ST CDN. INF. DIV.

5TH CDN.
ARMD. DIV.

Coriano

5TH BRITISH CORPS

Borgo Santa Maria

Montecchio

Foglia R.

1ST CDN.
INF. DIV.

2ND POLISH CORPS

GOTHIC LINE

1ST CANADIAN CORPS

Crotone

Catanzaro

STRAIT OF MESSINA

Reggio Calabria

SICILY

Regalbuto
Agira

Adrano

Valguarnera

CATANIA

Piazza
Armerina

Catenanuova

Caltagirone

Grammichele

Modica

Churchill tanks of the Calgary Highlanders were unable to manoeuvre on the large pebbles; the Essex Scottish and Royal Hamilton Light Infantry were left virtually unprotected. To the east at the village of Puys, the Royal Regiment of Canada and the Black Watch ran into withering fire; on the west flank at Pourville, the South Saskatchewan Regiment and the Cameron Highlanders got ashore easily enough, but inland the casualties mounted. The South Sask's commanding officer, Lieutenant-Colonel Cecil Merritt, repeatedly led his men across a bridge swept by enemy fire – "Come on over, there's nothing to it," he said – and Merritt's heroism was one of the few bright spots in a day of death and disaster. Merritt won the Victoria Cross as did Padre John Foote of the Royal Hamilton Light Infantry who stayed on the beach helping to care for the many wounded. The German High Command had not been overly impressed by the fighting capacity of the Canadians, all in action for the first time. One after-battle report noted that they had "fought badly and surrendered afterward in swarms." That was too harsh; another German observed that the Canadian soldier "fought – so far as he was able to fight at all – well and bravely." Perhaps the best judgment was that Canadian training methods had yet to meet the cruel requirements of this war. Still, better training alone could not have prevented the collapse of a badly conceived plan.

The result of the ghastly few hours ashore recalled the charnel house of France and Flanders in the Great War. Whole battalions, regiments with famous names and proud traditions, were lost. Of the 4963 Canadians who set off from England, only 2211 returned; half of the survivors had never gone ashore. Only 300 or so had been evacuated from the main beach and another 600 from Pourville. On the beaches 907 men died and 586 were wounded; 1946 became prisoners of war – more than the First Canadian Army lost in northwestern Europe from D-Day to the German surrender.

The tragedy of Dieppe presumably taught the Allies some lessons about amphibious warfare. The failure of the raid presumably persuaded Marshal Stalin of the Soviet Union that the Allies were serious about the war, something he hitherto may have doubted. Such intangible benefits were a terribly high price to pay for the Canadian casualties.

Nonetheless the war was beginning to go better. American entry put a huge industrial machine fully at the Allies' service, and vast armies were soon in the field under the American flag. The Russians, to universal astonishment and awe, held against the Wehrmacht, while in North Africa General Montgomery's victory at El Alamein marked the turning

Canadian bodies and equipment litter the beach at Dieppe. In 1942, this German photograph made splendid propaganda about the strength of Fortress Europe.

C-14160/NATIONAL ARCHIVES OF CANADA.

of the tide, as did the almost simultaneous Allied landings in Algeria and Morocco. It was the end of the beginning.

Sicily was the next stage, and over McNaughton's protests a Canadian division was assigned to that invasion. The Italian island fell fairly quickly, and there followed an invasion of the mainland and, inevitably, an increased commitment of Canadian troops to the campaign. Casualties began to mount, and the hometown newspapers had their lists of the dead, wounded, and decorated each week. The war at last began to hit home to Canadians. For those at the front, slogging their painful way up the Italian boot, the fighting was extraordinarily difficult. The terrain favoured the defenders, and every river crossing, every mountain was contested. The Wehrmacht must have known that they no longer held the upper hand, but that seemingly only made the German soldiers fight more fiercely, and the Canadian, American, and British armies paid dearly for every inch of ground.

Rome was captured in June 1944, just at the time that the Allies launched their long-awaited invasion of France. The 3rd Canadian Infantry Division was in the initial landing force, and R.C.A.F. squadrons

The invasion of Normandy on June 6, 1944, happily was more successful than Dieppe. These infantry in their landing craft anxiously await touchdown on Juno beach.

PA-132796/NATIONAL ARCHIVES OF CANADA.

and R.C.N. ships also participated as the Canadians quickly seized most of their D-Day objectives. A new slogging match began as the bridgehead was slowly expanded and Allied forces augmented. The culmination came in the great Canadian struggle for Caen and in the near-successful effort to close the Falaise Gap and trap a large part of the Nazi armies. Had that effort succeeded, the Germans in France might have succumbed immediately, but since it did not, the Canadians and their allies had to battle through France. The First Canadian Army, a massive formation under the command of General H.D.G. Crerar, a professional soldier who had graduated from the R.M.C., served in the trenches in the Great War, and worked his way up the promotion ladder in the tiny prewar Permanent Force, was in reality an international army with Polish, British, and a few other national contingents serving under Canadian command. The army had the left flank of the Allied advance, a position that involved the clearing of the Channel ports (including a joyful liberation of Dieppe by the reconstituted Second Division), the freeing of Holland, and the clearing of the great Scheldt estuary. Again, casualties were heavy, and soon it became apparent that there was a growing shortage of infantry.

In one sense this was inexplicable. The Canadian army had enlisted 650 000 men in the course of the war and had sent overseas five divisions and ancillary troops. But because Canada insisted – and properly – on controlling its own forces in this war, a long supply line and reinforcement chain was necessary. That absorbed manpower, as did the need, both political and military, to keep forces in Canada, most notably in British Columbia. The result was that the army's "teeth-to-tail" ratio – or its balance of fighting to supporting troops – was low, probably the lowest of any of the Allied forces. It was also true that misjudgments had been made by British planners, who had overestimated the effectiveness of the Luftwaffe and had prescribed a heavy quota of reinforcements for rear-area troops and such supporting arms as the artillery. Happily, the German air force was controlled, but the infantry took heavier casualties than expected, and reinforcement shortages arose. Soon, recently wounded Canadians were being returned to the front, and claims that untrained men were being posted to infantry battalions also began to be heard by the late summer of 1944. The final crisis over conscription had arrived.

The Politics of Conscription

Mackenzie King was not ready for it. He had watched events in Europe with some satisfaction since D-Day. Canada's forces had served with distinction and valour, and no one doubted that Hitler was doomed, squeezed between the Russians moving westward and the Allies coming from the south and east. And, King believed, he had brought Canada through this titanic struggle without a divisive internecine struggle over compulsory mulitary service. Who could call for conscription now, with the war all but won?

Colonel Ralston, the minister of national defence, had gone to the front in September 1944 to see for himself if the complaints of infantry shortages were true. To his horror, he found that they were, and the minister returned to Ottawa in October, tired, ill at heart, but determined to press for the necessary reinforcements for the fighting men overseas. After all, had Mackenzie King not promised in 1942 that there would be conscription if necessary? Of course he had, a startled King admitted, but he had meant necessary to win the war, and the war clearly was already won. The battle lines were drawn for one of the greatest cabinet struggles in Canadian history.

Ralston had a steely determination to get his way, and he was prepared to resign and to take as many of his colleagues as possible along with him if he could not. Mackenzie King had a similiar determination, masked though it was by his soft, puffy appearance and reputation for indecision. He was committed to preventing the destruction of his country, cabinet, and party. King was to prevail when, as we have seen, in a stunning move he sacked Colonel Ralston at the cabinet meeting on November 1, 1944, and put in his place General McNaughton, the former army commander in England who had been returned to Canada because of ill-health and British dissatisfaction with his command capabilities. Andy McNaughton, nonetheless, was a man with a very powerful personality, extremely popular in the country and with the forces, and King believed that the general could persuade enough of the 68 000 N.R.M.A. home defence conscripts to volunteer for service overseas. For that was the government's chosen – and seemingly only – course.

The most popular military cartoonist of the Canadian army here illustrates scrounging, a favourite activity of Canadian soldiers in Europe.

TORONTO TELEGRAM COLLECTION, YORK UNIVERSITY ARCHIVES.

McNaughton failed, despite his best efforts. The N.R.M.A. men were as determined to resist volunteering as men could be, telling their pleading chaplains and commanding officers that they were willing to fight if the government had the courage to send them but they would be damned if they would let King off the hook by going voluntarily. For McNaughton, this was personally shattering, and, finally advised by the military staff that volunteers could not be secured, he told Mackenzie King so. King's problem now was to justify a change of policy to himself, first, and then to his cabinet, party, and country. Characteristically, he managed to do so, persuading himself that the military advice to McNaughton amounted to a challenge to civil authority, one that could only be countered by imposing conscription for overseas service on the N.R.M.A. That did the trick with King and with his ministers, many of whom were on the very verge of resignation, and the political crisis was resolved by the decision to send 16 000 N.R.M.A. men overseas. The military crisis was resolved when casualties at the front, fortuitously, were less than anticipated, and only 2463 of the N.R.M.A. soldiers reached the front lines. Those that did, by all reports, fought and died as well as any other soldiers. Sixty-nine N.R.M.A. soldiers were killed, a tiny proportion of the army's 22 917 dead, the navy's 2204, and the R.C.A.F.'s 17 101.

The crisis had been caused by planning failures far more than anything else, but it was a crisis nonetheless. King had survived with his cabinet more or less intact, and above all he had prevented French Canada from deserting the Liberal Party and, King was convinced, abandoning faith in the promises of their federal leaders. Still, the reaction in Quebec was sharply critical, many apparently believing that the betrayal of 1942 (for so the plebiscite was seen) had produced its inevitable result. Nonetheless, bad as he was, Mackenzie King still seemed the best of a bad lot of Anglo politicians to French-Canadians. Could they support the Conservatives, that party that was ferociously in favour of compulsion and pressed for it to be used in the war with Japan as well? Could they support the C.C.F., a socialist party that, while no longer condemned by the Church, still seemed too radical for a traditionalist society? Could they support the Bloc Populaire Canadien, a protest party that had sprung into existence as a result of the plebiscite campaign of 1942? The B.P.C. had some able leaders in men such as André Laurendeau, but its policies mixed reformism with nationalism in a way that seemed forced to many. Provincially, French-Canadians had taken out their frustrations by returning Maurice Duplessis and the Union Nationale to power in August 1944, but there was no apparent desire to isolate Quebec from the rest of the country.

If Quebec made Mackenzie King nervous for the fate of his government, so too did English Canada. Feelings were high on the conscription issue, and many in Ontario and the West were convinced that they had been gulled by King in 1942 and betrayed by him in 1944. The Conservatives fed on this resentment, but the party was in some difficulties of its own. In 1942, after Meighen's defeat in Toronto, the party was left leaderless, convinced that its fate was sealed unless it could find a new base of support. That turned Conservatives to the West and to social reforms simultaneously, and in December 1942, the assembled party faithful picked John Bracken as leader and changed the party's name to the Progressive Conservative Party. Bracken had been a very successful Liberal-Progressive premier of Manitoba, a skilful and shrewd operator who had come to power at the beginning of the 1920s directly from the faculty of the Manitoba Agricultural College. But Bracken, who was really more conservative than progressive, foolishly decided not to seek a seat in Parliament, and, thus deprived of a national forum, he devoted himself to delivering dry speeches across the land. Conservatives quickly became disillusioned and many looked wistfully to George Drew, the Ontario leader who had led his party to a minority victory in 1943. The ideologically divided and weakly led Tories seemed stronger than they were.

The Move to the Left

J.S. Woodsworth, the saintly socialist of the Co-operative Commonwealth Federation, was dead and gone, and the C.C.F. was led now by M.J. Coldwell, a decent and able man; the party organization was directed largely by the forceful, brilliant David Lewis. The defeat of Meighen had put the socialist party into the news, and the next year the C.C.F. had risen from zero to thirty-four seats in the Ontario provincial election and to a narrow lead over the old parties in the national opinion polls. Something was happening to Canada as the war went on. The C.C.F. began to win federal by-elections and astonishingly, under Tommy Douglas's leadership, it captured control of Saskatchewan in 1944, the first elected Socialist government in North America. The challenge from the left was a real one.

Mackenzie King was fully aware of this, although the demands of the war forced his and his government's attention away from political and domestic affairs. Tired ministers wrestling with intractable problems of state had little time for politicking. But by 1943 the Liberals had to reorganize and rethink their role if the party was to survive the war. The direction that people wanted to go seemed clear – virtually every opinion poll taken openly by the Canadian Institute of Public Opinion and secretly by the government's Wartime Information Board demonstrated that Canadians were afraid that depression conditions would return with the peace. People wanted jobs, security, a good standard of living, and if the C.C.F. promised those things, then people would vote C.C.F. King himself had always claimed to want similar things – after all, he had written *Industry and Humanity* in 1918 as a virtual manifesto of social welfare – but the times had never before been right. Now the war had demonstrated that Canada could produce goods in profusion and that billions of dollars worth could be given away to our allies. Could the country not do as much for its own citizens?

More to the point, perhaps, the federal bureaucracy had become converted to Keynesian economics, convinced that a prosperous Canada could be erected only if the federal government played a major role in directing the economy. When times were tough, officials in the Department of Finance now believed, the state should prime the pump with money. And as everyone believed that the reconstruction period was certain to be difficult, that it would strain the country to reintegrate the servicemen and to convert industry from producing tanks to once again building automobiles, preparation had to be made now. One step had been taken in 1940 with the establishment of a contributory scheme of unemployment insurance. Another came in 1944 with the creation of a great plan for family allowances. The "baby bonus," as some sneeringly described it, was deliberately designed to give mothers (and not fathers) a monthly payment for each child. This money would buy milk, shoes, and clothing; it would help raise the standard of living for everyone; it would lead to healthier children; and it would put money in the hands of those who would spend it and thus stimulate the economy. It would also convince millions of Canadians that the Liberal party was their salvation, that Liberals – and not C.C.F.ers or Tories – were the party that delivered the goods. It would and did. So too did a whole series of additional government measures to move toward the welfare state, to re-establish industry and stimulate exports, to encourage housing construction, to resettle veterans in the cities or on the land, and to give demobilized servicemen a chance for an education or all the medical care they needed. The country had changed with the war, and the ideas of state intervention that in the 1930s had been denounced as unjustified interference with the laissez faire tradition were now hailed as essential.[7]

The Liberals were the beneficiaries of all this, in part because they happened to be in office when the shift in attitude occurred and could react to it, in part because they had the good sense to listen to the advice of an extraordinarily able bureaucracy. Whatever the reason, the Liberals stole the social welfare planks away from the Opposition, and in the election of June 1945, they were returned to power. The Tories won only 67 seats, a reflection of the party's lack of wisdom in harping on conscription for the Japanese war while Canadians, fresh from victory in Europe in May, were looking only to the peace. The C.C.F. – badly battered by a sometimes vicious anti-socialist campaign that denounced

Tommy Douglas campaigned for the C.C.F. in the Saskatchewan election of 1944. Douglas's victory frightened the old parties and helped push the federal government along the road to social welfare programs.

SASKATCHEWAN ARCHIVES/R-A7917(1). PHOTOGRAPHER: WEST'S STUDIO, REGINA.

---

[7] On reconstruction, see Bothwell and Kilbourn, *C.D. Howe*; Granatstein, *Canada's War*; R. Bothwell, I. Drummond, and J. English, *Canada Since 1945, 2nd ed.* (Toronto, 1989); and Leonard Marsh, *Report on Social Security for Canada 1943* (Toronto, 1975).

them as both Nazi and Communist, authoritarian and academic – won only 28. It was the socialists' best showing yet, but it was a far cry from the party's expectations. And King and the Liberals received 127 seats, a bare majority in a House of 245 members. Quebec, restive and unhappy, had nonetheless opted for King, giving him 50.8 percent of the vote and 53 seats. Considering that such a leader as Winston Churchill was deposed by an ungrateful British electorate as soon as possible after the war, King's triumph might fairly be seen as one of the most remarkable in our history. He had been saved by Quebec, to be sure, but he had deserved to be. He had guided the country through a long and terrible war, he had produced an astonishing military and industrial war effort, and he had remade Canadian society in the process. In 1939 Mackenzie King seemed an eminently forgettable prime minister; by 1945 he had to rank with Macdonald and Laurier, although both his contemporaries and historians have been grudging with this judgment.

A Nation on the World Stage

The coming of peace was a tremendous relief and release to Canadians. At last the killing was over, at last the boys and girls would come home. But the atomic bombings of Hiroshima and Nagasaki, however necessary they had seemed to the president of the United States and his political and military planners, and however they had been hailed as casualty-saving weapons in Allied countries, heralded a new and dangerous world. So too did the defection of a Soviet cipher clerk, Igor Gouzenko, from the Russian embassy in Ottawa. Carrying with him documents that irrefutably demonstrated that the Soviet Union had been operating major spy rings in Canada throughout the war, Gouzenko's flight might be said to have launched the Cold War.

Almost as surprising as the revelation that the U.S.S.R. had been spying in Canada was the realization that there might be something worth spying on here. That surely would not have been the case in 1925 or 1935, but by 1945 Canada had suddenly blossomed forth as a Middle Power, an important ally of Britain and the United States, and as the nation that had put together the third largest navy and fourth largest air force and a large, powerful, and well-equipped army in the course of the Second World War. By itself, that made Canada important, but so did its close relationship with its Anglo-American allies on atomic research, its co-operation with them in other scientific research and in intelligence matters, and the general friendliness with which Canada, the United

States, and the United Kingdom worked and co-operated as partners. That too was a change from the prewar years or even from the opening years of the war.

In 1939, for example, Canada had gone to war for much the same reasons and in much the same way as it had in 1914. There was little Canadian involvement in the events preceding the British and French declaration of war, notwithstanding the long process of Canada's movement toward autonomy and the Statute of Westminster of 1931. Canada went to war not because Hitler was a monster who had invaded Poland, not to fight for democracy, not to save the Jews of Europe but simply because Britain had gone to war. If the Chamberlain government had managed to welsh on its commitments to Poland (promises made without any consultation with Canada), then Canada would have stayed out of the war too. But Chamberlain's cabinet insisted on honouring its

The victory in Europe produced a great celebration all across the country. This Toronto mother's display, showing photographs of her sons in Europe and an effigy of a German soldier, must have been among the most impressive.

TORONTO TELEGRAM COLLECTION, YORK UNIVERSITY ARCHIVES.

pledges, and after a week of semi-neutrality that let Mackenzie King honour *his* promise that "Parliament will decide," Canada was at war. It was almost as if the long struggle for autonomy, from 1914 to 1939, had never occurred.

Nor did matters alter much with the first years of war. Canada was occasionally feisty and jealous of its rights, but Ottawa never claimed or sought any share in Anglo-French strategic or economic planning, contenting itself with the right to a say only in how Canadian troops could be employed. London took Canada for granted, and while Mackenzie King grumbled about this, he did little to rectify it, although on economic questions he and his ministers sometimes struggled forcefully with Whitehall.

Relations with the United States prior to Pearl Harbor were, as we have seen, friendly and close on both economic and defence fronts, but that was as much a function of the American desire to make the hemisphere inviolate as it was a genuine concern for Canadians. And as war in the Pacific threatened in mid-1941, and as the British and American military staffs began secret consultations about actions in the event that America entered the war against the Axis, Canada began to find itself forgotten in Washington too. After Pearl Harbor matters grew worse, for the Anglo-American leadership created a whole series of combined agencies, boards, and military planning staffs, blithely forgetting Canada and all the other junior partners in the struggle against Hitler.[8]

For the first time in the war the Canadian government – or its civil servants – began to be upset at the treatment the country was receiving. In the Great War, Sir Robert Borden had complained that London could not expect Canada to put a half million men into the field and then treat it like a colony; the same thing might have been said in 1942. But in the Second World War, Canada already had won its formal autonomy from Britain, and its efforts this time were directed at achieving genuine influence in the councils of the Great Powers.

The chosen tactic was the functional principle. The idea had been developed in academic journals, but the way Ottawa used it was uniquely Canadian. The approach was developed by Hume Wrong, the

---

[8] On wartime foreign policy, see the volumes in the *Canada in World Affairs* series (Toronto); John Holmes, *The Shaping of Peace: Canada and the Search for World Order, 1943-57*, vols. I, II (Toronto, 1979, 1982); Stacey, *Canada and the Age of Conflict*, vol. II; Granatstein, *Canada's War*; Cuff and Granatstein, *Ties that Bind*; and Granatstein, *A Man of Influence*.

very able professional diplomat who was then serving at the Canadian legation in Washington, and refined by Norman Robertson and Lester Pearson, the two most senior officers in the Department of External Affairs and both men of great ability. The functional principle conceded that Canada was no overall great power – no nation of ten million could ever be. But in some specialized areas, Canada ranked with the great powers, and in those, Ottawa demanded, Canadian wishes and concerns had to be heard. This was true of food, mineral production, the provision of relief supplies to war-ravaged areas, and civilian air transport, to cite only four areas. The Canadians mounted a skilful political attack on Britain and the United States, and occasionally on France, the U.S.S.R., and China, as well, with the intention of achieving a larger voice. In the end, after very tough bargaining that saw Canada threaten to cut off wartime financial assistance to Britain, the point was won. Alone among the lesser powers, Canada received a place on some of the Anglo-American combined boards that directed war supply; alone among the smaller countries Canada received a crucial role in the United Nations Relief and Rehabilitation Administration. And in a very real sense, those achievements amounted to a declaration of responsibility. For the first time, Canada was seeking a share in carrying out tasks, not simply autonomy for its own sake, not status alone.

This could be seen in the discussions and negotiations that led to the creation of the United Nations. The Canadian argument, advanced as well by such other countries as Australia, New Zealand, the Netherlands, and Belgium, was that there were a number of Middle Powers with special capabilities, nations that had shown during the war that they could carry their own weight and more. Surely such countries were entitled to a place in the new world organization that distinguished them from small countries that had not contributed much to the Allied victory. The Big Four – the United States, the United Kingdom, the Soviet Union, and China – were not particularly receptive to this, being more interested in securing a veto for themselves, and Canada had little success. A Canadian delegation was slightly more successful at the United Nations Conference on International Organization in San Francisco in the spring of 1945 when it sought to secure guarantees that the U.N. Security Council would not be able to commit Canadian forces to collective security operations without Canadian participation in the decision-making. The long history of Canadian resistance to Whitehall's imperious demands required such a guarantee, and although Ottawa won its point, it turned out to be a hollow victory, as the relevant clause has never been employed.

The San Francisco conference was also an eye opener to many Canadians in what it told them about the Soviet Union. The Russian delegation was large and able, but the Soviet stonewalling tactics sometimes seemed disruptive and reprehensible. The good feelings of the war, the great admiration of the West for the U.S.S.R.'s doughty resistance to Hitler (even if it had involved forgetting the excesses of Stalin's Russia in the 1930s), were rapidly beginning to dissipate, a casualty of mutual Soviet and western suspicions and of the powers' postwar jockeying for control in eastern and central Europe, the Balkans, and Asia. This posed serious problems for Canada, situated as it was on the direct bomber route between Moscow and Washington, and Canadi-

After twenty years' service as a diplomat, L.B. Pearson became secretary of state for external affairs. His reputation at home and abroad was high, and he led Canada's foreign policy in its "golden age."

UNITED NATIONS/NATIONAL ARCHIVES OF CANADA, C-18532.

an planners – for the first time ever there *were* planners in Ottawa and this fact deserves to be noted – had already carried out staff studies on Canada's role in the cold peace. There was no doubt that Canadian interests were seen to require co-operation with Washington, for the United States, in its own defence interests, would require this of us in any case. The Gouzenko revelations made the point more clearly still.

The result was that Canada quietly began to ready itself to play a part in the defence of the western world. This was a slow process of accommodation to the new realities, and the Canadian forces, rapidly demobilized after 1945, were in no condition to undertake operations against any enemy, however weak. But to Ottawa's officials, the need, by 1947, was becoming clear: the West had to organize itself to resist Soviet communism and, above all, the United States had to be dragged out of its self-satisfied isolationism and made aware of its responsibilities to the rest of the world. In other words, Ottawa was not dragged into the Cold War, kicking and screaming, by Washington; the reverse was more nearly the case, and officials in External Affairs, National Defence, and the Department of Finance were present at the creation of the postwar world as participants. The North Atlantic Treaty of 1949, the result of an idea first advanced by Escott Reid of External Affairs in August 1947 and advocated again and again by others such as Louis St. Laurent, the secretary of state for external affairs, and his deputy minister, Lester Pearson, was in many senses a Canadian creation. To Ottawa and to most Canadians, the treaty seemed the definitive burial of the old prewar years of evasion of responsibility. The war had altered Canada and Canadians dramatically.

Dollars and Trade

This was also demonstrable in postwar Canadian trade policy. Officials and politicians alike had realized by 1944 that while postwar trade was certain to be disrupted, there were opportunities to be seized. Europe and Asia were in ruins, their industrial plant and agricultural production virtually destroyed. What should Canada do in these circumstances? One plan was to press for a great measure of free trade to end the prewar system of tariff barriers that had done so much to breed suspicion and enmity, and that plan culminated in 1947 in the General Agreement on Tariffs and Trade that brought together all the great trading states. Canada also realized that most of its traditional trading partners had no money to buy Canadian goods, their scanty resources being necessary to rebuild homes, factories, and lives. In such circumstances, the answer was clear: Canada had to give credits to Britain, France, and the Low Countries. However, this was not charity, although it involved the realization that our allies had suffered greater hardships in the war than we; instead, this policy was pragmatically based on the hard-headed understanding that unless Canada could trade, the nation would face massive unemployment and unrest at home. In the circumstances, and in keeping with the wartime policy of mutual aid that had seen us give away goods when Britain could no longer pay for them, and also in keeping with the conclusion, arrived at during the war, that the most important task of a nation was to give its people work and security, the Canadian government in 1946 offered $2 billion in credits to Britain and western Europe. It was purposeful generosity, it was good business, and it demonstrated more than anything else could that Canada had grown up.

Trade with the United States was also vitally important because the majority of Canada's exports and imports travelled in a north-south direction. With the peace, and after ten years of depression and six years of war, the Canadian people, their pockets stuffed with dollars earned from wartime overtime pay or veterans' re-establishment grants, wanted some of life's little luxuries once more. And in the postwar world, luxuries seemed to be American: trips to California, American-made automobiles, possibly even an automatic washer, or one of the new-fangled television sets. But all those things cost American dollars, and, although Canada had emerged from the war with its reserves of American currency in good shape, it did not take long before there was a major exchange crisis facing Douglas Abbott, the minister of finance in 1947, and Clifford Clark, his deputy minister and one of the ablest civil servants in Canadian history. The situation was strikingly similar to that of 1941. Then Canada had been caught in a situation where every effort we made to support Britain with munitions forced us to import more from the south and to slide deeper into debt, largely because we were unable to convert the sterling surplus that our large trade balance with Britain had earned into U.S. dollars. In 1947, the Canadian government was paying almost the entire cost of its exports to Britain and Europe, getting almost nothing back in return, and imports from the United States were skyrocketing. The crisis must have seemed inevitable.

How to resolve it was unclear. One response was to restrict the flow of imports as a dollar conservation measure, but that produced little more

TABLE 4

PERCENTAGE OF TOTAL NONRESIDENT INVESTMENT

	U.S.	U.K.	Other
1914	23%	72%	5%
1920	44	53	3
1939	60	36	4
1945	70	25	5
1947	72	23	5
1949	74	22	4
1952	77	18	5

INVESTMENT BY NONRESIDENTS IN DOLLARS (MILLIONS)

	U.S.	U.K.
1914	$ 881	$2778
1920	2128	2577
1939	4151	2476
1945	4990	1750
1947	5201	1647
1949	5906	1717
1952	7997	1886

SOURCE: F.H. LEACY, ED., *HISTORICAL STATISTICS OF CANADA* (OTTAWA: STATISTICS CANADA, 1983).

than nickels and dimes. Another was to initiate discussions with Washington for a full-scale free trade agreement. Those discussions, in 1947 and 1948, had been agreed to by Mackenzie King and conducted in great secrecy, but when the Canadian negotiators came back to Ottawa with the draft agreement, suddenly the hitherto favourable climate altered when the prime minister began to suffer doubts. He was at the end of his career, he knew, and he did not want to go into history as the prime minister who had tied Canada irrevocably to the United States – or as the leader who repeated the Liberal disaster of 1911. For King, the decision to veto the free trade deal was finally reached when he pulled a book down from his shelves and opened it by chance to a page discoursing on the spiritual meaning of the Empire. That was fate, and

King closed off the talks, perhaps saving the country, as he believed, or losing the opportunity of the century, as many in the bureaucracy argued.

What then could rescue Canada from its dollar shortage? The answer again reproduced the events of the war. Then the Hyde Park Agreement had allowed Canada to import components from the United States and to have these charged to the British Lend-Lease account. This time, skilful Canadian negotiators in Washington persuaded the Americans to allow European countries, and mainly Britain, to use funds allocated by Congress under the European Recovery Program – better known as the Marshall Plan – to cover purchases in Canada. That was clever, and in the inflationary postwar years, when genuine shortages existed, the Truman administration was willing to agree. The result was that almost a billion dollars flowed north in 1948 and 1949 to pay for wheat shipments to Britain and food and manufactured goods for countries as diverse as France, Norway, and Italy. That proved enough to restore equilibrium to the Canadian economy and to put the country's postwar boom on firm foundations.

Korea and Suez

The economy also received an extraordinary incentive as a result of war in an unlikely place, the small Asian peninsula of Korea. Korea had been under Japanese control until 1945; then, by a wartime agreement, it was divided into a northern zone, to be under the control of the Soviet Union, and a southern zone under the United States. While it had been anticipated that the two zones would be merged into a single, independent country, the Cold War had frozen matters, and when the two great powers departed in 1948 they left two mutually antagonistic states behind. On June 25, 1950, the armies of North Korea invaded the south, sweeping the disorganized armies of Syngman Rhee's Republic of Korea before them. The United States intervened, bringing the United Nations in its train, and many in the West perceived the struggle as the first shot in a world war against communism. The North Koreans could not have attacked, people in the West – and in Canada – believed, without the go-ahead from Moscow and/or Peking, where the Communists now ruled also. If Moscow was prepared to go to war in Korea, could western Europe not expect a similar fate? The answer was massive rearmament and the enlistment of new armies.

For Canada, this meant the raising of a brigade group to fight in Korea, a decision squeezed out of a government somewhat reluctant to fight in Asia only by substantial American pressure. Had Mackenzie King been the prime minister, Canadian participation would have been unlikely; King was always too worried about conscription and national unity to consider such a foreign adventure. But King was gone, retired in the fall of 1948 and, by a striking coincidence, dead and buried in Toronto at the very height of the Korean crisis. Indeed, it was on the way back from King's funeral that most of the cabinet, gathered in a private rail car, decided that Canada had to participate in the Korean conflict. The new prime minister, Louis St. Laurent, although a Quebecker, had none of his countryman's worries over conscription and much more confidence in the strength of Canada's unity than Mackenzie King. To him communism was an evil, the anti-Christ, and if it had to be stopped in Korea, so be it. But even St. Laurent must have become alarmed at the impact of the Cold War on Canada. Korea sparked fears that the U.S.S.R. might strike in Europe, and these fears prompted the decision to raise an additional brigade for service in Germany with the North Atlantic Treaty Organization's forces, the first permanent peacetime commitment of troops abroad in Canadian history. The brigade was to be joined by an air division of the R.C.A.F., flying 12 squadrons of Canadian-made F-86 Sabre jets in an interceptor role. The R.C.N. was strengthened as well, its destroyers plying the waters of the Atlantic and Pacific. The armed forces' strength rose rapidly – the army increased from 20 369 in July 1950 to 42 622 a year later, and the other services' numbers increased similarly – and costs increased more rapidly still. In 1949, Canadian defence spending had been $361 million, or 2.2 percent of G.N.P.; in 1951 it was $1157 million, or 5.5 percent; and in 1953 it was $1907 million, or 7.6 percent of G.N.P., the highest level in peacetime Canada to that point.

Many of the volunteers for Korea or N.A.T.O. were old "sweats" from the Second World War, and very quickly they were whipped into shape. The Korean brigade did not fight as a unit until well into 1951, although one battalion of the Princess Patricia's Canadian Light Infantry, arriving in Korea before the main body, saw action early in that year. The Canadian brigade served as part of a Commonwealth division and fought well, especially the Princess Patricia's at Kap'yong in April 1951, and the Royal Canadian Regiment on the Sami-ch'on River in May 1953. In all, 22 000 Canadians served with the brigade in Korea under the United Nations flag; 309 were killed, 1202 were wounded, and 32 became prisoners of war. "By way of comparison," the official army history of Korea notes a bit drily, "in 1950, 2289 persons in Canada were killed in traffic accidents."

That U.N. service in Korea was something of a foretaste of future efforts to keep the peace. Korea had been described by President Truman as a police action; but the United Nations was also playing different military roles in other parts of the world. A war, after independence, between Pakistan and India had resulted in a truce, and a U.N. observer group, on which Canadian personnel served, was involved. There was a similar situation along the borders of the new state of Israel after 1948. And in 1956, after President Nasser of Egypt nationalized the Suez Canal,

Though initially reluctant to commit troops to ground fighting in Korea, Canada ultimately sent a brigade group. Here infantry move through a village in 1951.

PA-110828/NATIONAL ARCHIVES OF CANADA.

an act symbolic of an irresistible upsurge of Third World nationalism against the old imperialist and colonial powers, U.N. peacekeeping reached its pinnacle in the attempts to resolve matters when Britain, France, and Israel combined to attack Egypt.

The Suez crisis caused a dramatic series of events. For the first time ever, the Canadian government found itself deeply opposed to actions undertaken by its two mother countries, for to Ottawa the Anglo-French attack – and the collusion between Paris and Tel Aviv – seemed like nothing so much as a foolish attempt to reverse history, one that was certain to rebound to the discredit of the West's position in the Middle East and throughout the Third World. Ottawa's policy, largely directed by Lester Pearson, the secretary of state for external affairs since 1948, was to salvage as much face as possible for the British and French, to preserve what remained of the N.A.T.O. alliance, and to keep Washington, itself bitterly opposed to the invasion that occurred in the final few days of a presidential election campaign, talking with London and Paris. A subsidiary, but no less important goal, was to preserve the Commonwealth, for nations such as India were on the verge of breaking all ties with London. Difficult as those tasks may have been, Pearson's splendid and supple diplomacy largely accomplished them.

The locus of action was the United Nations in New York. Heading the Canadian delegation, Mike Pearson worked tirelessly to improvise a U.N. peacekeeping force that could be interposed between the combatants and preserve a truce. Indeed, Pearson got cabinet support to offer a Canadian battalion for the U.N. force, an effort that was well intentioned but more than a little maladroit. Egypt had been invaded by the Queen of England's soldiers, English-speaking and wearing uniforms and flying flags not at all dissimilar to those carried by Canadians. No one should have been surprised when Nasser refused to have the Canadian battalion, but the shock to Canadian pride was terrible. It was only with the greatest of difficulty that Nasser was persuaded to permit Canadian logistics troops to be part of the United Nations Emergency Force. The Canadian triumph in creating the U.N.E.F. and easing the tense situation was recognized with a Nobel Peace Prize for Pearson; the humiliation of Nasser's rejection of the Canadian infantry and the resentment of some English-Canadians that Canada had let down Britain were possibly reflected in the general election results of 1957.

But in a sense, the anger in Canada over the government's treatment of Britain was a last gasp of the old Anglocentrism. Too many of Canada's business, trade, and defence ties were with the United States now, and the arrival of television was bringing American culture directly and intensely into all parts of the country. The population mix was altering as well under the impact of postwar immigration, and although Canadians of British ancestry still occupied the key places in the business, media, and political elites, demographic power was shifting. The old Canada was going, and the Suez crisis and the responses it provoked demonstrated that fact.[9]

Postwar Immigration

Immigration had been one of the central facts of the Canadian experience before the Great War, and it had been a moral question in the 1930s. But after the Second World War, immigration became less contentious and more accepted. The newcomers brought skills and wealth, different religions and cultures, and they immeasurably altered the Canada they found. The first waves after the war were refugees from Hitler or Stalin – Jewish survivors of the death camps or anti-Communist Poles, Ukrainians, and others who had not wanted to return home after the war. By the time of the Cold War, security considerations were beginning to become important, and applicants for admission to Canada could be denied entry for political reasons – a policy that was little known but one that probably would have been enthusiastically accepted by Canadians. Who wanted former Nazis in Canada? Who wanted Reds? However, members of both of those groups sometimes slipped through the cursory checks.

The checks had to be cursory because the numbers coming were enormous – even though many Canadians were unenthusiastic about accepting more foreigners. From 22 722 in 1945 (a number that included thousands of war brides, married to soldiers overseas), immigration to Canada increased to 64 127 in 1947, 125 414 in 1948, and 194 391 in 1951. Thereafter, for every year of the 1950s, immigration was above a hundred thousand, and in 1957, a year that saw Hungarians who had fled

---

[9] On foreign policy to 1956, see Holmes, *The Shaping of Peace*, vols. I, II; Stacey, *Canada and the Age of Conflict*, vol. II; L.B. Pearson, *Mike: The Memoirs of the Rt. Hon. Lester B. Pearson*, vols. I, II (Toronto, 1972, 1973); Pickersgill, *The Mackenzie King Record*, vols. III, IV (Toronto, 1970); Granatstein, *A Man of Influence*; R.D. Cuff and J.L. Granatstein, *American Dollars/ Canadian Prosperity: Canadian-American Economic Relations 1945-50* (Toronto, 1978); James Eayrs, *In Defence of Canada*, vols. III, IV (Toronto, 1972, 1980); Denis Stairs, *The Diplomacy of Constraint: Canada, the Korean War, and the United States* (Toronto, 1974); and the biennial volumes of the *Canada in World Affairs* series.

their homeland after the abortive revolution of 1956 admitted along with thousands of Britons, disillusioned by the Suez fiasco and declining economic opportunity in England, immigration reached the amazing total of 282 164. In all, between 1945 and 1957, 1.7 million people left their homes in Europe and came to the New World, firmly expecting to find the streets paved with gold.

Most of the newcomers went to Ontario, almost half heading for the factories of Toronto, the mines of the North, or the booming construction industry of the cities. The next largest group chose Quebec, but as many were British in origin or opted to send their children to English-language schools, the demographic implications were serious for French-Canadians, ever conscious of their language and culture and sensitive to their declining relative numbers within Confederation. There was little support in Quebec for mass immigration if the children of Italian workers after one generation became part of the Anglophone community. The rest of the country, less threatened, was more tolerant. British Columbia received more than a hundred thousand immigrants between 1945 and 1957, and many, such as the entire forestry faculty and student body of Sopron University in Hungary, brought crucially needed skills. J.W. Pickersgill, the minister of citizenship and immigration in the St. Laurent government, had arrived in Vienna to administer Ottawa's crash program of assistance to Hungarian refugees, heard about the Sopron foresters, and sprang into action. "I telephoned Jimmy Sinclair [a cabinet colleague] who was in Vancouver, and he succeeded in a few hours in making arrangements to have the Forestry Faculty of Sopron affiliated with the University of British Columbia. Through Harold Foley of Powell River Paper Company, Sinclair was able to arrange to have a lumber camp at Powell River provided as a reception centre for the faculty and students from their arrival in British Columbia until the university term opened in September 1957." The foresters came and greatly benefited the country.

Not everyone was happy at the influx of Hungarians, of course. In Toronto, Pickersgill noted, Gordon Sinclair, a popular broadcaster, was bemoaning the costs to the taxpayers, and the provincial government, too, was worried about the costs of integrating into Canadian society people who arrived with little but the clothes on their backs. "These people are arriving with absolutely nothing," one Ontario minister complained, "not even an extra suit of underwear. Who is going to pay for the underwear?" Pickersgill paused for breath and then said, "We will." Ottawa did. In all, 35 000 Hungarians came to Canada as a result of the revolution's failure.

If the Hungarians brought skills, so too did many others. Over 50 percent of British immigrants arriving between 1946 and 1963 were professionals. However, the percentage of professionals was infinitesimal among Italian immigrants, most of whom were destined for the labour force. The Italians amounted to the second largest national group to come to Canada, 139 000 entering the country between the war and 1957, and most settling in Toronto, Montreal, and Vancouver. But if the Italians were not managers or doctors or lawyers when they arrived, their children would be. Hardworking and industrious, the Italian immigrants quickly began to play a role in the cities they were helping to build. The Toronto subway, opened in 1954, was largely built by Italian labourers, as were most of the skyscrapers that began to sprout in the downtown.[10]

Federal-Provincial Wrangling

Immigration, particularly when it involved a crash program such as the one organized for the Hungarians in 1956-57, demanded close federal-provincial co-operation. That co-operation increasingly was required across a wide range of activities, and co-operation between Ottawa and the provinces had never been easy to secure. The report of the Royal Commission on Dominion-Provincial Relations (usually called the Rowell-Sirois Commission after its first and second chairmen) was received in Ottawa only in 1940, at a time when the war was absorbing everyone's attention. A federal-provincial conference in 1941 to consider the subject of the report collapsed in disagreement, and Ottawa, desperate for money to finance the enormous costs of the war, soon announced its intention to take the areas of personal and corporate taxation from the provinces and to offer the provinces an annual payment in return. This had been one of the major recommendations in the Rowell-Sirois report, and the provinces grumbled but went along. At war's end they would not be so accommodating.

The wartime tax rental agreements expired in 1947, and while no one

---

[10] On immigration policy, see Freda Hawkins, *Canada and Immigration* (Montreal, 1989); Alan G. Green, *Immigration and the Postwar Canadian Economy* (Toronto, 1976); and Gerald E. Dirks, *Canada's Refugee Policy* (Montreal, 1977). There is a substantial literature on various ethnic groups, most notably in the *Generations* series, published by McClelland and Stewart in association with the Multiculturalism program of the Department of the Secretary of State, and in the publications of the Multicultural History Society of Ontario. The best periodical in the field is *Canadian Ethnic Studies*, published at the University of Calgary.

wanted to return to the prewar system where the two levels of government levied taxes without reference to each other, the provinces insisted on receiving a high price for their abandonment of certain rights of taxation. The federal proposals, usually called the Green Book proposals, aimed at securing a continuation and broadening of Ottawa's control of corporate and income taxation so that it could implement a series of national programs with the revenues gained. The Green Book laid out a complex and interrelated program of public works and social welfare. T.C. Douglas, the C.C.F. premier of Saskatchewan since 1944, later called the federal plan "one of the most comprehensive pieces of work that has ever been done in Canadian history – in laying out a blueprint for establishing the beginning of a planned economy in Canada. . . . The general idea was that in times of prosperity we should be pulling money out of circulation, and in times of depression we should be pumping money into circulation. . . . Both the provincial and federal governments should have a whole series of public works projects on the shelf – already drafted with all the specific details – which could be taken off the shelf at any time that unemployment began to reach menacing proportions." In addition Ottawa proposed a series of social welfare plans – universal old age pensions financed by Ottawa alone for those over 70 years, and a program shared with the provinces to finance pensions for those from 65 to 69 years who qualified after a means test; assistance for the able-bodied unemployed to be administered by Ottawa through the existing unemployment insurance system; and plans for the beginnings of a system of health insurance with Ottawa picking up 60 percent of the costs. Ottawa also offered unconditional subsidies to the provinces in return for their giving up the levy of corporation and income taxes (and now succession duties as well) for a trial period of three years. The subsidies were to be determined by comparing the gross national product per capita in each of the three years with that of 1941. Most of the have-not provinces – the Maritimes and the Prairies – stood to gain from renting their tax fields to Ottawa, but Ontario and Quebec did not. Both believed their taxpayers would be subsidizing the rest of the country, and neither Premier Duplessis nor Premier Drew (joined by Angus L. Macdonald of Nova Scotia, who hated King) were willing; Duplessis, in addition, saw in Ottawa's proposals yet another attempt to centralize power and to destroy the autonomy of Quebec. The failure to reach agreement led to the shelving of the federal proposals for social security. In the end, Ottawa drafted tax rental agreements with seven provinces, Ontario and Quebec refusing to the end. A great opportunity had been lost.

Louis St. Laurent addressing an outdoor meeting, probably in the 1957 election campaign.

MATHESON PAPERS, QUEEN'S UNIVERSITY.

One opportunity was seized, however. On April 1, 1949, Newfoundland joined Canada, at last making the country's motto "A Mari Usque Ad Mare" a reality. The great island had been a dominion until the Depression of the 1930s forced it into virtual bankruptcy and back to the status of a Crown Colony of Britain. The war had brought tens of thousands of Canadian sailors and troops to Newfoundland and the close links they forged had helped to erode centuries of suspicion. But the war had also brought visiting British delegations and free-spending American soldiers, and in a real sense the postwar fate of Newfoundland was a problem of the old North Atlantic triangle. The Americans probably had some desire to get the island, but in Washington's eyes Newfoundland was not worth a bitter fight with Ottawa so long as they could keep bases there; the war-ravaged British wanted out as cheaply as possibly – austerity demanded that; making no bones about it, the Canadians wanted Newfoundland to be the tenth province. And the people of the island? They were torn. Many wanted dominion status back again, others sought a link to the United States, while still others, led by the redoubtable broadcaster and labour leader, Joey Smallwood, wanted Confederation. After two plebiscites and after a narrow victory for Confederation on the second one, hard negotiations produced a bargain. Smallwood became the leader of the new province's Liberal Party and the first premier, and for a time, as baby bonus cheques and unemployment insurance poured in to help redress the island's seasonal unemployment, Newfoundlanders thought they had struck the mother lode at last. Those feelings would alter over time, as new defence costs strained the federal treasury.

The provinces and the federal government met again in December 1950 in the shadow of the Korean War. Prime Minister St. Laurent made it clear that this government hoped to renew the tax rental agreements, and Ontario, this time led by Premier Leslie Frost, went along with the plan, thus preserving the possibility of double taxation only for taxpayers in Quebec. In addition, St. Laurent won the support of all the premiers for the implementation of a program of old age security, universal for everyone over 70. Ottawa would in addition share the costs of pensions for needy citizens between 65 and 69 with any province willing to join in such a scheme. All the provinces agreed to this, and a constitutional amendment that provided for concurrent jurisdiction over old age pensions was duly passed. The old age pension was fixed at $40 a month, with the supplemental scheme of the province also providing the same sum.

There was one final and major federal initiative in the area of social welfare – hospital insurance. The idea of freeing Canadians from the crippling costs of hospitalization had first been legislated in Saskatchewan in 1946, and Tommy Douglas's government had long been pressing Ottawa for assistance with the costs, which rose each year. In the end, and thanks to the efforts of Paul Martin, the minister of national health and welfare, Ottawa had committed itself to supporting such a scheme whenever a majority of the provinces, representing a majority of the population, were ready to put into effect programs to provide hospital insurance. The Hospital Insurance and Diagnostic Services Act of 1957 came into effect on July 1, 1958, and committed the federal government to paying 50 percent of the cost of provincial hospital insurance plans covering a basic range of in-patient services. Eventually every province was compelled by public opinion to offer hospital insurance to its people; the province of Saskatchewan and its C.C.F. government had led the way.

St. Laurent and Duplessis finally resolved the differences over taxation between their two governments in 1954. Duplessis had announced his intention to impose personal income taxes – as he had not yielded that right to Ottawa, he could certainly do so – but the result would be that a taxpayer in Montreal, for example, would pay 15 percent more than one in Ontario and have two forms to fill in. That was not Duplessis' position, however; the premier argued that as the Constitution gave taxation powers to the provinces, Quebec had priority, and taxpayers there could deduct their provincial taxes from their end-of-April payments to Ottawa. A war of speeches between Ottawa and Quebec City went on for some months, until the two leaders met in Montreal on October 5, 1954. The resulting agreement saw Duplessis withdraw his claim of provincial priority. In response, St. Laurent offered Duplessis – and all the other premiers – the right to reduce their federal taxes by 10 percent; since a federal tax abatement of 5 percent was already in place, this meant that Quebeckers escaped double taxation. Duplessis had probably won the day, yielding a spurious constitutional premise to St. Laurent in return for substantial cash benefits.

In 1956 St. Laurent suggested a new system of revenue sharing with the provinces. In effect, he proposed to offer a choice to the provinces – tax rentals as before, or a system of provincial taxation of up to 10 percent of federal personal or corporate income taxes and 50 percent of federal succession duties. In any case, most of the provinces would receive a new equalization grant that represented the difference between what any province could collect at the standard rates and the average that could be collected by the two wealthiest provinces, Ontario and British Columbia. One advantage of the scheme was that Quebec could continue to impose its own taxes and still be eligible for equalization grants, something that St. Laurent believed essential to the unity of the country. The very word "equalization" also suggested that all citizens, wherever they happened to live, had a right to equivalent services and standards of living. That too would assist unity. In the end the new system was accepted by Parliament, and eight of the provinces made tax rental agreements for all their taxes; Ontario made an agreement covering personal income taxes alone; and Quebec, though it made no agreement, accepted the equalization grant.[11]

The Postwar Boom

One reason that Ottawa could afford to be generous was that the country was riding the crest of a great, almost unprecedented boom. The

---

[11] Studies of federalism and federal-provincial relations for the period from 1939 to 1957 include *The Rowell/Sirois Report/Book 1* (Toronto, 1963); R.M Burns, *The Acceptable Mean: The Tax Rental Agreements, 1941-62* (Toronto, 1980); Wilfrid Eggleston, *The Road to Nationhood* (Toronto, 1946); F.R. Scott, *Essays on the Constitution* (Toronto, 1977); and A.R.M. Lower et al., *Evolving Canadian Federalism* (Durham, 1958).

difficulties that had plagued the economy after the war had largely disappeared, thanks initially to a billion dollars in American Marshall Plan money, but thanks, too, to vast quantities of American investment capital that poured into Canada. By 1950, the United States was beginning to worry about its own resources and sources of supply in the uncertain world of the mid-twentieth century. If China expanded in the East, if Russia expanded its frontiers, where could America turn for crucial minerals and metals? One answer was Canada, and, pressed by strategic necessity – as well as by geographical proximity, common attitudes and ideals, and the unwavering eagerness of the Canadian government – American corporations poured billions of dollars into Canada. Oil gushed from the ground in Alberta and most of the money for exploration, drilling, and development was American. Iron ore from Quebec was developed by American corporations, loaded on American ships, and transported to the blast furnaces of Pittsburgh, Cleveland, or Gary. New industries leapt the tariff wall (a leap that was no longer as high as it had been under the National Policy or under the tariff revisions of the late 1930s, thanks to the General Agreement on Trade and Tariffs) and set up shop in Montreal, Toronto, Hamilton, and a hundred other communities, providing employment and good wages. The country was booming, and every index reflected this. The gross national product increased from $11.8 billion in 1945 to $18 billion in 1950 and to $31.9 billion in 1957. The average wage of a male factory worker increased over the same period from $30.47 per week to $44.03 and then $64.96.

The good times encouraged organized labour to try to heal the wounds in its ranks. The Canadian Congress of Labour and the much more conservative Trades and Labour Congress of Canada had been feuding for years, and in 1954 the two organizations, representing some 960 000 of the 1.25 million unionized workers in the country (a record 33.8 percent of the workforce), began negotiations to put labour's house in order. By 1956, as the C.C.L. and the T.L.C. emulated the peace between the American Federation of Labor and the Congress of Industrial Organizations in the United States, the Canadian Labour Congress had come into being. Approximately three-quarters of the C.L.C.'s membership were affiliated with American unions. The bulk of the country's unaffiliated workers were in Quebec, members of the Canadian and Catholic Federation of Labour (which in 1960 changed its name to the Confederation of National Trade Unions) which chose not to join the C.L.C. There was great optimism for the future.

Women workers did not fare so well. The gains women had made during the war when a range of hitherto closed jobs had suddenly been opened to them evaporated. Women, always lower paid than male workers, had been the first to be laid off to make room for demobilized veterans, and the percentage of women in the labour force dropped rapidly, as many seized the chance to return to being full-time home-makers and to raising children after the interruption of the war years (the birth rate after 1945 remained high for almost twenty years). By 1948 only 23.5 percent or 835 000 women were in the non-farm workforce – and there were only tiny numbers in managerial jobs and in professional positions (other than nurses and teachers). By 1957, after years of boom, the situation was not much better. Labour force participation was up only to 25.8 percent, or 1 263 000 women workers, and the small numbers in managerial and professional posts, while higher all across the board, demonstrated that Canadians still remained overwhelmingly a patriarchal society, resistant to change in relations between the sexes.

The Americanization of Canada

But in view of the general prosperity, few questioned the direction of the country or its economic policies. In a sense, this was understandable. Everyone could remember the Great Depression and its catastrophic impact on the living standards of the population. In a time of unrelieved boom, when everyone's life was improving each year, surely the government's policy was proving itself. But some were looking askance at the unchecked influx of American capital that seemed necessary to fuel the boom. One such was Walter Gordon, a wealthy Toronto businessman and chartered accountant who had worked in Ottawa in the senior bureaucracy during the war and who had the best of connections with the Liberal Party and the government. From the mid-1950s Gordon had become fretful about the dangers to Canadian economic independence from unchecked foreign investment, and he had begun to believe that economic control could lead to American political control as well. Some of those concerns were advanced in an article he drafted for an academic journal, one calling for a royal commission to investigate the state and direction of the economy. The article was not to be published, for the government, to which Gordon had sent a draft, took over the idea and appointed Gordon as chairman of the Royal Commission on

Canada's Economic Prospects in the spring of 1955. His investigation, carefully based on the best academic research then available, demonstrated the extent of American penetration of every sector of the economy. An interim report was issued before the election of 1957, and it probably fed the growing feeling that Canada had somehow become too close to the United States and, for some, strayed too far from her British roots – an idea intensified by the Suez crisis.

The extent of American cultural penetration also worried many. A Royal Commission on National Development in the Arts, Letters and Sciences had been created in 1949 and put under the chairmanship of Vincent Massey, the former minister to the United States and high commissioner to Britain from 1935 to 1946. Massey's report, released in June 1951, bemoaned Canadian culture's struggle to survive on the fringes of society and called for the creation of a Canada Council, an arm's-length federal agency that could use tax dollars to foster the arts in Canada. Massey also called for strengthening such agencies as the Canadian Broadcasting Corporation, formed by the Bennett government in the 1930s, and the National Film Board, created by Mackenzie King just before the Second World War, to make them carriers of Canadianism in the face of massive American intrusions in cultural areas. There was some real need for concern. American magazines held an increasing share of the market and absorbed high percentages of the advertising revenues in Canada. *Time* and *Reader's Digest* led the way. American radio stations near the border captured much of the Canadian audience, and the advent of television, seductive in its appeal and particularly mindless in its content, worsened matters. From the end of the 1940s Canadians in cities near the border purchased expensive television sets and erected high antennae to bring in the CBS, NBC, or ABC stations from nearby American cities. The advent of Canadian broadcasting in 1952 – the CBC first appeared on Toronto screens with its logo upside down – partially redressed the balance, but increasingly the public corporation found itself compelled to buy American programs to hold a satisfactory share of the viewing audience. Massey's prescriptions would be hard to achieve. One of his recommendations was finally implemented in 1957 when the Canada Council was set up, its revenues being provided by succession duties from the huge estates of two recently deceased millionaires, Isaac Walton Killam and Sir James Dunn. The Council, over the years, would alter the lot of Canadian artists and scholars; it would also, by helping such nascent organizations as the Stratford Festival (started in 1953), the National Ballet (1951), Le

Théâtre du Nouveau Monde (1951), and Toronto's Crest Theatre (1951), foster and encourage the development of a Canadian culture that was often vigorous and experimental. American cultural penetration, nonetheless, continued.

 ## Liberal Arrogance

The parties that worried most about the American presence in Canada were the C.C.F. and the Progressive Conservatives. The socialist party was still led by M.J. Coldwell of Saskatchewan, one who fought the good fight every day in the House of Commons. The C.C.F. had made little headway nationally – although in Saskatchewan Tommy Douglas continued to lead his government to election victory after victory – but the party could be counted upon to speak out for democratic socialist alternatives. The C.C.F. supported Canada's adherence to N.A.T.O., and it went along with participation in the Korean War, but it fretted about American policies and strategy and called for distinctively Canadian positions.

So too did the Progressive Conservatives, although often that party's idea of a distinctive position was for Canada to follow Britain's course. The Tories had chosen John Bracken as their leader in 1942, but when Bracken only marginally improved the party's position in the general election of 1945, unrest in the ranks increased. The answer in 1948, after Bracken's resignation, was the election of George Drew, the premier of Ontario since 1943. Tall, good-looking, a man with a good record from the Great War, Drew had easily defeated a little-known Saskatchewan M.P. named John Diefenbaker on the first convention ballot. The difficulty was that Drew, too, failed to improve the party fortunes. In June 1949, running against Louis St. Laurent, the new prime minister, he suffered a grievous defeat as St. Laurent swept to the largest majority in Canadian history to that point. Only 41 Conservatives and 13 C.C.F. M.P.s were returned to the House of Commons, against 193 Liberals. Drew, with his central Canadian attitudes, his seeming inability to understand French Canada or the West, and his stiff, rather shy exterior (one that was said to mask a warm personality), simply was no match for "Uncle Louis," a smooth Liberal machine, and prosperity. The same thing proved to be true in August, 1953, when St. Laurent again enjoyed a comfortable majority with 171 seats, the Conservatives taking 51 and the C.C.F. 23. The Liberals seemed able to go on forever.

But cracks were developing. The debate in 1955 on the renewal of the Defence Production Act of 1951, a measure that gave C.D. Howe, St. Laurent's "Minister of Everything," quite extraordinary potential powers over the economy, revealed some of them. There seemed less need for sweeping powers than there had been at the peak of the Korean War two or three years before, and that stirred the Opposition and public concern. So too did Howe's stubborn and almost arrogant defence of *his* need for the act's renewal. Drew and his front-benchers, Donald Fleming, a Toronto M.P., Davie Fulton from British Colmbia, and Diefenbaker harried and harassed the government, delaying other business with a filibuster. In the end St. Laurent caved in, agreeing to a compromise with Drew that renewed Howe's powers only for a limited four-year term. The unbeatable government had suffered a tactical defeat.

The next year there was to be another and more serious blow. Howe had become convinced that a pipeline had to be built to carry Alberta's natural gas to central Canadian markets, a good idea but one that was to be carried out by a largely American-controlled corporation. That was bad enough for the increasing number of Canadians concerned with American investment in Canada, but the company, Trans-Canada Pipelines, was in financial trouble and needed government assistance if its project was to be completed on schedule. One plan was to create a Crown corporation to build a pipeline through the difficult (and financially unrewarding) terrain of Northern Ontario. Another was to loan the company enough money to build its western section of pipeline. Most Canadians probably understood few of the details of the contract or even of the supposed necessity of the pipeline. But what all understood, what the combined Conservative and C.C.F. Opposition made them understand, was that the Liberal government was using improper methods to ram its pipeline bill through the House. Using Parliament's rules to advantage, the Opposition resisted at every turn, consistently outmaneuvring the government. With irrevocable deadlines approaching, Howe, in desperation, resorted to closure, a legitimate but unpopular measure, to cut off debate and force a vote. The ensuing struggle, characterized by the apparent abandonment of impartiality by the Speaker, by the expulsion of Conservative Donald Fleming from the House and the draping of his seat with a Union Jack, and by a long, unruly series of sittings, resulted in the bill's passage and the government's disintegration. The Liberals had won, but their highhandedness had shocked the country. C.D. Howe had served Canada well during the war and after, but by 1956 Canadians were beginning to wonder if he had overstayed his welcome in the arena of power.

Still, no one truly expected the government to be defeated in the election of 1957. St. Laurent remained as prime minister and leader of the Liberal Party, and, although he was 75 years old and clearly tired, he still projected personal decency and integrity. Coldwell also remained in his place at the head of the C.C.F., his party bolstered by its sterling performance in the pipeline debate. But the Tories had changed leaders, Drew resigning after the pipeline affair because of ill-health. At a convention in Ottawa at the end of 1956, the assembled Progressive Conservatives chose John Diefenbaker as their leader. In Parliament since 1940, Diefenbaker had a reputation as a fierce partisan, a civil libertarian, and a fine orator. Many in his party also thought of him as a prima donna, but because the new chief was 61 years old, those who worried over the Prince Albert lawyer's stewardship doubtless thought he would not stay long. Certainly, few thought him likely to amount to much, and *Maclean's* magazine, caught by a deadline that forced it to produce an election editorial before the votes were cast on June 10, took what it believed to be a safe gamble and noted that Canadians had once again returned the most powerful government in the western world. For once, events did not proceed the way the editors – or the Liberals – had planned.[12]

---

[12] Works on Canadian politics from 1948 to 1957 are not numerous. The first volume of Diefenbaker's memoirs, *One Canada* (Toronto, 1975), and Dale Thomson's *Louis St. Laurent: Canadian* (Toronto, 1967) are useful guides; so too is J.W. Pickersgill's *My Years with Louis St. Laurent* (Toronto, 1975). Academic studies include Whitaker's *The Government Party*, John Meisel's *The Canadian General Election of 1957* (Toronto, 1962), Bothwell et al., *Canada Since 1945*, and Donald Fleming's memoir, *So Very Near*, vol. I (Toronto, 1985).

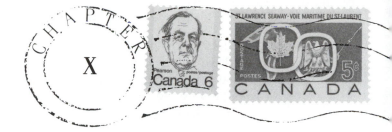

THE GOLDEN AGE OF
FOREIGN POLICY

August 1947: Escott Reid, a senior official of the Department of External Affairs, goes to the Conference on Public Affairs at Lake Couchiching, Ontario, and delivers a speech that urges "the peoples of the western world" to create an international security organization "with teeth." In September, Secretary of State for External Affairs Louis St. Laurent says much the same thing to the United Nations General Assembly. Early the next year, after a coup in Czechoslovakia turns that little eastern European country into a Soviet satellite, the British government proposes that Canada and the United States meet with it to discuss a mutual assistance pact. Prime Minister Mackenzie King agrees and tells the Canadian people and the world that all "may be assured that Canada will play her full part in every movement to give substance to the conception of an effective system of collective security by the development of regional pacts under the Charter of the United Nations."

Mackenzie King pledging support for collective security? Officials of the Department of External Affairs flying trial balloons in public speeches? The country's foreign minister taking a lead at the United Nations? A quarter century before, such things would have been almost inconceivable. But Canada had grown up fast in the second quarter of the twentieth century, and Canadian foreign policy had altered dramatically from the days of "Parliament will decide."

Beginnings

When the Dominion of Canada came into existence in 1867, it was a British colony, in fact and in law. In terms of foreign policy, that meant that Prime Minister Sir John A. Macdonald had no right to make foreign policy for his new nation; that power lay with the bureaucrats and ministers of the Foreign Office in Whitehall. Such a situation could cause problems for Her Majesty's government in Canada. When the British and the Americans sat down in 1871 to resolve a host of problems that had sprung up between them before, during, and after the American Civil War, a number of the questions directly concerned Canada, notably, fisheries and the losses suffered in the Fenian raids of 1866 and 1870-71.

Macdonald thus became a member of a five-man British delegation and, as it turned out, one voice against four. For their own imperial reasons, the British desperately wanted a treaty with Washington, and inevitably they seemed ready to sacrifice Canada's interests for the sake of those that concerned Great Britain directly. Macdonald was frustrated: "I stand alone," the prime minister wrote, "the Americans are constantly depreciating the value of our property and making absurdly low offers, which my colleagues, in their anxiety for a settlement, are constantly pressing me to yield to." The resulting Washington Treaty, signed in May 1871, was unsatisfactory, but Macondald nonetheless had to present it to Parliament – and take the blame for it.

There were lessons in that experience, though most Canadians were slow to grasp them. The United States was so big, so aggressive, and so near that few Canadians relished the idea of an independent foreign policy, let alone genuine independence for their country. Britain might be needed to help defend Canada against the United States, an idea that seemed credible as late as the 1890s when an obscure dispute between Britain and the United States over the boundary of Venezuela seemed to bring the powers close to battle. Everyone in Canada recognized that the Americans would strike north if they went to war against England, and the hopelessly inefficient Canadian militia hurried to prepare. Once again, few drew the less obvious conclusion that Canada would not have been threatened were she not a British colony.

Sir Wilfrid Laurier's government was cooler than its Conservative predecessors to imperial entanglements, but even Laurier proved completely unable to resist the pressure in the country (and within his own cabinet) to send contingents to the South African War in 1899.

Imperial sentiment remained a powerful force – after all, was Canada not the senior dominion in the greatest Empire the world had ever seen? But Laurier carefully refused to make commitments when Joseph Chamberlain, Britain's aggressive colonial secretary, pressed him to do so at Colonial Conferences in London. And he and the country were furious when Lord Chief Justice Alverstone, the British member of an arbitration panel set up to adjudicate the boundary between Alaska and Canada, voted for the American position. Even before the final vote on the panel, Laurier had cabled London that "if we are thrown over by the Chief Justice, he will give the last blow to British diplomacy in Canada." After the decision, the prime minister told the House of Commons "that so long as Canada remains a dependency of the British Crown the present powers that we have are not sufficient for the maintenance of our rights. It is important," Laurier added, "that we should ask the British Parliament for more extensive powers so that if we ever have to deal with matters of similar nature again, we shall deal with them in our own way. . . ." That was no ringing cry for independence, and, when the governor general pointed out that if Canada increased its powers in foreign affairs it would have to assume responsibility for its own defence, Laurier grumpily subsided.

In 1909, however, Laurier did establish the Department of External Affairs, an essential first step toward a Canadian foreign policy. The department was tiny, its primary role being to catalogue the British treaties that committed Canada and to store the dispatches that the Foreign Office or Colonial Office occasionally passed on to Ottawa. Relations with Britain continued to be handled by the governor general, and Canada continued to be a colony in law and in fact.

The Great War did not change Canada's status, but it changed the reality. Sir Robert Borden played an important role on the Imperial War Cabinet, and he pressed very hard for increased autonomy, using his nation's massive contribution to the war as his ace in the hole. But Borden did not want independence, though he pressed very hard for Canada to be a signatory to the peace treaty that brought the war to a close and a member of the League of Nations. Borden instead looked to a common imperial foreign policy, one that Canada would help to make and one for which Canada would have to assume some of the responsibility. After the horrible casualties of the Great War, however, the war weariness in Canada was profound, and the country turned inward.

The new Liberal prime minister, Mackenzie King, better suited the Canadian mood. King recognized one fundamental truth about Canada:

imperial commitments and foreign policy could be divisive. After all, had Canada not gone into the war in 1914 and had the need for reinforcements not led to conscription and to terrible racial divisions? For King, the lesson was obvious: the best foreign policy was the most invisible foreign policy. The prime minister set out to move toward increased autonomy within the Empire. When the Chanak crisis between Britain and Turkey erupted in 1922, King refused to commit Canada to assist the mother country. Parliament was not in session, he said, and only the elected representatives of the people could agree to any commitment. The next year, Canada signed a treaty with the United States covering halibut fisheries, a simple document of concern only to Canadian-American relations, but an important one because it marked the first time that a British representative had not scrawled his signature on a treaty affecting Canada. And after the King-Byng affair of 1926, the prime minister set out to hamstring the powers of the governor general and to create a new channel of communication between London and Ottawa. Britain and Canada exchanged high commissioners, in effect ambassadors, thus normalizing the relationship. No longer was the vice-regal representative in Ottawa the channel of communication with London. Soon, Canada and the United States exchanged representatives, and Canada sent diplomats to Tokyo and Paris as well. In 1931, finally, the Statute of Westminister, a piece of British legislation, recognized the reality King had created: Canada had full control over its foreign policy, just as it did over domestic matters.[1]

These steps toward autonomy looked impressive on paper, but they did not affect Canada's true place in the British Empire in any major way. The dominion still acknowledged the British sovereign as the King of Canada, and there was some genuine doubt about the situation that would arise if the King of Great Britain went to war. Did that mean that Canada automatically was at war too? Theorists argued, but the issue was resolved in September 1939 when Canada went to war one week after Great Britain, and only when George VI accepted the advice of his Canadian ministers to so declare.

Undoubtedly, Mackenzie King had made major strides toward a situation in which Canada had the capacity to create its own policy. But

---

[1] On Canada's road to autonomy, see Philip Wigley, *Canada and the Transition to Commonwealth* (Cambridge, 1977); C.P. Stacey, *Canada and the Age of Conflict*, vol. 2: *1921-1948* (Toronto, 1981); R.M. Dawson, *William Lyon Mackenzie King*, vol. I: *1874-1923* and H.B. Neatby, *William Lyon Mackenzie King*, vol. II: *1924-32* (Toronto, 1958, 1963).

caution remained the watchword, and no Canadian initiative abroad could be permitted lest it stir trouble at home. That was evident in the fall of 1935 (as the federal election that returned King to power took place) when Canada's permanent representative at the League of Nations in Geneva lent Canadian support to the imposition of oil sanctions against Italy for its invasion of Ethiopia. Fearful of the response in Quebec where Mussolini, the Fascist dictator, was much admired, King quickly disavowed the diplomat. Nothing in foreign policy that upset domestic tranquility could be permitted, and the relative ease with which the prime minister brought an acquiescent Canada into the war in 1939 lent credence to his tactics.

Building a Foreign Service

Canadian foreign policy, therefore, amounted to not much. To create a policy took time, and above all, it took people. First, Canada had to assemble a corps of diplomats to learn the craft of diplomacy. Britain, France, and the United States had had hundreds of years to learn the arcane techniques of statecraft; Canada was starting from scratch.

The real beginning of Canadian foreign policy came in 1924 when Mackenzie King brought Dean Oscar Douglas Skelton from Queen's University to Ottawa to become a counsellor in the Department of External Affairs. Skelton was a political economist, the biographer of Galt and Laurier, and one of Canada's leading writers on the economy and public affairs. He was also a Liberal, someone who had worked for Mackenzie King during the 1911 reciprocity election and who had assisted the prime minister at the Imperial Conference of 1923 that dealt with the aftermath of the Chanak affair. But Dr. Skelton was no patronage appointee. He came to Ottawa because he believed that the creation of a Canadian foreign policy and a department to shape it were worthy goals. In 1925, Skelton became undersecretary of state for external affairs, the senior civil servant in the department, and thus he found himself in a position to do something toward achieving those goals.

His first task was to find good candidates for his fledgling foreign service. He was in a good position to do it: he knew the universities intimately, then a repository of intelligent generalists and good ideas, and he could draw on his contacts to recruit. He was, as undersecretary, the prime minister's deputy in the department. But King was cautious, fearing that if the Department of External Affairs expanded too quickly his critics in the House of Commons would cry that he was expanding his personal empire and squandering the public's funds to do it, and so Skelton had to move carefully. His recruiting was slow but of high quality.

Skelton persuaded the Civil Service Commission, the watchdog body for appointments and staffing, that he should run a competition for a first secretary and a third secretary for his department. Those competitions in 1928 attracted a host of applicants and resulted in the eventual appointments of Lester Pearson, Norman Robertson, and Hugh Keenleyside, three uncommonly able men who were as far removed from the kinds of civil servants who had preceded them in Ottawa as one could imagine. All were young and well educated, with graduate degrees in history or economics from the best institutions in the United States or Britain. All were generalists, men with the capacity to apply their broad intelligence to differing problems and to improvise solutions. All were willing and – thanks to Skelton's guidance – unafraid to propose policy to their political masters. Their advice was often declined, but that it was offered was the key. In a few years Skelton had turned the Department of External Affairs from a post office that filed British dispatches and sent back form replies into a policy agency, one that had the capacity to offer advice to the prime minister and cabinet, who were desperately in need of it. Skelton had made himself and his men indispensable, something that R.B. Bennett, taking power in 1930, was quick to discover. He had probably intended to sack Skelton, a Grit, but, perhaps to his surprise, Bennett found that he received prompt and effective advice from the undersecretary, and as a result he kept him on. An important milestone on the road to the ideal of an impartial public service had been reached.

If the public service was now becoming impartial, it was also remaining completely masculine and English-speaking at the top. No women filled senior posts in the bureaucracy and none would for more than 30 years. Women were the secretaries and clerks, the necessary cogs in the wheels of bureaucracy, but no one seemed to believe that they might ever help make policy. In a sense, that omission is understandable for the era; less so is the complete absence of French-Canadians from the corridors of power. There were French-speaking civil servants in Ottawa, but as with women, most were junior functionaries without power. Quebec ministers surrounded themselves with aides and offered patronage posts on boards and commissions to their friends, but only a rare Québécois could crack the policy-making upper levels of the public service; if one managed the trick, he was certain to be fluently bilingual – all the government's work was carried out in English. That lack of consideration was to have serious consequences for Canada before too many years passed.

Skelton's Department of External Affairs was surprisingly tiny. When Skelton came to Ottawa in 1924 (for one year, he said), there was only Sir Joseph Pope, the undersecretary, and an assistant, and both men were little more than clerks. Once Skelton took over as undersecretary in 1925, he very quickly made himself into King's senior adviser on foreign policy – and on domestic questions too. But the staff at his command remained small. A few appointments were made and one or two missions abroad opened up before the onset of the Depression. A legation in Washington was opened in 1927 with the millionaire dilettante Vincent Massey as minister and Hume Wrong, Laurent Beaudry, and Tommy Stone as officers, all men that Massey had personally selected. A legation in Paris was in the care of Philippe Roy, a long-time Canadian government employee in France. In Tokyo, the millionaire Sir Herbert Marler was in charge. And in London the Canadian high commissioner was Peter Larkin, yet another millionaire who had assisted King and his party. The one additional post abroad was at the League of Nations in Geneva, where W.A. Riddell, an academic, was the advisory officer. That was Skelton's empire abroad; at home, by 1929, there was a counsellor, a legal adviser, and a first, second, and third secretary to watch over the entire world, to prepare and negotiate treaties, and to provide advice to the prime minister and his government, as well as to supply a "fire-fighting" crew that moved from job to job and crisis to crisis. Lester Pearson, for example, was the first secretary in Ottawa, and he handled disarmament questions, filled in at the Washington legation, served as secretary to two royal commissions, and took on a host of additional responsibilities before he was posted abroad in 1935. Others did much the same variety of work out of necessity.

And yet Skelton's department and his officers built up a splendid reputation in Ottawa. They were all professionals, educated, intelligent, sophisticated, and genuinely idealistic in a town that lacked such qualities. More to the point, they were all competent men in a civil service that desperately needed competence, and both Mackenzie King and R.B. Bennett after him came to rely on External Affairs. Skelton worked himself to the point of exhaustion trying to create a foreign service and a foreign policy while simultaneously advising the prime minister on the myriad questions of domestic policy. Perhaps Skelton's exhaustion was responsible for the administrative chaos that seemed to surround External Affairs and that led the caustic Hume Wrong, frustrated at what he saw as the do-nothing policies of his minister, Massey, and his prime minister, Mackenzie King, to characterize Canada's foreign service as farcical.

For someone like Hume Wrong, probably the most brilliant man in the foreign service, the fuzzy atmosphere in which policy existed in Ottawa was an affront. What would happen if Britain went to war once more? he asked in letters to Ottawa in the late 1930s. Skelton, who shared Wrong's concerns and felt even more deeply about them, was realistic enough to recognize that this was the ultimate political question. Mackenzie King had the task of bringing a reluctant French Canada into a war, of restraining an eager public opinion in English Canada, and of reconciling the two. Squaring a circle was easier. But King managed the job adroitly, issuing bellicose statements one day and cautionary ones the next, warning the British high commissioner not to count on Canada in an eastern European war, while telling Adolf Hitler that Canadians would swim the Atlantic to participate in a war that pitted Germany against Britain. Mackenzie King knew what he was doing, but his grand design was hidden from almost everyone else. The difficulty was, as Stephen Leacock put it in an article in the *Atlantic Monthly*, that if you asked any Canadian if he had to go to war if Britain did, the answer was certainly no. But if you asked him if he *would* go to war if Britain did, the answer was certain to be yes. If you then asked why, the answer, reflectively, would be, "Because we'd have to." In essence that was precisely true; Canada did not have to go to war, thanks to the Statute of Westminster, but it would go to war because English Canada, whose elites still controlled the media, business, and public opinion, would insist on going. King knew this, shared the same attitudes, and directed the process.

Wartime Nationalism

The Second World War altered all this and gave the officers of External Affairs their heads. Mackenzie King quickly became too busy to watch over every aspect of foreign policy or to concern himself with the location of telephone extensions and expense allowances. The prime minister's every waking hour was devoted to the manifold tasks of directing a fractious cabinet and a huge war effort, and he was soon reduced to meeting with the undersecretary once or twice a year to discuss departmental administrative matters. And after 1941, when Skelton was gone – he died on a January day at the wheel of his car while on his way home for lunch – and Norman Robertson was in charge, the department had a different cast to it. Robertson was only 36 when he took over as the top professional in the department, wide in his knowledge, realistic, and unafraid to try to have his country play a role in the world. Assisting him were Hume Wrong and Lester Pearson, both young and vigorous, extremely skilful diplomats, and men who similarly wanted Canada to have its proper place in the Allied councils. There can be no doubt that these three men, backed up by their colleagues in the department, effectively altered Canadian policy during the war and postwar years.

Their first task was to ensure that Britain and (once the Americans had come into the war after Pearl Harbor) the United States did not take Canada for granted. There was every sign that the great allies would do so when, for example, they created the Combined Chiefs of Staff to plan the war's fighting and a series of combined boards to plan the economic effort at the beginning of 1942. What was Canada's place to be in this scheme? No one in London or Washington had concerned themselves with this, simply expecting the Canadians to do as they were told, whatever that might be. But Hume Wrong, stationed in Washington at the time, was not about to let this pass. "The principle," he wrote to Ottawa, on which Canada and the Great Powers should operate was that "each member ... should have a voice in the conduct of the war proportionate to its contribution to the general war effort. A subsidiary principle is that the influence of the various countries should be greatest in connection with those matters with which they are most directly concerned."

That was very shrewd. There was no way that Canada could claim a position as a co-equal with the United States, Britain, the Soviet Union, or China, the acknowledged Great Powers. Their contribution to the war was simply too great for a country like Canada, with only 10 million people, to expect to match. Nonetheless, Canada had raised very substantial military forces and was straining every nerve to produce vast quantities of food, munitions, and raw materials for the common war effort. In the case of food, for example, the British and Americans had created the Combined Food Board to control the allocation of food; but Canada, as the greatest food producer in the Allied ranks next to the United States, had no place on that board. Wrong's principle, soon to be

Hume Wrong, one of Canada's ablest professional diplomats.

C-45196/NATIONAL ARCHIVES OF CANADA.

described as the functional principle, suggested that in such an area Canada had the right to be consulted and to participate in decisions. The same thing could be said of Canada's role in munitions production or even of its development of civil aviation. In certain areas, in other words, Canada had the attributes of a Great Power and should be treated as such.

But to claim this was different from securing it. British and American officials, harassed beyond measure by the demands of global war, craved peaceful co-operation more than anything else, and importuning Canadians quickly became pests. But the Canadians pressed their case. Ottawa was giving Britain vast sums in aid by 1942, a billion dollars in that year alone, and Canadian officials, most notably the nationalistic Clifford Clark in the Finance Department, began to tell visiting officials from London that the tap would be turned off unless Britain recognized Canada's new status. That had some impact, naturally enough, but in the crucial negotiations in Ottawa in the late summer of 1942, Mackenzie King caved in and accepted British support for Canadian membership on the Combined Production and Resources Board, already the one combined board of little consequence, instead of a place on the Food Board. Mike Pearson complained that all too often Canadian policy seemed to be the strong glove over the velvet hand.

But the next year the Canadians were back at the charge once more. There were too many difficulties in allocating food because Canada, a great producer, had no place on the Food Board, or so Ottawa officials claimed. The board dealt with commodities Canada produced in large quantities, and Canada's special place had already been recognized by putting Canadians on most of the board's subcommittees. Moreover, Canadian public opinion was demanding that Canada's contributions be recognized, and under this repeated, interminable hammering both London and Washington gave way. Canada won its place on the Combined Food Board in October 1943, adding this to its place on the Production and Resources Board.

In a very real way, the achievement of membership on the boards was important only as a symbol. No other country had achieved such recognition, not the Netherlands, France, Australia, or New Zealand. Clearly that appealed to Canadian nationalism. But what was more important than securing a place on the boards was that Canada had set out to fight for its rights. In the 1920s and 1930s, Canadian politicians had fought for and won autonomy – but then had to go to war in 1939 much as they had in 1914. Arguably, the nation had entered this war as much a colonial power as it had the last. But now Candian diplomats were beginning to take their autonomy seriously and were pressing the Great Powers for a greater Canadian share in decision making. In other words, it was no longer only *status* that was being sought (although that still remained important) but *responsibility* too. Give us a share and let us show what we can do, the Canadians argued, waving the banner of the functional principle aloft. And the Great Powers to some extent recognized the justice of the Canadian case. That was a marked advance.

The same arguments were advanced by Robertson, Pearson, Wrong, and their political masters at the United Nations Conference on International Organization at San Francisco in 1945. The San Francisco conference created the new world organization, and Canadians were concerned that the United Nations should not simply be a vehicle for the Great Powers. There had to be a role for the smaller states, and there should be some way of differentiating among those states, some method of enshrining the functional principle and establishing a category that Canadians were beginning to think of as Middle Powers. Canada had more international clout than Guatemala, for example, and it had proved its good faith by its contribution in the war; why not then give Canada and other countries of similar status more weight than nations whose major export was postage stamps?

It was a good argument, but not one that made much headway. The Great Powers were already beginning to create the Cold War and were more concerned with establishing their right to veto U.N. actions than with protecting the rights of lesser states. Canada won only a few token recognitions of its new power in the U.N. Charter, but again it was the effort that was important, not the results. The war had changed the country immeasurably, given it confidence and clout. No longer were Canadians afraid to speak up and speak out.[2]

Getting On With Washington

The war had changed Canada, but its effects on the United States were still more striking. Before the Second World War, the United States, like Canada, had been sunk in depression, often unwilling to play its part in world affairs, and certainly unwilling to assume the leadership of the western democracies. The events of 1940 and 1941 had altered that condition permanently, plunging Franklin Roosevelt and his adminstration pell-mell into the conflicts in the Atlantic and the Pacific theatres and obliging America to assume the role of the great citadel of

---

[2] On the development of policy, see H.B. Neatby, *William Lyon Mackenzie King*, vols. II-III; Stacey; J.W. Holmes, *The Shaping of Peace: Canada and the Search for World Order*, vols. I-II (Toronto, 1979, 1982); J.L. Granatstein, *The Ottawa Men* (Toronto, 1982), and *A Man of Influence: Norman A. Robertson and Canadian Statecraft, 1929-68* (Ottawa, 1981); also by Granatstein, *Canada's War: The Politics of the Mackenzie King Government, 1939-45* (Toronto, 1975).

democracy. That shift served the interests of Britain, the Soviet Union, and Canada during the war, but there could be no doubt that it posed problems for all of them, not least for Canada.

Before the war and for the first 18 months or so of America's neutrality, Canadians rested secure in the assumption that they were held in high regard in Washington as the best friends of the United States. Naturally, there had been difficulties on such matters as trade and tariffs, but the relations between the two countries had been conducted with a level of cordiality that was possibly unmatched in other international negotiations and that could lead Norman Robertson to write to Mackenzie King that Canadians "have tended to take it for granted" that the U.S. administration would "always regard Canadian interests as a close second to their own and appreciably ahead of those of any third country." The Ogdensburg Agreement and the Hyde Park Declaration of 1940 and 1941, both of which had resolved pressing Canadian defence and economic problems, had only confirmed that view, or so it seemed in Ottawa.

But Canadians had been startled by the way the United States had forgotten about Canadian concerns when the combined boards were set up and had even suggested on occasion that Ottawa should resolve its concerns in London so the Americans would not have to deal separately with Ottawa. All of this worried Ottawa, particularly the "rather abrupt and not too tactfully handled" shift in attitude, or so Robertson characterized it. The Americans had become convinced anew of their "enormous strategic imoprtance and strength," imbued with "a new sense of . . . 'manifest destiny' " and a corresponding willingness to make decisions and accept responsibility. "The change of attitude," Robertson noted at the end of 1941, a few weeks after the Japanese attack at Pearl Harbor at last had brought the U.S. into the war, "is very encouraging from the standpoint of the world in general, but it does imply quite an important modification of the special relationship in which Canada has hitherto stood with regard to the United States." So it did, and Canadian relations with the United States ever after would be at the top of Ottawa's agenda. Power had shifted in the world, and Britain clearly was never again to be a giant. The new empires were directed from Washington and Moscow; by the end of the war there was hostility between them; and Canada had to create a new relationship with its neighbour to the South. This was essential, first, because the war's demands had put substantial numbers of American troops into the Canadian North and because the coming Cold War had increased interest in the Pentagon in the defence of North America against threats across the Pole. It was also vital because of the way the war had established a web of interconnections between the two North American economies, tying them more tightly than ever before.

The Canadians were conscious of the problems, and on the economic front they tried to meet them with a generosity and creativity that deserve note. Most of the world, other than Canada and the United States, was in ruins in 1945, and Canada's trading partners in western Europe had little money to pay for the food, raw materials, and manufactured goods they needed to re-establish their economies. If Canada was to find markets for its products other than in the United States, and if it was to locate sources of the goods it needed elsewhere, then Canada had to treat trade in a very different fashion than it had before the war. In other words, if Canada wanted to avoid total dependency on Washington for its exports and imports, it had to give Britain and the Europeans credits with which to buy Canadian goods. Foreign aid was not yet in vogue, but spurred on by the economic analyses of Graham Towers in the Bank of Canada and a startling degree of consensus among the key officials in Finance, External Affairs, and the Privy Council Office, the Mackenzie King government offered substantial sums to its friends. The British were given $1.25 billion, a vast sum and fully one-third of that the United States proffered, although the American economy was at least ten times larger than the Canadian. An additional $750 million was offered to the western Europeans so they could buy wheat, timber, and manufactured goods. It was generosity of an unparalleled sort, but it was absolutely essential, or so the Ottawa planners believed. It was equally essential for the sake of the Canadian economy – all those returning servicemen and munitions workers had to have jobs to go to or else the Depression would return with a vengeance.

If only the plan had worked. The devastation in Britain and Europe was worse than anyone had calculated, and the Canadian credits did not go very far to rectify matters. Britain, the major importer of our wheat and foodstuffs, was very quickly into a state of financial emergency, desperate for dollars, virtually forced to cut back on the imports it needed for want of them. Worse, the British wartime ban on the conversion of sterling into dollars remained in place, thus preventing Canada from using any of the pounds it earned in London to pay the costs of the goods it imported from the United States. This was becoming a critical matter; Canadians, after 15 years of depression and war, wanted the luxuries they had been denied for so long. They wanted fresh fruit from Florida and winter vacations; they wanted new cars, refrigerators, jukeboxes, and radios, and they wanted them now.

The problem became apparent by the middle of 1947. The U.S. dollar reserves Canada had built up after the Hyde Park Declaration began to melt away to pay for the goods Canadians imported. During the prewar period those imports had been paid for by converting pounds earned in London into American dollars, but now that was impossible. Worse still, Canada was putting up $2 billion of its own money to assist its friends. Very quickly, because of generosity and a desire on the part of Canadians for a good life, the country was in the midst of a great foreign exchange crisis.

How could this be resolved? To Clifford Clark and Robert Bryce in the Department of Finance and to Graham Towers and Louis Rasminsky in the Bank of Canada, four of the officials most directly involved, the choices were few. Canada could opt for self-sufficiency, cutting its links with the world and living off its own resources. That approach pleased no one and was quickly dismissed. Or Canada could tie itself to the sterling bloc, to Britain and its dependencies. That choice too had little to recommend it – given the parlous state of the British economy, it was akin to tying oneself to a corpse. The remaining option was to take the American road, to recognize that the United States, in 1947 and for the immediately foreseeable future, was the strongest economy in the world.

But what did the choice mean? To most of the officers in the Department of Finance, and particularly to those who had been making regular trips to Washington to discuss Canada's difficulties with their counterparts in the Treasury Department, it meant striking a deal with the United States that saw the Americans give a loan to Canada and agree to purchase far more goods in Canada than hitherto. John Deutsch was the key Finance representative in these talks. The son of a German immigrant farmer in Saskatchewan, he had risen from dire poverty, working his way through Campion College in Regina and then through Queen's University in Kingston. Tough and solid, a man with the thick fingers of a farmer, Deutsch had one of the quickest minds in Ottawa, and he saw in Canada's difficulties a chance to strike a bargain with the United States that would ease long-standing domestic problems. What issue had wracked Western Canada for years? Deutsch might have asked. The answer was clear: high tariffs and a desire for reciprocity with the United States that would mean less expensive manufactured goods for prairie farmers. With the rest of the world gripped by economic dislocation and possibly prey to communism, surely now was the time for the United States and Canada to join economic forces in the interests of both.

Deutsch and his colleagues secretly put this proposition to Mackenzie King and received the go-ahead just days after the Canadian government had been obliged to put restrictions on American imports and on tourist travel to the United States in an attempt to stem the hemorrhage of U.S. dollars. Through January and February 1948, the Canadian and American teams met to discuss the free trade scheme, their secrecy precautions being severe. One American official privy to the talks believed that the Canadians were anxious for the arrangement because King was soon to retire and was the person best able to get public support for the package. (The import restrictions were unpopular and would, with time, build up vested interests that would make their removal very difficult.) That was probably true enough, and the Americans themselves had the international situation much in mind. Psychological factors, the official wrote, "favor immediate action. The widespread popular concern over Russian policy would undoubtedly lead to an acceptance of the international political and strategic implications which will override the supposed economic difficulties in the minds of many people."

The draft agreement negotiated by the officials by March 1948 was comprehensive. It envisaged the immediate removal of all duties by both countries, the prohibition of restrictions on imports after five years (though with important exceptions for both countries), and joint consultation on agricultural export marketing. Under the plan, Canadian manufacturers would have five years to adapt to U.S. competition, but almost all Canadian goods secured immediate access to the American market. Sir John A. Macdonald had said 70 years earlier that his National Policy was designed only to protect infant industries. Deutsch and his negotiating colleagues were saying that those industries had had time to grow, and if after five years of adaptation they could not survive, then they did not deserve to live.

However, by this point, Mackenzie King was beginning to have second and third thoughts. He was on the verge of retiring after more than two decades as prime minister. Would he go down in history as the man who had carried out Laurier's great dream – or would he be the traitor who had sold Canada to the United States? To King, ultimately, the latter concern was the more pressing, the feeling that the free trade arrangement would "absolutely destroy the significance" of the whole of his career. That was bad enough, but King soon persuaded himself as well that the proposal could lead toward the achievement of "the long objective of the Americans . . . to control this continent." And shortly after, his officials having tried once more to press the free trade deal on him, King complained bitterly in his diary that he got "alarmed beyond measure at the casual way in which a few officials take it into their hands to try and settle the great national policies; force the hands of the government, etc., without the least knowledge of the political side of matters of the kind or the least kind of political judgment." That judgment was grossly unfair; nonetheless, the free trade idea was dead, killed by Mackenzie King in his final months in office.

But Canada's dollar shortage still remained, and it had to be resolved. Thanks to skilful negotiation by the same officials with whom he was so furious, Mackenzie King and his country were rescued by the Americans. The great European Recovery Program – or the Marshall Plan, as it was usually called – was working its way through Congress in the winter of 1948, and the Canadians persuaded their friends in Washington to agree that funds from the plan could be used to pay for "off-shore purchases," that is, goods bought in countries other than the United States. The arrangement was sufficiently flexible, for example, that even Canada's contract to sell wheat to Britain could be covered. In other words, instead of using its own hard-earned dollars, or instead of paying with the $1.25 billion credit from Canada, Britain could get wheat from Alberta and the American taxpayer would pick up the tab. This generous arrangement rescued Canada, pouring a billion dollars in U.S. funds into the foreign exchange reserves by the end of 1949. The dollar crisis was over.

However, its legacy would not disappear so quickly. In the first place, the immediate result for Canada of the Marshall Plan's suport was that virtually all of Canada's exports were either to the United States itself or subsidized by the United States, a dangerous and vulnerable position for Canada. Second, in order to boost foreign exchange holdings, Canadian negotiators had been forced to urge the Americans to buy more and invest more in Canada, a situation that increased our dependency on the U.S. market and one that significantly increased American foreign investment – and economic control – in Canada. Perhaps Mackenzie King had been correct to resist free trade with the States. That was an emotive issue that could only have sharply divided Canadians. But the remedies selected by his government, the only remedies that could have been selected, had much the same effect as free trade might have had. By the end of the 1940s, Canada had become a virtual economic colony of the United States.

∼∼∼ Creating N.A.T.O.

Another plan that worked better had two purposes. One was to see the United States play an appropriate part in world events, a direct reaction to the interwar period when, in the eyes of Canadians and others, the United States had largely withdrawn and thus contributed to the coming of the Second World War. The second purpose of the plan was to see Canada take up its fair share of the load in an alliance of democratic states in the North Atlantic area.

The North Atlantic Treaty and its military product, N.A.T.O., were to a substantial extent Canadian creations. It was not that the Canadian officials in the Department of External Affairs were particularly prescient or that they assessed Soviet intentions with a perspicacity that others lacked; it was simply that an organization such as N.A.T.O. appeared to serve so many Canadian needs. The free trade initiative, launched from within the bureaucracy and scuppered by the aging Mackenzie King, had failed, and new efforts were needed to balance the Canadian export economy. What better way than to create an alliance that encompassed all of Canada's historic trading partners? The presence of the United States as a giant power immediately to the South invited the creation of some multilateral organization through which American direct influence on Canada might be moderated. What better way than in a North Atlantic alliance that reunited the democratic partners of the Second World War? And the threat exerted by the Soviet Union, and almost as important, by the Communist parties that operated – and seemed to thrive – in France, Italy, and elsewhere had to be checked. How better to do this than to revitalize the spirit of democracy in western Europe? The North Atlantic Treaty might have been designed to fill Canadian needs.

The key bureaucratic players in the Canadian service were Escott Reid and L.B. Pearson in Ottawa, Hume Wrong, the Ambassador to the United States, and Norman Robertson, the High Commissioner to Great Britain. These four men had all served in External Affairs during the war, and they had seen the United States and Britain arrogate all power to themselves in planning Allied strategy and economic policy. They had determined then that this could not be permitted, and they had invented the functional principle to serve their ends. They had worried about the United States as it became messianic and as they saw it, full again of a spirit of manifest destiny. But with the peace, paradoxically, the old-style isolationism seemed to be finding its feet again in Congress, and there was alarm in Ottawa at the abruptness with which Lend-Lease had been cancelled as soon as Japan surrendered and at the American reluctance to take up the burdens that Britain and France were so clearly unable to carry. President Truman seemed willing to press ahead, but Congress was the difficulty, and Wrong and other western ambassadors in Washington spent much time talking to senators and representatives, trying to persuade them of the urgency of providing money and energy to a Europe desperately in need of both.

The Marshall Plan, passed by Congress in the spring of 1948, was a sign that Washington was beginning to recognize the needs of western Europe. However, that great and generous plan had in it a desire to dispose of American surpluses and to bolster an economy that was beginning to sag, almost as much as it had a desire to prop up Europe. And the bill, seemingly stalled in Congress, had been sped through only because of the Soviet takeover in Czechoslovakia and the fear that event created and enhanced. That plan too had served Canadian needs, as we have seen, and the Canadians had pushed very hard for it, probably harder than a foreign mission in a national capital should ever do.

But what could be done to ensure that a fickle Congress could not change its mind tomorrow and go off half-cocked in a fit of either rabid anticommunism or Fortress America-style isolationism? An alliance that bound the United States to take its place in the defence of western Europe seemed the solution, a guarantee of commitment.

The idea of a treaty had been gaining ground ever since Escott Reid, the assistant undersecretary of state for external affairs, had raised it in a speech at the Canadian Institute of Public Affairs' annual conference at Couchiching, Ontario, in the summer of 1947. Still in his early forties, Reid was one of the brightest of the senior officials in Ottawa, a determined man with a crusader's zeal. He had been on the left in the 1930s, a strong neutralist and an advocate of Canadian isolationism from the follies of Europe. But the war had driven that out of him, and his new role in the creation of the United Nations had convinced him that the new world organization was the salvation of civilization. However, Reid had become increasingly alarmed over Soviet actions in eastern Europe and at the United Nations, and he had gradually become convinced that the U.S.S.R. was destroying the world body. Those concerns were probably in his mind when he told his Couchiching audience of academics and others that if "the peoples of the western world want an international security organization with teeth . . . they do not need to amend the United Nations Charter in order to create such an organiza- tion. . . . They can create a regional security organization to which any state willing to accept the obligations of membership could belong. In such an organization," he said, referring to the way in which the Soviet

Union had largely paralyzed the operations of the U.N. Security Council, "there need be no veto right possessed by any great power. In such an organization each member state could accept a binding obligation to pool the whole of its economic and military resources with those of the other members if *any* power should be found to have committed aggression against any one of the members." That was likely the first public call for an alliance of democratic states.

At the same time, Reid set out other aspects of his thinking in a secret memo to Pearson, the undersecretary, which he called "The United States and the Soviet Union." In it, Reid argued that Canada's major goal had to be to influence the United States to accept membership in a North Atlantic alliance. "In the event of war we shall have no freedom of action in any matter which the United States considers essential," he argued. "We shall be out-and-out belligerents from the day the war starts." That posed problems reminiscent of the Second World War, but Reid also noted that "if we play our cards well we can exert an influence at Washington out of all proportion to the relative importance of our strength in war compared to that of the United States. The game is difficult; the issues will be delicate, but with skill we can play it successfully."

The important point here is that Reid's assessment, ultimately accepted by Pearson and soon by the whole Canadian government, was based on an appraisal of the United States *and* the Soviet Union. The two superpowers, in their separate ways, were the Canadian problem. Equally important was that Canadians believed that the situation held some opportunities that could be exploited. Norman Robertson, the deepest thinker in External Affairs, noted this from his post in London when he wrote in April 1948 that Canada's problem had always been "the antinomies created by our position as a North American country and as a member of the Commonwealth, by our special relationship with the United Kingdom and at the same time, though in a lesser degree, with other countries in western Europe as well." Now, with the possibility of a North Atlantic treaty, there was a chance. "A situation in which our special relationship with the United Kingdom can be identified with our special relationships with other countries in western Europe and in which the United States will be providing a firm basis, both economically and probably militarily, for the link across the North Atlantic," he noted, "seems to me such a providential solution for so many of our problems that I feel we should go to great lengths and even incur considerable risks in order to consolidate our good fortune and ensure our proper place in this new partnership."

Norman A. Robertson, undersecretary of state for external affairs from 1941 to 1946 and high commissioner to England during the critical years of the Cold War.

In other words, Robertson was saying, Canada could solve its long-standing economic problems through creative use of a new alliance. A North Atlantic arrangement might be used to secure Canada permanent access to markets that were fragile, it could solidify links with western Europe, and it could even help to ease the problems involved in sharing a continent with the United States. The alliance, while necessary to deal with the Soviet Union and to put heart into western Europe, also could be an instrument of Canadian economic policy abroad.

Indeed, all through the long negotiations that eventually produced the North Atlantic Treaty in April 1949, that concern was at the forefront of the Canadian negotiating position. The Americans thought of the treaty as a simple military alliance and were impatient of the Canadian concerns that could cause them problems in the Senate; most of the other participants in the discussions were lukewarm; and even Hume Wrong, charged with the task of presenting the Canadian case in the day-to-day talks, believed that Ottawa's emphasis was misplaced. But Wrong, a superb bargainer, hid his concerns from the representatives of the other allies, and after a titanic struggle won acceptance for what came to be called Article II or "the Canadian article." That article bound the signatories of the North Atlantic Treaty to "seek to eliminate conflict in their international economic policies and ... encourage economic collaboration between any or all of them."

Article II was an effort to eliminate trade wars among the democracies as much as it was an attempt to achieve peculiarly Canadian aims. But its importance proved less than Robertson and Reid had hoped, for, particularly after the outbreak of the Korean War on June 25, 1950, N.A.T.O. was convinced that the U.S.S.R. was beginning to use force openly to achieve its ends and so became much more of a military alliance than some had expected or hoped. Indeed, it was not long after the onset of hostilities in Korea that Canada began to raise a brigade of troops for service with N.A.T.O. in Germany and to build a large fighter aircraft division for service there. N.A.T.O. had created a situation in which, for the first time, Canada stationed troops abroad as part of an alliance in peacetime. The era of isolationism, the days of "Parliament will decide" as the only policy Canadians had, were over for good – even if N.A.T.O. as the centrepiece of Canadian policy lasted no more than two decades. Now Canada was playing its part in the world, bargaining actively and with skill in negotiations with its friends, and using its resources and such clout as it could muster to make its case. Some, in fact, see the years from 1947 onward as a golden era in Canadian foreign policy, and they are likely correct.[3]

Suez: Pearson's Triumph

If there was a golden era in foreign policy, its very pinnacle came during the Suez crisis of 1956. Led by Lester Pearson, by this time the secretary of state for external affairs, the Canadian foreign service produced its most important intervention in world events, a difficult feat of mediation between Britain and the United States, a demonstration of enormous skill in politicking at the United Nations but also a rather risky venture in terms of Canadian public opinion.

The key figure unquestionably was Pearson. In 1956, Pearson was 59 years old, but his unwrinkled face still had a boyishness to it, and his legendary charm was as powerful as ever. Pearson had served in the Great War, he had attended university at Toronto and Oxford, he had taught history, and he had spent 20 years in the senior ranks of the

---

[3] On Canadian policy with regard to the formation of N.A.T.O., see J.W. Pickersgill and D. Forster, *The Mackenzie King Record*, vols. III–IV; Holmes; Stacey; James Eayrs, *In Defence of Canada*, vol. IV: *Growing Up Allied* (Toronto, 1980); Escott Reid, *Time of Fear and Hope: The Making of the North Atlantic Treaty 1947–49* (Toronto, 1977); and R. Cuff and J. Granatstein, *American Dollars/Canadian Prosperity* (Toronto, 1978).

Department of External Affairs before he abandoned the security of his civil service position for the vagaries of politics in 1948. Of course, Pearson had started at the top, entering the cabinet as secretary of state for external affairs. That had troubled some in the Opposition who were beginning to worry that the senior bureaucracy was too close to the Liberal government, but that storm had passed (although five years later, when J.W. Pickersgill resigned as clerk of the Privy Council to enter St. Laurent's cabinet, the concern, redoubled, would emerge again). As minister, Pearson had demonstrated the same skills he had shown as a diplomat and ambassador. He was the master of the compromise phrase, the helpful fixer who could cajole two or three sides into reaching a mutual accommodation that might leave no one happy but all more or less satisfied. He had shown his skills at the United Nations in negotiations that had led to a cease-fire in Korea, an action that angered some in the United States but that built lines of trust to India and even China. He was at the peak of his powers in 1956, a still-tireless man who understood how people thought and how nations worked.

He had to have that kind of broad understanding, for the Suez crisis stood the world – or at least the comfortable Canadian world – on its ear. Who could have envisaged a situation in which Britain and France would stage an invasion of Egypt in collusion with Israel? Who would have expected the United States, with President Eisenhower in the midst of his campaign for re-election, to have been misled by its senior European allies? Who could have expected that the breach in the ranks of N.A.T.O. could have occurred at precisely the moment that the Soviet Union was sending in its tanks to crush a democratic revolution in Hungary?

The world was in an uproar those days at the end of October and the beginning of November in 1956. London and Paris had virtually ceased to communicate with Washington, except through the medium of Ottawa. And the telegrams between Prime Minister St. Laurent and Anthony Eden, the British leader, had developed a tone of asperity that was unequalled in the long history of Anglo-Canadian relations. From London, Eden wired disingenuously that Britain and France had intervened in the Israeli-Egyptian war only to separate the combatants and to protect the Suez Canal, nationalized a few months earlier by Egypt's President Nasser. It had been a difficult, even agonizing decision, but Britain was certain it was right, Eden said. St. Laurent was not so sure. "I think we have a sympathetic understanding of you [sic] and France's position but we still regret you found it necessary to follow the course you are taking. Of course the motives and the known character of the actors do make a difference, but it is unfortunate that the events in the

Middle East have cloaked with a smoke screen the renewed brutal crimes of the Soviets." The cries of outrage from President Eisenhower and Secretary of State John Foster Dulles and from India's Jawaharlal Nehru were even more pointed.

In the circumstances, the task of Canadian diplomacy seemed clear. Canada had to work to rescue the British and French from the consequences of their folly; it had to restore communication between Washington and London and Paris; it had to try to save the Commonwealth, sorely tested in Asia and Africa by the reappearance of old-style gunboat colonialism; and, if possible, it had to work to make the Suez crisis a stepping-stone to a permanent resolution of the hostilities between Arab and Israeli in the Middle East. That was an agenda and a half; the astonishing thing is that Pearson and his colleagues largely carried off all but the last point.

Pearson was the heart and soul of the operation, but he was assisted by an extraordinary crew. In London, Norman Robertson was serving his second term as high commissioner, and there was no one with better entrée to high places or more wisdom among the array of foreign representatives there. In Washington, Arnold Heeney was ambassador, forthright, skilful at arguing cases, and a supremely organized man. At the United Nations, John Holmes served as Pearson's strong right arm, cajoling wary Third World delegates and arguing the Canadian case. And in Ottawa, the undersecretary of state for external affairs was Jules Léger, the senior Francophone in the public service and a man whose intelligence and character were recognized by all.

But Pearson was the key. His initial idea on hearing of the Israeli attack against Egypt and the subsequent Anglo-French ultimata was to go to New York and to suggest at the United Nations that the Anglo-French invaders be transformed into a U.N. force, "not to give United Nations respectability to the . . . intervention but to change its character and make it serve different ends." That idea was a nonstarter, Pearson discovered on arrival; the tone of the U.N. membership tended far more to branding the invaders as aggressors. In the early hours of November 2, an American resolution calling upon the "parties now involved in hostilities in the area" to accept a cease-fire was easily carried. Canada had abstained, and Pearson explained his vote:

I regret the use of military force . . . but I regret also that there was not more time, before a vote had to be taken, for consideration of the best way to bring about that kind of cease-fire which would have had enduring and beneficial results. . . . We need action, then, not only to end the fighting but to make the peace. . . . I therefore would have liked to see a provision in this resolution . . . authorizing the Secretary-General to begin to make arrangements with Member Governments for a United Nations force large enough to keep these borders at peace while a political settlement is being worked out. . . . My own Government would be glad to recommend Canadian participation in such a United Nations force, a truly international peace and police force.

That idea ultimately would get Pearson his Nobel Peace Prize, but his greatest achievement came as he worked out the details with U.N. Secretary General Dag Hammarskjöld over the next harrowing days.

Shuttling from delegation to delegation at the United Nations, flying back to Ottawa for consultations with the prime minister, the cabinet, and the officers of the Department of National Defence, Pearson seemed to be everywhere at once. Early in the morning on November 4, the U.N. General Assembly accepted Pearson's resolution that directed "as a matter of priority, the Secretary General to submit . . . within forty-eight hours a plan for the setting up, with the consent of the nations concerned, of an emergency international United Nations force to secure and supervise the cessation of hostilities. . . ." Because of Canadian lobbying, that resolution carried 57 to 0, with 19 abstentions. It seemed only logical, given the origins of the United Nations Emergency Force, or U.N.E.F. as it soon was called, that a Canadian officer, General E.L.M. Burns, who was in the area on U.N. duties, should be named commander of the force.

While the fighting around the Suez Canal intensified, the work at New York continued. Working with Hammarskjöld and an advisory group of U.N. members, Pearson prepared a major document for the General Assembly. Presented on November 6, the report made very clear that the British and French could have no place in the U.N.E.F.; neither could the United States nor the Soviet Union. Political control of the U.N. force was to be in the secretary general's hands, assisted only by the advisory group, and U.N.E.F. was to be more than a corps of observers but "in no way a military force temporarily controlling the territory in which it is stationed." Within days, troops were on the way to staging areas in Europe, wearing hastily painted U.N.-blue helmets.

It had been a triumph for Pearson and Canada thus far, a genuinely major achievement. The Suez fighting was halted, and if the face of the British and French had not been saved, at least they had not been irretrievably labelled aggressors. And Washington, its rage mollified by Eisenhower's sweeping election victory, was at last beginning to speak, if still sternly, to its friends overseas. But now for Canada the triumph began to turn into a farce.

The Department of National Defence had selected one of Canada's premier infantry regiments for service with U.N.E.F. The Queen's Own Rifles of Canada, with their British-cut battle dress and their British-pattern weapons, would proudly enter Egypt behind the U.N. flag and the Red Ensign, with the Union Jack occupying the upper corner. Curiously, no one had stopped to think that Nasser, under assault by the British, might object. After all, had Canada not worked so hard to save Egypt? But Nasser did object, and his foreign minister told General Burns that "the trouble was that Canadian soldiers were dressed just like British soldiers, they were subjects of the same Queen – the ordinary Egyptian would not understand the difference, and there might be unfortunate incidents." That was by no means a foolish response, but it could not easily be accepted by Canada.

The public response in the country to Pearson's role at the United Nations had not been completely favourable. Anglophile sentiment was still fierce in Canada in 1956, and the Conservative Party was sharp in its criticism, denouncing Canada for letting down its friends and declaring Nasser to be another Hitler. Arthur Meighen, the former Tory prime minister who had said in 1922 that Canada should have been "Ready, aye, ready" at Chanak, had not allowed 34 years to alter his views and he regretted that Canada had not followed Australia in backing Britain. And the Toronto *Globe and Mail* charged that Canada had "added nothing to its prestige . . . by its conduct" at the United Nations. In the circumstances, if Egypt rejected Canadian soldiers in U.N.E.F., the political costs would be incalculable.

Pressure was put on Cairo from every direction. The Canadian ambassador, Herbert Norman, was trusted by Nasser, and Norman argued the Canadian case. In New Delhi, Escott Reid, the Canadian high commissioner, spoke fervently to Nehru, who had been impressed by Canadian efforts at the U.N. – and by Reid's arguments that the Commonwealth deserved to survive, notwithstanding the British action – and Nehru, the senior statesman of the nonaligned world, added his support to the Canadian case. So too did Hammarskjöld, although the secretary general had to be more interested in seeing U.N.E.F. created than he was in rescuing a Liberal government in trouble with its English-speaking voters. The result was a compromise, accepted and papered over by General Burns, who told Pearson in writing that "the most valuable and urgently required contribution that Canada could make to the force at the present time would be to supply an augmented transport squadron of the R.C.A.F. to lift the troops assembling at Naples to Egypt. It would also be of great assistance if the administrative elements of the army contingent could go forward at an early date in order to help in

L.B. Pearson and his wife, Maryon, just after he received the Nobel Peace Prize in 1957.
C-94168/NATIONAL ARCHIVES OF CANADA.

organizing the administration at the base of the force in Egypt." In other words, instead of the Queen's Own, Canada would be represented on the ground in Egypt by administration, supply, and signal troops. Temporarily, Canada's face had been saved.

But if U.N.E.F. was a great achievement for Pearson and his officials, its results were probably damaging to the St. Laurent government in the election of June 1957. Although the Conservatives, now led by John Diefenbaker, did not assail the creation of the U.N. force as such (Diefenbaker, in fact, claimed to be the originator of the idea), they took every advantage of what they saw as an anti-British cast of mind on the part of the Liberals. In the House of Commons, St. Laurent had remarked in anger that the British and French were among "those supermen of Europe whose days are about over," giving the Opposition a large target. There were cries that the Liberals had made Canada into the chore-boy of the United States, and Howard Green, a British Columbia M.P., said it was "high time Canada had a government which will not knife Canada's best friends in the back." To what extent this affected the election results is uncertain. There were innumerable other issues, particularly the perceived arrogance of the entrenched government. But it seems probable that the U.N.E.F. episode had not helped the Liberals.[4]

Still, it was a great achievement; even if it failed to produce permanent peace, it was the absolute culmination of Canadian influence and power. In the postwar world, Canada *had* influence and power, it had idealism and skilled diplomats, it had money and the willingness to spend it in the furtherance of its aims. Suez had brought all this together, and if the Egyptians had not trusted the Queen's Own, they seemed to be almost the only nation that didn't. But the world was already altering, and the events of 1956 probably marked the end of Canada's golden age. The ruined countries of Europe and Asia were largely rebuilt, and Germany and Japan were already playing important roles. The Europeans were moving toward the creation of the Common Market to pool their strength. The Third World countries were becoming both more numerous and more concerned to play off East against West, and the United Nations, as a result, was altering too. Never again could a country such as Canada have quite so much influence.

---

[4] On Suez and U.N.E.F., see Holmes; Granatstein, *A Man of Influence*; Alastair Taylor et al., *Peacekeeping: International Challenge and Canadian Response* (Toronto, 1968); L.B. Pearson, *Mike: The Memoirs of the Right Honourable Lester B. Pearson*, vol. II (Toronto, 1973); Terence Robertson, *Crisis: The Inside Story of the Suez Conspiracy* (Toronto, 1964); James Eayrs, *The Commonwealth and Suez* (London, 1964); and Eayrs, *Canada in World Affairs 1955-1957* (Toronto, 1959).

1957-1990:
RESPONDING TO SOCIAL CHANGE

The huge crowd gathered in the city's Chinatown was festive. There were placards with the names of the local candidates, a few Canadian flags, and a host of posters with the leader's face and name boldly displayed. Advance representatives circulated through the throng handing out buttons to the children and teen-agers, of whom there were far more present – as well as many more young women – than one usually found at political meetings. When one of the organizers went to the microphone on the decorated stage and tested it, "Testing, one, two, three . . . ," he drew a cheer, a sign that the throng was becoming impatient.

At last the offical party appeared, suddenly emerging from the rear of the platform. There were the ritual speeches of welcome, the introductions of party notables, the exhortations to vote in the coming general election. But none of this was what the people had come to see or hear. They wanted the prime minister, and soon the crowd's shouts were almost drowning out the droning speakers.

Finally, the moment arrived. "Ladies and gentlemen, the prime minister of Canada." As the leader appeared from behind the official party, the crowd literally went wild, pressing even closer to the stage, shouting out the prime minister's name, throwing him kisses. Girls jumped and squealed, reaching out to try to touch him. Not even the prime minister's calming words could quiet everyone down, not even his speech, when he finally got a chance to deliver it. There was very little content in the leader's remarks; there didn't have to be much. The party strategy was simply to show the man to the country, to allow his style and grace – so very different from the politicians who had preceded him in power – to come across. It was the new Canadian politics of 1968 that was being tested, and it was working.

At the end of the prime minister's remarks, he hopped lightly down off the platform and moved into the crowd, much to the despair of his security men. But no harm would come to Pierre Trudeau unless a man could be hurt by kisses, by people reaching out to touch him. It was Trudeaumania, 1968, and the Canadian people had gone slightly mad with giddy excitement. Politics, the wise journalists covering the love-in sagely agreed, would never be the same in Canada.

Canada in 1957

The decade from 1957 to 1967 was the most turbulent decade in Canada's political history, with five federal elections, two changes of government, and four minority governments.[1] It is tempting to explain this in terms of the rivalry between John Diefenbaker and Lester B. Pearson, the respective leaders of the Progressive Conservative and Liberal parties, who differed sharply in personality as well as policies. However, this rivalry was made possible by profound changes in the attitudes and the aspirations of Canadians in these years. Political leaders did not initiate these changes. They could only respond to them and attempt to give a new sense of common purpose to a society that seemed open to change without knowing where it was going.

Technology helped to create the impression that a new world was emerging. Canadian children of the late 1950s and early 1960s were the first to grow up with television, to see satellites and space ships and a man on the moon. It was the age of supersonic jets and supertankers, of photocopying and the computer. Closer to home, it was the age of instant foods, automatic dishwashers, and polyester suits, of transistors, and tapedecks, and stereophonic sound. Medical science held out the promise of revolutionizing human behaviour, beginning with tranquilizers and

---

[1] R. Bothwell, Ian Drummond, J. English, *Canada Since 1945: Power, Politics and Provincialism* (Toronto, 1989) is a good study of the postwar years, especially for economic issues. The best reference for events is the *Canadian Annual Review*, founded and directed by J.T. Saywell from 1960 and edited by R.B. Byers since 1978. Statistical data can be found in the *Canada Year Book*, in various publications of Statistics Canada, and in F.H. Leacy, ed., *Historical Statistics of Canada* (Ottawa, 1983).

birth-control pills. There seemed no limit to the ability to control the environment and to shape human existence.

The rising expectations based on this technological revolution were also encouraged by the apparent capacity of governments to direct the national economy. The postwar administrations had concentrated on maintaining full employment and averting another depression; success had shifted the emphasis to economic growth. There were some disturbing economic indicators, however. In 1958 and again in 1960 unemployment reached 7 percent, the highest rate since the Depression, and the cost-of-living index, which rose at an average rate of less than 2 percent throughout the 1950s and early 1960s, rose to an average of over 4 percent for the last half of the decade. But unemployment could be attributed to a rapidly expanding labour force and a government that had been slow to apply Keynesian remedies, while inflation could be blamed on profligate politicians spending too much money. It was still assumed that competent governments applying wise fiscal and monetary policies could ensure sustained economic progress.

Associated with this faith in material progress was a demographic revolution with far-reaching consequences. The baby boom of the postwar period and the immigration of the 1950s had produced a population with an unusually large proportion of young people; by the mid-1960s almost half of Canadians were under 25 years of age. Even more significant was the decision of young parents to have small families. The birth rate, which had remained just above 27 births per thousand since the war, dropped abruptly in the 1960s until it was just below eighteen per thousand by the end of the decade. The contraceptive pill made family planning easier, but the decisive factor appears to have been the desire of many Canadians to enjoy higher living standards.

The most obvious impact of these demographic changes could be seen in the labour force, which grew from 6.5 million to 8.6 million over the decade. The number actually declined in farming, lumbering, fishing, and mining, where machines replaced unskilled labour while increasing production. Manufacturing and construction absorbed only a small proportion of the additional workers with the major increase coming in the service industries. Changing family patterns also affected the labour force. Women had more time to work outside the home and could contribute directly to family income, and the number of women in the labour force rose from 1.8 to 2.9 million. By the end of the decade, 40 percent of all Canadian women and one-third of married women were working. Two-income families were no longer unusual and day-care centres were beginning to be seen as a necessity. However, in one area there was little change. Women were still concentrated in the clerical and service jobs where wages were relatively low, and within those occupations they earned about half as much as male workers.[2]

The 1960s are best remembered as the decade when adolescents became associated with a distinctive lifestyle. Young Canadians of both sexes adopted long hair and jeans, experimented with marijuana, and hitchhiked across the country in the summer. What set them apart more than anything else, however, was the music. For the first time, teenagers were singing to teenagers about being teenagers, and doing it in a way that adults found disturbing and even objectionable.

The popularity of rock and roll had its roots in many of the developments of the 1960s. The baby-boomers had become teenagers, and more of them were staying in school. As adolescents trying to come to terms with the physical and social implications of puberty, they were often resentful of the discipline at home and at school. At the same time, their numbers and the nation's sustained prosperity made them a growing market for consumer goods. Technology, in the form of transistors, helped to make music the most dramatic symbol of this youth culture. Television was now providing much of the adult entertainment and, with the distinction between FM and AM radio, there was radio time available. Transistor radios were portable, and some radio stations were soon catering to this special audience, which seemed prepared to spend most of its waking hours listening to the top 40. In the competition for sales of long-playing records, the eventual success of the 33 r.p.m. records left record companies looking for a special market for their 45s, and again popular music was the answer. Older fans still listened to Frank Sinatra, but the young responded viscerally to the heavy beat and the suggestive gyrations of Elvis Presley and then to the fun-loving brashness of the Beatles. Canadians were mainly consumers of rock, but Canadian rock groups such as the Guess Who and Bachman-Turner Overdrive did top the charts. Canadian adults were not impressed. The appearance and the music of young rock stars were seen as a deliberate challenge to established social patterns. Parental objections confirmed the conviction of the young that they were different and that they were misunderstood.

---

[2] The best study on the impact of economic changes on Canadian women is Pat and Hugh Armstrong, *The Double Ghetto* (Toronto, 1984). See also Micheline Dumont et al., *Histoire des femmes au Québec depuis quatre siècles* (Montréal, 1982).

In retrospect, the 1960s was a pivotal decade. The apparent radicalism of the young attracted the most attention but labour, native peoples, and women also affirmed their distinctive identity and demanded to be heard. Rising expectations did not bring agreement on how the benefits should be distributed. In a country that had gained confidence in its political leaders during the war and postwar era, Canadians looked to politicians to provide leadership in this age of change. The politicians shared in the rising expectations, in the faith that sound administration would ensure sustained economic growth. Naturally enough, they promised more than they could deliver. More damaging to their fortunes, growth proved to be divisive. Technology was altering the Canadian way of life, but the adjustment was not easy. Some Canadians resented any changes, while others reacted against a political system that accepted nuclear weapons, pollution, and poverty. Even for the majority, there was the uncertainty of a society in which material prosperity seemed linked to unpredictable disruptions. It was a decade that undermined the traditional social patterns and left most Canadians with an uncertain sense of what should be tolerated and what should be encouraged.

The greatest impact was in Quebec. There the technological advances coincided with radical changes in French Canada. A society that had survived by resisting change suddenly decided to join the modern world and share in its benefits. The result was revolutionary for French Canada and for the federal union.

Dief the Chief

The Conservative victory of 1957 was a stunning upset. It was also difficult to assess. John G. Diefenbaker had campaigned against an arrogant and insensitive Liberal government and his apocalyptic intensity had tremendous impact. A million more Canadians went to the polls than in the previous election. The freshness, vigour, and charisma of the new leader seemed to account for the public's interest in politics and for the increased support for the Conservative Party, but the victory was far from decisive. The Conservatives won only 112 of 265 seats; they faced an Opposition of 105 Liberal, 25 C.C.F., 19 Social Credit, and 4 independent seats. And although it was clear that Diefenbaker was against the Liberals, it was less clear what he was for – other than a change. It was difficult to predict what the new government would do, or indeed, whether it would be able to survive.

John Diefenbaker captured the Conservative leadership – on his third try – in 1957. Here defeated leadership hopefuls Donald Fleming and Davie Fulton raise the Chief's hand in triumph.

PA-112695/NATIONAL ARCHIVES OF CANADA.

Diefenbaker soon showed himself to be a masterful tactician.[3] He attracted favourable publicity at a Commonwealth prime ministers' meeting in the summer of 1957 with a promise to divert Canadian trade from the United States to Great Britain. He humiliated Lester B. Pearson, the newly chosen Liberal successor to Louis St. Laurent, then his government lowered taxes and increased housing loans and old age pensions. He then promptly dissolved Parliament and went back to the hustings in search of a majority.

The election of 1958 was a rout. Diefenbaker promised to end unemployment and regional disparities and waxed eloquent about

---

[3] The best survey of the Diefenbaker era is J.L. Granatstein, *Canada 1957-1967* (Toronto, 1986). Peter Newman, *Renegade in Power* (Toronto, 1963) provides a journalistic account of the Diefenbaker administration; H. Basil Robinson, *Diefenbaker's World* (Toronto, 1989) focuses on foreign policy but offers a sensitive view of the populist politician.

developing northern resources. It did not matter that his "vision of the north" lacked substance and that his "roads to resources" were (foolishly) ridiculed by Pearson as running from "igloo to igloo"; Canadians responded to his old-style, evangelical rhetoric because they wanted to believe. The total number of voters rose by another half million, and this time the Conservative support was overwhelming. The party swept Prince Edward Island, Nova Scotia, and the four western provinces and won decisive majorities in every other province except Newfoundland. The most startling results were in Quebec, where Maurice Duplessis' Union Nationale organizers openly supported the Conservatives; the fifty Conservative seats in Quebec were the most since the days of John A. Macdonald. In all, the Conservatives won 208 seats, with the Liberals reduced to 49 and the C.C.F. to 8. John Diefenbaker had won the most decisive election victory in Canada's history.

The Diefenbaker government released this advertisement in the first months of the new administration.

Diefenbaker had stressed regional economic grievances in his election campaigns, a testimony to his sound political instinct – regional grievances had intensified during the St. Laurent administration. The federal government had relied on broad fiscal and monetary policies to maintain a high level of employment. These measures stimulated manufacturing and the exploitation of natural resources, but the economic benefits had been unequally distributed. Some sectors of the economy, such as farming and fishing, had suffered from declining prices for their products. They could only share in the national prosperity by becoming more efficient, which meant enlarging their scale of operations, investing heavily in machinery, and reducing labour costs. The point was bluntly made by the Royal Commission on Canada's Economic Prospects under Walter Gordon, a Liberal accountant from Toronto. The Gordon report, released in 1958, paid special attention to the Maritimes, where incomes

had been consistently below the national average; its long-range solution was for more capital investment in the rural and fishing communities in the Maritimes, with the displaced workers migrating to central and Western Canada where there were jobs and higher wages. This economic argument may have been right, but it ignored the social consequences. It was proposing the death of the old-fashioned family enterprise and the end of the stable lifestyle of traditional rural and fishing communities. The Conservative government rejected this social revolution, and the party swept the Maritimes.

In Nova Scotia, Robert L. Stanfield, the slow-speaking but able Conservative premier who had taken office in 1956, was already undertaking a different approach to economic recovery. He was concerned with rural communities where small farms and marginal lands kept incomes low, with fishing villages where the inshore fisheries were less and less productive, and also with the mining towns of Cape Breton where antiquated equipment and less accessible coal seams were increasing the costs of production. His response was to lend government funds to entrepreneurs who would establish local industries in these communities and so provide employment for the surplus labour force. Over the next decade the Nova Scotia government helped to establish small textile, hardboard, and fishpacking plants across the province with mixed success. The Diefenbaker government provided support for such projects through a $25 million annual adjustment grant to the Maritime provinces.

Such projects did provide jobs and income for local communities, but they were not a long-range solution to the economic problems of the family farm. Alvin Hamilton, the innovative minister of northern affairs and later of agriculture, introduced a more direct approach with the Agricultural and Rural Development Act (A.R.D.A.), which initiated a wide range of shared-cost programs to increase rural incomes. Much was done to improve farming procedures and to make farm lands more productive. However, the problem of rural poverty was not so easily resolved. In the Maritimes and in many rural areas in other parts of Canada, the unpalatable fact was that profitable farming now depended on large farms. Farm improvements and efforts to stimulate tourism could increase rural incomes, but a long-range solution had to involve more fundamental changes in the rural economy.

In Newfoundland the problem was the modernization of the logging industry. The major pulp and paper mills relied on the part-time work of farmers and fishermen to supply many of their logs. The International

Woodworkers of America successfully organized the full-time loggers in 1959 and called a strike to win the wages and working conditions of loggers elsewhere in North America. These demands had far-reaching social implications. The higher labour costs would inevitably lead to mechanization and reliance on a small corps of highly paid professional woodsmen. The part-time jobs, the supplementary income on which many farmers and fishermen depended, would disappear.

The strike was broken by the intervention of Joey Smallwood, the volatile and partisan provincial premier. Smallwood, once a socialist, may have sympathized with the strikers, but he could not face the disruption in the farming and fishing communities. After the strike had gone on for a bitter six weeks, Smallwood decertified the I.W.A. and certified a rival union that promptly signed a less favourable contract with the mills.

The federal government became involved when violence broke out during the strike. The R.C.M.P. acted as both the provincial and federal police force in Newfoundland, as they did in all provinces except Ontario and Quebec. Smallwood asked for R.C.M.P. reinforcements to maintain order. After some hesitation, Diefenbaker refused the request, despite a clear legal obligation, because he did not wish to appear to support strike-breakers.

The political consequences of the strike attracted the most attention. In Ottawa, Diefenbaker's refusal to send reinforcements led the commissioner of the R.C.M.P. to resign. In Newfoundland, Smallwood's reputation as the champion of the underprivileged was tarnished, and this was a factor in his eventual defeat years later. But in the logging industry the political intervention had little effect in the long run. Within a few years mechanization had arrived, and logging had become the monopoly of a few specialized, full-time workers, in spite of the reluctance of politicians and businesspeople and the unwelcome consequences for farmers and fishers.[4]

The federal policy of transfer payments to the Atlantic provinces was not a resounding success. Average per capita income rose in the four eastern provinces, as it did in all Canadian provinces, but in relative terms it improved only slightly and remained well below the national

---

[4] Geoffrey Stevens, *Stanfield* (Toronto, 1973), and Richard Gwyn, *Smallwood: The Unlikely Revolutionary* (Toronto, 1968) are well-written biographies by journalists without access to private papers. Allan McDougall's *John P. Robarts* (Toronto, 1985) and David Mitchell's *W.A.C. Bennett and the Rise of British Columbia* (Vancouver, 1983) are useful.

average. The sense of regional grievance may have grown even stronger in these years. Television programs and advertising, as well as political campaigns, helped make the less privileged regions aware of their relative poverty, and the rising standard of living only whetted their appetites for more. There was also some backlash because prosperity tied the Maritimes to an industrial economy that rewarded adaptability but also brought insecurity and eroded the traditional values of family and community.

In contrast to the Maritimes, some regions in Canada were prospering greatly. In British Columbia, the growing demand for minerals and forest products in the United States stimulated economic development. Confident that a depression was no longer a threat, businesspeople and politicians on the West Coast advocated rapid expansion; capital investment in resource industries would create jobs and exports. British Columbians were critical of federal transfer payments that taxed the wealthier provinces to subsidize the less fortunate ones. From their point of view, federal funds would contribute more to the national income if they were invested in growth industries. Not surprisingly, this would mean federal support for industries in British Columbia.

W.A.C. Bennett, the Social Credit premier of the province from 1952 to 1972, was the most vocal exponent of this regional approach. Bennett was flamboyant and brash, but his free-enterprise rhetoric came from an authoritarian politician, and the perennial smile concealed a tough-minded negotiator. His commitment to vast water-power projects on the Columbia and Peace rivers brought him into direct conflict with an unsuspecting federal government.

The growing demand for industrial power in the American northwest had already led to major hydro-electric installations on the Columbia River south of the border. Dams on the Canadian side could store the spring runoff and increase the power developed at these downstream installations, as well as contribute to flood control. An American proposal for a storage dam that would flood Canadian territory led to international negotiations for joint development of the entire Columbia watershed. The discussions were conducted on the Canadian side by the federal government, but provincial jurisdiction meant that any final agreement would require British Columbia's consent. A major breakthrough in the negotiations came when the Americans agreed to pay for a portion of the downstream benefits from storage dams in Canada.

The treaty was delayed because the federal and provincial governments disagreed over how this payment should be made. The federal government favoured low-cost electricity that could be delivered from the state of Washington to the Vancouver area, where there was a growing demand for power. The provincial government preferred to sell the downstream benefits for cash, which could then be used for yet another huge development on the Peace River to supply the needs of the lower mainland. Ottawa, convinced that its solution would mean cheaper power and that it would have the support of most British Columbians, nonetheless signed a treaty with the United States that provided for the construction of three large storage dams in Canada in return for low-cost power.

Bennett rejected the agreement. He strengthened his bargaining position by suddenly expropriating B.C. Electric, the private utility serving Vancouver, which then agreed to buy power from the proposed Peace River installation. The premier ultimately had his way because the majority of British Columbians supported his ambitious projects. The newly elected Liberal government recognized that Bennett held the trump cards, and a new treaty was finally ratified in 1964 that gave Bennett what he wanted.[5]

Going Wrong

Federal relations with Quebec also deteriorated. The Conservative hopes of 1958, when they won fifty seats in Quebec, were never fulfilled. In large measure, this was the result of developments within Quebec. Maurice Duplessis, whose support probably accounted for most of the Tory gains, died in 1959 and the Union Nationale government was defeated by the Liberals under Jean Lesage in the following year. This was more than a transfer of power from one party to another. Duplessis had defended the traditions of rural Quebec, whereas the Liberal Opposition increasingly drew its support from French-Canadians who believed that this policy was misguided. The Liberal victory in 1960 marked the beginning of the Quiet Revolution, when French-Canadians rapidly began adapting their institutions to meet the needs of an urban and industrial society. There were differences in the new government and in the progressive sectors of the society about what changes were

---

[5] Neil A. Swainson, *Conflict over the Columbia* (Montreal, 1979), is a detailed study of the negotiation of the Columbia River Treaty. Additional material is available in the Diefenbaker and Fleming memoirs.

necessary and about the speed of change, but there was general agreement on the final objective. The aim was still the survival of French Canada as a cultural entity, but now the goal was survival by becoming a modern society rather than survival by rejecting the modern world. Among the changes was a shift from the Roman Catholic Church to the state as the major instrument of *la survivance*. In this case, the state meant the provincial government, and inevitably this implied conflict with Ottawa over respective spheres of authority. Any federal government, Conservative or Liberal, was bound to clash with the government of Quebec under these circumstances.

John Diefenbaker, nonetheless, aggravated the situation because he never understood French-Canadian aspirations. He knew that political support from Quebec was important, and so he made some gestures toward the province. He spoke some French on public occasions even though he was far from fluent in the language, and he introduced long-needed simultaneous translation into the House of Commons. However, his French-Canadian ministers held only minor portfolios and none exercised much influence. It was easy, therefore, for French-Canadians to believe that the government in Ottawa represented English Canada and that only the government in Quebec represented them. Diefenbaker's failure to understand French Canada was also illustrated by his Canadian Bill of Rights, which he considered the greatest achievement of his political career. In his Saskatchewan experience, ethnic minorities wanted to eliminate invidious distinctions and merge with the English-speaking majority. His bill reflected this experience by protecting all citizens against the exercise of arbitrary power by the federal government, regardless of their race or ethnic origin. It was limited in scope because it gave no protection against the actions of provincial governments and because it could not bind future federal Parliaments, but the objectives were certainly commendable in an era of expanding government activities. But to French-Canadians, Diefenbaker's emphasis on individual rights ignored their rights as a cultural group, and his ideal of "unhyphenated Canadianism" seemed to them to be a policy of assimilation.

In an earlier era, the consequences of this insensitivity to French-Canadian aspirations would have been less serious. However, in these turbulent years, with French-Canadian nationalism rising, the political results were disastrous. The 50 Conservative seats of 1958 plummeted to 14 in 1962 and to 8 in 1963. The Progressive Conservative Party was once more confined largely to English Canada.

John Kennedy's first presidential visit was to Ottawa in May of 1961. The result was a developing antipathy between him and Prime Minister Diefenbaker.

JOHN F. KENNEDY LIBRARY/ST-120-21.

Diefenbaker was more in sympathy with those Canadians who felt a sentimental attachment to Great Britain. Sentiment is not always a clear guide to what should be done, and Diefenbaker's rhetoric about the Commonwealth was not always consistent with his actions. He was also apprehensive about Canada's close economic and military associations with the United States. He was not anti-American – on the contrary, he had great respect for the United States's political and economic achievements – but he was concerned that its dominance as Canada's trading partner and the integration of continental defence under American control were threats to Canadian autonomy. His concern was well founded, but his policies were vacillating and inconsistent. The problems may have been insoluble, but they could have been more fully understood.

Diefenbaker had a romantic view of the British Empire – he took a world tour in 1958 that included an elephant ride in Ceylon, a tiger hunt in Bengal, and a side trip to the Khyber Pass – but he also saw Great Britain as a counterweight to the United States. Shortly after taking office in 1957, he proposed shifting 15 percent of Canada's imports from the United States to Great Britain. It was a well-meaning but irresponsible proposal because there were no available incentives to create the necessary market in Canada for British goods. His response to the British application for entry into the European Economic Community in 1961 was no more constructive. Membership in the Common Market would certainly weaken Britain's economic links to the Commonwealth and hurt Canadian trade, but to the British the alternative seemed to be a continuing economic decline. The Liberal Opposition in Canada accepted the British decision and tried to make the best of it by arguing that the E.E.C. could become a major trading bloc and a counterbalance to the United States. But the Conservative government publicly insisted that Britain had an obligation to the Commonwealth that was inconsistent with E.E.C. membership. Charles de Gaulle ended the debate in 1963 by vetoing the admission of the United Kingdom, delaying its entry for almost a decade, but Diefenbaker's position showed only a nostalgic longing for a Commonwealth that no longer had much meaning.

The British economic difficulties only aggravated the concern for Canadian economic independence. American firms continued to invest in the development of Canada's natural resources, and Canadians continued to debate the implications of American ownership in newspapers and academic journals. There were even isolated cases of American branch plants in Canada conforming to restrictive American trade legislation directed against countries such as China or Cuba. More significant for Canada's long-term economic development was the argument that American firms would conduct all their research and development in the United States, leaving Canada far behind in the competition for technical innovation. There was not much consolation in the counterargument that Canadian-owned firms did even less research than American subsidiaries in Canada. On the other hand, the rate of economic growth was levelling off, and higher than usual rates of unemployment in 1958 and again in 1960 meant that the Conservative government, sensitive to any suggestion of economic mismanagement, saw advantages in any investment, foreign or domestic.

In the summer of 1961 the debate over American ownership focused on the activities and policy prescriptions of James Coyne, governor of the Bank of Canada. Coyne was convinced that foreign investment should be discouraged, but his reasons apparently had more to do with his personal philosophy than with economic theory. Canadians, he argued, should live within their means by tightening their belts and investing their own savings instead of borrowing from the United States. He advocated "tight money" – restraining credit by raising interest rates. Most Canadian professional economists disagreed with Coyne: they favoured economic growth, and the national origin of the investment dollar seemed irrelevant to them. A more telling argument was that even if the government accepted Coyne's objective, his proposal would be self-defeating because higher interest rates would actually attract foreign capital. His monetary policies would probably have had to be accompanied by rigid import regulations and a level of government intervention that almost no one favoured.

However, the debate quickly shifted from monetary policy to the role of the governor of the Bank of Canada. The government had no clear policy of its own and Coyne's public statements were an embarrassment. Diefenbaker and his finance minister, Donald Fleming, seized on the fact that the governor of the Bank of Canada should not be discussing monetary policies in public. His duty, they argued, was to advise the government and then to administer and defend government policy. A bill for his dismissal was introduced in the House of Commons, but it proved to be a major political blunder when the Liberal majority in the Senate gave Coyne an opportunity to defend himself before a Senate committee. The Coyne affair had no apparent effect on Canadian monetary policy, but it did have political consequences. It created an image of a vacillating Conservative government, looking for scapegoats to blame for its own shortcomings and indecision.

The government did agree with the objective of reducing imports and encouraging domestic production. But instead of tight money, it eventually opted for a tentative policy of inflation. The difficulty was to control the value of the floating Canadian dollar so that it would drop, but not drop too far. Confidence in the government had been weakened by the prolonged debate over monetary policy and by the government's growing reputation for indecision in a number of spheres. Investors began to hedge by exchanging Canadian dollars for foreign currencies. In May 1962, in the middle of the federal election campaign, there was a sudden run on the Canadian dollar, and the government was forced to peg it at 92.5 American cents. It was a difficult and embarrassing political decision at the time, but in retrospect it showed sound judgment. The dollar stayed at that level until 1970, when once more it was allowed to float and to find its own level against the U.S. dollar.

The Diefenbaker government found defence policy even more controversial than monetary policy. The logic of a continental defence policy seemed self-evident when technological advances in atomic weapons and missiles made co-operation all the more necessary. However, the need for more rapid response to any attack would make it more difficult for Canadians to be consulted before the button was pushed. The North American Air Defence Agreement of 1957 was one answer to technological changes; it integrated the air defence forces of the two countries under an American commander and a Canadian second-in-command. The N.O.R.A.D. agreement provoked little controversy at the time – it was negotiated by the St. Laurent government and quickly ratified by the Diefenbaker government as soon as it took office. But it was not safe to assume that Canadians would always agree with American decisions. In 1962 the Americans uncovered Russian missile sites in Cuba and demanded their immediate withdrawal. The American defence forces were alerted during the crisis; the Canadian government, slow to admit that there was a crisis, hesitated. This could be seen as an affirmation of Canadian autonomy, but it left the American government – and many Canadians – wondering about the reliability of its defence partner.[6]

National defence was also intimately linked to economic strength. Defence research and development could lead to technological innovations and the development of skills that could spawn profitable high-technology industries. In the 1950s the Liberal government had invested heavily in the CF-105 Arrow, a supersonic fighter, in an attempt to foster the aeronautics industry in Canada. The Arrow was an ambitious project, but its success depended upon sales to other countries, and production delays and spiralling costs eventually made foreign sales less and less likely. In 1959 the Diefenbaker government cancelled the project, provoking an outcry from those who believed that Canada needed an aircraft industry in order to have access to the high technology it involved. The cancellation of the Arrow was, in fact, a tacit admission that the stakes were too high for Canada to compete with the superpowers in this high-risk game. The alternative was an agreement that allowed Canadians to share in American defence projects. There would

---

[6] There is no standard survey of Canadian foreign policy since 1957. Two volumes of essays by John Holmes in the *Carleton Library Series*, *The Better Part of Valour: Essays on Canadian Diplomacy* (1970) and *Canada: A Middle-Aged Power* (1976), touch on the major issues. The same series has published two volumes of documents, edited by Arthur Blanchette, *Canadian Foreign Policy 1955-1965*, and *Canadian Foreign Policy 1966-1976*. Stephen Clarkson, ed., *An Independent Foreign Policy for Canada?* (Toronto, 1968), gives the tenor of the debate in the 1960s. Robinson, *Diefenbaker's World*, is an excellent study of foreign policy under Diefenbaker. See also Granatstein, *Canada 1957-1967* and Dale Thomson, *Jean Lesage and the Quiet Revolution* (Toronto, 1984).

be Canadian jobs but defence production would be organized on a continental basis, with the major decisions on military equipment being made in the United States.

Prime Minister Diefenbaker, Governor General Vincent Massey, and the new Secretary of State for External Affairs Howard Green after his swearing-in in 1959.

PA-114895/NATIONAL ARCHIVES OF CANADA.

The devaluation of the dollar during the 1962 election led the Liberals to issue "Diefendollars."

In the 1963 election, the Conservatives belatedly countered the "Diefendollar" with their own version. The economic claims were true, but Diefenbaker lost power, nonetheless.

Under the impact of the Arrow, the Coyne affair, and a shaky economy, the Diefenbaker charisma of 1958 had faded by 1962. In the federal election of that year the Conservatives elected only 116 members, a stunning loss of 92 seats. The results also showed intensified regional divisions. The Atlantic provinces continued to support the government, and the Prairie provinces remained overwhelmingly Conservative, a reward in part for wheat sales to China, which had compensated for declining markets in Europe. Local issues played a part in these results, but it was no coincidence that these two Conservative strongholds were less urban and less industrialized than the rest of the country. The same pattern emerged in Ontario, where most of the 35 seats that Diefenbaker retained were in rural ridings. The 30 Ontario seats lost to the Liberals, on the other hand, were mainly in urban communities. There was a growing cleavage between smaller, more traditional communities and larger industrial centres. The pattern showed clearly with the New Democratic Party, the reorganized and

In the 1963 election the Liberals concentrated on attacking Diefenbaker's indecision. This cartoon from *The Election Colouring Book* had an impact on the Liberals, who were denounced for lowering the tone of the campaign.

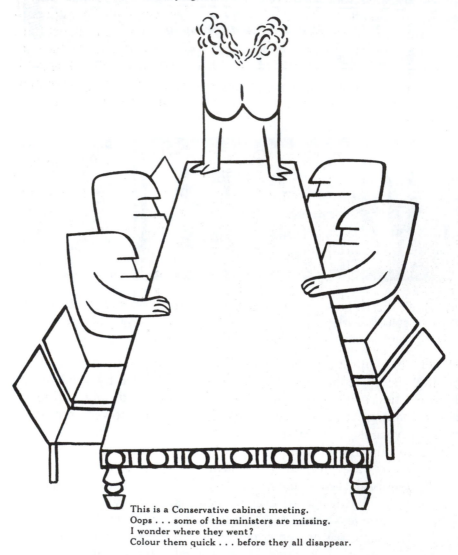

This is a Conservative cabinet meeting.
Oops . . . some of the ministers are missing.
I wonder where they went?
Colour them quick . . . before they all disappear.

revamped C.C.F., which appealed directly for labour support and whose 19 seats came mainly from industrial ridings in Ontario and British Columbia. The Liberal Party still retained some support in smaller communities, but its strength now clearly lay in the industrial areas of central Canada. The same divisions emerged in Quebec, although there the Conservatives were not the beneficiaries in the rural areas. The Social Credit Party under Réal Caouette, a fiery orator and an immense campaigner, came from nowhere to take 26 seats in northern and eastern Quebec. The Créditiste slogan – *Il n'y a rien à perdre* – was an appeal to voters disoriented by the changes of the Quiet Revolution to reject both major parties in favour of one that offered a simple monetary panacea to restore the good old days. The Conservatives retained only 14 seats in Quebec. A divided House of Commons and a minority government mirrored an uncertain country divided by regional and social differences. The bloom was off the roses of 1958.

An enthusiastic crowd cheers at an N.D.P. rally in Toronto's Maple Leaf Gardens during the 1965 election.

TORONTO TELEGRAM COLLECTION, YORK UNIVERSITY ARCHIVES.

Prime Minister Diefenbaker continued in office, but even within his party there were growing doubts about his ability to regain some of the support he had lost. A controversy over defence policy provoked an open challenge to his leadership. The continental defence plans against Soviet bombers included the construction of a number of Bomarc missile sites, two of them in Canada. Canada had agreed in 1959 to install the Bomarcs; by 1962 construction was almost completed and all that remained to make them operational was to install the nuclear warheads. However, by this time the antinuclear movement had gained adherents. Diefenbaker's relations with President John F. Kennedy had deteriorated, and the prime minister found excuses not to arm the Bomarcs. The American State Department took the unusual step of a press release to refute some of his statements. Then in February, 1963, his minister of national defence, Douglas Harkness, resigned in protest, and the three Opposition parties combined to defeat the government. After the pariamentary defeat other ministers resigned as well.

The Conservatives were defeated in the following election, although the results could hardly be called decisive. Diefenbaker ignored a divided cabinet and a sharply hostile press and conducted an emotional and effective campaign against "them" – an omnibus group that included the Liberals, the Americans, and big business. To the surprise of the pundits, the Conservatives again swept the Prairies, held most of their seats in the Maritimes, and survived in rural Ontario. The Liberals won 128 seats, just short of a majority, while the number of N.D.P. and Social Credit seats was almost unchanged.

John Diefenbaker was not a man to accept defeat gracefully. Though he was now almost 68 years old, the Chief rallied his followers in the House and attacked the Pearson government with a force and viciousness that were surprising. The Liberal government's errors provided the target, and Diefenbaker, always good in Opposition, was at his destructive best. As a result, in the election of 1965 the fragmented Conservative Party came together once more, many of the rebels of 1963 returning to work for the defeat of Pearson. But when the results demonstrated that Conservative support was more than ever confined to rural Canada, and when Diefenbaker still showed no sign of being willing to step down as party chieftain, the grumbling increased. Led by Dalton Camp, the party president, a movement began for a change in leadership; it became a struggle that tore the old party apart. Finally, after many vicissitudes and a long fight, the challenge to Diefenbaker succeeded. At the Progressive Conservative Party's leadership convention in Toronto in September

1967, the Chief belatedly decided to attempt to succeed himself, but his decision came so late and his organization was so weak that he ran a humiliating fifth on the first ballot. Robert Stanfield, the premier of Nova Scotia and Camp's choice for the succession, won out on the fifth ballot, but the party remained sorely divided. John Diefenbaker himself remained a member of Parliament, his very presence a rebuke to the new leader.

Pearson at the Helm

The Liberal Party in 1963 was a sharp contrast to the dispirited Conservatives. The Liberals had attributed their earlier defeats to their own inadequate public relations and to Diefenbaker's demagogy. They were convinced that the Diefenbaker administration had been indecisive and incompetent and that any regional dissatisfaction could soon be resolved by restoring economic growth; grievances would disappear with rising incomes. In the election campaign of 1963 they boldly promised "60 days of decision" as an alternative to Conservative ineptitude.

The social policies of the Pearson government over the next five years were a far-reaching effort to adapt both to the demands and to the insecurities of an industrial economy. The need for a skilled labour force was obvious, and although education is a provincial responsibility in the Canadian federal system, federal governments had been convinced that labour training was too important to be left to the provinces. In 1960 the Conservative government had offered generous financial incentives for technical and vocational training. But sociologists were talking of a "postindustrial" society in which the benefits of high technology would go to countries with highly trained researchers and skilled technicians. The Economic Council of Canada, appointed in 1963 to advise the government on economic policy, explained in its first annual report that "the potential Canadian economy we visualize for 1970 is a high-standard-of-living and a high-employment economy, and it must therefore be a high-education economy, a high-resource-mobility economy, a high-research economy, a high-investment economy, and a highly competitive economy." The emphasis under the Liberal administration shifted to university education.

There were dramatic changes in Canadian universities in the 1960s. Full-time undergraduate enrolment rose from 100 000 in 1960 to 300 000 by 1970. There were more young people reaching university age and an ever higher proportion sought university education, encouraged by parents, by governments, and by an economy that offered financial rewards for higher educational qualifications. It was also important that much of this increased enrolment was accounted for by women who were preparing to compete for more remunerative jobs. The demand for advanced training had an even greater impact at the graduate level, where enrolment rose from 6000 to 30 000 over the decade. Old universities expanded and new universities – Simon Fraser, York, the Université de Québec and others – were built. The costs of this expansion were more than provincial governments were willing or able to meet. The federal government had introduced per capita grants to the provinces for university education in 1951; the grants had risen to $1 per capita by 1957, had been doubled by the Conservatives in 1962, and increased again to $5 in 1965. In 1967 the federal government changed its policy to encourage further expansion and undertook to reimburse the provinces for half the costs of all postsecondary education. The cost to the federal government in the first year of the program almost doubled to more than a billion dollars.

The government tried even more to provide economic security in an industrial society. The Canada Assistance Plan of 1965 was a major restructuring of federal grants-in-aid for "the further development and extension of assistance and welfare service programs." Under this plan, the federal government agreed to share the costs of a wide range of income-support programs, including child care, mothers' allowances, health care for the needy, and the costs of welfare administration. Special programs included rehabilitation and work projects to prepare individuals for employment. The plan removed a substantial financial burden

Although Judy LaMarsh was not the first woman cabinet minister, she was the first to hold significant portfolios – health and welfare and secretary of state in the Pearson government.

PA-108053/NATIONAL ARCHIVES OF CANADA.

from provincial and municipal governments and also reduced the demands on private charity.

This major extension of social assistance was supplemented by other social security programs. Hospital insurance had done nothing to protect individuals against other medical costs. In 1962 the N.D.P. government of Saskatchewan once more took the initiative when it introduced a comprehensive medical insurance scheme. The plan provoked a bitter doctors' strike in the province, but a compromise was negotiated that made some minor concessions to the medical profession while preserving the major outlines of the scheme. Three years later, the Pearson government adopted the broad outlines of the Saskatchewan plan and offered to share the costs of any provincial medical insurance scheme that provided universal coverage for "all medically necessary services." Some provinces would have preferred to encourage the expansion of voluntary insurance plans, but the demands of their people, the lure of federal funds, and the federal insistence on universal coverage meant

The introduction of medicare into Saskatchewan caused enormous controversy. This photograph shows a rally at the legislative buildings in Regina sponsored by the Keep Our Doctors Committee, an anti-medicare group.

SASKATCHEWAN ARCHIVES R-B39801(1).

that all provinces were virtually forced to participate in the program by the end of the decade.

Government programs paid special attention to young people because throughout the western world restless youth seemed a threat to social stability in the 1960s. Affluence allowed the children of middle-class families to postpone their careers, and idealism led some of them to challenge the discrimination and inequities in their society. Canadians found no cause in Canada comparable to the civil rights movement in the United States, but Canadian youth did agitate in support of native peoples and the poor and showed an interest in the emerging nations of Africa. Ironically, young English-Canadians were less interested in French Canada. University students were at the centre of most of the agitation, and the federal government made special efforts to placate them. Ottawa established the Canada Student Loan Fund in 1963. A much more imaginative response was the Company of Young Canadians, designed to channel youthful enthusiasm into projects for the underprivileged. The experience of the C.Y.C. showed that idealism has its problems: local officials protested when young people encouraged the Métis or slum tenants to organize, and federal bureaucrats complained when the C.Y.C. workers ignored proper accounting procedures. Funds for the company were cut, and after some years it was disbanded.

The aged also presented a special problem in Canada in these years because improved health care had increased life expectancy. The federal government had taken over the full responsibility for old age pensions in 1951, but in 1963 it proposed a radical shift to a universal and contributory pension plan. Individuals and employers would contribute to a fund that would then provide a retirement pension after the age of 65 or benefits for the contributor's widow or dependents. The Canada Pension Plan was accompanied by a federal Guaranteed Income Supplement for the benefit of the elderly with low incomes who retired before establishing full benefits under the plan. The plan itself was generous, and it avoided the humiliating means test, with its taint of charity.

There was almost no opposition in Canada to these extensions of social security; the costs did not seem excessive in a period of economic growth, and aid to the less fortunate had general approval in an egalitarian decade. However, the federal initiatives did provoke strong criticism for constitutional reasons, since they encroached on the legislative powers allocated to the provincial governments. Prime Minister Pearson stressed the efficiency and equity of uniform social security measures across Canada, and his constitutional justification was that his government was not imposing any programs on provincial administrations; it was merely offering assistance to provinces that agreed to introduce the programs. The provincial governments were not impressed with this argument. The Ontario government of John Robarts, for example, had made it clear that it was strongly opposed to the federal Medicare Plan. But once the offer was made and accepted by other provinces, it was difficult to resist federal generosity and deprive the people of a popular program. Federal initiatives, in fact, were imposing federal priorities on provincial administrations.

Not surprisingly, the strongest opposition came from Quebec, where provincial autonomy was linked to cultural survival. When the federal government first proposed its pension plan to the provinces, the Liberal government in Quebec responded with its own plan. The eventual compromise was a Canada Pension Plan that accepted some features of the Quebec proposal and a separate Quebec plan that was parallel to Ottawa's and permitted workers to carry pension rights from one plan to the other. In lieu of the federal grant paid to the other provinces, the Quebec government received an equivalent sum through an increase in the provincial income tax balanced by an equal reduction in the federal income for Quebec residents. This opting-out procedure was adopted for a number of other federal measures. It had the advantage of maintaining broadly uniform programs across the country while conceding formal administrative control to Quebec. Critics did argue that opting out would weaken the links of Quebec residents with Ottawa and dilute their sense of belonging to a national community, but in these years of militant nationalism in Quebec, some special recognition of provincial autonomy seemed inevitable.[7]

This debate was part of the larger problem of the future of French-Canadian society within Canada. The problem had become more acute with the sense of alienation from the Diefenbaker administration in Ottawa and with the social changes produced by the Quiet Revolution in Quebec. Pearson had committed the Liberal Party to fuller recognition of the French fact in Canada, and in 1963 the government appointed a Royal Commission on Bilingualism and Biculturalism "to recommend what steps should be taken to develop the Canadian Confederation on the basis of an equal partnership between the two founding races."

---

[7] Richard Simeon, *Federal-Provincial Diplomacy: the making of recent policy in Canada* (Toronto, 1972), is a detailed study of constitutional discussions from 1963 to 1971.

The Commission adopted as basic the principle that Canadian citizens should have the right to be served by the federal administration in either English or French. This principle seemed obvious and straightforward, but it required major changes within the federal public service before it could be put into effect. English had always been the language of work. Documents now would have to be translated, and communication with citizens would have to be available in the two languages. Within the civil service this meant that supervisors would often have to be bilingual. Furthermore, if French-Canadians were to be attracted to the public service and were to have equal chances of promotion, their language had to have a status equivalent to that of English. This meant a massive second-language training program for both anglophones and francophones (two new words that appeared in the 1960s).

The federal government accepted the principle of federal services in both languages and began the slow process of altering language patterns within the public service. There was strong resistance from unilingual anglophones who saw their careers threatened, and progress was slow. But there was progress, and in 1969 the government passed the Official Languages Act, which established the legal right of citizens to federal services in either English or French.

The principle of "equal partnership between the two founding races" also had constitutional implications, but here the Commission was less helpful. The survival of French-Canadian society depended on more than linguistic rights: its distinctive cultural identity would have to be assured. The Quebec government under Premier Jean Lesage claimed to represent the interests of French Canada as the only government in which French-Canadians were a majority, and Lesage demanded expanded legislative and administrative powers in recognition of this special status without clearly defining what those powers should be. However, in 1966 the provincial Liberal government was defeated by the Union Nationale under Daniel Johnson. The Quiet Revolution had lost some of its impetus and a rural backlash against sweeping educational reforms contributed to the election results. The new government was more cautious about social change, but it was equally determined to extend Quebec's constitutional powers. The choice, according to Johnson, was equality or independence.[8]

---

[8] For a discussion of French Canada and the Quiet Revolution, see Thomson and Kenneth McRoberts, *Quebec: Social Change and Political Crisis*, third ed. (Toronto, 1988). For additional readings, see Chapter 12.

Some English-Canadians feared that equality would mean independence. Pearson advocated "co-operative federalism" and was willing to make substantial concessions to meet Quebec's demands. But each concession seemed to be followed by further demands. Would it be possible to satisfy Quebec and at the same time preserve the federal system? Opposition grew to any further concessions to this creeping separatism.

French-Canadian representation in the federal Parliament was also a matter of concern because, whatever the powers allocated to Quebec, the federal government would still exercise substantial jurisdiction over French-speaking citizens. Pearson did not make any formal changes in the structure of the federal legislature, but through his choice of cabinet ministers he did give French Canada an influence in Ottawa it had never had before. This influence was further strengthened when, in 1965, he persuaded Jean Marchand, Gérard Pelletier, and Pierre Trudeau, three French-Canadians who had played prominent roles in the Quiet Revolution in Quebec, to join the federal Liberal Party. Their arrival in Ottawa

The Canadian flag, displayed here by Prime Minister Pearson and adopted in 1964, was the choice of a parliamentary committee and the occasion of extraordinarily bitter public debate.

PA-136153/NATIONAL ARCHIVES OF CANADA.

after the election of that year and their obvious influence meant that the federal government could no longer be dismissed as an English-Canadian government, and the Quebec government could no longer claim to be the sole interpreter of the interests of French-Canadians.

Social security and French-English relations were not the only controversies of the Pearson years. The flag debate of 1964 was a debate over Canadian identity. The British Commonwealth was one of Canada's windows on the world, but it was no longer a major factor in Canadian foreign policy. Canadian autonomy had gradually evolved into Canadian independence, although no decisive incident or confrontation had marked the change. When Pearson proposed a maple leaf flag to symbolize this new status, some Canadians saw it as a rejection of the British heritage. The Opposition, led by Diefenbaker, fought for the inclusion of the Union Jack. The bitter debate was only ended by the adoption of closure. And yet, in retrospect, the debate can be seen as a turning point. Popular acceptance of the new flag reflected the emerging pride in Canada as a separate nation.

Immigration also provoked discussion about Canadian identity. At a time when the dominance of the white race was being challenged by anticolonialism in Africa and southeast Asia, Canadians became more aware of their own racism. Canada had welcomed immigrants after the war because of industrial expansion, but white immigrants were given preference. This bias was reinforced by allowing established immigrants to sponsor their relatives. When unemployment rose in the 1950s, this privilege was restricted to members of the immediate family. In 1967, partly in response to criticisms from the Third World, a point system was adopted for selecting immigrants, based on such factors as education, language skills, and occupational demand. The number of immigrants was based on annual economic forecasts, but colour was no longer a barrier. By the end of the decade, half of the immigrants were from the West Indies and Asia, and visible minorities were becoming part of the urban pattern. The Canadian majority, as well as the newcomers, are still coming to terms with the racial and cultural consequences.

For Canadians in the 1960s, however, relations with the United States were of more immediate concern. The declining influence of Great Britain and the strength of the European Economic Community focused attention on American investment in Canada and our increasing dependence on American markets. On these issues, the Pearson government had an ambivalent record. Walter Gordon, the minister of finance when the Liberals returned to office in 1963, was a spokesman within the government for Canadian nationalists who wanted to limit American investment in Canada. His first budget, part of the promised "60 days of decision," included discriminatory taxes on Canadian company shares sold to nonresidents and on Canadian dividends paid to nonresidents. Aside from businesspeople and their press, there was general approval in Canada for these takeover and withholding taxes, but they became a major embarrassment to the government when they proved to be uncollectable and had to be withdrawn. Gordon was further embarrassed when a proposed American tax on foreign loans threatened to weaken the Canadian dollar, and he had to beg the American government to exempt Canada from the tax. In 1965 Gordon's budget attempted to limit the distribution of American journals in Canada by disallowing income tax deductions for advertising in non-Canadian publications. But as a result of pressure from the United States, the two leading American magazines, *Time* and *Reader's Digest*, were exempted. Gordon's economic nationalism was frustrated by the interdependence of the Canadian and American economies – and by Pearson's unwillingness to risk a confrontation with the United States or with those in the cabinet who favoured close links with the United States.

Relations with the United States had broken down under John Diefenbaker; one of Prime Minister Pearson's first tasks in May 1963 was to visit President John Kennedy at Hyannisport, Mass., to restore the status quo ante. He succeeded, for a time, but economic questions and the Vietnam War soon caused new difficulties.

JOHN F. KENNEDY LIBRARY.

The Auto Pact of 1965 actually fostered an even greater integration of the two economies. Canadians had long objected to a branch-plant automotive industry in which most parts were manufactured in the United States and only assembled in Canada. The United States in turn objected when the Canadian government subsidized Canadian car exports at the expense of American exporters. A distinctively Canadian automotive industry was out of the question; existing Canadian plants built American cars and, equally important, Canadian buyers wanted the choice of models that international corporations could offer. The government's solution was an even more closely integrated automotive industry. The Auto Pact established continental free trade in automobiles and parts, limited only by guarantees that Canadian production would be equivalent to Canadian sales. The agreement made economic sense – and in 1965 provided substantial benefits to Canada – but it bound the Canadian economy more closely than ever to that of the United States.

Misgivings about Canadian autonomy were not restricted to matters of trade. At the diplomatic level, the two governments had long discussed problems freely while avoiding public confrontations. This "quiet diplomacy" assumed a community of interests and a basic accord on major issues, an assumption that was to be sorely tested by the American involvement in Vietnam. Canadians feared that major Communist powers might be drawn into the conflict there and that Canada would be forced into a wider war as a reluctant participant. Massive American bombing of North Vietnam in 1965 increased this concern. In a speech in Philadelphia, Pearson had the temerity to suggest a halt in the bombing as an invitation to negotiations for a peaceful settlement of the war. President Lyndon B. Johnson was furious at this criticism, and he made no bones about telling Pearson so. If there was a lesson to be learned from this affair, it was that Canada's influence on American foreign policy was limited. Since any public confrontation ran the risk of American economic retaliation, Canadian government representatives became more guarded in their public comments on the American conduct of the war. This, in turn, led Canadian critics of the war to denounce their own government's spinelessness.

In five years the Pearson government had some major accomplishments to its credit, but the high hopes of 1963 were never fulfilled. It had introduced major social security programs, had adopted the principle of linguistic equality within the federal administration, and had altered the division of powers within the federal system. And yet the government,

Gerda Munsinger, captured here on a TV screen in 1965, was the central figure in a Canadian "sex and spy" scandal that besmirched political reputations and lowered Canadians' esteem for Parliament.

PA-112770/NATIONAL ARCHIVES OF CANADA.

which came into office as a minority government, never significantly broadened its popular support. Pearson called a snap election in 1965, assured by his advisers that he would win a clear majority. The odds were in his favour; with the Conservatives under Diefenbaker deeply split, pollsters and journalists disagreed only on the margin of victory. But the voters had minds of their own, and the results were almost a repeat of the previous election. Only a small number of constituencies changed hands, and the Liberals, with 131 seats, were still in a minority position. It was a political setback from which the Pearson government never recovered.

Part of the explanation lay in the intensely partisan politics of those years. The Liberal claims of administrative competence were thinly veiled attacks on what they considered to be Diefenbaker's incompetence and indecision. Their scorn for him partially blinded them to the new complexity of the nation's problems and, beginning with the first

Gordon budget, they projected an image of both arrogant overconfidence and vacillation. The Conservatives, faced with internal divisions that could not be resolved, seized every opportunity to embarrass the government, and in the charged atmosphere of those years their attacks often went beyond discussions of policy to concentrate on allegations of corruption and personal dishonesty. Had Department of Justice officials tried to win bail for Lucien Rivard, a criminal with Mafia connections? Had Yvon Dupuis, a minister without portfolio, accepted a bribe? Were political favours exchanged when two other ministers acquired furniture with no down payment? Evasive answers by Pearson hinted at an awareness or tolerance of corruption that even a royal commission investigation and the resignation of some ministers could not dispel. The partisan bitterness was sharpened when the Liberals retaliated by drawing attention to an alleged breach of security by one of Diefenbaker's ministers who had consorted with a German prostitute and potential spy. It was all very sordid and had little to do with national policies.[9]

However, the inability of the Liberals to gain wider support also had its roots in the deep divisions within Canadian society. The erratic pattern of the government's relations with the United States frustrated both nationalists and continentalists. The sweeping social security measures provoked debates on the distribution of powers between the federal and provincial governments. But the most striking division was over the place of French Canada within the union. The government's efforts to respond to Quebec's demands had convinced some French-Canadians that the federal system, with its inevitable compromises, could never be satisfactory. The survival of French Canada, they concluded, required a separate, independent Quebec. The emergence of separatist parties in the province was an ominous sign. At the same time, the concessions to Quebec had provoked a backlash among those English-Canadians who resisted the idea of linguistic or cultural duality in Canada. The election of three minority governments within three years was the response of a society that could not agree on its future.

The divisions might well have been more serious. Mike Pearson was a diplomat, even as prime minister, and his instinct was to search for consensus rather than to impose a solution. Many Canadians interpreted his willingness to compromise as weakness, and there were many

---

[9] For an account of the partisan debates, see Richard Gwyn, *The Shape of Scandal* (Toronto, 1965); Granatstein, *Canada, 1957-67* (Toronto, 1986); and Peter Newman, *The Distemper of Our Times* (Toronto, 1968).

occasions when policy reversals strengthened the image of bumbling indecision. However, in the 1960s, Canadians were faced with major changes. Decisive policies might well have led to confrontations; compromises at least provided time for discussion and debate and a wider appearance of the issues involved. Pearson had no dramatic solutions, but he was sensitive to the social changes, and he did begin the painful process of adjustment.

The culminating event of the Pearson years, the celebration of Canada's centennial in 1967, gave a different perspective. Despite their political controversies, Canadians had enjoyed a decade of rising living standards, and this affluence had provided the impetus for impressive development in the arts. The endowment income of the Canada Council was handsomely supplemented by large annual grants from the federal government. Canadian theatre groups, orchestras, and ballet companies established loyal audiences at home and the best of them toured the United States and Europe where they usually received good reviews. Canadian playwrights, composers, and choreographers received less

Canada's centennial was celebrated at Nepean Point, Ottawa. Among those in attendance were the Queen, Prime Minister Pearson, and former prime minister John Diefenbaker.

TORONTO TELEGRAM COLLECTION, YORK UNIVERSITY ARCHIVES.

acclaim than Canadian performers, but there was beginning to be a conscious effort to produce Canadian works. Both English and French Canada showed a heightened interest in the works of Canadian poets and novelists. However, the widest international recognition went to two literary scholars: Marshall McLuhan, who articulated the sense of a revolutionary electronic age, and Northrop Frye, who provided an analytical framework for the whole of literature. The developments on so many fronts seemed to mark the passing of a colonial and derivative culture and to portend the emergence of a culture that would be uniquely and distinctively Canadian.

Expo 67, for a brief and heady moment, was seen as a showcase for Canada's cultural maturity. It not only opened on schedule, despite the well-publicized problems of the project, but it was an exhilarating success from the beginning. The architecture and environmental design reflected a modern and sophisticated society, but there was also a human and personal scale and even a playful whimsy that seemed distinctively Canadian. The pageant of the opening ceremonies was impressive without being solemn, and the artistic performances and films over the summer seemed to show an essential vitality beneath the characteristic Canadian restraint. Expo 67 was clean and efficient – no mean accomplishment – but it also had the friendly atmosphere of a national birthday party.

But even Expo 67 could not be isolated from unresolved problems. General Charles de Gaulle, president of France, was one of the many heads of state to visit Canada, but his triumphal journey from Quebec City to Montreal, carefully staged by the Quebec government, ended in a deliberate provocation of the federal government when de Gaulle publicly proclaimed "*Vive le Québec libre,*" the rallying cry of the Quebec separatists. The enthusiasm of many Quebeckers and the outrage of many federalists showed the depths of the cultural division. Expo 67 would also be remembered for its cost. This was partly the resentment of some English-Canadians at being taxed for the construction of roads and pavilions in Montreal, but it was also a dawning recognition that there were limits to what governments could afford.

Modern Canada

The high hopes of the 1960s became the frustrations of the next generation. Technology showed no signs of losing its momentum – satellite communications, the silicon chip, and microbiology were extending

Expo '67 in Montreal was Canada's first World's Fair. It was an enormous success and a fillip to Canadian and Quebec nationalism.

C-18536/NATIONAL ARCHIVES OF CANADA.

the revolutionary potential of science – but there was a growing scepticism about the benefits. Innovations were now associated with costly consequences: atomic power meant radioactive wastes, industrial growth meant acid rain. The zeal for warring against poverty at home and abroad was tempered by the apparent failure of research or financial aid to have much impact on economic inequities. The world seemed more complex and more resistant to change, and the crusading zeal was gone.

Economic developments reinforced the concern for security. Average family income rose during the 1970s and 1980s even after inflation, but the statistics could be misleading. Husband and wife were both likely to be working, and even the combined incomes could not keep up with the price of houses in major Canadian cities. Housing costs were aggravated by fluctuating interest rates, which rose briefly to an astonishing 20 percent and remained at double-digit levels. Unemployment rates were at their highest levels since the war, and a sharp recession in the early 1980s was a reminder that the Canadian economy was vulnerable. In Western Canada falling prices for oil and wheat, and then a sustained drought, brought on a depression that in some ways was worse than the 1930s. Every farmer suffered heavy losses. Many with large mortgages lost their farms, and others only survived because of huge federal subsidies. Industrial Canada had recovered from the recession by the mid-1980s, but there was little confidence in the future at a time when North American industrial giants were losing out to European and Asian competitors.

Demographic changes contributed to this shift in emphasis. By the 1980s there were 25 million Canadians, but the low birthrate meant an aging population. Pensions and medicare attracted more attention than youthful idealism. Students were less inclined to take time off to meditate or agitate when they had to compete for admission to a professional school or for a job. Reforming the world, for most, seemed less urgent than personal security.

There was no return to an earlier age; the deference to traditional institutions was not restored. Radicals became even more militant, turning to confrontation rather than gradual reforms to bring on the revolution. The more common pattern was a shift from broader social concerns to narrow self-interest. Physical fitness became almost an obsession: books on jogging became best-sellers; smoking in public buildings was banned; families took up bicycling and cross-country skiing. Religion, too, reflected this new self-absorption. Evangelical preachers attracted large crowds and television audiences; even conservative and middle-class congregations had charismatic groups that stressed individual religious experience. It was a decade of credit cards and lotteries. University students, who had been on the cutting edge of social criticism, showed more interest in high marks and the professional degrees that might bring them material rewards in a tight job market.

Music continued to be the symbol of the youth culture, but in the 1970s and 1980s the mood changed. The fantasies of love and fun did not disappear, but now many of the hits had explicit references to sex, social change, and violence. A number of subcultures could be identified, with almost no cross-over between disco, heavy-metal, or punk-rock. Technology supplied the synthesizers and the amplifiers that shaped the sound on tapes and in concerts. Technology also supplied the portable tape-players, which provided the market with a new means for listening to these specialized songs. In 1971 a federal regulation requiring

Canadian radio stations to play 30 percent Canadian music led to the expansion of the recording industry in Canada. Canadian performers, however, still depended upon continental popularity for success, and no definable Canadian sound emerged. Successful Canadian rock groups such as Rush or the Guess Who became part of the North American musical scene. Canadian folk-artists like Gordon Lightfoot, Leonard Cohen, and Bruce Cockburn somehow continued to seem more Canadi-an, but it was not clear whether this was because of their style, their message, or because they had never made it as big as was hoped in the United States. Only in Quebec, where language and traditions were different, did a distinctive popular music evolve. There the words had more importance, because singers like Robert Charlebois and Pauline Julien, as well as rock groups such as Beau Dommage and Harmonium, articulated the nationalist aspirations shared by many French-Canadi-ans. In Quebec, popular music was not the monopoly of the young because nationalists of all ages could respond to it.

The changes in the trade union movement illustrate the economic uncertainties of the period. The major expansion came from teachers, white-collar workers, and public servants, who in the past had consid-ered themselves closer to professionals than to workers. Now, however, they found themselves squeezed by inflation and government retrench-ment; they swallowed their pride and joined trade unions in an effort to protect their standard of living. Teachers and hospital workers, once so proud of their devotion to their charges, staged strikes to win better contracts. Even doctors united to protect their economic status. It was beneath their dignity to join a union, but their professional associations did negotiate with governments for higher medicare fees and threatened to withdraw medical services to support their demands. The family doctor of an earlier age would not have approved.

Industrial unions were affected by developments in the United States, where unions lost members in industries that were moving to the sunbelt or were forced to accept contracts on less favourable terms. Some Canadian workers, with better legal protection, preferred to negotiate on their own. The Canadian auto-workers withdrew from their international union and won expanded benefits including indexed pensions. In the Canadian Labour Congress, the presence of Canadian industrial unions, as well as powerful public service unions, brought a more national perspective to a congress that had been dominated by international unions.

The new public service unions created problems that were not easily solved. In the private sector, the strike could be an effective tool because it reduced the employer's profits, but governments do not have profits. Strikes in the public sector inconvenienced the employer only indirectly. The people directly affected were the citizens who had to rely on services provided by postal workers or air traffic controllers and whose protests encouraged the governments to reach a settlement. Federal and provincial governments were also unlike private employers because they could declare a strike illegal and pass back-to-work legislation, a tactic that became increasingly common. Such laws were temporarily successful, but they embittered labour relations for the future. While it was obvious to everyone that the strike was an unsatisfactory negotiating tool in the pubic service, it was not easy to find a satisfactory alternative. With almost one-third of the workers employed directly or indirectly by governments by the 1980s, labour relations were a major concern.

The most remarkable social changes were related to the status of women. The Divorce Act of 1968, which had accepted mental cruelty and a three-year separation as grounds for divorce, gave women a protection they sorely needed. Even more important were the provincial laws over the next decade that gave divorced wives a claim to half the property acquired during the marriage. Less progress was made in the workplace. By 1980, half of the women over the age of 15 worked outside the home, but generally they earned only two-thirds of the average man's income, and their unemployment rates were usually higher. The labour codes of most provinces guaranteed equal pay for equal work, but the principle of equal pay for work of equal value was more difficult to enforce. It was encouraging that more women were graduating from university with professional degrees, but at the higher income levels they were still trying to break into a man's world. There were glaring economic disparities. Among single-parent families, those headed by a woman were three times more likely to be below the poverty line, and among senior citizens women had the lowest average incomes. The feminist movement had made Canadians, men and women, more aware of the problems, but there were still many men and even some women who did not welcome the changes.[10]

The striking feature of these and other changes was that, more and more, personal and social concerns had become matters of public

---

[10] The last four chapters and many of the tables in Alison Prentice et al., *Canadian Women: A History* (Toronto, 1988) provide a survey of women in Canada for the postwar years.

concern, with governments or courts expected to establish and enforce social norms. The emphasis of the 1960s on individual liberties had shifted to an emphasis on the elimination of discrimination. Equality, in the words of the Charter of Rights and Freedoms incorporated into the Constitution in 1982, meant the equal protection and benefit of the law "in particular, without discrimination based on race, national or ethnic origin, colour, sex, age, or mental or physical disability." The social implications of this equality would not be clear for at least another generation but the changes would certainly be profound. Homosexuals had equal rights to jobs and apartment leases. The disabled were entitled to access facilities to public buildings. But was it discriminatory if girls could not play on boys' hockey teams? Was abortion discriminatory? Was it discriminatory if women or Jews, or Anglo-Saxons for that matter, were not proportionately represented in the public service or the professions? And could positive action to establish a desirable gender or ethnic balance be interpreted as discrimination against otherwise qualified candidates? Canadians have opted for equality before the law, but politicians and judges are under constant pressure to extend the law to forbid or punish behaviour that was formerly seen as falling within the private sphere.

Governments found it even more difficult to deal with regional rivalries. Canadian politics had always been structured along regional lines, but regional divisions were sharper than ever before. Quebec's Quiet Revolution was part of the explanation. The federal government was unwilling to give special status to Quebec, but this meant that any concession to that province of increased legislative authority or a larger share of tax revenues meant a similar concession to other provincial governments. As one example, the federal government under Pearson matched provincial expenditures in health and postsecondary education and thus influenced provincial priorities. In 1977, these matching grants were replaced by federal funds transferred directly to provincial governments without strings. By the 1980s, 20 percent of federal expenditures went to these and other provincial transfer payments over which the federal government had no control. Provincial premiers, not surprisingly, welcomed the federal funds and asked for more.

Regionalism was strengthened even more by the claims of all regions for economic assistance. Every level of government encouraged economic development by offering subsidies, tax rebates, or other benefits to prospective investors. The federal government found it difficult to mediate between the almost limitless regional demands on its budget.

Regional development was popular, but an economic incentive to stimulate investment in one region provoked demands from other regions. There were no effective countervailing pressures. Political support in each region became more and more closely associated with support for regional demands. With a newly volatile electorate, federal parties quickly learned that any reductions in welfare programs or regional subsidies were a formula for political disaster.

Political leadership was complicated by the increasing sophistication of opinion polls and of television. Political organizers came to rely on opinion polls to assess voters' interests and attitudes, and political policies and political campaigns were planned on the basis of these surveys. The pollsters consistently reported regional biases, which politicians could hardly ignore. The other major development was the use of television. Politicians still campaigned, but their primary concern was now the television audience. They hopped from one region to another, and rushed from one organized rally to the next, with brief statements and much handwaving, all in the hope of appearing in a favourable light on the evening news broadcast. Press releases and interviews became carefully orchestrated to project the image and the message that opinion polls indicated would be the most effective. In the federal campaigns of 1984 and again in 1988, the television debates between the party leaders significantly affected the election results. The voters had the advantage of seeing the leaders in their own living rooms, but the leaders they saw were staging a carefully planned performance. Both political polls and television fostered a sense of immediacy and of short-range planning, which tended to postpone risky decisions.

The Coming of Trudeau

In 1968 the Liberals chose Pierre Trudeau as Pearson's successor. In many ways he was a surprising choice. Trudeau had been an activist in the Quiet Revolution and a harsh critic of many federal policies before entering federal politics in 1965. However, being a newcomer was an advantage in the 1960s. Many Canadians were looking for an alternative to the indecision and the compromises of recent years and were attracted to this unorthodox bachelor who expounded philosophy or talked slang in both French and English, whose lifestyle included sandals, beautiful women, and sports cars, and who seemed attuned to the modern world. He had attracted attention by easing abortion and divorce laws ("The state," he said, "has no place in the bedrooms of the nation") and by a televised debate with Premier Daniel Johnson of Quebec in which he had argued for a strong central government. At the Liberal leadership convention he was the overwhelming favourite of the media, and, although Liberal delegates had some reservations, he was elected on the fourth ballot.[11]

Trudeau dominated the election of June 1968. Journalists coined the word "Trudeaumania" to describe the response of the large and enthusiastic crowds who seemed more fascinated by his personality than his policies. But political issues were also a factor. Trudeau was an outspoken critic of separatism and even of special status for Quebec, and English-Canadians unsympathetic to the demands of the minority saw a leader who would end the concessions to that province. But the election

Pierre Trudeau first made his mark on the Canadian consciousness at a constitutional conference in early 1968 when, as justice minister, he sparred with Quebec's Premier Daniel Johnson. Here Johnson and Trudeau shake hands before a smiling Mike Pearson.

PA-117460/NATIONAL ARCHIVES OF CANADA.

---

[11] The most useful of the many biographies of Trudeau is George Radwanski, *Trudeau* (Toronto, 1978). See also Richard Gwyn, *The Northern Magus* (Toronto, 1980); Christina McCall-Newman, *Grits* (Toronto, 1982); and Trudeau's *Federalism and the French Canadians* (Toronto, 1968).

results showed that Trudeau's popularity had not effaced the regional and social differences. The Liberals won 155 seats, most of the gains coming in Ontario and the West, to form the first majority government since 1958. But it was by no means a landslide victory: less than half the voters had supported Liberal candidates.

Pierre Trudeau did bring a new style to Ottawa. For all his uninhibited manner, he was an intellectual who believed that government policies should be based on a definition of social objectives and a logical analysis of how to achieve them. He appeared to welcome debate and confrontation as part of the process of participatory democracy, and he was seemingly prepared to consider untried measures to achieve social goals. It was not a style to which Canadians were accustomed.

The government's policy for native peoples illustrated the strengths and, even more, the limitations of this approach. The plight of these people was documented in statistics on income, unemployment, health, suicide, law-breaking, family breakdown, and dependence on welfare. Whether status or non-status Indians, Métis or Inuit, the majority of them lived in conditions that would have been unacceptable for any white group. By the 1960s, northern development had reduced their isolation, and improved medical services and a high birthrate had combined to increase their numbers without improving their living conditions. The White Paper on Indian Affairs in 1969 adopted the goal of social and economic equality for individual Indians. It proposed to end discrimination by gradually eliminating any special status, until the Indians merged with other Canadians as equal citizens. Equality of status, however, was no guarantee of social and economic equality. The Indians, who had not been consulted, were shocked by a policy based on cultural assimilation and by measures that brushed aside their rights under the Indian Act. They protested so vehemently that the White Paper was shelved.

The debate nonetheless had far-reaching consequences. The native peoples became more conscious of their collective identity and more insistent on their special status. The federal government, made painfully aware of the need for consultation, funded native organizations to defend native claims. In the 1970s, the debate focused on the issue of aboriginal land claims to areas not formally ceded by Indian treaties. The claims of British Columbia Indians were given some recognition by the courts in the Nishga case, and the Cree and Inuit of northern Quebec were compensated for the infringement of their hunting and fishing rights by the James Bay hydro-electric development. A royal commission on the impact of a proposed pipeline in the Mackenzie Valley drew attention to native claims there when the chair, Thomas Berger, consulted the inhabitants of small northern communities. A combination of sympathy for the natives and concern for the environment, plus the falling price of oil, effectively blocked the pipeline. Over the decade the native peoples developed a new consciousness of their common interests and a new militancy, and most Canadians became aware of the need for special measures. The new awareness, however, has as yet done little to resolve the social and economic problems that the White Paper addressed.

A study of Canadian foreign policy had similar results. Trudeau was sceptical of Pearson's emphasis on Canada's role as a peace-keeper and "helpful fixer" in international affairs. He was specifically critical of Canada's participation in N.A.T.O., being less impressed than the Department of External Affairs with the dangers of Soviet aggression. He favoured a less ambitious foreign policy tailored to fit Canada's national interests. But how could these national interests be defined, and how could they be balanced against the interests of other nations?

In *Foreign Policy for Canadians*, a study prepared in the Department of External Affairs and completed in 1970, the emphasis was placed on economic interests. The new approach to foreign policy was illustrated by the recognition of mainland China in that year, an indication of China's growing importance as a market for Canadian wheat. But economic interests were not easily isolated from other concerns. The talk of withdrawal of Canada's N.A.T.O. forces from Europe brought strong protests from N.A.T.O. allies. The government eventually reduced the N.A.T.O. forces, but left some Canadian troops in Europe. Economic interests were used to justify increased aid to less developed countries, with much of the aid linked to their purchase of Canadian goods, but there was also a sense of obligation to the less privileged. "Canada's foreign policy," Trudeau declared in 1974, "would be nothing if it were not caring." In the long run, the hard-headed talk of economic considerations proved to be less radical and less innovative than it sounded.[12]

French-English relations in Canada did have a direct impact on foreign relations. The provincial government of Quebec wanted special economic and cultural ties with France, but the federal government insisted on its constitutional monopoly in international diplomacy. An uneasy

---

[12] On this reappraisal of Canadian foreign policy in the early Trudeau years, see especially Bruce Thordarson, *Trudeau and Foreign Policy* (Toronto, 1972) and J.L. Granatstein and R. Bothwell, *Pirouette: Pierre Trudeau and Foreign Policy* (Toronto, 1990).

modus vivendi saw the federal government appointing provincial nomi-nees to federal delegations when provincial matters were to be discussed abroad. The changes were more clear-cut in the area of foreign aid. Membership in the British Commonwealth had created links with some African countries, and, in the 1960s, most of Canada's foreign aid to Africa went to former British colonies. Under Trudeau the emphasis on cultural duality led to increased contacts with French Africa, and by the end of the decade, Canadian aid was divided almost equally between former French and British colonies.

Canada's relationship with the United States was one example of a constant in foreign policy. The importance of this relationship – and Canada's vulnerability – was underlined in 1971 when the United States, facing a serious balance of payments crisis, levied a special tax on imports. This time, when Canada asked for an exemption, it was bluntly refused. The Canadian government advocated strengthening trade rela-tions with other countries in order to reduce dependence on the United States, but this was more easily said than done. Two-thirds of Canada's foreign trade continued to be with its North American neighbour. American investment in Canada also continued to attract attention. In 1973 the government established a Foreign Investment Review Agency that could intervene to block the takeover of any Canadian company or any foreign investment that was not considered to be of any "significant benefit" to Canada. F.I.R.A. was much resented by Americans and by expansionists in Canada, but it had little impact. Americans owned just over 25 percent of the shares of all Canadian corporations, excluding financial institutions, and this proportion remained almost unchanged over the decade.

The foreign policy developments in Africa reflected the high priority given to domestic issues and particularly to the French-Canadian question. Trudeau had been one of the leading advocates of moderniza-tion in Quebec; as a liberal he had consistently argued that French-Canadians must be prepared to compete on equal terms with their compatriots. He had no sympathy for a narrow French-Canadian nationalism, which he saw as restricting individual rights and isolating Quebec, and he had entered federal politics in reaction to Quebec's demands for a special status. He saw the need for a strong central government to regulate the national economy, and he understood French-English relations largely in terms of civil liberties. French-Canadians would become loyal Canadians, he believed, when they were no longer treated as second-class citizens outside the province of

Quebec. The solution, according to Trudeau, was not a transfer of powers to the provinces or special status for Quebec, but the provision of education and other services in French in all parts of Canada where French-Canadians lived. Trudeau's accession to power set the stage for a confrontation with the Quebec government, which was demanding broader economic powers. The election of a Liberal government in Quebec in 1970, under Robert Bourassa, eased tensions only slightly because the separatist Parti Québécois, under the former Liberal René Lévesque, was now the official Opposition and the champion of *nationaliste* sentiment in Quebec.

Attention was distracted from the constitutional issue by the October Crisis of that year. For some time, a handful of Quebec's extremists had advocated the use of violence in the fight for the "liberation" of their province. Terrorists had dynamited some federal buildings and blown up a few mailboxes in Westmount. The tension grew in October 1970 when they kidnapped James Cross, a British trade commissioner, and demanded the freeing of some "political prisoners" from jail as a condition for his release. Five days later, Pierre Laporte, a provincial cabinet minister, was abducted. The most disturbing aspect of all this was the apparent support for the kidnappers among Quebec's *nationalistes*. The fear of widespread civil disorder even led some provincial leaders to suggest negotiating with the terrorists.

Other leaders, including Trudeau, rejected any compromise. When police forces failed to find the kidnappers, Ottawa declared "a state of apprehended insurrection" in Quebec and invoked the War Measures Act, which permitted the arbitrary arrest and detention of suspected sympathizers. This suspension of civil liberties was widely supported in English and French Canada, and it effectively ended the demonstrations of support for the terrorists. It was less effective in apprehending the kidnappers. Over 400 persons were arrested, of whom 60 were brought to trial and only 20 convicted, but no useful information was obtained. Laporte was murdered and his body found two days after the War Measures Act was proclaimed. Eventually Cross was located and his release was arranged in exchange for a safe passage to Cuba for his abductors. The murderers of Laporte were later caught and convicted. Public opinion, in retrospect, concluded that the fears of insurrection were exaggerated and that the federal government had overreacted.

When constitutional discussions reopened at Victoria in 1971, a tentative accord was reached. The federal government obtained the extension of French language rights, although the western provinces were not included, and in exchange it conceded greater provincial authority in social legislation. An amendment procedure would give a veto to Quebec and Ontario and to a majority of the Atlantic or western provinces. However, popular opinion in Quebec interpreted the agreement as an obstacle to further extensions of provincial authority, and Premier Bourassa eventually refused to ratify the agreement. A decade would pass before the next constitutional agreement.

Economic problems could not be shelved so easily, especially with an election in 1972. The unemployment rate, which had fallen below 4 percent in the mid-1960s, rose to over 6 percent in the early 1970s. This could be attributed to an expanding labour force or even, as some argued, to the generous social security measures that encouraged "welfare bums." Far more disturbing was the rate of inflation, as measured by the consumer price index, which rose to an average of 4 percent per year despite the high unemployment. In the election campaign, the Liberals shrugged off the economic difficulties as temporary and offered only a banal slogan – "The Land Is Strong." David Lewis of the N.D.P. tried to shift attention from the poor to the "corporate welfare bums" – wealthy corporations thriving on tax exemptions. The Conservatives, under Robert Stanfield, concentrated on the Liberal government's economic mismanagement. The election results were the closest in Canadian history. The Liberals lost some urban support in Ontario and British Columbia and dropped to 109 seats compared to 107 for the Conservatives, 31 for the N.D.P., and 14 for the Créditistes in Quebec. The Liberal losses were widely interpreted as a protest against the insensitivity of the party and its leader to the economic problems of individual Canadians.

Over the next two years, the Liberal minority government tried to regain political support by showing its concern. The emphasis was once more on social security. Unemployment insurance benefits were extended, and, in response to inflation, family allowance and pensions were increased and linked to the consumer price index. Even income tax exemptions were to rise with the cost of living. However, in economic terms the situation grew worse. Unemployment came down only slightly and inflation shot up to over 10 percent by 1974, partly because an international cartel, the Organization of Petroleum Exporting Countries, dominated by Arab countries in the Middle East, doubled the price of oil. In political terms the N.D.P. supported the Liberal measures and kept the minority government in office until opinion polls encouraged Trudeau to call another election.

The election of 1974 seemed to offer voters a clear choice. Robert Stanfield, the Conservative leader, had reluctantly come to the conclusion that the economy was out of control, that traditional fiscal and monetary policies were ineffective, and that wage and price controls were needed to meet the crisis. Many Conservatives were dubious, but the party was officially committed. The Liberals, on the other hand, believed the crisis was a temporary result of the jump in oil prices. Canada was almost self-sufficient in oil, with imports to Eastern Canada balanced by exports to the United States from Western Canada, and so Canada could cushion the shock by keeping domestic oil prices well below the world price. It seemed probable that within a few years Canada would be relatively better off than other industrialized countries. Trudeau himself treated Conservative arguments rather flippantly (what was Stanfield going to say to Americans and to Arab sheiks: "Zap, you're frozen"?), but differences between the two parties seemed clear. It was less clear whether Canadians voted for policies or personalities, but the results, at least, were beyond dispute. The Liberals won a clear majority with 141 seats, most of the gains coming in Ontario at the expense of both the Conservatives and the N.D.P.

A year later, in a stunning flip-flop, Trudeau announced the imposition of wage and price controls. With double-digit inflation continuing and with unemployment rising sharply to 7 percent, even the government had lost confidence in the orthodox response of fiscal and monetary restraint. The problem seemed to be psychological. The expectation of high rates of inflation led businesspeople to raise prices and trade unions to negotiate higher wage settlements, and this in turn fuelled further inflation. When voluntary appeals for restraint had no effect, the government appointed the Anti-Inflation Board to limit wage and price increases in accordance with certain guidelines. It was seen as an emergency measure, an attempt to stop the wage and price spiral and to end the expectations of continuing inflation. The anti-inflation program did have some effect. Wages were held in check and the rate of inflation dropped below 10 percent, although it was difficult to determine how much of this could be attributed to the program and how much to other economic factors. However, political events in Quebec, culminating in the provincial election of 1976, diverted attention from economic problems.

In 1972 the Bourassa government had been re-elected on a platform of job creation and continuing economic growth. But the stress on economic issues did not silence the fears of Quebec's *nationalistes*, who were convinced that the combination of the low French-Canadian birth rate and the tendency of newly arrived immigrants to become part of the English-language community was a direct threat to French-Canadian survival. Bourassa attempted to placate his critics by proposing some tentative restrictions on admission to English-language schools, but his response only angered English-Canadians without satisfying the *nationalistes*. His government became even more unpopular when its economic initiatives failed to prevent higher rates of unemployment.

The language issue in Quebec was greatly exacerbated by a strike of English-speaking air traffic controllers in 1976. The controllers argued that air safety was endangered by the increased use of French at Quebec's airports, although concern for their own careers was clearly a factor also. The strike became a major political issue when English-Canadians across Canada supported the strikers; the support was so strong that the federal government reluctantly yielded and appointed a commission to study the problem. French-Canadians, who believed that air safety could only be improved by giving instructions in French to French-speaking pilots, were shocked at this evidence of English-Canadian prejudice against their language. By 1979 reason prevailed and the commission report, which unequivocally supported bilingual air traffic control in Quebec, was accepted without any protests. But the incident had some substantial bearing on the election in Quebec in November 1976.

In this election, the Parti Québécois focused on the shortcomings of the Bourassa government. René Lévesque promised an honest and competent administration and reassured the uneasy by promising a referendum on the question of independence before any other steps were taken. The verdict, a large majority for the P.Q., was a stunning defeat for the Liberals and a vote of confidence in Lévesque, who was an enormously engaging personality. Whether it was a vote for an independent Quebec was less certain.

The first step of the P.Q. government was to deal with the language question. Bill 101 established French as the official language in Quebec and made it compulsory for all children to attend French-language schools; only the children of parents who themselves had attended English-language schools in Quebec were exempted. The legislation was criticized outside of the province as an infringement of individual rights, but it was generally popular among French-Canadians in Quebec, who saw it as a guarantee of their survival as a people. However, there was less support in Quebec for independence, and so the P.Q. government postponed the referendum. The fate of Canada remained undecided.

The End of the Trudeau Era

The Trudeaumania of 1968 was only a bitter memory ten years later. Inflation was up, unemployment was rising, and regional antagonisms were intensified. The federal government, apparently stunned by the election of the Parti Québécois in Quebec, tried to re-open the constitutional question. Trudeau proposed a bill of rights, but the premiers demanded increased provincial powers, and the negotiations ended in frustration. Even events in Quebec, however, could not divert Ottawa's attention for long from the pressing economic problems. The rate of inflation was still unacceptably high – in 1977 it was at 8 percent – and with lower wage settlements it was necessary to look elsewhere for the cause. For some the answer was to be found in the federal deficits. By 1975 the combination of tax concessions, federal projects to fight unemployment, and the spiralling federal contributions to the provincially administered social security and education programs had begun a series of federal deficits that by 1978 had risen to 10 billion dollars. The auditor general had already warned that "Parliament – and indeed the government – has lost or is close to losing effective control of the public purse." The deficits were surely inflationary, but in a time of high unemployment it seemed inappropriate to reduce expenditures or to raise taxes. The Canadian dollar, which had been floating since 1970 and had stayed close to par with the American dollar, began to drop sharply in 1977 and by 1979 was worth about 85 American cents. Foreign investors had lost confidence in the financial administration of the Canadian government.

A controversy over oil prices that year reinforced the impression of a federal government with no clear economic objectives and no sensitivity to regional interests. When O.P.E.C., the oil cartel, had raised oil prices sharply in 1974, the Canadian government had protected Canadian consumers by keeping the domestic price below the world price. The cost had been shared by the Western producers and by the federal government, which subsidized imports. In 1979 when O.P.E.C. raised the price sharply to $35 a barrel, the domestic price had to rise accordingly, but by how much? Alberta would benefit from the world price, but Ontario was unhappy about increased manufacturing costs and higher unemployment. Federal efforts to limit the price increase angered Premier Peter Lougheed of Alberta and provoked the semi-facetious western bumper sticker that taunted: "Let the eastern bastards freeze in the dark." An agreement was eventually negotiated for annual increases whereby the federal government would receive 10 percent of the additional revenue, and the rest would be shared between the oil companies and the province in which the oil was produced.

The election of 1979 seemed to bring the Trudeau era to an end. The Liberals tried to appeal to national sentiment by stressing Trudeau's personality and the need for a strong central government, but most voters were not convinced. Liberal support increased in Quebec, presumably for a native son, but the party was almost wiped out in Western Canada and even lost some support in Ontario. The Trudeau government resigned, and later that year Trudeau himself resigned as party leader.

The Conservative Party under Joe Clark formed a minority government. Clark, labelled "Joe Who?" by journalists, had been a compromise choice as a successor to Stanfield in 1976. His emphasis on cultural harmony and regional equality contrasted with Trudeau's confrontational style. It was unfortunate for him that inflation grew worse after he took office. Regional rivalry, however, proved more durable than he had expected. Lougheed, although a Conservative, insisted on re-opening negotiations on the price of oil, and Clark's concessions won no friends in Ontario. The granting of off-shore petroleum rights to the Maritime provinces was variously interpreted as generosity or weakness. The new government, in its first budget, did show courage by imposing an unpopular 18 cents-a-gallon tax on gasoline despite provincial protests. The Opposition parties, after reading the public opinion polls, combined to defeat the budget and force an unexpected election.

The election of 1980 offered a confusing choice to the voters. The Conservatives defended a record that had not yet clearly taken shape. The Liberals persuaded Trudeau to return to lead the campaign but left policies and future leadership for a further date. The election results followed the political pattern that had emerged over the previous 20 years. The Conservative Party was almost eliminated in Quebec; the Liberal Party barely survived west of Ontario. There was a slight shift in popular support in the Atlantic provinces and Ontario, this time toward the Liberals. The shift was nonetheless enough to return the Liberals to office with a small majority. Pierre Trudeau was back! "Welcome to the 1980s," he told the country.

The political consequences were more dramatic than anybody could have predicted. The Trudeau administration, possibly affected by the criticism that it had accomplished little in its previous term of office, attempted to resolve some long-standing national problems by unilateral action. Its controversial policies on energy and the Constitution dominated Canadian politics for the next few years.

The National Energy Policy, based on the assumption that oil prices would rise, was an attempt to ensure a larger share of future profits for the federal government while at the same time increase Canadian ownership in the petroleum industry. It provoked bitter opposition from the oil-producing provinces, but it had the restrained support of Premier William Davis of Ontario because it held out the prospect of controlling energy costs for manufacturers and residents of the province. It was a dramatic political initiative, but it broke down because, instead of higher prices, increased world oil production and a world recession led to lower prices. The federal government was forced to make financial concessions to the producing provinces and to the oil companies in order to maintain domestic production. The incentives to Canadian companies did increase domestic ownership, but again the low oil prices had an effect. Dome Petroleum, the most ambitious Canadian company, went bankrupt. The N.E.P. was quietly dismantled by the next federal government. Possibly the most lasting consequence was western hostility to Liberal centralists and Ottawa bureaucrats.[13]

The attempt to revise the Constitution was even more controversial. The impetus for constitutional change had been lost with the rejection of the Victoria charter, but for Trudeau the election of the Parti Québécois in 1976 had given the issue new life. Some revision of the existing federal constitution seemed necessary to win a majority of the French-Canadians to the federal cause. Trudeau had convened a series of federal-provincial conferences, but the results had been disappointing. The provinces differed among themselves over the desirability of a charter of rights, over the distribution of powers between federal and provincial levels of government, and over an amendment procedure for a new constitution. Nor was there a sense of urgency; as one western premier candidly explained, out of one hundred items of concern to his province, constitutional amendment was the hundred and first. By 1979 constitutional revision once more seemed a dead issue. The Conservative government took no new initiatives, and the Constitution was scarcely referred to in the election campaign of 1980.

Quebec's referendum in May of 1980 revived the issue. The referendum itself was far from decisive. The provincial government was careful not to pose the question of independence directly; the question it put to the voters was whether the Quebec government should begin negotiations with Canada for "sovereignty-association." The federalists in the

---

[13] G. Bruce Doern and Glen Toner, *The Politics of Energy* (Toronto, 1985), provides an informed and judicious assessment of the National Energy Policy.

Joe Clark, a 37-year-old Alberta M.P., was selected Conservative leader in 1976. Three years later, his party won a minority victory over Pierre Trudeau's Liberals.

PA-116450/NATIONAL ARCHIVES OF CANADA.

referendum campaign, who included some politicians from English-language provinces and Ottawa, were also cautious. They appealed for support while reassuring Quebeckers that the existing Constitution would be revised. The result, with 60 percent voting against negotiations, could be interpreted as a rejection of independence, but it could not so easily be interpreted as a vote for the existing federal union.

Trudeau interpreted the federalist campaign as a commitment to constitutional revision. Since previous negotiations with the provincial governments had accomplished nothing, he now decided to act unilaterally. In October of 1980 he introduced a resolution in the House of Commons to patriate the Constitution, while at the same time adding a charter of rights and a formal amendment procedure. This arbitrary action was bitterly denounced by the Opposition and by most of the provincial premiers, although Ontario and New Brunswick supported the federal measure. A reference to the Supreme Court delayed any decision but did not end the controversy; the Court ruled that unilateral action by the federal government was legal but also affirmed that the agreement of most of the provinces was a constitutional convention. Eventually the federal government and nine provincial premiers reached an eleventh-hour compromise. René Lévesque was the isolated opponent.

Public protests forced the premiers to make some minor modifications. At the insistence of the New Democratic Party, a guarantee of the aboriginal rights of native peoples had been added to the federal government's original proposal. Some western premiers were fearful of the land claims that these rights might entail, and this clause had disappeared in the last-minute negotiations. Public sympathy for the native peoples' claims forced the premiers to agree to the insertion of a clause guaranteeing the "existing" aboriginal rights. Women's organizations were also concerned about the guarantee against legal discrimination on the basis of sex. Earlier in the year they had forced the federal government to insert a special section to strengthen this guarantee. One of the compromises of the last-minute revision, however, had been a clause that would permit provincial governments to override some sections of the charter. Did this include the clause on women's rights? Nobody was sure until a public campaign by women forced the premiers to affirm that this clause could not be overridden. By December 1981, the modified resolution was passed by the House of Commons and the Senate, and in the spring of 1982 for the last time the British Parliament passed the necessary legislation. Canada possessed its own Constitution and the power to alter it.

The debates over the National Energy Policy and the Constitution seemed to have exhausted the government. Canada felt the impact of the world recession acutely because its manufacturers suffered from foreign competition and because its exports were affected by the trend toward protectionism. The record levels of inflation subsided but unemployment rose beyond 10 percent and showed no sign of declining. It was widely believed that structural changes were needed to reduce unemployment to an acceptable level, but there was no agreement on how these changes could be introduced. In the meantime, decreased revenues and increasing social security costs produced record government deficits and limited the initiatives that governments could take.

Politicians were blamed for the economic frustrations. In part it was their own fault; they made promises that they could not keep, and they seemed more concerned with public opinion polls than with economic strategy. On the other hand, regional and class divisions made it difficult for any party or any leader to defend economic initiatives or even to receive a hearing in all parts of the country. In Western Canada, for example, a combination of resentment against French-Canadian influence in Ottawa and economic exploitation by central Canada crystallized into a virulent personal hostility to Pierre Trudeau and made any policy introduced by his government suspect from the beginning. Trudeau's confrontational approach only confirmed the suspicions.

Mulroney's Canada

The Liberal Party responded in 1984 by replacing Pierre Trudeau with John Turner, a Liberal cabinet minister who had left federal politics a decade before for a business career. Turner was not identified with Trudeau and so, it was hoped, might regain the confidence of westerners and businesspeople, or so Liberal convention delegates hoped. The Conservative Party had also changed its leader. Joe Clark was blamed for his government's defeat in Parliament and for failing to win support in Quebec. Brian Mulroney, a bilingual Quebecker, challenged Clark and in 1983 won the party leadership in a bitterly contested convention. In

In 1976, Joe Clark defeated Brian Mulroney at the Conservative leadership convention. But *Time* had prepared this cover in case Mulroney won; seven years later, Clark was out and the bilingual Quebecker was in.

DUNCAN CAMERON/NATIONAL ARCHIVES OF CANADA, C-85896.

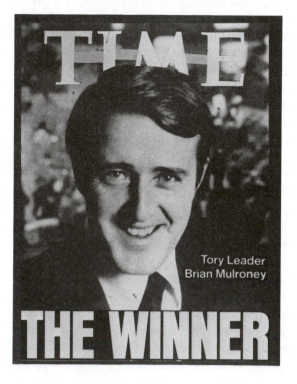

Tory Leader
Brian Mulroney

THE WINNER

1984, when the newly installed John Turner called a snap election, the stage was set for a choice between new leaders.

The sweeping victory of the Conservatives, with over 200 seats, marked the end of the Trudeau era. The confrontational style gave way to the more traditional style of negotiation and trade-offs. But the issues had also changed. Some of the contentious concerns of the Trudeau years had been settled or, at least, there was a consensus on what needed to be done. On constitutional issues, however, and on the broad question of the development of the Canadian economy, the Mulroney administration brought a different perspective.

Trudeau's policy of two official languages was now firmly established. All three federal parties were committed to bilingualism; it was even taken for granted that the three leaders, all of them Anglophone, would debate in French and English during the election campaign. The provincial government of New Brunswick was officially bilingual and Ontario offered a wide range of government services in French. And in all provinces there were public French-language immersion schools, the unique Canadian experiment in second-language instruction where English-speaking children were taught in French beginning in the first grade. Some Canadians still resented having French "stuffed down their throats," but official bilingualism was securely entrenched.

Other issues that had attracted attention in the Trudeau years were by no means resolved, but the commitment had been made and the debate would focus on putting theory into practice. It was significant that the Mulroney cabinet had more women than any previous one and that some of the women members held important portfolios responsible for economic policies. In 1985, publicly owned corporations were instructed to implement plans to end discrimination against women, minorities, and the disabled. It was not a radical measure; women's groups had hoped for more, but at least it was another step toward equality. It was also a reflection of the changed perspective of women in the workforce. By 1988 the government had enunciated an expanded policy of federal funding for day-care centres. Sexual equality would require more than legislation, but the guidelines were being established.

There was not the same consensus on the rights of native peoples. In 1982, the first ministers had guaranteed aboriginal rights without having defined them. A series of subsequent conferences could reach no agreement. The native leaders, however, did draw attention to their claims that aboriginal rights went beyond land title and land usage to include some form of self-government. Local band councils were already being given greater autonomy and, in the Northwest Territories, increased autonomy meant a cabinet responsible to a legislature with a native majority. The economic and social conditions of many of the native peoples were still a national disgrace, but the political concessions at least held out some hope for future measures based on collaboration between political and native leaders. An exhibition at the Calgary Winter Olympics in 1988, "The Spirit Sings," fostered public interest in the artistic traditions of Canada's first peoples. The boycott of the exhibition by native leaders, on the other hand, underlined their frustrations.

Immigrants continued to join the visible minorities, especially in Canada's major cities, limited only by the capacity of the economy to provide jobs. The policy for political refugees was more controversial. Refugees were defined as immigrants whose lives would be in danger if they returned home. In the past, Canada had admitted refugees from Hungary, Czechoslovakia, and Uganda, and in 1986 had even received a United Nations medal for its generosity. But the number demanding political asylum increased, especially from Southeast Asia and Central America, and it was not always easy to distinguish between political and economic motives. The regulations were tightened to limit the number admitted as refugees, but every attempt was made to grant sanctuary to those in danger of torture or death if denied entrance and forced to return to their homeland.

On the constitutional front, the Meech Lake agreement of 1987 marked a change from the approach of 1982. The Constitution of 1982 was bitterly resented by the Quebec government because it denied an opting-out clause with compensation, which would have permitted a special status for the province, and because it eliminated the veto that Quebec had customarily exercised over constitutional amendments. Mulroney, the "boy from Baie-Comeau," had won the Conservative leadership by promising a foothold for the party in Quebec. The Conservatives did sweep the province in 1984, but these gains would have to be consolidated. In 1987 Mulroney reached an agreement with the provincial premiers on a constitutional amendment that recognized Quebec as "a distinct society" and that would give all provinces substantial input into the nomination of senators and federal court judges. The subsequent debate showed that Canadians still disagreed about Canadian identity. The Meech Lake accord was seen in Quebec as a recognition, though limited and grudging, of the province's special place in the Canadian federation. Outside of Quebec, some Canadians accepted the accord as the price of national harmony. Critics, however, argued that national unity would be weakened by the tacit recognition of special status for Quebec and by permitting provincial influence in federal institutions. The Meech Lake amendment required unanimous consent. The federal government and eight of the ten provincial governments eventually approved the accord, but its adoption was blocked by the opposition of Manitoba and New Brunswick and by serious second thoughts in Newfoundland. This opposition could be explained partly by personal and partisan factors, but it also reflected the concern, especially outside of central Canada, that decentralization had serious drawbacks. By mid-1989, after the Quebec government had insisted on limiting the use of English on commercial signs, it seemed unlikely that the Meech Lake agreement would ever be officially adopted.

The Mulroney government also differed from the previous administration in its economic policies. Without being doctrinaire, it preferred to rely on market forces rather than government intervention. It dismantled the ailing National Energy Policy and sold government-owned de Havilland Aircraft of Canada to an American firm. But its "privatization" was still tentative. Canada Post became a Crown corporation, and, when Air Canada shares were sold to the public, the government retained majority control. The government was even prepared to invest public funds in such enterprises as the Hibernia fields off Newfoundland for the sake of regional development. Canadians were not exposed to the more rigorous conservatism of Reagan in the United States or Thatcher in Great Britain.

The government's fiscal policy showed the same tentative conservatism. In 1984 government revenues were $60 billion, and expenditures exceeded revenues by a record $30 billion. The government might have reduced the deficit by raising taxes, but it was reluctant to increase the tax burden on private enterprise. Initially, at least, its tax reform measures, which lowered corporation taxes and intended to replace the sales tax by a value-added tax, were not implemented to bring in more money. The deficit might also have been reduced by reducing expenditures. Mulroney had talked of Canada's social security programs as a "sacred trust," but his government did make an ill-fated effort to lower old age pension costs in 1985 by limiting annual cost-of-living increases. The government was forced to back down when pensioners roundly denounced this move. As a result, deficit reduction was limited to avoiding new commitments and relying on economic growth to provide higher revenues. After four years the annual deficit was still almost $30 billion. It was not an impressive achievement.

Other issues were eventually overshadowed by the debate over free trade with the United States. Canada had strongly supported multilateral tariff reductions under the General Agreement on Tariffs and Trade, but the prospects of another round of GATT reductions were not promising, and many countries, Canada included, regularly circumvented lower tariffs by nontariff barriers. Canadian exporters found it difficult to compete in major markets such as the European Common Market and the increasingly prosperous Pacific rim. Trade with the United States met with fewer barriers, and by the 1980s, almost three-quarters of Canadian trade was confined to this one trading partner. Canadians fretted about this increasing integration into the American economy but seemed unable to do anything about it. In the 1970s the Trudeau government had outlined the options of protectionism, continentalism, and increased trade with the rest of the world. At that time, it had favoured world trade – the so-called Third Option – but its weak efforts failed to reverse the continental trend. The problem became acute in the 1980s when the success of the Japanese automotive and electronic industries strength-ened protectionist forces in the United States. To protect access to the American market, the Canadian government entered into negotiations for a free trade agreement.

The eventual Canada-U.S. Free Trade Agreement eliminated tariff barriers and imposed some limits to nontariff barriers. As with any trade agreement, there were sharp differences of opinion about the conse-quences. Most economists and prominent businesspeople supported it because it offered some assurance of wider access to the American market. Critics, on the other hand, argued that access was not assured and that the economic benefits were illusory. Neither side suggested that the impact on trade or employment would be dramatic. The debate over free trade, however, became more than a debate over economic consequences. It became a debate over Canadian identity.

When the election of 1988 was called, nobody had expected a one-issue campaign. The government intended to run on its record, with emphasis on prosperity, financial responsibility, and Meech Lake, as well as the trade agreement. The opposition parties hoped to capitalize on the excesses of government patronage and ministerial conflicts of interest, on environmental and welfare issues, as well as the faults of the free trade agreement. The television debates changed all that. Turner accused Mulroney of having negotiated an agreement that endangered medicare and other welfare policies, one that would undermine Canada's regional

In October 1987, Canada and the United States signed a historic Free Trade Agreement that lowered tariffs and bound the two economies more tightly. The FTA became the main issue in the election of November 1988, and Brian Mulroney's victory ensured its implementation.

THE INTERNATIONAL TRADE COMMUNICATIONS GROUP, EXTERNAL AFFAIRS CANADA.

economic policies and limit public support in the future for Canadian cultural activities. Many Canadians took these allegations seriously. In the final weeks of the campaign, Canadians debated the implications for Canada's future with an emotional intensity that seemed almost un-Canadian. Opponents of the agreement talked of a dramatic choice between a distinctive Canadian identity or assimilation by the United States. In the words of the Liberal slogan: "It's more than an election; it's your future."

After the intense campaign, the election results were almost anticlimactic. A majority of the voters supported the two parties opposed to the free-trade agreement, but the Conservatives were returned to office with significant levels of support in all parts of the country. As emotions subsided, the election looked less like a turning point in Canadian history. Even on social and economic policies, the parties had not offered radically different choices. There would be free trade, but most of Canadian trade was already with the United States; increases in trade would be incremental. The future looked very much like the past.

What had Canadians been shouting about? The election had focused attention for a fleeting moment on the visceral sense of Canadian identity. In 1911, a Reciprocity Agreement with the United States for free trade in natural products had also provoked an emotional response. At that time, increased trade with the United States was seen by many as a threat to Canada's identity as a British dominion. In 1988, some voters saw the prospect of closer economic ties with the United States as a threat to an identity based on distinctive social and regional policies. The danger may have been exaggerated, but the concern showed what Canadians considered to be important.

FROM CANADIENS TO QUÉBÉCOIS

In the Paul Sauvé arena a delirious crowd sang "Gens du Pays" and waited for their leader. When a diminutive, balding man finally approached the microphone, the cheering audience drowned out the amplifiers. René Lévesque tried in vain to silence them, shrugged his shoulders, and waited with a look of benevolent resignation. It was now official. That day, November 15, 1976, the voters of Quebec had elected the Parti Québécois, a party committed to making Quebec a sovereign and independent country. When his followers finally quieted down, Lévesque attributed the victory to the pride of Quebeckers, to their determination to complete the work of the Quiet Revolution and to become truly *"maîtres chez nous."* It was the birth of a new country. A stunned Pierre Trudeau, watching events from Ottawa, offered a different explanation. The people of Quebec, he argued, had only elected a new provincial government. "I am confident," he said grimly, "that Quebeckers will continue to reject separatism because they still believe their destiny is linked with an indivisible Canada."

By 1976 nobody would have expected Lévesque and Trudeau to agree on the destiny of Quebec. They had been associates in the early years of the 1960s, sharing an intense dislike of the reactionary regime of Duplessis and the desire to bring French Canada into the twentieth century, but they had never agreed on how this was to be done. Lévesque was a democrat and a *nationaliste*, convinced that only French-Canadians could decide how French Canada should adapt to survive in the modern world. As a consequence, Quebec must have as much autonomy as it needed to make the necessary decisions. Trudeau, on the other hand, was a liberal with a deep respect for individual rights, one who mistrusted the arbitrary and discriminatory power of nationalism and saw federalism as a safer way to become a modern society. In the 1960s they had gone their separate ways, and by 1976 they had become bitter political opponents. And yet, each in his way was a spokesman for Quebec.

The election of 1976 was not decisive for Quebec. It was clearly a victory for Lévesque, but the war was far from over. For almost twenty years, French-Canadians had been debating their past and their future, and in those years there had been dramatic changes in the way French-Canadians saw themselves. There had been a revolution – the Quiet Revolution – in which people and institutions had been altered. But what did Quebec want? Neither Lévesque nor Trudeau nor anyone else could be sure. The only thing on which everyone could agree was that French-Canadians in 1976 no longer wanted what they had wanted twenty years before.

Quebec Nationalism

French-Canadians had long thought of themselves as a distinctive society. In the nineteenth century, they reached the consensus that they were essentially and fundamentally a Roman Catholic society. This distinguished them and set them apart from the rest of the continent, which they saw as Protestant and increasingly secular. Survival in this context meant reinforcing and strengthening their Catholic identity. Even the fact that they spoke French in a predominantly English-speaking country was of secondary importance. The language was useful because it was a barrier to heretical ideas – *la langue, gardienne de la foi* – and protected them from alien influences. In the 1860s, Bishop Laflèche had talked about the destiny of French Canada and of its sacred mission "to expand the Kingdom of God by developing a predominantly Catholic nationality." In the twentieth century, the Abbé Groulx had rewritten the history of French Canada as a stirring epic of martyrs and patriots carrying out the will of God. Religion gave this minority a sense of purpose and a justification for survival.

But it was not enough merely to want to survive as a Catholic society. There also had to be agreement on how this was to be achieved. French-Canadians, not surprisingly, looked to the clergy for leadership;

its authority was based on training in the faith and dedication to Catholicism. But survival was also associated with the rejection of the values and patterns of the rest of North America. In Quebec, according to Maria Chapdelaine, nothing would change and nothing should change. On a continent that was becoming urban and industrial, French-Canadians held to the folkways of a rural society. The ideal for the leaders of French Canada became the rural parish, where citizens could live simple Christian lives under the paternal guidance of the parish priest, far from the temptations of the godless, alien cities.

This ideal required the adaptation of social institutions. Education provides the most striking example. Nineteenth century English-speaking North America had developed a system of nondenominational, tax-supported public schools that reflected the values of a liberal and secular society. With different values, French Canada developed a much different system. Instead of one publicly supported system, it created two systems divided along religious lines, thus separating Roman Catholic from Protestant students. The Catholic schools were tax-supported, but they were not run by a department of education under a cabinet minister; instead a Catholic committee controlled by the Catholic bishops in the province set curriculum and standards. The Church was even more dominant at the secondary level. There were no French-Catholic high schools, only classical colleges that were religious institutions, often residential, offering eight years of liberal arts instruction based on Latin and Greek language and literature. Only a small minority attended these colleges. The graduates became an elite who dominated the liberal professions and became the leaders, clerical and lay, of French-Canadian society.

The system was well suited to the needs of rural, Catholic French Canada and its leaders. The curriculum was imbued with traditional values. The classical colleges reinforced the hierarchical social pattern by limiting the number of students beyond the elementary level; they did not offer the technical and vocational options appropriate to an industrial society that had found a place in the curricula of secondary schools elsewhere in North America.

None of this meant that Quebec had truly remained a rural province. There were major developments in pulp and paper and in mining, and Montreal became a major manufacturing centre. By 1921, half the population of the province lived in urban communities. However, it did mean that this industrial development was unique in one way. In Quebec the entrepreneurs and the managers were almost all English-speaking;

the unskilled workers were mainly French-Canadians drawn from the surplus rural population. The division between management and labour, a feature of all industrial societies, was more marked in Quebec because it was based on language as well as status.

Not all French-Canadian leaders were hostile to industrial growth. Most clerical leaders extolled the rural life and saw urban society as immoral and corrupt, but French-Canadian politicians regularly co-operated with English-Canadian entrepreneurs, offering privileges and concessions to attract capital investment and providing a number of technical and vocational institutes to train the labour force, a task that the traditional school system ignored. Maurice Duplessis, for example, was a French-Canadian *nationaliste* who co-operated with the Church and the rural elite, and his Union Nationale drew its political strength from the rural ridings. But Duplessis saw no contradiction between this and the encouragement of industrial development in Quebec. Revenues from the industrial sector would reduce taxes or improve government services in the rural areas. In northern Quebec, the exploitation of natural resources could even provide part-time jobs and encourage agricultural settlement. Industry, it was assumed, could exist in Quebec without endangering the values of rural French Canada.

However, this political system left the industrial workers with little protection. The traditional French-Canadian elites, committed to the survival of a rural society, showed little interest in the health or welfare of the urban proletariat. The provincial government under Duplessis was no better. Eager to attract new industries, Duplessis was unsympathetic to any labour demands that would increase costs. His Padlock Law of 1937 was used against labour "agitators" who tried to organize industrial workers, and postwar legislation restricted the right to strike and outlawed any unions with Communist officials. It was a striking anomaly of the system that in labour disputes a *nationaliste* government consist-ently sided with English-speaking industrialists against French-Canadian workers.

The Church authorities similarly showed little sympathy for these workers. The clergy continued to extol the virtues of rural life long after most French-Canadians lived in urban communities, and it encouraged opening up new farming communities long after most of the arable land in the province was occupied. Some priests did organize Catholic trade unions as a desirable alternative to international unions, but the objectives were more cultural than industrial. They were benevolent associations, guided by a chaplain, but were often little better than company unions when it came to negotiating contracts.

The focus on a Catholic society isolated from the rest of North America also shaped Quebec's place within the federal system. Provincial governments in Quebec advocated a federalism of watertight compartments in which the federal and provincial governments were autonomous.

There were crises in French-English relations when other provinces tried to assimilate their French-speaking minorities; Quebec protested any attempts to limit the religious or linguistic privileges of these minorities. There were also crises in both world wars over conscription, which French-Canadians interpreted as an attempt by the English-Canadian majority to force them to fight in British wars. But for most of the time, French-Canadians within the province of Quebec lived within the federal system with very little friction. The federal government did not interfere with Quebec's distinctive institutions and respected its cultural identity – by entrusting federal patronage in Quebec to French-Canadians, for example. Quebec, in turn, ordinarily allowed the federal government a free hand in its economic policies. Provincial autonomy was a policy of isolation.

The federal context changed after the Second World War. Wartime experience and the economic theories of John Maynard Keynes encouraged the federal government to play a more active role in planning the national economy. This expanded role included a federal monopoly of income taxes in exchange for larger federal subsidies to the provinces, massive federal projects such as the St. Lawrence Seaway, and a wide range of measures to improve industrial skills and to provide more social security. Almost all of the English-Canadian provinces broadly agreed with the federal objectives and even encouraged an expanded federal role. Maurice Duplessis, premier of Quebec from 1944 to 1959, had a different reaction. He saw the federal policies as a threat to the traditional way of life in Quebec and consistently opposed federal initiatives. The financial costs were not insignificant – Duplessis spurned lucrative tax agreements with Ottawa and prevented Quebec's universities from accepting federal grants – but he accepted the costs as part of the price of French-Canadian survival.

Prelude to the Quiet Revolution

In 1949 there was a strike in the asbestos mines in Quebec. It was not the first and it would not be the last. Technically it was an illegal strike because when negotiations broke down the workers set up picket lines instead of following provincial procedures and waiting for arbitration.

The companies involved appealed to the provincial government, and Duplessis responded by denouncing the strike and sending in his provincial police to break up the picket lines and arrest the strike leaders. The workers, nonetheless, held firm and stayed out for four months until a new contract was signed.

In the history of Quebec's industrial relations, the Asbestos Strike was no more violent and no more significant than many other strikes, but it has since been given a huge symbolic importance and has come to be seen as a turning point in the history of the province. It was noteworthy that one of the unions involved was a Catholic union and that this union was among the most militant in its defiance of its employer and of the provincial government. Even more unusual was the fact that leading clergymen, including Archbishop Charbonneau of Montreal, openly supported the strikers. *Le Devoir*, another pillar of French-Canadian nationalism, also gave its approval. French-Canadian university students joined the workers on the picket lines. Still, French Canada was far from unanimous. Duplessis and the provincial government had the support of many clerical and nationaliste leaders, who saw the strike as a challenge to all the established authorities. But to have *any* support for a strike seemed significant. It was interpreted as evidence that, slowly but surely, the social perspective of French-Canadians was changing.

It was also noteworthy that English-Canadians in Quebec were not divided. Their leaders and press strongly supported Duplessis and his repressive measures. In Quebec the English minority was clearly on the side of the industrialists.

The shifting attitudes within French Canada must be linked to important changes in the province during the postwar years. Quebec had become an urban, industrial province even before the war, but during and after the Second World War the shift from rural to urban accelerated. In two decades, from 1941 to 1961, the rural farm population dropped from one million to half a million. In the same period the urban population doubled; Montreal alone had a population of two million by 1960. But the changes were more than numerical, for in these years people not only migrated to the cities, but the cities, by way of radio and television, moved out to the smaller communities and eroded the traditional values held there. The leaders of French-Canadian society might deplore the changes, but they could not turn back the clock. French Canada had become an urban, industrial society. The Quiet Revolution of the 1960s was a consequence of the tardy recognition of this fact.

By the 1950s a growing number of social critics were responding to these social changes. They realized that rural French Canada, even if it could be preserved, would have no vitality; it would be no more than a quaint survival of a bygone age. The future lay with the world that French Canada had rejected for so long. A group of historians at the University of Montreal reflected this new perspective by their reinterpretation of the past.[1] French Canada, they argued, had no providential mission. New France had been a colony like other European colonies in North America, with a commercial base and a developing middle class. Under normal circumstances it would have developed much like the British colonies in North America, with a partnership of local politicians and businesspeople promoting local commerce and industry. But circumstances had not been normal. The colony had been conquered and British entrepreneurs had replaced the French-speaking middle class. French-Canadians were left in control of only the rural communities and the Roman Catholic Church. According to the Montreal historians, this accounted for the myth that French-Canadians were an agricultural people with a religious mission and for their rejection of the modern world. "It must never be forgotten," wrote Michel Brunet, one of these historians, "that the fundamental weakness of French-Canadian thought stems from the inability or the refusal to understand the real meaning of the Conquest of 1760."

Brunet's was a pessimistic view of the past. He and his colleagues offered an explanation for French Canada's economic inferiority but held out no hope for the future. The Conquest could not be undone, and French Canada seemed fated to remain a backward society. However, some younger critics found this pessimism unacceptable. They shared the historian's view that a modern society required a strong industrial base and that the ideal of a rural Catholic society was absurd. But they refused to believe that French Canada's future had been determined forever on the Plains of Abraham. They believed that, given the opportunity, French-Canadians could compete successfully in the modern world and could provide the economic basis for social and cultural development.

---

[1] The viewpoint of the Montreal school is most readily accessible in two Canadian Historical Association pamphlets: Guy Frégault, *Canadian Society in the French Regime*, and Michel Brunet, *French Canada and the Early Days of British Rule 1760-1791*. Ramsay Cook, "La Survivance French Canadian Style," in *The Maple Leaf Forever* (Toronto, 1971), is a brief essay on French-Canadian historiography. The articles in this collection and in Cook's earlier *French Canada and the Canadian Question* (Toronto, 1966) provide an essential historical context for French Canada and French-English relations in the 1960s.

One group of critics was associated with Pierre Trudeau, a wealthy young law professor and intellectual with a talent for debate, self-contained, reputed to be something of a dilettante, but deeply committed to individual freedom.[2] Trudeau and Gérard Pelletier, a journalist who had been active in the Catholic youth movement, founded a journal, *Cité Libre*, in 1950. *Cité Libre* expressed a liberal point of view, with an emphasis on individual rights and democratic procedures. It assumed that political power and cultural development depended on economic power and that this in turn depended on exploiting technology in a world increasingly subject to automation, computers, and nuclear energy. *Cité Libre* was harshly critical of the traditional French-Canadian elites who had turned their backs on the modern world. Its most scathing criticisms were directed against the paternalistic and authoritarian attitudes of these elites and their insistence on conformity. The Asbestos Strike was seen as proof that French-Canadian workers could act responsibly and effectively, and social reforms would follow if these workers gained more political power. A liberal and democratic regime, responsive to the urban voters, would encourage and train French-Canadians to compete within the industrial system and eventually to share in the direction of the industrial economy. The workers were seen as the key to the modernization of French Canada.

Cité Libre saw no need for constitutional reform. Trudeau argued that the federal system was the best guarantee of a liberal regime because it diffused political power. But it was also the essence of Canadian federalism that each province should be responsible for its own social policies. *Cité Libre* insisted that a more centralized federal system was not a short-cut to reform. Thus, Trudeau approved of more money for universities but he opposed federal grants to universities; education was a provincial responsibility and it was up to the voters of Quebec to persuade the provincial government to provide the funds. At the same time he opposed separatism for Quebec; the provincial government already had all the powers it needed to introduce social reform, and nationalist passions seemed to him more likely to bring despotism than liberty. However, in the 1950s the main target for *Cité Libre* was the

---

[2] The best biographies of Trudeau are George Radwanski, *Trudeau* (Toronto, 1978) and Richard Gwyn, *The Northern Magus* (Toronto, 1980). Trudeau's own view of the traditional ideology can be found in his long introduction to P.E. Trudeau, ed., *The Asbestos Strike* (Toronto, 1974). Some of his comments on French Canada in the 1950s and 1960s are available in P.E. Trudeau, *Federalism and the French Canadians* (Toronto, 1968).

Duplessis regime, which was both reactionary and corrupt. The first step toward social reform in Quebec was a democratic government, and this meant defeating Duplessis.

Others were equally critical of the traditional view of French Canada and equally committed to French-Canadian participation in the modern industrial world, but they were less willing to trust a federal system in which French-Canadians were a minority. They feared that competing within a Canadian economy would mean adopting English-Canadian patterns and that success could mean assimilation. It was not enough to exercise economic power in a modern, industrial society; that society must be distinctively French-Canadian. For these critics the provincial government was of crucial importance because it could be the agent of economic planning and because it was the only government that French-Canadians controlled. Few of these *nationaliste* critics were separatists in the 1950s, but, like André Laurendeau, editor of *Le Devoir*, they defended provincial autonomy.

These neo-nationalists were ambivalent about Duplessis. They shared his concern for provincial rights and his suspicions of any extension of federal authority. At the same time they deplored his co-operation with English-speaking businesspeople at the expense of French-Canadian workers. For them the Asbestos Strike was significant not only because the workers had united against their employers but also because the workers were French and the employers were English. By the mid-1950s, *Le Devoir* had ended its ambivalence and decided that provincial autonomy was no longer enough. Laurendeau compared Duplessis to the "negro-king," the figurehead allowed by the British to govern a colony despotically so long as he protected British property and British economic interests. *Le Devoir* became a leading advocate of an interventionist provincial government, one that would use its autonomy to enhance the economic power of French-Canadians.[3]

The municipal government of Montreal became yet another focus of opposition to Duplessis in the 1950s. Camilien Houde had been mayor in the early postwar years, kept in office by his popularity in the working-class districts of the city and by his willingness to co-operate with business interests and the provincial government in keeping down

---

[3] Philip Stratford, ed., *André Laurendeau: Witness for Quebec* (Toronto, 1973) is a collection of Laurendeau's writings, including some editorials from *Le Devoir*. See also Ramsay Cook and M. Behiels, eds., *The Essential Laurendeau* (Toronto, 1976). See Michael Behiels, *Prelude to Quebec's Quiet Revolution* (Montreal, 1985).

the costs of municipal administration. A combination of civic reformers who wanted improved services, especially in transportation, and moral reformers who wanted to eliminate prostitution and gambling elected Jean Drapeau in 1954. Drapeau's demands for greater autonomy for Montreal were frustrated by Duplessis, and soon Drapeau was numbered among the critics of the provincial regime.

The French-Canadian clergy did not play a decisive role in this criticism of the old regime. For almost the first time, some priests, disturbed by the poverty and alienation of the urban proletariat, wanted the Church to identify itself with the cause of the workers and to fight for their economic as well as their spiritual needs. Archbishop Charbonneau forcefully expressed these sentiments. "The working class is the victim of a conspiracy . . . ," he declared, "and it is the duty of the Church to intervene." Other bishops were more conservative. They deplored the insidious materialism of the modern world and preached the need to return to the Christian virtues of humility and submission. Rome, for reasons that are still a matter of controversy, removed Charbonneau from office, but his successor, Cardinal Léger, eventually became identified with the reform wing within the Church. Individual priests also contributed to the attacks on the regime – two of them denounced political corruption in the province, and a teaching brother, in a bestseller called *The Impertinences of Brother Anonymous*, described with bitter wit the fearfulness of a people who hid behind authority rather than thinking for themselves – but these priests spoke as individuals. The Church as an institution was divided and uncertain. This in itself was significant. The Church was not in the vanguard of reform but neither did it lead a rearguard action against change.

The evolution that occurred in the Catholic trade unions illustrates the declining role of the Church. These unions had been organized and supervised by priests who were reacting to the secular materialism of international unions, but by the 1950s laypeople had taken over union leadership and their objectives had become more worldly. The emergence of lay leadership coincided with an increasing militancy in both industrial and political disputes. In the years after the Asbestos Strike, the Catholic unions played a prominent part in the organized opposition to the provincial labour policies and became a significant element in the anti-Duplessis coalition.

By the end of the decade, the Liberal party had united most of the dissident elements within the province. Jean Lesage, who left a successful career in federal politics to become provincial leader in 1958,

Liberal Jean Lesage instituted Quebec's "Quiet Revolution" with his 1960 election victory. The beaming premier greets federal Liberal leader L.B. Pearson in 1962, while Mrs. Lesage looks on.

PA-113500/NATIONAL ARCHIVES OF CANADA.

managed to retain the support of the moderates while winning the confidence of those committed to change. This might not have been enough to unseat the entrenched Union Nationale government, but in 1959 Maurice Duplessis died, and six months later his successor died. Even under these circumstances the reformed Liberal Party did not win an overwhelming majority in the provincial election of 1960. Only a bare majority of Quebeckers had voted for what would become known as the Quiet Revolution, and Lesage held only 50 of the 95 seats in the legislature.

La Revolution Tranquille

The election of Lesage was much more than a change of governments. In politics it meant a shift from a defensive nationalism to an active government committed to change. However, the revolution in government was only part of the story. Almost every part of Quebec's society was affected. A pattern was quickly established of criticizing existing institutions and customs, of rejecting the past and identifying change with progress. For many French-Canadians it was an intoxicating experience. There was a sense of liberation, of being freed from suffocating traditions and of suddenly living in a society where there were no limits, where innovation was welcomed and talent would be rewarded. In an era of rising expectations, French-Canadians were doubly optimistic. For a few exhilarating years it was possible for them to believe that they could shape their own destiny.

The rejection of the past included a sharp turning away from religious faith and from clerical leadership. Church attendance dropped precipitously. Young people showed little interest in taking religious vows, and an increasing number of priests and nuns left their orders. At the same time, responsibility for education, welfare, and health shifted from the Church to the state. French Canada, which had once seen itself as essentially Catholic, was becoming a secular society.

The reforms in education were the most striking as well as the most controversial examples of this transformation. It had long been obvious that the system of elementary schools and classical colleges was inadequate for an industrial society. A bewildering number of separate technical and vocational institutions had appeared to supplement the public schools, and new colleges had been founded and the curricula adapted in response to social pressures. But in the changed mood of the 1960s it was no longer enough to adapt the established system. Instead, the old institutions were discarded and a new system was erected in their place.

The Lesage government began by appointing a royal commission to study the problem. For the next five years the Parent Commission was never far from the headlines. The public debate began with the commission's hearings, continued with the release of its report in five volumes between 1963 and 1966, and then focused on the legislation that followed. Emotions ran high and sometimes obscured the issues, but the public concern was justified. French-Canadians were debating what kind of education was most appropriate for the modern world.

The first volume of the report dealt with the thorny question of the roles of church and state. The commission advocated an integrated educational system, planned and co-ordinated to meet the diverse needs of a complex society, and it concluded that only the provincial government could administer such a system. The commission accepted the existing pattern of separate Catholic and Protestant school systems, but it recommended that ultimate control of both be given to a ministry of education. To devout Catholics the commission promised that this did not mean secular schools. So long as French-Canadians remained Catholic, their government would reflect their religious beliefs. The government promptly introduced a bill based on these recommendations.

The measure was bitterly debated. The representatives for the traditional point of view – and there were still many – denounced government control as the first step toward eliminating religion entirely. They were not satisfied with the Church's control over the teaching of religion as a subject; if the schools were to be Catholic, there must be some assurance that the other subjects and the teachers who taught them would reflect their religious character. This opposition forced the government to withdraw the bill and to negotiate a compromise with the Roman Catholic bishops. The revised bill muted the criticisms by establishing an advisory committee on religious matters, but the government nonetheless remained the final authority. Control of education in Quebec had shifted from church to state.

The subsequent recommendations of the commission led to a radically restructured educational system. It argued that "modern man no longer lives in the same universe as his ancestors," and concluded that Quebec needed a system that would train young people for a world transformed by science and technology. Education was to be democratic, in the sense that all children should acquire some essential skills and should then have the opportunity to develop their individual talents. The major change was at the secondary level, where the classical colleges were replaced by five-year secondary school and two-year colleges offering technical and vocational as well as academic programs.

Naturally enough, such sweeping changes threw the educational system into chaos. By the end of the decade enrolment at the secondary level had increased by almost half a million students, and there were almost 40 000 students attending the two-year colleges. The young found themselves in new institutions without established traditions, still in the process of defining goals and procedures. They faced teachers who were either novices or who had been trained for traditional institutions. It did not help that in Quebec, as elsewhere, the 1960s was also a decade when students and faculty were resentful of any authority. The immediate results were predictable. Classes were held in schools still under construction, programs were constantly being revised, and students and faculty were frequently on strike. Social change can be disruptive, but more important in the long run was the fact that the aims and structures of education were reformed.

Another area of controversy was hydro-electricity. René Lévesque, Lesage's minister of natural resources, was the key figure in this debate. Lévesque, an intense chain-smoker with an extraordinary talent for simplifying complex ideas, had come to politics after a brilliant career as a television journalist with his own program on current events.[4] He was a *nationaliste*, convinced that the provincial government was the instrument through which French-Canadians could direct and control their economic future. Electricity in Quebec had initially been generated and distributed by private power companies, and although the provincial government had taken over the Montreal Light, Heat and Power Company during the war, most of the power was still generated by foreign-owned private companies. Lévesque, who wanted the government to plan and direct industrial growth, saw the need for more electricity to power industrial growth. His solution was to expropriate the private power companies and to give Hydro-Québec a monopoly and allow it to develop new water power sites. He persuaded a reluctant Lesage to agree to the takeovers and to fight a provincial election on the issue with the nationaliste slogan of *"maîtres chez nous."* The Liberals won the provincial election of 1962 with an increased majority.

Hydro-Québec quickly became one of the success stories of the Quiet Revolution. This provincial power company, after taking over the private power companies in the province, undertook power installations to produce some five million kilowatts on the Manicouagan River. The significance of Manicouagan was, in part, that it was a French-language enterprise. The private power corporations had operated in English, and it was widely assumed that English was the only possible language for major engineering projects in North America. However, with Hydro-Québec, the language of work became French, and the construction on the Manicouagan was planned and carried out in French by French-Canadian engineers and managers. The experience contributed greatly to French-Canadian self-confidence.

Not all of the government's projects were as successful. The Société Générale de Financement (S.G.F.) was a provincial agency set up to

---

[4] Peter Desbarats, *René: A Canadian in Search of a Country* (Toronto, 1976) is an informative biography. Lévesque's *Opinion Quebec* (Toronto, 1969) is a useful statement of his views at the time of the founding of the Parti Québécois. Graham Fraser, *P.Q.: René Lévesque and the Parti Québécois in Power* (Toronto, 1984) is an excellent study of the events and personalities associated with Lévesque's career.

encourage French-Canadian entrepreneurs by providing capital for industrial and commercial enterprises. An even more ambitious project was the establishment of a steel mill. Sidérurgie Québec (Sidbec) produced steel from the iron ore of Labrador; it was also a status symbol because heavy industry was considered the hallmark of an industrial nation. Both S.G.F. and Sidbec were high-risk enterprises undertaken by a government eager to foster French-Canadian industry; both projects lost money.

Reaction in Quebec to the provincial government's initiatives was varied. There was a new-found assurance, especially among the middle-class youth, better educated than their parents, with confidence in technology and the social sciences, and eager to apply the new skills of computing and management. They were the privileged beneficiaries of the Quiet Revolution. As technocrats, they replaced clerical administrators in education, welfare, and health services. Even more encouraging, if French Canada was to win its proportionate share of economic power, they were the French-Canadians who would succeed to the management posts in Hydro-Québec, in the bureaucracy, and in industry, which until now had been a virtual monopoly of English-Canadians. For ambitious young French-Canadians, the Quiet Revolution was the road to power.

Others were ambivalent. Most French-Canadians probably shared the satisfaction of belonging to a society that no longer thought of itself as an insecure minority and that was affirming its place in the modern world. But for some, the Quiet Revolution was disruptive in a negative sense. The questioning of tradition and the challenge to authority was unsettling, especially to those for whom religious and social institutions brought order and meaning to life. In the areas outside of Montreal there was a growing resistance to change.

Some French-Canadian workers had a different reaction. The Liberals in Opposition had championed the rights of labour and, once in office, had encouraged the growth of trade unions. Much of the growth came in the public sector, with unions for public servants, hospital employees, and teachers. A reluctant Lesage was even persuaded to concede the right to strike to public servants. However, by the mid-1960s, the trade union leaders were losing confidence in the Quiet Revolution. The technocrats might be prospering, but workers were finding that it was almost as difficult to bargain with the Quebec government as it had been with English-language corporations in the private sector.[5] A number of

---

[5] Pierre Fournier, *The Québec Establishment* (Montreal, 1976) is a class interpretation of the links between business and government in Quebec.

strikes in the public sector were ended by back-to-work legislation, and it became clear that the Quiet Revolution did not mean power to the workers.

But much of the publicity relating to the Quiet Revolution focused on the clashes between Quebec and Ottawa. Disputes between the two levels of government were inevitable. Duplessis had resisted the encroachments of the federal government, but under Lesage it was no longer a matter of resisting federal intervention. It was no longer enough to defend provincial autonomy – the provincial government was now required to take the initiative in economic and social matters. Quebec City needed increased revenues to achieve its aims, and Lesage peremptorily demanded a larger share of income taxes and succession duties to finance his projects. To this point Lesage could count on the support of other provinces that also wanted more money from Ottawa.

But Lesage could not stop there. His government represented Quebec, but it also considered itself the representative for some four million French-Canadians, and the survival of French Canada was still the ultimate objective. The rules and regulations of the industrial milieu would have to be consistent with and should even reinforce French Canada's distinctive cultural identity. With its English-speaking majority, Ottawa could not be expected to discriminate in favour of the French-speaking minority or even to understand its needs. Quebec, therefore, was not a province like the others. Its provincial government had a special obligation to preserve the cultural identity of its French-Canadian citizens. It must have jurisdiction over all matters that touched on their cultural identity.

Lesage favoured opting out as a solution. Quebec would not participate in national programs that had cultural implications but would receive equivalent funds in the form of federal grants and so be able to finance similar programs of its own design. However, federalist critics argued that in the long run opting out would weaken the federal union. Fewer and fewer federal programs would operate in Quebec, and the provincial government would have a virtual monopoly of the legislation for the province.

Proposed pension legislation led to a major confrontation in 1964. The Liberal government under L.B. Pearson had proposed a contributory pension plan. Quebec had objected to this federal initiative in a provincial field and had devised a pension plan of its own, one that had the advantage of quickly accumulating a large reserve fund upon which the provincial government could draw for other purposes. Given

Lesage's constant need for revenue, this was a most attractive aspect of provincial control. On the other hand, Ottawa was committed to a national scheme that allowed workers to move from one province to another without losing their pension rights. Both Pearson and Lesage wanted to avoid an open breach, and at the last minute Ottawa proposed a funded pension plan that gave all provincial governments the right to draw on the funds. Quebec insisted on administering its own pension fund, but agreed to introduce a plan that would be compatible with the federal plan and so permit labour mobility.

The participants on both sides believed that the compromise had saved the federal union, and there certainly had been significant concessions on both sides. However, the pension plans did not provide a blueprint for future disagreements. The federal government might not want to adapt another program to suit Quebec, and the Quebec government might not always be willing to restrict its autonomy by conforming to a national plan. It was still by no means clear how a dynamic Quebec could be accommodated within a federal constitution.[6]

The War Between Ottawa and Quebec

The Quiet Revolution had lost its impetus by the mid-1960s. The exhilaration of a new beginning was tempered by experience. Reformers who had made common cause against Duplessis now found it less easy to agree on positive measures. French Canada, which for so long had been a cohesive minority, obedient to its leaders, was now a pluralist society, divided into groups and factions, each with its own aims and ambitions. For the next ten years the changes of the early 1960s were consolidated, but there was no consensus on further reforms. There were still debates and confrontations, but now the focus shifted. Differences over the nature of French-Canadian society were muted by a growing emphasis on the status of that society within the federal union. Decisions over what kind of society it should be were put aside until the relations between French and English Canada were more clearly defined.

---

[6] The best account of federal-provincial relations from 1963 to 1971 is Richard Simeon, *Federal-Provincial Diplomacy* (Toronto, 1972). Claude Morin, *Quebec versus Ottawa: The Struggle for Self-Government 1960-72* (Toronto, 1976), is the personal interpretation of an active participant.

English-Canadians outside of Quebec had already been drawn into the debate. English-Canadian commentators and academics had expressed sympathy for the critics of Duplessis and for the shift from a clerical to a more secular society. But the Diefenbaker government showed little awareness of French Canada. The Liberal government of L.B. Pearson, however, was more sensitive. In 1963 Pearson appointed a Royal Commission on Bilingualism and Biculturalism – the Laurendeau-Dunton Commission, after the co-chairmen – to advise on how the federal system could accommodate "an equal partnership between two founding races."

The commission offered only a partial answer. It made recommendations on behalf of the French-Canadian minorities outside of Quebec, and its main thrust was for a federal public service that would reflect the cultural duality implicit in an equal partnership. These were complex and controversial problems, but increased services for French-Canadians did not involve a direct reduction of services for the majority. A thornier problem was the redistribution of legislative powers between Ottawa and Quebec to reflect the more active role of the provincial government. Giving to Quebec meant taking away from Ottawa. In the end, the commission never did present its views on constitutional reform.

The commission ended abruptly because Pierre Trudeau succeeded Pearson as prime minister in 1968, and Trudeau already had firm opinions on the Constitution. Along with Gérard Pelletier and Jean Marchand, a prominent trade union leader, Trudeau had joined the federal Liberal Party in 1965 in reaction to the growing nationalism in Quebec. He was convinced that this nationalism would create an isolated Quebec, which would be as conformist and as intolerant as it was under Duplessis. His alternative was a federalism that provided equal opportunity regardless of individual differences of language and culture. Trudeau, therefore, favoured a constitution that guaranteed linguistic and educational rights for French- and English-Canadians in all parts of Canada. His emphasis was on individual rights and not on minority rights, and as a consequence he was opposed to any special constitutional status for the province of Quebec. This was a popular view in English Canada, where the continuing demands of Quebec for greater autonomy were widely seen as a threat to national unity. The extraordinary Trudeaumania in the federal election of 1968 was largely a response to his personal style, but it was far from irrelevant to English-Canadians that Trudeau seemed prepared to end the concessions to Quebec, or, as some saw it, to put Quebec in its place.

Separatist sentiment had deep roots in Quebec, even before René Lévesque galvanized the movement and led it to power. Here supporters of the Rassemblement pour l'independance nationale demonstrate.   C-5306/NATIONAL ARCHIVES OF CANADA.

Meanwhile, the political situation in the province was becoming more confused. Lesage had always been a cautious reformer, ready to do what was necessary to keep his party united but not entirely sure where the Quiet Revolution was taking him. The initiatives had come from *nationalistes* within his government – René Lévesque, for example, was convinced that the "powers of the nation-state that is Quebec must become as broad and autonomous as the federal system can stand." When provincial ministers could not persuade their more conservative colleagues in cabinet, they regularly discussed the issues in public and appealed for public support. Lesage's government soon gave the impression of being divided and irresolute.

The Union Nationale was also ambivalent. Daniel Johnson, party leader after 1961, had been associated with the Duplessis regime, but as leader of the Opposition he sought support where he could find it. He showed concern for those who found the Quiet Revolution disruptive, but at the same time he spoke for the *nationalistes* by criticizing Lesage for not being more forceful in his negotiations with Ottawa. He put more emphasis on provincial status than on social change, and his

slogan – "Equality or independence; a new constitution or separation" – deliberately failed to define the kind of society he envisaged.

The shift toward nationalism was also illustrated by the founding of
two separatist parties before the provincial election of 1966. The
Ralliement national looked to a state in Quebec that would return the
province to its traditional values; the Rassemblement pour l'indépen-
dance nationale, at the other extreme, advocated a socialist state.

The election was an unexpected victory for the Union Nationale. The
Liberals received a larger popular vote than Johnson's party, but much of
their support came from Montreal, which was under-represented in the
legislature. Only 9 percent of the popular vote went to separatist
candidates, but the results suggested that Quebec voters were as
undecided about their future as their political leaders.

Johnson and his successor, Jean-Jacques Bertrand, tried to ride the
whirlwind. The costs of the educational reforms and the economic
initiatives of the Liberal government meant heavy deficits despite
increased taxes. Demands for more generous terms from the federal
government fell on deaf ears; the federal government had deficits of its
own to worry about, and, after 1968, with Trudeau in power, it was
hostile to any suggestion of special status for Quebec. The Johnson and
Bertrand governments did not initiate any new major programs and
blamed the federal government for their own inactivity. The excitement
and the optimism of the Quiet Revolution were gone.

One sign of the change was the emergence of the new term *les
Québécois*. Until the 1960s French-Canadians in Quebec had called
themselves les Canadiens, implicitly including French-speaking minorities outside Quebec in the same category. But the attitude toward these
minorities changed with the Quiet Revolution. The French-Canadians in
Quebec increasingly thought of themselves as citizens of the province,
with the provincial government as their government. The distinction was
even more marked because French-Canadians outside Quebec looked to
the federal government for support and showed no interest in champion-
ing provincial rights. The new provincial perspective required a new
vocabulary, and within a remarkably short time les Québécois was in
general use, and les Canadiens had almost disappeared.

For les Québécois the problem of survival once again became a
pressing concern. The danger was two-fold. French-Canadians had long
had the highest birth rate in Canada. This birth rate had dropped slowly
after the Second World War, but suddenly, in the 1960s, it plummeted
until, by the end of the decade, it was the lowest in Canada. The postwar

period had also been one of massive immigration to Canada, with many of the immigrants settling in Montreal. The majority of these immigrants, with an eye for economic opportunity, sent their children to English-language schools. The combined effect of the low birth rate and high immigration threatened to produce an English-speaking majority in Montreal by the end of the century.[7] It did not matter that the danger was greatly exaggerated. For a group that now associated its survival with a greater role in industry and commerce, even the possibility of becoming a minority in Montreal was frightening. There was little inclination to return to large families, so the only solution was to make the newcomers join the French-speaking community.

The issue flared up in St. Léonard, a district in Montreal with a high proportion of Italian immigrants. The Catholic school board, at the request of the Italian parents, had provided bilingual schools with both English and French as the languages of instruction. Militant Québécois *nationalistes* objected to this compromise and demanded unilingual French-language schools. Disturbed by the increasing nationalism, Montreal's English-Canadians denounced this as an infringement on the right of parents to choose between English- or French-language schools. The provincial government attempted to defuse the issue in 1969 by reaffirming freedom of choice but, at the same time, undertaking to improve the teaching of French as a second-language in the English-language schools. The *nationalistes* rejected the compromise. They could not feel secure until the law gave French a privileged status.

A few young French-Canadians were not prepared to wait. To them the language issue was part of the broader issue of economic imperialism. They saw Quebec as a colony, still controlled by English-speaking capitalists, and they believed that cultural inferiority was the inevitable consequence of this economic servitude. In many parts of the world, the end of the decade was marked by student demonstrations and violence; in Quebec some young radicals saw violence as a necessary part of the crusade for Quebec's liberation. They organized demonstrations, supported strikers, and exploded bombs in federal armouries and Westmount mailboxes. The authorities, especially in Montreal, were deeply disturbed. They exaggerated the number of terrorists, but there was some justification for their concern because of the number of young

---

[7] Richard Joy, *Languages in Conflict* (Toronto, 1972), is a clear account of demographic developments, although it does not go beyond the 1961 census data. See also the many volumes published by the Royal Commission on Bilingualism and Biculturalism.

people who vociferously expressed approval of the resort to violence.

Quebec's nationalism found wider expression in the arts. The decade of the 1960s was remarkable for the outpouring of songs, poems, plays, and films, and even more remarkable for the popularity of the artists. This cultural explosion was an aspect of the Quiet Revolution, linked in some way with the release from conformity and the sense of shaping a new society. The songs of Gilles Vigneault and the plays of Michel Tremblay gave common experiences and popular language a cultural significance and became a celebration of the distinctive identity of les Québécois. From there it was but a short step to politics, and most of these artists were open advocates of independence for Quebec.[8]

The October Crisis and After

The political situation changed significantly with the provincial election of 1970. The Union Nationale, with its balancing act in constitutional and domestic affairs, was crushingly defeated. The Liberal Party, under Robert Bourassa, a young economist, offered a different choice. It attempted to divert attention from controversies over language and culture by stressing economic goals, and Bourassa promised to make federalism profitable. The alternative to the Liberal Party was now the Parti Québécois, a party that united a number of separatist groups under the leadership of René Lévesque. The new party included a wide range of conservative and radical *nationalistes*, but Lévesque, who had been frustrated by the constraints of the federal system, gave the new party an instant credibility. The Liberals won the election, but the Parti Québécois received almost a quarter of the popular vote. Quebec's electorate was becoming polarized.

The newly elected government was quite unprepared for the October Crisis of 1970. In that month terrorists kidnapped James Cross, a British trade commissioner, and then Pierre Laporte, the minister of labour in the Bourassa government. Bourassa had no sympathy for the kidnappers, for his "profitable federalism" depended on foreign investment that, in turn, depended on social stability. But Bourassa did not want to defy the moderate *nationalistes*, who seemed prepared to negotiate with the

---

[8] Malcom Reid, *The Shouting Signpainters* (Toronto, 1972) is an essay on the links between French-Canadian literature and nationalism in the 1960s. Also helpful is F. Dumont et al., *Idéologies au Canada Français 1940-1976* (Quebec, 1981) in three volumes.

terrorists. His hesitation was interpreted as weakness, and there was talk of a coalition to resolve the crisis. Bourassa's reputation as a leader was further eroded when federal authorities under Trudeau invoked the War Measures Act and took charge. Subsequently, when many French-Canadians concluded that the federal government had over-reacted, Bourassa was criticized for his collaboration with Ottawa. It was a difficult initiation for a government that had hoped to divert attention from divisive constitutional questions by concentrating on economic issues.[9]

The Québécois response to a constitutional accord in 1971 confirmed the wisdom of avoiding constitutional controversies. Trudeau and the provincial premiers, meeting in Victoria, British Columbia, proposed a constitution that would extend French language rights in the eastern provinces and concede a wider provincial authority in social legislation. The amendment procedure would give a veto to Quebec, as well as to Ontario and to a majority of the Atlantic and western provinces. After initially accepting the Victoria Charter, Bourassa soon discovered that many in his province objected vehemently to an agreement that might inhibit further extension of Quebec's autonomy in the future, and he soon refused to ratify the proposal. As a result, constitutional change was stalled for more than a decade.

Bourassa's major undertaking was the development of hydro-electric power in the James Bay region. It was a massive project, with three rivers to be diverted, installations to a total of 10 000 MW, and 1000 km of high-voltage transmission lines to bring this power to southern Quebec. Critics objected to the estimated cost of $15 billion, although ten years later, when the first turbines turned, the high cost of oil helped mightily to justify the project. In the meantime, the enterprise did mean investment and construction jobs.

The emphasis on economics did not prevent a confrontation with trade union leaders. By the 1970s prominent trade union leaders had lost confidence in governments, whatever their political colouration, and had concluded that the capitalist system was to blame for their problems. In 1972 the Confederation of National Trade Unions, an association of the

---

[9] Gérard Pelletier, *The October Crisis* (Toronto, 1971) presents the federal position; Denis Smith, *Bleeding Hearts . . . Bleeding Country* (Edmonton, 1971) is a criticism of federal policy. Other titles include Ron Haggart and A. Golden, *Rumours of War* (Toronto, 1971); Pierre Vallières, *The Assassination of Pierre Laporte* (Toronto, 1977); and M. Bellavance et Marcel Gilbert, *L'opinion publique et la crise d'octobre* (Montréal, 1971).

former Catholic unions, together with the Quebec Federation of Labour, representing the international unions, and the Quebec Teachers Corporation formed a common front in their negotiations on behalf of government employees. A massive strike, including hospital workers and teachers as well as public servants, provoked yet another law ordering the strikers back to work. This time both sides were intransigent. The presidents of the three labour federations, using references to the class struggle and to colonialism, advised the workers to ignore the law. They were arrested, convicted, and jailed. The government won that battle, but it lost some friends.

To take advantage of the popular reaction against labour disruptions and radicalism Bourassa called a snap election in 1973. The Liberals painted a frightening picture of the dire economic consequences of a separatist victory, graphically symbolized by the departure of a fleet of armoured cars on the eve of the election, supposedly carrying the contents of safety-deposit boxes to the security of Ontario. The polarization of the electorate was more marked than before. The Liberals won a

REPRINTED WITH PERMISSION – THE TOR-
ONTO STAR SYNDICATE.

majority of the votes and a vast majority of the seats, but the Parti Québécois vote rose to 30 percent.

The emphasis of the Bourassa government on economic growth could not suppress the language controversy for long. In 1974 Bourassa tried to resolve the issue by legislation to encourage the use of French as the language of work and to restrict admission to English schools to those children able to show proficiency in English. Bill 22 was intended to reassure the nationalistes without worrying the federalists, but it was a failure on both counts. As the consequence of a decade of agitation, both French- and English-Canadians were suspicious of a law whose impact depended upon how it was administered. The controversy over Bill 22 continued until the next provincial election.

The economic policies of the government were also criticized after 1973. Rapidly rising oil prices contributed to a higher cost of living and to unemployment. The James Bay development continued, but there was disturbing evidence of corruption and excessive costs. In an effort to avoid disruptive strikes, the government had given a monopoly to some construction unions that had then taken advantage of their position. Rivalries between unions and factions within unions had led to sabotage and violence, and public hearings on these events discredited both the government and the unions.

A dispute over air traffic control in the summer of 1976 raised the language issue in a new form and to new heights. Communications between pilots and their controllers had been in English, but there were now more French-speaking pilots, and they found it easier to communicate in French, especially at some of the smaller airports in Quebec. English-speaking traffic controllers protested that the use of French was a safety hazard, but Quebeckers were outraged by opposition to French-speaking pilots communicating with French-speaking controllers in their own language in their own province. They were more incensed still when the federal government yielded to massive English-Canadian pressure and appointed a commission to study the question. Three years later the commission would approve the use of French, and the government would establish bilingual air traffic control, but for the moment the entire province of Quebec only saw that the use of French was being restricted.

The Parti Québécois took full advantage of the situation. It tried to broaden its appeal by promising honest and efficient administration, a clear contrast to the corruption and favouritism of the Liberals. It tried to defuse the constitutional issue by denying that a vote for the party was necessarily a vote for independence, and Lévesque promised, if elected, to hold a referendum on the issue. He would negotiate sovereignty-association (a common-market arrangement with Canada) only after a majority of Quebeckers had voted for it. It was a concession that the militants within the party accepted only because of Lévesque's prestige – and the possibility of gaining office. On November 15, 1976, the Parti Québécois did win the election. Its share of the popular vote rose to 41 percent, while the Liberal vote dropped to 34 percent. Federalists could argue that it was not a vote for independence. Lévesque, on the other hand, could promise that "we will have the Quebec of which our ancestors dreamed." Whatever else the election results were, they were not a vote for the existing union.

P.Q. in Power

By this time, the French language had unquestionably replaced the Catholic religion as the essence of French-Canadian identity, and survival had become directly linked to the preservation of French. The two previous administrations had tried to reassure les Québécois, but their legislation had not allayed their fears. The first measure introduced by the new government attempted to resolve the language issue once and for all. Bill 101 declared French to be the official language of Quebec; it was to be the language of the courts, of government, and of business in the province, and English-language firms were given a limited time to give priority to French. The educational changes were also drastic. All children would attend French-language schools except the children of English-speaking parents who had themselves been educated in Quebec. The Liberal Opposition wanted the exemption extended to children of English-speaking parents educated elsewhere in Canada but, significantly, no party in Quebec argued on behalf of the children of immigrants to Canada. For those children, French schools would be obligatory: the survival of French Canada seemed to depend on forcing foreign newcomers to become French-speaking. Even Lévesque expressed regret for this illiberal policy. "There is an unhealthy aspect to it," he conceded with the frankness that was his most attractive characteristic, "but what the hell can we do – just go down the drain?"

The threat to survival may have been exaggerated. The Québécois birth rate, which had dropped so dramatically, levelled off at a rate close to that of Ontario, and immigration, which had threatened to flood

Montreal, declined sharply from the peak of the 1950s as the economy slowed. Bill 101 also coincided with a shift of corporate head offices from Montreal to Toronto and even to Calgary, a westward migration that was a North American phenomenon. The legislation accelerated or even precipitated the shift in some cases since the working language of most head offices was English. Whatever the reason, there was a net decline of English-Canadians in the province over the decade. Quebec was becoming more French, and, economically, Montreal was becoming more and more a provincial city with the entire province as its hinterland. However, psychologically, Bill 101 did give the assurance that French was to be the dominant language. In that sense the legislation was effective.

The long-term effects of Bill 101 may be more complex. French-language schools in the past had been culturally homogeneous and had played a major role in strengthening the sense of cultural identity. These schools now include children of diverse ethnic origins, with a wide range of customs and traditions. The school language is French, but the cultural milieu is more cosmopolitan.[10]

In other areas the years after 1976 were anticlimactic. Even with a separatist government the sky did not fall, for the new administration was cautious. The successive budgets were austerity budgets, limiting expenditures in an effort to control the size of the deficits. The government did introduce some reforms – "no fault" automobile insurance, a higher minimum wage, and supplements to family income – but these were not *nationaliste* and not very controversial. Nor did Lévesque accede to trade union demands. In its negotiations with the Common Front in 1979, his government obliged the union negotiators to submit its proposals to the workers, and when Hydro-Québec went on strike it passed back-to-work legislation. Lévesque had promised sound and honest government, and public opinion polls showed that Quebeckers believed he had kept his word. But for the new government this was not enough. Québécois – and Canadians in the rest of Canada – were holding their breath until the constitutional status of the province was settled.

The promised referendum was seen as crucial. All policies and public statements from Quebec and Ottawa were coloured by and directed toward the promised referendum. The in-fighting was not always

---

[10] Dominique Clift and Sheila McLeod Arnopolous, *The English Fact in Quebec* (Montreal, 1980) deals with the impact of the Quiet Revolution on Anglo-Quebeckers.

For the referendum campaign the Lévesque government established stringent rules that obliged proponents of federalism, whatever their political inclinations, to organize one committee and to channel all financing through that body. The illustration shows the cover of a pamphlet explaining the set-up.

edifying. When the provincial government declared June 24, St-Jean Baptiste Day, as Quebec's national holiday and funded the celebrations, the federal government reacted by making even more generous contributions to the celebrations on the first of July. When the federal budget offered compensation for reductions in the provincial sales tax, Quebec responded to this federal intervention by a selective reduction and a demand for reimbursement; when Ottawa instead sent income tax rebates directly to Quebec's residents, the provincial government altered the provincial income tax exemption so that it ended up with the money. There would be no co-operative federalism until the fate of the federal union was resolved.

The referendum was long delayed. Lévesque was doubtless discouraged by opinion polls that showed that, although most Québécois favoured changes in the federal system, only a minority wanted separation. In the meantime, the federal government talked of revising the terms of union, but a federal task force and a federal proposal to the provincial premiers failed to produce a consensus. The situation was further confused when the provincial Liberal Opposition, now led by Claude Ryan, a distinguished journalist, produced its own blueprint for a new federation along lines known to be unacceptable to Trudeau. When the provincial government finally set the date of the referendum in 1980, the wording of the question showed its uncertainty. Instead of asking Quebeckers to vote for or against independence, the question merely asked whether voters would authorize the provincial government to begin negotiations with the federal government for sovereignty-association.

The question was ambiguous but not the results. Almost 60 percent voted *non*. Even among the French-speaking Quebeckers a bare majority had voted against negotiations for a mitigated sovereignty. The results could not be interpreted as a vote for the status quo, but they did imply a commitment to continued association with the rest of Canada. The referendum effectively rejected separation as an option.

Pierre Trudeau considered that the federalists were now committed to a constitutional change. When the provincial premiers failed to agree on a revised Constitution, he decided to act unilaterally. In October 1980, he proposed a charter of rights that included educational rights for the provincial minorities. Lévesque bitterly denounced changes that gave Quebec no additional powers and actually limited its jurisdiction in the area of civil rights. The provincial election of 1981 showed that, even if Quebec had rejected separatism, it was still concerned about provincial autonomy. The Parti Québécois returned to power with an even larger majority than before.

This chart from the Parti Québécois referendum literature illustrates the declining influence of French-Canadians in Canada, in terms of population.

UN CANADA DE PLUS EN PLUS ANGLAIS

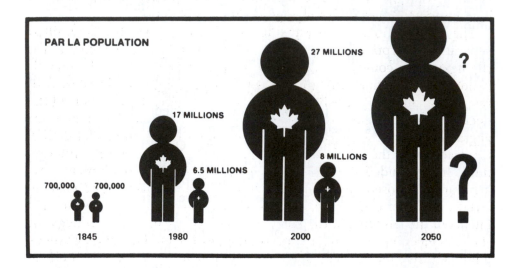

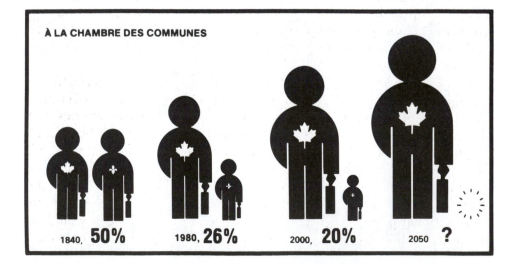

In Ottawa in the summer of that year, the Supreme Court ruled that unilateral action by the federal government, while legal, violated constitutional convention. In a last-minute attempt to reach some agreement, Trudeau and the nine English-speaking premiers hammered out a modified version of the federal proposal. The education rights for the minorities were included, but the new amendment procedures required the consent of the legislatures of two-thirds of the provinces, representing at least half of Canada's population. It was a slap in the face for Lévesque. Not only had the other provincial premiers left him isolated, but the new procedure meant that Quebec would have no automatic veto over future changes in the Constitution.

The constitutional revision split the Parti Québécois. Committed separatists interpreted it as a deliberate affront and passed a resolution at the next party convention opting for independence without the qualification of association with the rest of Canada. Lévesque threatened to resign. A mail vote – derisively known as the Renérendum – reversed the decision but did not unite the party. The internal divisions were aggravated by increasing unemployment and a rising provincial deficit. Contracts with the public service unions, negotiated before the referendum, had included generous annual increases. The government now arbitrarily imposed new contracts with salary roll-backs. The ensuing strikes were broken by back-to-work legislation, but Lévesque had alienated the left wing of the party. An open split came over strategy for the next election. What did the party stand for? Should it campaign on its administrative record, with some chance of winning, or should it affirm its separatist principles and go down to honourable defeat? When Lévesque opted for the former, hard-core separatists resigned from the government and even from the party. A beleaguered Lévesque then resigned and left it to the party to choose a new leader for the next provincial election.

The Liberal victory in the 1985 provincial election underlined the changes that had taken place in Quebec over the previous half-century. The future of French Canada was still undecided but the outlines of a distinctive society had emerged. Its foundation would be the French language. In 1988 when the Supreme Court rejected the section of Bill 101 that banned the use of any language other than French on commercial signs on the grounds that this was inconsistent with both the provincial and federal charter of rights, the Liberal government used its constitutional power to override the charters. Bilingual signs would be permitted within commercial establishments, but external signs would have to be in French only. The Liberal government, like the Parti Québécois before it, would use its political power to ensure the predominance of French in the province.

The place of Quebec within Confederation was still ambiguous. The federal political parties recognized the French fact. Party leaders spoke French as well as English and made deliberate efforts to win support in Francophone Quebec. In 1987, Prime Minister Brian Mulroney persuaded the first ministers to agree on a constitutional amendment that recognized Quebec as a "distinct society," and John Turner and Ed Broadbent, leaders of the Liberal and New Democratic parties respectively, persuaded their parties to support the accord. The Meech Lake agreement, however, did not seem likely to receive the required unanimous consent of the provincial legislatures, and many critics roundly denounced the Quebec government's decision to limit the use of English on commercial signs. The French fact might be better recognized, but it was not yet universally acclaimed.

Within Quebec and within Canada, the changes had been profound and apparently irreversible. *La survivance* had been given a new meaning. The provincial government had replaced the Church as the institution to which French-Canadians looked for strength and guidance. Instead of the Catholic religion, the French language had become the touchstone of cultural identity. A French-speaking society that had revered the traditions of a simple rural existence now had a frame of reference that was urban, industrial, and secular. Independence had been rejected as an option, at least for this generation. What was clear was that French Canada had survived a quarter century of profound change and that, although the linguistic and cultural patterns in Quebec were still being defined, French-Canadians were confident that they could meet the challenges of the future.

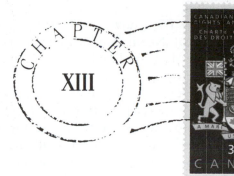

CANADA IN THE 1990s

Canada, as we have seen, has evolved throughout its entire post-Confederation history, but particularly in the years since the beginning of the Second World War. Of the changes in society since 1939 there can be no doubt. By the beginning of the 1990s, the nation at last seemed to find its identity; it industrialized and prospered; it created a safety net of social security measures; it patriated its Constitution and entrenched a Charter of Rights; and it tried to resolve the persistent problem of Quebec's place in Confederation. The millenium was at hand – or was it? Paradoxically, although Canadians were generally prosperous and contented with their lot, every one of those great achievements seemed in jeopardy as the nation entered the last decade of the twentieth century.

Both Canada's image of itself as an independent nation in North America and the Canadian manufacturing sector, ardent nationalists argued, have been placed in jeopardy by the Free Trade Agreement with the United States, which came into effect on January 1, 1989. The 1988 general election focused almost exclusively on the FTA, much to the surprise of the politicians, and the electorate, by returning Brian Mulroney and the Progressive Conservative Party to power with a very comfortable majority, seemingly expressed popular approval of the deal. (A majority in seats in the House of Commons did not mean a majority of the votes cast – the opposition parties in total outpolled the Conservatives.) But plant closings soon followed, especially in Ontario, as industries relocated south of the border. Whether those were a product

of the FTA, however, or simply part of the consolidation and contrac-
tion of North American industry was much less clear. In truth, the
FTA's full implications for Canadian manufacturing would take years
to determine.

Psychologically, however, the meaning of the FTA seemed clear. By
accepting reciprocity with the United States, the first such agreement to
go into effect since the abrogation of the 1854 Reciprocity Treaty by the
United States in 1866, Canadians acknowledged that the lines of force in
North America, and not just the economic ones, ran north-south rather
than east-west. That realization may have been inevitable, to be sure, but
it was not until the FTA and the 1988 general election that the Canadian
people's decision was absolutely clear. We had always claimed to be
different from Americans; most had been willing, as Vincent Massey put
it forty years earlier, to pay the price of being Canadian. The acceptance
of the FTA, whatever else it did, demonstrated that Canadians would not
pay that price indefinitely. A major prop of the Canadian identity, the
consciousness of being a separate nation with a distinct personality in
North America, had been weakened.

Moreover, by endorsing the FTA, Canada threw its economic lot in
with the United States, looking for prosperity in the world's largest and
richest consumer market. Unfortunately, that market was no longer quite
so dynamic or innovative as it had once been, especially when compared
with Japan's or the European Community's. Some people asked face-
tiously during the general election what the sense was in shackling the
country to a corpse. The image was not entirely off base. Seventy-five
years earlier, in Canada's last election that hinged on reciprocity with the
United States, Laurier Liberals had argued that the prosperity brought by
trade would guarantee Canada's remaining a separate, happy nation in
North America. Brian Mulroney's Conservatives implicitly argued the
same way. The Liberals had been rebuffed in 1911, but prosperity
eventually came; Canada was prosperous in 1989, but there seemed
fewer ways open to the nation to preserve a strong Canadian identity.

Another aspect of that national identity was also under attack. The
social security system, which included old age pensions, unemployment
insurance, family allowance, medicare, and the Canada Pension Plan,
was marked for attack by the Mulroney government soon after its
election in 1984. It was not so much that the government disliked the
idea of a safety net – Mulroney himself is basically a small-l liberal. But
the costs of operating it were high and rising to keep pace with inflation.
In an era of staggering budget deficits and a skyrocketing national debt,

the *universality* of welfare programs seemed to be too inviting a target for the Finance Department to pass by. During the 1988 election, critics of the FTA charged that Canada's social programs would be jeopardized if the agreement came into force. Unemployment insurance and even medicare could be put in doubt by the system of Canadian-American tribunals and appeals created by the FTA. Undoubtedly there was alarmist talk in this; but it was also equally certain that Canadian industries, hard-pressed to pay higher taxes needed to support this country's more generous social welfare programs, wanted a "level playing field," to use the jargon of the day, on which to compete for markets with American manufacturers. The FTA probably exacerbated a trend toward cutbacks that was underway already.

In 1985, the Mulroney government had been forced by angry senior citizens to withdraw a measure to de-index Old Age Security pensions. ("You lied, prime minister," one little old lady said to Mulroney in full view of the TV cameras, "you lied.") But four years later, unemployment insurance was cut back, and the de-indexing of other programs, as well as the recovery of payments through taxation, proceeded apace. There were complaints, but not enough to do anything more than mark the passing of the idea of universality. An era, one that had started in the Second World War, had come to an end.

The Constitution and Quebec's place in Canada were also under siege. The great achievement of the Trudeau years had been the patriation of the British North America Act and the entrenchment of the Canadian Charter of Rights and Freedoms. But Quebec, promised a new federalism if it rejected the separatist nostrums of the Lévesque government's referendum in 1980, did not sign the Constitution. Properly and wisely, Brian Mulroney made it a major task of his new government to bring Quebec aboard, something he achieved with the Meech Lake accord in 1987. Initially, all the provincial premiers accepted the arrangement (after an all-night bargaining session), agreeing that Quebec was a distinct society, that the unanimous consent of all ten provinces would be needed to alter the Constitution, and that the provinces would have a large voice in the selection of senators and Supreme Court justices. But the unanimity quickly disappeared as the critics began to pick at the accord. Women and native peoples felt that their concerns had been shunted aside by the all male, all white first ministers; historians (but, curiously, not political scientists) pointed to the holes in the Meech Lake text, and many argued that the agreement weakened the central government's power just at the time that the Free Trade Agreement made it all the more essential; and an English-Canadian backlash, strongest in the West but by no means limited to that region, focused on the "distinct society" provisions. The result was that the ratification of the accord, set for completion by mid-1990 and once a certainty, soon appeared in serious trouble. The voters of Manitoba and New Brunswick tossed out the governments that had agreed to the Meech Lake deal and expressed serious reservations. So did Newfoundland, its newly elected Liberal government threatening to rescind its predecessor's support.

The delay in implementing the provisions of the accord and the assault on the distinct society clause deeply troubled Quebec. For editorial writers and for those Québécois willing to give federalism a chance, the ratification of the Meech Lake agreement without a single altered comma or colon soon became a touchstone of the value Canada and Canadians placed on Quebec's presence in Confederation. If you English-Canadians want us to stay, Quebec politicians at the provincial and federal levels repeatedly argued, then you had better pass the accord. That litany shrilly swelled to a crescendo during and immediately after the Quebec election of September 1989. Robert Bourassa's Liberals were returned to power with a huge majority, but the Parti Québécois captured 40 percent of the popular vote – and it had campaigned on a straight separatist platform.

The difficulty was that an equally shrill anti-Quebec mood was running strongly through English Canada as the 1980s came to a close. Quebec's language law upset many English-Canadians, not least those in Quebec, with its rigidity. Even bilingual signs were forbidden under the law. And when the Supreme Court tossed out the act, Premier Bourassa overrode the justices, as was his right, and found demonstrators in front of the national assembly demanding even tougher action "to protect" the French language. Why, many Canadians outside Quebec asked, should we struggle any longer to keep *those people* in Confederation? Why should we be blackmailed into accepting Meech Lake by threats that Quebec will separate? Let them go, many said.

That response, while understandable as a heated emotional response, was shortsighted and destructive. What distinctiveness Canada retained in post-FTA North America surely resided in the bilingual character of the nation. The Québécois were an essential part of Canada, so much so that every effort had to be attempted – in the 1990s as in the 1890s, 1910s, 1940s, 1960s, 1970s, and 1980s – to making them and keeping them full partners in Confederation. The Meech Lake agreement may well be just as flawed as its critics maintained; but, if not Meech Lake, then some other accord had to be drawn up to which Canadians, French-and English-speaking could subscribe. It should not be beyond the wit of Canadians to find the appropriate formulas. For if they cannot, then Quebec will separate. And if Quebec separates, then Canada's existence will be in jeopardy. The 1990s promise to be a challenging decade.

However, the 1990s promise to be physically safer. For the first time since the onset of the Cold War in 1945, the superpowers were moving toward an accommodation. The Soviet Union and its satellites, once the models of communist orthodoxy, were experimenting with *glasnost* (openness) and *perestroika* (reform) and with different economic and political models. The Poles held free elections that put Solidarity in power, the Hungarians opened up their economy and their borders, the Czechs, East Germans, Bulgarians, and Romanians tossed out their reactionary regimes, and President Mikhail Gorbachev's Soviet Union faced widespread ethnic unrest in the republics that made up the great confederation that comprises the USSR. (Perhaps Canadian federalism could serve as a model for Russia?) Impelled by the crises that gripped his country, and also by his clear belief that any nuclear war was madness, Gorbachev made repeated signals that he wanted a change in the frozen hostility that had ordinarily marked relations with the West. Hesitantly, presidents Ronald Reagan and George Bush moved toward conciliation with the Soviets; hesitantly, the nuclear arsenals and the masses of conventional weaponry were set aside. In a fashion that no one could have predicted in 1985, the world seemed to draw back from the brink. There were still threats to peace in the Middle East and in the Far East, and the instability in the Soviet empire was dangerous in itself, but the prospect of war between the superpowers suddenly was replaced by the promise of co-operation.

What this miraculous outbreak of peace meant for Canada was the leisure to deal with its own internal problems. Those, as we have seen, are many. But Canadians and their leaders have historically shown the ability and patience to resolve the difficulties of region against region and people against people. The challenge this time, the great federalist test of the 1990s, might well be as trying as anything in our past.

Canada always has been God's country for the millions of immigrants, fleeing the troubles of their homelands, who came here – and still come here every year. But God's country too can be lost without wisdom, good sense, and tolerance. We have a country to save.

INDEX